FOUNDATIONS OF
CRIMINAL
JUSTICE

FOUNDATIONS OF
CRIMINAL
JUSTICE

Stephen S. Owen
Radford University

Henry F. Fradella
California State University, Long Beach

Tod W. Burke
Radford University

Jerry W. Joplin
Guilford College

New York   Oxford
OXFORD UNIVERSITY PRESS

Oxford University Press, Inc., publishes works that further Oxford University's
objective of excellence in research, scholarship, and education.

Oxford New York
Auckland   Cape Town   Dar es Salaam   Hong Kong   Karachi
Kuala Lumpur   Madrid   Melbourne   Mexico City   Nairobi
New Delhi   Shanghai   Taipei   Toronto

With offices in
Argentina   Austria   Brazil   Chile   Czech Republic   France   Greece
Guatemala   Hungary   Italy   Japan   Poland   Portugal   Singapore
South Korea   Switzerland   Thailand   Turkey   Ukraine   Vietnam

For titles covered by Section 112 of the US Higher Education Opportunity
Act, please visit www.oup.com/us/he for the latest information about
pricing and alternate formats.

Published by Oxford University Press, Inc.
198 Madison Avenue, New York, New York 10016
http://www.oup.com

Library of Congress Cataloging-in-Publication Data
Foundations of criminal justice /
by Stephen S. Owen . . . [et al.]. — 1st ed.
     p. cm.
ISBN 978-0-19-538732-2
1. Criminal justice, Administration of—United States.
I. Owen, Stephen S.
HV9950.F68 2012
364.973—dc23   2011036773

9 8 7 6 5 4 3 2 1

Printed in the United States of America
on acid-free paper

Dedications

Steve: To my parents, teachers, and students, all of whom have taught me much.

Hank: To my lifelong, dear friend: Justin Spitzer.

Tod: In loving memory of my father; to my mother, sisters, and family; and to my current and former students.

Jerry: With thanks to the many students who took Introduction to Criminal Justice with me and encouraged me to move criminal justice education in this direction.

Brief Contents

Contents

Unit V: Overview of Criminal Justice Institutions

Chapter 11: Core Concepts of U.S. Policing 289

Chapter 12: Core Concepts of U.S. Court Systems 316

Preface

Understand the core ideas of justice and law. Make better
real-world decisions in criminal justice.

What This Book Is

Criminal justice is the study and practice of society's responses to crime. Within criminal justice, discretion is inevitable. Whether the police officer on patrol, the prosecuting attorney making a charging decision, the judge determining a sentence, or the parole board considering the early release of an inmate, criminal justice professionals are faced with making countless decisions on a daily basis. Most of these decisions involve applying professional judgment (within the bounds of the law) to arrive at the best answer.

To place criminal justice within its most meaningful context, students must engage in the study of two overlapping areas. The first area is *analytical,* focusing on the theories that underlie the practice of criminal justice and the crafting of laws and policies. These include ideas about the nature of law, the meaning of justice, the philosophies of idealism and pragmatism, the history of justice practice, the theoretical foundations of policing, corrections, and judicial decision making, and more. The second area is *descriptive,* focusing on the structure of the criminal justice system and the particulars of the laws that it enforces. This book explores both and provides students with a foundation for further study of issues related to crime, law, and justice.

The former study necessarily enlightens the latter. Without *analyzing* the foundations of criminal justice, it is difficult to *describe* the laws and policies that criminal justice professionals are asked to enforce (and the rationale for doing so) or understand the full range of ideas that shape—implicitly or explicitly— the discretionary decisions inherent in criminal justice practice. We hope that the study of these ideas will serve to enrich the study of the criminal justice system and also prepare students to be thoughtful practitioners, decision makers, and scholars of criminal justice.

Why We Wrote It

We believe it is imperative for students to study the foundations of criminal justice from their first course in the discipline. Because these ideas underlie so much of current criminal justice policy and practice, they form the bedrock on which subsequent study is grounded. Indeed, the foundational concepts of criminal justice are ideas that apply across the criminal justice curriculum.

We have titled the book *Foundations of Criminal Justice* not because these are the *only* ideas that are central to the theory and practice of the discipline but because they are among the most significant conversations that have contributed to the field. Although discussion of the theoretical roots of criminal justice will no doubt continue and should continue, the ideas and topics surveyed in this text help present a view of criminal justice that can inform the subsequent study of criminal justice structures and processes.

The challenge in teaching the foundations of criminal justice in an introductory course is twofold. First, some of the key ideas are complex, particularly those drawing upon the interdisciplinary roots of criminal justice in areas that may not be very familiar to students, such as policy theory, legal theory, sociology, philosophy, and psychology. Second, there is no single source that collects these ideas, leaving instructors either to assign primary source readings (which can be even more challenging than the ideas) or to summarize materials in lectures without an accompanying textbook.

In writing this text, we have attempted to remedy both of these problems. We have included within the book a collection of ideas that are important for beginning criminal justice students to consider. Furthermore, we have worked to cover complex ideas in a manner that is engaging and accessible but without diluting their meaning. It is our hope that this will contribute not only to criminal justice pedagogy but also to promoting conversations—among students, professionals, and scholars alike—about the theoretical roots of the discipline of criminal justice and their application in practice.

Organization

The balance among three ideas represents the basis of our book: (1) the overarching and competing ideas of what our society should be; (2) the daily practices of an immensely complex collection of agencies described as criminal justice; and (3) the individual needs of a student going on to become a responsible citizen and perhaps a criminal justice professional. In Chapter 1, Introducing Crime and Criminal Justice, we outline various perspectives on criminal justice and explain how they relate to the "big ideas" explored in the rest of the book.

In Unit I, Perspectives on Law, we begin exploring the ideas that have vexed societies across the globe throughout history. That is, how should people live together in a society? What is right, what is wrong, and how can we act to ensure desired behavior? Working through the very practical ideas of police discretion and activities you might see on any street corner, we explore the concepts of law, morality, and formal ways of questioning those concepts.

In Unit II, Perspectives on Deviance and Crime, we explore the critical distinctions between behaviors society generally condemns and behaviors society classifies as criminal. It is extremely important to consider how social preferences can change the flow of criminal law and criminal justice policy.

In Unit III, Perspectives on Justice, the ideas in the earlier chapters about law and social control come together in an even bigger fundamental idea: what is just, and how do we find it as a society? Furthermore, how do harried professionals facing budget cuts, shifting policy priorities, high stress, and split-second decisions find justice in their daily work? In addition, recognizing the potential harm to people through race, class, and other forms of discrimination is an important responsibility of all those working in criminal justice.

In Unit IV, Penal Social Control, we focus on the process of developing and refining laws and how punishment is used to enforce society's priorities.

Finally, in Unit V, Overview of Criminal Justice Institutions, we introduce students to the terminology and procedures that are relevant to the police, courts, and corrections. In some schools, much of this information will be covered in later courses on each of these institutions. In other schools, students will need a working knowledge of each institution either because this is the only course they take in criminal justice or because they need this course as a direct gateway to other courses. These chapters are available for those who need them, and we have tried to keep the focus on the terminology, the structure, and the motivating ideas of each institution rather than on ever-changing fads and statistics.

How to Teach with This Book

Chances are, each individual instructor may not make use of every chapter in this book. Courses seeking a foundation of criminal justice grounded in the liberal arts may focus more heavily on Units I, II, and III, with less time dedicated to material in Units IV and V (which is often covered elsewhere in the criminal justice curriculum, in courses on police, courts, corrections, and criminal law). Conversely, courses more heavily focused on the components of the criminal justice system (particularly in programs for which there is not subsequent required coursework in police, courts, corrections, and criminal law) may use Units I, II, and III to "set up" a more detailed examination of material from Units IV and V. Still other instructors may bring in many more examples from local criminal justice policies and practices than appear in this book.

Of course, these options are not mutually exclusive. Content about the criminal justice system is easily integrated across discussions of Units I, II, and III, and references to philosophical underpinnings of criminal justice is easily integrated into discussions pertaining to Units IV and V. Some courses will give equal weight to all chapters over the course of a semester. We felt strongly, however, that it was important to offer flexibility for instructors and to keep the key information unique to a foundations course all available in one concise volume. Through years of consultation with instructors at a wide variety of schools across the United States, we have settled on this balance between conciseness and exhaustiveness that we hope will serve as a firm foundation for a course that still allows individuality and student discussion.

How to Study from This Book

We have designed this book to make the study process very active. Just as a professional in criminal justice will always need to be actively curious and observant in the field, studying the discipline requires curiosity and inquiry.

Each unit in the book is introduced by a photo essay, containing a series of photos accompanied by a narrative and discussion questions. The topics, photos, and discussion questions were selected to survey the broad range of issues included in each unit. Think about how you would respond to these issues before you read the chapters in the unit. Afterwards, you may consider how material from the chapters relates back to the issues in the photo essays.

Each chapter begins with a realistic situation that the criminal justice system has encountered or could encounter. In that Case Study, all the ideas that will be examined in the chapter are relevant. Read this case carefully and discuss the questions at the end with your classmates, your instructor, or in notes to yourself. Your understanding of the rest of the chapter will be enriched by considering this case.

Each main section of the text opens with a Focusing Question. These straightforward questions are meant to help you think about the main idea to come in that section and provide you with a framework for the ideas you will examine. The Focusing Questions can help you see the problem to be solved rather than reading the chapter as a simple stream of data to memorize.

Each main section of the text concludes with several in-text questions. These questions are designed to allow you to reflect upon, analyze, or apply the material you have just read.

At the end of each chapter, you will find a section called Criminal Justice Problem Solving. Introductory textbooks can sometimes give readers the mistaken impression that all the answers are already set in stone and that there is nothing new to discover in a discipline. These Problem Solving sections focus on a real-life issue the criminal justice system is still struggling to solve. Chances are, if you become a criminal justice professional, you will in some way personally be part of the efforts to solve these types of issues. If criminal justice is not your own career path, you may still be affected by these issues as a private citizen.

Ancillaries

Oxford University Press is proud to offer a complete and authoritative supplements package for both instructors and students. When you adopt *Foundations of Criminal Justice*, you will have access to a truly exemplary set of ancillary materials to enhance teaching and support students' learning.

INSTRUCTOR'S RESOURCE CD

The Instructor's Resource CD contains an enormous variety of materials to aid in teaching, whether at a four-year university or community college, online, or in person. In addition to general ideas for using *Foundations of Criminal Justice* in an introductory course, the CD includes **teaching tips and ideas** customized for instructors working in community colleges and online courses, as well as for those teaching out of sociology departments. New teachers, and those teaching the introductory course in a general education context, will also find specialized suggestions. The disc includes **sample syllabi** and long-term **integrative assignments** to help instructors plan for the entire semester.

Detailed **lesson plans, in-class activities**, and **homework assignments** are provided for each of the book's thirteen chapters. To help you assess your students, the package includes a robust **test bank**, offering multiple-choice, true/false, matching, short answer, and essay questions. In addition to the traditional answer key for objective questions, the essay questions are accompanied by **grading rubrics** laying out detailed criteria for evaluation. **PowerPoint-based lecture slides** and **clicker questions** are provided as well and are fully editable to meet your needs.

Finally, a complete **course management cartridge** is available to qualified adopters. Contact your Oxford University Press sales representative for more information.

COMPANION WEBSITE

Foundations of Criminal Justice is also accompanied by an extensive **companion website (www.oup.com/us/owen)**, which includes materials to help students with every aspect of the course. For each chapter, you will find:

- **Objectives for learning** that identify, in a clear, concise way, the concepts and subjects that students should understand after reading a given chapter
- A **brief summary** of the broad themes of each chapter, to help students organize their thinking and reading
- **Additional links** to websites providing supplemental information on the topics and ideas covered in the chapter
- **Additional recommended readings** that delve more deeply into the topics discussed in the chapter
- **Self-grading review questions** to help students review the material and assess their own comprehension
- **Case links** to the original text of every case cited in the book
- **Glossary flashcards** to assist students in studying and review

Thanks and Acknowledgments

We would like to thank John Challice, Sherith Pankratz, Sarah Calabi, Danielle Christensen, Amy Krivohlavek, Whitney Laemmli, Taylor Pilkington, Rich Beck, Tierra Morgan, and Keith Faivre at Oxford University Press for their exceptional guidance and encouragement in this project. We would also like to thank the anonymous reviewers at the *Journal of Criminal Justice Education* whose insights helped us in the development of our article, "Conceptualizing Justice: Revising the Introductory Criminal Justice Course," which, in turn, provided the impetus for this book. Finally, this book would not have "come together" without the hard work of the lead author, Dr. Stephen Owen. Hank, Tod, and Jerry express their heartfelt thanks to Steve for serving as the unifying voice among us.

In addition, the authors and the publisher would like to thank the following reviewers, focus group and webinar participants, and class testers for their invaluable time and feedback. Their comments and suggestions were instrumental in the development of the text.

Kristine Artello, Penn State University–New Kensington

Thomas Babcock, University of Texas at San Antonio

Sarah Bacon, Florida State University

Allan Barnes, University of Alaska–Anchorage

Kevin Beaver, Florida State University

Jay Berman, New Jersey City University

Michael Bush, Northern Kentucky University

Frank Butler, La Salle University

Mark Byington, Jefferson College

Amy Cass, California State University–Fullerton

Tammy Castle, James Madison University

David Clark, University at Albany–SUNY

Charles Crawford, Western Michigan University

Michael Cretacci, University at Buffalo–SUNY

Mengyan Dai, University of Baltimore

Randal Davis, Santiago Canyon College

Mary Louis Davitt, University of Maine–Augusta

Peggy DeStefano, Bakersfield College

Kristen DeVall, University of North Carolina–Wilmington

Heather Donovan, University of Massachusetts–Dartmouth

George Eichenberg, Tarleton State University

Patricia Erickson, Canisius College

Aaron Fichtelberg, University of Delaware

Linda Fleischer, The Community College of Baltimore

Laurin Flynn, Guilford College

Michelle Foster, Kent State University

Alan Frazier, Glendale Community College

Natasha Frost, Northeastern University

Christie Gardiner, California State University–Fullerton

Lior Gideon, John Jay College of Criminal Justice

Kay Gillespie, Weber State University

Julie Globokar, University of Illinois at Chicago

Andrea Hampton, Truman State University

Barry Harvey, Alvernia College

Stacy Haynes, Mississippi State University

Deborah Howard, TESST College of Technology

Cyndy Hughes, Western Carolina University

Patrick Ibe, Albany State College

Fred Jones, Simpson College

Mark Jones, East Carolina University

Delores Jones-Brown, John Jay College of Criminal Justice

Antonia Keane, Loyola University

Ashmini Kerodal, John Jay College of Criminal Justice

David Keys, New Mexico State University

Fred Kramer, John Jay College

Peter Kraska, Eastern Kentucky University

Christina Lanier, University of North Carolina–Wilmington

Lonn Lanza-Kaduce, University of Florida

Minna Laurikkala, Shenandoah University

Brian Lawton, George Mason University

William Lay, University of Bridgeport

Lynette Lee, California State University–Sacramento

Jason Levy, Virginia Commonwealth University

Elizabeth Lewis, Virginia Western College

Sean Maddan, University of Tampa

Elisha Marr, Calvin College

Sanjay Marwah, Guilford College

Mary Ellen Mastroilli, Boston University Metropolitan College

Carol Mathews, Century College

Greg Matoesian, University of Illinois at Chicago

Bruce McBride, Utica College

Karen McCue, University of Minnesota

Alida Merlo, Indiana University of Pennsylvania

Eric Metchik, Salem State University

Emil Moldovan, Radford University

Thomas O'Connor, Austin Peay State University

David Orrick, Norwich University

Allison Payne, Villanova University

Terrylynn Pearlman, Marist College

Amy Pinero, Baton Rouge Community College

Hillary Potter, University of Colorado–Boulder

Elaine Rizzo, Saint Anselm College

Manuel Roman, Consumnes River College

Dennis Santore, Indian River State College

Joseph Schafer, Southern Illinois University–Carbondale

Donna Schuele, University of California–Irvine

Michael Scott, Kaplan University

Todd Scott, Schoolcraft College

Diane Sjuts, Metropolitan Community College of Omaha

Alisa Smith, The University of Tampa

Hayden Smith, University of South Carolina

Susan Smith-Cunnien, University of St. Thomas

Jason Sole, Metropolitan State University

Paul Steele, Morehead State University

Mark Stelter, Lone Star College–Montgomery Campus

Quanda Stevenson, University of Alabama

David Struckhoff, Lewis University

L. Paul Sutton, San Diego State University

Chloe Tischler, ITT-Technical Institute

Pamela Tontodonato, Kent State University

Sheryl Van Horne, Widener University

Tim Wadsworth, University of Colorado at Boulder

Arnold Waggoner, Rose State College

Kenneth Wagner, Lynchburg College

Kevin Walsh, Aurora University

Stephanie Whitus, Aurora University

Tracey Woodard, University of North Florida

Brian Woodworth, Olivet Nazarene University

Richard Wright, Bridgewater College

Class Test Participants

Brian Woodworth, Olivet Nazarene University, and his students:

Kevin Arthur, Benjamin Backstrom, Seth Barrigear, Amanda Bender, Earl Bentley, Sarah Bodner, Faith Cavender, Simone Coburne, Howard Coleman-Patton, Cassandra Collins, Matthew Compton, Victoria Conley, Sarah Cook, Jonathan Damron, Justin Fahy, James Funk, Bradley Giamalva, Jessica Hafner, Tyler Hamilton, Erica Hammond, Luke Hasselbring, Jarad Holbrook, Samantha Holmes, Ross Johnson, Andy Knol, Erin Koehn, Randall Koehn, Kim Kratz, Ryan Lalone, Marcel Maiden, Gina Martin, Jerett Martin, Alan Meyers, Bradley Miller, Rhandyl Morris, Kristin Nichols, Andrew Pfundstein, Amy Preston, Jacob Ryan, Lukas Schindler, Laura Shickles, Tim Siadak, Joshua Smarrella, Benjamin Tobey, Lindsey Tobias, Jaclyn Travnik, Amanda Vanderpool, Jessica Voss, Marcus Washington, Michael Williams, and Jeremy Woods.

Alisa Smith, The University of Tampa, and her students:

Ian Berry, Kristina Egitto, Laura Fogg, Taylor Glatzer, John-Patrick Haney, Zachary Iacovino, Brittany Morgado, Miranda Nordell, Leah Paddock, Megan Podschine, Joshua Ratliff, David Saucedo, Allison Streeker, Laura Worrell, Zachary Yaeger, and Kristine Zambito.

A Guide to Using This Book

CASE STUDIES. At the beginning of each chapter, you will find a case study that explores an issue related to the field of criminal justice. Some are hypothetical, but most are based on actual court cases or policy debates. We encourage you to read these case studies, to think critically about the issues they raise, and to work through the questions that follow. Each has been carefully selected to illustrate one or more key points in the chapter, and other material in the chapter will often refer back to the opening case study.

CASE STUDY

Sexting

Before reading this case study, take a few moments to reflect on the following question. Make some notes about your answer and be prepared to explain it and share it with your instructor and classmates.

> What is justice? Think carefully about what justice means to you, how justice can be achieved, and how you might recognize justice.

Assume that a 16-year-old male (Max) and a 16-year-old female (Frieda), both of whom attend the same high school, have been dating for approximately two years. In the past year, the couple has regularly engaged in consensual sexual intercourse. Under the laws of the state in which they reside, it is legal for two 16-year-olds to engage in consensual sexual activity.

Both Max and Frieda have their own cell phones. From time to time, one sends the other a nude photograph accompanied by a sexually explicit text message. The decision to send the photograph and text message is consensual, and both Max and Frieda enjoy receiving and responding to these materials. This practice is known as *sexting*.

...nd Frieda decides to end the rela-
...etaliate. He does so by forwarding
...rieda had sent him several months
...e, as other students at her school
...Frieda reports the situation to the
...ifies the school resource officer (a
...same time, Frieda's mother hears
...Frieda's mother also notifies the

CASE STUDY

Working the Corner

You are a police officer beginning your evening shift patrol with your partner, who is driving the squad car. At roll call, your sergeant reminded you that complaints about prostitution were increasing in your patrol area. In particular, citizens have expressed concern about prostitutes who openly solicit clients on the street and who perform sexual acts in alleyways and parked cars.

That evening, you find a young woman, whom you and your partner have previously arrested for prostitution, occupying her usual street corner. Your partner stops the squad car and confronts the woman, asking her, "What are you up to tonight?" The young woman responds, "You know what I do." Your partner interprets this as an admission of guilt for solicitation of prostitution and arrests her for that offense, although he did not witness any specific illegal behavior other than perhaps loitering. Later, your partner explains to you that he was just doing his job by giving the people what they want, which is streets free of immoral behavior. He knew the charges would likely be dismissed, but said, "At least she'll be off the streets for a while."

FOCUSING QUESTIONS. At the beginning of each major section of the chapter, we will pose a "focusing question," which will be addressed in the coming pages. Focusing questions are meant to provide a roadmap for chapter content. As you read, consider how the material in the chapter leads toward an answer to the question.

Psychological Theories of Crime and Criminality

FOCUSING QUESTION 5.3

How can psychological theories explain crime and deviant behavior?

Psychological theories focus on individuals and their thinking processes. With origins in the work of Sigmund Freud, psychological theories have since developed to include a wide range of explanations for deviant behavior.

Some Explanations of Criminal Deviance

FOCUSING QUESTION 5.2

Why do some people engage in criminal deviance?

Think back to the case study at the beginning of the chapter. How did you answer the question about the factors that may have influenced Panzram to commit his criminal acts? In this section, we discuss **criminology**, which is the scientific study of the etiology (i.e., nature and causes) of criminal behavior. Many theories have been developed to explain why people commit crimes. Some of the most common are summarized in the following sections; see how they compare to your ideas about the causes of Panzram's behavior.

How would each essential tension influence policy about weightlifting in prison?

Are there remedies to the conflicts posed by the essential tensions? Why or why not?

What factors could explain the increase in the number of recognized mental disorders? To what extent is mental illness objective? To what extent might it be socially constructed?

Other than the example used earlier concerning the Victorian views on masturbation, think of a behavior that has been medicalized. What type(s) of medical social control might address the behavior? What might be the consequences of the medicalization?

What do you think ought to be the role of therapeutic social control, or the medicalization of deviance, in criminal justice? Why?

How do the media, interest groups, and bureaucracies influence the creation and enforcement of criminal law? Provide examples beyond those described in this section.

Try your hand at problem definition. Brainstorm as many responses as you can to this statement: "Marijuana is a _____ issue." Describe what kinds of policies or laws each response would suggest.

REVIEW QUESTIONS. Periodically, you will find questions within the text. These are not questions that will ask you to repeat information that you've just read. Rather, the questions are designed to promote intellectual interaction between you (and possibly your classmates and your instructor) and the text. When you reach these questions, pause and consider them. Doing so will help you process and reflect on what you've just read.

Criminal Justice Problem Solving: DETAINING COMBATANTS

In response to the terrorist attacks of September 11, 2001, then President George W. Bush authorized the indefinite detention and military trial of suspected terrorists or enemy combatants at "an appropriate location" outside the United States (3 C.F.R. § 918, 2002). As a result, roughly 500 prisoners had been detained at the U.S. military base in Guantánamo Bay, Cuba. Although the U.S. government denied these detainees access to the U.S. courts, the U.S. Supreme Court ruled in 2004 that enemy combatants had the right to have their detentions reviewed by an impartial judge as part of the guarantees of both due process and *habeas corpus* (*Hamdi v. Rumsfeld*, 2004; *Rasul v. Bush*, 2004). In response to these ruling
Status Review Tribunals (CSRTs) to revi
Guantánamo. These were *ex parte* pr
the detainee or his or her counsel pres
in *Hamdan v. Rumsfeld* (2006) becaus
Code of Military Justice and part of t
governing the treatment of prisoners of
these grounds, it declined to consider t
the CSRT process violated the *habeas*
of the U.S. Constitution.

Congress responded to the *Hamd*
military commissions to hold CSRTs w
included in the tribunals originally creat
cally provided that the decisions of the
habeas corpus. Congress extended thi
Act of 2006. It provides similar CSRTs f
batants anywhere in the world. In *Bou*
the justices on the U.S. Supreme Cour
amounted to an "unconstitutional susp

Criminal Justice Problem Solving: THE DEATH PENALTY

The most controversial current issue pertinent to criminal punishment deals with the death penalty. The very existence of the death penalty raises philosophical questions about the right of the government to take a human life. Concerns about the death penalty are varied, including:

1. The disproportionate use of the death penalty against members of minority groups;
2. Debates about the death penalty's effectiveness as a deterrent;
3. Concerns about whether or not defendants receive adequate legal representation;
4. Strong international pressure to abolish capital punishment; and
5. Fear of executing innocent persons.

Drawing on the ideas raised throughout thi
ment both for *and* against the death penalt
disagreement and debate? Go to the library
these issues.

How would you answer what is quickly beco
facing the criminal justice system: what sh
penalty?

PROBLEM SOLVING EXERCISES. Each chapter closes with a criminal justice policy issue that relates to ideas presented within the chapter. These are current questions or controversies that lawmakers and practitioners in the field consider as part of their work. They are the types of real issues that new criminal justice graduates may encounter in the field.

Criminal Justice Problem Solving: JUVENILE GANGS

Assume that you have been assigned as the supervisor to a gang task force. There have been numerous complaints from concerned community members, teachers, and parents that gang members have been recruiting extensively in your city. The police chief has requested that you and your officers take immediate action to rectify the situation. Based on your knowledge of criminal deviance and criminological theory, design a juvenile gang prevention program. In your prevention strategy, address the following by drawing upon the theories described in this chapter:

What factors might influence juveniles to join gangs?

What factors prevent juveniles from joining gangs? That is, why do some juveniles not join gangs?

Based on your responses to the preceding, what kind of program(s) could reduce the likelihood that juveniles will join gangs?

FOUNDATIONS OF
CRIMINAL
JUSTICE

Photo Essay: Policing Intimate Partner Violence

The practice of criminal justice requires striking many balances. We must safeguard society while maintaining individual rights. We must balance ethical decisions, effective resolution of problems, and cost efficiency. And we must balance competing philosophies about what the law ought to accomplish. The real decisions about how to strike these balances often lie with the criminal justice practitioners in the field, who must make judgments (often quickly) about how to resolve a situation. In many ways, this makes police officers, correctional officers, attorneys, and judges the philosophers of justice who profoundly shape how criminal justice is practiced in the United States. However, their work is no easy—or simple—task.

Consider the difficulties in police responses to incidents of intimate partner violence. Intimate partner violence refers to assaults between persons in intimate relationships, such as those who are dating, married, and so on. Determining the proper response has been a challenge for the criminal justice system.

Participants in this candlelight vigil remember the victims of intimate partner violence. The average yearly rate of intimate partner violence is 4.2 per 1,000 for females and 0.9 per 1,000 for males (Bureau of Justice Statistics, 2011). In addition to harming victims, police officers regard intimate partner violence calls as among the most dangerous calls to which they may respond (Hess & Wrobleski, 2003). Why do you think intimate partner violence calls pose risks to police officers? Can you think of any policies or tactics that would reduce the risk to officers?

Police officers responding to an incident of intimate partner violence must consider how to address the crime that has been committed. In the past, law enforcement did not treat intimate partner violence as a serious problem. This changed in the mid- to late twentieth century. One key event was a 1984 court case in which a police department was held accountable for failing to adequately protect a victim of intimate partner violence (*Thurman v. City of Torrington*). As intimate partner violence has come to be recognized as a serious problem, one question has been what the best or most appropriate police response should be. Criminologists Lawrence Sherman and Richard Berk (1984) published a study that attempted to shed light on this question. In Minneapolis, police officers responding to intimate partner violence calls were randomly assigned to make one of three responses (each of which some officers had previously used) described in the following paragraphs.

The first potential response was mediation (left). Officers would attempt to mediate the dispute between the two parties, hoping to reach a nonviolent resolution that would dissipate the violence and address any conflicts. What do you think are the risks and benefits of this response? In what cases, if any, do you think it would be appropriate?

The second potential response was separation of the two parties. Officers would require that the abuser leave the home and not return for eight hours. In part, the rationale was that this would provide a cooling-off period for the abuser, which would lead to the cessation of violence. What do you think are the risks and benefits of this response? In what cases, if any, do you think it would be appropriate?

The third potential response was the arrest of the abuser. Officers were required to automatically arrest the abuser and charge him or her with a criminal offense. This was grounded in the idea that assault was assault, and it merited arrest regardless of whether it occurred in the home or elsewhere. What do you think are the risks and benefits of this response? In what cases, if any, do you think it would be appropriate?

Sherman and Berk's (1984) research found that arrest was the only option that led to a reduction in reoffending. Based in part on the study, many states passed laws requiring an arrest to be made in cases of intimate partner violence. However, subsequent research has found that a variety of factors may affect whether or not arrest actually leads to reductions in repeat offending—for instance, arrest appears to reduce offending for employed offenders more than it does for those who are unemployed (see Dixon, 2008).

Assume you are a police officer responding to an incident of intimate partner violence. Further assume that in such cases the law allows you to make an arrest, but that you are not *required* to do so. If you do not make an arrest, you are required to file a report explaining why you did not, and if you are called back within 12 hours to another incident involving the same persons, then you *must* make an arrest (see Arrest for Violation of Order, 2010). As a police officer, this leaves you with tremendous discretion. You have just arrived on the scene of an incident. What factors do you consider as you determine how you might respond to a case of intimate partner violence?

Chapter 1 introduces some of the factors that shape decision making in criminal justice. These include viewing criminal justice as a system, a profession, a bureaucracy, a moral agent, and an academic discipline. In addition, the chapter defines the concept of crime and explores its prevalence in modern American society.

Introducing Crime and Criminal Justice

Policing, then and now. What do you think the future of criminal justice will hold?

Key Terms

criminal justice
criminology
emergency management
forensic science
homeland security
law and legal studies
security administration
victimology
criminal justice system
nonsystem
discretion
profession
craft
bureaucratic agency
morality
codes of ethics
Law Enforcement
   Assistance Administration
   (LEAA)

Law Enforcement Education
   Program (LEEP)
deviance
nullum crimen sine lege
nulla poena sine lege
crime
socially constructed
mala prohibita
mala in se
blue laws
infractions
prohibition
typical crime
Uniform Crime Report (UCR)
National Incident-Based Reporting
   System (NIBRS)
rate
clearance rate
social capital

National Crime Victimization
   Survey (NCVS)
dark figure of crime
self-report study
Youth Risk Behavior Study (YRBS)
DNA databases
nolle prosequi
initial appearance
pretrial release
preliminary hearing
grand jury
indictment
information
arraignment
nolo contendere
bench trial
jail
prison
parole

Key People

Max Weber
J. Edgar Hoover
Ronald Dworkin
August Vollmer
Orlando W. Wilson

Nils Christie
Marcus Felson
Jeffrey Reiman
Franklin Zimring
Gordon Hawkins

CASE STUDY

How Would You Spend $10 Million?

Assume that you have been elected to the state legislature (congratulations). The public is clamoring for you to "do something" about crime. Statistics indicate that the amount of crime in your state has been steady—no dramatic increases, but no dramatic decreases either. You will soon have to decide how to allocate state funds for criminal justice. You have the following seven options for spending $10 million.

1. Construct a new prison that will hold 188 inmates (see Clear, Cole, & Reisig, 2009, for information on the cost of prison construction).
2. Allocate the funds to local police departments to purchase equipment and to hire 100 new officers across the state, whose primary task will be the enforcement of drug laws.
3. Fund early education (preschool) programs for low-income families who would not otherwise be able to afford them. Over time, children who

participate in these programs are 40% less likely to be arrested for a violent crime by the time they are 18 and are 80% less likely to become chronic offenders in adulthood (see van der Does, Newman, & Dawson, 2004).

4. Hire additional judges, public defenders, and prosecuting attorneys so cases can proceed more quickly through the court system.

5. Fund the placement and monitoring of security cameras (also known as CCTV, or "closed circuit television" cameras) on city streets. Cameras are associated with a 7% reduction in crime on the streets where they are placed (Welsh & Farrington, 2009).

6. Allocate the funds to state crime labs so that DNA evidence may be processed more rapidly to aid in identifying offenders in unsolved cases. Currently, there are not sufficient resources to process all DNA evidence, which has resulted in a considerable backlog of cases. One study estimated that up to 550,000 unsolved crimes, nationwide, could be solved if more resources are allocated to DNA testing (Pratt, Gaffney, Lovrich, & Johnson, 2006).

7. Use the funds to create a Positive Futures sports program based on similar programs in England. The program, designed for at-risk youth aged 10 to 16, provides a variety of sporting opportunities while also promoting education, leadership, and mentoring. Research from England suggests that the program is effective in reducing crime (Sport England, 2002).

State funds are limited, so you can select only one of these options. It would not be feasible to "mix and match" by combining options, as doing so would minimize the overall effectiveness and return on investment.

> How would you rank order these options? Which one do you think is best and should receive the highest funding priority? Which do you think should receive the lowest funding priority? Why? What factors have shaped your answers? Compare your answers with those of your classmates.
>
> Realistically, most states don't have an extra $10 million to throw around. Look back at your top funding priority. Would you be willing to cut other items in the state budget (e.g., roads, education, social services, public health, state parks) to fund it? Why or why not? If so, what would you cut? Why?

Introducing Criminal Justice

FOCUSING QUESTION 1.1

What is criminal justice?

At its most basic, **criminal justice** may be defined as society's response to crime. The response may come after the crime has occurred while an offender is being processed through the criminal justice system, such as options number 1 and 4 in the scenario at the beginning of the chapter. It may be to facilitate the investigation of criminal activity, leading to the apprehension of offenders, such as options number 2 and 6 in the opening scenario. Or it may be designed to prevent crime from happening in the first place, such as options number 3, 5, and 7 in the opening scenario. Criminal justice also includes other elements, such as maintaining order in society and providing community services (e.g., police officers giving a presentation to an elementary school about bicycle safety).

While the police, the legal system, and correctional agencies play a key role in criminal justice, so do members of the community. Whether through volunteering in youth crime prevention programs, organizing neighborhood cleanup days and neighborhood watch programs, or advocating for policy change, community members are coproducers of criminal justice. Increasingly, criminal justice agencies seek community involvement, including such programs as community-oriented policing (Skogan & Hartnett, 1997; see Chapter 11 in this text), restorative justice (Hahn, 1998; see Chapter 10 in this text), and justice reinvestment (Tucker & Cadora, 2003; see Chapter 13 in this text). In each of these programs, community residents work with criminal justice agencies to determine priorities, goals, and solutions to community crime problems.

Again, criminal justice pertains to society's response to crime. The study of criminal justice is an interdisciplinary endeavor that overlaps with several related areas of inquiry, including the following.

- **Criminology** is the study of why persons commit crime. This is useful to criminal justice because understanding why crime occurs can aid in developing prevention or rehabilitation programs. Criminology also studies and attempts to explain trends in the amount and type of criminal activity.
- **Emergency management** is the study of how to prepare for, respond to, and recover from disaster or crisis situations. Criminal justice agencies are often at the forefront of emergency response operations.
- **Forensic science** is the application of scientific principles to cases progressing through the legal system. Most forensic science work is done in laboratories, where scientists analyze material that was collected by others (police officers, investigators, or evidence technicians) at crime scenes. Forensic science aids in identifying offenders and in making necessary evidence available for trials.
- **Homeland security** involves identifying and responding to threats to national security with a particular emphasis on terrorism. Criminal justice agencies often conduct investigations and disseminate information pertinent to homeland security and respond to identified concerns.
- **Law and legal studies** is a broad subject area, typically presented in law schools or in prelaw programs. In many ways, criminal law forms the basis for criminal justice because when laws are broken, the criminal justice process begins.

- **Security administration** focuses extensively on the identification and management of risk in residential or commercial settings. The use of private security has grown over time (Cunningham, Strauchs, & Van Meter, 1990) and has much in common with public criminal justice professions.
- **Victimology** is the study of why persons or entities (e.g., businesses) become victims of crime. This can aid in developing crime prevention and risk management programs.

As you can see, there are many potential issues that are relevant to the field of criminal justice. In turn, there are many careers that are related to criminal justice. Box 1.1 provides some tips for planning a career in criminal justice.

BOX 1.1.

CRIMINAL JUSTICE CAREER TIPS

Preparing for a career in criminal justice requires careful planning. Start thinking now about how you can begin working toward your career goals, including the following activities:

- *Internships:* If you have the opportunity, seek an internship with an agency of interest. An internship will allow you to witness firsthand the expectations of the job. It will also give you experience that you can reference when you begin to go on job interviews.
- *Visit Your Institution's Career Center:* If your institution has a Career Center, stop in and visit. Let the staff know your career interests. The Career Center can also provide assistance in your job search, in preparing a résumé, and more.
- *Attend Career Fairs:* Many colleges offer career fairs, which employers attend to recruit potential employees. Often, criminal justice agencies are represented. This is a great opportunity to speak with the recruiters and obtain valuable information about job opportunities and application requirements for their agencies.

Also remember that you need to make yourself marketable to criminal justice agencies. Here are some ways to do so.

- *Work Toward Physical Fitness:* Some criminal justice agencies (especially in the field of law enforcement) require applicants to pass a physical fitness test as part of the hiring process. Don't wait until your senior year to begin a fitness program, including a healthy diet. This should be started immediately and maintained throughout your career. Also, if you smoke—quit! Many criminal justice agencies now require employees to maintain a "tobacco-free" lifestyle.
- *Study a Foreign Language:* Become proficient in a foreign language that is valued by criminal justice agencies. Take a sequence of courses in the same foreign language to acquire proficiency. Agencies may differ in the languages they most value, so do some research to see which language would be most beneficial for you to study.
- *Enroll in Elective Coursework Related to Criminal Justice:* If you have the opportunity to take elective (nonrequired) courses, select those which are related to criminal justice, generally, or to your desired career, specifically. This could include, but is certainly not limited to, courses in constitutional law, first aid, geographic information systems, physical anthropology, professional

ethics, psychology, martial arts, sociology, and much more. Your advisor can help you select meaningful courses to supplement those required for your criminal justice program.

• *Obtain Leadership Experience:* Join clubs and organizations. This not only includes student organizations in the field of criminal justice but also those in other areas of interest. Pursue opportunities to hold offices, to do community service, and to build your leadership skills. Employers value this type of experience—but it's also something that you can enjoy and to which you can make a meaningful contribution during your college career.

• *Consider Graduate Education:* It's not too soon to think about attending graduate school. Many criminal justice agencies prefer (or require) applicants with a graduate degree; it can also be beneficial when seeking promotion within an agency. To be admitted to a graduate program, you will need to maintain high academic standards throughout your undergraduate experience.

• *Stay Out of Trouble:* It is likely that, as part of the job application process, you will undergo an extensive background investigation (including a polygraph examination). During the hiring process, a background investigator will inquire as to your previous life experiences, including your frequency and duration of legal and illegal drug and alcohol use; any prior record of illegal activity, whether or not it resulted in arrest (from childhood to current day); and your financial status (e.g., Do you live within your means? Are you in debt?); to name just a few.

• *Be Careful with Social Networks:* Be extremely careful about what material you place on social networking sites (e.g., Facebook, MySpace). Employers may check your site as part of their background investigation! Remember, the entire world can see and read what you place on the web as well as what others post to your site(s).

Visit Dr. Thomas O'Connor's website (http://www.drtomoconnor.com/employ.htm) about criminal justice employment. Research a career that you find interesting. What did you learn about it?

What do you most hope to learn about criminal justice? What topics most interest you? Why?

Are there any criminal justice career areas that interest you more than others? Why?

Perspectives on Criminal Justice

FOCUSING QUESTION 1.2

How do understandings of criminal justice vary based on whether it is viewed as a system, a profession, a bureaucracy, a moral agent, or an academic discipline?

As a complex societal response to crime, there are multiple ways we can view criminal justice. The following discussion identifies several theoretical lenses that may be used to do so. Each represents one way that criminal justice professionals can understand their work or that criminal justice scholars can understand criminal justice processes and policies. The purpose is not to suggest that any single approach is better or worse than another but instead to see how, taken together, these viewpoints provide a broad context for the field of criminal justice in both theory and in practice. A consideration of these perspectives can also help us understand disagreements that sometimes occur about justice policy based on differences of opinion about how the criminal justice system should be viewed.

CRIMINAL JUSTICE AS SYSTEM

You will often hear of the **criminal justice system**. This refers to the ways criminal justice agencies—that is, the police, courts, and corrections—work together to process a case from start to finish. The concept of a system suggests several important ideas. First, labeling criminal justice as a system implies that there is a process through which all cases progress, defined by a series of steps or activities that must occur in each case. Second, the system is perceived as orderly and predictable, meaning that the steps do not change and that there is clear communication between agencies as a case is processed. Third, viewing criminal justice from a systems perspective suggests that agencies carefully collaborate to ensure that cases are processed efficiently, which also requires that all agencies share a common set of goals and philosophies about what criminal justice should (or should not) do and how it should (or should not) operate. A diagram of the criminal justice system is included in Figure 1.5 (Chapter Appendix 1), with accompanying explanation from the Bureau of Justice Statistics (2010). You should take some time to familiarize yourself with this model.

There are advantages and disadvantages to a systems perspective. The primary advantage is that it does outline the basic criminal justice process with a common vocabulary that professionals within the criminal justice system do indeed use.

On the other hand, some scholars have argued that criminal justice is a **nonsystem** (see Cohn, 1974, p. 32). There are (at least) three observations that may support this view. First, in reality, criminal justice agencies are not neatly networked into a cohesive single unit; indeed, there is no single authority that oversees all of criminal justice practice in the United States. In fact, there are sometimes tensions between agencies. Geller and Morris (1992) observe that, while better in recent years than in the past, there have been conflicts between law enforcement agencies over which agency should have primary responsibility for an investigation, which agency should receive more resources, and so on.

Second, although the systems model appears fairly rigid, it is important to recognize that there is discretion at every decision point. **Discretion** refers to a criminal justice professional's ability to decide how the case should proceed at each turn rather than mandating a certain outcome. Of course, no laws or rules can be violated in making discretionary decisions, but criminal justice professionals usually have fairly wide latitude. For instance, a police officer can decide whether to give a speeding motorist a ticket or a warning; a prosecuting attorney can decide what the formal criminal charge should be in a case; a judge can decide whether to sentence an offender to prison or probation. Because each case presents different circumstances, it is generally accepted that discretion is an unavoidable part of criminal justice, but this also means that the process is not quite as systematic as it might initially appear.

Finally, agreement does not exist on philosophies or system goals among all criminal justice agencies or even among all persons within an agency. For instance, some judges may believe strongly in working to rehabilitate offenders, whereas others may believe equally strongly in sending offenders to harsh prison environments. Assume that a judge believes in sentencing offenders to prison time because he believes that prison environments ought to be harsh environments focused on punishment. However, the warden of the prison to which offenders are sent could decide to offer counseling and recreational programming to reform (rather than just punish) inmates regardless of what the judge thinks should happen. Diversity of ideas can and does exist within criminal justice.

Competing goals are not necessarily bad (and full agreement on goals may be impossible). In fact, discussions and debates about competing goals could be helpful for the criminal justice system, as they might generate new ideas for policies or programs. These new ideas can lead to innovative and effective strategies, advancing criminal justice as a result—due, in part, to the initial lack of consensus about the criminal justice system (see generally Wright, 1981).

CRIMINAL JUSTICE AS PROFESSION

The term *profession* is often used as a synonym for "job" or "career." However, it is not entirely accurate to do so. To qualify as a **profession**, a career field must meet a set of criteria, including those that follow (from Henry, 1995; Wilson, 1989). Well-established professions, such as law and medicine, meet each criterion listed here.

- *Require a common educational background, generally associated with a college degree.* In fact, the completion of required education is often viewed as the primary credential for entry to the profession.
- *Adopt an ethical code to guide professional practice.* Professional fields generally come with a great deal of discretionary decision-making powers. A code of ethics can help guide discretionary decisions and establish the broad values and principles of the profession.
- *Engage in specialized tasks that cannot be accomplished by those outside the profession.* Through their education and experience, professionals acquire expertise in their fields that is not easily available to others. As a result, they are the experts upon whom others must rely when their professional services are required.

- *Contain internal mechanisms for quality control.* Accreditation may be available in which members of the profession themselves certify that a particular agency has met specified standards of quality. Likewise, individual members of a profession may need to be certified or licensed—by other professionals in the field—to show that they meet their profession's standards.
- *Be members of the profession for their lifetime, unless they are removed due to professional misconduct.* This does not mean that persons will work in the same office or for the same agency for the duration of their careers (although some do). Rather, it signifies that once persons have entered the field, they have the rights and privileges to continue their work within it.
- *Acquire prestige based on their status as a member of the profession.* Being a member of a profession carries prestige in the community. The profession, as a whole, generally carries respect, and members of the profession are likewise presumed to receive respect.

There has long been debate about whether criminal justice occupations are (or should be) professions. In the past, criminal justice occupations have often been regarded as **crafts** based on the view that "it is best to have the majority of training/mentoring undertaken by experienced officers in a master/apprentice arrangement" (Murray, 2005, p. 352). The benefit of such an arrangement is that it allows experienced practitioners to disseminate their knowledge in an applied setting. For this reason, even in professions, there is sometimes a period of mentoring or field training to orient a new employee to the job.

Some concerns arise, however, if criminal justice were to be treated purely as a craft with the majority of training conducted in on-the-job mentorships. The educational background (focused on theory as well as practice, so professionals can understand the "why" of the job in addition to the "how to"), emphasis on ethics, and standards for peer review that underlie a profession can go a long way toward guiding both discretionary decision making and the development and implementation of effective justice policy. This can then help to promote public trust and confidence in the criminal justice system and its processes.

CRIMINAL JUSTICE AS BUREAUCRACY

As noted earlier, the criminal justice system (or nonsystem, if you prefer) is comprised of a variety of police, court, and correctional agencies. Those agencies spend approximately $214 billion per year, with a workforce of more than 2.4 million employees (Bureau of Justice Statistics, 2008). Criminal justice agencies are usually organized along a bureaucratic model. As defined by sociologist Max Weber ([1946] 1997), a **bureaucratic agency** is governed by many rules, policies, and procedures; is organized in a hierarchy with clear lines of supervision of employees; requires substantial amounts of paperwork to document activities; and requires training of employees. This is true of criminal justice agencies. All have fairly detailed statements of policy and procedure as well as rules to govern the agency's business. There is generally a rank structure with a leader (e.g., chief in a police department, warden in a prison), with midlevel managers (e.g., sergeants), and with line employees who are responsible for conducting most of the day-to-day business and interactions with the public or agency clients (e.g., officers). Paperwork is unavoidable within criminal justice, as there is seemingly a form or report for every action, all of which must be completed before the end of a shift. Furthermore, all employees must undergo training when they are hired and continue attending annual training sessions throughout their careers.

At one time, bureaucracies were considered separate from, or even above and immune to, politics. As Woodrow Wilson ([1887] 1997) wrote, "The field of administration is a field of business. It is removed from the hurry and strife of politics" (p. 20). This was understood as an advantage because it would allow bureaucracies to focus on their business without the worry of changing political contexts or the desires of politicians. The result was believed to be an effective bureaucracy driven by the agency's vision rather than political desires. However, Goodnow ([1900] 1997) observed that "practical political necessity makes impossible the consideration of the function of politics apart from that of administration" (p. 29). A yearly justice system expenditure of $214 billion from taxpayer funds can hardly avoid being political. Out of practical necessity, then, bureaucracies must be involved in politics. For instance, agencies must advocate for the legislature to allocate sufficient resources to them and can also lobby the legislature to enact policies and laws that benefit the agency.

The nature of bureaucracy contributes to understanding why there are different goals among criminal justice agencies. The accumulation of an agency's decisions and communications creates the agency's culture, "a persistent, patterned way of thinking about the central tasks of and human relationships within an organization" (Wilson, 1989, p. 91). Agency culture is sometimes political, responding to pressures of the time. Other times, agency culture is entirely internal and can shape how an organization goes about its business. Wilson (1989) explains why, until the 1980s, the Federal Bureau of Investigation resisted adding drug enforcement to its agenda.

> There were several reasons . . . but one was that these cases seemed to require FBI agents to behave in ways that judged by the standards of the bureau's culture were deemed too risky . . . [The agency's work was] in accordance with the strictest rules governing arrests, searches, and interrogations and in ways that permitted the agent to conform precisely to the image (that is, the mission) of the FBI that J. Edgar Hoover had been at such pains to develop—clean-cut, above board, nonpartisan . . . Undercover work [required for narcotics investigations] is not only risky for the agent, it is risky for the

bureau—it exposes it to the possibility that in going undercover an agent will break the law, become corrupted, or otherwise create embarrassment or controversy for the FBI. For decades the culture of the bureau led many of its key officials to oppose using undercover measures and for that reason (among others) to oppose investigating narcotics cases. (p. 108)

Things did change for the FBI, however, when "in 1982 the Reagan administration reorganized drug enforcement . . . by placing [the Drug Enforcement Administration] under the control of the FBI" (Wilson, 1989, p. 267). After a brief clash between the two agencies' organizational cultures, collaboration began, for which both were stronger. Although the DEA no longer reports to the FBI, the historical example illustrates the role that organizational culture can play in agency operations.

There is sometimes conflict between bureaucracies, especially if they have different organizational cultures; likewise, conflict can develop between professions and bureaucracies. Professionals would rather work in the system without the constraints of extensive rules limiting their professional choices and paperwork documenting (or requesting permission for) every move, much less dealing with politics. Yet, the bureaucratic model is the reality and, as such, poses some constraints within which the criminal justice system and its employees must work.

CRIMINAL JUSTICE AS MORAL AGENT

It is impossible to separate the study of criminal justice from the study of moral philosophy. Quite simply, criminal justice practitioners—whether working in a system or a nonsystem, as bureaucrats or as professionals—make decisions that both influence and are influenced by notions of morality. At its most basic, **morality** is about what behaviors and actions are right and wrong in a society's view. Behaviors that run afoul of moral judgments are labeled as deviant (see the discussion of crime that follows) and, in some cases, may be made illegal.

Morality goes beyond the concerns that are codified into a profession's statement of ethics. **Codes of ethics** are specific to the working environment in which professionals find themselves, whereas moral questions are broader and of greater interest to society as a whole.

Consider a debate about needle exchange programs, in which intravenous drug users can exchange dirty syringes and needles for clean ones. Needle exchange involves questions about morality on both sides of the issue. For instance, opponents could argue that such programs lend tacit approval to drug use, which they view as morally wrong. Supporters could argue that it is morally wrong to ignore the preventable public health risks (through transmission of blood-borne diseases, including HIV/AIDS) posed by dirty needles. Or the sides could compromise, arguing that rehabilitation and drug treatment are morally right and that needle exchange programs could provide a platform for offering treatment to persons addicted to drugs (see Kirp & Bayer, 1999; Sharp, 2005). These debates could result in new laws and policies allowing needle exchange, or they could lead to an affirmation of existing laws and policies that do not allow needle exchange.

Therefore, decisions about which policies to enact or which laws to create often involve moral questions. This is because these decisions are fundamentally about attempting to define (or regulate) conduct that is viewed as right or wrong. Criminal justice agencies then become responsible for implementing those policies and enacting those laws, meaning that the criminal justice system is, in part, responsible for enforcing socially accepted notions of what is or is not moral. Of course, this begs a larger question, which is how moral decisions are made in the context of justice policy. Future chapters will explore this issue more fully.

At the same time, as described earlier, there are many points at which criminal justice practitioners—police officers, judges, correctional officers, and so on—can exercise substantial amounts of discretionary decision making. Discretion underlies the criminal justice system and its processes. Discretion likewise involves moral philosophy. Discretionary decisions are a profound part of how society prioritizes and resolves questions involving morality—focused on what's right, what's wrong, and the most appropriate way to resolve dilemmas. But how does a police officer or other justice practitioner balance this complexity?

In exercising this discretion, the police may be considered "streetcorner politicians" (Muir 1977:271), "street level bureaucrats" (Lipsky 1980:3) or problem solvers (Goldstein 1990). Therefore, the exercise of the law enforcement function necessarily requires officers to think and make decisions, rather than acting solely based on a set of formalized rules. And, in the course of that decision-making process, officers become philosophers.

In the 2000 New York Council for the Humanities Scholar of the Year Lecture, legal scholar Ronald Dworkin commented about judges: "In the ordinary course of their work, judges make decisions about many matters that are also, at least on the surface, the subjects of a great philosophical literature" (2000:para 1). Could we not extend his arguments to police officers? After all, police officers make judgments about issues of liberty (and its curtailment), about what acts and persons are more deserving of sanction than others, and more. (Owen, Fradella, Burke, & Joplin, 2006, pp. 6–7)

The role of the criminal justice system in addressing moral dilemmas is a substantial informal power that merits considerable thought. Indeed, the theory and practice of criminal justice involve careful thinking about philosophical topics. You will find that this theme appropriately runs throughout this book.

CRIMINAL JUSTICE AS ACADEMIC DISCIPLINE

In an article about criminology, Nicole Rafter (2010) laments the lack of historical study of the field, observing that "knowing our history teaches us about not only where our ideas came from but also where we are going and who we are" (pp. 342–343). The same is true of criminal justice. By reviewing a history of the field of criminal justice, we can refresh knowledge about past theories and ideas and place current situations in their historical context. Rather than viewing current issues in a vacuum, we can see how the past has informed the present and consider long-term trends in the production of knowledge. For this reason, many of the chapters in this book will provide historical background to current areas of study.

In this introductory chapter, we consider the development of criminal justice as an academic discipline and its importance. The earliest roots of criminal justice education were in the 1920s, when a very small number of universities began offering criminal justice courses and programs. These early programs were primarily motivated by a desire to promote police professionalism and were established through the leadership of two progressive police chiefs who became college professors: August Vollmer (former chief of Berkeley, California) and Orlando W. Wilson (former chief of Wichita, Kansas). Over time, the number of programs and faculty increased somewhat (for a good history, see Morn, 1995), but it was not until the 1970s that dramatic growth occurred. As part of a major 1968 crime bill, Congress created the **Law Enforcement Assistance Administration (LEAA)**, an agency designed to distribute federal funds to improve criminal justice administration and practice in the United States. The LEAA created the **Law Enforcement Education Program (LEEP)** to fund college-level criminal justice education. In the decade of the 1970s, LEEP funded over 300,000 persons to complete college coursework and degrees in criminal justice. Through this influx of money, "LEEP helped create a fast growing segment of academia by backing the establishment of criminal justice training departments in universities nationwide" (Gest, 2001, p. 159). In 1979, LEEP was restructured for political reasons and disappeared soon thereafter (Gest, 2001). However, its legacy remains a long-lasting one, as criminal justice is now a program commonly offered at many colleges and universities.

Note the use of the word *training* in the preceding quotation. In the 1970s, many criminal justice classes focused more on vocational training than on an academic study of criminal justice theories and policy debates. At the time, criminal justice was still a new and growing academic discipline with only a limited body of theory and scholarship. However, since that time, criminal justice has matured into a robust academic discipline. It draws upon a variety of theoretical ideas to offer sophisticated coursework and to produce innovative scholarship that helps us better understand the foundations of criminal justice policy and practice. This transition is one that helps criminal justice move from craft to profession, as described earlier.

This change—from vocational education to theory-driven academic discipline—is also important because the scientific study of theoretical perspectives on crime and justice can help shape the development of effective criminal justice policy. These theoretical perspectives are advanced by the work of criminal justice scholars. Being able to understand the theoretical basis for why certain policies work but others don't, or being able to understand the theoretical basis for how (and why) the criminal justice system functions, can also help justice practitioners better understand their roles, responsibilities, and tasks. For instance, is it not useful for those enforcing the law to appreciate the reasons for having law in the first place, to better understand their role in pursuing justice? In addition, having a sound theoretical understanding of criminal justice issues can also help practitioners and policy makers design the most effective policies to respond to or prevent crime. For instance, a consideration of the respective roles of law, rehabilitation, public health, morality, and more could better help practitioners understand how to approach the needle exchange debate described in the previous section.

The development of criminal justice as an academic area of study has increased the number of persons—including public and private researchers and faculty at colleges and universities—who can conduct studies and develop theoretical understandings about crime and justice. As you continue reading this text, you will see multiple citations to the work of these scholars; we encourage you to review the research related to your areas of interest.

Whether viewed from the lens of system, profession, bureaucracy, moral agent, or academic discipline, criminal justice is fundamentally about how we address the problem of crime in society. Taken together, the five perspectives described above illustrate the ways in which criminal justice approaches its sometimes daunting task.

> Consider the policy option that you identified as most preferred from the scenario at the beginning of the chapter. How could each of the five perspectives described above impact or influence the policy?
>
> What goals do you think the criminal justice system should meet? How can each of the five perspectives promote (or challenge) the accomplishment of those goals?

Defining Crime

FOCUSING QUESTION 1.3

In what ways can we understand the concept of "crime"?

Recall the definition of criminal justice as society's response to crime. This naturally raises the question, "What is crime?" In this chapter, we introduce the concept of crime. In subsequent chapters, you will learn more about how specific criminal offenses are defined.

WHAT CRIME IS

It is important to distinguish crime from deviance. **Deviance** refers to any behavior that runs counter to society's expectations, beliefs, standards, or values (see Chapters 4 and 5). This may include acts ranging in seriousness from chewing gum in class, to talking too loudly in the library, to motor vehicle theft, to murder. However, not all deviant behaviors are crimes. There is an important principle that underlies an understanding of crime. As with many legal principles, it is expressed in Latin, the traditional language of the law: *nullum crimen sine lege, nulla poena sine lege*. Translated, the statement is that there can be no crime without a law, and there can be no punishment without a law. A deviant act is a crime (and can be punished by the criminal justice system) *only* if there is a specific law against it. Therefore, a **crime** is any behavior that the government chooses to define as such by passing a law against it. For instance, if there is no law that prohibits chewing gum in class, then it is not a crime, and a person may not be arrested, prosecuted, or sent to prison for it (although a teacher could impose routine classroom discipline, such as withdrawing recess privileges, if gum chewing violated a school rule). On the other hand, there is a law against murder, so a person who commits murder may be arrested, prosecuted, and sent to prison for that act.

One key task is for the government to determine which acts cause sufficient concern or are serious enough to define as criminal. Determining which deviant acts to criminalize requires substantial thought. Criminologist Nils Christie observed, "Crime does not exist. Only acts exist, acts often given different meanings within various social frameworks . . . Our challenge is to follow the destiny of acts through the universe of meanings . . . their meanings are created as [the acts] occur" (2004, pp. 3, 8).

Christie's argument is complex, but the basic idea is that there are many potentially deviant acts to consider. Some are simply viewed as unpleasant, but others are labeled as "crimes" under the law. Which acts are so labeled is based on what meaning society attaches to them. Therefore, societies decide which acts should or should not be defined as a crime, based on factors such as societal values, history, philosophies (such as those you will encounter in later chapters), and more. Another way of expressing this idea is to say that crime is **socially constructed**, meaning that societies construct their own understandings of which behaviors should be prohibited by law and defined as criminal. This is a significant point because it helps explain why we see variations over time and places in terms of what is or is not defined as a crime.

In explaining why certain acts are criminalized, scholars sometimes draw a distinction between (more important Latin phrases) *mala prohibita* and *mala in se* crimes. Crimes labeled as *mala in se* are acts that have been criminalized because they are inherently bad; that is, the characteristics of the act itself lead to near universal agreement that it is wrong by its very nature. These are typically the more serious crimes, including murder, rape, robbery, assault, and so on. Crimes labeled as *mala prohibita* are not viewed as inherently bad but rather are crimes only because the legislature (or public) decided that they should be. That is, the act is not so bad that it *must* be illegal, but a decision was made to criminalize it nonetheless. These often include victimless crimes (so named because persons consent to these activities) such as illegal gambling, prostitution, drug possession, and so on.

However, this distinction is far from precise, leading some to question its usefulness. Furthermore, interpretations can change over time, as "crimes which were originally solely *mala prohibita* may come to be universally recognized as *mala in se*" (Wolfe, 1981, p. 139). This could be the case when an act is initially defined as a *mala prohibita* offense, but over time, society comes to view the act as being *mala in se* and inherently wrong, even if they did not originally. As an example, domestic violence was once, while illegal, viewed as a private matter into which the law did not need to intrude (*mala prohibita*); today, it is viewed as a form of assault (*mala in se*) to which the police have an obligation to respond (Friedman, 1993). Likewise, crimes that were once viewed as *mala in se* can, over time, come to be viewed as *mala prohibita;* laws against such acts are sometimes even abolished. For instance, at one time, **blue laws** (the origin of the name is debated, but these laws required businesses to be closed and prohibited other activities on Sundays) were viewed as very serious moral imperatives (*mala in se*) with strict penalties for violation. Over time, however, blue laws were repealed as perceptions of the issue changed (Laband & Heinbuch, 1987).

In short, crimes are acts that are prohibited by the laws of a country, state, city, and so forth. Legislators and the public must consider which acts they want to define as crimes and which acts they do not. In this way, each society defines its own concept of crime. In the United States, there are a series of constitutional limitations on what can and cannot be made criminal. You will learn about these limitations as well as how specific criminal offenses are actually defined in Chapter 9.

WHAT CRIME IS NOT

When reading the preceding section, perhaps you thought that chewing gum in class isn't deviant and should never be defined as a crime. That is an entirely reasonable position to take, and it illustrates a lesson drawn from the discussion of crime—namely, that *definitions of crime are not universal*. Even within the United States, there are variations. Consider physician-assisted suicide as an example, in which physicians prescribe a lethal dose of medications to terminally ill patients who wish to end their lives (for a case study exploring the issues involved, see Kade, 2000).

In 1994, voters in the state of Oregon approved the Death with Dignity Act, which decriminalized physician-assisted suicide. As long as physicians follow specified procedural guidelines, they may prescribe medications that allow terminally ill patients to end their lives. There is no criminal penalty for physicians who do so (Gostin, 2006). In 2008, Washington became the second state to pass such a law (Steinbrook, 2008). Therefore, while most states do not allow the practice (and in fact prohibit it under the law), voters in two states have determined that it is acceptable and should not be within the criminal realm.

Cross-national research has further confirmed that definitions of crime are not universal. Acts commonly defined as being *mala in se* were prohibited differently across cultures. For instance, a study (Brown, 1952) of 110 societies found variations in the definition of sexual crimes. The two offenses that were universally prohibited and punished by all societies studied were "incest" and "abduction of [a] married woman." Other acts included "rape of [an] unmarried woman" (p. 138; 95% of societies punished those who committed this act), adultery (89% of societies punished those who committed this act), and seducing a female who is not yet sexually mature (77% of societies punished those who committed this act). Therefore, research indicates that crime is not universally defined across societies or even within a single society, as different governing bodies may reach different decisions about what behaviors to make criminal.

As illustrated by blue laws and physician-assisted suicide, *definitions of crime are not static*. Rather, they are constantly changing. Each new legislative session, whether in city council chambers, state legislatures, or the U.S. Congress, brings new laws defining new crimes and new laws decriminalizing old crimes. For instance, some states have taken steps to decriminalize possession of small amounts of marijuana, particularly for medical reasons (Hoffmann & Weber, 2010). At the same time, many states have enacted legislation to create new traffic offenses (technically speaking, traffic offenses are known as **infractions**) that prohibit certain cell phone and text messaging behaviors while driving (Governors Highway Safety Association, 2010).

After it is defined under the law, *crime is not automatically enforced*. Simply deciding that something is a crime does not automatically put a stop to the behavior in question, nor does it guarantee that the law will be enforced as it was intended. For instance, research on **Prohibition** in the United States, during which alcohol was banned by a constitutional amendment from 1920 to 1933, found that at the state and local level,

> enforcement was never very intense. The states mostly refused to devote any significant effort to the matter; only 18 appropriated money for a prohibition unit, and three appropriated less than $1,000, a derisory amount even then. New York made 7,000 arrests in 1921, but this produced only 20 convictions. (MacCoun & Reuter, 2001, p. 159)

Criminal justice agencies, and primarily the police, are responsible for enforcing the law. But remember from earlier discussions that criminal justice agencies have a great deal of discretion in how they enforce the law. And the police must balance multiple tasks and prioritize them according to their importance and the availability of resources. Typically, the greatest attention is devoted to the most serious crimes and to those which generate the most concern among community members. Other crimes may be less vigorously enforced.

When thinking about crime, it is also important to consider the persons who commit criminal acts. There is sometimes a temptation to think that it is possible to label individuals as either "criminal" or "noncriminal" based on their behavior. This is erroneous, as *crime is not something that is committed by a few easily identifiable persons.* Criminologist Marcus Felson (2002) calls this "the not-me fallacy" (p. 6), arguing that "You don't have to be bad to do bad. Indeed, empirical research has virtually destroyed the claim that victims and offenders are from separate populations . . . Most people violate at least some laws sometimes" (pp. 6–7). Consider this: "When 1,700 New York City adults without a criminal record were surveyed, 99 per cent admitted to committing at least one of forty-nine offences listed in a questionnaire (the men averaged eighteen, and the women eleven, different *types* of offences)" (Gabor, 1994, p. 5). The opposite is also true; perhaps with the exception of fleeing a crime scene, it is not unusual for offenders to stop at red lights, to obey traffic regulations, and so forth. Quite simply, an offender does not violate all laws all the time (e.g., Sykes & Matza, 1957).

Jeffrey Reiman (2001) argues that the criminal justice system focuses much more heavily on what he calls "**typical crime**," meaning *"one-on-one harm—where harm means either physical injury or loss of something valuable or both"* (p. 69). Certainly, it is important to respond to typical crime, but Reiman also argues that the criminal justice system neglects the enforcement of white-collar crime (e.g., fraud, embezzlement, corporate crime, etc.), although yearly losses in white-collar crime are "more than *10,000 times* the total amount taken in all bank robberies . . . and more than *20 times* the total amount stolen in all thefts" (p. 121) that are reported to the police on a yearly basis. This suggests that crime and criminal behavior extend beyond the scope that we may originally imagine and beyond the street crimes that are portrayed so frequently by the media.

Understanding crime as a concept, then, requires careful analysis that goes beyond the notion that it's simply "against the law." That is why it is important for criminal justice practitioners to study both the substance and the philosophies that underlie the creation of criminal law.

What factors do you think might influence a society's decisions about what acts should or should not be defined as crimes?

Are there any acts currently defined as crimes that you do not think should be? Are there any acts that are currently legal that you think should be defined as crimes? Why? Does your answer illustrate any of the ideas presented here about what crime is or what crime is not?

The Extent of Crime

FOCUSING QUESTION 1.4

How much crime occurs in the United States?

Crime can be measured in a variety of ways. In this section, we consider official and unofficial crime data and what they tell us about the frequency of crime in the United States.

OFFICIAL CRIME DATA

The **Uniform Crime Report** (**UCR**) is the official source of crime data in the United States. The UCR is compiled by the Federal Bureau of Investigation (FBI). Law enforcement agencies report to the FBI a variety of crime data. The FBI then prepares a yearly report called *Crime in the United States,* which provides annual information about the amount of crime. The UCR counts the number of crimes but does not provide detailed information about those crimes. However, another FBI process, the **National Incident-Based Reporting System** (**NIBRS**), collects more detailed data about individual criminal events. The NIBRS data, which include information about the victim, offender, and incident, are available to researchers and government agencies so they can research issues related to crime and victimization. Here, the focus is on data from the UCR.

Figures 1.1 and 1.2 show how the violent crime rate and the property crime rate have changed over time. A **rate** is calculated by the following formula: (number of offenses ÷ population of area) × 100,000. The result allows us to determine how many offenses occur per 100,000 residents of an area. This, in turn, allows us to compare data over time and between different places by presenting them in a standardized format.

The offenses included in the violent crime rate are murder, rape, robbery (i.e., taking another person's property through the use or threat of force, such as a holdup), and aggravated assault. The offenses included in the property crime rate are burglary (i.e., breaking and entering), larceny (i.e., stealing another person's property, such as shoplifting), and motor vehicle theft (Federal Bureau of Investigation, 2009a). The graphs in Figures 1.1 and 1.2 tell an important story. In the 1990s, the violent crime rate decreased dramatically, and that decrease continued (though less dramatically) through the 2000s. Over the same time period, property crime rates have also declined noticeably.

Criminologists and criminal justice scholars and practitioners are very interested in why crime has declined. As with many issues in criminal justice, no absolute answer fully explains it. However, research (Blumstein & Wallman, 2000; Conklin, 2003) has identified a variety of factors that have contributed to the reduction in crime, including more effective gun control and gun crime enforcement measures; increased prison sentences; improvements in

Figure 1.1. Violent Crime Rate in the United States, 1989–2008

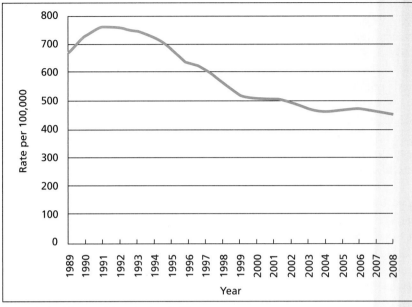

Source: Federal Bureau of Investigation, 2009a

Figure 1.2. Property Crime Rate in the United States, 1989–2008

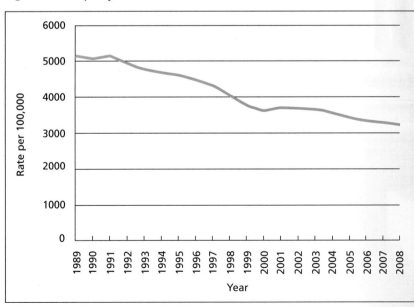

Source: Federal Bureau of Investigation, 2009a

services to victims; a decline in the popularity of crack cocaine, a drug associated with violence; more effective policing strategies; the strong economy of the 1990s; and a decline in the 18- to 25-year-old segment of the population, which statistically is at the greatest risk for offending. There may be other reasons as well. Criminologists will continue to study the various forces that affect the crime rate and the effect of criminal justice policy decisions on the level of crime in society.

The UCR also provides data about **clearance rates**, referring to the percentage of cases that are solved, or cleared, usually by arresting a suspect. Figure 1.3 shows the clearance rate for the major crimes included in the UCR. Murder has the highest clearance rate because homicide cases are often given the highest priority in terms of investigative resources.

The above data are for the United States as a whole. However, it is important to recognize that there are regional variations in the amount of crime. Figure 1.4 shows the amount of crime by region. The southern United States experiences the highest crime rates (both violent and property crimes), followed by the western United States, the Midwest, and the Northeast. There has long been a debate among criminologists as to why this is the case, much of it focused on whether there are attributes that lead the southern states to experience higher crime rates. Although there is not a firm resolution on this question, the following explanations have been proposed: a southern subculture that favors violence (Cohen, 1996); higher temperatures in the South (Cohn, Rotton, Peterson, & Tarr, 2004), perhaps because more potential offenders and

Figure 1.3. Percent of Crimes Cleared for Arrest or Exceptional Means, 2008

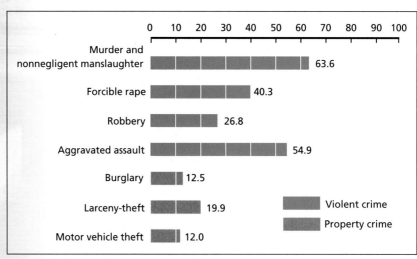

Source: Federal Bureau of Investigation, 2009b

Figure 1.4. Violent and Property Crime Rates in the United States by Region, 2008

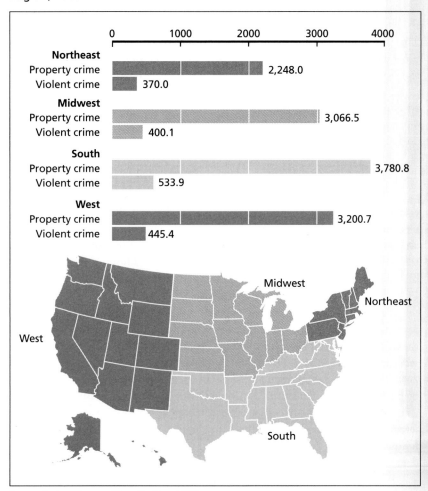

Source: Federal Bureau of Investigation, 2009c

victims venture out when the weather is nice or because hot weather makes tempers flare; differences in patterns of social relationships among people, known as **social capital** (Rosenfeld, Messner, & Baumer, 2001); and regional differences in poverty levels (Huff-Corzine, Corzine, & Moore, 1986).

Finally, in a global society, it is useful to consider how crime rates in the United States compare to those in other countries. Criminologists Franklin Zimring and Gordon Hawkins (1997) observe,

> Other industrial democracies have rates of crime comparable to those found in the United States . . . But the death rates from all forms of

violence are many times greater in the United States than in other comparable nations. *Lethal violence is the distinctive American problem* [emphasis added]. (p. 51)

The rate of lethal violence in the United States is a concern that policy makers must work to address. Its causes are complex and its solutions elusive, although the reduction in violent crime since the mid-1990s is encouraging.

OTHER SOURCES OF CRIME DATA

The UCR provides useful data to help us understand the nature and prevalence of crime in the United States. However, one substantial limitation is that it relies on data from crimes that were actually reported to the police. If a crime occurred that was not reported to the police, it was not included in the UCR data (for a useful overview of measurement issues related to crime data, see Lynch & Addington, 2007). Evidence suggests that not all persons report their victimizations to the police. Reporting rates vary by crime. Here are a few examples of the percentages of victims who report the crime to the police: motor vehicle theft, 85.3%; robbery, 65.6%; burglary of a home, 50.1%; rape and sexual assault, 41.6%; and theft of an item costing under $50, 14.9% (*Criminal Victimization in the United States*, 2010).

To gain a more complete perspective on the amount of crime in the United States, there are two methods other than the UCR that can be used. The first of these is a victimization survey in which researchers ask members of the public whether they have been victimized by crime (see generally Cantor & Lynch, 2000). The Bureau of Justice Statistics, an agency within the U.S. Department of Justice, conducts the annual **National Crime Victimization Survey** (**NCVS**). The NCVS is not directly comparable to the UCR because it uses a slightly different system for classifying offenses. In addition, the NCVS does not measure homicide because the victim is deceased. However, it does provide informative data about the amount of crime that occurs in the United States.

For instance, according to the NCVS (*Criminal Victimization in the United States*, 2010), of every 100,000 persons, 2,150 would be victimized by a violent crime and 14,650 would experience a property crime. Note that these figures are considerably higher than those detected by the UCR, as presented in Figures 1.2 and 1.3. The gap between the official UCR crime rate and the NCVS victimization rate is one measure of the **dark figure of crime**, meaning the volume of crime that goes unreported to authorities. Although NCVS rates are higher than those in the UCR, they do illustrate the same trend over time, showing a substantial decrease in crime since the mid-1990s.

The NCVS provides other interesting facts about victimization as well. Persons in the age group of 16–19 years old have the greatest risk of being victimized by a violent crime, as do persons with a family income below $7,500. Violent crimes are almost equally likely to involve offenders known to the victim (48.6%) as they are to involve strangers (51.4%). The greatest percentage of violent crimes occurs during the daytime (55.2%), and the most frequent location is at or near the victim's home (30.1%). When a weapon is used in a violent crime (20.4% of all cases), it is most likely to be a firearm (used in 7.1% of all cases). The sorts of data that the NCVS provides can be informative in developing crime prevention programs and in making decisions about criminal justice agency strategies and priorities.

A second form of crime data is the **self-report study**. This, too, is a survey administered to the public, but instead of asking about whether persons have been victims of crime, it asks whether persons have committed certain criminal acts. Research suggests that, with some exceptions, persons completing the surveys are generally truthful about their participation in illegal activities (for additional background, see Thornberry & Krohn, 2000). Unlike official crime data and victimization studies, there is no single survey recognized as the designated national self-report study for the United States.

One example of a self-report study is the **Youth Risk Behavior Study (YRBS)**, conducted every other year by the Centers for Disease Control. The YRBS is administered to high school students and has found that, of the students who completed the study, 9.7% reported driving under the influence of alcohol, 31.5% reported being in a fight, 5.6% reported carrying a weapon on school property, 6.4% reported having used cocaine, and 20.2% reported taking a prescription drug without having a prescription for it (Eaton et al., 2010). Follow-up questions on self-report studies can also gain useful information about what factors are associated with engaging in illegal behavior and why individuals are motivated to do so.

> Do you find the crime data presented in this section surprising? Why or why not?
>
> What do you think are the advantages and disadvantages of each method for collecting crime data?
>
> Look back to the scenario at the beginning of the chapter. If you wanted to gather a fairly comprehensive set of data to measure the amount of crime before and after the implementation of your preferred policy, what sort of crime data would you utilize? Be as specific as possible in your answer.

Looking Ahead

You will see from the Contents that the book is divided into five units. This chapter introduces the concepts of crime and criminal justice in preparation for the later units. Unit I explores how philosophies of criminal justice and law influence decisions about which acts to criminalize and about the strategies for responding to crime. Unit II focuses on the concept of social control, considering how individual behavior is regulated and why persons sometimes turn to deviant activities. Knowledge of social control may lead to more effective justice policy by helping justice agencies develop strategies that focus effectively on the root causes of crime and on forces that control criminal activity. Unit III asks the question, what is justice? There is no single definition, but this unit explores various models of what justice means as well as how justice policy is actually made. Unit IV considers the role of criminal law and punishment in accomplishing social control and achieving justice. Finally, Unit V turns to the agencies of criminal justice themselves, exploring the work of the police, the courts, and corrections.

Conclusion

As illustrated in this chapter, criminal justice can be understood from a variety of perspectives, each of which has the potential to shape the field in different ways. Ultimately, criminal justice centers on the study of society's responses to crime. The good news is that, as of this writing, crime in the United States has declined substantially since the mid-1990s. The challenge for criminal justice students and professionals alike is to consider what policies are most promising to continue reducing crime, while also protecting the rights and liberties valued by Americans. Understanding criminal justice as a system, profession, bureaucracy, moral agent, and academic discipline is a starting point for meeting this challenge. Also important is a survey of the key foundational ideas in criminal justice presented in subsequent chapters. Throughout the text, examples will draw connections between theory and practice and illustrate how philosophical concepts are applied in policing, law, corrections, and more.

    We encourage you to think critically about the ideas in each chapter and to work through the case studies and questions that are presented in the text. In addition to providing interesting and important points for reflection and discussion, this will help you become a sophisticated observer of the criminal justice system and its workings.

Criminal Justice Problem Solving: DNA EVIDENCE

Deoxyribonucleic acid (DNA) contains individualized genetic material that can, after scientific testing, be used to identify persons. You may have seen news reports, television shows, or movies that illustrate its use in criminal justice settings as a valuable tool of forensic science. If an offender leaves at the scene of the crime any material containing DNA, that DNA can potentially be matched to a sample taken from the offender at a later time. A DNA match between an offender and material left at the scene of a crime does not result in an automatic guilty verdict, but it can be used to establish that an offender was present or that an offender left biological material behind (e.g., blood, semen, saliva), which could be instrumental in linking the offender to the crime.

There are many unsolved crimes for which DNA evidence is available. However, without a suspect to whom the DNA sample from the crime scene can be compared, the DNA is of little use by itself. All states, as well as the federal government, have established **DNA databases** that archive samples from known offenders. When DNA is retrieved in an unsolved case, it can then be compared to the profiles in the database. If there is a match, or "hit," a formerly cold case (i.e., one that was not solved and for which investigators had insufficient leads to continue the investigation) can potentially be solved.

This is the foremost advantage of DNA databases—the potential to solve cold cases, increasing the clearance rate. In addition, the use of DNA databases is cost efficient as an investigative tool, particularly when balanced against the costs—both social and financial—of crime to society. Finally, DNA databases can in some instances help to ensure that the correct offender is identified and charged with the crime. For instance, a match acquired through a DNA database analysis could, depending on the circumstances of the case, result in the exoneration of other (actually innocent) suspects against whom there was circumstantial or questionable evidence (Grinnell & Burke, 2005).

At the same time, there are concerns about DNA databases. Consider the following questions:

> If a DNA database is used, who should be required to submit samples to the database? Persons convicted of certain serious crimes? Persons convicted of any crime? Persons arrested, whether or not they were convicted? Persons accused of traffic violations? The general public as a whole? Why?

> Would any moral concerns arise from the use of DNA databases? Why or why not?

> How could concerns about DNA databases be balanced against benefits that databases may offer? What factors weigh most heavily in your analysis?

> Is there any further information about DNA and its role in criminal justice that you would want to know before making a decision? Why?

Chapter 1 Appendix: The Criminal Justice Stystem

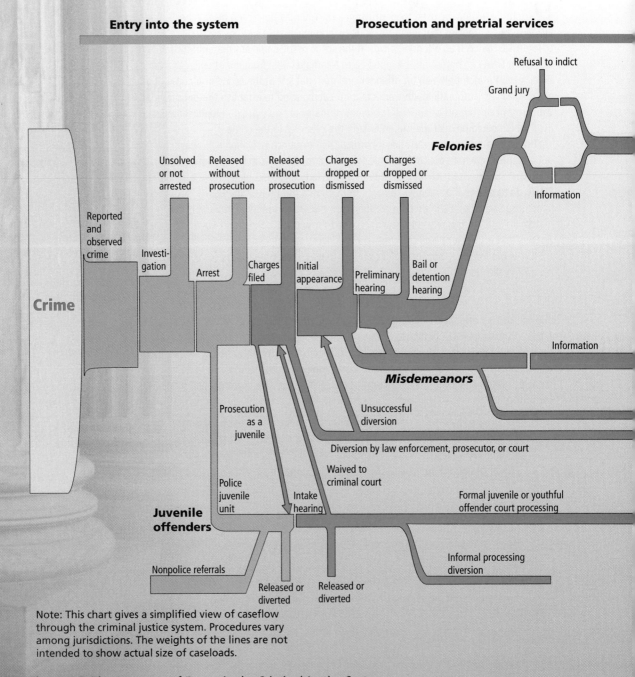

Entry into the system

Prosecution and pretrial services

Note: This chart gives a simplified view of caseflow through the criminal justice system. Procedures vary among jurisdictions. The weights of the lines are not intended to show actual size of caseloads.

Figure 1.5. The Sequence of Events in the Criminal Justice System

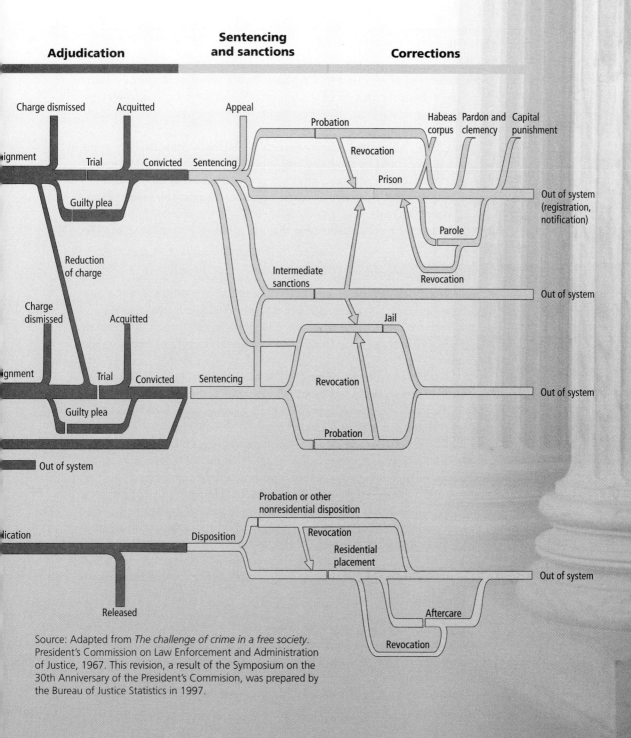

Adjudication   **Sentencing and sanctions**   **Corrections**

Charge dismissed   Acquitted   Appeal   Probation   Habeas corpus   Pardon and clemency   Capital punishment

ignment   Trial   Convicted   Sentencing   Revocation   Prison

Guilty plea

Reduction of charge   Intermediate sanctions   Parole

Charge dismissed   Acquitted   Revocation   Out of system (registration, notification)

ignment   Trial   Convicted   Sentencing   Jail   Out of system

Guilty plea   Revocation   Out of system

Out of system   Probation

Probation or other nonresidential disposition

lication   Disposition   Revocation

Residential placement   Out of system

Released   Aftercare

Revocation

Source: Adapted from *The challenge of crime in a free society*. President's Commission on Law Enforcement and Administration of Justice, 1967. This revision, a result of the Symposium on the 30th Anniversary of the President's Commision, was prepared by the Bureau of Justice Statistics in 1997.

Further Explanation of Figure 1.5

ENTRY INTO THE SYSTEM

The justice system does not respond to most crime because so much crime is not discovered or reported to the police. Law enforcement agencies learn about crime from the reports of victims or other citizens, from discovery by a police officer in the field, from informants, or from investigative and intelligence work.

Once a law enforcement agency has established that a crime has been committed, a suspect must be identified and apprehended for the case to proceed through the system. Sometimes, a suspect is apprehended at the scene; however, identification of a suspect sometimes requires an extensive investigation. Often, no one is identified or apprehended. In some instances, a suspect is arrested and later the police determine that no crime was committed and the suspect is released.

PROSECUTION AND PRETRIAL SERVICES

After an arrest, law enforcement agencies present information about the case and about the accused to the prosecutor, who will decide if formal charges will be filed with the court. If no charges are filed, the accused must be released. The prosecutor can also drop charges after making efforts to prosecute (*nolle prosequi*).

A suspect charged with a crime must be taken before a judge or magistrate without unnecessary delay. At the **initial appearance**, the judge or magistrate informs the accused of the charges and decides whether there is probable cause to detain the accused person. If the offense is not very serious, the determination of guilt and assessment of a penalty may also occur at this stage.

Often, the defense counsel is also assigned at the initial appearance. All suspects prosecuted for serious crimes have a right to be represented by an attorney. If the court determines the suspect is indigent and cannot afford such representation, the court will assign counsel at the public's expense.

A **pretrial-release** decision may be made at the initial appearance, but may occur at other hearings or may be changed at another time during the process. Pretrial release and bail were traditionally intended to ensure appearance at trial. However, many jurisdictions permit pretrial detention of defendants accused of serious offenses and deemed to be dangerous to prevent them from committing crimes prior to trial.

The court often bases its pretrial decision on information about the defendant's drug use, as well as residence, employment, and family ties. The court may decide to release the accused on his/her own recognizance or into the custody of a third party after the posting of a financial bond or on the promise of satisfying certain conditions such as taking periodic drug tests to ensure drug abstinence.

In many jurisdictions, the initial appearance may be followed by a **preliminary hearing**. The main function of this hearing is to discover if there is probable cause to believe that the accused committed a known crime within the jurisdiction of the court. If the judge does not find probable cause, the case is dismissed; however, if the judge or magistrate finds probable cause for such a belief, or the accused waives his or her right to a preliminary hearing, the case may be bound over to a grand jury.

A **grand jury** hears evidence against the accused presented by the prosecutor and decides if there is sufficient evidence to cause the accused to be brought to trial. If the grand jury finds sufficient evidence, it submits to the court an **indictment**, a written statement of the essential facts of the offense charged against the accused.

Where the grand jury system is used, the grand jury may also investigate criminal activity generally and issue indictments called grand jury originals that initiate criminal cases. These investigations and indictments are often used in drug and conspiracy cases that involve complex organizations. After such an indictment, law enforcement tries to apprehend and arrest the suspects named in the indictment.

Misdemeanor cases and some felony cases proceed by the issuance of an **information**, a formal, written accusation submitted to the court by a prosecutor. In some jurisdictions, indictments may be required in felony cases. However, the accused may choose to waive a grand jury indictment and, instead, accept service of an information for the crime.

In some jurisdictions, defendants, often those without prior criminal records, may be eligible for diversion from prosecution subject to the completion of specific conditions such as drug treatment. Successful completion of the conditions may result in the dropping of charges or the expunging of the criminal record where the defendant is required to plead guilty prior to the diversion.

ADJUDICATION

Once an indictment or information has been filed with the trial court, the accused is scheduled for **arraignment**. At the arraignment, the accused is informed of the charges, advised of the rights of criminal defendants, and asked to enter a plea to the charges. Sometimes, a plea of guilty is the result of negotiations between the prosecutor and the defendant.

If the accused pleads guilty or pleads *nolo contendere* (accepts penalty without admitting guilt), the judge may accept or reject the plea. If the plea is accepted, no trial is held and the offender is sentenced at this proceeding or at a later date. The plea may be rejected and proceed to trial if, for example, the judge believes that the accused may have been coerced.

If the accused pleads not guilty or not guilty by reason of insanity, a date is set for the trial. A person accused of a serious crime is guaranteed a trial by jury. However, the accused may ask for a **bench trial** where the judge, rather than a jury, serves as the finder of fact. In both instances the prosecution and defense present evidence by questioning witnesses while the judge decides on issues of law. The trial results in acquittal or conviction on the original charges or on lesser included offenses.

After the trial a defendant may request appellate review of the conviction or sentence. In some cases, appeals of convictions are a matter of right; all States with the death penalty provide for automatic appeal of cases involving a death sentence. Appeals may be subject to the discretion of the appellate court and may be granted only on acceptance of a defendant's petition for a writ of certiorari. Prisoners may also appeal their sentences through civil rights petitions and writs of habeas corpus where they claim unlawful detention.

SENTENCING AND SANCTIONS

After a conviction, sentence is imposed. In most cases the judge decides on the sentence, but in some jurisdictions the sentence is decided by the jury, particularly for capital offenses.

In arriving at an appropriate sentence, a sentencing hearing may be held at which evidence of aggravating or mitigating circumstances is considered. In assessing the circumstances surrounding a convicted person's criminal behavior, courts often rely on presentence investigations by probation agencies or other designated authorities. Courts may also consider victim impact statements.

The sentencing choices that may be available to judges and juries include one or more of the following: the death penalty; incarceration in a prison, jail, or other confinement facility; probation—allowing the convicted person to remain at liberty but subject to certain conditions and restrictions such as drug testing or drug treatment; fines—primarily applied as penalties in minor offenses; restitution—requiring the offender to pay compensation to the victim.

In some jurisdictions, offenders may be sentenced to alternatives to incarceration that are considered more severe than straight probation but less severe than a prison term. Examples of such sanctions include boot camps, intense supervision often with drug treatment and testing, house arrest and electronic monitoring, denial of Federal benefits, and community service.

In many jurisdictions, the law mandates that persons convicted of certain types of offenses serve a prison term. Most jurisdictions permit the judge to set the sentence length within certain limits, but some have determinate sentencing laws that stipulate a specific sentence length that must be served and cannot be altered by a parole board.

CORRECTIONS

Offenders sentenced to incarceration usually serve time in a local jail or a State prison. Offenders sentenced to less than 1 year generally go to **jail**; those sentenced to more than 1 year go to **prison**. Persons admitted to the Federal system or a State prison system may be held in prisons with varying levels of custody or in a community correctional facility.

A prisoner may become eligible for **parole** after serving a specific part of his or her sentence. Parole is the conditional release of a prisoner before the prisoner's full sentence has been served. The decision to grant parole is made by an authority such as a parole board, which has power to grant or revoke parole or to discharge a parolee altogether. The way parole decisions are made varies widely among jurisdictions.

Offenders may also be required to serve out their full sentences prior to release (expiration of term). Those sentenced under determinate sentencing laws can be released only after they have served their full sentence (mandatory release) less any "goodtime" received while in prison. Inmates get goodtime credits against their sentences automatically or by earning them through participation in programs.

If released by a parole board decision or by mandatory release, the releasee will be under the supervision of a parole officer in the community for the balance of his or her unexpired sentence. This supervision is governed by specific conditions of release, and the releasee may be returned to prison for violations of such conditions.

Source: Preceding paragraphs quoted from Bureau of Justice Statistics, 2010, para. 9–34

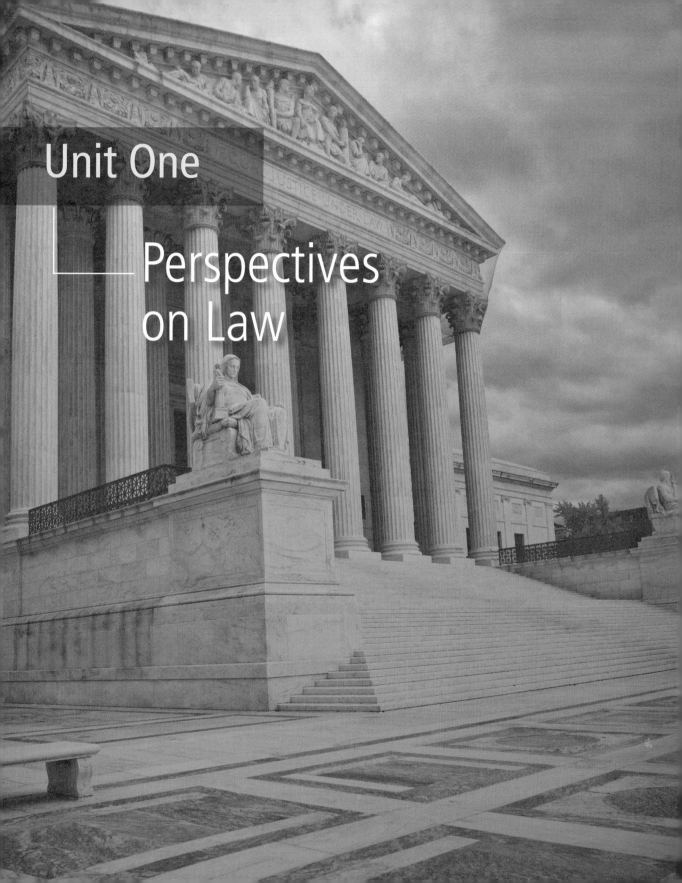

Unit One

Perspectives on Law

Photo Essay: Morality, Law, and Justice

Chapter 1 described the variety of perspectives through which criminal justice may be viewed. Consistent across these perspectives is the reality that the criminal justice process contains many points where discretionary decisions can be made, indicating the need to make decisions that are ethical and informed by research. In reality, discretionary decisions can pose challenging dilemmas, many of which lie at the heart of debates about philosophies of morality and law. It is a consideration of these ideas, and their effects on criminal justice theory and practice, to which Unit I will turn.

To what extent should notions of morality influence the law and criminal justice? In his book *Hellfire Nation,* political scientist James Morone suggests that American politics (and by extension, American law and its enforcement) has been profoundly shaped by moral forces "entangled in two vital urges—redeeming 'us' and reforming 'them'" (2003, p. 3). In this way, he argues, law and policy are shaped by sequential "moral storm[s]" (2003, p. 10), as public debate rages over moral ills and their remedies. However, what is defined as a moral ill—and who and what need to be reformed—changes over time.

THE UNJUST SENTENCE.

The response to crime has always contained a moral element. To borrow from Morone's argument, punishment was applied to the "them" who had violated social expectations that had been encoded into law. Whether it was a debtor being placed in stocks (as shown here) or a murderer being hanged, it was perceived as a justified response to the problem of crime in colonial days. Not all punishment was meted out equally, however. For instance, "In Massachusetts . . . anyone guilty of drunkenness was fined five shillings; offenders unable to pay spent three hours in the stocks. If . . . the criminal was an outsider to town, he would most often be whipped and then banished" (Rothman, 1995, p. 112). What concepts of morality do the Massachusetts punishments illustrate? How do you think morality was defined at that time and place?

Criminal laws in the colonial era were often grounded in religious morality. This included laws punishing blasphemy, heresy, and inappropriate conduct on the Sabbath day (e.g., traveling, drinking, shopping, and in some cases, failure to attend religious services). In addition, some colonies used the law to enforce adherence to their desired religion, prohibiting members of other religious groups from even entering the colony. For instance, the Massachusetts colony at one time required the banishment of Jesuits and Quakers; those who returned to the colony after being banished were executed (Friedman, 1993), such as Quaker Mary Dyer, pictured here, who was hanged in 1660. To what extent do you think laws should be driven by religious morality? Why?

As time progressed, the means of punishment turned more toward the use of prison but with a slightly different moral justification. In this era, a moral punishment became one that provided an opportunity for the offender to repent for his or her sins that had led to the commission of a crime. As one observer noted at the time, "Can there be a combination more powerful for reformation than that of a prison which hands over the prisoner to all the trials of solitude, leads him through reflection to remorse, through religion to hope" (de Beaumont & de Tocqueville, [1833] 1964, p. 84). At Eastern State Penitentiary in Philadelphia, pictured here, inmates were confined in solitary cells for the duration of their sentences, but the goal was for each inmate to experience a religious reformation as a result of a monastic life in the penitentiary. How would you assess this idea of punishment?

As society became more scientifically oriented, views of morality became less dependent on religion and more focused on social conditions. Crime came to be understood not just as a matter of failing to be pious, but rather as being driven (at least in part) by social conditions that could influence individual behavior. In

particular, criminologists began to seriously consider the impact on crime of issues such as poverty, social status, education, medical conditions, mental capacity, and more (see Chapter 5 for a survey of various perspectives on explanations for crime). If these issues are related to crime, does society have an obligation to ensure that education, health care, housing, or a minimum wage are available to all citizens? What do you think? Why?

As views of crime changed, so did views of punishment and its morality. Punishment became less about religious reformation and more oriented toward other goals. Among the goals for modern correctional agencies are the rehabilitation of offenders through programming, including education, vocational training, recreational activities, health care services, and more (see Carlson & Garrett, 2008). What would you identify as the characteristics or qualities that make punishment moral? Is there a moral obligation to provide these types of correctional programming?

Ideas about morality still underlie debates about law and justice in America and are often the subject of substantial controversy. However, there is not always agreement about how to decide what is or is not moral. Often in today's society, some people will attempt to discover a version of morality drawing upon historical roots. Others will advocate new conceptions of morality. What will morality mean in our future? Although that is difficult to predict, we find ourselves confronted by choices from the past as well as designing new options for the next gen-

eration. As we strive for consistency, fairness, and justice under the law, continued debates about morality will no doubt shape our response to crime, the laws we make, and how we decide to enforce them. How can you contribute to these conversations? What difference can your work make in the criminal justice system?

The chapters in Unit I explore the intersections between morality and law, including how philosophies of idealism and pragmatism shape the criminal justice system. Given the tremendous power that is accorded to justice professionals through their use of discretion, it is most important to consider the theoretical ideas that have shaped and will continue to shape the reality of criminal justice practice.

Concepts of Law and Morality

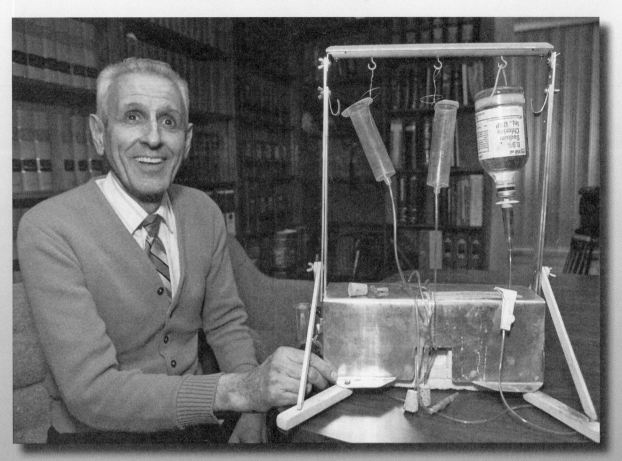

Assisted-suicide advocate Dr. Jack Kevorkian and his "suicide machine." Do you think physician-assisted suicide violates social morality?

Key Terms

state of nature

social contract theory

sneak and peek warrants

legitimacy

data

empiricism

morality

strategy

tactics

idealists

pragmatists

harmony

ultimate truth

a priori

a posteriori

self

spirituality

teleology

paradigms

Key People

Thomas Hobbes

John Locke

Plato

Charles Sanders Peirce

CASE STUDY

Justice on Lover's Lane

You are a police officer assigned to patrol Lover's Lane. Numerous assaults and robberies have recently occurred in this area. While on evening patrol, you notice a van that appears to be rocking. As a tactically trained officer on patrol, you know how to approach suspicious persons and suspicious vehicles. Should you stop to investigate the van that's rocking? Why or why not? If so, how far would you take the investigation?

If you decide *not* to stop, you fear the possible headlines in the news: MAYOR'S DAUGHTER RAPED IN VAN AS OFFICER DRIVES BY. It is not just the potential for personal embarrassment or harm to your professional integrity that requires you to stop. Rather, you have an obligation to obey your department's orders, which include instructions from your sergeant to "keep a close eye on Lover's Lane." Therefore, you decide to investigate the van.

You discover that the van was rocking because the two teenagers inside the vehicle, a male and a female, were engaged in sexual activity. Both teenagers were of legal age to engage in sexual activity, and the behavior was completely consensual. How would you handle the situation? Why?

There is no single correct answer to this scenario (nor will there be for many other scenarios you encounter in this book). Although police officers are required to implement an agency's strategies by using acceptable tactics, they have much discretionary judgment in deciding *how* to best do so. This makes policing, and all criminal justice professions, very complex. In rendering their decisions, police officers and other criminal justice professionals must work only within the bounds of law and agency policy. They also act in ways that illustrate morality.

> Consider your response to this scenario. Did your beliefs about the morality of sexual activity or the morality of other issues affect your decision? If so, how and why? If not, why not?

Does your response differ from that of your friends or classmates? Why or why not? If it does differ, what factors might have influenced the different decisions?

How strongly do you feel that your response is the best way to handle the situation?

Do you believe your answer could be viewed as a decision involving morality? Explain.

Criminal Justice and Society

FOCUSING QUESTION 2.1

Why do societies need criminal justice systems?

Consider for a moment why society needs police departments—or for that matter, other criminal justice agencies, such as courts and prisons. Another way of thinking about this is to ask the question: what would society be like if we *did not* have police departments, courts, and prisons? As you think about this question, you would probably reach one of two answers.

One possible answer is a society so perfect that there is no crime, no disorder, and therefore, no need for the agencies of criminal justice. While such a society may be theoretically possible, it can be difficult to envision. French sociologist Émile Durkheim (1938) observed that a truly crime-free society would require unanimous agreement on all aspects of life, something that is difficult to imagine given the variety of human opinions, tastes, and preferences.

Another possible answer is that a society without police, courts, and prisons would operate in a **state of nature**, a free-for-all environment where there is little order. After all, if there are no police to enforce rules, no courts to resolve disputes, and no prisons to punish wrongdoers, what would life be like? In describing a state of nature, British philosopher Thomas Hobbes suggested that life would be "solitary, poor, nasty, brutish, and short" ([1651] 1963, p. 143). Individuals would be responsible for enforcing their own self-interest, potentially by taking revenge against wrongdoers, while also fearing that they would accidentally offend others and then be the victim of revenge. Without a justice system, there would be little to protect the weak from being victimized by the strong, who could take or do what they wished without fear of punishment. Certainly, the chaotic state of nature is not an ideal lifestyle.

Let's return to the question posed earlier: why do we need criminal justice agencies? The simplest and most direct answer is that we need the police, courts, and corrections so we can *maintain order* in society. We do not live in a crime-free utopia. And we do not want to live in a Hobbesian state of nature. The criminal justice system helps us live in an orderly society that is a middle ground between the two extremes.

This notion is actually a fairly sophisticated concept called **social contract theory**. Several philosophers have written about different perspectives on social contract theory (including Hobbes, [1651] 1963; Locke, [1689] 1963; Rousseau, [1762] 1963), but the basics go something like this. In a state of nature, individuals have the complete freedom to do whatever they want to do, good or bad—that is, until a stronger person or group stops them—because there are no agencies to enforce laws or maintain order. Because this is an undesirable way to live, individuals agree to give up some of their freedom in exchange for security. That is, individuals no longer have complete freedom but instead are bound by a series of laws governing their behavior, which are enforced by a government. This is the social contract between the government and the governed, promising security in exchange for compliance with the law and its processes.

The social contract is dynamic, as the amount of freedom exchanged for the amount of security received may vary over time. For instance, after the attacks of September 11, 2001, the public and politicians seemed willing to accept more regulation in exchange for greater security (see Newman, 2003). Since that time, however, there have been many debates about the scope of government control under measures such as the controversial USA PATRIOT Act. Debate has centered on issues such as **sneak and peek warrants**, which "allow the government to conduct searches without notifying the subjects" (American Civil Liberties Union, 2003, para. 10), and provisions that allow the Federal Bureau of Investigation to require "anyone at all—including doctors, libraries, bookstores, universities, and Internet service providers—to turn over records on their clients or customers" without documented probable cause (American Civil Liberties Union, 2003, para. 6).

Therefore, the social contract is a *metaphor* that helps us explain the role of government, of which criminal justice is one part, in society. An important feature of a social contract is the notion that the government must be responsive to the people. English philosopher John Locke ([1689] 1963) quoted the Latin dictum *"salus populi supreme lex"* (p. 193), meaning "the good of the people is the supreme law." This is important because it leads to the concept of **legitimacy**. A government has legitimacy when the people accept that it has the right to govern them.

When a government does not have legitimacy, there may be protest, widespread disobedience of laws, or revolution. It is important for us to consider the philosophies that underlie our criminal justice system because debates about these ideas shape understandings of the criminal justice system and perceptions of its legitimacy.

CRIMINAL JUSTICE: POPULAR CONCEPTIONS
VERSUS ACADEMIC SCHOLARSHIP

Again flowing from the notion of a social contract, it is in everyone's best interest to have a criminal justice system to maintain order. In a democracy, where government agencies must be legitimate and responsible to the public, that criminal justice system must meet a number of ideals, including fairness, equality, and effectiveness. But how do we judge whether the criminal justice system is meeting its obligation? How do we determine the appropriate strategies and tactics for criminal justice agencies to use? Often, there is disagreement between members of the general public, to whom the criminal justice system must answer, and criminal justice scholars, who have dedicated careful study to the system and its functioning.

To the public, it is tempting to focus only on the goals of the criminal justice system without considering precisely how those goals are accomplished and with what implications. For instance, if prisons are meant to promote public safety by locking up offenders, persons might believe that what happens inside the prison is inconsequential as long as they also believe that prisons can meet their goals of keeping society safe. This leads some to give common-sense but overly simplistic responses to the complex questions of criminal justice. When asked about inmate rights or privileges (e.g., visits, education, recreation, etc.), a typical response would revert back to the perceived purpose of prisons—to promote public safety—leading to responses such as, "But how does *that* keep society safe?" An outcry could result, perceiving rights and privileges as unnecessary and extraneous. Little evidence is typically offered beyond what is reported in the media. As a result, much of the argument relies on notions of what the system should accomplish ("lock 'em up to keep us safe") without considering what must occur for that to happen. Much popular discourse on criminal justice, then, relies on moral arguments about the purpose of criminal justice agencies without careful analysis of how agencies go about their work. That is, the ends (i.e., the actual or desired outcomes) are the focus rather than the means (or methods) by which those ends are achieved.

Compare this approach to that of criminal justice scholars. First and foremost, scholars are concerned with **data**. The answers to all questions are grounded in the collection of data, such as statistics, careful observations, and in-depth interviews. This is also known as **empiricism** (see Box 2.1). To continue with the prisons example, a scholar may take as a starting point that the role of prisons is to protect society. But the scholar would then consider what would need to happen within prisons for them to truly serve as protection for society. The scholar might find, for instance, that most individuals who are sentenced to prison commit a new offense when they are released (Langan & Levin, 2002). The scholar would then conclude that prisons do not fully provide protection from future crime. However, the scholar would also find that data indicate that inmates are less likely to commit new offenses if they utilize the right to receive visitors while in prison (Bales & Mears, 2008) and that artistic programming may contribute to offender rehabilitation (Johnson, 2008). On the basis of empiricism, then, the scholar might reach a different moral conclusion than the public. For the scholar, it is the means that are of the

BOX 2.1

PROBLEM-SOLVING METHOD

Pragmatists have a five-step method for solving problems. The method is the basis for social science research as well as evidence-based criminal justice tactics and strategies (e.g., problem-oriented policing; Goldstein, 1990). Anyone can use the method for any problem; however, problems that are more difficult require more research and analysis.

- Step 1—Become aware of a problem. (*Example: Citizens complain to you about neighborhood disorder.*)
- Step 2—Locate, define, and analyze the problem. (*Example: You find that the disorder comes from a group of juveniles loitering in a nearby parking lot on weekend nights.*)
- Step 3—Entertain possible hypotheses for addressing the problem. (*Examples: Implement a curfew; play loud classical music on speakers in the parking lot; increase police patrols; provide alternative weekend entertainment.*)
- Step 4—Choose one hypothesis to test. (*Example: Play loud classical music on speakers in the parking lot.*)
- Step 5—Collect data to verify the results. (*Example: Observe how many juveniles congregate at the parking lot the weekend before the speakers are installed; compare that to how many juveniles congregate at the parking lot after the speakers are installed.*)

If playing loud classical music on speakers in the parking lot causes the juveniles to stop loitering there, you have implemented a successful solution (as long as they haven't just relocated to another parking lot!). If it turns out that the juveniles groove on classical music and now more of them loiter at the parking lot, you have not implemented a successful solution, and you would return to Step 3 (for a discussion of the actual impact of this type of solution, see Lucas, 2009).

How much of this process did you use to resolve the Lover's Lane scenario? Can this process be applied to that scenario?

How could this method be applied to other criminal justice problems? Compare this pragmatic approach to idealistic decision making.

Can you use this process to resolve a moral dilemma? For instance, how would a pragmatic police officer use this method to resolve the dilemma presented in Box 2.5? How would this differ from the way an idealistic police officer might resolve it?

most interest. The means may determine how the ends are accomplished and whether the ends themselves are valid.

Determining what criminal justice agencies should do is indeed a difficult task. It is sometimes complicated when the public and scholars use different processes to answer moral questions about the complexities of ends and means in the criminal justice system.

Do you agree with Durkheim that a crime-free society would be impossible? Explain why or why not.

What are some factors that you think would contribute to government legitimacy? How could the criminal justice system promote them?

What role should researchers play in making criminal justice policy? What role should public opinion play? How can they be reconciled when there are disagreements?

Morality and Justice Studies

FOCUSING QUESTION 2.2

How are philosophical arguments about morality related to criminal justice?

Morality and debates about it underlie the foundations of criminal justice. It is important to understand what the term **morality** means in this context. As McCollough (1991) explains, *"morality* refers to commonly accepted rules of conduct, patterns of behavior approved by a social group, values and standards shared by the group. It consists of beliefs about what is good and right held by a community with a shared history" (pp. 6–7). As such, this definition of morality does *not* assume that there is a master list of moral or immoral actions against which all others are judged. Nor does the definition assume that morality is grounded in any particular ideology, be it religious, political, economic, or any other. Rather, morality may be viewed as an ongoing *process* in which society continuously reflects on the items in McCollough's definition with the goal of determining the best solution to a dilemma.

Of course, finding the "best solution" is easier said than done, and it is typical to see spirited debate over criminal justice issues that raise questions of morality. For instance, consider physician-assisted suicide, as described in Chapter 1. In some U.S. states, there is a process by which terminally ill patients may obtain drugs for the purpose of ending their own lives. What beliefs, values, and standards may help us understand the moral implications of this issue? Some would argue that physician-assisted suicide for terminally ill patients protects an individual's dignity and freedom to choose how to end one's life. Others would argue that life is sacred and no life should be voluntarily terminated, even if in the course of a serious illness. Still others might argue that physician-assisted suicide gives too much power to the medical industry in determining who does or does not have a terminal illness and that society should instead value the role of family or nontraditional therapy in end-of-life decisions. Yet others might argue that, because physician-assisted suicide was approved by a public vote, it is an example of democracy in action and that the will of the people should prevail. Certainly, many other perspectives exist as well.

How, then, do we assess the morality of physician-assisted suicide? The answer lies in considering issues such as those raised earlier, by carefully studying what scholars, practitioners, and the public have to say about the issue, and by seeing how the arguments develop over time. As such, determining morality is much more complex than a first gut reaction of "that's right!" or "that's wrong!" But understanding the morality of criminal justice issues is essential, for it provides the foundation—albeit a foundation that shifts over time—for our criminal justice system and its operation.

Criminal justice practitioners make seemingly routine decisions on a daily basis that require them to grapple with difficult and complex issues, and the collection of those decisions (and the debates surrounding them) helps shape the moral conceptions that serve as the foundation of criminal justice. It is to these sorts of decisions that our attention will now turn.

> What questions of morality are raised by the case study at the beginning of the chapter? How do they reflect debates about beliefs, values, and standards?
>
> Can you think of other examples, besides physician-assisted suicide, in which there are debates about differing moral perspectives on issues of law and justice?

Choosing Strategies and Tactics

FOCUSING QUESTION 2.3

What judgments are involved in making decisions about criminal justice strategies and tactics?

Discretionary decisions help clarify the meanings of law and morality. With each accumulated decision, we gain a better understanding of how moral decision making proceeds and how the law is implemented in practice. An examination of strategies and tactics will provide further insight to this discussion. Concepts of morality influence each of these categories of judgment.

Reflect on your decision in the Lover's Lane case at the beginning of this chapter. There are numerous ways you could have responded. It would be within your authority as a peace officer to make an arrest for fornication or public indecency or to simply advise the couple to "move along." However, the couple in the van will perceive your decision, whatever it is, to be *the law* on the matter. In this way, through your actions, you have defined what the law means in practice (by choosing from a set of possible responses), at least as far as the couple in this case is concerned. Because you are an officer of the law, your decision will likely hold legitimacy. And in making your decision, you have consciously or unconsciously invoked notions of morality, as defined earlier. Of course, other officers in similar situations might make different choices, resulting in a different definition of law. Consider the responses in Box 2.2 as alternatives for the chapter's opening scenario.

It quickly becomes clear that in studying the law, it is as important to consider how the law is enforced and defined by criminal justice professionals as it is to consider what is written in legal codes. This is yet another example of

BOX 2.2

THE VAN ON LOVER'S LANE

Using information from the Lover's Lane scenario in this chapter, what would you do with the teenagers in the van? Consider the pros and cons of each approach.

1. Call both of their parents
2. Call the female's parents only
3. Call the male's parents only
4. Impound the van and insist that the parents must come and get it
5. Arrest one or both for fornication (i.e., sex outside marriage, which is illegal in some states although the laws against it are generally not enforced)
6. Arrest one or both for public indecency
7. Lecture them about the immorality of premarital sexual relations
8. Lecture them about the dangers of premarital sexual relations
9. Give them a condom if they do not already have one
10. Give them both a warning
11. Give them some advice about how not to get caught
12. Take one or both home in your vehicle
13. Take them to an area where they can safely engage in sexual activity
14. Lecture them about the dangers in the area
15. Allow them to continue and stay in the area until they are finished
16. Allow them to continue and move on with your patrol
17. Other (e.g., combination of the above or different solutions)

How would your decision differ if:

You knew one of the teenager's parents and knew that they would not approve of (or would be angry about) this activity?

The teenagers were consuming alcohol? Marijuana? Cocaine?

The teenagers were disrespectful or angry when you stopped them?

Rather than a male and a female, it was two males engaged in sexual activity? Two females?

Explain your responses.

the significant role that discretionary decision making plays in criminal justice as professionals consider the most appropriate strategies and tactics to use in a particular situation.

STRATEGIES

Strategy refers to the overall approach that a criminal justice agency may use to address crime. For instance, what strategies could a police department use to address driving under the influence of alcohol or drugs (DUI)? One strategy might be to take steps to drive DUI offenders home. Another strategy might be to publicize the dangers of DUI. Still another strategy might be to aggressively enforce

DUI laws. Strategic decisions of this sort are typically made by agency supervisors or administrators, and agency employees are expected to carry out the strategy. Strategies have moral consequences stemming from value debates. Is it fair to take DUI offenders home instead of holding them accountable for their actions? Is it a good use of police resources to spend money on an advertising campaign rather than to spend it on other things? Would aggressive enforcement strategies violate anyone's constitutional rights? These are important questions to consider when weighing the various strategies. An individual's values and beliefs would likely influence how he or she would answer these questions and would shape strategic decisions accordingly.

Strategies develop the big-picture plan for an agency to address a particular problem or conduct its business. However, even when strategies are established, they rely on individuals' judgments and decisions to carry them out. And again, this includes questions about morality in criminal justice practice.

TACTICS

Tactics consist of deciding *how* to implement a strategy. That is, strategies broadly identify problems and how to address them, while tactics identify specific ways to put the strategy into effect. Tactics are often developed by experienced supervisory personnel, but individual officers may also make valuable suggestions about how best to handle specific problems in specific locations. A reasonable strategy coupled with sufficient tactics should result in effective criminal justice policies.

Tactics involve moral decisions because they must be evaluated in terms of fairness, justice, equality, and other overarching values and philosophies. For instance, assume that an agency adopts a *strategy* of aggressively enforcing a state's law requiring seat belts to be worn by the occupants of a vehicle (and that failure to do so results in a $50 fine). Now assume that one *tactic* used to implement this strategy is to pull over all vehicles and then to arrest any persons who are not wearing seat belts. What beliefs, values, and standards need to be balanced to assess this tactic on moral grounds? Certainly, you would want to consider issues such as officer safety, whether an arrest for a such a minor offense would infringe on a person's rights, the value to society of ensuring that seat belts are worn, and how far an officer's right to make an arrest should extend in a democratic society (to see how the Supreme Court ruled in a similar case, see *Atwater v. City of Lago Vista*, 2001). Therefore, as you make decisions about tactics, you simultaneously shape the moral foundations of criminal justice. Box 2.3 will help you think more about tactics, using the Lover's Lane case from the chapter's opening as an example.

Select a criminal justice issue of your choice. What are the possible strategies that could address it? What tactics might accompany each strategy? What do you think is the best solution? Why?

BOX 2.3

TACTICS ON LOVER'S LANE

Refer back to the case study at the beginning of the chapter. The department's strategy has been to "keep a close eye on Lover's Lane." When you see the van, you must decide what tactics to use in approaching it so you can figure out what's going on. Remember, it is nighttime, you do not know how many people are in the van, you do not know who is in the van, and you do not know for sure what they are doing in the van. Assume that the van has tinted windows and that the interior is not lit. Here are some of the resources you have in your police vehicle: flashing police lights; siren; spotlight; headlights; loudspeaker; in-car video camera; two-way radio; handcuffs; mace; Taser; nightstick; sidearm; and shotgun.

Write a description of your tactics that includes these issues:

Where will you park your car in relation to the van?

How will you approach the van?

How will you get the attention of the occupants?

Will you ask them to leave the van? If so, how? If not, why?

What precautions will you take for your own safety?

What precautions will you take for the safety of the persons in the van?

What questions will you ask?

If you believe that sexual relations were occurring in the van, how would you determine whether it was consensual?

Discuss your tactics with those of your classmates. (You may also wish to discuss your solutions with a trained law enforcement officer. What do you think you would learn if you did so?) How do your tactics reflect ideas about morality, as described in the chapter?

What you have done in this exercise is engage in tactical decision making. But in the development of tactics, as you receive new information, your tactics may change. How would the following information change your tactical approach? Why?

- It is daytime instead of nighttime.
- The area is a suburb instead of a Lover's Lane.
- When you shine your lights on the van, five heads pop up.
- As you approach the van, you receive a radio call alerting you to a prowler in the area.

Three Tendencies of Idealists and Pragmatists

FOCUSING QUESTION 2.4

How do idealistic and pragmatic philosophies influence criminal justice?

To better understand the foundations of criminal justice, we will compare and contrast the philosophical perspectives of idealism and pragmatism. Not everyone agrees on what morality means or how it is established. Understanding the differences between idealism and pragmatism can help us understand why there are disagreements on questions involving morality, crime, and justice.

The preceding discussion of the difference between public and academic conceptions of criminal justice lays the groundwork for the distinction between idealism and pragmatism. Like many members of the public, **idealists** are concerned with the overall goals of the criminal justice system. Any idealist would first identify what he or she believed to be the broad goals of the system (perhaps that the police should keep the public safe and prisons should punish offenders). These goals would become the basis for the idealist's analysis of morality. The idealist would structure strategies and tactics toward meeting these goals, however they may be defined. Anything perceived (rightfully or wrongfully, based on evidence or not) as contrary to these goals would be criticized and disavowed.

Pragmatists, on the other hand, more closely represent most scholars. They are primarily interested in using empiricism to assess the performance of the criminal justice system, using the results of their analyses to inform moral discussions and decisions. To the pragmatist, the goals of the system are important, but equally important is information and evidence about how the system actually works and how that, in turn, informs discussions about strategy, tactics, and discretion.

As a simple example, consider the concept of a *dog*. The idealist might think of the grand concept of an ideal dog—perhaps a heroic dog like Lassie or a beloved childhood pet. This would then be the standard against which all dogs would be judged. The pragmatist might think of a more scientific notion of dog—perhaps distinguishing canine from feline or considering what biological characteristics define a dog. This would then be the standard against with the pragmatist would judge a dog.

To take a criminal justice example, consider the death penalty, which is (as of this writing) utilized by 34 states and the federal government (Death Penalty Information Center, 2011). A liberal idealist might see preservation of life and rehabilitation of offenders as the goals of the criminal justice system; accordingly, such an idealist would oppose the death penalty, making the moral argument that because it does not achieve either goal, it is unacceptable. A conservative idealist might see "eye for an eye" punishment of wrongdoers as a key goal of the criminal justice system; accordingly, such an idealist would support the death penalty, making the moral argument that because it does achieve the desired goal, it is acceptable. Disagreement between idealists would obviously result, and indeed, such disagreement has surrounded discussions of the death penalty for many years (see Mooney & Lee, 2001). As this example illustrates, both sides of the political spectrum can function as idealists. And regardless of their views, idealists use the same basic method: identifying a grand goal as moral doctrine and then judging all details based on whether or not they meet that goal.

The pragmatist, on the other hand, would acknowledge that there are goals that drive the criminal justice system. But the pragmatist would want to study the death penalty in practice. The pragmatist would use data and statistics to reach conclusions about the death penalty, which would likely include the following: most research indicates that the death penalty does not deter crime and in some cases may actually increase the homicide rate (e.g., Bailey, 1998); serious errors have been made in two-thirds of all death penalty cases (Gelman, Liebman, West, & Kiss, 2004); significant racial disparities exist in the use of the death penalty (e.g., Williams & Holcomb, 2001); there are concerns about the risk of executing innocent persons (Turow, 2003); implementing the death penalty is very expensive, more so than life imprisonment (e.g., Maryland Commission on Capital Punishment, 2008); and European democracies have banned the death penalty as a human rights violation (Zimring, 2003). These findings would be made solely on the basis of data. If scholars were to disagree, it would be about how the data were analyzed and not about their individual opinions about the death penalty as a form of punishment. However, these data would inform moral decisions about the death penalty, including how it does or does not support the traditional American values of equality, fairness, and efficiency. Whether or not a pragmatist chooses to support the death penalty remains a moral decision, but it is based on data and analysis rather than adherence to broad goals.

As noted earlier, the purpose of these discussions is not to dictate what is or is not moral but rather to examine the processes by which individuals decide for themselves. This helps us understand how working criminal justice professionals reach their decisions about strategy, tactics, and discretion and why different professionals may reach different decisions.

In Table 2.1, the philosophical tendencies of idealism and pragmatism are compared. As we proceed, we will see how this relates to criminal justice.

HARMONY

Harmony is the idea that when things are in their proper order, it represents beauty. The ancient Greek philosophers believed that true justice would result when groups of people were in harmony with one another (Grube, 1992).

Table 2.1 Tendencies of Idealists and Pragmatists

Philosophical Concept	Idealism's Tendencies	Pragmatism's Tendencies
Harmony	Serves as the verification of truth and the ultimate goal	Not relevant because it is not based on experience
Truth	Truth is found beyond normal experience	Truth beyond experience cannot be verified
Mind/Body Connection	Split	Connected

While we all may *hope* for harmony in our own lives and in society, the idealists truly consider it a natural guiding principle for making moral criminal justice decisions. Idealists seeking harmony sometimes draw upon philosopher Immanuel Kant's ([1785] 2002) categorical imperative, which states that people should only engage in an action if they would also be willing for others to do so as a universal rule. Kant's classic example is that, under the categorical imperative, it would not be acceptable for one person to lie because it would not be desirable to have a society in which all persons felt that it was appropriate to lie. It would be difficult to achieve harmony when it was unclear whether any particular statement is a truth or a falsehood, so Kant's solution was to define lying as morally wrong.

The officer responding to the Lover's Lane example might see the rocking van as out of place and therefore threatening to social harmony, be unwilling for it to be a universally accepted norm of behavior, and as a result, feel the need to take whatever actions are necessary to restore harmony. (However, the persons in the van might feel that their actions were harmonious and should be imitated by all—so you can see how disagreements about harmony can arise!) Therefore, it is harmony with universal principles—whether religious, ideological, or otherwise motivated—that guides an idealist's moral reasoning. This has resulted in profound expressions in American government of beautiful ideas that are indeed central to moral reasoning about justice issues, including the Declaration of Independence (harmony exists when all persons have rights to life, liberty, and pursuit of happiness) and the Bill of Rights (harmony exists when all persons may live according to their rights).

Conversely, pragmatism does not seek harmony. To the pragmatist, harmony is an *idea,* but its truth cannot be *verified.* Just because two or more things seem to fit together or appear to be pleasant does not mean that they are correct or appropriate. For instance, a correctional theorist might believe that all offenders benefit from hard work and discipline, leading to harmony by instilling universal values in offenders. If, on this basis, the theorist implemented a correctional boot camp in which offenders participate in military-style drills and discipline, she would be functioning as an idealist. The pragmatist, on the other hand, would not find this belief a satisfactory reason to implement a program. Instead, the pragmatist would seek to gather data about the programs to verify their usefulness or appropriateness (and in so doing would find them substantially flawed; see MacKenzie, 2006). If harmony happens to result from a pragmatist's analysis, that is fine, but harmony need not be a required outcome.

TRUTH

For years now, you have probably been taught to tell the truth. This is an important concept to criminal justice. After all, criminal justice seeks to determine the truth in various venues, including investigations (with their interviews and analyses of evidence), trials, and interpretations of law. But what is truth? This is actually a profound question. For our purposes, we will consider two perspectives, one from the idealists and one from the pragmatists.

Idealists believe there is an **ultimate truth** that guides, or should guide, human action. As an example, recall that the Declaration of Independence stated, "We hold these truths to be self-evident, that all men are created equal . . ." This is a statement grounded in idealism. By being held as self-evident, the truth is something that is accepted as a statement of how things ought to be, but it cannot be "proven" with data. You either accept or do not accept that all persons are equal; there is no mathematical equation that proves or disproves the proposition. As such, an idealist's truths are often used as the barometers by which harmony is judged. If something is in line with the accepted truth, whatever it may be, then the world is harmonious.

This is a very important argument to understand. For instance, idealists who accept as self-evident truth the idea that people commit crime because of the environment in which they are raised would advocate a range of social policies aimed at child rearing (improved schools, adequate childhood health care, parent training, positive after-school activities, etc.) in the hopes that these policies would make a person less likely to commit crime later in life. Criminal justice solutions that run contrary to this idea would be viewed as neither harmonious nor acceptable. On the other hand, if a person accepted as self-evident truth the idea that crime was caused by an offender's free will, in which he or she makes the conscious choice to commit a crime, then the aforementioned solutions would be irrelevant, and that person would likely advocate for harsh punishments to deter offenders from committing crimes. Therefore, disagreement about policies, especially among idealists, often occurs due to disagreements about what constitutes the truth.

Pragmatists tend not to focus on the ultimate truths. Rather, pragmatists define as truth only observations that could be verified in some way, whether through observation or through the analysis of data. Agreeing that something is a reasonable argument, a good idea, or an important value is not enough to constitute a truth. Therefore, the concept of truth is much narrower to the pragmatist, referring only to that which is verifiable. In considering why people commit crime, a pragmatist would likely avoid broad statements such as "environment causes crime" or "biology causes crime," instead preferring more nuanced, specific, and empirically verified findings, such as that low blood glucose (Virkkunen, 1987) or childhood abuse (Widom & Maxfield, 2001) has been found to be related to crime among some individuals. Because crime is so complex, any broader claims seeking to explain all crime with a simple statement would go beyond what could be verified empirically. Pragmatists and idealists sometimes disagree about issues because of differences in perceiving truth. The idealist might become frustrated with the pragmatist's focus on empirical verification, arguing that it loses sight of the "big picture"; conversely, the pragmatist might become frustrated with the idealist's desire to work from philosophical ideas that may not be precisely verified with data.

THE MIND/BODY CONNECTION

Not only can debates on criminal justice policy be clouded by different under-standings of truth, but these disagreements eventually run into the concept of reality. This raises a question: is the reality as perceived in our mind different from the reality in the physical world, as idealists might believe (a mind/body split)? Or is there only one true reality based on observable truth, as pragma-tists might believe (a mind/body connection)? It's important to explore these concepts further.

Idealists believe in a mind/body split. Recall the example from earlier in the chapter about how we know what a dog is. This goes back to ancient Greek philosophy in Plato's book, *The Republic*. Plato argued that for any object or concept (be it a dog, a chair, a triangle, or justice), there exists in the mind a perfect example (or model) of that concept. When identifying an object or concept in the physical world, we do so by comparing it to our notion of what the perfect example looks like. Reality, then, is whatever conforms to these perfect examples or models (Plato called them "forms"). This helps account for the passion with which idealists argue for their positions. When advocating for a concept (e.g., justice, rehabilitation, morality, or anything else), idealists are advocating for the perfect version of that concept, and anything short of that is both unacceptable and ultimately unreal.

Pragmatists believe in a mind/body connection and do not accept Plato's idea that there are perfect examples beyond the physical world. To the pragma-tist, the world is what it is, and reality is that which can be directly observed. When advocating for a concept, pragmatists are less concerned about the per-fect version of the concept but instead base their ideas on observations and data. A pragmatist arguing for rehabilitation, for instance, would be less con-cerned about the "perfect" version of rehabilitation but would be much more interested in whether or not particular programs work and what could be done to strengthen them.

> Do you think criminal justice professionals should follow idealism, pragmatism, neither, or both? Why?
>
> How can differences in idealistic and pragmatic understandings of harmony, truth, and the mind/body connection help to explain differing opinions on controversial issues? Provide an example.

Five Concepts of Morality

FOCUSING QUESTION 2.5

How do the five concepts of morality illustrate the distinction between idealism and pragmatism?

Idealism and pragmatism are competing philosophies with very different ideas about morality. Whether drawing upon idealism, pragmatism, or a combination of each, these decisions about morality are of great consequence to the justice system and the persons it affects.

Idealists and pragmatists have different ideas about knowledge, self, the nature of the universe, spirituality, and death, as illustrated in Table 2.2. These five concepts form the basis for their decisions about morality. We will consider each concept to show how they relate to idealism, pragmatism, and criminal justice.

KNOWLEDGE

Addressing questions about morality requires us to consider the logic that we apply when seeking answers to moral questions, whether they are questions of fact, questions of legal interpretation (i.e., what a law means), or questions about values. Idealists generally pursue these questions in an a priori manner. **A priori** reasoning occurs without empiricism and may stem from a number of sources, including tenacity, authority, or "common-sense" arguments offered without evidence. As long as the decision is in accord with harmony and truth as perceived by the idealist, it is acceptable. On the other hand, pragmatists rely on **a posteriori** reasoning. Even abstract ideas about morality draw upon actual experience and actual conditions in the world. Empirical verification is the hallmark of a posteriori reasoning in that it is grounded in observations, data, and experiences. Charles Sanders Peirce, a renowned American pragmatist philosopher, identified four ways by which we can know something (Peirce, 1877) that elaborate upon those described earlier; see Box 2.4 for a description.

For instance, consider analyses about whether burglary is right or wrong. The idealist would likely reason that burglary is wrong because it violates principles of security in one's property, thus leading to disharmony in the world. A pragmatist would likely reason that burglary is wrong based on the observable harm to others that it directly causes.

Table 2.2 **Five Concepts of Morality**

Moral Concept	Idealism	Pragmatism
Knowledge	a priori	a posteriori
Self	Higher purpose	Independent organism
Spirituality	Important role	Less important role
Universe	With overall purpose	Without purpose
Death	New beginning	The end

BOX 2.4

FIXATION OF BELIEF

Charles Sanders Peirce, a nineteenth-century pragmatic philosopher, developed an idea that still influences education today in the twenty-first century. In his article "The Fixation of Belief" (1877), he claimed there are four ways of knowing something. Every social science student is expected to understand the scientific (*a posteriori*) way of fixing a belief and to distinguish it from the other methods. The methods are:

1. Tenacity—Believing that something is true based on sheer desire to believe it so. In this case, something is true because you want it to be true. Individuals often use tenacity to support positions that are *intractable,* or not subject to empirical measurement (e.g., "justice is good").

2. Authority—Someone that you (or others) believe to be an authority figure claims something is true, and because of this person's authority, you believe it to be true as well. For instance, if a police chief tells you that crime rates have increased, then you would likely accept that as true without investigating data yourself.

3. Common-sense argument—You develop an argument that sounds logical but without the use of actual data or observations. For instance, you might believe that, because no one would want to be executed, using the death penalty would deter people from committing the crime of murder. On the surface, these arguments sound logical and well thought out. However, this can cause some questionable arguments to masquerade as reasonable when in fact they are not supported by the weight of the evidence (as is the case with arguments about the death penalty and deterrence, which research has not tended to support; e.g., Bailey, 1998).

4. A posteriori logic—This is a scientific way of knowing that verifies knowledge based on actual experience or data. The advantage of a posteriori logic is that it can demonstrate the truth or falsity of a proposition with evidence. For instance, if you were interested in drug courts (a rehabilitation program for drug offenders), you could determine the proportion of drug court participants who reoffend and compare that to the number of other offenders who reoffend. Your data would likely indicate that, on average, individuals who go through drug court are less likely to reoffend than those who do not (MacKenzie, 2006).

If you were to explain fixation of belief to a friend, what other examples could you use?

SELF

The concept of **self** represents how one views humanity. Does humanity have a timeless higher purpose or goal? Or is humanity primarily concerned with the day-to-day matters of the present time? Idealists see humanity as subject to rules that are not necessarily of their own making. The author of the rules could be a supreme being or it could be other forces in the universe, including a deep belief in certain values or ideas. By extension, idealists also believe that there is some sort of meaning or purpose to life. However, pragmatists believe that humanity is composed of organisms capable of thought, and as a result, they create their own individual meanings about what life is or should be. These meanings may change from time to time and are generally based on the pragmatist's experiences.

In the Lover's Lane scenario, did you consider the nature of humanity before deciding what to do? Perhaps or perhaps not. Regardless, differing views of self become important to consider. The ways criminal justice professionals view the nature of humanity, its purposes, and its goals can influence perceptions of justice and the exercise of discretion. This can also help explain disagreements about decisions involving morality.

SPIRITUALITY

Various notions of spirituality might affect how people make moral decisions and how they think they (and others) should behave. **Spirituality** may refer to belief in an organized religion (of any faith) or to a personal spirituality separate from a specific religious tradition. Idealists tend to believe not only that spirituality is important but that their spiritual traditions should be important in guiding the use of discretion, the development of law, and the overall conduct of society. It is important to note that pragmatists are not necessarily nonspiritual; in fact, pragmatists may have the same sort of deeply held spiritual beliefs as idealists. However, the role of spirituality in pragmatists' professional lives does differ from that of their idealistic peers. Pragmatists tend to view their personal spirituality as separate from their use of discretion, the development of law, and the overall conduct of society. Their personal spirituality is exactly that—personal and separated from their public lives.

In the Lover's Lane case, an idealistic officer might draw upon his or her spiritual tradition's approach to issues of sexuality, whatever it may be. A pragmatic officer might or might not have similar spiritual beliefs but would not incorporate them into the response to the situation. Pragmatists are more likely to believe in separation of church and state. This has been a contentious political issue in American history.

UNIVERSE

Some may see the universe as a natural entity with orderly processes and purposes. Others may see the universe as a chaotic environment with a disorienting series of problems. Idealists tend to see the universe as vast and purposeful, with an underlying order that, even if not directly observable, creates meaning (in philosophy, this is known as a **teleology**). Idealists also believe that humanity struggles to understand the principles that govern the order of the universe and to abide by those principles in making moral decisions. Pragmatists are more likely to believe in a universe without a recognizable purpose. This is consistent with the pragmatist's emphasis on that which is observable. To the pragmatist, it is irrelevant whether or not the universe has a purpose because it does not change either the universe itself or the problems that arise and must be resolved on a daily basis.

In the Lover's Lane example, an officer working from an idealistic perspective might consider (subconsciously, at least) the situation in terms of universal ideals. Of course, there are different possible interpretations of the universe's purpose. One idealist might see the universe as promoting the message "if it feels good, do it" and therefore feel that the proper moral decision is not to interfere with the couple's happiness and instead allow them to continue their activities. Another idealist might see the universe as requiring a celibate lifestyle outside marriage and therefore feel that the proper moral decision is to arrest the couple to stop the sexual activity and to deter them from engaging in similar behavior later. Both approaches could be justified as uses of discretion, and both involve making moral decisions. The pragmatist, on the other hand, would not see larger universal purposes as relevant, instead focusing on the harm that could come from the situation at hand, what rights could be affected, and how to respond accordingly.

DEATH

Appropriately, understandings of death are the final concept of morality. One unique quality among human beings is that we know, to borrow from Benjamin Franklin, that "nothing can be said to be certain, except death and taxes" (Isaacson, 2003, p. 463). Idealists often believe in an afterlife in some form (heaven, nirvana, reincarnation, or something else), which often includes being judged by a greater or higher force (which may or may not be a deity depending on their belief system). This leads some idealists to believe that in making moral decisions, they should judge others by the same criteria against which they believe they will be judged (this also relates to the pursuit of harmony). Pragmatists do not see death as having any special significance to moral decisions or actions. The pragmatist takes death seriously, especially when it results from a crime, negligence, or as a form of punishment. However, in these cases, it is the death itself that is important in the pragmatist's construction of a situation, and what happens after death is not significant. Events after death are not subject to direct observation and therefore do not play a strong role in the pragmatist's decision-making processes.

APPLYING PHILOSOPHY AND MORALITY TO CRIMINAL JUSTICE

Criminal justice is complex because it relates to complex human behavior. The criminal justice practitioner must be prepared to make difficult decisions about strategy, tactics, and discretion, and those decisions are fundamentally about morality. In making these complex decisions, individuals often follow the philosophical tendencies of idealism or pragmatism. These tendencies serve as **paradigms**, or worldviews that help individuals make decisions. By relying on idealism and pragmatism as paradigms, an individual does not start from scratch when addressing a problem. Rather, the paradigm—through its conception of harmony, truth, the mind/body connection, and the five concepts of morality—aids the individual in choosing the preferred methods and philosophies to apply in a situation.

Idealism and pragmatism may be viewed as endpoints on a continuum. There is much variation in human behavior and human thought. Some idealists may not believe in *all* of the elements of idealism that have been described, and some pragmatists may not believe in *all* of the elements of pragmatism described. Nonetheless, the descriptions do approximate two common perspectives on how to engage in the sorts of moral decision making necessary to address criminal justice questions. It is important to understand both models because doing so can help you understand why disagreements about criminal justice policy and practice occur and how they might be reconciled based on an individual's philosophical position.

The ultimate question for the criminal justice professional is, what is the right thing to do? Clearly, it is not as simple as making a choice that can be defended based merely on the situation at hand; instead, one must develop a consistent philosophy that produces the type of criminal justice best suited for a democratic society.

BOX 2.5

STERLING V. MINERSVILLE

On April 17, 1997, a police officer observed a vehicle in a parking lot with its lights off adjacent to a beer distribution center. The officer indicated that he was concerned about recent burglaries in the area and found the vehicle to be suspicious for that reason. Upon investigation, the officer found two males in the vehicle, an 18-year-old adult and a 17-year-old juvenile. The officer found no signs of a burglary to the establishment but did determine that the young men had been drinking. When questioned, the occupants of the vehicle were evasive with their answers. A legal search of the vehicle revealed two condoms, at which point the officer questioned the boys as to their sexual activity. Although the testimony remains debated, the officer testified that both boys acknowledged that they were gay and were in the parking lot to engage in consensual sexual activity. There was no law in the jurisdiction that prohibited either homosexuality or same-sex sexual behavior, and the two were both of legal age in their jurisdiction to engage in consensual sexual activity. However, because they were under the required drinking age of 21, the two boys were arrested for alcohol violations and taken to the police station.

While at the stationhouse, the officer lectured them on the Bible and counseled them against homosexual activity. The officer then told the 18-year-old that if he did not inform his grandfather he was gay, the officer would do it for him. Shortly after that statement, the 18-year-old confided to his friend he was going to kill himself, and upon release from custody, he committed suicide in his home. The Third Circuit Court of Appeals ruled that the officer had violated the young man's right to privacy (see Owen & Burke, 2003).

Consider the issue of capital punishment (the death penalty). How can it be analyzed through the five concepts of morality?

Drawing upon the five concepts of morality, explain how an idealist and a pragmatist would differ in their handling of the case presented in Box 2.5. How would you respond to the case. Why?

Do you think the criminal justice system more closely represents idealism or pragmatism? Provide examples.

Conclusion

Criminal justice professionals are called upon to make discretionary decisions on a daily basis. Whether addressing broad strategies or the tactics to implement them, these decisions have the potential to impact individuals and society in profound ways. This chapter has considered the role that academic scholarship, morality, and idealistic and pragmatic philosophies may play in shaping decisions about the practice of criminal justice. In the next chapter, we will draw upon the ideas presented here—particularly about idealism and pragmatism—to consider the different ways law can be understood and how these understandings can further shape the goals and activities of the criminal justice system.

Criminal Justice Problem Solving: **ALCOHOL POLICY**

American alcohol policy has had a long and varied history. "In early America, drink-ing was no vice" and was in fact common and accepted (Morone, 2003 p. 283). The importance of alcohol may be illustrated by the 1794 Whiskey Rebellion. In response to a national tax on whiskey levied in 1791 (to pay down the national debt), one congress-man stated that citizens in his district "have long been in the habit of getting drunk and that they will get drunk in defiance of . . . all the excise duties [taxes] which Congress might be weak or wicked enough to pass" (Boyer et al., 1993, p. 220). In 1794, citizens in Pennsylvania took up arms to resist the whiskey tax, and George Washington himself commanded federal troops to put down the uprising. This became a notable event in American history because it helped to establish the power of the federal government in the new republic.

However, there have also been numerous antialcohol movements in American history (Morone, 2003), the most notable leading to the prohibition of alcohol between 1920 and 1933. While there have been few calls to return to the Prohibition era, with its in-consistent enforcement, corruption, and attendant increase in crime (MacCoun & Reuter, 2001), debates about the legality of alcohol have continued, with a particular focus on the age at which individuals should be permitted to drink.

Worldwide, there is not a clear consensus on the appropriate drinking age. Some countries have no minimum drinking age. For those that do, the age tends to vary from 16 to 21 years old (Stimson, Grant, Choquet, & Garrison, 2007). And some countries prohibit the consumption of alcohol entirely.

In the United States, state governments are responsible for establishing the drinking age. Prior to 1988, there was variation in state laws: some set the drinking age at 18, others at 21. In 1984, Congress passed a law stipulating that states whose drinking age was lower than 21 would lose federal highway funding. By 1988, all 50 states had set their drinking age at 21 (Richardson & Houston, 2009). Recently, there has been consid-erable debate about lowering the drinking age to 18. In 2008, seven state legislatures considered measures that would lower the drinking age (Jolley, 2008). Also in 2008, more than 100 college and university presidents publicly expressed a desire for the drinking age to be lowered (Fain, 2008).

Lowering the drinking age from 21 to another age (most likely 18) would represent a substantial change in criminal justice policy. Would you be in favor of or opposed to this change? Why?

Discuss how an idealist would approach the answer to this question based on any of the concepts in this chapter.

Discuss how a pragmatist would approach the answer to this question based on any of the concepts in this chapter.

How would this change in law change criminal justice strategies, tactics, and discretion?

3

Concepts of Legal Philosophy

A "No cursing" sign in Virginia Beach, Virginia. Why do you think a locality would want to prohibit cursing?

Key Terms

six concepts of law
Hart-Devlin Debate
Wolfenden Report
legal moralism
collective judgment
harm principle
initiative or referendum elections
legal positivism
jurisprudence
idealistic theories of law

legal naturalism
natural law
critical theories of law
legal paternalism
parens patriae
legal pragmatism
legal realism
attitudinal model
majority opinion
dissenting opinion

Key People

Patrick Devlin
H. L. A. Hart
John Stuart Mill
Joel Feinberg

Richard Posner
Jeffrey Segal
Harold Spaeth
Michael Lipsky

CASE STUDY

Working the Corner

You are a police officer beginning your evening shift patrol with your partner, who is driving the squad car. At roll call, your sergeant reminded you that complaints about prostitution were increasing in your patrol area. In particular, citizens have expressed concern about prostitutes who openly solicit clients on the street and who perform sexual acts in alleyways and parked cars.

That evening, you find a young woman, whom you and your partner have previously arrested for prostitution, occupying her usual street corner. Your partner stops the squad car and confronts the woman, asking her, "What are you up to tonight?" The young woman responds, "You know what I do." Your partner interprets this as an admission of guilt for solicitation of prostitution and arrests her for that offense, although he did not witness any specific illegal behavior other than perhaps loitering. Later, your partner explains to you that he was just doing his job by giving the people what they want, which is streets free of immoral behavior. He knew the charges would likely be dismissed, but said, "At least she'll be off the streets for a while."

Do you agree with your partner's attitude and actions? Why or why not? If not, how would you have handled the situation differently?

Do you agree with your partner's description of a police officer's job: "giving the people what they want"? Why or why not?

Should police officers consider their own personal morality when they make discretionary decisions? What about the public's sense of

Chapter 3: Concepts of Legal Philosophy

morality concerning issues? Should legislators consider morality when determining what acts to define as crimes? Why or why not?

Studying Approaches to the Law

FOCUSING QUESTION 3.1

Why is it important to study the various philosophies of law?

It is important for criminal justice scholars, professionals, and policy makers to understand the distinctions between idealism and pragmatism and how they relate to questions of law and morality. We live in a diverse society where there is disagreement about what the law ought to accomplish and how it should do so, and debates grounded in idealistic and pragmatic thought certainly influence perceptions about the law.

The legal philosophies presented in this chapter also influence perceptions about the law, while building on the foundation of idealism and pragmatism introduced in Chapter 2. The goal of this chapter is to survey some of the classic and significant theories about the role of law in society. As you read, do not presume that there is a single legal philosophy that all persons agree upon. Likewise, do not presume that individuals simply select one philosophy and follow it when making all of their own personal decisions about what the law should accomplish. In reality, there is not uniform agreement about the role of law in society, and individuals may reflect on multiple legal philosophies when making a decision pertaining to law. The world is a complex place, but understanding a variety of (competing) legal philosophies will help to make some sense of it—at least in terms of the role of law in society.

This study is important because the perspective that an individual holds about the role of law in society can have several implications. It can affect how an individual enforces the law or thinks it should be enforced. It can affect how an individual behaves or thinks others should behave. It can affect how an individual votes or advocates for policies and helps explain why there are sometimes differences that are difficult to reconcile on controversial policy issues. And it can affect an individual's satisfaction with the legal system based on whether or not he or she believes the legal system, in practice, matches his or her concept of what the law should be. This, in turn, affects perceptions about whether the system is legitimate or whether it is in need of reform.

Consider the consequences of the latter point. If individuals perceive that the law has failed, they may lose confidence in the legal system. They may protest or engage in civil disobedience (deliberately disobeying a law they believe is unjust). They may simply ignore the law. Or they may engage in vigilantism and enforce the law themselves in the way they think it should be done rather than relying on the criminal justice system.

For all of these reasons, it is essential for criminal justice professionals, as well as policy makers and legislators, to give careful consideration to the role of law in society. For instance, it would not be enough for the police officer in the scenario at the beginning of the chapter to argue that he is "just enforcing the law." To appreciate the development of law and the pursuit of justice, we must understand the ideas that underlie them, which can also help us better understand our own positions.

> How can conflicts be resolved when two (or more) persons have differing philosophies of law that lead to differing opinions on a legal issue?
>
> Before reading about the various legal philosophies in this chapter, how would you explain what role you think the law should play in society? How would you apply your ideas to the scenario at the beginning of the chapter?

Analyzing the Law

FOCUSING QUESTION 3.2

What are the six concepts of law?

The chapter's opening scenario suggests an important question: should the law regulate morality? In the previous chapter, we saw that criminal justice decisions are often moral decisions because practitioners must, in the course of their jobs, resolve difficult questions about what is right and wrong. Here, we are interested in a slightly different question. When *making* the laws and determining what behaviors should or should not be punished under the law, should *legislators* (or the public or others) consider morality? If a group of legislators believe that prostitution is an immoral activity, is that a sufficient reason to make it illegal? Or should prostitution only be made illegal if it is found to harm persons? In fact, prostitution is not an issue on which there is unanimous agreement under the law. For instance, in some counties in Nevada, prostitution is not only legal but also regulated by the state (Brents & Hausbeck, 2001). In part, this stems from different understandings about the role of law in society.

This chapter will utilize **six concepts of law**, which provide a full understanding of the role law plays in society, from its creation through its actual use in guiding behavior. Too often, we may think of the law as doing only one thing or having one use without realizing that it is a much more complex concept. The six concepts of law help us organize that complexity. They are:

1. What is the *foundation of law*? On what ideas or notions is the law based?
2. What is the *rationale for law*? What purpose does the law serve in society?
3. How do we conceptualize the *formation of law*? How is the law created?

4. What is the application of law to actual problems? How is the law applied?

5. What is the *focal point of law*? What does one focus on to determine whether the law is successful?

6. What is the role of *discretion in law*? Is it to be encouraged or discouraged?

There is no single correct answer to these questions. Legal philosophers disagree about the proper approach to the law, as illustrated by the Hart-Devlin debate. The **Hart-Devlin debate** refers to an intellectual exchange between Patrick Devlin and H. L. A. Hart, both British legal scholars who wrote in the mid-twentieth century. Devlin fit the philosophical model of an idealist, and Hart fit the philosophical model of a pragmatist. The debate focused on the question of whether the law should attempt to regulate morality. We begin with this debate because it helps lay the groundwork for other idealistic and pragmatic legal theories.

The Hart-Devlin debate was sparked by the *Wolfenden Report* (1963), which was issued by a British government commission studying laws about prostitution and homosexuality. The report recommended legalizing private acts of homosexuality between consenting adults, in part because of "the importance which society and the law ought to give to individual freedom of choice and action in matters of private morality" (*Wolfenden Report*, 1963, p. 48). The recommendations regarding prostitution were more complex but essentially drew a distinction between public acts of prostitution, which were to be prohibited, and private acts of prostitution, which were to be tolerated. The report noted that the prostitution law "should confine itself to those activities which offend against public order and decency or expose the ordinary citizen to what is offensive or injurious" (*Wolfenden Report*, 1963, p. 143). Note that for both issues, the report recommended drawing a distinction between public and private behavior, and in the case of prostitution, the report was more concerned about disorder and harm than about the morality of the act. As you read, you may wish to refer to Box 3.1, which illustrates the difference between Hart's ideas and Devlin's ideas.

What do you think should be the relationship between the law and morality?

Do you agree or disagree with the *Wolfenden Report*'s recommendations? What criteria did you consider in making your decision?

Patrick Devlin's Legal Moralism

FOCUSING QUESTION 3.3

What did Devlin believe was the law's role in society?

Devlin ([1965] 1977) disagreed with the recommendations of the *Wolfenden Report* because he believed that the law should enforce public morality, a

BOX 3.1

RELATIONSHIPS OF LAW AND MORALITY

The relationships between law and morality in Figure 3.1 illustrate the differences between the theories of Patrick Devlin and H. L. A. Hart. Devlin believed that law and morality are inextricably joined. Hart believed that there is no necessary connection between law and morality.

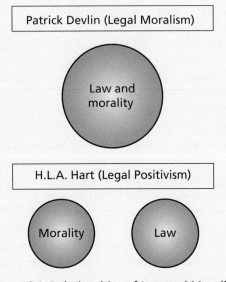

Figure 3.1. Relationships of Law and Morality

Which of these illustrations best represents your idea of how law and morality are connected? Can your ideas be illustrated in a better way?

Discuss which model would offer the best approach to the issue of animal abuse. Explain your answer.

philosophy known as **legal moralism**. To Devlin, religion and morality were linked because he believed that morality must be the basis for law and that religion must be the basis for morality. While religious foundations shaped Devlin's thinking, his philosophy was articulated through his consideration of three questions.

Devlin's first question was, "Has society the right to pass judgment at all on matters of morals?" (Devlin, [1965] 1977, p. 54). He answered this in the affirmative. To Devlin, a society's "**collective judgment**" (p. 55) would create a sense of public morality in which the members of a society would reach consensus about which behaviors are morally acceptable and which behaviors are morally unacceptable. Even *private* behavior could violate the *public* morality if it was perceived to affect society negatively in some way. And if it did, Devlin would argue that society could indeed pass judgment on it.

We will briefly compare Devlin's perspective to the work of John Stuart Mill, a nineteenth-century British philosopher. Mill ([1859] 1981) argued that society should only concern itself with actions that pose a direct harm to others. This notion has come to be known as the **harm principle**. Mill was not concerned about actions that might cause persons to harm themselves, nor was he concerned with actions that might *indirectly* lead to the potential for harm to occur. Also, Mill did not believe that society should concern itself with morality because he believed that doing so promoted conformity while discouraging the individuality that was necessary to allow a society to progress. Mill's position was reflected in the *Wolfenden Report*.

In contrast to Mill, Devlin believed that regulating public morality was necessary to allow a society to progress, as we see in the discussion of his second question, which was: "Has [society] also the right to use the weapon of the law to enforce [morality]?" (Devlin, [1965] 1977, p. 54). Devlin answered with a resounding "yes." To Devlin, a shared public morality was the bedrock of any society, and without this moral bedrock, the society would collapse. As a result, he believed that morality was essential to the very survival of society. Devlin noted that "societies disintegrate from within more frequently than they are broken up by external pressures" (Devlin, [1965] 1977, p. 59), and this could occur through two means—treason against the government and immorality. Because both means could promote the downfall of society, Devlin argued that both should be addressed with equal aggression through the law. Therefore, Devlin's philosophy does not distinguish between public and private acts; if the public believes the act is immoral, then Devlin would argue it threatens society and must be addressed in law.

Devlin's third question asked about how the government should go about creating a legal code reflecting moral interests. He recognized that there was the risk of creating a society in which *all* individual behavior is controlled by the public's opinion of morality, which would be undesirable. Devlin defines public morality as that "about which any twelve men or women drawn at random might after discussion be expected to be unanimous" (Devlin, [1965] 1977, p. 61). The unanimity should be guided by feelings of "intolerance, indignation, and disgust" (Devlin, [1965] 1977, p. 62) toward the issue in question. Without such strong feelings, Devlin believes it would be inappropriate to restrict an individual's behavior. Thus, he thought that the criminal law could be used to control behaviors that "lie beyond the limits of tolerance" (Devlin, [1965] 1977, p. 62).

Devlin also issued cautions in developing a morally driven legal code, as follows. First, it is important for the law (and for society) not to be overly restrictive but instead to focus only on aspects of morality that meet the rather strict criteria provided earlier. Otherwise, individuals should have freedom in their personal lives. Second, laws based on morality must be carefully considered and not made in haste. Over time, laws prohibiting a practice may remain on the books even if society no longer deems the practice immoral. It is then difficult to remove these laws "without giving the impression that moral judgment [overall] is being weakened" (Devlin, [1965] 1977, p. 63). Therefore, lawmakers should work to ensure that only the most significant moral issues are addressed by the law. Third, when enforcing laws based on morality, law enforcement should respect the legal requirements for privacy, such as procuring a warrant based on probable cause before entering a person's home to search for evidence of a crime. Finally, while the law can tell individuals not to engage in certain immoral acts, that does not mean that all people will then act morally in all other circumstances.

As an example of Devlin's legal moralism, consider a brief history of gambling law in the United States. From the early years of the United States into the twentieth century, collective judgment expressed a public morality opposed to gambling. In part, the moral objection to gambling was that it flouted the individual work ethic that was part of the national fabric: "Gambling was odious, then, because it was the wrong way to make money: it mocked the ideal of slow, steady progress through hard work" (Friedman, 1993, p. 134). As a result, laws against gambling of all sorts were enacted in the American states. Even private gambling was prohibited as a violation of society's morals. Gambling laws could not ensure that all financial transactions were moral, but they did help alleviate concerns that gambling would undo the stability of society. As the twentieth century unfolded, however, attitudes about gambling began to change. For instance, lotteries were increasingly viewed as engines for enhancing state budget revenues (Pierce & Miller, 2004), and riverboat casinos became popular strategies for localities to increase tourism and to stimulate the economy (Deitrick, Beauregard, & Kerchis, 1999). As Devlin predicted, changing the laws to permit lotteries and casinos proved difficult because some persons believed that doing so indicated an abandonment of social morality. However, the collective judgment on the issue clearly had shifted, as many laws were changed not by elected officials but by votes of the public as a whole (known as **initiative or referendum elections**) (Pierce & Miller, 2004).

DEVLIN AND THE SIX CONCEPTS OF LAW

Devlin's legal moralism can be assessed using the six concepts of law presented earlier. Table 3.1 summarizes how Devlin's theory fits the concepts. The left column lists the concepts of law. The middle column identifies the basic positions of the theory which, in Devlin's case, is idealistic, drawing upon the elements of idealism as described in the prior chapter. In particular, it seeks the truth in terms of a higher moral code, and it works to ensure that society is

Table 3.1. Devlin's Six Concepts of Law

Concepts	Idealist Perspective	Devlin's Position
Foundation of Law	*Public Morality*	Law is based on morality derived from religion
Rationale of Law	*Enforce Morality*	To preserve society by maintaining its morality
Formation of Law	*Nonempirical*	Underlying morality is the key principle to consider
Application of Law	*Rational*	Logical principles to ensure careful application
Focal Point of Law	*Product*	If society is preserved, then the law is successful
Discretion Within the Law	*Discouraged*	One person's private moral judgments should not replace society's views of public morality

in harmony with that moral code as enforced through the law. The third column provides further description of Devlin's position. Exploration of the six concepts of law will help you to compare and contrast the various theories presented in this chapter, to assess others as you discover them, and to arrive at your own philosophy about what the law should be.

Foundation of Law. Public morality is the foundation of law for Devlin. For legal moralists, the morality on which law is based often (though not always) has its base in religious beliefs of some sort. Devlin asserts that the public is duty bound to follow morality. This firm grounding in morality causes idealists to perceive great legitimacy in their efforts and to pursue them vigorously because they believe the stakes include not only the moral welfare of society but also its very survival.

Rationale of Law. For Devlin and legal moralists, the purpose of law is to preserve society by maintaining its underlying morality, arguing that a failure to do so would allow a society to crumble as its moral foundation shatters beneath it. Because proponents of legal moralism believe strongly in their underlying values, they often advocate firmly for laws supporting their values with only a limited willingness to compromise (see Sabatier & Jenkins-Smith, 1993). This is coupled with arguments that a failure to adopt a particular morality-driven law or policy will be a step toward society's decline.

Formation of Law. As conceptualized by Devlin, the legal moralist forms law by considering what the average person believes is morally offensive and then criminalizing it. This is a nonempirical method because it does not involve careful and systematic study of the issue that is being criminalized (which a pragmatist would favor); rather, it relies on beliefs about ultimate values and truths, which in their own right cannot be proven or disproven.

Application of Law. For Devlin and the legal moralists, the law must be applied carefully. Recall Devlin's principles to be considered as the law is implemented: that it permit freedom, that it is made carefully with a recognition that things may change over time, that it account for privacy in enforcement, and that it is realistic in recognizing that law will not cause all people to be virtuous all the time. This balances law and liberty and rationally considers the realities of what law can and cannot accomplish.

Focal Point of Law. Idealists tend to judge the success of the law by assessing its products, or end results. For instance, if the law punishes those who tamper with society's moral code and as a result the moral code remains intact, thereby preserving society, then the law has been successful. It is of less consequence whether or not the means (or techniques) used to accomplish the ends (or products) were proper, or appropriate, as long as the ends themselves are accomplished. Of course, this is an ethical question which has challenged criminal justice for centuries: What happens if a good result is obtained using improper or questionable methods? As Devlin perceived the law's regulation of morality as essential to society's survival, it is the outcomes that matter the most to legal moralism.

Discretion Within the Law. As discussed in Chapter 1, the use of discretion is an unavoidable component of criminal justice practice. The legal moralist does not take the position that there should never be discretionary decision making because that would be unrealistic. However, the legal moralist would discourage discretion, instead arguing that criminal justice practitioners should follow the public morality underlying the law rather that replacing it with their own individual views of morality. If the rationale of the law is indeed to preserve society by maintaining its underlying morality, then legal moralists would want that underlying morality to be uniformly enforced.

What is your opinion of the theory of legal moralism? Why?

Can you identify any examples of legal moralism? How do they meet the six concepts of law described in this section?

Do you believe there are any issues today that "lie beyond the limits of tolerance" using the criteria of "intolerance, indignation, and disgust"? Should they be controlled under the law? Explain your answer.

H. L. A. Hart's Legal Positivism

FOCUSING QUESTION 3.4

What did Hart believe was the law's role in society?

Legal positivism has been profoundly influenced by the work of British legal philosopher H. L. A. Hart ([1961] 1994). **Legal positivism** views the law solely as a human creation and not as an attempt to discover, confirm, or enforce higher moral standards. The legal positivist would not accept Devlin's notion that the law should even attempt to regulate morality. Hart (1958, pp. 601–602) identified five criteria for law that further illustrate the theory of legal positivism:

1. "Laws are commands of human beings";
2. "There is no necessary connection between law and morals";
3. "The analysis (or study of the meaning) of legal concepts is . . . worth pursuing and . . . to be distinguished from" . . . an assessment of morals;
4. "A legal system is a 'closed logical system' in which correct decisions can be deduced by logical means from predetermined legal rules" alone; and
5. "Moral judgments cannot be established or defended, as statements of fact can, by rational arguments, evidence, or proof."

Let's work to understand the meaning of these five criteria. It will become apparent that Hart is not an idealist because truth, harmony, and morality play little role in his theory. Hart's beliefs draw upon the pragmatic tradition because of his emphasis on viewing law as a rational creation of humans designed to address the observable reality of society, rather than nonempirical moral codes.

We will use gambling as an example to explore the five criteria. If a state were to pass a law against gambling based on legal positivism, it would be only because a group of individuals decided that such a law was necessary. There would be no presumption that the law was derived from any higher source (criterion 1). Simply believing that gambling is immoral would not be a sufficient reason to pass a law prohibiting it. Further, the mere fact that gambling is illegal is not necessarily an indicator that the behavior is immoral (criterion 2). The law could be based on evidence about facts pertaining to gambling, whether positive (such as economic development, e.g., Koo, Rosentraub, & Horn, 2007) or negative (such as gambling addiction, e.g., Room, Turner, & Ialomiteanu, 1999). However, evidence cannot prove or disprove the morality of gambling, which is a judgment not subject to empirical proof (criterion 5). When passed, the law should be clear enough so that a criminal justice professional would understand what it meant, to whom it applied, and how it should be enforced (criterion 4). And the law, its creation, and its impact could be subjects of legal scholarship and writing, **jurisprudence** (the study of law) being recognized as a legitimate area of academic study (criterion 3).

Hart's approach differs greatly from Devlin's. Hart himself wrote about his differences with Devlin, making several observations. Hart ([1959] 1971) observed that Devlin's approach is based largely on feelings, or emotions, in determining what is immoral. This means that, for Devlin, the law is also based on these feelings. Hart believed that feelings are not enough on which to base morality and not enough on which to base the law. In addition, Hart noted that emotionally based decisions about morality may infringe on individual liberties. This is problematic when "the popular limits of tolerance . . . shift" (p. 51)—that is, when a behavior is no longer viewed as immoral but remains illegal because people are reluctant to change the law (as Devlin predicted). At that point, the law continues to infringe on individual liberties but without a moral basis.

As a result, Hart believed that making decisions about the law must be more complex than reducing it to questions about perceptions of morality. Instead, he suggested that the first question should instead be whether the issue causes some sort of harm aside from concerns about morality. Hart did not believe society is threatened by acts that pose no harms aside from being viewed as immoral. To return to the recommendations of the *Wolfenden Report*, Hart wrote that there is no reason to believe society would be threatened because consensual sexual acts that are unpopular with the public are permitted to occur. In fact, Hart suggested that permitting legislation solely on the basis of Devlin's "intolerance, indignation, and disgust" ([1965] 1977, p. 62) can have dangerous results, as he illustrated with a striking example: "We once burnt old women because, without giving our reasons, we felt in our hearts that witchcraft was intolerable" (Hart, [1959] 1971, p. 53).

Hart ([1959] 1971) ended his critique of Devlin by issuing a caution to democratic societies: "it is fatally easy to confuse the democratic principle that the *power should be in the hands of the majority* with the utterly different claim that the majority, with the power in their hands, *need respect no limits*" [emphasis added] (p. 54). The concern is that Devlin's approach places no limits on lawmakers; if something is viewed as immoral, it can (and to Devlin, must) be made illegal. Hart was not opposed to morality. However, he believed that morality is not a *sufficient* reason to enact law, even if the majority is morally opposed to a practice. Instead, Hart believed it is important for government to protect the rights and freedoms of the public.

Let's consider one more example, this time about swearing (e.g., cursing or foul language). In some jurisdictions, cursing in public is against the law, and individuals have been arrested and cited for violating such laws (Associated Press, 2002). Some of these laws date back to early American history and are clearly grounded in concerns about public morality (Parkes, 1932). How would

Hart assess this kind of law? He would likely raise several objections. First, Hart might wonder what harm cursing actually causes and whether it would damage the fabric of society. Second, he might wonder what would happen if cursing later became an accepted behavior, as evidence suggests that it has, in particular judging from the mass media content (Jay, 1992). Could the law then be used against individuals whose behavior is no longer viewed with "intolerance, indignation, and disgust"? Third, Hart might be concerned about the impact of this law. What, exactly, is considered a curse word or inappropriate language? Could the law infringe upon free speech? These sorts of questions are those that Hart would want lawmakers to consider *before* making a law to ensure that it addresses legitimate concerns beyond general notions about the morality of swearing.

HART AND THE SIX CONCEPTS OF LAW

Hart's legal positivism can be assessed using the six concepts of law presented earlier. Table 3.2 summarizes how Hart's theory fits the concepts, reflecting the pragmatic approach described in the previous chapter.

Foundation of Law. Whereas Devlin believed that a public morality accepted by society is the foundation of law, Hart found the foundation in private morality. Hart believed that individuals should be entitled to follow their own morality as long as it is not "harmful to the legitimate interests of others. People have . . . a legal right to do (what others consider to be a) moral wrong" (Raes, 2001, p. 31).

Table 3.2. Hart's Six Concepts of Law

Concepts	Pragmatic Perspective	Hart's Position
Foundation of Law	*Private Morality*	Allow individuals the right to create their own morality
Rationale of Law	*Protect Individual Rights*	Individual needs are valued, even if scorned by society
Formation of Law	*Empirical*	Laws are formed based on careful study and analysis
Application of Law	*Irrational*	Professionals may reach different conclusions based on imperfect data
Focal Point of Law	*Process*	If the law follows its own rules, then it is successful
Discretion Within the Law	*Encouraged*	Discretion is inevitable and can strengthen the system

This notion sets clear limits as to what the law can and cannot do. Again, Hart was not opposed to morality, but he found morality, *by itself*, to be an insufficient reason for enacting a law.

Rationale of Law. Following from his foundation of law, Hart was concerned about protecting individual rights. Devlin would be willing to sacrifice individuals' rights by prohibiting them from doing things they would like to do, if doing so was necessary to protect society's moral views. On the other hand, Hart believed that individuals should have the freedom to do as they please as long as they do not harm others. For Hart, the law is not designed to create a model society (as Devlin believed) but rather to protect people's rights so they can live freely, but safely, within society.

Formation of Law. In creating law, Hart and legal positivists follow a rational process that is both logical and empirical. Rather than relying on feelings about what is moral and immoral, crafting the law about a particular issue requires careful study of that issue, its nature, its impact, its causes, and so forth. This demonstrates a desire for the empiricism that is characteristic of pragmatists. In doing so, lawmakers must work to identify the line between individual rights and harm to society, to strike the balance described in Hart's foundation of law, and to respect the rights described in Hart's rationale of law.

Application of the Law. Legal moralists discourage the use of discretion in law. This is sometimes accomplished through the development of guidelines for criminal justice professionals to follow (see Box 3.2 for one example). Rather than relying on guidelines, legal positivists would want to collect multiple data points (e.g., information about the offender's background, needs, employment, schooling, nature of the crime, etc.) and analyze them to reach the best decision in each individual case. This is also consistent with how legal positivists approach the formation of the law based on a careful study of data.

Table 3.2 labels this as irrational. In the application of law, the legal positivist is driven by two noble ideas. First, life's most important decisions are often made with insufficient information, and this should be remedied whenever possible. Second, human judgment should not be taken out of the law. As to the first observation, data will always be imperfect, especially when trying to make sense of complex human behavior. As to the second observation, infusing human judgment raises the possibility that different people will reach different conclusions based on the same data. For these reasons, the discretionary application of law becomes irrational in that outcomes are not driven by a strict set of rules and guidelines that guarantee the same result across different cases.

Focal Point of Law. For legal positivists, the law is successful only if it follows a clearly articulated, fair, and accepted process. Therefore, the means by which

BOX 3.2

SENTENCING GUIDELINES

In some jurisdictions, judges are required to utilize sentencing guidelines when deciding the appropriate punishment for an offender. Most sentencing guidelines incorporate two factors: an offender's prior record and the seriousness of the crime committed. Based on these pieces of information, a judge consults a grid to arrive at the appropriate sentence. A sample appears in this box. Across the top are column headings based on an offender's prior record. Down the left side, there are six rows (labeled A through F) representing the seriousness of the offense. The most serious offenses fall in the A category, and the least serious offenses are in the F category.

Let's say that trespassing is an F-level offense, and that it is the second offense for a particular trespasser. Looking at the table, this would indicate that the punishment should be a term of probation. All judges using this table would reach the same conclusion based on the facts.

Sentencing Matrix

Offense Seriousness	1st Offense	2nd Offense	3rd Offense	4th Offense
A	360	Life	N/A	N/A
B	120	240	Life	N/A
C	72	144	240	Life
D	36	72	144	240
E	18	36	72	144
F	Fine	Probation	18	36

There are more sophisticated sentencing models than the one presented here, but the idea is generally the same. To the idealist, this helps reduce discretion, ensuring that laws are enforced equally to protect the morality of society. To the pragmatist, tables such as this omit other information that would be useful in sentencing the offender, therefore reducing not only discretion but also empiricism in sentencing.

Do you think judges should be required to utilize sentencing tables such as this? Why or why not? If not, what alternatives would be more appropriate?

Which system would you prefer if you were a judge? If you were an offender? Explain.

the law operates become more important than the end results. This is not to say that the effectiveness of the law in responding to harmful behavior is unimportant—quite the contrary. Like good pragmatists, legal positivists want to collect data to see if the law is helping to reduce harms in society. However, remember that for legal positivists, promoting a private morality and protecting individual rights are most important and that careful study is required when forming and applying the law. For this all to occur, the process *must* be carefully followed, and if the process is not carefully followed, the law will likely not fully reflect the wishes of the legal positivist.

Discretion Within the Law. Hart acknowledges that the substantive criminal law, as written, cannot cover all possible scenarios of human behavior. This makes the use of discretion inevitable for criminal justice professionals. Furthermore, Hart would argue that the use of discretion could actually produce a better criminal justice system. For instance, better judgments, more informed by data and analysis, can be made by the criminal justice professional who is closest to the behavior or issue in question. This is closely related to the legal positivist's application of the law, discussed earlier, which relies on this sort of discretion. Discretion then becomes part of the process to ensure that the law is properly implemented and that individual rights are acknowledged.

> What is your opinion of the theory of legal positivism? Explain.
>
> Compare and contrast how Hart and Devlin would approach a law regulating foul language. Which approach do you most agree with? Why? You may wish to review the Michigan Court of Appeals case *Michigan v. Boomer* (2002).
>
> How do legal moralism and legal positivism compare to the characteristics of idealism and pragmatism described in the previous chapter?

Other Schools of Legal Philosophy

FOCUSING QUESTION 3.5

What are some other idealistic and pragmatic ideas about law?

Societies have long struggled to develop orderly legal systems. Two foundational approaches are those advocated by Devlin and Hart. Other theorists have also written about the law. Table 3.3 lists additional theories of law beyond legal moralism and legal positivism that we will briefly consider.

The theories are grouped according to whether they most closely reflect idealism or pragmatism. Although we do not attempt to cover all possible theories of law, this discussion will give you the flavor of some theoretical variations. The theories described serve as excellent examples that further distinguish between legal idealism and legal pragmatism. Expanding your understanding with these additional theories will help you to further appreciate others' ideas about law and justice, to see how those ideas lead to the creation and interpretation of laws, and to give you the opportunity to reflect on your own ideas about what the law should do.

Table 3.3. Legal Theories

Legal Idealism	Legal Pragmatism
Legal Moralism	**Legal Positivism**
Legal Naturalism	Legal Realism
Rights and Interpretive Jurisprudence	Everyday Pragmatism
Critical Theories of Law	
Legal Paternalism	

THEORIES OF LEGAL IDEALISM

Our discussion begins with **idealistic theories of law**. While all subscribe to the basic tenets of idealism, there is variety in how they do so. However, the theories tend to share the following ideas:

1. A systematic method is used to develop a legal system based on beliefs held as truths without empirical evidence.
2. Legal decisions draw upon history and tradition, attempting to reflect long-held understandings of the truth.
3. The purpose of the legal system is to create and serve a moral society (however "moral" may be defined), and if it does not do so, the law has failed.
4. Laws that do not correspond to the standards of public morality, and which do not work to create and serve a moral society, are viewed as invalid.
5. The legal system should consistently follow precedents (i.e., prior decisions) when dealing with similar cases rather than treating similar cases differently.
6. Legal idealism competes with other legal theories, and proponents of the theory work to demonstrate its superiority to other theories.

Individual philosophers vary in the degree of emphasis they give to each idea, and some may even alter the ideas or add new ones. However, your ability to recognize these concepts will help you to explain and interpret idealistic legal thought and behavior.

LEGAL NATURALISM

Proponents of **legal naturalism** believe in the concept of natural law. So far, you have read about theories in which humans create law either by attempts to define the public morality on which individuals agree (for legal moralists) or by more empirical processes focusing on the prevention of harm (for legal positivists). A belief in **natural law**, on the other hand, presupposes that there are *universally* *accepted principles* of human behavior that are meant to apply to all persons everywhere. For instance, a natural law theorist would argue that just as gravity is a natural law of physics applicable everywhere on Earth, there also exist standards of human behavior that should apply to all persons without exception.

But how does a natural law theorist know what these universal standards of behavior are? Because natural law assumes that these principles are inherent within the universe and not created by humans, there is no easy answer to this question. Some base their answers on what they believe to be universal religious principles, but others draw upon various conceptions of the state of nature to distill basic principles necessary for the peaceful coexistence of multiple persons. As an example, some natural law theorists might argue that universal principles suggest that all persons have a right to live without fear of violence. This principle would suggest that murder, assault, and war must be prohibited under law (interestingly, in 1928, the Kellogg-Briand Pact unsuccessfully attempted to criminalize war under international law; Paterson, Clifford, & Hagan, 1991). Therefore, laws against murder, assault, and war would not be made by humans but rather would be implemented because it was natural to do so and would be presumed to apply in all societies across the globe. It is worth reiterating the distinction from legal moralism. Law is not made because a group of people gathered to decide what was moral or not. Here, law is made because it is simply following the natural principles, design, order, or intent of the universe.

Philosopher Mortimer Adler (1947) argued that to make law "without a foundation in natural law is purely arbitrary" (p. 83) because doing so would mean that any legislator or politician could propose any law for any reason without having to reference grander truths. This could make the law appear very subjective, responding to the whims of the time. There would be nothing to prevent arbitrary changes to the law. At the same time, Adler noted that natural law, by itself, "is ineffective for the purposes of enforcing justice and keeping peace" (p. 83). Even if natural law issues moral absolutes (e.g., "stealing is bad"), someone must still identify those principles and incorporate them into a written legal code—a process which can be sidetracked by politics, debates about legal philosophies, or other distractions, resulting in outcomes other than the reflection of natural law in the legal code. This is a dilemma that is difficult to resolve, perhaps because once again it illustrates the differences between idealists in search of overarching principles and pragmatists seeking to make law based only on what is measurable and directly observable in the world. Table 3.4 describes how legal naturalism corresponds to the six concepts of law.

RIGHTS AND INTERPRETIVE JURISPRUDENCE

American legal philosopher Ronald Dworkin may be classified as an idealist due in part to his position on the role of morality in law. Although Dworkin was not quite as adamant as Devlin about the risks that immoral behavior

Table 3.4. Legal Naturalism and the Six Concepts of Law

Concepts	Idealistic Perspective	Legal Naturalism
Foundation of Law	*Public Morality*	Universal principles of human conduct
Rationale of Law	*Enforce Morality*	Law should promote universal standards
Formation of Law	*Nonempirical*	Laws should be made after identifying natural principles
Application of Law	*Rational*	The law should be clear and enforced uniformly
Focal Point of Law	*Product and Process*	Follow a natural process to achieve a moral outcome
Discretion Within the Law	*Discouraged*	Law should not be individualized, but should be enforced uniformly

posed to society, he did believe that legislators and judges could not ignore moral considerations when framing and interpreting law. Another point of difference between Devlin and Dworkin is in how morality is defined. Dworkin strongly criticized Devlin's methods of determining public morality, instead advocating for a more rational and even empirical approach:

> The claim that a moral consensus exists is not itself based on a poll. It is based on an appeal to the legislator's sense of how his community reacts to some disfavored practice. But this same sense includes an awareness of the grounds on which that reaction is generally supported. If there has been a public debate involving the editorial columns, speeches of his colleagues, the testimony of interested groups, and his own correspondence, these will sharpen his awareness of what arguments and positions are in the field. *He must sift these arguments and positions*, trying to determine which are prejudices or rationalizations, which presuppose general prejudices or theories vast parts of the population could not be supposed to accept, and so on. It may be that *when he has finished this process of reflection* he will find that the claim of a moral consensus has not been made out. [emphasis added] (Dworkin, 1966, p. 1001)

Therefore, we see that Dworkin shares the idealist's emphasis on morality in the foundation and rationale of law. He also shares idealistic tendencies in the application, focal point, and discretion of law. In his "right answer thesis," Dworkin (1978) argues that there is a correct answer even to the most difficult legal problems. It is the obligation of a judge to strive for identifying that right answer through a careful interpretation of legal materials (and that interpretation includes the consideration of moral contexts in which the law was made). Dworkin disavows the idea of having judges create their own versions of the law to fill in gaps in the written legal code, meaning that Dworkin is focused on a single proper (or correct) outcome as the focal point of law and does not advocate for frequent use of discretionary decisions. Although Dworkin has a well-respected moral theory, his critics note that he appears to rely on a single interpretation of morality to determine what the law should be (Tamanaha, 2004).

The protection of rights is important to Dworkin, and he believes that society should take rights seriously (1978). Should a legal conflict come down to the question of whether or not rights should be protected, Dworkin would generally favor protecting the rights. Therefore, his emphasis on morality is tempered by an appreciation for individual rights, which was less prominent in Devlin's theory. However, the formation of law may still be considered nonempirical because it does focus on the identification of a common morality which plays an important role in idealistic philosophy—even though the identification of morality is achieved through the rational process quoted earlier. Table 3.5 describes how Dworkin's theory corresponds to the six concepts of law.

CRITICAL THEORIES OF LAW

Critical theories of law represent a relatively new field with roots in the 1970s. It is also a somewhat diverse field comprised of a variety of different—but

Table 3.5. Interpretive Jurisprudence and the Six Concepts of Law

Concepts	Idealistic Perspective	Dworkin's Position
Foundation of Law	*Public Morality*	Morality discovered after careful interpretation
Rationale of Law	*Enforce Morality*	Law is grounded in morality but with protection of rights
Formation of Law	*Nonempirical*	Morality is the key principle in the creation of law
Application of Law	*Rational*	Interpret laws to identify the single correct answer
Focal Point of Law	*Product*	Discovering the proper answer leads to better law
Discretion Within the Law	*Discouraged*	Deviation from reasoned morality is avoided

overlapping—perspectives. According to most critical theorists, the law was created by powerful individuals to help them remain in power. Here are a few ideas shared by critical theorists.

1. Throughout American history, laws have been created by those with wealth and power to maintain their interests.
2. The interests of those with power differ from the interests of those without power.
3. The motives and hidden meanings of the law should be questioned to determine whether (and how) they marginalize and dehumanize those without power.
4. Developing a critical theory of law can raise awareness to these concerns, articulate the value of all persons, and prevent the law from being used to restrain or harm those without power in society.

Critical legal theorists have undertaken two distinct but related tasks. One task is to be critical of the status quo as described in the first two items on the list. Another task is to offer a better approach and to remedy problems they have identified in the law by accomplishing the third and fourth items on the list. Critical theory is often associated with calls for larger social reforms beyond the law, including the consideration of an array of social problems and the promotion of justice in law and society. This means that the focal point of law for critical theorists is in the outcomes, by accomplishing the reforms and achieving the move toward justice and equality that they desire.

While some critical theorists would disagree, it seems that critical theory fits more neatly in an idealistic framework than in a pragmatic framework, although there is some degree of overlap. Critical theorists are attempting to accomplish and enforce morality under the law, which places them in the framework of idealism. However, the morality that they draw upon is precisely focused, exploring issues related to the values of justice, fairness, and equality for all persons, and how they are related to societal power structures. These values are held as ultimate truths that are used in the pursuit of harmony in the world.

The formation of the law is listed as both rational and irrational. Some theorists hold their beliefs as a matter of value that is not subject to empirical verification. Other theorists draw upon sophisticated bodies of empirical evidence to structure their arguments, such as providing evidence about poverty, inequalities in arrests and sentencing, and so forth.

The application of law and use of discretion also follow idealistic principles. Critical theorists are generally fighting inequalities, and permitting widespread use of discretion or flexible application of law would have the potential to exacerbate those inequalities. In fact, discretion could be perceived as one tool that is utilized to favor those in power and punish those who are not.

You may sense that critical legal theory is controversial; it is. One example that illustrates critical theory is the disparity in sentencing between white-collar crimes and street crimes. White-collar crimes can result in injury and death, largely due to negligence or toxic environments (see Kappeler & Potter, 2005). However, sentences for white-collar crimes are often lenient, especially when compared to sentences for street crimes that cause less harm financially or otherwise (Reiman, 2001). Is this because the law was deliberately structured to protect the wealthy and financial wrongdoings? Some critical theorists would argue that to be the case. Or does society perceive street crime as more serious? In either case, critical theorists would work toward promoting fairness in the system, but doing so requires that they challenge the status quo, its assumptions, and its values, which can raise controversial questions. Table 3.6 summarizes the six concepts of law for critical legal theory.

LEGAL PATERNALISM

Under the philosophy of **legal paternalism**, the government can pass laws "to protect individuals from self-inflicted harm or, in its extreme version, to guide them, whether they like it or not, toward their own good" (Feinberg, 1971, p. 3). That is, if a person engages in a behavior that is likely to harm him or her but not harm anyone else, should the law intervene? Legal paternalists would answer that the law should. Some laws do attempt to protect people from making dangerous decisions, such as requiring a prescription for medications about which individuals might not know the proper uses and side effects.

All behavior, even something as routine as crossing the street, carries some risk of harm. Therefore, the challenge for the paternalist is to determine which

Table 3.6. Critical Legal Theory and the Six Concepts of Law

Concepts	Idealistic Perspective	Critical Theory
Foundation of Law	*Public Morality*	Morality emphasizing the needs of all citizens rather than the elite
Rationale of Law	*Enforce Morality*	Protect individuals with an emphasis on justice, fairness, and equality
Formation of Law	*Rational and Irrational*	Law may be based on empirical evidence or on notions of truth
Application of Law	*Rational*	Strict adherence to law to ensure fairness for all
Focal Point of Law	*Product*	Harmonic society for all citizens, not just the elite
Discretion Within the Law	*Discouraged*	Enforce law fairly without bias or special treatment

behavior is sufficiently risky to need regulation. Feinberg (1971) notes several factors that can be considered in this decision, including whether the behavior is voluntary, whether the risks are known or unknown, and the probability and severity of the potential harm. When a behavior is deemed risky enough to be regulated, legal paternalism can proceed in two ways. The first is a weak paternalism in which the law may intervene to ensure that individuals understand the potential risks of their behavior and are indeed willing to accept them; if they are, they may engage in the behavior. The second is a strong paternalism in which the law discourages (through higher taxes to discourage purchases of risky items, limiting where risky behavior can take place, etc.) or actually prohibits a risky behavior.

As an example, consider whether or not motorcycle riders should be required to wear helmets. A weak paternalistic response might be a state-funded media campaign alerting drivers of the risks, with the hope that it would increase their awareness to ensure that a choice not to wear a helmet was made voluntarily and with full information. A strong paternalistic response might be to require that helmets be worn while a motorcycle is in operation and fining drivers who fail to do so.

Legal paternalism meets the general criteria of an idealistic legal philosophy. The morality that paternalists perceive as the foundation and rationale of law is a belief that society has a moral obligation to protect its citizens, with the metaphor of the law acting as a parent to its subjects (a concept known as *parens patriae*). The formation of paternalistic law is generally rational in that it must be based on a consideration of the risks of the behavior. Paternalistic law does not support discretion. The focal point of law lies in its outcomes because the assumption is that all persons engaging in a prohibited risky behavior must be stopped for their own safety no matter what their intentions might be. This makes for a clear but rigid application of the law. Table 3.7 summarizes the six concepts of law for legal paternalism.

THEORIES OF LEGAL PRAGMATISM

Richard Posner (2003) is a leading spokesperson for **legal pragmatism**. Posner and other legal pragmatists would prefer to see the law based on empirical evidence rather than grand concepts such as morality. Again, this is consistent with Hart's approach as well. We will consider two additional legal philosophies that have their roots in the ideas of legal pragmatism.

LEGAL REALISM

Legal realists give their primary focus to the decision-making processes of the courts because they believe that the courts *create* law through their accumulated decisions. The law, then, becomes whatever the courts say it is.

A modern perspective related to the roots of legal realism is the **attitudinal model**, which was developed by political scientists Jeffrey Segal and Harold

Table 3.7. Legal Paternalism and the Six Concepts of Law

Concepts	Idealistic Perspective	Legal Paternalism
Foundation of Law	*Public Morality*	Value of protecting all citizens from harm
Rationale of Law	*Enforce Morality*	Views law and government in the role of a "parent"
Formation of Law	*Rational*	Based on study and analysis of what behaviors are risky
Application of Law	*Rational*	Law must be applied to all persons, as written, to minimize risks of harm
Focal Point of Law	*Product*	Minimizing risk
Discretion Within the Law	*Discouraged*	It is morally wrong to pick and choose who to protect through enforcement of law

Spaeth (1993) to explain Supreme Court behavior. The attitudinal model argues "that the Supreme Court decides disputes in light of the facts of the case vis-à-vis the ideological attitudes and values of the justices" (p. 65). Almost any Supreme Court case provides an example. When the Supreme Court decides a case, it issues a **majority opinion** that becomes the law of the land. Justices who disagree with the majority can write a **dissenting opinion**, which does not become law but serves as a statement of a justice's beliefs. For instance, in a 2001 case *Kyllo v. United States*, the Supreme Court addressed the question of whether a search warrant should be required before taking thermal images outside a home (e.g., the use of infrared images to detect heat emanating from a structure, which could indicate whether marijuana was grown inside). Five justices agreed that a warrant should be required; four justices argued that it should not. Each side issued a written opinion supported by facts, law, and rational argument. How could the justices reach opposite conclusions based on one body of facts and law? Because, as the legal realists suggest, the law is what the judges *interpret* it to be, and different judges may reach different (though legitimate) interpretations.

Legal realists focus primarily on the courts. However, similar questions could be asked of other criminal justice professionals. Do a police officer's discretionary decisions on the street serve to create law? Are a correctional officer's discretionary decisions in a prison based on interpretations of what policies mean or ought to mean? This is the basis of Michael Lipsky's (1980) theory of street-level bureaucracy in which he argues that the individual decisions made by practitioners do in fact create policy, which may be different from or serve to interpret what written laws and policies actually say. Discretion and independence in the application of law are key values to the legal realist.

Unlike idealists, legal realists do not claim that the law has a specific foundation. They believe it may be presumptuous to assume what the foundation of law might be. Legal realists do not rely on public morality as a foundation for law because they are more likely to rely on interpretive and problem-solving skills to discover the meaning of the law through the consideration of individual cases. Legal realism does ask whether the law makes society a better place to live by solving problems. A successful law does not need to determine the morality or immorality of an offense. A successful law is one that (through the interpretive actions of criminal justice professionals) provides a meaningful answer to the victim of the crime, to the offender, and to society. Table 3.8 summarizes the six concepts of law for legal realism.

EVERYDAY PRAGMATISM

Richard Posner, a judge on the U.S. Seventh Circuit Court of Appeals, argues that the pragmatism of everyday people has become the basis of the law (2003). The law is capable of functioning in our society because the citizenry allows it to do so. If the law was unsatisfactory, everyday people could protest or rebel against it, at which point the law would no longer be legitimate (i.e., no longer have the public support it needs to be effective). Posner is not suggesting that the people have assembled and agreed upon any legal concepts. Rather, the law is dynamic and has evolved into its present form, which is acceptable to the public's interests.

Table 3.8. Legal Realism and the Six Concepts of Law

Concepts	Pragmatic Perspective	Legal Realism
Foundation of Law	*Private Morality*	Morality need not be the basis for law; realists do not focus on foundations of law
Rationale of Law	*Protect Individual Rights*	Balance rights, societal needs, and other factors to provide meaningful results
Formation of Law	*Rational*	Analyzes the immediate situation under review
Application of Law	*Irrational*	The law as written is not always clear or applicable and must be interpreted
Focal Point of Law	*Process*	Outcomes depend on the process that is followed by professionals
Discretion Within the Law	*Encouraged*	Professionals make judgments to give law meaning

One of Posner's ideas is that the law is an *activity* (1993). The importance of this idea is that, again, law is dynamic, changing over time as a result of the interactions between people. It would be a dramatic oversimplification to suggest that law is adopted and then enforced. Law is created through negotiations, often in a political context, and then shaped by the discretionary decisions of criminal justice professionals. And as the public, the media, interest groups, scholars, and others see areas that are in need of reform or revision, they are raised and reconsidered, all of which involves human interaction. The law, then, in addition to being an activity, is shaped by a multitude of individuals, and the responsibility for the law ultimately lies with all people in a democratic society.

We do not present the six concepts of law for this perspective because it is more centered on a realistic view of the process by which law is developed than on a full exposition of the six concepts. However, it is a perspective that is important to appreciate when considering how the law has been constructed.

Of the theories presented, which do you think are useful perspectives on shaping or implementing the law? Which are not useful? Why?

How would each of the theories address the case study at the beginning of the chapter? What are the differences and similarities?

Conclusion

Whether police officers, attorneys, judges, correctional officers, or serving in other areas of the justice system, criminal justice professionals are charged with upholding the laws of society. On the surface, this sounds simple enough, but the complexities reveal themselves when we discover that there are multiple—sometimes conflicting—opinions about what the law should accomplish. Before attempting to enforce the law, it is important to reflect on its purpose(s) by considering perspectives such as those described in this chapter. Although it is not likely that there will ever be complete agreement about the role of law in society, understanding the debates can help place into context the variety of laws that are on the books or that are proposed in legislatures each year. As we move to Unit II, we will consider why some persons violate the laws that have been established and the forms of social control that attempt to regulate behavior.

Criminal Justice Problem Solving: **NUDIST CAMPS**

The previous chapter was about moral reasoning pertaining to criminal justice under the idealistic and pragmatic models. This chapter was about legal theory under the idealistic and pragmatic models. This material need not be considered in isolation but should be integrated. Consider *White Tail Park v. Stroube* (2005), a case from the Fourth Circuit of the U.S. Court of Appeals.

> AANR-East [American Association for Nude Recreation—Eastern Region, Inc.] is one of several recreational organizations affiliated with the American Association for Nude Recreation, a national social nudism organization. In June 2003, AANR-East opened a week-long juvenile nudist camp at a licensed nudist campground operated by White Tail near Ivor, Virginia. AANR-East leased the 45-acre campground that ordinarily attracts about 1,000 weekend visitors who come to engage in nude recreation and interact with other individuals and families who practice social nudism . . .
>
> Modeled after juvenile nudist summer camps operated annually in Arizona and Florida by other regional divisions of AANR, the 2003 AANR-East summer camp offered two programs: a "Youth Camp" for children 11 to 15 years old, and a "Leadership Academy" for children 15 to 18 years old. The camp agenda included traditional activities such as arts and crafts, campfire sing-alongs, swimming, and sports. The camp also included an educational component designed to teach the values associated with social nudism through topics such as "Nudity and the Law," "Overcoming the Clothing Experience," "Puberty Rights Versus Puberty Wrongs," and "Nudism and Faith." A total of 32 campers attended the 2003 summer camp [and AANR-East planned to operate the camp the subsequent year].
>
> Prior to the scheduled start of AANR-East's 2004 youth camp, the Virginia General Assembly amended the statute governing the licensing of summer camps specifically to address youth nudist camps. The amended statute requires a parent, grandparent or guardian to accompany any juvenile who attends a nudist summer camp (p. 455).

Prior to this new law, there was no requirement that guardians accompany their children at nudist camps. AANR-East, White Tail, and three sets of parents sued Robert B. Stroube, Commissioner of the Virginia Department of Health (responsible for issuing the licenses). The complaint stated that the new law violates parents' rights to raise their children as they see fit. In other words, the complaint alleges that parents should have the right to send their children to a properly licensed nudist summer camp, without having to accompany them for the duration of the camp.

Using the concepts presented in Chapter 2, describe the perspectives you could use to engage in moral reasoning about this issue. Explain your response.

Using the concepts presented in this chapter, describe the perspective of law you would use to resolve this issue. How would it resolve the issue?

In what ways are your responses to the preceding questions connected? Do you see any common themes that might be important in guiding your own interpretation of the law?

Do any of the five concepts of morality (Chapter 2) or six concepts of law (this chapter) strike you as more important than the others? How would they affect your decision in this case?

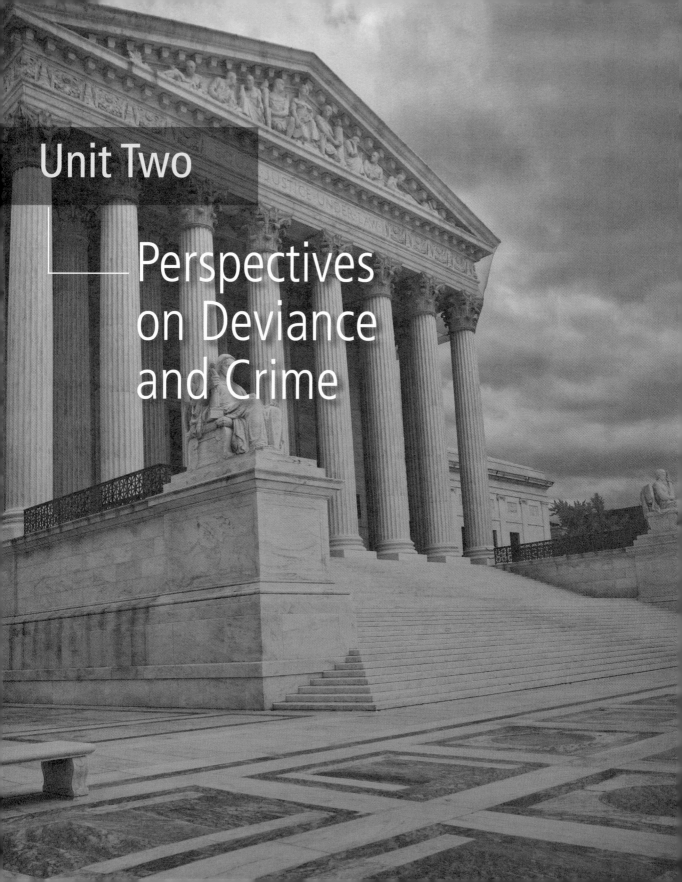

Unit Two

Perspectives on Deviance and Crime

Photo Essay: What Behaviors Are Deviant?

The study and practice of criminal justice involve pragmatic and idealistic questions about the relationship between law and morality and the role of law in society. These ideas help shape decisions about how the law ought to be developed and enforced. This unit continues the discussion by exploring how societies decide what behaviors should be permitted and what behaviors should be prohibited. We also consider competing explanations for reasons individuals engage in behaviors that society has labeled as deviant or illegal.

What makes us describe some behaviors as acceptable and others as unacceptable? There is no simple answer to this question, nor is there a consensus about what is deviant and what is not. Although there is consensus that serious crimes such as murder, rape, robbery, and assault should be labeled as deviant and criminalized, other behaviors have been the subject of legal debate, as the following examples illustrate.

Would you wrestle a bear? Should you? In 1998, the citizens of Missouri went to the polls to, among other issues, vote on whether to make bear wrestling a criminal offense. They voted to make it a crime (Bear Wrestling, 2010). But is it deviant? Statistically, it is safe to assume that not many individuals have wrestled a bear—but that does not automatically make it illegal. In Ohio, bear wrestling is legal (as of this writing). At least one venue in the state has allowed members of the public to wrestle bears (Associated Press, 2006). What do you think are the arguments on either side of bear wrestling? What principles would you consider in determining whether the practice is deviant? How would this shape your opinions about what, if any, laws should govern the practice? How does this compare to issues such as dog fighting or cockfighting?

Let's consider a practice that, unlike bear wrestling, is very common but still the subject of legal debate. Estimates are that over 90% of the American public has been spanked during childhood (Straus, 2001), a number that some say is too high. In fact, in 2007, laws were proposed in California that would have banned physical discipline of children three and younger as well as the use of belts, paddles, or other implements to spank any child (Vogel, 2007). This is not without precedent, as a number of European countries have banned spanking altogether, including Germany and Sweden. The rally shown here is part of a European antispanking campaign. Conversely, in 2008, the

Indiana Supreme Court upheld the legality of a punishment in which an 11-year-old was struck "five to seven times with either a belt or an extension cord" (*Willis v. State*, 2008, p. 179). Clearly, there is not an American consensus on this issue. Should spanking be defined as deviant? Why or why not? Again, reflect on what principles you would consider in making your decision.

Bear wrestling and spanking may have little in common, except that both may inflict pain and possibly injury, depending on the circumstances. But is the causation of injury a consistent principle that is used to define deviance? The answer is "no." The law is generally willing to accept, or even encourage, some harmful practices. For instance, athletes may participate in activities that can result in or cause physical harm, even for juveniles (high school football games can be rough!). But is there a limit? What is the dividing line between physical harm a player consents to as part of the game and physical harm that crosses the line into an unacceptable assault? Even for those acts that go too far, where is the line between wagging a finger and saying, "That's bad sportsmanship," versus deciding to file criminal charges (see Yates & Gillespie, 2002)?

Part of the dilemma about injuries related to sporting activities stems from the fact that athletes know that there is a risk of harm and accept it as part of the game. Does consent, then, become a significant aspect of defining deviance? If an adult voluntarily chooses to wrestle a bear but a juvenile does not choose to be struck with a belt as a form of punishment, does it influence perceptions of whether that behavior is socially or legally acceptable? Consent

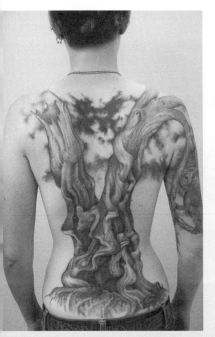

is a complex issue, but it, too, is inconsistent as a predictor of what is deviant. Like sports, the law is generally willing to allow individuals to modify their bodies through tattooing, piercing, and other practices, although doing so may cause pain, physical alteration, scarring, or other outcomes that, without consent, would certainly be viewed as criminal (Egan, 2007).

Compare body modification, such as piercing and tattooing, to sadomasochistic sexual practices, also known as S&M. One definition of S&M practices is: "The knowing use of psychological dominance and submission, and/or physical bondage, and/or pain, and/or related practices . . . in order for the participants to experience erotic arousal or personal growth" (Egan, 2007, p. 1616).

Generally, the law has been reluctant to allow individuals to consent to injuries that result from S&M, unlike those which result from body modification or sports (Egan, 2007). Does this reflect inconsistencies in law and in definitions of deviance? Or does it reflect a divergence in attitudes about the sexual versus the nonsexual, the mainstream versus a subculture, or other distinctions? It becomes clear that there is not a so-called "bright line," to borrow a legal term, that distinguishes what is deviant from what is not, and much less a line that determines when the law should get involved and when it should not.

Much of this photo essay has focused on activities that have some potential for harm. But what about behaviors that are not inherently harmful; may they be defined as deviant and subject to social control? "Sagging" is the colloquial term to describe the practice in which individuals, usually male, wear their pants low enough that their undergarments (or lack thereof) are readily visible. Those who believe that it is deviant have used a variety of strategies to curtail the behavior. For instance, one New York legislator sponsored billboards, such as the one pictured on the previous page, to use informal social control to encourage individuals not to sag (Peltz, 2010). Others have promoted more formal social control, as local ordinances have been passed in some communities that would punish sagging through fines and jail time (Koppel, 2007). Is sagging deviant? What arguments do you think could be made on either side?

The focus of this unit is deviance. As you will see, there is no single explanation as to why certain acts are labeled as deviant whereas others are not. Nor is there a single explanation for why some behaviors that are labeled as deviant are controlled through the law (prisons and fines), whereas others are controlled more informally (through peer pressure or scolding). And there is no single explanation for why some individuals choose to engage in behaviors that have been labeled as deviant. However, all of these topics are essential to the study of criminal justice because a natural starting point is understanding the behaviors to which the criminal justice system ultimately responds (or equally important, does not respond) through its law enforcement powers. As you read the chapters in this unit, pause to consider issues like these, reflecting on the human behavior (and debates around it) that is the central focus of criminal justice.

Deviance and Social Control

A drug user injecting heroin. What are some ways that deviant behavior can be controlled?

Key Terms

deviance
social norms
prescriptive norms
proscriptive norms
mores
folkways
subcultures
socialization
social control
informal social control

internal or self-control
external or relational social control
formal social control
agents of ideological social control
agents of direct social control
stratification
penal social control
compensatory social control
conciliatory social control
therapeutic social control

medical model of deviance
medicalization of deviance
medical technologies
medical collaboration
medical ideology
deinstitutionalization/decarceration
vindication
putative backlash

Key People

Edward A. Ross
D. Stanley Eitzen and Maxine Baca-Zinn
Donald Black
Talcott Parsons
Peter Conrad and Joseph Schneider

CASE STUDY

Crime and Mental Illness

In the early hours of June 21, 2000, Officer Jeffrey Moritz of the Flagstaff Police responded in uniform to complaints that a pickup truck with loud music blaring was circling a residential block. When he located the truck, the officer turned on the emergency lights and siren of his marked patrol car, which prompted petitioner Eric Clark, the truck's driver (then 17), to pull over. Officer Moritz got out of the patrol car and told Clark to stay where he was. Less than a minute later, Clark shot the officer, who died soon after but not before calling the police dispatcher for help. Clark ran away on foot but was arrested later that day with gunpowder residue on his hands; the gun that killed the officer was found nearby, stuffed into a knit cap (*Clark v. Arizona*, 2006, p. 2717).

Eric Clark suffered from paranoid schizophrenia. He believed that his hometown was under invasion by aliens. Furthermore, he believed that some of the aliens impersonated government officials and were out to kill him. In fact, Clark rigged a fishing line with beads and wind chimes as part of an alarm system at his house to alert him to when alien invaders came near. Similar unusual behavior included his insistence on keeping a bird in his truck to ward off airborne poisons. On the day he killed Officer Moritz, Clark believed that the officer was an alien who was trying to kill him. Clark was convicted because the court concluded that his mental illness "did not . . . distort his perception of reality so severely that he did not know his actions were wrong" (p. 2718).

Clark was sentenced to 25 years to life in prison. His conviction and sentence were upheld by a sharply divided U.S. Supreme Court.

> Do you think Eric Clark's actions were the purposeful commission of an act that he knew to be a serious crime, or were they due to a mental illness?
>
> Do you think the punishment in this case "fits" the crime? Why or why not?

An Overview of Deviance

FOCUSING QUESTION 4.1

How are the concepts of deviance, social norms, and socialization related?

Deviance refers to any departure from behaviors that are typical, acceptable, or expected. It is often confused with crime. However, these concepts are distinct, as crime is only one form of deviant behavior. For example, shoplifting is both a crime, because it is prohibited under criminal law, and an example of deviance, because it is viewed as an unacceptable behavior. On the other hand, consider door-holding behavior. Holding the door open for the person immediately behind you is often viewed as an acceptable, even expected, behavior. Failure to do so could then be viewed as deviant—though certainly not criminal. Therefore, deviance refers to a range of behaviors including, but not limited to, crime.

This broad definition does not capture the negative connotation that the term deviance has come to have in everyday use. We tend to restrict our everyday usage of the term "deviance" to refer only to behaviors that are negatively viewed or condemned by society (Conrad & Schneider, 1980). However, deviance can also refer to atypical or unexpected behaviors that are, in fact, positive. For example, men who become Buddhist monks are "deviant" under the broadest definition of the term because separating oneself from mainstream society to live in a religious community is a departure from "typical" social behavior. Yet, we do not condemn these monks for their lifestyle; indeed, they are held in high regard. Therefore, although their behaviors may meet the *definition* of deviance, the monks would not be *labeled* by society with the negative term "deviants."

NORMS

Many of the social sciences define deviant behaviors as those that depart from accepted social norms (McCaghy, Capron, Jamieson, & Harley Carey, 2007). **Social norms** are societal rules. The norms that tell us what we *ought* to do—become educated, respect our elders, obey the law—are **prescriptive norms**. The norms that tell us what we *ought not* to do—commit crimes, lie, drop out of high school—are **proscriptive norms**.

Norms are based on widely shared values regarding that which is "good" or "correct" and, conversely, that which is "bad" or "incorrect." Norms may be formal or informal. Formal norms, also known as **mores**, tend to have moral underpinnings. The values expressed in the Ten Commandments (not killing or stealing, not committing adultery, etc.) or other religious doctrines are examples of mores. In contrast, informal norms, also known as **folkways**, do not have as strong a moral foundation. Folkways include rules governing etiquette and acceptable standards of behavior, like how to dress for a particular occasion.

Norms vary across both situation and time (Curra, 1999). For example, language that may routinely be used while hanging out with your friends after school might be inappropriate to use at home with your family. Similarly, behaviors that may be considered perfectly acceptable by today's standards, such as teenage males wearing earrings, would have been taboo, or unacceptable, to many of our grandparents or great-grandparents.

Norms also vary across cultures. For example, belching at the dinner table is considered rude in many Western cultures but is considered a compliment to the host or cook in some African and Asian countries (see Sinha, 1996).

Even within a given culture, there may be subcultures that have their own set of norms. **Subcultures** are groups that share a set of norms that are different from those of the larger society. Subcultures may exist based on race, ethnicity, religion, sexual orientation, and occupation. For example, in certain ethnic subcultures, wine is routinely served with dinner, even to family members under the legal drinking age. Similarly, certain professions have their own subculture. Police, for example, tend to socialize among themselves, often socially isolating themselves from people who do not work in law enforcement. As you will learn in Chapter 11, this behavior in the policing subculture fosters a type of solidarity in which the officers come to value bravery, secrecy, and loyalty (see, e.g., Cochran & Bromley, 2003; Van Maanen, 1974).

It is important to note that the norms and behaviors of members of subcultures may or may not be criminal. For example, the members of a biker gang may be deviant (i.e., have norms different from the larger society) in the way they act and dress. However, these same members may be law-abiding citizens. In contrast, "swingers" are members of a deviant subculture, with norms (different from the larger society) that permit having multiple sexual partners other than one's spouse (Walshok, 1971). In some jurisdictions, this would constitute the crime of adultery. However, in other jurisdictions, it may be legal behavior (remember that norms vary between places). As you can see, identifying social norms, identifying subcultures and their norms, and defining deviance, both criminal and noncriminal, can be a complex process, indeed.

SOCIALIZATION

In legal and justice-related studies, we tend to think of the law as the primary means of controlling human behavior. It is easy, after all, to imagine that passing a law against an undesired behavior will make people stop doing it.

However, there are many other and arguably more important factors that account for human behavior besides the law. These range from genetics and the biochemistry of the brain to the influences of friends, families, teachers, religion, the media, and so on (see Mohr, 1996). Different social sciences focus on different causes of behavior. For example, psychology tends to focus on the individual, whereas sociology tends to focus on the role of social institutions (family, religion, peers, etc.). Two related processes, socialization and social control, are key concepts in understanding the role that "society" plays in shaping our behavior. As you read about these concepts, bear in mind that they are as important, *if not more so*, as law in controlling human behavior (see Black, 1976).

Socialization is the process by which "people learn to conform to social norms; a process that makes possible an enduring society and the transmission of its culture between generations" (Abercrombie, Hill, & Turner, 2006, p. 363). Socialization works in two ways: internally and externally. Internal socialization occurs when a person learns social norms from others so the norms become a part of the individual's own personality. When we internalize norms, our own behavior is guided by the rules we have learned. For example, when we learn that it is wrong to steal, we refrain from stealing even though there may be opportunities to do so with no one around to catch us. Our own moral compass or conscience guides our behavior because societal norms have been "internalized" to become a part of us. Thus, our behavior is controlled by self-imposed regulation rather than by external forces.

In contrast, external socialization occurs when interactions with other important people cause us to behave in accordance with social norms so that we gain "acceptance and status in the eyes of others" (Abercrombie et al., 2006, p. 363). *Primary socialization* takes place at home in early childhood when social norms are taught to children by family members, especially by parents. Gender roles, including how to act and dress according to gender-specific norms, are examples of primary socialization. Later, *secondary socialization* occurs throughout childhood and adolescence. Secondary socialization occurs through our interactions with the educational system, religion, peer groups (first in neighborhoods, then at school), and the media—especially through television, cinema, music, and the Internet (e.g., Saracho & Spodek, 2007). Keep in mind, though, that secondary socialization is not a separate process. Rather, it is a continuation of the process initiated by primary socialization. The key distinction is that primary socialization is provided by family members, while secondary socialization is provided by people and institutions with which we do not have as close a relationship. For example, learning how to interact socially with other people starts with primary socialization, as family members model and teach these behaviors. As children grow older, their social skills are refined by secondary socialization through interactions with classmates, in clubs and organizations, and so on. This process continues into adulthood through *adult socialization*, when new work environments socialize people into "roles for which primary and secondary socialization may not have prepared them fully" (Abercrombie et al., 2006, pp. 363–364).

A failure of normal socialization processes is one of the most widely accepted ways in which sociology explains deviance (Deflem, 2006). Under this view, the institutions of socialization, primary and/or secondary, fail to properly "impart the knowledge and opportunities that result in rule-abiding behavior" (Heitzeg, 1996, p. 38). Another sociological explanation for deviance is that people may be socialized into a deviant subculture rather than being socialized with widely accepted social norms. This may cause people to be deviant for two reasons. First, through the process of internalization, the deviant norms may become a part of a person's personality. Second, if socialized into a deviant subculture, a person may conform to that deviant subculture's norms to win social approval from the other members of the group (Akers & Jensen, 2007; Deflem, 2006).

> Provide an example of a deviant behavior that is not a crime but is viewed negatively by society. Provide an example of a deviant behavior that is viewed positively by society.
>
> What are some examples of norms that likely shaped your grandparents' behavior as teenagers that would not be viewed as norms today?
>
> Who or what were the most important agents of primary socialization in your life? How did the influence of secondary socialization change your own behavior from the ways in which you were first brought up?

The Social Control of Deviance

FOCUSING QUESTION 4.2

How do informal and formal social controls affect human behavior?

Social control refers to the processes by which society controls individual and group behaviors. It was originally defined by Edward A. Ross (1901) as "virtually all of the human practices and arrangements that contribute to social order and . . . that influence people to conform" (Ross, as cited in Black, 1998, p. 4). However, largely due to the work of Talcott Parsons (1951) and Donald Black (1984; 1989), the term is now used to refer to the ways deviant behaviors are controlled both informally and formally.

INFORMAL VERSUS FORMAL SOCIAL CONTROL

Informal social controls are the tools used to control behavior in everyday social life—"within families, friendships, neighborhoods, organizations, and groups of all kinds" (Dawson, 2006, p. 1435). As such, informal social controls form the basis of the socialization process. They are both internal (often referred to as "self-control") and external (often referred to as "relational controls").

Internal or self-control is akin to one's conscience—one's "internalized norms, beliefs, morals, and self-concept" (Conrad & Schneider, 1992, p. 7). Sociologists explain the development of conscience via the socialization process, which is similar to the way psychologists explain its development. **External or relational social control** depends on a person's interactions with others. Virtually any type of positive or negative reaction from others constitutes informal social control. Positive reactions from others—such as praise, a smile, tangible rewards, and emotional support—encourage and positively reinforce desired behaviors. Such positive responses are designed to cause the recipient to continue to engage in behaviors that are encouraged or accepted by society. In contrast, negative reactions from others—such as ridicule, gossip, corporal punishment, shaming, ostracism, and even something as simple as a stern, disapproving look—discourage and punish undesired behaviors. Such negative responses are designed to cause the recipient to change his or her behaviors by conforming to desired social norms. See Box 4.1 for a discussion of informal social control of drinking and driving.

BOX 4.1

THE SOCIAL CONTROL OF DRUNK DRIVING

Laws against drinking and driving have been around since shortly after the advent of the automobile. However, drinking and driving were not considered a particularly important social problem for much of the twentieth century. In fact, it was not until the early 1980s that widespread public attention was given to the problem of drinking and driving. It was at that time that Candy Lightner, whose daughter was killed in an alcohol-related traffic accident, formed Mothers Against Drunk Driving (MADD). Through MADD's activism, drinking and driving "gained recognition as a prominent social concern" (see Applegate et al., 1996, p. 57) and were addressed by politicians and policy makers (see Reinarmann, 1988).

In response to the increased recognition of the DUI (driving under the influence) problem in the United States, policy shifted "toward an increased emphasis on deterrence, retribution, and incapacitation . . . the common thread of this social climate [being] harsher punishment of offenders" (Applegate et al., 1996, p. 58). For example, in the years following the establishment of MADD, specifically between 1980 and 1989, the number of DUI arrests nationwide increased nearly 22% while the number of licensed drivers increased only 14% (Bureau of Justice Statistics, 1992). Yet, the increasing severity of criminal punishments for DUI had little effect on drinking and driving. Rather, research has found that the activities of grassroots organizations like MADD, SADD (Students Against Destructive Decisions, originally known as Students Against Driving Drunk), and anti-DUI educational and public service campaigns are far more effective at curtailing drunk driving than the criminal law (e.g., Fradella, 2000; Ross, McCleary, & LaFree, 1990).

Why do you think informal social controls are more effective than formal ones in controlling drunk driving?

What do you think should be done to reduce drinking and driving? What kinds of solutions could utilize informal social control? Formal social control? Both?

Formal social controls are mechanisms exercised by the government to control human behavior. Although criminal justice tends to focus on criminal law, which is the most important tool of formal social control, other forms of law (e.g., constitutional law and civil law, which are discussed later in this text) are also tools of formal social control.

Clearly, the criminal justice system represents the ultimate in formal social control, with its government-authorized power to arrest, hold trials, and punish as a means of regulating behavior. Nevertheless, the criminal justice system increasingly bridges formal and informal social control with policies such as community policing, community courts, victim–offender reconciliation programs, and the like. As you read this book, look for examples of how modern criminal justice utilizes elements of both formal and informal social control.

AGENTS OF SOCIAL CONTROL

The institutions of social control are similar to those of socialization. Eitzen and Baca-Zinn (1998) classified the institutions of social control into two types of agents: agents of ideological social control and agents of direct social control.

Agents of ideological social control attempt to shape the consciousness of people in society. Such agents include the family, educational institutions, religion, organized sports, media, and the government. These agents influence ideas, attitudes, morals, and values. In doing so, they help to maintain the status quo by reinforcing governing ideologies and persuading citizens to comply willingly with laws.

According to Eitzen and Baca-Zinn, the family teaches the child to "fit" into society. Educational institutions uphold the behavioral standards of the community and indoctrinate in their students social norms about work, respect for authority, and patriotism. Most major religions support the status quo in American society by honoring the American way of life and by teaching acceptance of an imperfect world, with the promise of rewards in the next life if believers strive to achieve what society defines as "good." Sports promote local, regional, and national pride; allow for a cathartic and productive channeling of aggressive energies; provide an avenue for upward social mobility; and build character. The media similarly promote adherence to basic social values by shaping how we evaluate others and ourselves; by influencing, through advertising, what we view as desirable; and by molding how the public perceives and interprets events. Finally, the government sets educational standards, acts in the name of national security, and promotes solidarity and patriotism through public services and the public appearances of elected leaders. In acting as they do, these institutional agents of social control successfully promote social norms in a manner that leads most Americans to accept the legitimacy of the social, political, and economic order. Moreover, even when the status quo is questioned, it tends to be done in an "acceptable" manner, such as through critical commentary and peaceful demonstration.

In contrast, **agents of direct social control** attempt to punish or neutralize both organizations and individuals who deviate from society's norms. These need not be "bad" people. Rather, they may be deviant only insofar as their behavior departs from what is expected by others in society. Examples include the poor, the mentally ill, and political dissidents. In each case, the behaviors and norms of individuals in these groups may, sometimes through no fault of their own, run counter to social norms or expectations. The agents of direct social control include welfare agencies, science and medicine, and government. Welfare agencies provide and administer public assistance programs that function to prevent social unrest. However, they also may exert social control through the stigmatization that is often associated with being on such public assistance programs. This may reinforce and legitimize the norms of work and self-sufficiency. Science and medicine have developed a number of devices that are aimed at controlling the behavior of some members of society. These devices will be explored in more detail later in this chapter. Finally, the government also acts as an agent of direct social control. When the government does so, it acts in one of the four styles that we will explore next.

> Which type of informal social control do you think is the most powerful—internal self-controls or external relational controls? Explain. Do you think the answer might vary depending on the behavior in question? Why or why not?

> Legal sociologist Donald Black (1984, 1989) argued that there is an inverse relationship between informal and formal social control. That is, as one goes up, the other goes down. Why do you think this happens? Give examples to support your reasoning.

> Educational institutions are generally classified as an ideological agent of social control. Yet, they have the ability to punish students who violate norms. Do you think schools serve as agents of ideological social control, agents of direct social control, or both? Explain.

Styles of Social Control

FOCUSING QUESTION 4.3

What are the four main styles of formal social control?

Donald Black, a leading scholar of law and society, has argued that law is used as a tool of formal social control in four related, yet distinct, ways. He termed the four styles of formal social control penal, compensatory, therapeutic, and conciliatory (Black, 1984). These four styles are summarized in Table 4.1.

Black argued that there is an inverse relationship between law (as formal social control) and informal social control. That is, in societies where informal social control is strong and effective in controlling behavior, there is less need to rely on law to do so. Conversely, in societies lacking strong and

Table 4.1. Donald Black's Styles of Social Control

Style of Social Control	Summary of Style
Penal	Views the violator of a social norm which has been codified into criminal law as an offender who deserves official condemnation. Four main justifications are proffered for using criminal law as a tool of formal social control: retribution, deterrence, rehabilitation, and incapacitation. These concepts are explored in depth in Chapter 8.
Compensatory	Focuses on providing restitution to the victim of an act. That is, it attempts to compensate wronged or aggrieved individuals in a way that restores them as closely as possible to the "status quo ante"—the way they were before the deviant person wronged them. This is typically accomplished via the civil justice system. The victim sues the rule breaker and is compensated for his or her injuries and/or losses, usually financially.
Therapeutic	Views the deviant person as someone who needs help to become nondeviant or "normal." This is often accomplished via science and medicine, especially psychology and psychiatry. Because of this fact, it is clear that science and medicine are major institutions of social control.
Conciliatory	Attempts to create and preserve social harmony via dispute resolution. Mediation is an example of conciliatory social control. The focus is on allowing both sides to express their displeasures and then work toward a compromise that allows not only the removal of the irritants in a relationship but also perhaps restores some semblance of social harmony.

consistent systems of informal social control, it becomes necessary to have a greater reliance on law to control behavior (Black, 1976).

For example, in tightly knit, highly structured communities, the need for formal social control should be very low because both socialization and informal social control should be highly effective. In contrast, as societies become larger and more complex, close relationships with family and community become less important and more difficult to maintain. In addition, stratification increases. **Stratification** refers to differences between members of a society that occur when persons or groups are divided in a hierarchical manner. This results in levels of inequality for which persons at the top of the hierarchy benefit whereas those at the bottom suffer (from discrimination, reduced opportunity, etc.). Examples may include differences based on "social class, race, gender, birth [order], age," ethnicity, or any other characteristic which might be associated with prestige or social status (Abercrombie et al., 2006, p. 381). Simply having differences does not automatically result in stratification; rather, stratification occurs when individuals are judged on the basis of the differences.

In societies where people share similar belief systems or have similar backgrounds, there tends to be little stratification (because there are few differences or persons are not judged based on differences that do exist). As a result, there is greater consensus on behavioral norms, and socialization and informal social control may be effective in teaching and enforcing those norms. When informal social controls fail, then the formal mechanisms of social control used tend to be compensatory and/or conciliatory, relying on the tight bonds between community members. Consider, for example, the Amish. This group of Swiss-German ancestry is known for very simple living, primarily in rural, self-contained communities. They dress plainly and resist most modern conveniences like electricity, telephones, and automobiles. They value humility, family, community, and devout adherence to their religious beliefs. As you might imagine, informal social controls are quite effective in bringing about conformity with desired behavior.

In contrast, complex and stratified societies may produce less consensus about social norms, in part stemming from perceived or actual inequalities produced by stratification. Socialization then becomes less consistent and complete, and informal social controls less effective, as communities are less tightly bound together. Formal social controls in such complex societies tend to be more punitive and more therapeutic than in less complex societies. Life in contemporary urban areas is a good example of this. Few people may care what others think of them. In fact, in a large city, you may not even know the other people who live on the same block or on the same floor of your apartment building. In such an environment, informal social controls would have little effect in changing people's behavior. Hence, there is a greater need for more formal social controls.

All four styles of formal social control are important for the justice system. **Penal social control** is exclusively the province of the criminal justice system and is explored throughout this text. **Compensatory social control** is usually achieved through lawsuits brought in the civil justice system, which will be discussed in Chapter 7. **Conciliatory social control** is increasingly being integrated into the criminal justice system through programs emphasizing restorative justice or restitution, as described in Chapters 6 and 10.

In the balance of this chapter, we will consider **therapeutic social control**, as it is not covered elsewhere in the book. To best understand therapeutic social controls, it is necessary to explore the roles that medicine, especially psychiatry and psychology, play in defining and treating deviant behavior.

Provide a specific example of each of the four styles of social control. What do you think are the advantages and disadvantages of each?

Eric Clark was subjected to penal social control for killing a police officer. How might the other styles of formal social control have been applied to Clark? Which (alone or in combination) do you think is most appropriate? Why?

The Medicalization of Deviance

FOCUSING QUESTION 4.4

What is "the medicalization of deviance" and what are its consequences?

The **medical model of deviance** is, historically speaking, a relatively new way of explaining deviance and one that underlies therapeutic social control. The emergence of the medical model was made possible by the development of medicine as an established science. The medical model defines deviance objectively as a disease. As such, the medical model advocates treatment of the underlying disease in accordance with the therapeutic style of formal social control.

Talcott Parsons (1951) was the first to conceptualize medicine as an institution of social control. Parsons viewed illness itself as a form of deviance, primarily because the sick could not perform their normal roles in society (and thereby threatened the stability of the social order). Sick individuals are viewed as ill through no fault of their own. They are viewed as needing treatment so they can get well. Such treatment is sought from a health care professional, with whom a sick person is expected to cooperate. The health care professional, especially the physician, seeks to return the sick person to wellness, thereby removing the deviance and allowing the sick person to resume his or her normal role in society. In this way, health professionals promote social control.

One of the most comprehensive treatments of medicine as an institution of social control was Peter Conrad and Joseph Schneider's (1980) book entitled *Deviance and Medicalization: From Badness to Sickness*. Conrad and Schneider traced the history of how "moral-criminal definitions of deviance [changed] to medical ones" (p. 32). For example, the excessive consumption of alcohol was once considered sinful and/or immoral, and it required punishment. Through the process of medicalization, such behavior is now understood as the disease of alcoholism, which requires treatment. Similarly, in the past, an unruly, unfocused child was thought to need discipline. Today, however, such behaviors may be symptoms of a condition called attention-deficit disorder (ADD), which may be treated instead of punished. Defining a deviant behavior as an illness, or a symptom of an illness, and then providing medical intervention to treat the illness are what Conrad and Schneider mean by the **medicalization of deviance**.

Consider the implications of the medicalization of deviance. Much of the criminal justice system is based on the assumption that offenders have free will to choose their actions, with the assumption that they will be held accountable for any actions they take which violate the criminal law. Compare this to medicalization, which suggests that an individual's behavior may be controlled or determined, at least in part, by a medical condition. This, then, raises questions about the extent to which individuals can or should be held accountable for their actions, if those actions were the product of a medical condition rather than an entirely voluntary free choice.

The medicalization of deviance is most apparent in the behavioral sciences of psychiatry and psychology. In criminal justice settings, the behavioral sciences play an important role in determining criminal responsibility. For example, when a psychiatrist or psychologist diagnoses an offender with a serious mental illness that prevents the person from appreciating the difference between right and wrong, we classify that person as legally insane. We then excuse what might otherwise constitute criminal conduct on this basis of insanity and excuse criminal punishment for it; however, a court may require the person to undergo some sort of treatment for the underlying mental illness.

The behavioral sciences are also powerful in civil law. Diagnoses of mental illnesses are important to legal determinations regarding involuntary hospitalization or child custody placements. Such diagnoses also may affect a person's capacity to enter a contract, make a will, or manage one's financial affairs or health care decisions.

TYPES OF MEDICAL SOCIAL CONTROL

Scholars have offered varying explanations of the ways medicine may act as a direct agent of social control. Conrad and Schneider (1980) assert that medicine acts as a tool of social control in three distinct ways: through medical technology, medical collaboration, and medical ideology.

Medical Technologies. **Medical technologies** refer to the techniques available to treat many forms of illness and/or deviance. For instance, the administration of psychotropic drugs to people who have schizophrenia or tranquilizers to people who have anxiety disorders constitutes routine treatment for mental illness.

Essential to understanding the role of medical technologies, however, is understanding the importance of what conditions get "medicalized." Only when a condition is medicalized can it be treated (as opposed to punished) with available medical technologies. Medical experts, specifically through the American Medical Association (AMA) and the American Psychiatric Association (APA), control the definitions of illness. The primary tool for defining deviance under the medical model is the *Diagnostic and Statistical Manual of Mental Disorders (DSM)*. The most recent edition of the *DSM* (referred to as the *DSM-IV-TR*) contains diagnostic criteria for 410 psychiatric disorders. This represents more than a 580 percent increase in the number of recognized mental disorders since the first edition of the *DSM* was published in 1952. See Box 4.2 for a debate about media intoxication as a psychological diagnosis.

In addition to holding the power to define illness, medicine often holds the exclusive ability to treat the illnesses it has defined. Tranquilizers may treat anxiety. Methadone helps keep addicts off heroin. People whose mental conditions

BOX 4.2

MEDIA INTOXICATION?

In *Florida v. Zamora* (1978), a 15-year-old boy was accused of killing an 82-year-old woman after breaking into her house and stealing a gun and money. Zamora's attorney pleaded insanity on his behalf. In support of the insanity claim, the defense offered evidence that Zamora acted under a state of pseudo-intoxication that resulted from watching hours of violent television programs which, in turn, drove the boy to kill the woman. The trial court refused to allow testimony on television intoxication, finding it to be irrelevant to the question of Zamora's insanity.

In a provocative article, Patricia Falk (1996) reviewed the extensive body of literature addressing the nature and effects of media intoxication and addiction. She noted, "[t]he primary, and almost unanimous, finding common to this extensive body of research is that a positive correlation exists between viewing violent television programs and subsequent aggressive behavior" (p. 767). Similar research findings have linked violence against women to the viewing of pornography. In 1987, serial killer Bobby Joe Long asserted in the sentencing phase of his murder trial that his addiction to violent pornography should have constituted a mitigating factor against the death penalty. The jury rejected this argument, and he was sentenced to death.

In *Schiro v. Clark* (1992), the defendant "argued that he was a sexual sadist and that his extensive viewing of rape pornography . . . rendered him unable to distinguish right from wrong" (p. 971). The defendant produced the testimony of two leading experts on the link between violence and pornography. He sought to have this link used as evidence of insanity and as a type of intoxication that Florida law would recognize as a mitigating factor. The defendant was convicted, and his subsequent appeals were denied, on the rationale that it would be absurd to excuse criminal conduct due to the defendant's exposure to materials that are, in fact, legally acceptable and protected by the First Amendment.

Similar reasoning resulted in an unsuccessful defense involving music lyrics. Nineteen-year-old Ronald Ray Howard killed a police officer and sought to avoid the death penalty by arguing that his addiction to "gangsta rap" was a mitigating factor. The argument was rejected by the jury, which sentenced Howard to death.

> Should media intoxication be accepted as a "diagnosis" that excuses or reduces criminal responsibility in U.S. courts of law? Explain your reasoning based on the concepts presented in the chapter's discussions of medicalization.

> Assume that media intoxication was recognized as legal defense to rape (or other crimes). What would be the public policy consequences of such a defense?

pose a danger to themselves or to others can be involuntarily hospitalized for in-patient treatment. Sex offenders can be chemically castrated. Health care professionals have the exclusive authority to prescribe these medications and to deliver these treatments. Therefore, the medical profession holds substantial power as an agent of social control seeking to treat conditions that lead to undesired or deviant behavior (whether criminal or noncriminal behavior). It should be noted, however, that some of the medical technologies used to treat deviance are not always benign. For example, a lobotomy is a form of surgery in which certain nerve connections in the brain are severed. The surgery results in a "calming" of patients who suffer from a wide range of mental illnesses by rendering them nearly comatose. Lobotomies are an example of a medical technology that was once considered "state of the art" science, but they are rarely used today.

Medical Collaboration. Medical collaboration refers to how the medical profession works with other institutions of social control. Two examples offered by Conrad and Schneider (1980) illustrate medical collaboration. Work and school environments, both institutions of social control, require the attendance of employees and pupils, respectively. A physician's note, however, can excuse a person from those obligations. Medical excuses work similarly in a wide variety of settings, such as in worker's compensation claims, social security disability benefit claims, exemptions from military service, placement in prisons, and so on. Perhaps the clearest example of medical collaboration occurs in the legal system when someone raises the insanity defense to excuse criminal liability. Although the determination of insanity is a legal one, it is made with great deference to medical experts and their opinions. Therefore, the judgments of medical professionals may help other social control agents evaluate whether a person is deviant and, if so, what the most appropriate response or treatment may be.

Medical Ideology. Medical ideology concerns "the social and ideological benefits accrued by conceptualizing [a behavior or condition] in medical terms" (Conrad & Schneider, 1980, p. 245). This can work in two ways. First, by labeling something as a disease, the moral blame is shifted away from the individual. An individual may be viewed as "sick" and in need of treatment instead of being viewed as "bad" and in need of punishment. Second, the label of disease and associated medical treatments can reinforce the dominant values of society, making it difficult to enact social change.

The Victorian view of masturbation provides an example. Victorian society viewed masturbation as both an illness and as a cause of other illnesses, like epilepsy (see Baker-Brown, 1866). For women, the so-called "cure" was a gruesome medical technology called a clitoridectomy—the removal of the clitoris. By treating masturbation as an illness, the moral condemnation was removed from the person masturbating. However, the "treatment" repressed sexuality, especially in women. Thus, medical ideology reinforced sexually repressive views and male dominance in society.

SOCIAL CONSEQUENCES OF MEDICALIZATION

Positive Effects of Medicalization. Conrad and Schneider identify five beneficial consequences of the medicalization of deviance. First, a rehabilitative focus, as opposed to a punitive one, is more humanitarian, which may lead to a more compassionate society. Second, reducing moral blame increases understanding of the deviant behavior, which is attributed to illness. Rather than condemning the individual, medicalization can make it easier to reintegrate a deviant individual into society after treatments have been administered. Third, the therapeutic ideology is optimistic, helping the deviant individual's recovery by promoting hope for successful recovery and termination of deviant behaviors. Fourth, medicalization increases the power and prestige of the "beneficent and honorable" (Conrad & Schneider, 1980, p. 248) people in the medical profession. Fifth, medicalization may be the most efficient form of social control because it identifies and responds to the specific needs of each individual rather than assuming there is a single simple solution (e.g., imprisonment) that fits all deviant persons.

Negative Consequences of Medicalization. It is important to note that medicalization may also pose harms to society. Conrad and Schneider (1980) identify seven negative consequences to the medicalization of deviance. First, it removes personal responsibility for behaviors. If individuals commit deviant behaviors for which they are not personally responsible, they may be viewed as second-class citizens who must depend on others to take care of them. Indeed, by implication, others *must* take care of them to prevent future deviant behaviors from occurring.

Second, while the medical model claims objectivity, it is not morally neutral. Although "cloaked in the mantle of science . . . [and therefore] assumed to be objective and value-free, . . . the very nature of medical practice involves value judgment" (p. 249). For example, homosexuality was once viewed as socially unacceptable and therefore was classified as a mental illness. This was a value judgment once made by the medical profession, but it has since been reversed.

Third, allowing highly educated experts to control the definition of deviance and to specify its treatment takes power out of the hands of the public. Ordinary citizens are often unable to discuss the technicalities of scientific matters, which "decreas[es] the accessibility of public debate" (p. 249). Conrad and Schneider (1980) argue that public discourse on deviance should be fostered and not squelched.

Fourth, medical social control allows treatments to be undertaken that would not ordinarily be socially acceptable. The forced administration of medications is an example of a social control that would not be possible without the involvement or encouragement of medicine.

Fifth, medicalization focuses on the individual at the expense of solving larger social problems. Rather than addressing societal ills, such as poverty and inadequate educational systems, we focus only on the individual and his or her problems. This is important because individual problems are often related to societal ills. However, the medical model does not attempt to solve larger problems beyond those of an individual. For instance, individual drug users may receive treatment for drug addiction, but the socioeconomic pressures that may have caused them to start using drugs in the first place remain unresolved.

Sixth, and related to the other concerns, medicalization and the individualization of social problems perpetuate the political status quo. By focusing on the individual, we fail to see that the politics of the dominant culture might be a cause of the deviance at issue. For example, labeling children as hyperactive shifts attention away from the politics and policies surrounding the educational system against which students may be rebelling.

Finally, Conrad and Schneider (1980) offer the "exclusion of evil" as an important negative effect of medicalization. Medical explanations render unnecessary any notions of sin and evilness. Illnesses explain behavior, even if certain individuals and behaviors are inherently evil or bad. For example, defining Adolph Hitler only as sick "portrays the horror of the Holocaust as a product of individual pathology" (p. 251), failing to capture the actual horror and evil it entailed. This "detracts from our ability to see and confront the evils that face our world" (p. 252).

> What factors could explain the increase in the number of recognized mental disorders? To what extent is mental illness objective? To what extent might it be socially constructed?
>
> Other than the example used earlier concerning the Victorian views on masturbation, think of a behavior that has been medicalized. What type(s) of medical social control might address the behavior? What might be the consequences of the medicalization?
>
> What do you think ought to be the role of therapeutic social control, or the medicalization of deviance, in criminal justice? Why?

Medicalization and Public Policy

FOCUSING QUESTION 4.5

How does the medicalization of deviance affect public policy?

SHIFTS IN THE STYLE OF SOCIAL CONTROL

Conrad and Schneider (1980) noted the impact that the medicalization of deviance has had on social policy. As decisions are made about which behaviors to address through penal social control and which behaviors to address through therapeutic social control, public policies change accordingly.

Conrad and Schneider pointed to the **deinstitutionalization/decarceration** movement of the 1960s and 1970s as a dramatic shift in social control. People were released from mental hospitals and prisons in favor of community-based, often therapeutic, social control. Social service agencies, diversion programs, halfway houses, and group homes are examples of social controls that were to be created or strengthened in response to deinstitutionalization. For example, as public drunkenness was widely decriminalized (i.e., controlled by tools other than the law), outpatient medical treatment of alcoholism increased dramatically. Deinstitutionalization resulted in a substantial change in how social control was supposed to be accomplished in the United States, and it reflected an increased use of medical technologies and medical collaborations.

However, the principles of deinstitutionalization were not completely realized in practice. Advocates of deinstitutionalization hoped that community-based treatment would be more effective and more economical, particularly as new medications were available to manage even fairly serious mental illnesses. The community-based treatment facilities, however, never fully materialized due to inadequate planning, a lack of funding, a lack of assistance in helping deinstitutionalized persons find the variety of programs they needed, and disagreements about what deinstitutionalization was supposed to accomplish in the first place (Talbott, [1979] 2004).

Hence, the deinstitutionalization movement failed to achieve its goals. Many persons who were released from mental institutions became homeless because they did not have access to treatment services, and as a result, the symptoms of their illnesses worsened (Talbott, [1979] 2004). The criminal justice system then sometimes became involved, as homelessness created "more opportunities for [persons with mental illness] to come to the attention of the police for what is perceived to be criminal behavior. Such behavior is often a manifestation of their illness" (Lamb & Bachrach, 2001, p. 1042).

Consider what has happened in the deinstitutionalization/decarceration movement. The approach taken by the medical model shifted as new medical technologies developed (in the form of prescription medications) and as the mental health community recommended the promotion of community-based medical collaborations as an alternative to mental hospitals. This was grounded firmly in notions of therapeutic social control. However, due to imperfect implementation of necessary programs, mental illness has become, at least in part, regulated through penal social control, as there is a "pressure to institutionalize persons who need 24-hour care wherever there is room, including jail" (Lamb & Bachrach, 2001, p. 1042). Contrary to public perceptions, persons with mental illnesses who are confined in jail or prison often do not have access to a full range of treatment services, creating a dilemma that is addressed in further detail in the case study at the end of this chapter. What the future holds and whether there will be a return to a therapeutic emphasis remain to be seen.

The deinstitutionalization/decarceration movement is but one example of how styles of social control may shift over time. Clearly, social control is not static but rather changes in response to social, political, and economic contexts.

PUTATIVE BACKLASH

Some behaviors may be decriminalized and demedicalized—that is, removed from the control of either law or medicine. When this happens, Conrad and Schneider (1980) predict two possible outcomes. The first possibility is that the underlying behavior will become "vindicated." **Vindication** occurs when the behavior is no longer viewed as deviant. Alternatively, some **putative backlash** may occur that either recriminalizes the behavior or redefines the deviant nature of the behavior.

In support of this proposition, Conrad and Schneider used the example of homosexuality. Homosexuality was removed from the *DSM* in 1973. As a result, homosexuality was no longer viewed as a mental illness as it once had been. Between 1971 and 2000, 34 states removed their sodomy laws (which were essentially laws against same-sex sexual activity). Moreover, in the 2003 Supreme Court case of *Lawrence v. Texas*, the remaining sodomy laws in the United States were ruled unconstitutional as violations of the right to privacy and personal liberty embodied in the Fourteenth Amendment's Due Process Clause. Therefore, homosexuality has been both demedicalized (as it is no longer viewed as a mental illness) and decriminalized (as it is no longer a criminal offense). Both vindication and putative backlash have occurred.

A fair argument can be made that homosexuality has been vindicated, at least in part. The arrival of the twenty-first century brought a new social perspective on homosexuality. No longer does it hold the social stigma that it once did. By the middle of 2008, laws banning discrimination based on sexual orientation had been enacted in hundreds of counties and cities nationwide as well as in 17 states and the District of Columbia (AFL-CIO, 2008). Nearly 90 percent of all Fortune 500 companies have policies that prohibit discrimination based on sexual orientation, and close to 60 percent offer domestic partnership benefits (Human Rights Campaign, 2011). Of the top 125 colleges and universities as ranked by *U.S. News & World Report*, 90 percent have written nondiscrimination policies that include sexual orientation (Luther & Herrschaft, 2007). Massachusetts, Connecticut, Iowa, Vermont, New Hampshire, New York, and the District of Columbia have legalized same-sex marriage; Hawaii, Illinois, and New Jersey offer civil unions. California, Oregon, Nevada, and Washington offer legal recognition of domestic partnerships that confers many of the same state rights associated with marriage. Maine and Wisconsin offer limited rights to same-sex couples in registered domestic partnerships (National Conference of State Legislatures, 2011). Also, gay and lesbian characters on television and in movies have become increasingly commonplace (Anderson, 2005). This is indeed evidence of vindication.

On the other hand, there can be no doubt that putative backlash has also occurred. For instance, antigay violence remains, as evidenced by the killings of victims such as Matthew Shepard, Diane Whipple, Lawrence King, and Simmie Williams, to name just a few. Antigay violence in the form of assaults and batteries often goes unreported in the mainstream press even though it occurs in significant numbers (National Coalition of Anti-Violence Programs, 2005). Antigay initiatives seeking to repeal hate crime laws, domestic partnership laws, and nondiscrimination laws are one of the hottest topics in politics. Furthermore, the legal status of same-sex relationships has proven to be one of the most divisive issues of our time. Thus, as Conrad and Schneider predicted in 1980, putative backlash has occurred as debate continues about rights that are not completely vindicated.

MEDICINE AS SOCIAL CONTROL

There can be no argument that medicine acts as a powerful institution of social control. The medicalization of deviance has produced what the *New York Times* described as "a veritable epidemic of mental illness," as the U.S. Surgeon General asserted in 1999 that "22 percent of the population has a diagnosable mental disorder" (Sharkey, 1999, para.1). Critics have noted that, as the *DSM* has expanded its definitions of mental illness, there has been a corresponding increase in the number of routine behaviors now labeled as mental illness, including excessive drinking, over- and undereating, and compulsive gambling. This medicalization of deviance has real consequences. The medical model of deviance is driven, in part, by a profit motive. As more behaviors qualify as sickness, more specialists are needed to diagnose and treat those sicknesses. More clients mean more money. That is not to say that the members of the AMA or APA are not acting with the best of intentions, but there can be no doubt that the medicalization of deviance has been a major contributor to the ever-rising costs of health care.

In addition to the economic consequences of medicalization, putative backlash against medicalization has created many other problems with real costs—both economic and human. Consider the fact that at least since the 1990s, we have heard repeated calls for people to "take responsibility" for their own actions, as science has continually offered excuses for their deviant behavior (e.g., Dershowitz, 1994). In spite of the fact that insanity defenses rarely work, people often get angry when they see high-profile criminal defendants arguing that they should not be held responsible for their actions. This backlash against medicalization has led to significant changes in the legal definitions of insanity for a host of criminal and civil justice proceedings (Fradella, 2007). For example, for the insanity defense to be used successfully today, it is no longer sufficient to demonstrate that the defendant suffers from a mental illness that causes him or her to be unable to know right from wrong. Rather, in some U.S. jurisdictions, the mental illness must be so "severe" that the defendant did not even know what he or she was doing.

These definitional changes affect due process. People adjudicated as sane and guilty who were criminally incarcerated sometimes find themselves labeled as mentally ill upon their parole. This can result in continued involuntary incarceration in a mental health setting in the name of therapeutic social control (Miller, 1997).

> Do you think there are any types of deviance that should be medicalized? Are there any types of deviance that you think should be decriminalized and/or demedicalized? If they are, do you think vindication or putative backlash will occur?
>
> How has the debate regarding same-sex marriage been shaped by the process of the medicalization of deviance? Would national legalization of same-sex marriage vindicate homosexuality as a nondeviant behavior in the twenty-first century, or would there be further putative backlash? Why?

Conclusion

Human behavior is the complex product of many forces, both internal and external. Bringing behavior into compliance with a society's norms is the function of the socialization process and of social control mechanisms, as described in this chapter. The social control function is not limited to criminal justice but can also include family, peer groups, the medical profession, and more. Sometimes, however, socialization and social control do not result in full compliance with social norms, in which case deviance results. The next chapter will further explore the nature and causes of deviant behavior.

Criminal Justice Problem Solving: MENTAL ILLNESS AND CORRECTIONS

There are more than seven million people under correctional supervision in the United States, more than two million of whom are incarcerated in prisons and jails (as described in Chapter 13). Estimates of the percentage of incarcerated people with serious mental disorders range from a conservative 7.2 percent to upward of 20 percent in certain metropolitan jails (Butterfield, 1998; Slate & Johnson, 2008).

Various explanations are proffered for the prevalence of mentally ill persons in correctional institutions. The most frequent include the lack of treatment provided to individuals deinstitutionalized during the 1960s and 1970s, the economic shift from mental health spending to correctional spending in the 1980s and 1990s, the lack of insurance coverage for the mentally ill, and "aggressive prosecution and incarceration for drug-related offenses" (Stone, 1997, p. 291).

Regardless of the reasons for the high proportions of mentally ill inmates, research indicates that mentally ill offenders often do not receive adequate treatment while incarcerated. "The lack of adequate mental health resources exacerbates existing serious mental conditions for inmates, resulting in decompensation in inmate mental and physical health, inmate suicides, and related complications in inmate management for correctional officials" (Stone, 1997, p. 285).

There have been numerous books and articles published on the lack of adequate treatment for mentally ill jail and prison inmates. Many such scholarly works point out that we have a national crisis on our hands in dealing with mentally ill inmates. These scholars have also conducted a detailed examination of inmate legal rights in their calls for reform. Yet, their calls have largely gone unheeded. The conditions faced by inmates with untreated mental illness usually prevent them "from obtaining access to prison programs or rehabilitation plans which could facilitate release and improve post-release success. As a result, inmates with severe mental disorders are virtually condemned to a cycle of criminal offending" (Stone, 1997, p. 357). Thus, mentally ill inmates may serve longer sentences because of their inability to qualify for early release, and without treatment and upon their eventual release, mentally ill offenders are likely to find themselves yet again involved with the criminal justice system. We must recognize that this is a problem not only for the individual but also for society at large.

> Do correctional institutions have an obligation (legal, ethical, or otherwise) to provide treatment to mentally ill inmates? Why or why not?
>
> In light of what you learned in this chapter, do you think we should create a special court system to handle offenders with mental illnesses using a therapeutic, rather than penal, style of social control? Explain your reasoning.
>
> What role should medical professionals play in sentencing decisions and in the administration of correctional institutions? Does the medical model replace other forms of social control in instances when mental illness is present?

Deviance and Criminal Behavior

A group loitering and drinking in public. Why do you think individuals or groups might engage in deviant behavior?

Key Terms

serial murderers
criminologists
deviance
criminology
demonology
phrenology
atavism
somatotypes
mesomorphs
eugenics

classical criminology
rational choice theory
routine activities theory
psychodynamic theory
differential association theory
neutralization theory
antisocial personality
social disorganization theory
concentric zone theory
strain theory

delinquent subcultures
social bond theory
labeling theory
conflict criminology
Marxist criminology
feminist criminology
peacemaking criminology
life course theory

Key People

Kai Erickson
Émile Durkheim
Franz Gall
Cesare Lombroso
Charles Goring
William Sheldon
Richard Dugdale
Henry Goddard
Francis Galton
Karl Christiansen
Lawrence Cohen
Marcus Felson

Sigmund Freud
August Aichhorn
Edwin Sutherland
Gresham Sykes
David Matza
Hans Eysenck
Michael Gottfredson
Travis Hirschi
Robert Park
Ernest Burgess
Roderick McKenzie

Clifford Shaw
Henry McKay
Robert Merton
Albert Cohen
Walter Miller
Richard Cloward
Lloyd Ohlin
Robert Agnew
Edwin Lemert
Frank Tannenbaum
Richard Quinney

CASE STUDY

The Case of Carl Panzram

Serial murderers (also known as serial killers) are offenders who have killed two or more victims over time (i.e., not in the same incident). Serial killing is rare when compared to other crimes. In fact, between 1800–2004, there have been more fictional serial killers (well over 500 in novels and movies) than actual offenders (approximately 430). Nonetheless, the investigation of serial murders is a high priority for law enforcement agencies (Hickey, 2010).

Carl Panzram may not be the most infamous serial killer, but he did leave "behind a remarkable listing of his crimes and misdeeds" (*Serial Killers . . .*, 1991, p. 85). Born in Minnesota in 1891, Panzram began his life of crime at an early age.

When only eight years old, Panzram was arrested for disorderly conduct and drunkenness. He was arrested for a number of robberies by age 11 and was sentenced to reform school at age 12. While serving his time, he burned the school down. Not long after his release, he set another fire, this time to a warehouse in Minnesota, which prompted another reform school sentence.

As an adult, Panzram joined the army and received a dishonorable discharge after serving 37 months in a military prison. Following his discharge, he became a serial killer, traveling the world in search of victims. He later wrote, "In my lifetime I have murdered 21 human beings. I have committed thousands of burglaries, robberies, larcenies, arsons and last but not least I have committed sodomy on more than 1,000 male human beings. For all these things I am not in the least bit sorry . . ." (*Serial Killers . . .*, 1991, p. 85).

After being sentenced to prison, Panzram killed another inmate, for which he received a death sentence. In 1930, after a lifetime of criminal activity both inside and outside correctional institutions, Panzram was executed. While an extreme example, Carl Panzram's life and activities beg for explanation. Can criminologists provide it?

- Even without further biographical information about Panzram, brainstorm a list of factors—possibly including individual characteristics, social conditions, negative influences, and so on—that *could have* influenced him to commit his deviant acts.
- Look back at the list you just created. Why would these factors lead an individual down the path of criminal activity?
- Look back at your list once again. Is there anything that society could do through laws or policies to reduce the harmful impact of these factors?

Conceptualizing Deviance

FOCUSING QUESTION 5.1

What are the characteristics of deviance in society?

There are many activities that are viewed as socially unacceptable, or deviant. These activities range from relatively minor indiscretions (e.g., speaking too loudly in a library) to very serious criminal activities (e.g., murder). **Criminologists** are scholars who study why people commit these types of acts. Criminologists generally seek to answer questions similar to those that you answered following the opening scenario of this chapter. These may be summarized as follows: What causes deviance? Why do these things cause deviance? What steps can we take to reduce deviance?

Unfortunately, there is not a simple answer to these questions. In fact, many criminologists disagree about the causes of deviant behavior and the policy implications that flow from them. The reality is that there are many theories that contain partial answers, but there is no single correct answer that applies in all cases. Therefore, it is important to have a broad understanding of the possible answers, which this chapter will provide (for more thorough evaluations of each theory, excellent sources include Akers & Sellers, 2008, and Shoemaker, 2004). First, however, it is important to review and expand upon the concept of deviance, as introduced in Chapter 4.

As defined in Chapter 4, **deviance** is any departure from behaviors that are typical, acceptable, or expected. Norms and laws, as enforced through the various forms of social control, help identify behaviors labeled as deviant. Therefore, deviance is "any behavior that is likely to be defined as an unacceptable violation of a major social norm and elicit strong negative reactions by social control agents" (Best & Luckenbill, 1994, pp. 2–3). It is important to have a thorough understanding of deviance before attempting to understand why it occurs. Consider the essentials of the definition just presented.

First, deviance is a behavior. To be deemed a behavior, an *action* must occur, such as when Carl Panzram burned down the reformatory. *Traits*, on the other hand, are not deviant. A trait is a characteristic over which a person has no control. To draw out this distinction, consider hair color as an example. Having naturally blonde (or any other color) hair is a genetically determined trait and, as such, is not deviant. Some people may prefer one hair color to another; this is a personal judgment. But the trait of hair color is not a behavior, and thus, it is not inherently deviant. However, styling hair is an action, and as a result, some hairstyles may be viewed as deviant. For instance, if a person decides to dye his or her hair shamrock green, then this is an action that some might label as deviant because it runs counter to social expectations about hairstyling.

The important point here is that to be deviant, a person must do something. This also illustrates that deviance is a social phenomenon rather than one that is defined by physical characteristics. This is what separates the concept of deviance, which is an action in violation of social norms, from personal biases and discriminations targeting physical traits over which a person has no control.

Second, deviant behaviors violate social norms, as discussed in Chapter 4. But social norms vary over time and place (see Box 5.1), as Kai Erikson (2005) described:

> [B]ehavior that is considered unseemly within the context of a single family may be entirely acceptable to the community in general, while behavior that attracts severe censure from members of the community may go altogether unnoticed elsewhere in our culture . . . A man may disinherit his son for conduct that violates old family traditions, a woman may ostracize a neighbor for conduct that violates some local custom, but neither of them are expected to employ those standards when they serve as jurors in a court of law (p. 9).

Therefore, there is no single and universally agreed-upon list of social norms. However, there are some social norms that society feels so strongly about that they are codified into laws. For instance, Panzram's actions violated norms of behavior on which there is little disagreement and which have been

BOX 5.1

PARADE STRIPPERS

In his article, "Parade Strippers: A Note on Being Naked in Public," Craig Forsyth (1992) described the practice of females (and some males) exposing their breasts and other intimate body parts during the New Orleans Mardi Gras celebration (essentially, a street party with parades) in exchange for glass beads and other trinkets thrown by parade float riders and parade observers. This form of public nudity has been compared to nude sunbathing, joining a nudist colony, "streaking," and "mooning."

This is a behavior that is prohibited by criminal law, usually through statutes against indecent exposure. However, "on Mardi Gras day in New Orleans, many things normally forbidden are permitted. People walk around virtually nude [and] women expose themselves . . . Laws that attempt to legislate morality are informally suspended" (p. 395).

> Do you consider this form of public nudity to be deviant behavior? If so, explain how it meets the definition of deviance and whether you think it should be classified as crime, sin, and/or poor taste. If not, explain why not.
>
> What factors might contribute to making this behavior acceptable during one time of year (Mardi Gras) but not others?
>
> If you were a police officer in New Orleans, how would you respond to indecent exposure during Mardi Gras? During other times of the year? Is there a difference in your answers? Why or why not?

codified into law. Obviously, arson and murder are viewed as both illegal and unacceptable in most, if not all, circumstances. On the other hand, an unusual hairstyle may be viewed as a deviant violation of norms among some persons but not others, making it a much more situational judgment and not something that is codified into law.

In the study and practice of criminal justice, the focus is primarily on social norms that have been codified in law. However, the explanations of deviance discussed in this chapter apply to any deviant behaviors, whether they are illegal or simply viewed as distasteful or undesirable. This is important to consider because over time, new laws may be passed that increase the scope of social control by criminalizing behaviors that were once merely viewed as distasteful. As a contemporary example, consider smoking in public places. Once acceptable, the behavior is now often viewed as undesirable and has, in fact, been made criminal in some jurisdictions (see Glantz & Balbach, 2000).

Third, deviant behaviors elicit negative reactions from social control agents. This may include formal social control (e.g., police officers arresting Panzram for arson) or informal social control (e.g., a parent expressing disapproval of an unusual hairstyle). In fact, these negative reactions complete a feedback loop. When a norm is violated and a punishment is issued, the punishment serves to further communicate the unacceptability of the behavior (Feinberg, 1965), which reinforces the strength of the norm.

Therefore, defining deviance is sometimes complex, as norms vary and different social control agents treat similar behavior differently. Also, behaviors that were previously considered deviant may be acceptable today, and those that were previously considered acceptable may now be viewed as deviant.

CRIME, SIN, AND TASTE AS A FORM OF DEVIANCE

As noted in the earlier quote from Erikson, not all deviance is criminal. Behaviors that violate a tradition or custom may violate norms and elicit negative reactions but are not necessarily criminal. Smith and Pollack ([1976] 1994) suggest that there are three categories of deviance: crime, sin, and poor taste.

As you learned in Chapter 1, crimes are behaviors that are specifically prohibited by the law. This makes crime a unique form of deviance because it is the only form in which the government (as opposed to other agents of social control) may punish individuals for their deviant behaviors. In addition, crimes are often the most serious of deviant acts, including behaviors such as murder, rape, and robbery.

Sin as a form of deviance stems from behaviors that are religiously prohibited, as described by religious texts, doctrine, or clergy. Sinful behavior may be regulated by clergy (e.g., through expulsion from a religious group) or through informal control exerted by members of religious groups. As you will learn in Chapter 9, in the past, there was little distinction between what was a sin and what was a crime. In fact, religious courts were once the primary legal authorities, and some countries still utilize religious legal systems (e.g., the use of Islamic law in Saudi Arabia; see Bracey, 2006).

Although the United States has a secular (i.e., nonreligious) legal system, there are instances in which religious beliefs have been reflected in the criminal law. For instance, the prohibition of alcohol in the early twentieth century was partially motivated by religious beliefs opposing alcohol, and until fairly recently, religious beliefs underlay the blue laws that required stores and businesses to remain closed on Sunday.

Poor taste as a form of deviance is regulated by informal social control, which is in turn based on understandings of social norms. In the past, some societies relied on unwritten understandings about what was (and was not) tasteful or acceptable behavior as a basis for law. These were known as traditional legal systems. In the United States, legal codes have always been written, but taste may still influence criminal law. As an example, consider cursing. To some people, foul language is no more than a form of expression. However, to others, foul language is not in good taste, and agents of informal social control may discourage it (through a raised eyebrow from a passerby, a reprimand from a teacher, etc.). In some jurisdictions, this distaste has been formalized by the creation of laws against cursing.

Therefore, the various forms of deviance—crime, sin, and taste—overlap to some extent. Smith and Pollack ([1976] 1994) argue that only the most serious deviant acts should be made criminal, and "in regard to those whose conduct really harms no one but themselves, *we should let them alone*, recognizing that to some extent we are all deviants" [emphasis in original] (p. 20).

DEVIANCE IN SOCIETY

What functions does deviance serve in society? Kai Erickson (2005) argued that one function of deviance is to help communities maintain boundaries. Each deviant act is considered along with the norm that was violated; this "sharpens the authority of the violated norm and restates where the boundaries of the group are located" (p. 13). Thus, with each deviant act, the community has an opportunity to reflect on the deviance and decide whether the boundaries of acceptable behavior need to be strengthened, kept the same, or relaxed.

For instance, assume that panhandling (i.e., requesting money from passersby in public places) is viewed as a violation of a community's social norms. With each instance of panhandling, communities may affirm their opposition to it and their resolve to do something about it. As a result, tougher laws against panhandling could be enacted. The community may also refine the norm, such as drawing distinctions that would permit charitable groups to request money in public but prohibit homeless persons from doing so. Furthermore, how the agents of social control respond to panhandling also may change. Whether the police should ask the panhandler to move along, issue a summons, or make an arrest is a tactical decision that reflects community priorities (for additional reading on this example, see Kelling & Coles, 1996). Therefore, the nature of deviance and its evolution directly impact the job of the police officer on the street.

The presence of deviance therefore permits the definition of deviance to evolve, and as it does, persons and communities may revise and redefine their understandings of their norms. Norms and laws are indeed dynamic, continually being revised based on new understandings.

Émile Durkheim ([1938] 1980) had a different perspective on the role of deviance and crime—namely, that crime is a normal and functional part of society. Durkheim first noted that all human societies have crime, even if there are differences in terms of what acts are criminalized. This makes crime a normal, though obviously not desirable, part of society (or what Durkheim called a *social fact*). The only way that any particular crime could be eliminated would be if every single person in society agreed that it was a bad act and that they would never commit it. Durkheim then argued that even if serious crimes were eliminated in this way, people would then turn their attention to criminalizing less serious actions. The process would continue until the law controlled even trivial behavior. For instance, to return to a prior example, if violent crime was eliminated, some might turn their attention to less serious issues, such as criminalizing unusual hairstyles instead of viewing them as a matter of taste.

Durkheim argued that this sort of process would likely not occur because there is a natural diversity of human ideas that makes it impossible for unanimous opinions to develop. This means that there will never be complete agreement on an issue. As long as this is the case, people will continue to disagree (regardless of what the law says) about whether certain behaviors are or are not acceptable, and crime will exist. This makes crime the normal, but undesirable, feature that Durkheim described.

Durkheim also saw crime as necessary to society. His logic was based on the idea that, for society to progress, it needs a diversity of ideas rather than unanimous opinions. However, he believed that it would be impossible to prohibit the diversity of ideas that leads to crime, just described, while permitting the diversity of ideas that leads to progress. Consider the implications of Durkheim's theory: crimes and other forms of deviance are virtually impossible to eliminate because they are created by natural variations in human thought—ironically, the same type of natural variations in human thought that also permit the development of new ideas that allow society to advance.

The arguments set forth by Erickson and Durkheim serve to illustrate that deviance, while appearing to be a simple concept at first glance, is actually a very complex phenomenon. The discussion next turns to explaining why individuals engage in acts of deviance.

> How should we decide which behaviors to regulate through the criminal law? Do you agree with Smith and Pollack's argument, quoted in this section, about what should be criminalized?
>
> Provide examples of various forms of deviance. Are they a crime, sin, or bad taste? How have their definitions changed over time? Has social control of the issues (formal or informal) reinforced the strength of the norm being violated?
>
> One implication of Durkheim's argument is that as society comes to agreement on the prohibition of serious crimes, attention increasingly turns to the regulation of less serious behaviors. Do you believe this is true? Why or why not?

Some Explanations of Criminal Deviance

FOCUSING QUESTION 5.2

Why do some people engage in criminal deviance?

Think back to the case study at the beginning of the chapter. How did you answer the question about the factors that may have influenced Panzram to commit his criminal acts? In this section, we discuss **criminology**, which is the scientific study of the etiology (i.e., nature and causes) of criminal behavior. Many theories have been developed to explain why people commit crimes. Some of the most common are summarized in the following sections; see how they compare to your ideas about the causes of Panzram's behavior.

HISTORICAL PERSPECTIVES ON CRIMINOLOGY

Early theories attempted to explain crime based on the supernatural or on physical characteristics or by defining crime as an inherited behavior. It is important to note that these theories have been discredited and are presented only to provide historical context.

Demonology. One of the earliest forms of criminology was **demonology**, which attributes criminal behavior to the influence of evil spirits or demons. Blaming crime on witchcraft is one example. The concept of an evil witch emerged in fourteenth-century Europe. Since that time, witches have been blamed for a variety of social ills. Witchcraft as an explanation for criminal behavior made its way to the New World in the Puritan colony of Massachusetts Bay. Spiritual explanations of crime surfaced when the community believed it had been invaded by a large number of witches (Erikson, 2005). The Salem Witch Trials resulted, including the execution of individuals labeled as witches. Ben-Yehuda (1985) has observed that campaigns against witchcraft served to strengthen the power of the religious authorities who waged them. This is an illustration of the link between sin and crime as conceptualizations of deviance as well as the connection between informal social control (i.e., religion) and formal social control (i.e., courts of law) in responding to perceptions of deviance.

A number of explanations have been offered to understand the panic over witchcraft in the Massachusetts colony. However, one dominant theme that cannot be overlooked is the role that gender played in the construction of witchcraft. As criminal justice historian Lawrence Friedman (1993) observed, "In some subtle and not so subtle ways, the war against witches was also a war against women" (pp. 46–47). Women who were perceived as violating social norms in a patriarchal (i.e., male-dominated) society have been subjects of persecution not only in the Massachusetts witch trials but also in other witch-hunts worldwide (Levack, 2001).

Phrenology. This is the study of personality traits as revealed by examining bumps and grooves in the skull. This pseudo-science, led by Franz Gall (1758–1828), argued that criminal traits could be determined by the study of the skull's size, weight, shape, and other facial features.

Atavism. Cesare Lombroso (1835–1909), known as the "father of criminology," believed that criminal behavior was the result of inherited traits. That is, he believed a person could be born as a criminal. Lombroso, a physician with a specialty in psychiatry and legal medicine, "proposed that criminals were biological throwbacks to an earlier evolutionary stage, people more primitive and less highly evolved than their noncriminal counterparts. Lombroso used the term **atavistic** to describe such people" (Vold, Bernard, & Snipes, 1998, p. 32).

Somatotypes. Building on Lombroso's theory, Charles Goring (1870–1919) believed that a person's height and weight were associated with criminal behavior and that offenders tended to be shorter and lighter than nonoffenders. Similarly, William Sheldon claimed that people with different physical builds (what he called different **somatotypes**) possess different temperaments. He believed that persons who are muscular, active, and aggressive, known as **mesomorphs**, were more likely to engage in delinquent behavior (see Figure 5.1).

The theories of phrenology, atavism, and somatotype have two commonalities. First, they all deal with the relationship between physical characteristics and deviance. Second, there is no scientific support for these ideas, and they are generally discarded by modern criminologists. Research continued along biological lines described next.

Family Criminality and Eugenics. Richard Dugdale (1877), while visiting county jails in New York, discovered six incarcerated persons who were blood relatives. He traced their family genetic lines back hundreds of years and reported that the family had a history of criminal activity, including attempted murder, attempted rape, burglary, and theft, to name a few. Based on his findings, Dugdale concluded that the Jukes (a pseudonym for the family) were a family of degenerates whose environment and heredity led to criminality. This had an impact on thinking about a practice known as eugenics.

Eugenics is the study of genetic factors that may influence future generations. Francis Galton, Charles Darwin's cousin, was considered by most to be the founder of the eugenics philosophy. Galton believed that eugenics was a means to positively influence human evolution by assuring that only the finest reproduced. Galton also argued that persons possessing "bad" genes should be discouraged from reproducing.

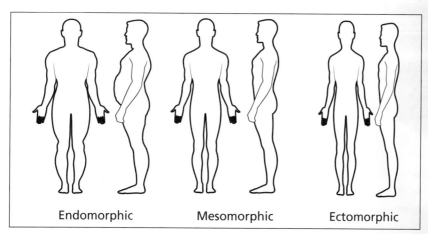

Endomorphic   Mesomorphic   Ectomorphic

Figure 5.1. Sheldon's Somatotypes

Research continued to examine the relationship between crime and genetics. In the twentieth century, psychologist Henry Goddard told a tale of the Kallikak (again, a pseudonym) family. The Kallikaks produced a genetic line of illegitimate children, persons deemed sexually immoral by standards of the time (mostly prostitutes), alcoholics, and assorted criminals. "Goddard thought that mental weakness and other undesirable traits were handed down from father and mother to daughter and son" (Friedman, 1993, p. 335).

This led some to advocate sterilization as a means of protecting society from criminals, including even those who had the *potential* for violence and criminality. Eugenics is not limited to sterilization. Other policies derived from eugenics include execution, incarceration for *future* bad acts, and lobotomies for crime prevention, to name a few (Lanier & Henry, 1998).

Box 5.2 provides additional information about state-mandated sterilization and legal challenges to it. It is important to note that eugenics and notions of biological familial inheritance of criminality have been disregarded. These theories were based on overly simplistic notions that bear little resemblance to what modern biological science has learned about the nature of genetic influences on behavior.

XYY Chromosomes. Later research focused more specifically on chromosomal differences and their impact on criminal behavior. Recall from your biology coursework that humans possess 23 pairs of chromosomes. Female chromosome pairs are labeled XX and male chromosome pairs are labeled XY. During the early 1960s, the discovery of an XYY chromosome in some males raised concern about the relationship between the extra Y chromosome and criminality. Some feared that the extra chromosome would lead to aggression and violence. However, subsequent research revealed that there was no relationship between the extra chromosome and criminal violence.

MODERN BIOLOGICAL PERSPECTIVES ON CRIME AND CRIMINALITY

Criminologists have continued to pursue the relationship between biology and crime. After its shaky beginning, the biological perspective on crime and criminality has made a resurgence. Interestingly, research suggests that one explanation of the witchcraft panic in Salem had a biological component—the effects on the body of intoxication from a poison called ergot that sometimes grows on various grain crops (Caporael, 1976). Many modern biological theories focus on genetics but in the context of inherited traits that are conducive to crime. The biological perspectives described in this section have been scientifically validated.

Researchers have examined the relationship between crime and heredity by comparing the criminality of identical twins with the criminality of fraternal twins of the same gender. Researcher Karl Christiansen (1977) found that if one identical twin had a criminal conviction, the other twin also had a

BOX 5.2

BUCK V. BELL, 274 U.S. 200 (1927)

In 1924, Virginia adopted a statute authorizing the compulsory sterilization of the mentally retarded for the purpose of eugenics. Carrie Buck, an 18 year old, was described by the superintendent of the Virginia State Colony for Epileptics and Feebleminded as "feebleminded" (an archaic term used to label individuals who were mentally retarded or who had certain cognitive impairments) and a genetic threat to society. Carrie was housed at the same institution as her mother, who was also labeled as feebleminded. In addition, Carrie was the mother of an illegitimate child who was classified as feebleminded.

The superintendent requested that Carrie be sexually sterilized so she would be unable to have additional children, arguing that it was for the betterment of society. The Supreme Court agreed. In an 8–1 decision, Justice Oliver Wendell Holmes stated:

> It is better for all the world, if instead of waiting to execute degenerate offspring for crime, or to let them starve for their imbecility, society can prevent those who are manifestly unfit from continuing their kind . . . Three generations of imbeciles are enough (274 U.S. 200, p. 208).

Do you agree with the Supreme Court ruling? Why or why not?

Eugenic sterilization programs were eventually abolished. However, debate continues about castration (usually through the administration of drugs) of criminal sex offenders. Do some research to find out what arguments have been made for and against this practice. Which side do you think has the better arguments?

conviction in 35% of the cases (see also Rowe & Osgood, 1984). More recent twin studies have detected a genetic component for committing acts of intimate violence (Hines & Saudino, 2004) and for juvenile aggression (Elev, Lichtenstein, & Moffitt, 2003).

Studies such as these suggest there may be a genetic component to criminal behavior. Unlike prior work, however, the focus is not on specific families passing *crime* directly to their offspring. Rather, the focus is on identifying particular genes that may influence a variety of behaviors that are associated with a *propensity* to commit crime. "No single gene can deterministically make a person into a criminal. Instead, complex traits are subtly influenced by a great number of genes, the exact number of which is unknown" (Rowe, 2002, p. 100). For instance, genetic differences in the production of neurotransmitters (chemicals in the brain) may produce aggressive tendencies in some persons, which if acted upon inappropriately can lead to crime (see Ishikawa & Raine, 2002). Other genes have been associated with a propensity for personality characteristics such as "novelty seeking" (Guo, Roettger, & Cai, 2008, p. 547), which again could lead to criminal activity (committed as a "novelty") if acted upon inappropriately.

Modern biological researchers are also careful to acknowledge that these traits do not cause crime by themselves; rather, the environment in which an individual lives has a significant impact as well (e.g., Guo, Roettger, & Cai, 2008) through processes described later in this chapter. Also, some persons may channel tendencies toward aggression or novelty seeking through socially acceptable activities, such as sports or skydiving. The social environment can impact how individuals respond to such tendencies. Therefore, the relationship between biology and crime is extraordinarily complex, and new discoveries regularly emerge about the interaction of genes, environment, and human behavior.

THE CLASSICAL SCHOOL OF CRIMINOLOGY

Classical criminology is based on the concept of *free will*, which is the idea that people may choose whether or not to commit a criminal act. This idea has its origins in the eighteenth-century writings of Jeremy Bentham ([1789] 1970). Bentham argued that people are hedonistic, being motivated by the pursuit of pleasure and the avoidance of pain. Therefore, persons who commit criminal acts believe that the potential rewards from their actions will outweigh the potential consequences.

Rational Choice Theory. A modern version of classical criminology is **rational choice theory**. Using free will as the philosophical base, rational choice theorists believe that offenders use a strategic thinking process to evaluate rewards and risks. In choosing to commit a criminal act, offenders engage in a rational decision-making process that includes a consideration of factors such as the type of offense to be committed to achieve the desired goal, the selection of the victim, the best strategy to utilize in committing the crime, the risk of being caught, the potential sanction (if apprehended), the potential rewards (if successful), and so on. If the benefits outweigh the risks, the offender decides to commit the crime.

Note that the rational choice decision-making process is similar to the hedonistic calculus proposed by Bentham, although rational choice includes consideration of a wider range of variables than pain and pleasure. Rational choice theory also underlies the concept of deterrence, which suggests that crime may be prevented (or deterred) if offenders know they will be caught and swiftly punished for their offenses. Such knowledge could cause a rational offender to decide against committing a crime. Deterrence theory will be more fully discussed in Chapter 10.

Routine Activities Theory. A logical outgrowth of rational choice theory is routine activities theory. Based on research conducted by Lawrence Cohen and Marcus Felson (1979), **routine activities theory** views crime and victimization as a function of individuals' everyday behavior, habits, lifestyle, living conditions, and social interactions. According to Cohen and Felson, crime occurs when three elements converge: a motivated offender, a suitable target, and a lack of capable guardians.

To be a *motivated offender*, an offender must be willing to commit the offense and be capable of committing it. There are any number of reasons offenders may choose to offend. Although some offenders engage in "deviance as fun" (Riemer, 1981, p. 39) or enjoy the "seductions of crime" (Katz, 1988), motivations often go beyond the statement, "I *want* to commit a crime." Some offenders believe they have nothing to lose or few legitimate alternatives to crime; others have external motivations for committing a crime. For example, if an offender addicted to drugs needs money to buy them, he might decide that robbery is the most effective means to obtain the money.

A *suitable target* can be an object or person. The offender will often select a target that is both vulnerable and that produces the greatest rewards. For example, an armed robber may select a potential robbery victim (or target) based on the time of day, location of the crime, age of the victim, and demeanor of the victim. For instance, when considering the commission of a robbery, an offender may notice two targets: one a physically weak individual openly counting a large amount of money while walking down an empty, unlit alley and the other a bodybuilder on a busy street with no visible sign of valuables. The former would likely be judged the more suitable target. Based on signals of this sort, the potential offender will make the decision of whom, if anyone, to victimize.

Capable guardians are people or objects that may serve as a deterrent to criminal activity. These may include police officers, watchful parents, concerned neighbors, and crime prevention security devices (e.g., alarms, effective lighting, fences), to name a few. When these people or objects are absent, the likelihood of crime increases. For example, if the potential victim of the robbery was walking in a well-lighted area with a group of friends, the potential offender may decide that the risks of being identified and apprehended are too great, thereby deterring the robbery.

> What are the strengths and weaknesses of the genetic approach to explaining criminal deviance? How does this relate to the medicalization of deviance, as discussed in the previous chapter?
>
> Do you believe that classical theories explain Carl Panzram's criminal activity? Why or why not?

As a police officer, your sergeant informs you that a number of adult males have been the victim of pickpockets. The crimes are occurring on Main Street during nonbusiness hours. Based on your newly acquired knowledge of the routine activities theory, how might you resolve the problem?

Psychological Theories of Crime and Criminality

FOCUSING QUESTION 5.3

How can psychological theories explain crime and deviant behavior?

Psychological theories focus on individuals and their thinking processes. With origins in the work of Sigmund Freud, psychological theories have since developed to include a wide range of explanations for deviant behavior.

PSYCHODYNAMIC THEORIES

Developed by Sigmund Freud (1856–1939), **psychodynamic theories** (also known as psychoanalytic theories) propose that human behavior is controlled by a variety of mental processes. Freud believed that the mind could be divided into three levels. The first was the conscious mind, which refers to one's current awareness. The second was the preconscious mind, where many memories are stored. The third was the unconscious mind, which is a warehouse of troublesome memories and feelings that are hidden from immediate awareness. Freud argued that "behaviors could be explained by traumatic experiences in early childhood that left their mark on the individual despite the fact the individual was not consciously aware of those experiences" (Vold et al., 1998, p. 91).

To Freud, human behavior was driven by unconscious mental processes involving the id, superego, and ego (Seigel, 2002). The *id* represents the hedonistic side of people, seeking instant gratification and pleasure regardless of the consequences. The id includes urges, impulses, and intense energies (known as the libido, which includes sexual drives) that may influence criminal activity. The superego represents the extreme opposite of the id. The *superego* is the moral compass of a person influenced by parental values and societal norms. The ego represents the "umpire" between the id and superego. The *ego* attempts to keep both the id and superego balanced, resulting in appropriate behaviors.

Based on his many years of running an institution for delinquent youth, psychologist August Aichhorn "found that many children in his institution had *underdeveloped* superegos, so that the delinquency and criminality were primarily expressions of an unregulated id. Aichhorn attributed this to the fact that the parents of these children were either absent or unloving, so that the children failed to form the loving attachments necessary for the proper development of their superegos [emphasis in original]" (Vold et al., 1998, pp. 93–94).

Aichhorn also noted that delinquency could result when a child received an overabundance of love, thereby spoiling the child by succumbing to the child's requests and demands.

DIFFERENTIAL ASSOCIATION

Edwin Sutherland introduced **differential association theory**, which proposes that criminal behavior is learned from others. Sutherland argued that learning occurs most effectively as a result of face-to-face interactions, usually among intimate social contacts such as family members and close friends. Individuals may learn how to commit crime as well as attitudes that promote criminal behavior (Sutherland, 1947). It is important to note that criminal behavior does not need to be learned solely from other offenders. One can learn criminal behavior from law-abiding people who simply approve of the illegal activity.

Learning may occur in a number of ways. Social learning theory (also known as observational learning) holds that individuals learn behaviors by watching others. This was illustrated in a classic study by Albert Bandura, Dorothy Ross, and Sheila Ross (1961) in which the authors determined that children who watched aggressive behavior subsequently behaved aggressively themselves by hitting an inflatable toy. Learning may also occur as a result of reinforcements and punishments in what is known as operant conditioning. According to the theory, behavior can be influenced through four techniques:

- Giving a positive reinforcement (i.e., a desirable reward) after a desired behavior;
- Giving a negative reinforcement (i.e., removing something that a person does not like) after a desired behavior;
- Giving a positive punishment (i.e., administering an unpleasant consequence) after an undesired behavior; or
- Giving a negative punishment (i.e., taking away something that a person likes) after an undesired behavior.

When criminal behaviors are reinforced or when noncriminal behaviors are punished, individuals may learn to commit crime. This often occurs through peer pressure or through association with peers who engage in criminal activity.

TECHNIQUES OF NEUTRALIZATION

Gresham Sykes and David Matza (1957) argued that offenders learn to justify their behavior through **neutralization theory**. That is, offenders learn to neutralize or suppress accepted social values and attitudes, which allows them to drift into criminal behavior. Sykes and Matza identified five techniques that may neutralize accepted norms; in essence, these are excuses that some offenders may use to justify their criminal behavior. They include: (1) denial of responsibility, (2) denial of injury, (3) denial of the victim, (4) condemnation of the condemners, and (5) appeal to higher loyalties. Table 5.1 describes each in further detail.

Table 5.1. Five Techniques of Neutralization

Neutralization Technique	Description	Statement Example
Denial of responsibility	This blames forces beyond the control of the individual. The offender views himself or herself as a victim of circumstance.	"It wasn't my fault."
Denial of injury	The offender does not believe that he or she has caused any great harm to the victim, even if the act did violate the criminal law.	"The store can afford the loss."
Denial of the victim	Even when the offender accepts responsibility, admitting his or her illegal activity, the actions are viewed as rightful retaliation.	"They deserved what they got."
Condemnation of the condemners	Offenders may shift focus from their own actions to judging those who disapprove. They believe that the condemners (i.e., agents of social control) are hypocrites because they also commit similar illegal acts.	"Everyone drives drunk."
Appeal to higher loyalties	The offender is conflicted between violating the law and violating a trust.	"I did it for my best friend."

Source: Sykes, G. M. & Matza, D. (December, 1957). Techniques of neutralization: A theory of delinquency. *American Sociological Review, 22*, 664–670.

Sykes and Matza also recognized that many offenders do not view themselves as criminals because they only selectively violate the law—disobeying some laws while obeying others. For instance, a rapist may obey the traffic laws, and a shoplifter might resist the idea of committing armed robbery.

PERSONALITY AND CRIME

What role does personality play in criminality? *Personality* refers to an individual's patterns of behavior, mental traits, thoughts, emotions, temperament, and feelings. Personality traits suspected as links to criminal behavior include aggression, hostility, impulsivity, and hyperactivity, to name a few.

Hans Eysenck (1964) proposed that criminals can be distinguished from noncriminals by their lack of conscience and other personality traits linked to antisocial behavior (to be discussed momentarily), such as extroversion and neuroticism. *Extreme extroverts* are thrill seekers and impulsive. *Neuroticism* occurs when a person lacks emotional stability and is viewed as irrational, moody, anxious, and tense. Eysenck argued that potential criminals possess both neurotic and extroverted personality traits because they may act in a self-destructive manner without viewing their behavior as harmful or dangerous (Eysenck, 1964).

Michael Gottfredson and Travis Hirschi (1990) have suggested that self-control is a key personality trait that can influence criminality. Specifically, they argue that persons with low self-control are "impulsive, insensitive, physical (as opposed to mental), risk-taking, short-sighted, and nonverbal, and they will tend therefore to engage in criminal and analogous acts" (p. 90). Low self-control is viewed as a stable trait, meaning that it does not change over an individual's lifetime, with its origins in childhood.

Psychoses are also associated with criminal activity. Persons with psychoses lose touch with reality. They may experience delusions (i.e., stable but false beliefs, such as believing that they are a deity or a famous historical figure) and/or hallucinations (e.g., false sensory perceptions, such as hearing voices that are not there in reality). "The psychosis that is most often linked to criminal behavior is schizophrenia, which involves disordered thought patterns characterized by fantasy, delusion, and incoherence . . . Schizophrenia is sometimes associated with acts of violence, including homicide, particularly against people who are thought to be threatening to the schizophrenic" (Conklin, 1998, pp. 175–176).

Finally, antisocial personality disorder is associated with criminal activity. This does not refer to persons who isolate themselves from others. On the contrary, many **antisocial personality** types, also known as *sociopaths* or *psychopaths*, thrive on personal contact but do so for the purpose of manipulation and deceit. Table 5.2 lists the characteristics of antisocial personalities.

Table 5.2. Diagnostic Criteria for Antisocial Personality Disorder

There is a pervasive pattern of disregard for and violation of the rights of others occurring since the age of 15 years, as indicated by three (or more) of the following:

- Failure to conform to social norms with respect to lawful behaviors as indicated by repeatedly performing acts that are grounds for arrest.
- Deceitfulness, as indicated by repeatedly lying, use of aliases, or conning others for personal profit or pleasure.
- Impulsivity or failure to plan ahead.
- Irritability and aggressiveness, as indicated by repeated physical fights or assaults.
- Reckless disregard for safety of self or others.
- Consistent irresponsibility, as indicated by repeated failure to sustain consistent work behavior or honor financial obligations.
- Lack of remorse, as indicated by being indifferent to or rationalizing having hurt, mistreated, or stolen from another.

Source: American Psychiatric Association, 2000, p. 706.

What do you see as the strengths and weaknesses of psychodynamic theories of crime?

How would the neutralization and personality theories apply to Carl Panzram? Explain your answer.

In what ways is crime learned through differential association theory? What prevention programs could be developed that use learning theories to reduce crime?

Sociocultural Theories of Crime and Criminality

FOCUSING QUESTION 5.4

How can sociological theories explain crime and deviant behavior?

The psychological theories just described focus primarily on individual-level explanations for deviant behavior. However, some conditions within society beyond the individual may also influence criminal deviance. Therefore, to more fully understand the causes of deviant behavior, it is important to consider the following sociocultural theories.

SOCIAL DISORGANIZATION THEORY

The work of sociologists Robert Park, Ernest Burgess, and Roderick McKenzie from the University of Chicago resulted in the development of **social disorganization theory**, which focuses on environmental conditions that lead to crime. Because of its association with the City of Chicago, this is sometimes called the *Chicago School* of criminology. Environmental factors leading to crime may include poverty, the breakdown of families and social institutions, a high turnover of residents (i.e., many persons moving in and then out of the neighborhood), and a lack of bonds to the community. Areas with these characteristics are identified as socially disorganized.

Popularizing social disorganization theory, Clifford Shaw and Henry McKay (1942) developed the **concentric zone theory** to explain criminality in cities. Shaw and McKay divided Chicago into five concentric zones (each two miles wide) to explain social development and crime patterns. Imagine a large circle, beginning at the city's core and spreading outward (illustrated in Figure 5.2). *Zone One* was the downtown, composed primarily of businesses. *Zone Two*, or the "transitional" zone, was formerly a residential community undergoing transition to commercial or industrial uses. *Zone Three* contained the "working-men's homes," occupied by the working class forced to move from Zone Two as its transition occurred. *Zone Four*, the "residential zone," is where the majority of suburban families resided. *Zone Five*, the "commuter zone," was the most desirable of residential locations, comprised of expensive single-family dwellings; residents could drive to the city for work but were far enough away to be distant from the hustle and bustle of city stress (Lanier & Henry, 1998).

Figure 5.2. Shaw and McKay's Concentric Zones

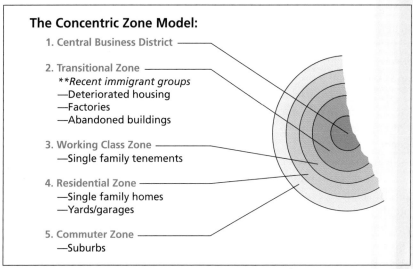

The Concentric Zone Model:

1. Central Business District

2. Transitional Zone
   **Recent immigrant groups*
   —Deteriorated housing
   —Factories
   —Abandoned buildings

3. Working Class Zone
   —Single family tenements

4. Residential Zone
   —Single family homes
   —Yards/garages

5. Commuter Zone
   —Suburbs

Source: http://www.csiss.org/classics/uploads/conzone.jpg

Shaw and McKay discovered that Zone Two produced the highest rate of crime and other social problems, including drug abuse, suicide, and mental illness. They theorized that as one resided closer to the business district in an area undergoing transition, there would be minimal community bonding and socialization, a lack of social resources, greater residential transition, and lower levels of security, thereby creating social disorganization.

STRAIN AND DELINQUENT SUBCULTURES

Strain theorists, such as Robert Merton (1968), argue that society defines certain goals (principally the accumulation of wealth) as worthy of attainment. When members of society, predominantly the lower socioeconomic class, fail to achieve those goals, frustration (or strain) results. To relieve this frustration, some indigent (i.e., poverty-stricken) persons may reject socially accepted norms and feel that they may only achieve society's valued goals through deviant means, including criminal activity.

Albert Cohen (1955) argued that juveniles seek to attain status, usually from their peers. Cohen noted that status could be *achieved* (i.e., that which is earned through competition among peers or accomplishments at school) or *ascribed* (that which is acquired through the status already held by family members). According to Cohen, strain occurs when neither ascribed nor achieved status is obtainable, in which case youth reject middle-class values and seek other means of achieving status. Sometimes, youth may create their own system of values and norms, known as **delinquent subcultures**, to acquire the status they seek. Cohen argued that this process might lead juveniles to turn to gangs and criminal activity.

Walter Miller (1958) proposed that delinquency resulted from efforts to achieve a *different* set of goals than those promoted by social norms—goals that he labeled "lower class culture" (p. 5). Miller highlighted six focal concerns of lower-class culture, including trouble, toughness, smartness, excitement, fate, and autonomy.

Getting into *trouble* or staying out of trouble is a concern in Miller's lower-class culture. While remaining clear of trouble minimizes contact with law enforcement authorities, non-law-abiding behavior may provide status among peers.

Toughness is based on bravery, masculinity, and physical prowess. Miller found that youth raised in single-parent female-headed households may lack positive male role models and, to avoid being called weak or soft, may exaggerate their male bravado.

Smartness is the ability to remain streetwise, including the ability to con others while being careful not to be conned. *Excitement* includes thrills and risks, legal or nonlegal, to avoid boredom. Excitement may take the form of gambling, drug and alcohol use, joining a gang, or other outlets.

Fate is a function of *external control*, which is a belief that life events are the result of luck and chance rather than hard work and effort. This stems from a belief that individuals possess little control over their lives, accepting the adage "whatever happens, happens." *Autonomy* is the desire to remain independent from authority figures. Authority figures may include parents, police, and teachers.

Criminologists Richard Cloward and Lloyd Ohlin (1960) integrated subcultural deviance and social disorganization theory. Cloward and Ohlin argued that in socially disorganized communities, juveniles may lack adult role models and opportunities for success, whether through legitimate or illegitimate means. They called these juveniles *retreatists*, who resort to drugs, sex, or other activities as a means to escape societal expectations.

Robert Agnew (1992) expanded the concept of strain theory by suggesting that it could apply to all persons regardless of their socioeconomic status. This was a departure from the preceding theories, which focused extensively on class-based differences. According to Agnew, anyone could experience the kind of strain that results from a failure to achieve a desired goal, loss of something that a person perceives as bringing value to his or her life, or being faced with unpleasant events or circumstances. The impact of these strains is heightened when "they are (1) greater in magnitude or size, (2) recent, (3) of long duration, and (4) clustered in time" (p. 64). Individuals (again, regardless of income) can address these strains through positive coping strategies or by turning to crime or deviant behaviors. Many factors, including those expressed in other psychological and sociocultural theories, may influence how an individual copes with strain.

SOCIAL CONTROL THEORY

According to criminologist Travis Hirschi (1969), criminal deviance occurs when an individual's bonds to society (i.e., **social bonds**) are weak or broken. Social bonds are provided by individuals, groups, and organizations that connect a person to the community, including parents, friends, religious groups, clubs, and others. Hirschi identified four components to social bonds: attachment, commitment, involvement, and belief.

Attachment is related to sensitivity. According to Hirschi, if a person is insensitive to the opinions of others and is willing to violate social norms, he or she is free to deviate. Conversely, being attached to family, friends, and other social institutions means a person is sensitive to their opinions and therefore less likely to violate norms (this is related to informal social control).

Commitment occurs when a person invests time and energy to meet a personal goal, such as attaining a college degree. Of course, one can be committed to accomplishing criminal activity as well by focusing attention on deviant behavior. Therefore, persons who are invested in *conventional* societal norms and values are less likely to engage in criminal conduct.

Involvement or participation in conventional activities is a key factor in social control. According to Hirschi, a person engrossed with work, deadlines, and other conventional activities does not have the opportunity to commit deviant acts. On the other hand, those with too much idle time are more likely to engage in criminal conduct. In addition, involvement with conventional activities may promote prosocial norms and foster informal social control.

Belief occurs when people share a common set of socially accepted norms, values and moral principles. Although most persons may understand that deviant acts are wrong, such acts are more likely to occur if the common set of beliefs and values is threatened or absent.

LABELING THEORY

The idea behind **labeling theory** (which developed from a sociological perspective called *symbolic interaction*) assumes that once society places a label on a person, that individual will self-identify with the label and behave accordingly. The label serves as a self-fulfilling prophecy. For example, if a parent repeatedly tells a child that he is a troublemaker, whether the label is accurate or not, the child will internalize the label and get into trouble.

Edwin Lemert (1951), a proponent of labeling theory, indicated that the labeling process includes two forms of deviance: primary and secondary. *Primary deviance* is an initial deviant act. Sometimes, committing a deviant act does not negatively stigmatize or label a person. For instance, assume that a criminal justice student successfully cheats on a final exam (don't even think about it!) but was never identified or apprehended. Years later, the student becomes the chief of police. Because the student was never labeled as a cheater, she was able to become a successful community leader.

Secondary deviance occurs when an individual commits a deviant or unlawful act—primary deviance—and the incident then comes to the attention of others, including family, friends, and police, any of whom may apply and reinforce a negative label. Unable to remove that negative label, the "deviant" heads in a downward spiral. After accepting and internalizing the label of deviant, the individual starts to act as though he or she actually is deviant, including the commission of further deviant acts. These subsequent deviant acts, committed as a result of the labeling, are known as the secondary deviance. For example, assume that the student who cheated was apprehended, called before the student conduct board, found in violation of academic dishonesty, and suspended from the university. The suspension for cheating became widely known and circulated among the student's friends and family. The student, like others, also considered herself to be a cheater. Unable to find employment in the field of criminal justice, the student might accept being labeled as deviant and therefore turn to alcohol, drugs, and other deviant pursuits. This is the essence of labeling theory.

Frank Tannenbaum (1938) described a process he called "the dramatization of the 'evil'" (p. 21), arguing that labeling a child as "evil" plays a vital role in that child's future criminality. The labeled child not only accepts the "tag" but also seeks others who are similarly labeled. Groups of labeled youth may then join together in delinquent enterprises—all as a result of the initial way the child was labeled.

CONFLICT CRIMINOLOGY

Conflict criminology, also known as *critical criminology, conflict theory, radical criminology,* or *new criminology*, holds that crime is a consequence of the oppression of the lower classes by the rich and powerful elites. In conflict criminology, "Unequal distribution of power produces conflict" (Seigel, 2002, p. 174), which becomes the foundation for criminal activity. There are many varieties of conflict criminology, several of which are profiled here.

Marxist criminology argues that there is a strong relationship between capitalism, class conflict, and crime. Individuals with political power and wealth create laws to keep the lower class "in their place." For instance, Marxist theorist Richard Quinney (1970) argued that definitions of crime are created and applied by the powerful elite to shape the enforcement and administration of the criminal law against members of the lower classes.

Feminist criminology (Arrigo, 1999) developed in the late 1960s and gained prominence during the Women's Movement in the early 1970s. Feminist criminologists examine the relationship between gender inequality, male dominance, and the exploitation of women under capitalism. Traditional criminology focuses primarily on male offenders and victims, ignoring gender differences in criminal activity, gender differences in victimization, and inequality in the division of labor (i.e., the exploitation of women in the work force, including salary disparities). Feminist criminologists attempt to address these issues.

Peacemaking criminology is grounded in social justice. "In the peacemaking frame of mind, all imbalances of power *over* . . . others are defined as 'violence' [emphasis in original]" (Pepinsky, 1999, p. 56). Therefore, traditional forms of punishment, such as incarceration, are considered counterproductive to justice because they reflect an imbalance of power. Peacemaking criminologists instead argue that the encouragement of communication and relationships can promote justice and heal social wrongs. "Peacemaking is the art and science of weaving and reweaving oneself with others into a social fabric of mutual love, respect, and concern" (Pepinsky, 1999, p. 59).

> What do you think are the strengths and weaknesses of the sociological theories of crime presented in this section? Are there any sociological theories that you think are more effective than others in explaining why crime occurs?
>
> Do you think any of the sociological theories explain Carl Panzram's criminal behavior? If so, explain how.
>
> Are there any programs that could be developed to prevent crime by addressing its causes as suggested by the sociological theories presented?

The Study of Deviance in Criminal Justice

FOCUSING QUESTION 5.5

Why is the study of deviance important for criminal justice?

This chapter has provided a foundational overview of criminal deviance and theories that explain it. Understanding criminal deviance is essential for the study and practice of criminal justice. After all, it is important for criminal justice students and practitioners to understand the origins of the laws they are studying and enforcing on a daily basis. An understanding of why individuals engage in deviant behavior—and crime, in particular—is equally essential.

If we can understand *why* people commit crimes, we can design policies and programs that will *reduce* crime by addressing its causes. Regrettably, as noted criminal justice scholar Samuel Walker (2006) observed, "most current crime control proposals are nonsense" (p. 11), in part because they "rest on faith rather than facts" (p. 22; see also Lab, 2004). Criminologist James Austin (2003) has gone so far as to label criminology "irrelevant" (p. 557) because it has not received much attention from those responsible for making criminal justice policies. Let this be a challenge to you as a future criminal justice practitioner and scholar: consider how theories of criminal deviance can be applied to prevent crime and then advocate those solutions that have a sound basis and the promise for effectiveness rather than those resting on mere speculation.

A word of caution is in order, though. Understanding the causes of crime is a complex area of study. In fact, there are many theories that were not presented in this chapter, and no single theory of deviance or crime is perfect. Different individuals commit deviant acts for different reasons. Some may be influenced by antisocial personality disorder (a psychological theory), others due to genetic factors (a biological theory), still others due to strain (a sociocultural theory), and many for other reasons altogether. Even the same offender may be influenced by different theories at different times. Therefore, it is important to resist the temptation to identify a single "right" theory but rather to consider how each can contribute to our understanding of criminal behavior.

Some criminologists have worked to develop integrated theories, which blend an array of theoretical perspectives to produce a more comprehensive explanation of crime. One type of integrated theory is known as **life course theory**, which explores how involvement in criminal activity changes as offenders grow older and encounter new life circumstances (e.g., marriage, full-time employment, and other major life activities). Life course theories posit that, over the course of a person's life, multiple forces (drawing upon biological, psychological, and sociocultural perspectives) can combine to influence behavior in different ways depending on the stage in life at which a person finds himself or herself (Akers, 2000).

Over time, new theories (e.g., integrated theories) emerge to explain crime and deviance as older theories are revisited. As theories change, their implications for criminal justice policy and practice also change.

> Having considered the variety of criminological theories presented in this chapter, are there any that strike you as particularly strong explanations of crime? As particularly weak explanations? Why?
>
> Do you think any of the theoretical perspectives presented in this chapter could be integrated to provide a more comprehensive explanation of why crime occurs? If so, how?

Conclusion

Deviant acts are those that violate social norms, including crime. As has been illustrated, there are many possible explanations for deviant behavior. Each explanation suggests its own policy recommendations for how to better prevent or respond to crime. Although it is unlikely that we will ever fully understand criminal behavior and it is virtually impossible to imagine that a single theory can definitively explain all crimes, it remains important to consider why crime occurs. As new theories continue to emerge, we simultaneously continue the quest of understanding how social control can better address crime. In doing so, however, the values of justice and fairness must be upheld, and it is to these issues that we will turn in Unit III.

Criminal Justice Problem Solving: JUVENILE GANGS

Assume that you have been assigned as the supervisor to a gang task force. There have been numerous complaints from concerned community members, teachers, and parents that gang members have been recruiting extensively in your city. The police chief has requested that you and your officers take immediate action to rectify the situation. Based on your knowledge of criminal deviance and criminological theory, design a juvenile gang prevention program. In your prevention strategy, address the following by drawing upon the theories described in this chapter:

What factors might influence juveniles to join gangs?

What factors prevent juveniles from joining gangs? That is, why do some juveniles not join gangs?

Based on your responses to the preceding, what kind of program(s) could reduce the likelihood that juveniles will join gangs?

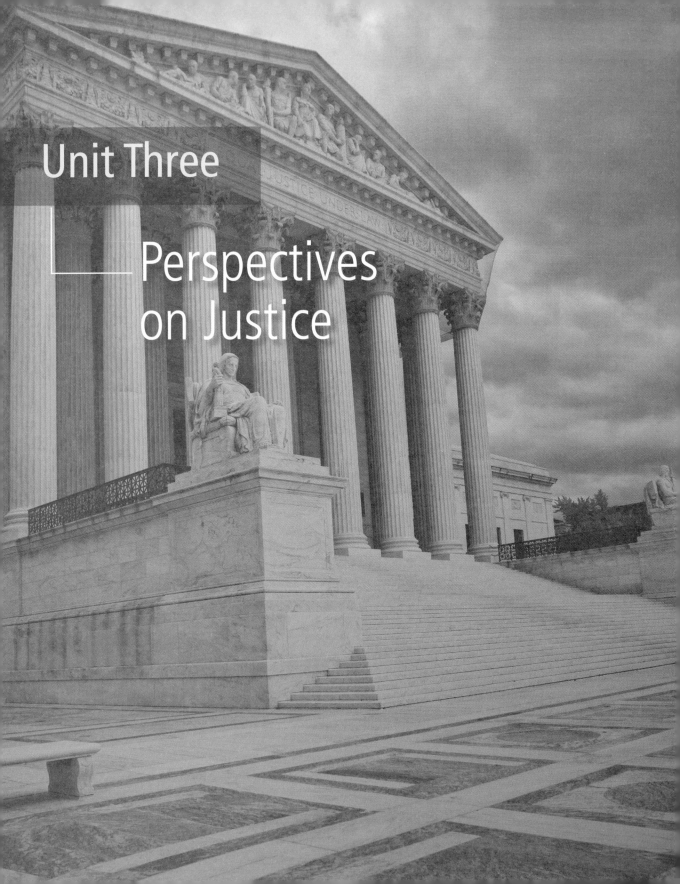

Unit Three

Perspectives on Justice

Photo Essay: Search and Seizure

Unit II showed that both the definitions of deviance and the explanations for it are complex. It is a challenge to understand the sometimes shifting distinctions between those behaviors that are largely viewed as acceptable, those that are viewed as unacceptable but controlled informally, and those that are viewed as unacceptable and regulated through criminal law. For criminal justice professionals, it is the law that guides action. Once a behavior is criminalized, regardless of the reason, the criminal justice system becomes responsible for addressing it, whether through prevention programs targeting the underlying causes of the behavior or through enforcement activities that result in criminal investigations, arrests, prosecutions, and punishments. The goal of the criminal justice system is to seek justice in these activities—a task significant enough that "establish justice" is listed second only to "form a more perfect union" in the goals contained within the preamble of the U.S. Constitution.

But establishing justice is no simple endeavor. It requires considerations about what justice means, how it is to be established, and what limits are imposed on its pursuit. Controversies related to search and seizure illustrate these dilemmas. Search and seizure is an area of law rooted in the Fourth Amendment to the U.S. Constitution, as you will learn in subsequent chapters. When should law enforcement officers be permitted to search property and seize

items that are found there? Typically, a search warrant issued by a judge or magistrate is required, but are there exceptions? Courts of appeals are generally the arbiters of these questions, as they hear cases about police practices. Each case requires careful consideration of what the pursuit of justice means. In many instances, the issue emerges as a conflict between notions of privacy, on the one hand, and the need for the police to acquire information about criminal cases, on the other.

A phone booth was at the center of one of the most famous cases about search and seizure. In the days before cell phones, phone booths dotted the landscape as sheltered locations from which a person could make a telephone call when away from home or work. In *Katz v. United States*, agents from the Federal Bureau of Investigation (FBI) affixed a device to the exterior of a phone booth, which monitored and recorded what was said inside the booth. This allowed the FBI to obtain evidence that led to Katz's conviction for violation of federal gambling laws, although no warrant had been obtained to permit this electronic surveillance. Was justice upheld in this case? The Supreme Court thought not, arguing that "the Fourth Amendment protects people, not places. What a person knowingly exposes to the public, even in his own home or office, is not a subject of Fourth Amendment protection. But what he seeks to preserve as private, even in an area accessible to the public, may be constitutionally protected" (*Katz v. United States*, 1967, p. 351). The Court viewed phone booths as areas of privacy, rendering inadmissible the recordings that were made without a warrant. How do you define privacy? Do you think a phone booth meets the definition? What about a pay phone that is not enclosed in a booth? Let's see how this precedent might apply to other cases that utilize newer technologies.

Should a warrant be required to search an arrested person's cell phone? The U.S. Supreme Court has held that, upon arrest, officers have a broad ability to search, without a warrant, a suspect and any containers that he or she may be carrying. The rationale is that such searches protect officer safety and help to preserve evidence. But does this extend to the digital information stored within a cell phone? The California Supreme Court ruled "yes," suggesting that all personal property under the suspect's control at the time of arrest was subject to search, whether a traditional container in which physical objects could be stored or an

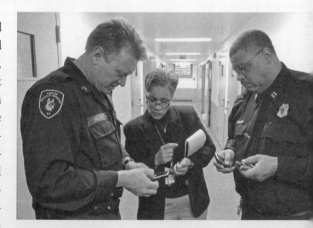

electronic container in which digital material was stored (*People v. Diaz*, 2011). The Ohio Supreme Court ruled "no," suggesting that cell phones are different from traditional containers, requiring a warrant before examination (*State v. Smith*, 2009). What do you think? How does this meet your definition of justice?

Does the Fourth Amendment protect your personal e-mail? To what extent should there be an expectation of privacy in e-mail communications? A recent case from the Sixth Circuit Court of Appeals held that law enforcement officers could not, without a warrant, obtain an individual's e-mails from his or her Internet service provider. Drawing upon the *Katz* case presented earlier, the court held that "given the fundamental similarities between email and traditional forms of communication, it would defy common sense to afford emails lesser Fourth Amendment protection" (*United States v. Warshak*, 2010, p. 19). Therefore, the court applied Fourth Amendment protections to e-mails, just as they are applied to telephone and postal communications. Police need a warrant to search for and seize computer materials like hard drives and to review the files and e-mails on them. Do you believe this is a just decision? How would you define privacy in a digital age?

The preceding cases have addressed privacy in communications. Is there a privacy right for bodily fluids? What if they may contain incriminating information? Consider the U.S. Supreme Court case of *Ferguson v. City of Charleston* in which a hospital administered drug tests to pregnant women without their consent. Women who tested positive were subject to arrest. What are the implications of this case for establishing justice? How would you assess the role, needs, and/or rights of the women, the hospital, the police, the fetuses, or the newborns? How would you balance the justice interests of each party? The Supreme Court held that the hospital's practice constituted unreasonable search and seizure, stating that "the threat of criminal sanctions to deter pregnant women from using cocaine" was not a sufficient reason to override the requirement of a warrant for this type of testing (*Ferguson v. City of Charleston*, 2001, p. 70). Do you agree or disagree with the decision of the Court?

Do you have a reasonable expectation of privacy regarding where you travel in your car? May the police, without a warrant, attach a global positioning system (GPS) device to your car that provides information about the locations of your travels? How would the precedent

in the *Katz* case shape the answer to this question? Actually, courts have issued differing answers to this question. One court, in a case where a GPS device was attached to a car for a month, held warrantless GPS searching to be unconstitutional, noting that "prolonged GPS monitoring reveals an intimate picture of the subject's life that he expects no one to have— short perhaps of his spouse"

(*United States v. Maynard*, 2010, p. 563). However, another court held that the monitoring was fine because it was similar to traditional forms of surveillance but with newer technology: "the amendment cannot sensibly be read to mean that police shall be no more efficient in the twenty-first century than they were in the eighteenth" (*United States v. Garcia*, 2007, p. 998). What do you think of these perspectives?

A recent controversy has emerged around the issue of body scanners in airports. The scanners are part of pre-flight screening and "provide a clear image of passengers under their clothes and are meant to find threats that existing metal detectors cannot, like ceramic knives and bomb components" (Wald, 2010, para. 12). How would this correspond with the *Katz* decision? Does it matter whether or not images would be saved or deleted? Does it matter whether the machines have image filters that blur the genital area? Does it matter whether the machine operator sees only the scan image or also the person being scanned? As technology continues to develop, so too will questions about the role of searches in establishing justice.

The focus of this unit in the book is on justice. As these search and seizure cases illustrate, it is important to consider the role of "justice" in "criminal justice." As you can see, there are disagreements about what constitutes justice and where the boundaries are between individual privacy and the pursuit of justice. It falls to the courts and to criminal justice agencies to grapple with the often blurry lines that delineate how justice is to be established. As you proceed through the chapters in this unit, you will learn more about the different meanings of justice, how justice policy is made, and how decisions about criminal procedure influence the pursuit of justice in American society.

Concepts of Justice

Curtis Sliwa (center) and other members of the Guardian Angels, a volunteer-based crime prevention group. How do you think justice can be achieved?

Key Terms

justice
just world
procedural justice
social justice
individual justice
restorative justice
ideology
libertarian
socialist

democratic socialism
transitional justice
apartheid
postmodernism
distributive justice
commutative justice
utilitarian justice
vigilante justice
Guardian Angels

veil of ignorance
original position
indigent
mechanical model
authoritarian model
compassionate model
participatory model
lever pulling

Key People

Lawrence Kohlberg
Nelson Mandela
David Schmidtz
Aristotle

Jeremy Bentham
John Rawls
Malcolm Feeley
Bob Altemeyer

CASE STUDY

Sexting

Before reading this case study, take a few moments to reflect on the following question. Make some notes about your answer and be prepared to explain it and share it with your instructor and classmates.

> What is justice? Think carefully about what justice means to you, how justice can be achieved, and how you might recognize justice.

Assume that a 16-year-old male (Max) and a 16-year-old female (Frieda), both of whom attend the same high school, have been dating for approximately two years. In the past year, the couple has regularly engaged in consensual sexual intercourse. Under the laws of the state in which they reside, it is legal for two 16-year-olds to engage in consensual sexual activity.

Both Max and Frieda have their own cell phones. From time to time, one sends the other a nude photograph accompanied by a sexually explicit text message. The decision to send the photograph and text message is consensual, and both Max and Frieda enjoy receiving and responding to these materials. This practice is known as *sexting*.

Over time, Max and Frieda grow apart, and Frieda decides to end the relationship. This upsets Max, who decides to retaliate. He does so by forwarding to 50 of his friends a nude photograph that Frieda had sent him several months earlier. Frieda soon learns what Max has done, as other students at her school begin to taunt and harass her. As a result, Frieda reports the situation to the school principal, and the school principal notifies the school resource officer (a police officer stationed in the school). At the same time, Frieda's mother hears what has happened and demands justice. Frieda's mother also notifies the news media about the situation, and the local television station runs a news story in which the anchor states, "Sexting is nothing short of an epidemic at this school, and the principal cannot control it." This leads to widespread public outrage.

> Pause briefly. You are the school resource officer. How do you handle this situation and why? Explain how this corresponds to your definition of justice.

The school resource officer reviews the state's legal code and discovers several provisions that may apply in this case: (1) Section 68a prohibits the production of child pornography, which includes sexually explicit images of persons under 18; (2) Section 68b prohibits transmitting child pornography to others through electronic means; and (3) Section 68c prohibits the possession of child pornography.

The school resource officer interviews Max and Frieda. The officer also obtains a search warrant for Max's cell phone as well as the cell phones of his friends to whom he sent the picture. Frieda voluntarily allows the officer to examine her cell phone. The officer determines that Frieda's cell phone contains 28 sexually explicit images of Max, that Max's cell phone contains 32 sexually explicit images of Frieda, and that Max's friends' cell phones each contain one sexually explicit image of Frieda. The officer then arrests Max, Frieda and Max's friends on the following charges:

Against . . .	Section and Counts . . .	Rationale . . .
Frieda	Section 68a, 32 counts	For creating 32 sexually explicit images of an underage person (in this case, herself)
	Section 68b, 32 counts	For transmitting each of those images to Max
	Section 68c, 28 counts	For possessing the 28 sexually explicit images sent to her by Max
Max	Section 68a, 28 counts	For creating 28 sexually explicit images of an underage person (in this case, himself)
	Section 68b, 78 counts	For transmitting each of those images to Frieda and for transmitting Frieda's image to his 50 friends

| Max (continued) | Section 68c, 32 counts | For possessing the 32 sexually explicit images sent to him by Frieda |
| Each of Max's 50 friends | Section 68c, 1 count | For possessing the sexually explicit image of Frieda sent by Max |

The prosecutor decides to try Max as an adult offender. Max is sentenced to three years of probation and six weekends in jail. He must also permanently register as a sex offender and will be barred from coming within 500 feet of areas where children gather, such as parks and schools (this also means that Max must attend a high school GED program for adults because he is banned from his high school). The prosecutor tries Frieda and Max's friends as juvenile offenders. Each receives one year of juvenile probation, required counseling, and 40 hours of community service; no sex offender registration is required for them.

> Is the outcome of this case just? Why or why not? How does it correspond to the definition of justice that you provided earlier?
>
> Assume that Max was 27 instead of 17. Would this change your answer? Explain.
>
> Assume that Frieda was 27 instead of 17. Would this change your answer? Explain.
>
> Assume that the parents of Max's friends are angered by the charges. They hold a community protest attended by hundreds of others, demanding that their children not be prosecuted. Should this influence the prosecutor's decision? Explain.

Justice: Fact or Fiction?

FOCUSING QUESTION 6.1

Why does justice matter?

Our ideas about **justice** have been influenced by the culture in which we live and by historical influences too numerous to acknowledge here. Defining justice has been a challenge to philosophers since the days of ancient Greece. The tendencies of idealists and pragmatists and the five concepts of morality (from Chapter 2) have helped shape debates about justice for centuries, as justice has been defined as harmony, as consistent with spirituality, as the quest for truth, and more.

However, for many people, justice is like art: they do not know what it is, but they know what they like when they see it. Some people believe that justice is a reality, something that has been achieved through a set of policies and laws.

Other people believe that all we can do is aspire toward justice, arguing that perfect justice is illusory and impossible to achieve. Still other people curl their lips mockingly when asked about whether justice exists, believing that there is much *injustice* in the world which may or may not be correctable. Even so, virtually everyone believes that justice, however it may be defined, is something worth achieving. Ultimately, the criminal justice system is charged with distributing justice throughout society, so it is important for us to give some careful thought to the meanings of justice.

Ideas about justice are also important because they lead to ideas about what is good. If society strives toward justice, then justice becomes a social benchmark. People's actions are weighed against the standards of justice that have been adopted by society. Actions perceived as just are viewed as correct or good, whereas actions perceived as unjust are viewed as incorrect or bad. Ideas about justice are complicated, yet they are not simply theories devoid of meaning. Instead, the quest for justice shapes individuals' lives, and in the case of criminal justice professionals, it shapes their life's work.

The quest for justice may be a natural phenomenon. Evaluating actions against a concept of justice helps fulfill the need to feel certainty about whether something is right or wrong. People strive for feelings of certainty, as doubt causes discomfort (Peirce, 1877). Believing in a **just world**, "in which individuals get what they deserve" (Hafer & Bègue, 2005, p. 128), can also serve several psychological functions. These include helping to provide order in life, maintaining a commitment to long-term goals (rather than abandoning them for hedonistic pleasures or in the face of adversity), and coping with anger and frustration (for a summary of this line of work, see Hafer & Bègue, 2005).

Psychologist Lawrence Kohlberg (1984) studied how individuals make decisions about moral dilemmas. One such dilemma posed the question of whether a man should break into a store to steal a medication that was necessary for his wife's survival but which they could not afford. Kohlberg found that individuals progress through various stages of moral reasoning during their lifetimes. The lowest stage (stage 1) is focused on obedience to legal authority, yielding the answer that the man should not steal the drug because doing so would violate a law. The highest stage (stage 6), which few persons reach in their lifetimes, is marked by a commitment both to justice and to protesting injustice, even if this requires breaking a law. A person at this stage would most likely indicate that the man should break in and steal the drug because doing so produces a just outcome valuing the preservation of life over the protection of property. Kohlberg's work suggests that a focus on justice is the highest point in the development of moral reasoning.

The importance of justice may not be limited to humans, as it may exist in the nonhuman animal kingdom as well. For instance, one study reported that dogs have an innate sense of justice against which they measure actions. When one dog in a pair is rewarded for a task and the other dog is not, the unrewarded dog appears able to identify that he has been treated unfairly (Range, Horn, Viranyi, & Huber, 2009). This could illustrate an irony—that injustice is significant enough to be recognized by a variety of creatures, but justice itself is so complex as to have generated centuries of discussion, only to arrive at tentative (and hotly debated) definitions of what it means.

From a sociological perspective, the quest for justice has a tremendous impact on society. Because there is no single definition of justice, there are (and always have been and always will be) ongoing debates about what justice is. In the context of these debates, society explores its most controversial issues of public policy. For instance, in debates on abortion, same-sex marriage, the use of the military to intervene in situations overseas, health care reform, and more, each side makes reference to arguments grounded in their concept of justice. As British philosopher John Stuart Mill ([1859] 1981) observed, the ability to engage in informed discussions of these complex issues is necessary for society to make decisions based on the most current ideas and philosophies.

For these reasons, it is important to study theories of justice. An awareness of various justice theories—understanding both those with which you agree and those with which you disagree—enables a full understanding of the multiple sides to a debate, particularly when all participants are arguing from different perspectives of justice. This can allow ideas about justice to be reviewed with full thought and results in an improved application and understanding of the law. Criminal justice professionals have the responsibility, and even the obligation, to understand what justice means and how it informs the workings of the criminal justice system, from a police officer's discretion to a judge's sentencing determinations. This chapter will aid you in this understanding.

> Compare your definition of justice to those of your classmates. How can different definitions lead to differing perceptions of what makes a just world? A just criminal justice system?
>
> How might differing definitions of justice shape what goals or strategies the criminal justice system, or those employed by it, seek to accomplish

The Justice in Criminal Justice

FOCUSING QUESTION 6.2

In what ways has justice been defined?

American statesman Daniel Webster once commented, "Justice . . . is the great interest of man on earth. It is a ligament which holds civilized beings and civilized nations together" (1914, p. 533). While a lofty sentiment, the importance of justice and its implications cannot be overstated. Consider American history. According to the Declaration of Independence, the American Revolution (1776–1783) was partially motivated because Great Britain was "deaf to the voice of *justice"* [emphasis added]. The American Civil War (1861–1865) was concerned in large part with the injustice of slavery (see Stampp, 1991). In the late twentieth and early twenty-first centuries, substantial debate has emerged about whether American military force should be used to combat injustices (generally contextualized as human rights violations) abroad. Justice, then, is a concept so highly valued that societies are willing to engage in life-and-death struggles about it.

Many of the decisions we make about criminal justice reflect our ideas about justice. Consequently, the type of criminal justice system we prefer is also shaped by our understandings of what justice is (or equally important, what justice is not). Sometimes, we realize that we are uncomfortable with a policy or an action but have difficulty in distinguishing the source of the discomfort. Considering the following perspectives of justice can help us distinguish where discomfort lies or where concerns about justice exist. Can you identify any of the following issues as causing concern in the case about Max and Frieda?

Procedural justice holds that justice is achieved when the proper procedures are followed. Of course, this begs the question, "What are the proper procedures?" The answer is that the proper procedures are those laid down in the Constitution, the Bill of Rights, court decisions, and legal codes. In Chapter 8, you will learn more about the various forms of procedural justice.

Social justice considers issues of equality and inequality in society. Is there discrimination—in society or in the criminal justice system—based on race, gender, social class, sexual orientation, or other factors (see generally Arrigo, 1999)? To social justice theorists, then, the pursuit of justice is the pursuit of equality. You will learn more about social justice in Chapter 7.

Individual justice is the focus of this chapter. Individual justice primarily focuses on the outcomes that apply to individual persons. The emphasis is less on group equality (as in social justice) or on legal procedures (as in procedural justice) than it is on whether or not the results are correct. For instance, what should be done if a person's home is burglarized? Certainly, we would hope there would not be discrimination based on who the victim or the offender was, which is a matter for social justice. And certainly, we would hope the police and courts would follow the proper procedures in handling the case, which is a matter for procedural justice. But in this chapter, we are most concerned about what happens to the victim and the offender as individuals.

The following sections describe several perspectives through which we can view individual justice. We begin with the theories of restorative justice, ideological justice, transitional justice, and postmodern justice. We then move to a discussion of what is arguably the most significant perspective: distributive justice.

RESTORATIVE JUSTICE

When a crime occurs, it causes harm to the victim. However, crimes also cause harm to the community and to the offender. For instance, the victim of a robbery has financial losses and the fear of bodily injury (or actual injury). The fabric of the community is harmed because after learning of the robbery, residents might subsequently fear or distrust others, leading to a decline in social interactions. The offender is harmed by virtue of having stepped outside the accepted bounds of social and legal behavior, which results in an emotional, psychological, or physical (in the case of incarceration) separation from the rest of the community. The goal of **restorative justice** is to take actions to restore the victim, the offender, and society to more desirable conditions that existed before the offense occurred (Hahn, 1998).

Restorative justice may be understood as an opportunity for the parties to a crime to heal. There are various mechanisms by which this can occur. One is the simple virtue and power of a sincere apology (Lazare, 2004). In some societies, an apology is powerful enough to render further legal action unnecessary (Haley, 1986). Another strategy is the use of mediation in which a mediator (a person with conflict management and resolution training) confers with the victim and offender to recommend a solution that takes into account the needs or interests of both (McGillis, 1998). A more dramatic example is the use of sentencing circles in which multiple parties come together to discuss a criminal incident and negotiate the appropriate solution. For instance, the offender and his or her family, the victim and his or her family, and community members would come together, each sharing his or her perspective. This enables the offender to understand the harms that resulted from the offense and to take accountability for them by accepting a sentence formulated in the group's discussions (Sentencing Circles, n.d.). Restorative justice has proven to be promising for some (generally minor) offenses.

Restorative justice can also be understood from a compensatory approach—that is, making efforts to repair the physical or financial damage caused by a crime. In many jurisdictions, there is a crime victims' fund through which the government can provide compensation to victims for their losses. Offenders can be required to pay into the fund, which then helps repair the individuals and the communities that were harmed by their actions. Offenders can also be required to compensate their victims directly, paying for lost items, medical bills, and so on. One judge in Tennessee even made national news for his controversial practice of allowing victims of burglaries to be compensated by taking items from the offender's home (Judge lets victim . . . , 1992).

IDEOLOGICAL JUSTICE

To some persons, justice is achieved when their desired ideological system is supported through government policy. An **ideology** is essentially a worldview to which a person subscribes. There are many ideologies with many different belief systems, but what binds them together under this heading is the notion that, to their adherents, society will not be able to achieve justice until its policies reflect those supported by the ideology. Rather than beginning by asking what justice is, the analysis begins by asking how can society be more like a preferred ideology, which will then *lead to* justice. That is, the ideology comes first as a collection of beliefs that are assumed to produce justice as a result. The supporters of an ideology may view those who oppose the ideology as standing in the way of justice. Here we will focus on two ideologies near the opposite ends of a spectrum: libertarianism and socialism.

A **libertarian** might believe that justice is best accomplished in a society that respects individual rights, particularly the right to own and do as one wishes with property with only the most minimal of government influences (Sargent, 1996). Therefore, any intervention of the law into private property or private rights is viewed as unjust. For instance, libertarians would likely argue that the state should not restrict obscene material, require seat belt usage, criminalize drug possession, or levy more than the most minimal of taxes. Libertarians object to policies that limit what individuals can do with property because they are counter to libertarian ideology and therefore ideologically unjust.

On the other hand, a **socialist** might believe that justice is best accomplished in a society with a large government that manages public ownership of industries that are viewed as most necessary for a productive society and that provides many services to all members of society. High tax rates are used not only to provide these industries and services but also to control the distribution of wealth. This model of government is known as **democratic socialism** (Sargent, 1996). Unlike the libertarian, the socialist would argue that an active government is required to promote justice—perhaps arguing that government-funded drug rehabilitation should be made available to any person who desires it, that all educational institutions should be public and well funded, or that economic inequality and social class distinctions should be eliminated.

There are many other ideologies that are beyond the scope of this book (see Sargent, 1996). However, the common theme of ideological justice is that the ideology to which one subscribes defines one's perception of justice.

TRANSITIONAL JUSTICE

As described by Teitel (2002), **transitional justice** applies only in a unique set of circumstances in which (1) a country's government changes and (2) the new government wants to move away from a set of human rights abuses that occurred under the old government. Therefore, as the name suggests, the concern is about ensuring justice during the transition from one governing regime to another, with a concern about human rights at the forefront. Two notable twentieth-century examples illustrate this concept.

A dramatic example was the case of Germany at the end of World War II. One question facing Germany was what the new government should look like after the fall of the Third Reich and the Nazi regime. The Allied nations (United States, France, Soviet Union, and United Kingdom) each occupied a zone of Germany to plan for rebuilding (Paterson, Clifford, & Hagan, 1991). Another question was what should be done to the remaining leaders, including individuals who had planned and implemented the Holocaust. The Allied nations conducted the Nuremberg Trials beginning in 1945, which tried and convicted numerous individuals of war crimes and crimes against humanity (see Marrus, 1997).

The transitional justice experienced by Germany and other post–World War II European countries has had a legacy for modern criminal justice. After the human rights abuses they witnessed during the war, Germany and other European countries moved to abolish the death penalty, labeling it as a human rights violation in its own right. The risk of another Holocaust was too terrifying a prospect to tolerate state-sanctioned penalties of death. Today, to join the European Union, member states must abolish their death penalties (Zimring, 2003). Interestingly, "demonstrations protesting against the United States death penalty have . . . been held in France, Spain, and Norway" (Bohm, 2000, p. 4), in which American capital punishment has been decried as an injustice and a human rights violation. This illustrates how global opinion has changed on this controversial issue, partially as an outgrowth of transitional justice.

A more recent example, also dramatic and one that garnered much attention on the world stage, was the collapse of **apartheid** in South Africa. Apartheid was state-sanctioned racial segregation in which the all-white government of South Africa repressed the rights, freedoms, and political participation of the majority of the population, who were black. The government's control over the population was sometimes marked by violence aimed at protesters and opponents. Control was also exerted through "the ban, an order from the justice minister" aimed at those who would protest the system, in which they might be prohibited from socializing with others, be given a curfew, be prohibited from working "in a large group (such as in a factory)," and more (Roskin, 2004, p. 510).

Apartheid lasted from the late 1940s to the early 1990s, at which time a new constitution and new government were put into place. Instrumental to the transition was the government's decision to release Nelson Mandela from prison, where he had served 27 years for his role in opposing apartheid in the 1960s. After his release in 1990, Mandela went on to be elected as president of South Africa in 1994. The transition to a new government, and the corresponding move away from the human rights abuses of apartheid, is an example of transitional justice. The transition was not the product of a war; rather, it was motivated by substantial dissent from within and by international politics (Roskin, 2004). As part of the transition, a Truth and Reconciliation Commission (1998) was established. Although the commission found that "the predominant portion of gross violations of human rights was committed by the former state through its security and law-enforcement agencies" (p. 212), the focus was also on the need for "reconciliation" and for "extensive healing and social and physical reconstruction at every level of society" (p. 350).

Transitional justice is rare, as it is limited to circumstances when a government undergoes substantial change. However, as these examples (and others) demonstrate, it is associated with remedying abuses of human rights.

POSTMODERN JUSTICE

Recall the discussion of pragmatism in Chapter 2. As you may remember, pragmatists utilize empiricism when structuring their arguments. For a pragmatist to accept something as true or as reality, he or she must observe it or see data about it. That is, for a pragmatist, truth and reality are grounded in measurable observations. This is very similar to the philosophy of modernism, which assumes that there is a *single* reality, and it is the reality based on rational and empirical study. The philosophy of **postmodernism**, on the other hand, holds that there are "many distinct and equally valid realities created by people from many different cultures and subcultures and from many different times and places" (Velasquez, 2002, p. 215). The postmodernist believes that different people create their own narratives (i.e., understandings) of what is real, and furthermore, if they *believe* it is real, then it indeed *becomes* real to them.

So, what does this mean for justice? One important implication is that, for a postmodernist, there cannot be one single definition of what is just or unjust (and one definition is not necessarily better than another). This is different from idealism because idealists do believe in a particular vision of truth and harmony. As a means for judging whether an action or outcome is just, postmodern justice does not provide much guidance. But perhaps that is its point; as Arrigo (1995) suggests, one goal of postmodern justice is to help understand why different persons and groups have varying definitions of justice, through an exploration of their narratives. In turn, this understanding can possibly help resolve conflicts that emerge based on differing views of justice.

In many ways, postmodern justice reflects the reality of what criminal justice professionals must deal with on a daily basis. While two witnesses to the same criminal event might report seeing very different things, each swears that his or her testimony is "how it really happened." Neither witness is lying. What has happened is that the *actual* reality becomes unimportant; what the witnesses *believe* they saw *becomes* the reality to them. It is the job of the criminal justice professional to figure out how to resolve the accounts in a way that represents the truth in order to pursue justice.

> How might these theories of justice influence the resolution of the sexting case described in the chapter's opening?
>
> How would you assess the strengths and weaknesses of each theory of justice? How closely do they correspond (or not correspond) to your definition of justice?

A Focus on Distributive Justice

FOCUSING QUESTION 6.3

How is distributive justice related to criminal justice?

It is easy to become overwhelmed when thinking about the multiple ways justice can be defined. The remainder of this chapter focuses on the broad form of justice that is arguably most relevant to the criminal justice system: **distributive justice**. Philosopher of justice David Schmidtz (2006) observed that, at its most basic, "justice concerns what people are due" (p. 7). Think carefully about this, as the implications of the quotation are substantial. First, we must consider the question of who is due what. From a criminal justice perspective, this means determining which acts or behaviors should be prohibited under the law. The individuals who commit those acts or behaviors (the "who") are then due something under the law, such as a punishment (the "what"). Second, we must determine what it is, precisely, that the individuals are due. From a criminal justice perspective, this means how to distribute the "results of justice processes—police stops, arrests, verdicts, and sentences—asking whether these results are legitimate" (Castelanno & Gould, 2007, p. 75). Because the end result of this process is a distribution of outcomes (i.e., the stops, arrests, verdicts, and sentences), it is known as distributive justice. There are several ways that we can conceptualize the best approach to giving individuals their due.

A CLASSIC APPROACH: ARISTOTLE'S COMMUTATIVE JUSTICE

The philosophy of **commutative justice** has its origins in Aristotle's *Nicomachean Ethics* (2000). Aristotle was concerned about proportionality in exchanges. He wrote, "What is just . . . is what is proportionate. And what is unjust is what violates the proportion" (p. 87). To Aristotle, this applied to voluntary exchanges, such as when a price is established for a good or service (voluntary because individuals can choose whether or not to make the purchase), and to involuntary exchanges, such as when determining the appropriate punishment for an offense (involuntary because the offender may not reject the punishment). Thus, if a good or service has a price that is proportional to its value and if a punishment is in proportion with an offender's crime, then justice has been achieved. The concept of proportionality is explored further in the discussion of punishment in Chapter 10.

AN ECONOMIC APPROACH: BENTHAM'S UTILITARIAN JUSTICE

In theory, **utilitarian justice** is simple. It has its roots in British philosopher Jeremy Bentham's 1776 work, *A Fragment on Government*, in which Bentham observes, "it is the greatest happiness of the greatest number that is the measure of right and wrong" (para. 2). To determine what is just, then, one must ask the question, *what produces the greatest good for the most people?* A technique called cost–benefit analysis, derived from economics, is often used to arrive at an answer. The first step is to identify the *costs* of an action and then to add up their value. The second step is to identify the *benefits* of an action and then to add up their value. The final step is to *compare* the value of the costs to the value of the benefits. If the benefits are greater than the costs, then the conclusion is that (to borrow from Bentham) more happiness will be derived than unhappiness, so the action is just.

It is possible to measure utilitarian justice in a purely mathematical fashion. For instance, a study by Cohen (1988) estimated that the average cost of a robbery, in terms of lost money or property as well as the monetary value of a victim's pain and suffering, was $12,594. Cohen then went on to calculate the cost and benefit of extending the length of an average robbery sentence by 10%. He calculated that the benefit, which was the value of the crimes that would be prevented as a result, would be approximately $300 million, whereas the cost of the added prison time would be approximately $336 million. From a utilitarian perspective, this would not be a rational outcome because the increased punishment would produce a loss rather than a benefit. Therefore, the increased prison time would be an unjust outcome on a cost–benefit basis.

It is also possible to conceptualize utilitarian justice as a metaphor instead of adding up actual numbers. Hart and Devlin (from Chapter 3) attempted to examine the costs and benefits of regulating morality, and then each reached his own conclusion about whether it was just to do so. Although not phrased directly in utilitarian terms of costs and benefits, the arguments employed by Hart and Devlin attempted to identify what they believed would produce "the greatest happiness for the greatest number." For Devlin, enforcement of morality produced the greatest happiness by protecting society. For Hart, maximizing freedom produced the greatest happiness by allowing individuals to pursue their preferred (noncriminal) behaviors.

OUTSIDE THE SYSTEM: A VIGILANTE APPROACH

When people decide to "take the law into their own hands" (Brown, 1969, p. 176), bypassing the criminal justice system (e.g., police, courts, and corrections), **vigilante justice** occurs. Individuals generally engage in vigilante justice (also known as vigilantism) when members of the community agree that it is necessary to do so to protect persons or property. Sometimes, this occurs because there is no established criminal justice system, such as in the early years of the American West. Other times, vigilantism exists alongside an established criminal justice system, perhaps because individuals lack confidence in the system or because they believe they have the right to take steps to protect themselves.

Some forms of vigilante justice operate within the bounds of the law. For instance, the **Guardian Angels** citizen group was created in 1979 to combat crime in the New York City subway system. Since that time, the group has expanded to other cities and other venues. Members of the Guardian Angels, who are recognized by their distinctive red berets, are citizen volunteers who organize unarmed patrols of public spaces. Research has found that the group has reduced fear of crime, has reduced the frequency of some crimes, and has provided role models for at-risk youth (Pennell, Curtis, Henderson, & Tayman, 1989). The Guardian Angels use legal means to accomplish their goals. Contrast this with vigilante justice that uses illegal means. For instance, if a crime victim chose to exact revenge by assaulting an offender (other than in legally recognized self-defense; see Chapter 9), then that victim could be held accountable through arrest and prosecution. The criminal justice system does not recognize a right to revenge or a right to use illegal means to engage in vigilantism. Rather, all criminal acts are viewed as crimes against the state, which the state then has the sole responsibility for prosecuting and punishing.

BUT IS IT FAIR? RAWLS ON JUSTICE

John Rawls was one of the leading contemporary philosophers of justice. Rawls defined "justice as fairness" (Rawls, 2001, p. xvi). Of course, this requires us to define fairness, which is perhaps no easier than defining justice. See Box 6.1 to try your hand at defining fairness. Rawls did, however, recommend tools that we can use in an effort to define fairness and thus justice.

Rawls (1999) described a philosophical approach to determining what is fair and just. Specifically, he asks us to use a **"veil of ignorance"** (p. 118) and to make decisions about justice and fairness from an "original position" (p. 15).

JUSTICE AS FAIRNESS

BOX 6.1

Think about your definition of fairness. What do you think is the fairest way to resolve the following dilemma (adapted from Stone, 2002)?

> Think about the class in which you are using this book. Assume that, one day, your instructor brings to class the most delicious chocolate cake that you can possibly imagine (if you don't care for chocolate cake, then substitute your favorite dessert or food). Of course, everyone in class wants a share. The question is, how should the cake be divided? Why is this the best approach?

Now, compare your answer to that of your classmates. What are the differences? The similarities? Does each answer provide an equally fair outcome? Finally, consider the following concerns (adapted from Stone, 2002). How would you respond to them from the perspective of fairness? It becomes clear that fairness may not be as simple as it appears.

1. Students who missed class complain that they were left out because they would have attended had they known there would be cake. Does it matter why they missed class?
2. Students who did not enroll in the class complain that they were left out because they would have registered for the class had they known there would be cake.

(continued)

BOX 6.1 (continued)

3. Perhaps the cake should be distributed by rank—faculty and teaching assistants with the biggest pieces, seniors with the next largest, juniors with the next largest, and so on. Does rank have its privileges?

4. "A group of men's liberationists stages a protest. Women have always had greater access to chocolate cake, they claim, because girls are taught to bake while boys have to go outdoors and play football" (p. 40). The men demand larger shares.

5. Some students have just come from lunch, where they had their own delicious desserts. Students who did not just come from lunch claim that they are more entitled to the cake because they need it more. But the students who had lunch claim they wouldn't have had dessert there had they known about the cake.

6. Students who don't like the cake volunteer to take a smaller share because they wouldn't enjoy it anyway.

7. But what if the students who don't like cake then demand an equally valuable reward of some sort?

8. Some students claim it would be fairest to put the cake in the middle of the room and just let the chips fall (or the pieces of cake fly) as they may. First come, first served; let the strongest prevail.

9. The cake is so delicious that one piece would hardly be satisfactory. A lottery should be conducted to award the cake as a whole to one lucky person (or large sections, perhaps one-quarter, of the cake to several lucky persons).

10. Some students suggest that a cake supervisor be elected from within the class to manage the distribution of the cake. Candidates for cake supervisor can announce their cake distribution plans, and the class can elect their preferred supervisor. What if the cake supervisor is paid by being given a share of the cake in advance?

Let's consider what this means. The veil of ignorance is a technique in which a person must assume that he or she knows nothing whatsoever about his or her background. While under the veil, a person would not know his or her gender, race, sexual orientation, socioeconomic background, nationality, religion, parentage, job status, education, or other information. Therefore, a person would not be able to make a self-serving decision at the expense of others. For example, under the veil of ignorance, a wealthy person would not be tempted to create a policy that would deliberately cause harm to others to increase personal wealth because under the veil no persons know their financial status. When this lack of knowledge about personal background is achieved, individuals are said to be in an **original position**, or a starting point, from which government and policy can then be developed.

Of course, there is no actual cloth that is a real veil of ignorance. Rawls's ideas are simply metaphors about how individuals should approach decisions about justice and fairness. Rawls believed that, while in an original position, individuals would agree on principles (see Box 6.2 for additional background on principles vs. rules) that are fundamentally fair because they are unable to act in a manner of self-interest that would be fair to some but unfair to others.

Rawls was not writing specifically about criminal justice but about justice in society as a whole. He argued that the veil of ignorance exercise would lead to two principles that should guide society. First, all persons should have equal access to the same basic rights, whatever they may be. For instance, to Rawls, an **indigent** (i.e., poor) defendant should not be denied the right to have an attorney during a trial if that right is available to a wealthy defendant. The U.S. Supreme Court agreed with this principle in *Gideon v. Wainwright* (1963; see Lewis, 1964), holding that indigent defendants in felony cases must be provided with legal representation, even if they cannot afford it. This right was later extended to indigent defendants in any crime, felony or misdemeanor, that carried potential jail time (see *Argersinger v. Hamlin*, 1972).

Second, Rawls argued that society must provide equality of opportunity. This means society must not discriminate and all persons should have the same opportunity to succeed. For instance, it is increasingly accepted that a good education is necessary to advance into many leadership positions. Therefore, Rawls's theory would suggest that all persons should have the opportunity to pursue a good education. If an individual is unable to attend a good school for reasons *other than* his or her merit—because, for instance, he or she lives

PRINCIPLES VERSUS RULES IN JUSTICE THEORY

Some high schools regulated hallway traffic with a special rule about stairway use. Specifically, certain staircases in the building were designated as "up" staircases, and others were designated as "down" staircases. This meant that if you wanted to go upstairs, you used the up staircase; if you wanted to go downstairs, you used the down staircase. Using the down staircase to go upstairs, and vice versa, would result in punishment. The rule was generally accepted during class change times because it did make the crowded traffic flow in an orderly way. However, before school, after school, and during classes, there was little traffic on the stairways. Yet, the rules were still enforced at these times. Even if the staircases were entirely empty, a student going "up the down staircase" (see Kaufman, 1991) was subject to punishment, and when this occurred, it was viewed as something less than fair.

To understand why this rule was enforced, it is necessary to distinguish rules and principles. Rules are externally imposed guidelines that shape our behavior (laws are one type of rule). We follow rules because an authority figure of some sort tells us to, and we know that there are consequences for not doing so. Rules are designed to provide order and consistency, but they sometimes may appear arbitrary or unfair, as is the case here.

Principles are the reasons for the rules. As such, they are generally expressions of broad ideas about how the world (or some part of it) ought to work. For instance, the principle guiding the staircase rule is that traffic should flow in an orderly manner. Once a principle has been agreed upon, rules are formulated to put it into effect. If the principle is understood and individuals accept it as a valid idea,

BOX 6.2

(continued)

BOX 6.2 (continued)

then the rules become acceptable. In our example, if the hallway traffic principle is accepted, the rules about stairway use become clearer. It is possible to see the connection between the principle and the rule, and it is easier to understand both how the rule provides order and why it must be enforced consistently (e.g., so people become and remain accustomed to the hallway traffic pattern, which is necessary for the order that the principle values).

For principles and rules to function effectively, though, they must be accepted by all persons. If students are required to follow the rules but teachers are not, then a sense of injustice can emerge because the rules and principles are not followed equally. If some persons are permitted to violate them, then rules lose their strength.

It is important to understand what principles individuals value and how rules are related to those principles. In many ways, this is what the study of justice theory is all about; theories of justice help provide us with the principles on which rules are based.

> Should officers driving police cars be permitted to disregard traffic laws (e.g., exceed the speed limit, go the wrong way down a one-way street, etc.) if doing so is necessary to enforce the law? Explain. How would this impact the principles on which the laws are based?

> Review the case study at the beginning of the chapter. What principles underlie the laws (i.e., 68a, 68b, 68c)? Do you think the laws (rules), as enforced in the sexting case, match the principles that you identified?

in an area where the schools are dilapidated or because he or she has been discriminated against in an admission decision—then Rawls sees an injustice. Of course, once individuals are given a fair opportunity, their success will vary based on their individual choices, aptitudes, and talents—but the opportunity must be there. See Box 6.3 for a policy debate on equality of opportunity.

To summarize, Rawls argued that justice is fairness. He then argued that fairness is achieved when society provides the same set of rights and liberties to all persons and when society allows persons an equal opportunity to succeed. If individuals receive their due in accordance with these principles, justice is achieved. Although Rawls's theory has its critics (e.g., Nozick, 1974; Walzer, 1984), it still stands as one of the more important perspectives on contemporary justice.

> How would any of the models of distributive justice described in this section apply to the resolution of the sexting case at the beginning of the chapter?

> Are there any features of distributive justice that you believe should form the basis of the criminal justice system? Why or why not?

> What features would a just criminal justice system have based on Rawls's principles? Explain.

BOX 6.3

EQUALITY OF OPPORTUNITY

What does equality of opportunity mean? Consider the following actual case.

On March 16, 1996, an individual applying to be a police officer (who will be referred to as the "plaintiff" in the rest of this narrative) completed a written test administered by the Law Enforcement Council of Connecticut, Inc. The Council collated test results and distributed them to 14 Connecticut towns, including New London. The towns used this information when considering candidates for employment in their police agencies.

Among other things, the test measured cognitive abilities. The plaintiff's score on the test was 33. The user's manual for the test suggested two different ranges of scores that it recommended for police patrol officers: 20–28 and 18–30. In either case, the plaintiff's score of 33 exceeded the recommended range.

After taking the test and receiving his score, the plaintiff wanted to apply for an open position with the New London police. However, the Assistant City Manager informed him that he was not eligible for employment with the town's Police Department, "because he scored too high on the written test . . .New London had decided to consider only applicants who scored between 20 and 27 on the written examination" (*Jordan v. City of New London*, 1999, pp. 2–3).

The plaintiff sued, arguing that his rights of equal opportunity for employment had been violated (see *Jordan v. City of New London*, 1999).

> If you were the judge, how you would rule in this case? Why?

> The court actually ruled that the city had rational reasons to deny the job to the applicant with the high score, including the argument that overeducated persons would not be satisfied in the job, causing them to leave the position after being hired and trained, and the argument that only considering applicants in a particular range of test scores could help narrow the pool of applicants to a manageable number. How does this compare to your ruling?

> Assess the court's ruling using your definition of justice, your definition of fairness, and your definition of equality of opportunity.

Individual and Community Interests in Distributive Justice

FOCUSING QUESTION 6.4

In distributive justice, how can offenders' needs and society's needs be balanced?

You may recall from Chapter 2 that the use of discretion plays a central role in the criminal justice system. For instance, research has found that police officers vary in their ideas about how the law should be enforced (e.g., Muir, 1977), and probation officers vary in their ideas about how probationers should be supervised (e.g., Seiter & West, 2003). These variations can lead two different officers to approach the same situation in very different ways. For instance, one probation officer might see a failed drug test as a reason to revoke probation and send a client back to prison, whereas another probation officer might respond by sending a client to a treatment program. In either case, the probation officer would be using discretion to provide distributive justice—that is, to decide how to provide the client what he or she is due and how to distribute the outcomes of the criminal justice system.

The application of justice may also differ based on place. The criminal justice system and the ideas about justice that underlie it may vary between states, counties, and towns. You may have heard of places where people believe that the law is applied very strictly, for instance, or of places where the justice system is not so strict. Again, the focus is squarely on distributive justice. Areas with strict enforcement might more freely distribute criminal justice outcomes (e.g., tickets, arrests, lengthy sentences) than areas with lenient enforcement.

In considering these kinds of variations in distributive justice, it is useful to address two questions: what is in the best interest of the individual? And what is in the best interest of the community? For instance, in the case of a noise violation, an individual's interest might be the right to play music at a desired volume, but the community's interest might be for peace and quiet. Of course, these two questions suggest a third: whose interests should receive the most attention and how should they be balanced?

The difficult task is to select the proper balancing point. It may be tempting to consider the balance on a continuum between two endpoints in which justice emphasizes either the individual or the community. If the balance moves toward the individual, then the needs of the community are sacrificed. If the balance moves toward the community, then the needs of the individual are sacrificed. Figure 6.1 illustrates this model.

However, the model presented in Figure 6.1 is an oversimplification. Instead, it is possible to place a high value on both the individual and on the community at the same time. This leads us to a two-dimensional model, illustrated in Figure 6.2.

The models in Figure 6.2 consider the community, labeled here as "societal needs," and the individual, labeled here as "offender needs" (because it is the offender who generally receives the most attention from the criminal justice system). Four models are illustrated in Figure 6.2 (drawing upon concepts

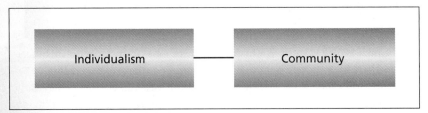

Figure 6.1. Balance Between Individual and Community

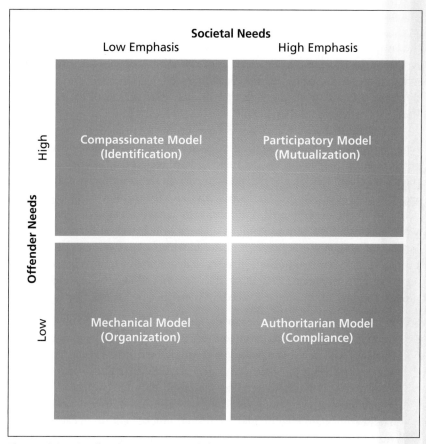

Figure 6.2. Distributive Justice Models

presented in Blake & Mouton, 1964). In parentheses, you will find the focal point of each model. This is the perspective that each model uses to resolve conflicts and to achieve justice. The sections that follow will provide a description of each model and its focal point.

MECHANICAL CRIMINAL JUSTICE

The **mechanical model** focuses neither on the needs of society nor on the needs of the offender. The intent of the model is to provide social order, and it does so through a focal point of organization. Rather than specifically considering anyone's needs, be they societal or individual, the model holds that society is static and unchanging—almost as though it could be permanently captured in a snapshot. All one needs to maintain order in this unchanging society is an organizational structure that implements the laws and policies that have already been put into place. As long as there is a written code of laws and policies, a police agency that enforces them, a court system that judges them, and a correctional system that punishes violators, the system is assumed to work. There is no need for discretion and little need for judgment beyond what the law says. The dispassionate enforcement of the laws precisely as they are written is the most important element of this model. Its measure of success is whether the laws and policies have been followed regardless of what outcomes they may produce or what effects they may have on society or on individuals. Processes matter more than people.

From a distributive justice perspective, criminal justice outcomes are allocated through a very mechanical process without consideration of individual circumstances. Individuals are assumed to have received what they are due if the law has been followed. A decision's impact on the community is also inconsequential, as processes matter more than the actual resolution of a problem. This model is best exemplified in the notion of assembly-line justice, particularly when addressing less serious criminal offenses, which will be discussed further in Chapter 8. Briefly, it is a type of justice in which a busy courtroom works to process as many cases as possible in as short an amount of time as possible, with a greater focus on moving cases along than on trying to identify, or much less address, individual and community needs. As described by Malcolm Feeley (1992),

> In the lower courts trials are rare events, and even protracted plea bargaining is an exception. Jammed every morning with a new mass of arrestees who have been picked up the night before, lower courts rapidly process what the police consider "routine" problems—barroom brawls, neighborhood squabbles, domestic disputes, welfare cheating, shoplifting, drug possession, and prostitution—not "real" crimes. These courts are chaotic and confusing; officials communicate in a verbal shorthand wholly unintelligible to accused and accuser alike, and they seem to make arbitrary decisions, sending one person to jail and freeing the next. (p. 3)

Feeley titled his book about lower courts *The Process Is the Punishment*. In many ways, this is an apt description of mechanical criminal justice.

AUTHORITARIAN CRIMINAL JUSTICE

The **authoritarian model** focuses on the needs of society but not on the needs of the offender. Justice is achieved by mandating compliance with the laws set forth by the government, which has authority over society. Authoritarianism most specifically refers to the mind-set of the masses that allows them to receive direction from someone who desires to provide leadership and authority to them. Altemeyer (1996), the leading expert on authoritarian thought, defines it as a combination of the following:

> Authoritarian submission—a high degree of submission to the authorities who are perceived to be established and legitimate in the society in which one lives; Authoritarian aggression—a general

aggressiveness, directed against various persons, that is perceived to be sanctioned by established authorities; [and] Conventionalism—a high degree of adherence to the social conventions that are perceived to be endorsed by society and its established authorities. (p. 6)

Let us consider how this applies to justice. Certain persons or groups in society have authority, which is simply the legal ability to do something. For instance, legislatures have the authority to pass laws, police officers have the authority to arrest persons who break those laws, and courts have the authority to sentence persons found guilty of violating the law. Unlike the mechanical model, outcomes are more important than process. Desired outcomes are those identified by persons or agencies with authority, and the measure of success is whether those outcomes are achieved. If the outcomes are achieved, then justice has been achieved as well. It is important to note that the authoritarian model has little tolerance for disagreement. The law and its enforcement, for instance, are considered absolute. An "us" versus "them" mentality develops in which persons who hold nonconventional values and persons who disagree with desired outcomes are ostracized or labeled as deviant. In addition, the voices of persons and groups without authority often go unheard.

Consider drug enforcement laws as an example. There are laws against certain kinds of drugs, the police enforce those laws, and the courts sentence offenders. So far, this sounds like the mechanical model. However, the authoritarian model does not simply specify that an orderly process should be followed to enforce drug (or any other) laws. The authoritarian model goes a step further, stating that the outcome desired by the law—that is, the elimination of illegal drugs—should be accomplished by any means possible (here we see the focus on the needs of society) whether or not it respects the rights of the offender or other individuals (here we see a lack of focus on the needs of the individual). Rights of procedural justice, such as those discussed in Chapter 8, are viewed negatively, sometimes even as annoyances to be circumvented. Persons who argue against strict enforcement, who are in favor of individual rights, or who advocate for changes in the law (e.g., decriminalizing medical marijuana) are viewed as suspect persons themselves for daring to question the conventional values established by those in authority. Their views are disregarded, and they are labeled as "dangerous" persons who challenge the stability of the system. As you can see, the tone of the authoritarian model is one that tolerates neither dissent nor disobedience.

From a distributive justice perspective, criminal justice outcomes are allocated through loyalty to and compliance with authority. That authority emphasizes that its goals must be accomplished, even if doing so minimizes individual rights and needs. Research has found that some criminal justice professionals demonstrate authoritarian tendencies (see Owen & Wagner, 2008), so an understanding of this model and its implications becomes important.

COMPASSIONATE CRIMINAL JUSTICE

The **compassionate model** places a higher emphasis on an offender's needs than on society's needs. However, neither society's needs nor public safety is ignored. The focal point of identification indicates that justice may best be achieved by identifying and correcting the needs of the offender that led him or her to commit crime. In this way, the compassionate model takes a two-tier approach. First, it emphasizes the importance of preventing crime by anticipating and responding to those needs in advance. For instance, research has identified certain characteristics that increase the risk of a child engaging in delinquent behavior, such as intimate partner violence, negative peer pressure, being "rejected by peers" (Wasserman et al., 2003, p. 7), and more. Programs could then be created to address these issues, leading to reductions in future criminality. Second, the model emphasizes the importance of rehabilitation. Helping offenders to identify their needs and address these concerns in a constructive manner helps to yield justice for the offender and, consequently, for society. This does not render punishment unnecessary but specifies that in the course of punishment, criminal justice professionals should identify and correct the underlying issues that led offenders to commit crime in the first place, thereby lowering the risk for repeat offending. The programs that are instrumental to compassionate justice require partnerships between criminal justice professionals and experts outside the criminal justice system in the fields of psychology, education, social work, and more. For instance, in seeking to prevent juvenile crime, the government might work with child psychologists to develop and staff a program.

If violations of law occur, it communicates that more effort needs to be placed in crime prevention and rehabilitation or that the law itself needs to be modified to reflect changes in societal norms or realities. Violations can also indicate a failure to understand the law and the rationales underlying it, placing the burden on the criminal justice system to educate the public. From a distributive justice perspective, individuals are given their due in an individualized manner after the identification of needs specific to a particular situation and for a particular offender. Justice is only achieved when criminal justice outcomes are distributed in a way that addresses these needs.

PARTICIPATORY CRIMINAL JUSTICE

The **participatory model** places a high value on both the needs of society and the needs of the offender. To do so, the model uses a focal point of mutualization. This means understanding that meeting one set of needs does not preclude meeting another set of needs. This understanding is based on a commitment to the principles of justice (recall Box 6.2), however they may be defined, and a subsequent commitment to applying those principles in a way that maximizes their value to society and to individuals. The success of the model is measured by the harmony between society and the individuals within it as they work together to promote justice.

An example might prove helpful. Community policing is a popular strategy that you will learn more about in Chapter 11. In short, it involves police officers forming partnerships with the community so they can work together to address issues of crime and disorder. This helps break down barriers that are perceived to exist between the police and the public. As in the compassionate model, the public works with the police to identify and address community needs that lead to an increase in order. However, societal needs are not abandoned, as the police continue their work of patrolling, investigating crime, and so on, but in doing so, the police learn and respond to the community's concerns about which issues should take the highest priority. An effective community policing partnership allows both the public and the police to work together in harmony to achieve justice, focusing both on individual needs and on larger-scale societal concerns.

In this model, all participants in the system must work together to create, understand, and apply the law. In turn, the law must reflect a thorough consideration of perspectives from the public, legislators, criminal justice professionals, and more. The result is a law that truly must be a balance as diagramed in Figure 6.1, providing rights and freedoms for individuals while also providing sufficient protection for society.

The participatory model achieves distributive justice through collaboration. Individuals are given their due in a system that allows for public participation in setting priorities and influencing law. As a result, the process that distributes criminal justice outcomes is one for which all members of society have accountability and ownership.

TOWARD JUSTICE

As you can see, justice theory involves many (sometimes conflicting) ideas. If "justice . . . is the great interest of man on earth" as Webster (1914, p. 533) suggests, then it is not an interest about which all persons agree. Different theories of justice can lead to different outcomes in the same case. Yet, it is important to appreciate the variations in justice theory for precisely that reason. The value of justice is powerful enough that "The never ending battle for truth, justice, and the American way" (see Karp, 2009, p. 1) is the call to action for comic book superheroes—and it is also powerful enough to motivate individual actions and societal priorities. Professionals and the public alike must explore the ways justice is defined so we may then understand our own actions and those of others. Doing so can help us look for areas of common agreement, even when disagreements occur about which outcomes are most just.

Of course, this material can only be an introduction to justice theory. As you go through your personal, educational, and professional lives, continue to reflect on what justice means, how it relates to established theories, and how the concept can be refined. Justice is a dynamic concept that makes static definitions difficult. However, continued reflections about justice can advance our understanding of the entire criminal justice enterprise.

What are the benefits, disadvantages, and consequences of each model of distributive justice that has been presented?

How would each model of justice discussed in this section apply to the sexting case at the beginning of the chapter?

Should all aspects of the criminal justice system (i.e., police, courts, corrections) subscribe to the same model of justice or to different models? Explain.

Conclusion

What is justice and how do we know when it has been accomplished? This is a question that has vexed humankind for millennia. As illustrated in this chapter, there are many ways to view justice. Certainly, distributive justice is one of the most central to criminal justice practice, with its emphasis on providing individuals what they are due. That is not to discount the other perspectives of justice provided in this chapter, however, as they also can inform the study of criminal justice policy issues. In the next chapter, we will turn to a comparison of different forms of justice (criminal, civil, and social) and also consider how criminal justice policies—strategies that attempt to achieve justice, broadly speaking—are actually made.

Criminal Justice Problem Solving:
DRUGS AND PROSTITUTION

Consider the following scenario as described by the police department in High Point, North Carolina (Fealy, 2006):

> High Point is a city of approximately 95,000 in central North Carolina (it adjoins the much larger city of Greensboro) with a furniture-industry industrial base. The city is 60% white and 30% African-American; some 13% of the population and 10% of families live below the poverty line. High Point started experiencing serious drug activity and gun violence in the mid 1990s, when its homicide rate climbed higher than Greensboro and nearby Winston-Salem . . .
>
> [The newly appointed police chief's] first tour of the city was enough to show chronic street-corner dealing, crack houses, prostitution, and drive-through drug buyers. These markets were exclusively in poor minority neighborhoods, though drug and sex buyers often came from outside. The markets drove a wide range of crime; community complaints were chronic. [The High Point Police Department] and its partners did a great deal of street drug enforcement, warrant service, and investigation of mid-level dealers, but to no effect; some of High Point's open-air markets dated back 40 years to the first heroin epidemic. (pp. 2–3)

The criminal behaviors in this description—drug sales and prostitution—are fairly common problems in many communities. In High Point, church leaders and other community members became frustrated. In fact, members of some congregations were unable to enter their respective parking lots on Sunday mornings because the cars of patrons waiting for prostitutes blocked the entrance. Appalled by the traffic congestion and the reason for the congestion, the pastors of the churches and their congregations sought assistance from the police as well as committing to help the police.

To address the situation, the police department used a strategy called **lever pulling**, which has several characteristics. The police identify a group of offenders that they wish to target. These offenders are then invited to attend a meeting at which they receive several messages. First, community leaders, clergy, and family members explain to offenders how their actions have caused them harm and pain. Second, offenders are offered resources to help them stop offending, such as treatment or employment programs. Third, offenders are told that if they do not stop offending, an aggressive enforcement campaign will be launched against them, including the use of "any and all legal tools (or levers) to sanction" them (Kennedy, 2006, pp. 156–157).

This strategy has been successful in a number of locations (Kennedy, 2006), and evidence indicates that it was successful in High Point. The police report that drug markets have disappeared and violent crime has declined. Furthermore, many of the former drug dealers responded to the strategy and are now leading crime-free lives while seeking and receiving employment (Fealy, 2006).

Why do you think this program was successful?

What philosophy or philosophies of justice does this program illustrate?

How does this program illustrate the relationship between justice and law, the public, the government, and criminal justice professionals? Which model(s) of distributive justice (e.g., mechanical, authoritarian, compassionate, participatory) does it illustrate? Explain your answer.

What is your opinion of this approach to law enforcement? Explain your answer.

Concepts of
Justice Policy

Robbie Callaway, former Chairman of the National Center for Missing and Exploited Children, shows an AMBER Alert kit at a Senate hearing. How do you think criminal justice policy should be made?

Key Terms

Marijuana Tax Act

victimless crimes

parens patriae

statute of limitations

civil justice

tort

preponderance of evidence

social justice

hegemony

political culture

liberty

equality

public policy

policy window

federalism

Dillon's Rule

National Supremacy Clause

Commerce Clause

agenda setting

problem definition

interest groups

bureaucrats

Key People

Harry Anslinger

David Miller

Thomas Dye

John Kingdon

Louis Brandeis

Theodore Lowi

Steven Lab

CASE STUDY

The Quagmire of State Marijuana Policy

The history of American marijuana law has come close to a full circle. Marijuana is derived from cannabis plants. In the nineteenth century, cannabis compounds were sold by pharmacists and traveling salespersons, offering to cure a variety of ailments. At that time, the criminal law did not restrict the use of marijuana (Inciardi, 1992).

By the mid-1930s, most states had passed laws regulating the distribution of marijuana, generally restricting it to those who had a prescription for its medical use (Ferraiolo, 2007). The laws were the product of a public panic about marijuana. The roots of the panic lay in a series of sensationalized and, by most accounts, inaccurate portrayals of marijuana use and its consequences, which appeared in newspapers and magazines. Also included was the original *Reefer Madness* film, released in 1936, which was specifically designed as an antimarijuana propaganda piece. The public came to fear marijuana and viewed it as a dangerous substance that led to violence and disorder and that was (reflecting the racism prevalent at the time) used by minorities to "have a corrupting influence on white society" (Inciardi, 1992, p. 21).

Enter Harry Anslinger, the director of the Federal Bureau of Narcotics, which was the forerunner of the Drug Enforcement Administration (DEA). In what some have argued was an attempt to gain power for his agency

(Inciardi, 1992), Anslinger led the charge against marijuana; in fact, he drafted the antimarijuana law that many states chose to adopt in the 1930s. In 1937, Anslinger was instrumental in the passage of the federal **Marijuana Tax Act**, which essentially outlawed marijuana nationwide by imposing a series of strict restrictions and taxes on its distribution. Subsequent federal laws further controlled and penalized marijuana possession and distribution, and in 1970, it was classified as an illegal Schedule I drug, which defined it as having "no accepted medical use and a high potential for abuse" (Ferraiolo, 2007, p. 158). Since the War on Drugs in the 1980s, federal laws against the possession, sale, and distribution of all illegal drugs, including marijuana, have been strictly enforced as part of "getting tough" on crime and drugs (see Walker, 2006).

Although *federal* law still defines marijuana as an illegal substance, some *states* have taken steps to legally permit marijuana possession and use in certain circumstances. In 1975, the Alaska Supreme Court ruled that individuals may possess small amounts of marijuana for personal use, noting "that citizens of the State of Alaska have a basic right to privacy in their homes . . . [which] would encompass the possession and ingestion of substances such as marijuana in a purely personal, non-commercial context in the home" (*Ravin v. State*, 1975, p. 29). In 1996, voters in California approved a measure that legalized medical marijuana (Brown, 2008). As of 2010, more than 40,000 California residents had been issued permission to possess medical marijuana (California Department of Public Health, 2010). In 2008, voters in Massachusetts approved a measure which decriminalizes any possession of up to one ounce of marijuana, even for recreational purposes. Rather than facing criminal charges, individuals who are caught in possession of an ounce or less will now pay a $100 fine that carries no criminal record and no criminal consequences (*Information for Voters*, 2008). Beyond these examples, the National Organization for the Reform of Marijuana Laws (NORML), an interest group advocating the decriminalization of marijuana, estimates that more than 12 states have decriminalized marijuana to some (even limited) extent and more than 14 states make some allowance for medical marijuana (National Organization for the Reform of Marijuana Laws, 2006). Of course, even with these *state* laws, marijuana remains illegal in *federal* law (more on this later).

> How do you think the law should regulate marijuana? Why? How do debates over the regulation of marijuana correspond to competing philosophies of law?
>
> Assume that a person in Alaska who possesses a small amount of marijuana for personal use is arrested by a federal DEA officer because possession is illegal under federal law (regardless of what Alaska law says). How would you resolve such a case? Why?

Criminal Justice and Civil Justice

FOCUSING QUESTION 7.1

What is the difference between criminal justice and civil justice?

As you learned in Chapter 6, justice is an elusive concept, difficult to define and perhaps equally difficult to fully achieve. In this chapter, we further refine our understanding of justice by exploring three broad venues in which justice can be achieved: criminal, civil, and social. The chapter will then turn to the making of criminal justice policy.

It is important to recognize that, although each accomplishes a different task, criminal, civil, and social justice are not entirely isolated from one another. For instance, the same action can fall under the purview of the criminal justice system and the civil justice system while raising social justice concerns. To help in clarifying the distinctions while highlighting the potential for overlap, this section will track the following hypothetical case.

Hoping for a rousing night "out on the town," Abel stops by his favorite tavern. After ordering and consuming several rounds of shots, Abel notices a female patron at the end of the bar and decides to strike up some conversation. The two hit it off. Their dialogue is interrupted, however, by the arrival of Baker, the patron's jealous ex-boyfriend. Baker takes exception to Abel's conversation (they were only discussing the weather!) and communicates this by breaking several beer bottles over Abel's head. As a result, Abel sustains a concussion (these were heavy beer bottles) as well as a number of cuts that require stitches. Abel's resulting medical bills exceed $10,000, and because Abel is uninsured, he has to pay these bills out of his own pocket.

CRIMINAL JUSTICE

Criminal justice is, most broadly speaking, the government's response to crime. Characteristics of criminal justice processes will be described and illustrated by Abel and Baker's case.

1. *Criminal justice processes apply only when a crime has been committed.* As described in Chapter 1, crimes are acts or omissions that are specifically listed in a state's criminal code. The criminal code defines the act and indicates whether it is a felony or a misdemeanor. If a person's behavior does not constitute one of the acts or omissions in the criminal code, then no crime has occurred and the criminal justice process is not utilized.

Assume that a statute states: "A person may not intentionally cause or attempt to cause serious physical injury to another," as doing so is the crime of assault in the first degree (Assault . . ., 2011). In the hypothetical example, Baker has intentionally wounded Abel and has done so with the intent of causing injury. Therefore, Baker's conduct meets the criteria for a crime as defined by the quoted criminal code, and the criminal justice processes may be initiated.

On the other hand, if Baker had only said, "Your shirt is ugly and your socks don't match, you contemptible knave," then no crime would likely have occurred, and the criminal justice system would probably not need to be involved in the incident. Next time, Baker will know.

2. *Criminal justice processes are initiated by the state against the accused.* Even though most crimes have victims who experience a direct harm (the exceptions being **victimless crimes**, in which no direct victim is readily identifiable, such as drug use, prostitution, gambling, and others), all crimes are technically considered crimes against the state, or government. If Baker was to be arrested and charged, the case would be *State v. Baker*. The government decides whether charges will be filed and a case will be brought. It is something of a misrepresentation in movies and television programs when a victim says, "I don't want to press charges," because that is not the victim's decision to make; again, it is up to the government. Having said that, it would be difficult for the government to prosecute a case if the victim does not cooperate with the prosecution, so often if a victim does not wish to press charges, the government does not do so.

The concept of crimes being against the state rather than against individual victims has its roots in the social contract theory described in Chapter 2. Recall that the theory is a metaphor for justice processes in which the state takes responsibility for protecting its citizens. This notion has further roots in English common law, under which the monarch was understood to be the parent and protector of his or her subjects (Custer, 1978), a concept known in Latin as **parens patriae**. Casting the state as victim also serves another purpose: it symbolically depersonalizes criminal incidents. It is the state's task, as government, to address and punish crimes. Victims are no longer responsible for producing their own justice. This removes the need for blood feuds in which victims would be responsible for enacting their own vigilante justice on an offender. This is of substantial importance because a government's ability to promote justice without blood feuds is associated with the degree of peace in a society (Otterbein & Otterbein, 1965).

3. *The agents responsible for initiating the criminal justice process are government employees.* The police investigate crimes and, based on probable cause, arrest persons believed to have committed crimes. The prosecuting attorney files the formal charges and works to resolve criminal cases either through guilty pleas or convictions at trial (the overwhelming majority of cases are resolved through plea bargains and guilty pleas). Both the police and district attorneys are public employees who work for the government.

In the hypothetical tavern situation, assume that someone from the bar calls the police. The police would come and investigate the incident to determine what happened. Upon completing their investigation, they would arrest Baker for his acts against Abel and file an initial charging document. A prosecutor would review the case and the charges against Baker and then would proceed with the case by attempting to secure a guilty plea or a guilty verdict in court.

4. *Because crimes are viewed as acts against society as a whole, there are few time limits placed on when charges may be filed.* For certain legal actions, there is a provision called a **statute of limitations**, which sets time limits on when court processes can be initiated. There is generally no statute of limitations for murder and other very serious crimes. For less serious offenses, there may be statutes of limitations, but generally speaking, the more serious the crime, the longer the time period in which charges can be filed.

Assume there is a 15-year statute of limitations for malicious wounding. If Baker had fled the scene after the incident, neither Abel nor the police may have known his identity. If, 10 years later, evidence surfaced (perhaps a long lost video surveillance recording) to indicate that Baker was Abel's assailant, then Baker could be arrested and charged with the crime—even though 10 years had passed.

As a general rule, the more time that elapses between a crime and the filing of charges, the more difficult it is to proceed. Witnesses will grow older and may forget details of the case, evidence may be misplaced or deteriorate, and the police and prosecutors initially involved in the case may have moved on in their careers. However, delayed prosecutions can occur. One such case was dramatized in the film *Ghosts of Mississippi*, which is the story of the trial of Byron De La Beckwith. In 1994, Beckwith was tried and convicted of first-degree murder in the assassination of civil rights leader Medgar Evers—a crime that occurred in 1963. The case was reopened when a prosecutor discovered new evidence in the early 1990s. Upon appeal, the Mississippi Supreme Court upheld the conviction because there was no statute of limitations for murder, which allowed the trial to occur even decades after the offense (*Beckwith v. State of Mississippi*, 1997).

5. *In the criminal justice system, proof of guilt must be beyond a reasonable doubt.* A criminal conviction carries with it many consequences. Depending on the crime and the jurisdiction, they may include, but are not limited to, deprivation of freedom through a prison sentence, inability to hold certain jobs, inability to vote, attaching the label of "convict" or "criminal," and more. Because of these consequences, the state sets a very high bar before it determines guilt. It is difficult to provide a precise definition of "beyond a reasonable doubt." It does not mean absolute certainty beyond any doubt, but at the same time, it does not leave much room for doubt. You will learn more about this concept in Chapter 12.

6. *Upon pleading guilty or being found guilty, a defendant may receive criminal punishment.* Each jurisdiction's legal code defines what that criminal punishment entails. In Baker's case, assume that the punishment specified for assault in the first degree is "imprisonment not exceeding 25 years" (Assault . . ., 2011). The judge could sentence Baker to prison for any amount of time with a maximum of 25 years or suspend part of the prison sentence and require that Baker serve that time on probation (Chapter 13 will explain probation in greater detail). Regardless of Baker's actual sentence, it is a criminal punishment issued by a judge after Baker's conviction.

These characteristics define the criminal justice process. As you can see, it is largely directed by the government and relies on addressing crimes as defined by the legal code.

CIVIL JUSTICE

Civil justice is distinct from criminal justice; it is an entirely different process. However, it is important to recognize that the same incident may be processed through both the criminal justice system and the civil justice system, sometimes with different outcomes. For instance, in 1994, former NFL player, sports commentator, and actor O. J. Simpson was criminally charged with the murders of his ex-wife Nicole Brown and her friend Ronald Goldman; in criminal court, he was found not guilty of those charges in 1995 (the case was *People of the State of California v. Simpson*). However, in 1997, Simpson was held accountable in civil court for the death of Goldman and for assault against both Goldman and Brown (in *Goldman v. Simpson* and *Brown v. Simpson*, cases filed by the survivors of the victims) (for further information, see Schuetz & Lilley, 1999). To understand how different outcomes can occur—one in criminal court, one in civil court—based on the same incident, you must understand the differences between criminal justice and civil justice. Consider the following characteristics of civil justice.

1. *Civil justice processes do not require that a crime has been committed.* Under civil justice, individuals may sue when they believe they have been harmed in some way, whether or not the harmful act is codified as a crime. Civil justice is very complex (and forms the basis for most study at law schools). To oversimplify, however, one instance in which individuals can pursue civil justice is when they have been physically or emotionally injured as the result of an act. Therefore, in addition to criminal action, Abel could bring a civil action against Baker, claiming that Baker committed actions that harmed Abel in some way. This type of action is known as a **tort**, or civil wrong. There is no precise statute that lists every specific type of harm that can be addressed in tort law in the way that there are precise statutes that list all types of crimes. Attorneys instead base their arguments, and judges base their decisions, on common law (i.e., established precedents from prior cases), on the particular circumstances of each case, and on how they match broad and general principles that define tort actions.

The Abel and Baker case is an instance of a crime that is also a tort. Let's consider a relatively famous case from 1992 in which a tort claim was raised but which was not a criminal act.

> [A woman] sitting in the passenger seat of her grandson's car holding a coffee that she purchased from a drive-through window of a

McDonald's . . . opened the lid of her coffee to add cream and sugar, [and] spilled the coffee on herself. The coffee cups were made of Styrofoam and were not particularly sturdy. The sweatpants that [she] was wearing absorbed the coffee and held it next to her skin. A vascular surgeon determined that [she] suffered third degree burns over 6% of her body, including her inner thighs, groin, buttocks, and genital areas. She was hospitalized for eight days, during which time she underwent skin grafting. As a result of the burns and surgery, [she] had permanent scarring on more than 16% of her body. (Ryan, 2003, p. 80)

While an unfortunate occurrence, this was not a criminal event, so it would not be resolved through the criminal justice system. However, as a result of the injury, the victim was able to pursue the case as a tort in civil court.

   2. *The civil justice process is initiated by individuals.* In civil justice, acts are not against the state or government; rather, they are against individuals. When one individual tells another person (or a company, or an organization, or whomever) "I'll *SUE* you," they are referring to the initiation of a civil case. Therefore, the civil justice process is only initiated when a person who has been harmed makes the decision to file a lawsuit in a civil court. If Abel were to decide that Baker's criminal punishment was not enough or if Abel wanted to hold Baker further accountable, he could do so by suing him in a civil tort action.

   3. *The agents responsible for pursuing civil justice lawsuits are private attorneys.* When an individual has decided to pursue a civil case, he or she generally must hire an attorney to help initiate the proceedings, to conduct necessary inquiries and investigations, and ultimately, to present the case in court (there are some exceptions, such as small claims court). This attorney is not a government employee but may be in private practice or a member of a law firm. Because attorneys generally charge by the hour or by the case, and cases generally take substantial time to prepare, the civil justice process is more available to those with financial resources than to those without. To pursue a civil case, Abel would have to make an appointment with an attorney to discuss the case. If the attorney agreed to accept the case, he or she would work with Abel to prepare the required documents and to present the case in court.

   4. *Civil court places more time limits on bringing a case forward.* There are generally stricter statutes of limitations in civil justice than there are in criminal justice. For instance, for a wrongful injury tort, it is not unusual for there to be a two-year time limit within which civil cases may be filed. If that was the time limit, it would mean that two years and one day after Abel's assault he would no longer be able to bring a civil case against Baker. Again, civil justice refers to private noncriminal disputes between individuals and/or organizations, and the courts do not want such issues to linger.

   5. *The burden of proof in civil court is by a preponderance of the evidence.* Proof beyond a reasonable doubt is not required. Because individuals will not be deprived of their liberty (by being placed in prison or on probation) and will not lose basic rights (e.g., voting) as a result of losing a civil case, the burden of proof is lower. A **preponderance of evidence** means the judge or jury believes it is "more likely than not" that the defendant injured or harmed the plaintiff. In addition, many of the protections that you will learn about in the next chapter apply only to criminal cases and not civil cases.

6. *Civil justice verdicts do not result in criminal punishment.* If a judge or jury "finds for the *plaintiff,*" it means the person bringing the case wins. However, as noted earlier, the defendant will not be sentenced to prison or probation or lose any rights. Instead, the defendant will generally be ordered to pay a financial settlement to the plaintiff. This is not a fine paid to the government; rather, it is a sum of money paid directly to the plaintiff. Financial settlements often cover the actual damages incurred in the case for physical injury, and they may also include money to compensate for emotional injury. The settlement can also include punitive damages, which is a sum of money designed to symbolically and publicly "punish" the defendant for the damaging acts.

Returning to the hot coffee case, a jury found for the plaintiff and also concluded "that McDonald's had engaged in willful, reckless, malicious, or wanton conduct" (Ryan, 2003, p. 82). The jury made the following awards (although the case was appealed and the total amount was later reduced):

> [Punitive damages were] the equivalent of two days of worldwide coffee sales, totaling $2.7 million. With respect to actual damages for medical bills, attorneys' fees, and compensation for loss, [plaintiff] was [also] awarded $200,000. However, the jury determined that [plaintiff] was also at fault in the way she handled the coffee. On this point, the jury determined that [plaintiff] was 20% at fault, which automatically reduced the $200,000 award by 20% to $160,000. (Ryan, 2003, p. 82)

As you can see, civil justice and criminal justice are very different. The primary focus of this text is on criminal justice, but it remains important for you to have a basic understanding of civil justice processes. Not only can the same incident be subject to a civil claim and a criminal case, but criminal justice personnel and agencies can also be sued under civil justice processes by individuals who believe they have been wronged.

Assume that a person was arrested for possession of marijuana. How would each of the elements of criminal law apply to the case?

One type of civil tort is "wrongful discharge" from a job. Assume that a person has a physician's prescription for medical marijuana but is fired for violating a company's "zero tolerance" substance abuse policy. How would this case proceed according to the six elements of civil justice that have been described?

Social Justice and American Values

FOCUSING QUESTION 7.2

How do social justice and political culture influence criminal justice?

Unlike criminal justice and civil justice, **social justice** does not refer to a legal process. Rather, it is an idea or a value to which individuals may subscribe and which, in turn, can shape decisions about civil justice and criminal justice policy issues. Social justice embodies concerns about fairness and equality, some of which you have already read about in previous chapters. Political theorist David Miller (1999) is one of the leading scholars of social justice theory; he states that social justice is

> how the good and bad things in life should be distributed among members of a human society. When, more concretely, we attack some policy or some state of affairs as socially unjust, we are claiming that a person, or more usually a category of persons, enjoys fewer advantages than that person or group of persons ought to enjoy (or bears more of the burdens than they ought to bear), given how other members of the society in question are faring. (p. 1)

Social justice often challenges **hegemony**. Hegemony refers to the influence that is exercised by powerful groups within society. Some debates about social justice stem from fears that those with power use their influence to make decisions that marginalize socially or politically unpopular groups either deliberately or due to a lack of awareness of those groups' needs and concerns. Social justice advocates raise attention to issues in which they observe unjust, unfair, or unequal treatment of persons.

There are many issues that can be raised under the umbrella of social justice. One conceptualization is to ask the question, can we have a just society without a particular benefit being available to all members of society? Or are there systematic inequalities or discriminatory behaviors that lead to unequal benefits, which in turn can lead to injustices? Social justice theorists would argue that both criminal and civil justice processes should strive to promote social justice through their decisions and that doing so ought to be a key focus for all legal processes.

In the case of Abel and Baker, one question pertaining to social justice is Abel's lack of health insurance. In the 2010 debates on health care, one pervasive question was precisely about whether it was a social injustice for some persons to be uninsured and to have limited access to health care. This debate emerged as a challenge to the hegemony of the health care system at the time. But how is social justice specifically related to criminal justice?

Social justice theorists (see Arrigo, 1999) argue that criminal justice should reflect social justice, linking the two concepts and requiring the criminal justice system to demonstrate fair and equal treatment of all persons under its control, with an emphasis on basic rights. This presumes that we ask questions about what makes a just, fair, and equitable society and then promote a criminal justice system that achieves those goals. Conversely, when an injustice is detected, affirmative steps must be taken to correct the system so it may more effectively promote social justice. Because social philosophies change over time, this can become a continuous process.

As an example, consider health care in prisons. Are inmates entitled to receive health care? And if so, what quality of health care should be provided? This is a social justice question because it considers the distribution of a resource (health care) and whether one group of persons (those in prison) is unfairly denied those resources. For many years, health care in correctional institutions was less than adequate. Consider the following description of one state's correctional health care system through the 1970s (*Ruiz v. Estelle*, 1980):

> Major problems pervade all aspects of the medical care . . . The personnel providing routine medical care are often unqualified; they are also wholly insufficient in numbers and deficiently supervised. The meager medical facilities, inadequately equipped and poorly maintained, do not meet state licensing requirements. Medical procedures are unsound and faulty at all levels of care. Initial processing, sick call methods, and transfer practices are all unnecessarily cumbersome, inefficient, and life-threatening . . . Medical records are so poorly maintained, and the entries made therein are so incomplete and inaccurate, as to be either useless or harmful in the day-to-day provision of medical care. (p. 1307)

In 1976, the U.S. Supreme Court ruled "that deliberate indifference to serious medical needs of prisoners" (*Estelle v. Gamble*, 1976, p. 104) is cruel and unusual punishment. One way of understanding this decision is through a social justice lens, with the Supreme Court indicating that provision of health care to inmates is necessary to meet the requirements of fairness and justice. As a result, correctional agencies must create policies that meet this requirement by allowing for proper inmate medical care.

As another example, consider a recent Arizona state law designed to address illegal immigration, which illustrates the dilemmas that can arise from the perspective of social justice. One of the most controversial provisions of the law is the following:

> For any lawful contact made by a law enforcement official or agency of this state or a county, city, town or other political subdivision of this state where reasonable suspicion exists that the person is an alien who is unlawfully present in the United States, a reasonable attempt shall be made, when practicable, to determine the immigration status of

the person. The person's immigration status shall be verified with the Federal Government. (*Senate Bill 1070*, 2010, p. 2)

One fear is that the law would lead to racial profiling by police. Opponents argue that it gives law enforcement too broad of an ability to detain virtually any persons, but in particular persons who appear to be Hispanic, for the purpose of verifying their citizenship. Shortly after the law was passed, President Barack Obama commented that the law could "undermine basic notions of fairness that we cherish as Americans, as well as the trust between police and our communities that is so crucial to keeping us safe" (Archibold, 2010, para. 5). Because of the concerns about discrimination and fairness, this issue invoked concerns pertinent to social justice. It also illustrates conflicts that may occur between criminal justice and social justice.

For instance, the criminal justice system might argue that the law was necessary to promote security and order and that social justice concerns are secondary. At the same time, social justice advocates might argue that the criminal justice system promotes inequitable outcomes. Meaningful dialogue between the two sides could be difficult because each is arguing from its core values (Sabatier & Jenkins-Smith, 1993). In 2011, the U.S. Court of Appeals upheld a preliminary injunction (i.e., a legal mechanism that temporarily prohibits enforcement of a law) against the section of the law quoted above (*U.S. v. State of Arizona*). As of this writing, the matter remains under legal review. In the meantime, arguments about the legislation and its social justice impacts continue.

There are many other examples of social justice issues. As a general principle, social justice involves concepts of fairness and equal treatment, particularly when there are concerns about differences between groups. It is also important to note that there are many social justice issues that have not traditionally been the focus of study in criminal justice but which have criminal justice implications nonetheless. Box 7–1 presents one such example pertaining to homelessness.

AMERICAN POLITICAL CULTURE

Before concluding a discussion of justice, it is useful to consider the broad range of values that are held as part of American political culture. A **political culture** refers to the broad set of values that underlie a particular political system (see generally Almond & Verba, 1989). In reality, the concept of a political culture is a philosophical oversimplification. There is not one single political culture in most jurisdictions. However, the notion of political culture is important because it is the broad political culture that tends to shape law and policy.

There is no central repository that officially lists or declares a nation's political culture. Rather, it is derived from the nation's documents (e.g., Constitution, Bill of Rights, Federalist Papers, and Declaration of Independence, among many others) and the nation's social, economic, and political history. Several components of American political culture are briefly surveyed here.

BOX 7.1

HOMELESSNESS, SOCIAL JUSTICE, AND CRIMINAL JUSTICE

There are approximately 3.5 million persons in the United States who are homeless—a number that has increased over the past 30 years (National Coalition for the Homeless [NCH], 2009d). Homelessness raises concerns about social justice because it involves a basic human need (i.e., shelter) that is unavailable to a substantial number of people. Homelessness as a social problem is also related to criminal justice. While not an exhaustive list, consider the following links between homelessness and criminal justice.

1. *Domestic violence is a significant cause of homelessness*. Research has found that "a majority of homeless women are victims of domestic violence" and that, of homeless families, "28% . . . were homeless because of domestic violence in 2008" (National Coalition for the Homeless, 2009a, p. 1). This raises a related concern for social justice and criminal justice in terms of whether female victims of domestic violence, in particular, receive adequate support.

2. *Persons who are homeless are at risk of being victims of crime*. From 1999 through 2008, there were 244 homicides committed against persons who were homeless. The homeless population is also at risk for being targeted as potential victims of antihomeless hate crimes (National Coalition for the Homeless, 2009c). It is the obligation of the criminal justice system to provide protection to persons who are homeless.

3. *Foreclosure is a cause of homelessness and is related to crime*. In the economic downturn of 2008–2009, there was an increase in the number of mortgage foreclosures. Generally, this means that the persons who were living in a foreclosed home had to vacate the property. It is estimated that 21% of persons whose homes were foreclosed spent at least some time living "on the streets" (National Coalition for the Homeless, 2009b, p. 2) and that as many as 10% of homeless persons became homeless because of a mortgage foreclosure. Neighborhoods with higher foreclosure rates experience higher crime rates (Bess, 2008).

4. *There are debates about the rights of persons who are homeless*. These debates often center on loitering and on the solicitation of money from passersby (sometimes known as "panhandling"). There have been a variety of court cases exploring the rights of homeless persons, but there is not a national consensus on the issue.

Again, homelessness is an issue with implications for social justice and criminal justice. Consider the following policy questions:

What can the police do to reduce victimization of the homeless?

What policies could be developed to reduce homelessness, especially when it results from a person leaving an abusive home?

What services should be provided to assist persons who are homeless?

From a social justice perspective, how could existing laws against loitering be balanced with the needs of homeless persons?

Certainly, two of the most preeminent values in American political culture are liberty and equality. **Liberty**, or freedom, is embodied in the first 10 Amendments to the Constitution, the Bill of Rights. From the emphasis on "life, *liberty*, and the pursuit of happiness" [emphasis added] in the Declaration of Independence, liberty has been a key American value. The criminal justice system must balance the need to promote order with a respect for and protection of the many rights that are afforded under the Constitution and Bill of Rights both to the innocent and to those accused of crime. You will learn more about these rights in Chapter 8 and Chapter 10.

Equality is also embodied within the Declaration of Independence, which notes that "all men are created *equal*" [emphasis added], and further protected by various constitutional protections and acts of legislation. There has been substantial change and progress over time in ensuring that the political system promotes equality. In the late 1700s, equality was only available to white male property owners who were over the age of 21. Through a series of constitutional amendments and law, equality is now accorded to all persons over 18 regardless of race, gender, or property ownership. In addition, efforts have promoted the expansion of equality to also consider disability status, veteran status, age, sexual orientation, citizenship status, religious affiliation, and more. The criminal justice system must ensure that it functions in a way that does not discriminate or deny rights to certain groups, which is the essence of the concern for social justice described earlier.

The final value to be discussed is important for the success of any political system. Legitimacy refers to the public's belief in the government's right to govern. That is, it refers to public faith in a particular government or political system. This is essential for criminal justice. If the actors in the criminal justice system—that is, the police, courts, and corrections—are to be effective, they must have the trust of the public. If the public does not place its faith in the criminal justice system, then the social contract is eroded and order may be diminished. Legitimacy may be built by tradition, the creation of policy outcomes that the public views as successful, a common identity shared by the government and the public (e.g., a shared history or a common belief system), and the use of "procedures in which many people have confidence" (Shively, 1999, p. 139). The latter point is particularly important for criminal justice. Indeed, procedural justice, in which criminal justice processes demonstrate fairness and social justice, is one factor that leads citizens to obey the law (Tyler, 2006). Legitimacy, in part through its impact on the effective functioning of the criminal justice system and in part on encouraging citizens to be law abiding, can lead to security in a society.

The values described provide a glimpse into American political culture. Understanding political culture can help place policy debates, including those about criminal justice, in a philosophical context.

> Discuss the ways marijuana law could be related to social justice and political culture.
>
> How can criminal justice promote social justice?
>
> How are the values described in the discussion of political culture related to criminal justice generally? Do you think there are other values that should be included as part of American political culture?

The Development of Criminal Justice Policy

FOCUSING QUESTION 7.3

How is criminal justice policy shaped by government structure?

How, then, is justice to be pursued? The criminal justice system is developed and shaped through public policy decisions, as new laws are created and new strategies and tactics are developed.

Political scientist Thomas Dye (1984) defined **public policy** as "whatever governments choose to do or not to do" (p. 2). Criminal justice policy, then, consists of the decisions that governments (whether local, state, or federal) make about what should be done to address crime. It is important to make one initial observation about American public policy, including criminal justice policy. That is, policies tend to be remarkably consistent over time. In what Robertson and Judd (1989) call "policy restraint" (p. 1), it is difficult to enact substantial and dramatic change in public policies. In short, the steps that are required to change policy are so difficult and require agreement from so many political actors that change is difficult to accomplish. For instance, laws must generally pass the muster of two legislative bodies, be signed by the chief executive, and not be struck down by courts. One positive argument for policy restraint is that it helps promote stability in public policy and therefore stability in the criminal justice process. Stability, in turn, can help build the historical roots that promote legitimacy. If criminal justice policies were to change often, dramatically, and quickly, the public might come to have skepticism in the authority of the system. At the same time, policy restraint can make it difficult to implement changes that are necessary to improve the criminal justice system.

This is not to say that there are never changes in criminal justice policy. However, dramatic change is rare, and once it happens, it tends to become established policy that lasts for a long time (see Baumgartner & Jones, 1993). For dramatic change to occur, political scientist John Kingdon (1995) argues that three factors must come together at the right time: public perceptions that a problem exists; the availability of a satisfactory solution to solve the problem (often, this solution is prepackaged or advertised by politicians); and a political climate that supports the change. When these factors come together, a **"policy window"** (p. 88) opens and change occurs. The policy window then quickly closes, at which time the policy becomes established and does not dramatically change until the three factors once again converge.

Consider the example of marijuana policy. The last major punctuation, or change, in marijuana policy occurred in the 1930s. There was public hysteria, driven by the media, about fear of marijuana, so there were clear public perceptions that a problem existed. The readily available solution, actively promoted by Anslinger, was to criminalize marijuana use. The political climate at the time was receptive to regulation of marijuana. In fact, only one witness (a medical doctor) testified against criminalization at congressional hearings about the law (Ferraiolo, 2007). Although there has been pushback in a small number of states that have allowed medical marijuana or limited degrees of decriminalization, there is not yet a national consensus in that direction. These variations among states have not yet met the three criteria to fully open a national policy window that would result in a dramatic and sustained national change in marijuana policy.

FEDERALISM

Variation in the law between states is not unusual. Indeed, aside from the most serious of crimes (e.g., murder, rape, robbery) and from rulings of the Supreme Court to which all must adhere (e.g., requiring Miranda warnings prior to custodial interrogation), there are often legal differences between jurisdictions in terms of what is (or is not) criminal, how offenses are defined, and so on.

This is because of an aspect of government structure called **federalism**, which means that we have two levels of government in the United States: the national (or federal) and the state. These two levels of government are provided for in the U.S. Constitution, each with its own (though sometimes overlapping) powers. There are additional layers of government below the state, including counties, cities or towns, and special districts (which are units that often cross over several local jurisdictions for a single purpose, such as a school district that serves students from several towns). However, the federal and state governments are the most powerful. In fact, a principle known as **Dillon's Rule** notes that a local government "is a creation of the legislature; it has only the powers which the legislature gives it; and nothing more" (Friedman, 2002, p. 411). This is important because it tells us that the states have very broad powers, but local governments do not. States may delegate to local governments the right, for instance, to have police agencies (as all states do), which may pursue their own strategies and tactics for responding to local crimes. On the other hand, states do not delegate to local governments the right to define criminal laws that would supersede those of the state, although localities do have a very limited ability to define ordinances such as speed limits, noise violations, and so on.

Consider the implications of federalism. One substantial disadvantage is that it leads to a lack of consistency in terms of the law and its enforcement between different places. For example, Virginia authorizes the death penalty in cases of first-degree murder, but neighboring West Virginia does not. In some counties of Nevada, state-regulated prostitution is legal (see Brents & Hausbeck, 2001); in no other jurisdiction in the United States is this true. Police in some jurisdictions follow an aggressive enforcement approach and arrest all persons found in possession of any marijuana; in other jurisdictions, casual marijuana use, even when criminal, may be ignored (see Johnson, Ream, Dunlap, & Sifaneck, 2008). There is no single pattern to criminal law and justice across the United States. Even in this book, much of what we write is general, and there are differences between jurisdictions too voluminous to list in a single source.

So why have federalism? One benefit of federalism is that it allows jurisdictions, within the bounds of state and federal law, of course, to shape their own responses to their own problems. This is illustrated in Justice Antonin Scalia's opinion in the case of *Harmelin v. Michigan* (1991). The state of Michigan enacted a law requiring a mandatory life sentence for persons in possession of 650 or more grams of cocaine. In upholding the constitutionality of the law after an appeal claiming it to be cruel and unusual, Justice Scalia wrote, "The Members of the Michigan Legislature, and not we, know the situation on the streets of Detroit" (p. 988). Thus, even though the punishment is indeed harsh (a subject for debate in its own right), the Supreme Court acknowledged respect for the judgment of the state of Michigan in determining what its own criminal laws and penalties should be (state legislators later revised this law to reduce the penalties).

Federalism also allows that, in the words of Supreme Court Justice Louis Brandeis, "a single courageous state may, if its citizens choose, serve as a laboratory, and try novel social and economic experiments without risk to the rest of the country" (*New State Ice Co. v. Liebmann*, 1932, p. 311). As some states experiment with medical marijuana or decriminalization, other states watch to see how it works. If, after watching, one state or city adopts a policy from another, then policy diffusion has occurred, which is defined as the transfer of a policy (or a law) from one jurisdiction to another (see Mooney & Lee, 1999).

STATE AND FEDERAL POLICY

Much of the preceding discussion focuses on differences among states. Let's turn our attention to the relationship between federal policy and state policy. Each state has its own complete criminal justice system. Likewise, the federal government has its own complete criminal justice system. Violations of state law are enforced by that state's law enforcement officers, are tried in that state's courts, and are punished by that state's supervised probation or by sentences to that state's prisons. Violations of federal law are enforced by federal law enforcement officers, are tried in federal courts, and are punished by federal-supervised probation or sentences to federal prisons. Therefore, there are really 51 separate criminal justice systems in the United States, each with its own processes. How a case is handled depends on whether it is a violation of a state law or a violation of federal law.

One question posed after the marijuana case study at the beginning of the chapter asked you to consider what should happen when a state law conflicts with a federal law—that is, when a state allows some marijuana possession even though it remains illegal under federal law. The **National Supremacy Clause** of the U.S. Constitution speaks to this issue: "This Constitution, and the Laws of the United States which shall be made in Pursuance thereof . . . shall be the supreme Law of the Land; and the Judges in every State shall be bound thereby, any Thing in the . . . Laws of any State to the Contrary notwithstanding." Simply stated, federal law trumps state law.

However, the question does become more complex than the clause just cited. Traditionally, the states have had primary authority over criminal law. There were originally very few federal criminal laws, and those that did exist were for instances when a crime was committed against the nation as a whole (i.e., treason), against a federal employee, or on federal property. Otherwise, the federal government stayed out of criminal justice (Miller, 2008). This changed in the twentieth century. Brickey (1996) observed, "In contrast with the 17 crimes that formed the entire body of federal criminal law two centuries ago, there are now more than 3000 federal crimes on the books today" (p. 28). Why the change?

In the twentieth century, the federal government began utilizing the **Commerce Clause** of the U.S. Constitution to define new federal crimes. The clause gives Congress the power "To regulate Commerce with foreign Nations, and among the several States." Here, commerce does not have to mean a business transaction, as we might normally define it. Instead, commerce can be understood more broadly to include any kind of transaction that crosses state lines. Stealing a motor vehicle and crossing state lines was one of the first federal crimes created under the auspices of the Commerce Clause. This law was passed, in part, to make the investigation and prosecution of such crimes more efficient (Brickey, 1996). The federal government could coordinate the investigation and prosecution, which saved states the burden of coordinating investigations, determining which state would prosecute, and so forth. Over time, federal crimes were defined that did not even require the actual criminal event to cross state lines, as long as it affected commerce in some way. As a result, the federal government has greatly expanded its role in criminal justice over the past century.

It is also important to note that, under federalism, the federal government can influence (though not require) states to adopt certain laws through the distribution of federal funding. As one example, the federal government provides money to states for the purpose of highway construction, and "the loss of federal highway construction funds has been a common threat issued by Congress if states do not adopt traffic safety laws . . . [such as] 21-year old minimum legal drinking age . . . and the 0.08 [blood alcohol content] law [for DUI cases]" (Richardson & Houston, 2008, p. 120). States comply and change their own laws so they can retain federal highway funding.

SEPARATION OF POWERS

Another significant feature of American government is the separation of powers. At the federal and state levels, there are three branches of government: legislative, which makes the laws; judicial, which interprets the laws; and executive, which enforces the laws. Separating powers into three branches (and at both the state and federal levels) is one feature that makes American government particularly complex, leading to the policy restraint described earlier. This was a deliberate decision by the founders, who were concerned that a single branch of government would gain too much power (see Madison, [1788] 1982). Through a system of checks and balances, each branch of government can counteract the other. (For example, the president can veto a bill from Congress; the courts can rule unconstitutional the acts of other branches; and Congress has authority to deny or confirm appointments of executive officers.) This helps each branch of government safeguard the other, the goal being that only the best policies will ultimately pass muster.

With the exception of the courts, criminal justice agencies typically fall under the executive branch of government. Consider how the legislative and judicial branches may impact policing and correctional agencies. It is the legislature that makes the very laws about what behaviors are or are not criminal. Police officers do not get to make up their own laws but instead must enforce only those that are created by the legislature. The legislature also is responsible for approving the state (or federal) budget. A prison warden must operate his or her facility without spending more money than was allocated by the state legislature; if the warden believes the funds are insufficient, he or she has little recourse other than to try to persuade the legislature to allocate more money in future years.

The courts hold trials and sentence offenders. A prison warden does not get to pick and choose who is sent to prison, nor does a probation officer get to select which persons will be assigned to his or her caseload. The courts make that decision, and the warden and probation officer must work with the persons who are sent to them regardless of what they may think of the decision. The courts also rule on constitutional and procedural issues, and in doing so, they establish guidelines that police and correctional agencies must follow. If the Supreme Court rules (as it has) that police officers may not use thermal imaging devices (which measure heat) to scan a home (e.g., to detect artificial lights that are used to promote marijuana plant growth) without a warrant, then police officers may not use thermal imaging devices in that way (see *Kyllo v. United States*, 2001).

The point of this discussion is to demonstrate that criminal justice agencies are constrained by the actions of multiple branches of government and must operate within those constraints. It quickly becomes clear that developing criminal justice policy involves not only a consideration of social justice and political culture but also political structure.

> What features contribute to restraint in American public policy? What do you think are the advantages and disadvantages of policy restraint? Of federalism?

> Select a criminal justice policy that interests you. How does it illustrate the features described in this section, including policy windows, federalism, state–federal relations, and separation of powers?

Forces Shaping Criminal Justice Policy

FOCUSING QUESTION 7.4

What forces have a role in shaping the development of criminal justice policy?

Within the political system, there are many forces that come together to shape the development of criminal justice policy. The following discussion highlights several of the most important, beginning with agenda setting and problem definition (see Rochefort & Cobb, 1994).

Agenda setting refers to the process by which an issue—any issue—is identified as one that needs to be addressed through policy or law. First and foremost, this is a political process. As Edelman (1988) notes, "conditions accepted as inevitable or unproblematic may come to be seen as problems" (p. 12). For instance, the history of marijuana policy illustrates that marijuana, once viewed as unproblematic, was later defined as a very serious problem—based less on a scientific study of the issue but more on a media-driven public panic and on political advocacy, including that by Harry Anslinger. Edelman (1988) also notes that some "damaging conditions may not be defined as political issues at all" (p. 12). For instance, homelessness is a serious problem with numerous implications for the criminal justice system (see Box 7.1), but it has not been at the forefront of public policy debates.

Once an issue is placed on the agenda for discussion, problem definition occurs. **Problem definition** is an attempt by interested individuals and groups to determine "where problems come from and, based on the answer to this question, what kinds of solutions should be attempted" (Rochefort & Cobb, 1994, p. 3). An example will help to illustrate; consider school violence. To determine where problems of school violence come from, fill in the blank: school violence is a _____ problem. Following the 1999 shootings at Columbine High School, an analysis of newspaper stories found that school violence was identified by the media as a "guns" problem (not enough gun control), as a "pop culture" problem (too much violent media), as a "security" problem (not enough security in schools), and as a "teen life" problem (negative school cultures)

(Lawrence & Birkland, 2004, p. 1197). Each of these is a different problem definition for school violence. Individuals and groups have the tendency to select the one definition that they most agree with and to promote it to the exclusion of other possible definitions. This is important because the most politically popular definition drives the types of policies that result. For instance, if "security" is the problem definition most accepted by legislators, then the policies and laws that result will focus primarily on strengthening school security (this indeed was the case; see Lawrence & Birkland, 2004), and less attention will be given to addressing the other aspects of the problem.

So where do agenda setting and problem definition come from? Although there are many players in politics and policy making, we will briefly consider three: the media, interest groups, and bureaucrats.

MASS MEDIA

The media include entertainment programming (movies, television programs, etc.) and news programming (newspapers, television newscasts, etc.). Both can influence perceptions of crime and criminal justice. Much entertainment programming focuses on crime, as the public seems to enjoy a good detective story. These programs tend to depict work in criminal justice professions as highly exciting, while omitting the routine or mundane parts of the job. The entertainment media also depict much more crime than actually exists; studies have estimated that the homicide rate is 1,000 times higher in fictional television programs than it is in real life. Entertainment programs can influence criminal justice policy by shaping inaccurate perceptions of crime and the criminal justice system. In fact, entertainment programs can "generate fear and reinforce popular support for harsher punishment" (Beckett & Sasson, 2004, p. 81).

Similarly, the news media can influence public policy outcomes. Complex news is that which offers "a balanced coverage of diverse viewpoints and ideas toward audiences' understanding of complicated issues" (Sotirovic, 2001, p. 313). When users consume complex news, they are more likely to carefully consider an issue, and this leads to support for criminal justice policies that emphasize efforts to prevent crime rather than only to punish offenders. On the other hand, when users consume noncomplex news, they are more likely to become fearful of crime, which leads to support for policies that punish offenders but do not prevent crime (Sotirovic, 2001).

Through editorial choices, the news media can also shape problem definition. For instance, in a study of gun control policy, Callaghan and Schnell (2001) found that the problem definition most often adopted by the media was that gun control debates reflected concern about a "culture of violence" (p. 193) in the United States. Neither politicians nor interest groups (on either side) identified this as their primary problem definition. The media may have utilized this problem definition because it was the one that generated the greatest audience interest and, in turn, the highest ratings.

INTEREST GROUPS

Interest groups are organized groups of individuals who advocate for a particular policy outcome. There are many interest groups pertinent to criminal justice. For example, the National Rifle Association and the Brady Campaign to Prevent Gun Violence are two interest groups on gun issues—the former to advocate for gun ownership rights and the latter to advocate for gun control. Theodore Lowi (1967) attributes significant power to interest groups, suggesting that they are a dominant force in modern politics. Indeed, Lowi envisions the political process as a struggle among competing interest groups, which sometimes eclipse the legislators themselves in terms of the attention they receive and the amount of policy making power they hold.

One notable example of interest groups is Mothers Against Drunk Driving (MADD). In 1980, MADD was created by Candy Lightner, whose daughter Cari had been killed by an intoxicated driver. The organization was able to raise national attention to the problem of driving under the influence (DUI). By developing and advocating a problem definition that placed the blame on individuals who drove under the influence, MADD's efforts resonated with the emphasis on victim's rights and personal responsibility that were part of the political culture in the 1980s. The alcohol industry also supported MADD, as the problem definition did not place blame for DUI on the alcohol itself but rather on how it was misused by some persons. As a result of MADD's efforts, many new laws and policies have developed both to prevent DUI and to punish those who do so (Reinarman, 1988).

BUREAUCRATS

Once policies have been made, they must be implemented, or put into effect. **Bureaucrats**, or persons working within the executive branch of government, have the responsibility for implementing policies. The way bureaucrats implement policy can subsequently shape what a policy actually means. As Michael Lipsky (1980) notes, "bureaucrats make policy in two related respects. They exercise wide discretion in decisions about citizens with whom they interact. Then, when taken in concert, their individual actions add up to agency behavior" (p. 13). As an example, consider police officers enforcing the speed limit. Assume that a stretch of highway has a 55 mile-per-hour (mph) speed limit. Would an officer be legally justified in stopping a motorist who was cruising at 56 mph? Of course. Now assume that officers, as a matter of practice, only stop motorists traveling faster than 60 mph, effectively giving a 5 mph "buffer zone." In practice, this means the *informal* policy is that 60 mph is the "real" speed limit. As citizens learn this (which they will, quickly), motorists will then routinely set their cruise control for 60 mph, confident that they will not be stopped. Consider what has happened here. The law still states that the speed limit is 55 mph. And officers may still stop individuals who travel at 56 mph or faster. However, because of the way the police officers have used their discretion, 60 mph is in perception and in practice functionally the speed limit. In this way, the officers have indeed created public policy.

> How do the media, interest groups, and bureaucracies influence the creation and enforcement of criminal law? Provide examples beyond those described in this section.
>
> Try your hand at problem definition. Brainstorm as many responses as you can to this statement: "Marijuana is a _____ issue." Describe what kinds of policies or laws each response would suggest.

Conclusion

Criminal justice and civil justice represent different means by which justice can be achieved, and social justice is an idea emphasizing fair and equitable treatment for all persons. Justice policies are made in an attempt to achieve justice, however it may be defined. There are many influences on justice policy, including political culture and values, government structure, the media, interest groups, bureaucrats—and of course, politics, which underlies them all. These forces come together in shaping the pursuit of justice in the United States. The next chapter explores procedural justice, pertaining to how justice is implemented in practice and the constitutional rights that must be safeguarded in the process.

Criminal Justice Problem Solving: PRESCHOOL CRIME PREVENTION

A study by the Washington State Institute for Public Policy (Aos, Miller, & Drake, 2006) found that the implementation of preschool programs for low-income children could reduce crime by approximately 14%. Furthermore, the program was estimated to save the state more than $12,000 per child who completed it after costs and savings (through reduced crime and corresponding reductions in criminal justice system expenses) were factored in. Have you heard of preschool crime prevention programs? If so, that's great. If not, why not? This is a question worth considering.

Steven Lab (2004), former president of the Academy of Criminal Justice Sciences, observed that politicians sometimes abandon programs known to be effective (including preschool) but adopt programs known to be generally ineffective (including Drug Abuse Resistance Education and three-strikes laws). Curious as to why, Lab offered four premises as potential explanations.

1. "Politicians look for immediate results that will help them to be reelected" (p. 684).
2. "The emphasis for politicians is on what can be easily counted" (p. 685).
3. "Politicians emphasize those policies and actions that play well in 15-second sound bites" (p. 685).
4. Political decisions are always focused on the 'issue of the moment'" (p. 685).

Indeed, these four observations would, if accurate, make it difficult for publicly funded preschool programs to gain a foothold. First, the results would not be immediate, as the crime prevention value would not be fully achieved until the preschoolers grew up and lived crime-free lives. Second, because of the time lag, there would not be an easily countable result—at least not for a number of years. Third, it would take more than 15 seconds to fully explain the dynamics that lead preschool education to have crime prevention value, especially when showing figures to demonstrate that its benefits exceed its costs. Finally, there is not a current public outcry (or "issue of the moment") for which preschool programs are the agreed-upon solution. In addition, there would likely be some philosophical or ideological objections to publicly funded preschool programs.

Lab's implication is that nonexperts set the agenda and define the problems and that, for political reasons, it is sometimes difficult to create policies that are based on research and empirical data. However, there is an alternative in evidence-based policy making. In this approach, policy is made "using the highest quality available research evidence on what works best to reduce a specific crime problem and tailoring the intervention to the local context and conditions" (Welsh, 2006, p. 305). This requires careful collaboration between policy makers and experts, including researchers.

What do you think are the challenges in implementing evidence-based policy making?

What do you think could be done to encourage the use of research in policy making?

How can political realities, such as those described by Lab, be balanced with evidence, notions of justice, and concern for liberty and equality when making policy? Use preschool programming for crime prevention, or another issue of your choice, as an example.

Concepts of Criminal Procedure

An officer and canine searching a school locker area. What principles do you think should guide searches by police officers?

Key Terms

substantive due process
procedural justice
perfect procedural justice
imperfect procedural justice
pure procedural justice
crime control model
due process model
Bill of Rights
habeas corpus
bill of attainder
ex post facto
treason
reasonable expectation of privacy

probable cause
stop and frisk
reasonable suspicion
protective sweep
exigent circumstances
exclusionary rule
fruit of the poisonous tree
standing
grand jury
indictment
preliminary hearing
double jeopardy
privilege against self-incrimination

Miranda rights
interrogation
custody
waivers
trial by jury
bench trial
Confrontation Clause
subpoena
effective assistance of counsel
equal protection
Due Process Clause
Equal Protection Clause
ex parte

Key People

John Thibaut and Laurens Walker
Tom Tyler
Herbert Packer

CASE STUDY

SUNY New Paltz

During the 2005–2006 academic year, three male students who were running for executive positions in the student government at the State University of New York (SUNY) at New Paltz confronted a female residence director. They accused her of using her administrative position in residential life to influence students to vote against them. Following the incident, the residence director filed harassment complaints against all three students under internal university procedures as well as by pursuing charges in criminal court. Following a campus disciplinary hearing, the students were determined to be responsible for harassment. The university expelled one student and suspended the other two. In criminal court, one student was criminally convicted of harassment, but the other two were acquitted (i.e., found not guilty) (see *Holmes v. Poskanzer*, 2008).

Two of the students filed a lawsuit in federal district court arguing that they had been denied due process in the campus disciplinary hearing. First, the students asserted that they were not permitted to have representation from legal counsel during the hearing. Second, they argued that the university prohibited them from directly questioning the witnesses who testified against them. Finally, they contended that the hearing committee was not impartial. Because the students were "simultaneously facing possible university expulsion and pending state criminal charges" (p. 22), the court was concerned with the denial of the students' request to have counsel present because the questions posed to the students during the university hearing had self-incrimination implications. The students also claimed that the charges filed against them were retaliatory in response to the exercise of their First Amendment free speech rights; the students had publically criticized the university administration during on-campus rallies and in the local press. Ultimately, the court ruled in favor of the university for technical legal reasons. In spite of the students' loss, the court made it clear that the procedures used by the university during the disciplinary hearing were unacceptable (*Holmes v. Poskanzer*, 2007).

What procedural rights do you think college students should have during campus disciplinary proceedings? Why?

Do you think the students' rights were violated in this case? Why or why not?

Concepts of Procedural Justice

FOCUSING QUESTION 8.1

What does the term "procedural justice" mean?

Due process is the cornerstone of American law. Due process is guaranteed through two clauses in the U.S. Constitution. The clause in the Fifth Amendment restrains the power of the federal government. The clause in the Fourteenth Amendment restrains the power of the state governments. Both due process clauses protect against the arbitrary use of government power in two ways: substantively and procedurally. **Substantive due process** protects against governmental infringement of important rights, like freedom of speech, religion, and the right to privacy (see Chapter 9). **Procedural justice** concerns the fairness of the processes used when applying the law. Procedural justice is grounded in the idea that fair procedures are the best guarantees for fair outcomes. Moreover, if everyone is treated fairly, then it is easier for people to accept outcomes with which they disagree (Deutsch, 2000; Thibaut & Walker, 1975). But how do we know when a procedure is fair?

THREE PHILOSOPHICAL MODELS OF PROCEDURAL JUSTICE

In his book *A Theory of Justice* (1971), legal philosopher John Rawls described three models of procedural justice: perfect, imperfect, and pure. A review of these models can help identify the key principles of procedural justice and the differing emphases that may be placed on each of them.

Perfect Procedural Justice: The Accuracy Model. **Perfect procedural justice** exhibits two characteristics. First, there must be some criterion for determining what a fair outcome is. Second, there must be procedures put into place that are designed to facilitate that fair outcome (Rawls, 1971). The first characteristic is supposed to define the "right" or "fair" result. The second sets

forth the mechanism to achieve that result. To illustrate this concept, Rawls uses the example of slicing a cake (think back to Box 6.1). He points out that the person slicing the cake normally chooses his or her piece last. As a result, the cake slicer is likely to make all of the pieces the same size because failure to do so could leave him or her with the smallest piece. "'Equal shares for each' is the independent criterion of a fair division; the slicer-picks-last rule is the procedure that reliably produces that outcome" (Solum, 2004, p. 239).

Perfect procedural justice is based on the accuracy model. This somewhat idealistic model strives for accuracy in searching for the truth. "Accuracy . . . is provided by elaborate trial procedures, including cross examination, neutral judges and juries, rules of evidence, and representation by counsel" (Solum, 2004, p. 245). Rawls argued that the U.S. system of justice is *not* based on the accuracy model. Instead, Rawls pointed out that legal doctrines often interfere with the accuracy in fact finding required of perfect procedural justice. For instance, the exclusionary rule is a good example. If police violate someone's Fourth Amendment rights by conducting an illegal search and seizure, the evidence seized during the illegal search will likely be inadmissible at trial—even if it is strong evidence of the person's guilt (see *Mapp v. Ohio*, 1961). A higher principle of public policy—namely, protection of constitutional rights—is addressed by this rule. However, it interferes with the overall accuracy of the trial process. Indeed, a guilty person may go free because of the application of the exclusionary rule. (The exclusionary rule is discussed in more detail later in this chapter.)

Imperfect Procedural Justice: The Balancing Model. **Imperfect procedural justice** occurs when the first characteristic of perfect procedural justice (i.e., the independent criterion for a fair outcome) is present, but the second characteristic—a procedure for guaranteeing the outcome—is missing. Rawls asserts that criminal trials in the United States represent this type of procedural justice. The independent criterion for a fair outcome is present—namely, that someone who is proven to have violated a criminal law should be convicted. Conversely, someone who is not proven to have violated a criminal law should be found not guilty. Yet, the procedures used in criminal courts do not *guarantee* this outcome. Consider the exclusionary rule again. Its use can sometimes make it difficult to accomplish the first characteristic by interfering with the ability to convict someone who is very likely guilty. But this is because imperfect procedural justice operates within a balancing model.

The balancing model assumes that procedures are designed "to strike a fair balance between the costs and benefits of adjudication" (Solum, 2004, p. 193). This involves a consideration of trade-offs in the judicial process. For example, what is the "cost" of a mistake, such as the wrongful conviction of an innocent person? A series of procedural rights are specified in the U.S. Constitution and the law of evidence to protect against this kind of error. Honoring the constitutional rights of the accused while also attempting to effectively control crime is, in itself, a delicate balance (see Packer, 1968). We will explore the attempt to balance these competing interests later in this chapter.

Pure Procedural Justice: The Participation Model. Finally, **pure procedural justice** focuses on creating a system with fair procedures that, if followed, are *likely* though not *guaranteed* to produce fair outcomes. The process is then more significant than the accuracy of the outcome. Rawls used gambling as an example. Assuming that a number of people place money on a fair bet, whoever winds up with the money is the fair winner. The fact that the winner may have already been a multimillionaire who did not need the money is irrelevant; the fact that one of the people cannot pay the rent as a result of having lost the bet is similarly irrelevant. The outcome, therefore, is not what matters in a system of pure procedural justice; rather, playing by a set of predetermined, mutually agreed-upon, fair rules is what is important.

To protect against adjudication procedures based on chance alone (like a coin toss), Rawls states that pure procedural justice must be based on a participation model. The participation model of procedural justice posits "those affected by a decision have the option to participate in the process by which the decision is made" (Solum, 2004, p. 259). Clearly, parties to a trial are guaranteed a series of rights designed to allow their meaningful participation in the justice process.

However, there are problems with the participation model. First, not all parties can participate equally (see Peterson, Krivo, & Hagan, 2006). For example, those who can afford to hire experienced attorneys and authoritative expert witnesses might have an advantage in court over those who cannot afford to hire such people. Second, racial, ethnic, gender, or sexuality stereotypes and prejudices can affect decisions made by judges and jurors. This, in turn, can give an unfair advantage to some participants while disadvantaging others. Finally, even if it were possible for all participants in the justice system to be on a truly level playing field, the need for accuracy must play a more prominent role than it does in the participation model. That is, participative processes are not enough, by themselves, to ensure justice; rather, there needs to be a "connection between participatory processes and correct outcomes" (Solum, 2004, p. 267). Table 8.1 summarizes Rawls's concepts of procedural justice.

This brief review of theoretical perspectives on procedural justice points to some important principles. First, accuracy matters (drawing upon perfect procedural justice). Second, accuracy is not the only important goal of the system; other principles, such as dignity and respect for people and their rights, must also be taken into account (drawing upon imperfect procedural justice). And third, meaningful participation in processes that adhere to fair rules is also important (drawing upon pure procedural justice). Social psychologists have

Table 8.1. Summary of Rawls's Three Concepts of Procedural Justice

Criterion	Type of Procedural Justice		
	Perfect	*Imperfect*	*Pure*
Independent criterion for a fair outcome	Yes	Yes	No
Procedure for guaranteeing the outcome	Yes	No	Yes
Model focused upon	Accuracy	Balancing	Participation

studied these philosophical principles as they apply to the criminal justice system. Their research teaches us some valuable lessons about what our justice system must do to be perceived as "fair."

SOCIAL PSYCHOLOGICAL FACTORS

In the mid-1970s, John Thibaut and Laurens Walker formed a theory of procedural justice that profoundly influenced research for decades. They argued that the *outcome* of cases (i.e., who "wins" and who "loses") was not as important to the participants' satisfaction as were their perceptions regarding whether the *processes* were fair (e.g., Thibaut & Walker, 1975, 1978). Building on their work, Tom Tyler and his colleagues (2002, 2003) developed a model of three interrelated claims, nicely summarized by O'Hear (2007, pp. 12–13).

> *First*, a person's perception of whether a decision-making process was fair does not depend solely on the outcome, but also on various attributes of the process used to reach the outcome. Those attributes include (1) whether people had an opportunity to state their case ("voice"); (2) whether the authorities were seen as unbiased, honest, and principled ("neutrality"); (3) whether the authorities were seen as benevolent and caring ("trustworthiness"); and (4) whether the people involved were treated with dignity and respect. *Second*, the extent to which decision-making processes are perceived as fair helps shape beliefs regarding the legitimacy of the legal authorities responsible for the decision. And, *third*, the perception that legal authorities have legitimacy enhances the sense that the authorities are entitled to be obeyed. Fair procedures thus promote cooperation with the authorities and compliance with their directives, as well as the development of a more general sense of obligation to obey the law.

Maiese (2004) added a fourth criterion requiring that the processes must be transparent. That is, decisions "should be reached through open procedures, without secrecy or deception" (para. 5).

Legitimacy in criminal justice comes only if procedural justice exists and if participants perceive the process as fair. Recall from Chapter 2 that the moral authority of law—the reason people should obey the law—is contingent upon legitimacy (see Raz, 1972). But what does legitimacy mean? Assume, for example, that the criminal justice system operated under the following four conditions that are supported by the research of Tyler and Maiese. First, assume that legal processes were consistently applied. Second, assume that these processes were adjudicated by impartial/neutral people. Third, assume these processes were participatory, meaning that those affected by the decisions have both voice and representation. And fourth, assume that the processes were transparent, meaning that they utilized open procedures without secrecy or deception. Would these criteria create legitimacy in law? Most scholars answer "no." Procedural justice is a necessary component to law's legitimacy, but it is not enough. Laws "must also comply with certain values, such as human dignity, liberty, equal concern for all, etc., in order to be fully legitimate" (Sadurski, 2005, p. 1). To address these concerns, the *substance* of law must also be fair. In criminal justice, this refers to decisions about which acts should be defined as crimes and what their punishments should be. These concepts are explored in greater detail in Chapters 9 and 10.

> Most people would argue that perfect procedural justice is not attainable in criminal trials. How might the criminal trial process be enhanced within a perfect procedural justice model? What obstacles might there be to achieving the solutions you propose?
>
> What form of procedural justice do you think the SUNY New Paltz case represents? Explain your answer.
>
> Other than those identified by Thibaut, Walker, Tyler, and Maiese, what other values do you think are essential to ensuring that fair procedures are used in the criminal justice system?

Two Models of the Criminal Process

FOCUSING QUESTION 8.2

How does the criminal justice system balance crime control with the rights of the accused?

Herbert Packer (1968) described two models of the criminal justice process. The **crime control model** can be viewed as assembly-line justice. Its focus is to move the offender through the criminal justice process as quickly and efficiently as possible. The idea is to arrest, try, convict, and punish with ease and finality. For example, traffic court judges sometimes minimize the time it takes to adjudicate cases. They ask if the defendants would be willing to plead guilty in exchange for a reduced fine, the minimum court costs, and perhaps even the reduction or dismissal of driving points. The people who agree are then pronounced "guilty" and sentenced. The violator benefits because he or she receives a lighter punishment. The judge benefits by having cleared the courtroom in a timely manner. Thus, the system functions quickly and with efficiency, though not with an attention to individual details.

The crime control model assumes guilt and the need for quick and effective punishment. Under this philosophy, the belief is that if accused persons were not guilty, they would not have been arrested in the first place. Furthermore, the prosecutor, the judge, and often the defense attorney believe the accused is guilty. Proponents of the crime control model recognize the possibility that some of those accused of criminal activity are in fact not guilty. However, punishing a few innocent people is viewed as an acceptable price to pay for controlling crime rapidly and efficiently.

The **due process model**, in contrast, focuses on the rights of the accused. This model assumes that the accused is innocent until proven guilty. If the crime control model is assembly-line justice, the due process model is obstacle-course justice. That is, there are numerous steps that the criminal justice process must go through to assure that only the guilty are punished. If at any point during these many steps there is reasonable doubt that the offender is guilty, then he or she should be removed from the system and set free.

The due process model advocates formal decision-making procedures. Accused persons should have their right to have their day in court. For example, if you wished to contest the traffic ticket in court, you would be able to do so without fear of reprisal. If you were found guilty, the judge should not impose additional fines, court costs, or driving points just because you decided to have your case heard rather than proceed through the assembly-line process.

The due process model supports the adversarial process, meaning that the prosecution and defense battle it out in a courtroom so that the truth will emerge. This model assumes that a person's freedom is paramount and that there must be conclusive evidence of guilt supported by valid and reliable information before a person can be punished. Furthermore, this evidence is only determined when both sides—the prosecution and defense—have the opportunity to put forward their best cases while contesting the case put forth by the opposing side. The system should be structured carefully to result in the punishment of only those who deserve it.

It should be evident that Packer's two models conflict with each other. Yet, elements from both models work simultaneously throughout the criminal justice process. As described earlier, striking a balance between the two models is one of the reasons John Rawls argues that our criminal justice system is one of imperfect procedural justice.

Which do you support more—the due process model or crime control model? Why?

How do the due process and crime control models correspond to the three theories of procedural justice described by Rawls? Which model is more consistent with the social psychological research on fairness described earlier? Why?

Procedural Justice and the U.S. Constitution

FOCUSING QUESTION 8.3

What procedural criminal justice rights are identified in the text of the U.S. Constitution?

The U.S. Constitution, comprised of a Preamble and seven Articles, was originally adopted in 1787. It was ratified by the states over the course of the three years that followed. In 1789, Congress adopted 10 constitutional amendments that were ratified by the states within three years. These first 10 Amendments to the Constitution are collectively referred to as the **Bill of Rights**. The Articles of the original Constitution were primarily concerned with the structure and powers of government. However, the text did contain a handful of procedural justice guarantees. The Bill of Rights expanded on these with a more comprehensive list of individual rights and liberties that restrain the powers of the government in both substantive and procedural ways.

PROCEDURAL RIGHTS IN THE ORIGINAL U.S. CONSTITUTION

Habeas Corpus. Suppose you were imprisoned for a crime you did not commit because, at a state court trial, you were not permitted to cross-examine the prosecution's witnesses against you. Such a trial would violate a number of your constitutional rights. Of course, such errors should not occur. However, if they did, you would have a great argument for the reversal of your conviction on appeal. But what if the appeals process failed to correct this injustice? Article I, Section 9 of the U.S. Constitution guarantees that you could file a petition for a writ of *habeas corpus* in which you ask a federal judge to order your release from state custody. Note that this reflects the concept of federalism discussed in Chapter 7, under which there are both state and federal governments—and under which the federal government has supremacy.

Literally, *habeas corpus* is Latin for "you have the body." A writ of *habeas corpus* is a court order directed at someone who has custody of a person (and therefore, "has" the person's "body"), ordering the release of that person because his or her incarceration was achieved through unlawful processes. Sometimes referred to as "The Great Writ," *habeas corpus* originated in the courts of England as a means of curbing the authority of the king (Sholar, 2007). Its importance grew over the centuries in England, and by the late 1700s, it was deemed so important that the framers of the U.S. Constitution included it in the first Article. Article I, Section 9, Clause 2 provides that "The Privilege of the Writ of Habeas Corpus shall not be suspended, unless when in Cases of Rebellion or Invasion the public Safety may require it." Since that time, it has been interpreted more broadly than it ever was in England. The Great Writ is considered "the fundamental instrument for safeguarding individual freedom against arbitrary and lawless state action" (*Harris v. Nelson*, 1969, pp. 290–291). The writ of *habeas corpus* is an important form of procedural justice because it provides the mechanism to challenge unlawful incarcerations.

Bills of Attainder. If Osama bin Laden had not been killed, suppose that Congress had passed a law declaring him guilty of many crimes, including thousands of murders for the deaths that occurred in the September 11, 2001, attacks. That law would have been an unconstitutional bill of attainder because it declared bin Laden's guilt without there having been a trial.

A **bill of attainder** is a legislative act declaring someone guilty of a crime and imposing punishment (see Reynolds, 2005) in absence of a trial. Because the determination of guilt is delegated only to the judicial system, and not to the legislature, Article I, Section 9, Clause 3 of the Constitution prohibits Congress from passing bills of attainder. Clause 10 of the same Article and Section similarly prohibits the states from passing bills of attainder. This ensures that all accused persons will have their day in court and that the court will hold all responsibility for determining whether or not persons are guilty based on evidence introduced at trial. This is important to the concept of procedural justice because it prevents "legislative oppression of those politically opposed to the majority in control" (Pound, [1930] 1998, p. 133). Guilt will only be adduced after a fair process and with an accounting for evidence.

Ex Post Facto **Laws.** Article I, Section 10 of the U.S. Constitution provides: "No State shall . . . pass any . . . *ex post facto* Law." An ***ex post facto*** law is any law that "punishes an act that was not criminal when committed" (West, 2007, p. 243). Say, for example, that you ate chocolate cake on Monday. Then, on Tuesday, a law went into effect criminalizing the eating of chocolate cake. The *Ex Post Facto* Clause would prohibit your prosecution and/or punishment for having eaten the cake *before* there was a law against doing so. The Supreme Court has also interpreted the *Ex Post Facto* Clause as barring laws that increase the possible punishment for a crime after it was committed or that change the "rules of evidence after the commission of the offense for the purpose of obtaining a conviction" (West, 2007, p. 243). The prohibition of *ex post facto* laws ensures that guilt can be assigned and punishments meted out only when offenders have the opportunity to know that their behavior was criminalized—certainly, a prerequisite for fairness.

Trial by Jury. Article III, Section 2 of the Constitution guarantees that trials for all federal crimes, other than impeachment trials, shall be by jury. The Supreme Court has ruled that this right does not apply to petty crimes, military tribunals, or when the defendant has waived the right to a trial by jury. This right was expanded upon in the Sixth Amendment, discussed later in this chapter in greater detail.

Trial for Treason. The only crime defined in the U.S. Constitution is **treason**. The framers were concerned that espousing unpopular views in a new democracy might be considered treasonous. Since the First Amendment's protection of free speech came later, they defined the substantive elements of the crime and procedures for proving it to ensure that simple speech could not be interpreted as the crime of treason. Article III, Section 3 states: "Treason against the United States, shall consist only in levying War against them, or in adhering to their Enemies, giving them Aid and Comfort. No Person shall be convicted of Treason unless on the Testimony of two Witnesses to the same overt Act, or on Confession in open Court. . . ."

PROCEDURAL RIGHTS IN THE BILL OF RIGHTS

The Fourth Amendment. Article 21 of the Code of Hammurabi (c. 1750 B.C.E.) stated: "If a man makes a breach into a house, one shall kill him in front of the breach and bury him in it." Some scholars consider this the first statement of law expressing the notion that a "man's home is his castle" (Lasson, 1937). This principle embodies the notion that one's home is sacred and should, therefore, be beyond the reach of unreasonable intrusions—especially from governmental actors, a principle embodied in the Fourth Amendment, which provides:

> The right of the people to be secure in their persons, houses, papers, and effects, against unreasonable searches and seizures, shall not be violated, and no Warrants shall issue, but upon probable cause, supported by Oath or affirmation and particularly describing the place to be searched, and the persons or things to be seized.

A comprehensive review of the Fourth Amendment is beyond the scope of this text. However, in the few pages that follow, we will explore some of the most important principles and cases related to the two clauses of the Fourth Amendment.

The first clause in the Fourth Amendment is referred to as the Reasonableness Clause. It prohibits unreasonable searches and seizures. "A 'search' occurs when an expectation of privacy that society is prepared to consider 'reasonable' is infringed. A 'seizure' of property occurs when there is some meaningful interference with an individual's possessory interest in that property" (*United States v. Jacobsen*, 1984, p. 113). Thus, for the protections of the Fourth

Amendment to apply, there must be some governmental invasion of a **reasonable expectation of privacy** (see Box 8.1).

The second clause of the Fourth Amendment is called the Warrants Clause. It specifies that warrants must (1) be supported by probable cause, (2) specify where a search is to take place, and (3) describe with particularity who or what is to be seized. **Probable cause** is defined as a "fair probability" based on facts and known circumstances (1) that seizable evidence will be found in a particular location or on a particular person (*Carroll v. United States*, 1925) or (2) that an offense has been or is being committed by the person to be arrested (*Brinegar v. United States*, 1949).

Although probable cause is usually necessary to conduct a search, seize evidence, or make an arrest, the Supreme Court has created several notable exceptions to this rule. The first important exception is commonly referred to as a **stop and frisk**. Police are permitted to "stop" suspects based on **reasonable suspicion** of criminal activity—a lower standard of proof than probable cause. Moreover, if they have reasonable suspicion that the suspect may be armed, they may "frisk" the suspect for weapons (*Terry v. Ohio*, 1968). Also, cursory

---

WHAT ARE REASONABLE EXPECTATIONS OF PRIVACY?

BOX 8.1

In *Katz v. United States* (1967), the Supreme Court ruled that the FBI had violated the Fourth Amendment by placing a recording device just outside a public telephone booth. The Court reasoned that the user of the telephone had a subjective expectation of privacy during the call he made from the phone booth. Moreover, the Court found that subjective expectation to be objectively reasonable. Do you think individuals would have a reasonable expectation of privacy in the following circumstances, thereby ensuring the protections of the Fourth Amendment in each circumstance?

- In abandoned property—property that someone has voluntarily discarded or left behind? The Supreme Court ruled "no" in *United States v. Jacobsen* (1984).
- In garbage placed in sealed plastic bags for collection outside your home? The Supreme Court ruled "no" in *California v. Greenwood* (1988).
- Your bank records? The Supreme Court ruled "no" in *United States v. Miller* (1976).
- The numbers dialed from your home telephone? The Supreme Court ruled "no" in *Smith v. Maryland* (1979).
- In your home? The Supreme Court ruled "yes" in *Payton v. New York* (1980), unless some emergency justifies an immediate warrantless entry or unless you grant consent for state actors (i.e., police officers) to enter your home. In *United States v. Kyllo* (2001), the Court said that the privacy expectation in one's home is so special that the Fourth Amendment protects people's homes from being scanned by thermal imaging devices.
- In face-to-face conversations you have with others? The Supreme Court ruled "no" in *United States v. White* (1971), unless the other person is someone with whom you may have a "privileged" (i.e., protected) conversation, such as your attorney, your priest, your psychotherapist, and so forth.

protective sweeps of the passenger compartment of a car may be made if an officer has reasonable suspicion "that the suspect is dangerous and . . . may gain immediate control of weapons" (*Michigan v. Long*, 1983). The same is true for a brief protective sweep of premises (*Maryland v. Buie*, 1990).

The Fourth Amendment does not tell us if warrants are *required* for searches and seizures to be deemed "reasonable" and, therefore, constitution-ally valid (see Davies, 1999; Lasson, 1937; Maclin, 1997). While an oversimplifi-cation, the courts have responded to the question with a generalized "yes" but have created a number of exceptions to the warrant requirement, which are summarized in Table 8.2. One overarching exception to the Fourth Amend-ment that should be noted concerns **exigent circumstances**. Exigent circum-stances are those "that would cause a reasonable person to believe that entry (or other relevant prompt action) was necessary to prevent physical harm to the officers or other persons, the destruction of relevant evidence, the escape of a suspect, or some other consequence improperly frustrating legitimate law enforcement efforts" (*United States v. McConney*, 1984, p. 1199). This is because the touchstone of the Fourth Amendment is reasonableness, and compliance with the usual requirements of probable cause and a warrant would be *unrea-sonable* in such emergency, or exigent, situations.

Because the Fourth Amendment originally applied only to the federal government rather than to the state and local governments that had primary responsibility for law enforcement, it had little effect for the first 100 years or so of our nation's history. It really was not until the era of Prohibition that federal law enforcement became so active that Fourth Amendment litigation began to become commonplace. In 1914, the Supreme Court had adopted the exclusionary rule in *Weeks v. United States*. The **exclusionary rule** is a remedy for violations of the Fourth Amendment. The rule stipulates that il-legally seized evidence may not be used in federal criminal trials. Moreover, if the illegal evidence led law enforcement officers to find additional evidence, then it too is also inadmissible. This is called the **fruit of the poisonous tree** doctrine. It provides that secondary evidence gathered as result of some ear-lier constitutional violation must also be excluded (*Silverthorne Lumber Co. v. United States*, 1920).

In *Wolf v. Colorado* (1949), the Supreme Court held that the Fourth Amend-ment protected against the actions of state and local officials. Within 11 years, the Supreme Court extended the exclusionary rule to state trials as the remedy for Fourth Amendment violations by state actors (*Mapp v. Ohio*, 1961). As a re-sult, illegally obtained evidence may not be used in trials at either the federal or state level. Courts, however, dislike the exclusionary rule because it sometimes excludes highly relevant evidence from the trial process. So starting in the early 1980s, as support began to shift from the due process model toward the crime control model, the Supreme Court created a series of exceptions to the exclu-sionary rule that are summarized in Table 8.3.

Table 8.2. Exceptions to the Warrant Requirement

Doctrine	Case(s)	Fourth Amendment Holding
Search Incident to Arrest	*Chimel v. California* (1969)	Police may search someone who is lawfully arrested "to remove any weapons that the latter might seek to use in order to resist arrest or effect his escape." Police may also search for and seize any evidence on the arrestee's person or in the area within his or her immediate control "in order to prevent its concealment or destruction."
Motor Vehicle Searches	*Carroll v. United States* (1925) *California v. Acevedo* (1991) *Florida v. Jimeno* (1991)	The mobility of motor vehicles justifies warrantless searches of them if there is probable cause to believe that the vehicle contains contraband. This includes any location where the particular contraband might be found, such as the trunk, the glove compartment, luggage, and other containers in the vehicle that could hold the contraband.
Consent Searches	*Schneckloth v. Bustamonte* (1973)	Fourth Amendment rights may be voluntarily waived. Thus, if police ask for permission to search without probable cause and/or a warrant and permission is granted, any evidence found may be used in a criminal prosecution. The person granting consent need not know that he or she may refuse consent; accordingly, unlike in the *Miranda* setting, police do not have to inform people that a request to conduct a consensual search may be denied (i.e., that people can refuse to give consent).
Border Searches	*United States v. Ramsey* (1977) *Illinois v. Andreas* (1983)	Searches conducted at any international border do not require a warrant, probable cause, or even reasonable suspicion. This is based on the "longstanding right of the sovereign to protect itself by stopping and examining persons and property crossing into this country" (*United States v. Ramsey*, p. 616).
Open Fields Doctrine	*Cady v. Dombrowski* (1973) *Oliver v. United States* (1984) *United States v. Dunn* (1987)	Because one cannot have a reasonable expectation of privacy in open areas, like fields, forests, open water, vacant lots, and the like, police do not have to comply with the Fourth Amendment's mandates of warrants and probable cause to search open areas, even if "no trespassing" signs are posted. Only areas within the "curtilage" of one's home (i.e., the areas immediately adjacent to a home that the owner has taken steps to keep private, like a detached garage, a locked shed or barn, etc.), receive Fourth Amendment protection.

(continued)

Table 8.2. Exceptions to the Warrant Requirement (continued)

Doctrine	Case(s)	Fourth Amendment Holding
Plain View Doctrine	*Harris v. United States* (1968) *Washington v. Chrisman* (1982)	When a law enforcement officer is legally in a place in which he or she sees contraband or other evidence that provides probable cause to believe criminal activity is afoot, the evidence may be seized without a warrant. The plain view doctrine has been expanded to cover other senses, such as "plain smell."
Special Needs Searches in Public Schools	*New Jersey v. T. L. O.* (1985) *Board of Ed. of Ind. School Dist. 92, Pottawatomie County v. Earls* (2002) *Safford Unified School District v. Redding* (2009)	While the Fourth Amendment applies to searches and seizures conducted by school teachers and administrators, neither probable cause nor a warrant is required. There need be only reasonable "grounds for suspecting that the search will turn up evidence that the student has violated or is violating either the law or the rules of the school" (*New Jersey v. T. L. O.*, 1985, p. 342). Moreover, to curb alcohol and drug abuse in schools, random drug testing of students who participate in extracurricular or athletic activities may be conducted without any individualized suspicion or a warrant. Strip searches of students, however, have been held to go too far.
Searches of Public Employers and/ or their Work Spaces	*O'Connor v. Ortega* (1987) *National Treasury Employees Union v. Von Raab* (1989) *Skinner v. Railway Labor Executives' Assoc.* (1989)	Neither probable cause nor a warrant is necessary for public employers to conduct searches either for work-related purposes or for investigations of work-related misconduct. This includes noninvasive seizures of bodily fluids to conduct random drug tests on public employees whose job functions make it particularly important for them to be drug-free, such as federal law enforcement agents and railroad conductors.
Administrative Searches	*Donovan v. Dewey* (1981) *New York v. Burger* (1981)	Neither probable cause nor a warrant is required to conduct administrative inspections for compliance with regulatory schemes such as fire, health, and safety codes (e.g., inspections of jetliners, mining operations, junkyards, pharmacies, gun stores, etc.).
Searches of People Under Correctional Supervision	*Hudson v. Palmer* (1984) *Sampson v. California* (2006)	Warrantless and suspicionless searches may be conducted of jail or prison cells as well as of the person of inmates in custody, on probation, or on parole.

Table 8.3. Exceptions to the Exclusionary Rule

Exception	Key Case(s)	Effect	Example
Independent Source	*Nix v. Williams* (1984) *Segura v. United States* (1984)	Evidence that is tainted by a Fourth Amendment violation is admissible if it is also obtained from an independent source—a source that had nothing to do with the underlying constitutional violation.	In *Segura*, police illegally entered an apartment and remained inside for nearly 19 hours until a search warrant arrived. Even though the entry was illegal, the evidence collected during the search was admissible because the warrant was supported by probable cause established by information independent (that is, separate) from the illegal entry.
Attenuation	*Nardone v. United States* (1939) *Won Sun v. United States* (1963) *United States v. Ceccolini* (1978)	If evidence is obtained in a manner that is so far removed from a constitutional violation that the initial illegality is sufficiently attenuated (meaning weakened), then the evidence is admissible.	In *Ceccolini*, police conducted an illegal search that led them to discover a key witness. That witness was allowed to testify at trial in spite of the illegal entry because the witness's voluntary cooperation with the police sufficiently attenuated the original violation from the testimonial evidence.
Inevitable Discovery	*Murray v. United States* (1988) *State v. Miller* (Supreme Court of Oregon, 1984)	Allows illegally obtained evidence to be admitted if it would have inevitably been discovered by lawful means.	In *Miller*, police violated a defendant's Miranda rights and got him to confess that he had "hurt someone" in his hotel room. During a warrantless search of the room, a dead body was found. The court ruled that the body would have inevitably been discovered by a hotel maid, so evidence from the room (including the body) was admissible in spite of the Miranda violation and the warrantless search of the room.

(continued)

Table 8.3. **Exceptions to the Exclusionary Rule (continued)**

Exception	Key Case(s)	Effect	Example
Good Faith	*United States v. Leon* (1984) *Arizona v. Evans* (1995)	If a police officer acts in good faith reliance on a warrant that he or she reasonably believes to be valid but later is determined to be invalid, the officer's good faith should allow the evidence to be admissible. There is no police misconduct to be deterred when an officer does not know that he or she is doing anything wrong.	In *Evans*, police lawfully stopped a motor vehicle and found that there was an outstanding arrest warrant for the driver. The officer therefore arrested the driver and searched the vehicle, finding marijuana. The warrant, however, had been dismissed. Thus, the arrest was invalid. But because the officer acted in good faith reliance on a warrant believed to be valid, the search of the vehicle was upheld.

It is important to note that the Fourth Amendment generally applies only to governmental actors (e.g., the police) but not private citizens (*Burdeau v. McDowell*, 1921). However, when private citizens act at the direction of police, they are considered governmental actors for the purposes of the Fourth Amendment (*Coolidge v. New Hampshire,* 1985). Moreover, the term "governmental (or state) actor" is not limited to police or correctional officers. Evidence gathered by governmental inspectors—even teachers in public schools—is covered by the Fourth Amendment and, therefore, may be subject to the exclusionary rule (*New Jersey v. T. L. O.*, 1985). Thus, it is important for all governmental actors to have a thorough understanding of the Fourth Amendment and of relevant Supreme Court cases to ensure that procedural requirements are met so relevant evidence is not excluded.

Finally, you should remember that to challenge a search or seizure on Fourth Amendment grounds, your *own* reasonable expectation of privacy must have been violated. That is, you cannot assert *someone else's* Fourth Amendment rights or raise a challenge on their behalf. In other words, the person whose rights were violated is the person who has to raise the challenge. This is known as the doctrine of **standing**. Standing is a requirement to make a challenge to any alleged violation of constitutional rights, not just Fourth Amendment violations.

The Fifth Amendment. The Fifth Amendment to the U.S. Constitution provides:

No person shall be held to answer for a capital, or otherwise infamous crime, unless on a presentment or indictment of a Grand Jury, except in cases arising in the land or naval forces, or in the Militia, when in actual service in time of War or public danger; nor shall any person be subject for the same offense to be twice put in jeopardy of life or limb; nor shall be compelled in any criminal case to be a witness against himself, nor be deprived of life, liberty, or property, without due process of law; nor shall private property be taken for public use, without just compensation.

A number of important procedural justice rights are contained in this Amendment: the right to indictment by a grand jury, the right to be free from double jeopardy, and the privilege against self-incrimination. We will briefly explore each of these concepts.

A **grand jury** is a group of citizens, often up to 23 people, who review the evidence against a suspect to make sure there is probable cause to believe that the accused has committed a felony. If there is probable cause, then the grand jury returns an **indictment** (sometimes also called a *true bill*). The indictment outlines the facts and circumstances surrounding the crime and the reasons for believing that the accused should stand trial on such charges. If, on the other hand, the grand jury concludes that there is insufficient evidence to make someone stand trial on felony charges, they can refuse to issue an indictment, a process sometimes referred to as issuing a *no bill*. In this case, the process would go no further (unless new evidence was presented), and the accused would not stand trial.

Because of the Fifth Amendment, all felony cases in the federal system are usually presented to a grand jury. However, the Supreme Court ruled in *Hurtado v. California* (1884) that the right to a grand jury indictment was not so important that it needed to be applied to the states via the Fourteenth Amendment's Due Process Clause. Accordingly, not all states use a grand jury system. Rather, some states have judges make determination of probable cause in open court at a judicial proceeding called a **preliminary hearing**. Similar to a grand jury, if a judge finds probable cause, the case proceeds; if not, the process stops and there is no trial. States that use grand juries often do so because their state constitutions or state laws require it.

Double jeopardy is a complex concept. In its most basic form, **double jeopardy** bars the same governmental entity from criminally prosecuting and bringing someone to trial twice for the same offense. It also bars "multiple punishments for the same offense" (*Justices of Boston Municipal Court v. Lydon*, 1984, p. 307). However, there are a number of exceptions to these general principles. For example, a second trial for the same offense may occur when the first trial results in a deadlocked jury being unable to reach a unanimous verdict. Retrial may also occur when a conviction is reversed on appeal and remanded for a new trial. Since the concept only limits successive prosecutions by the same governmental sovereign (e.g., the same state), it does not bar a second trial by a different sovereign government, like the federal government or that of another state. For example, assume that someone lies down across the state border between Iowa and Nebraska so that he is simultaneously in both states. If he were shot to death at that moment, both Iowa and Nebraska could place the shooter on trial for murder without violating the Double Jeopardy Clause. And finally, keep in mind that the doctrine only applies in criminal, not civil, cases. Therefore, someone acquitted of homicide charges in criminal court can still be sued for wrongful death in civil court, which uses a lower burden of proof.

The **privilege against self-incrimination** protects a person against being incriminated by his or her own compelled "testimonial communications." A testimonial communication occurs when persons disclose information verbally or in writing. Thus, the privilege against self-incrimination does not prevent the government from forcing someone to appear in a lineup; to give a voice, breath, blood, or handwriting sample; or to be fingerprinted, even if doing so would incriminate him or her. The privilege does, however, allow a person to refuse to testify against himself or herself at a criminal trial. It also allows someone to refuse to answer questions before a trial that might later be used against him or her.

You are probably familiar with the commonly known words of *Miranda v. Arizona* (1966): "You have the right to remain silent. Anything you say can and will be used against you in a court of law. You have the right to have an attorney present during questioning. If you cannot afford an attorney, one will be appointed for you." The Supreme Court ruled in *Miranda* that police had to inform suspects of their **Miranda rights** before starting to question someone who is in custody, to ensure that suspects knew of the privilege against self-incrimination. If the police fail to issue such warnings, then the information gained during the interrogation—even a confession—becomes inadmissible under the exclusionary rule. Such statements could not be used unless one of the exceptions listed in Table 8.3 applied.

Contrary to popular belief, Miranda rights do not need to be read to someone upon arrest. Miranda rights are designed to protect someone in custody from being forced to provide incriminating information about themselves while being interrogated. If there is no interrogation, then *Miranda* does not apply. **Interrogation** includes not only direct questioning but also any statements or actions that are designed to elicit an incriminating response from a suspect (*Rhode Island v. Innis*, 1980). Moreover, for *Miranda* to apply, the interrogation must occur while the suspect is in **custody**. Custody not only includes situations when someone is under formal arrest but also situations that are the "functional equivalent" of arrest. Such situations occur when a reasonable person would no longer feel free "to terminate the interrogation and leave" (*Thompson v. Keohane*, 1995, p. 112).

Once informed of Miranda rights, people are free to waive them. Valid **waivers** occur when people knowingly, intelligently, and voluntarily give up their constitutional rights. If police used physical force, intimidation, threats, deception, or other forms of coercion to get suspects to waive their rights, the waiver would be ineffective because it was not voluntary (*Moran v. Burbine*, 1986).

The law of self-incrimination is complicated. There are numerous rules, exceptions to those rules, and exceptions to the exceptions. Our goal here is not to provide you with a detailed understanding of Miranda or the privilege against self-incrimination. Rather, you should see that there are a series of procedures in place designed to make sure the criminal justice system treats suspects fairly—the core value of procedural justice.

The Sixth Amendment. The Sixth Amendment to the U.S. Constitution states:

> In all criminal prosecutions, the accused shall enjoy the right to a speedy and public trial, by an impartial jury of the State and district wherein the crime shall have been committed, which district shall have been previously ascertained by law, and to be informed of the nature and cause of the accusation; to be confronted with the witnesses against him; to have compulsory process for obtaining witnesses in his favor, and to have the Assistance of Counsel for his defence.

As you see, the text of the Sixth Amendment begins with the phrase "in all criminal prosecutions." That phrase is a bit misleading. It is accurate insofar as the rights in the Amendment are limited to criminal cases and, therefore, do not apply in civil court, including juvenile delinquency proceedings which are technically civil in nature (*McKeiver v. Pennsylvania*, 1971). However, the word *all* really should read *most*. For example, while *all* criminal defendants are entitled to a speedy and public trial (see *Barker v. Wingo*, 1972), the right to have a trial by jury depends on the type of case. As a rule, the right to a **trial by jury** exists only for felonies and misdemeanors that are not "petty offenses." In *Baldwin v. New York* (1970), the Supreme Court ruled that, for the purpose of the right to trial by jury, a petty offense is any misdemeanor case that carries a potential sentence of less than six months of incarceration. Accordingly, the right to trial by jury only exists when a defendant is facing jail time of six months or more. For crimes that carry lower penalties, a **bench trial** will be conducted—a trial in which the judge determines the verdict. A bench trial may also occur in cases when a defendant who is entitled to a trial by jury waives that right with the approval of the court.

Notice of the criminal charges someone is facing is an important right guaranteed by the Sixth Amendment. It provides the accused with an opportunity to prepare a defense. Notice is typically provided in two ways. First, written notice is provided in a *charging document*. There are three primary types of charging documents: *indictments* (issued by a grand jury), *informations* (filed by prosecutors), and *complaints* (signed and sworn by a police officer or victim of a crime). Second, oral notice is given during various pretrial court proceedings, such as the initial appearance and the arraignment. These procedures are discussed in more detail in Chapter 12.

To ensure the reliability of evidence, witnesses cannot provide testimony secretly. Rather, they must do so in open court and be subject to cross-examination (*Maryland v. Craig*, 1990). The portion of the Sixth Amendment that guarantees these rights is referred to as the **Confrontation Clause**. "The opportunity for cross-examination . . . is critical for ensuring the integrity of the fact-finding process. Cross-examination is 'the principal means by which the believability of a witness and the truth of his testimony are tested'" (*Kentucky v. Stincer*, 1987, p. 736). The Confrontation Clause significantly limits the use of out-of-court statements by people who are not testifying at trial (see *Crawford v. Washington*, 2004).

A defendant has the right to subpoena witnesses to testify on his or her behalf. A **subpoena** is a court order commanding a witness to appear in court at a specific date to provide sworn testimony in a case.

Finally, the Sixth Amendment guarantees the right to counsel. Historically, this right meant something very different than it does now. At the time the Sixth Amendment was adopted, the Right to Counsel Clause was included to ensure that people who could afford to hire lawyers were free to do so—a right people still enjoy to this day (Neubauer & Fradella, 2011). But the courts' interpretation of the Sixth Amendment has changed over time. Today, people who cannot afford to hire their own attorney must be provided with one free of charge. This right to free counsel applies to any criminal defendant facing potential jail time for either a felony or a misdemeanor offense (*Argersinger v. Hamlin*, 1972; *Gideon v. Wainwright*, 1963).

Of course, the right to counsel does a defendant no good if the attorney does not represent the defendant competently. The Supreme Court has therefore interpreted the Sixth Amendment as guaranteeing the **effective assistance of counsel** (*Strickland v. Washington*, 1984). Accordingly, when a lawyer's performance falls so far below the standard of reasonable competence that the outcome of the case is likely to be unfair or unreliable, the Sixth Amendment provides a remedy for a new trial to occur (*Lockhart v. Fretwell*, 1993).

The Fourteenth Amendment. The Fourteenth Amendment to the U.S. Constitution provides that:

> All persons born or naturalized in the United States, and subject to the jurisdiction thereof, are citizens of the United States and of the State wherein they reside. No State shall make or enforce any law which shall abridge the privileges or immunities of citizens of the United States; nor shall any State deprive any person of life, liberty, or property, without due process of law; nor deny to any person within its jurisdiction the equal protection of the laws. . . .

Arguably, no other provision in the U.S. Constitution is more important to procedural justice than the Fourteenth Amendment in light of its guarantees of due process and **equal protection**.

Recall that most of the provisions that have been discussed originally applied only to the federal government. Although an oversimplification, the **Due Process Clause** of the Fourteenth Amendment was responsible for making nearly all of the criminal procedural rights guaranteed in the Bill of Rights (and discussed earlier in this chapter) applicable to the states (e.g., *Gitlow v. New York*, 1925). Additionally, the Due Process Clause has been interpreted as providing an independent source for other procedural justice rights that are not specifically enumerated, or listed, in the Constitution or Bill of Rights. For instance, requiring proof beyond a reasonable doubt for criminal convictions (*In re Winship*, 1970) is grounded in the Due Process Clause. Forbidding a state from compelling a criminal defendant to stand trial before a jury while dressed in identifiable prison clothes is another example (*Estelle v. Williams*, 1976). The Due Process Clause has also been interpreted as the basis for providing substantive rights not explicitly guaranteed in the Constitution. Such substantive rights include the right to privacy (see *Lawrence v. Texas*, 2003), the right of the mentally ill to be free from undue restraints (*Youngberg v. Romeo*, 1982), and the right to refuse medical treatment even if that means a patient will die (*Cruzan v. Director, Missouri Department of Health*, 1990), just to name a few.

Similarly, the **Equal Protection Clause** of the Fourteenth Amendment is a cornerstone of procedural justice. Recall that Tyler's model of procedural justice required that people perceive the justice system as treating people alike, a concern shared by social justice advocates and instrumental to the equality promoted by American political culture. The Equal Protection Clause serves to guarantee equality, requiring that the law treat similarly situated people in a similar manner. Thus, the government may not discriminate based on characteristics like race, ethnicity, and religion (see *Brown v. Board of Education*, 1954).

Which of the preceding procedural rights did the SUNY New Paltz case illustrate? Which procedural rights were not part of the campus disciplinary system that you think should have been? Why?

Because the students in the SUNY New Paltz case were not being interrogated while "in custody" during their campus disciplinary hearing, Miranda rights were not a concern in that case. However, the larger principle of self-incrimination was. How? What protections, if any, should have been provided?

Are there any rights, beyond those discussed in this section, that you think should be provided in criminal proceedings? Explain your answer.

The exclusionary rule has been very controversial, leading some to call for abolishing it. What are the arguments for and against the use of the exclusionary rule? Do you think it should continue to be utilized in the criminal justice system? Why or why not?

Conclusion

Procedural justice is concerned about the ways laws are enforced. At the heart of this concern is the notion of "fundamental fairness." Philosophy and social psychology can inform us about perceptions of fairness, but the U.S. Constitution is what ultimately sets the minimum requirements for procedural justice. It does so not only by guaranteeing due process and equal protection of the laws but also by guaranteeing a number of specific procedural rights to all who are accused of committing a crime. The criminal justice system attempts to follow its procedures as closely as possible in an ongoing attempt to balance societal needs for crime control with the due process mandates of the Constitution. In Unit IV, we will continue to explore the pursuit of justice through the role of substantive criminal law and punishment.

Criminal Justice Problem Solving: **DETAINING COMBATANTS**

In response to the terrorist attacks of September 11, 2001, then President George W. Bush authorized the indefinite detention and military trial of suspected terrorists or enemy combatants at "an appropriate location" outside the United States (3 C.F.R. § 918, 2002). As a result, roughly 500 prisoners had been detained at the U.S. military base in Guantánamo Bay, Cuba. Although the U.S. government denied these detainees access to the U.S. courts, the U.S. Supreme Court ruled in 2004 that enemy combatants had the right to have their detentions reviewed by an impartial judge as part of the guarantees of both due process and *habeas corpus* (*Hamdi v. Rumsfeld*, 2004; *Rasul v. Bush*, 2004). In response to these rulings, the Department of Defense created Combatant Status Review Tribunals (CSRTs) to review the legality of enemy combatant detentions at Guantánamo. These were ***ex parte*** proceedings, meaning that they took place without the detainee or his or her counsel present. The Supreme Court declared the CSRTs illegal in *Hamdan v. Rumsfeld* (2006) because the process failed to comply with the Uniform Code of Military Justice and part of the Geneva Conventions (an international treaty governing the treatment of prisoners of war). Because the Court invalidated the CSRTs on these grounds, it declined to consider the underlying constitutional question of whether the CSRT process violated the *habeas corpus* provisions in Article I, Section 9, Clause 2 of the U.S. Constitution.

Congress responded to the *Hamdan* decision by passing legislation to authorize military commissions to hold CSRTs with additional procedural safeguards that were included in the tribunals originally created by the Department of Defense. The law specifically provided that the decisions of these commissions were not reviewable by means of *habeas corpus*. Congress extended this law when it enacted the Military Commissions Act of 2006. It provides similar CSRTs for all non-U.S. citizens being held as enemy combatants anywhere in the world. In *Boumediene v. Bush* (2008), a five-person majority of the justices on the U.S. Supreme Court determined that the Military Commissions Act amounted to an "unconstitutional suspension of the writ" of *habeas corpus*.

Which of Rawls's procedural justice models, if any, is applicable to CSRTs? Explain.

Clearly, the U.S. government's approach to enemy combatants is heavily weighted toward crime control in that it seeks to combat terrorism. Putting aside the issue of *habeas corpus* just for a moment, what procedural due process rights in the U.S. Constitution are being denied to enemy combatants? Should enemy combatants be entitled to any of the due process rights described in this chapter? Explain your answer.

Do you agree with the narrow majority in *Boumediene v. Bush* that the Military Commissions Act of 2006 violates the *habeas corpus* provisions in Article I, Section 9, Clause 2 of the U.S. Constitution? Explain your reasoning.

Unit Four

Penal Social Control

Photo Essay: Bullying

Unit III considered the various ways justice may be constructed: philosophically, politically, and procedurally. Unit IV will explore the two primary means through which justice may be achieved: substantive criminal law and criminal punishment. Substantive criminal law is the listing of acts that have been deemed illegal. This combines the definitions of deviance discussed in Unit II and the ideals of justice discussed in Unit III, as both shape the appearance of the laws that the criminal justice system is charged with upholding. Just as there are laws, there are inevitably persons who break them and who are then punished for doing so. There are many debates about what makes a punishment fair, just, and appropriate.

Consider the issue of bullying in schools. Although bullying has occurred for many years, it has only recently come to be viewed as a serious problem that school officials, legislators, and others have worked to address. While states have taken steps to address bullying in their legal codes, the most common response has been to require schools to develop bullying prevention programs and to address bullying in their own discipline codes. However, some have suggested that incidents of bullying should be criminalized. Consider how the law might regulate bullying.

Can bullying be distinguished from assault? For instance, consider this definition of third-degree assault: "A person commits the crime of assault in the third degree if . . . The person purposely places another person in apprehension of immediate physical injury" (Assault in the Third Degree, 2010). Would the scenario pictured meet this definition? Would it be preferable to use third-degree assault charges, or should there be a separate law against bullying? Or should bullying be dealt with through informal social control? Why?

If bullying were criminalized, the law would have to carefully define it so everyone would know what acts the law prohibited. How would you define

bullying? Here is one legal definition of bullying: "any written or verbal expression, or physical act or gesture, or a pattern thereof, that is intended to cause distress upon one or more students in the school" (Board of Education, 2010). How does this definition match yours? Would you change this definition in any way? In the cartoon, has either character committed an act of bullying? Why?

Legislators have begun to propose laws to address the problem of cyberbullying. It is important for all laws to be very clear and precise. If laws are not clear, they may be void for vagueness. This means that courts may strike down and render unenforceable laws that are not clear in their description of the prohibited behavior. Consider a cyberbullying law that prohibits communications "about another student . . . which a reasonable person under

the circumstances should know would cause the other student to suffer fear of physical harm, intimidation, humiliation, or embarrassment and which serves no purpose of legitimate communication" (Harassing Communications, 2008). Do you believe this law gives adequate notice of what behaviors are prohibited? Why or why not? If not, how could it be improved?

In addition to being clear and specific, laws must be crafted so they do not intrude upon any constitutionally protected freedoms. If they do, then they are said to be overbroad and unenforceable. For instance, consider shunning as a bullying behavior in which a group of students may deliberately decide to visibly ignore another student entirely, acting as though he or she is not there. Is this a behavior that should be prohibited by a bullying law? Where

is the line between the right to choose with whom one wants to associate and be friends, and engaging in behaviors that create a climate of bullying? What do you think?

Once a crime has been defined, a punishment must be associated with it. Some schools have identified themselves as bully-free zones, signaling a commitment to reducing bullying behaviors. There are multiple approaches to doing so. What if, under the law, the first incident of bullying resulted in a student's suspension and the second incident resulted in expulsion? This would be known as a zero-tolerance policy, imposing a quick and serious punishment regardless of the circumstances surrounding the incident (see Lyons & Drew, 2006). Do you think this would be a good punishment? Why or why not? What positive or negative effects do you think it might have?

Rather than zero tolerance, another approach is to prevent bullying through the work of school counselors, creating safe and inviting atmospheres within the school as a whole (Stanley, Small, Owen, & Burke, in press). Which do you think is the better approach: punishing, preventing, or counseling? Why? Ultimately, this is an issue that the criminal justice system must address in determining what role punishment ought to play.

Through the example of a single issue—bullying—it quickly becomes clear that criminal law and punishment are perhaps more complex than they may seem at first glance. Even after an act has been deemed deviant and worthy of formal social control, laws must be carefully crafted and punishments carefully considered. This unit will explore the nature of criminal law and the philosophies of criminal punishment, both of which ultimately shape the work of law enforcement, court, and correctional professionals.

Criminal Law

Tablet containing the Code of Ur-Nammu, the oldest known legal code. How do you think crimes should be defined under modern criminal law?

Key Terms

substantive criminal law
Code of Ur-Namma
Code of Hammurabi
lex talionis
restitution
trial by ordeal
Magna Carta
Model Penal Code (MPC)
actus reus
mens rea
strict liability
attendant circumstances
result
cause in fact

proximate cause
crimes against the person
crimes against property
inchoate crimes
defense
defenses of excuse
defenses of justification
procedural defenses
symbolic speech
overbreadth
Establishment Clause
Free Exercise Clause
substantive due process

CASE STUDY

Copyright Infringement

If you have purchased or rented a movie on DVD, you have probably seen this warning:

> The unauthorized reproduction or distribution of this copyrighted work is illegal. Criminal copyright infringement, including infringement without monetary gain, is investigated by the FBI and is punishable by up to five years in federal prison and a fine of $250,000.

In late May 2008, Barry Gitarts became the first person ever convicted by a federal jury for engaging in criminal copyright infringement involving the illegal online swapping of music. Mr. Gitarts was accused of running a server for an Internet-based piracy group known as the Apocalypse Production Crew (APC). The APC had hundreds of thousands of pirated songs, movies, and games on the server available for illegal downloading. He was sentenced to 18 months in federal prison, two years of supervised release, and a $2,500 fine (U.S. Department of Justice, 2008).

> Should copyright infringement be handled through the criminal justice system or through civil lawsuits for monetary damages? Why?
>
> In October 2007, the Recording Industry Association of America won a civil lawsuit for copyright infringement against a Minnesota woman who had illegally shared 24 songs online using a peer-to-peer Internet filesharing program (Leeds, 2007). The jury imposed $222,000 in damages—$9,250 for each song. Do you agree with the outcome of the case? Explain why. Why do you think this case was handled through the civil justice system and Gitarts's case was criminally prosecuted?

The History of Criminal Law

FOCUSING QUESTION 9.1

How did U.S. criminal law evolve into its present form?

Crime is defined as "an intentional act [or omission] in violation of the criminal law . . . , committed without defense or excuse, and penalized by the state as a felony or misdemeanor" (Tappan, 1947, p. 100). In this chapter, we focus on legal prescriptions and proscriptions—the "rules" of what one must do or must not do, respectively. These rules comprise **substantive criminal law**. The chapter first surveys the history of criminal law. It will then move to a discussion of criminal offenses, defenses to criminal charges, and constitutionally imposed limits on what behaviors may be made criminal.

CRIMINAL LAW IN ANCIENT CIVILIZATIONS

The earliest known written set of laws is the **Code of Ur-Namma** (often called Ur-Nammu) from Sumer around 2100 B.C.E. (Roth, Hoffner, & Michalowski, 1997). This ancient Sumerian code set forth its laws in an "if–then" manner. For example, *if* a man committed the act of kidnapping (the crime), *then* the code specified that he was to be imprisoned and pay a fine in silver (the punishment). This was the pattern in most of the legal codes that followed. In comparison to other ancient legal codes, the punishments in the Code of Ur-Namma were remarkably humane. The code used monetary fines as the predominant form of punishment, even for crimes that inflicted bodily injury. Only crimes viewed as most serious by ancient Sumerian society—murder, robbery, adultery, and rape—were punishable by death (Roth et al., 1997).

The better-known **Code of Hammurabi**, a codification of ancient Babylonian laws, was written approximately 300 years after the Code of Ur-Namma. Like the older Sumerian code, it did not distinguish between civil and criminal law. The Code of Hammurabi was tied to the theology of the time. Hammurabi believed these laws had been given to him by various gods, some of whom had personalities that led them to act arbitrarily. Hammurabi thought having his subjects abide by these divine laws would not only promote justice and fairness in his kingdom but also would keep capricious gods happy (Rosenblatt, 2003). To achieve these goals, the code provided punishments for all types of wrongs. However, unlike the Code of Ur-Namma, the Code of Hammurabi focused much more extensively on retribution, a philosophy of punishment grounded in notions of giving to offenders the type of pain they delivered to their victims (see Chapter 10). In fact, retributive punishment is often interpreted as embodying the principle of *lex talionis*—"an eye for an eye, a tooth for a tooth"—as stated in the code.

The principle of *lex talionis* was continued by the Hebrews in their adaptations of ancient Babylonian law. Indeed, the law of Moses as expressed in

Exodus 21:22–25 says: "eye for eye, tooth for tooth, hand for hand, foot for foot, burn for burn, wound for wound, bruise for bruise." However, unlike Babylonian law, compliance with Mosaic Hebrew law was not viewed as having magical powers to control the arbitrary acts of a deity. Rather, Moses saw the law as a moral code dictated by God that represented a contract. Under this covenant, God would not act capriciously but rather would protect His followers as long as they "held up their end of the bargain by adhering to a prescribed ethical tract" (Rosenblatt, 2003, p. 2127). In light of the nature of the covenant, scholars who study biblical law usually do not interpret the expressions of *lex talionis* in Exodus and similar biblical passages as advocating revenge. Instead, the principle represents "a measured and proportionate response to punishable conduct by a member of the community . . . [a] rationality as the defining features of . . . punishment [rather than] the unbridled and unchecked vengeance that had earlier prevailed" (Fish, 2008, p. 61).

CRIMINAL LAW IN ANCIENT GREECE AND ROME

Ancient Greek civilization is credited with being both the birthplace of democracy and of Western jurisprudence. The Greeks "invented the revolutionary idea that human beings are capable of governing themselves through laws of their own making, and seizing control of their destinies" (Rosenblatt, 2003, p. 2129). The Greeks conceptualized law as divinely inspired, not divinely given. Moreover, the Greeks did not see compliance with the law as being reverent to their deities. Rather, they saw obedience to the law as part of one's civic duty and, above all, as rational behavior necessary for the orderly control of the universe.

At first, there were few, if any, written laws in ancient Greece. Draco codified the first set of Greek laws in an era when Greece was an oligarchy (ruled by a small, wealthy class). His laws were so oppressive and punitive (indeed, death was the most common penalty) that today we use his name to refer to unduly harsh punishments as "Draconian." When Solon became the governor of Athens in roughly 594 B.C.E., Greece was transforming into a more democratic society. Due to Solon's work, the Greeks eventually came to conceptualize crime differently from other ancient civilizations. They began to distinguish between private wrongs, akin to our civil law, and offenses that harmed the community as a whole, akin to our criminal law (Calhoun, 1927). The city-state of Athens led the development of a system of criminal law and procedures. These included the creation of a system to prosecute specific acts before public courts comprised of citizens (keep in mind that neither women nor slaves were citizens in Athens). These citizens served in large numbers (often in excess of 500) on juries that decided both guilt and punishment (MacDowell, 1978). However, there was no public prosecutor; proceedings could be initiated by any Athenian citizen. Moreover, many acts that we think of today as crimes, such as homicide and rape, were not viewed as true crimes in ancient Greece (Calhoun, 1927).

Unlike punishments under other ancient codes, Greek punishments focused on **restitution**—the payment of money to the victim. Still, even after Solon's reforms, punishments for some crimes remained quite harsh, including death, imprisonment, fines, and exile/banishment. In addition, the Greeks used the deprivation of civil rights as a form of punishment, including the loss of the rights to vote, to serve as a juror, to speak in the public forum, or to have a proper burial (see Cohen, 2005).

The blur between civil and criminal law continued in ancient Rome. The *Lex Duodecim Tabularum*—Law of the Twelve Tables—marginally separated criminal law from other forms of law. However, the punishments for a number of acts that we think of as crimes today were often civil in nature. For example, thefts, assaults, and robberies were treated as civil property violations (see Robinson, 1990). As such, the remedies for these offenses were monetary compensation.

By the time of the Emperor Justinian, a clearer division between civil wrongs and true crimes had evolved. Crimes included "treason, adultery, assassination, parricide, kidnapping, and extortion, among others" (Lindgren, 1996, p. 39). Most crimes were punishable by death or by exile enforced by transportation to a far-off land. Other common criminal punishments in ancient Rome included flogging, torture, enslavement, and imprisonment (Lindgren, 1996).

CRIMINAL LAW CHANGES IN EARLY CHRISTENDOM

With the fall of the Roman Empire in the early fifth century, much of western Europe fell under the control of the kings of Germanic tribes from modern-day Scandinavia. Germanic tribal justice blended retributive and restorative justice. Their conceptualization of *lex talionis* was used to support blood feuds—killings to avenge killings. But blood feuds could be avoided through the payment of restitution, even for murder, rape, theft, and assault (Milsom, 1976).

Meanwhile, Christianity grew throughout the first century. This, too, affected criminal law. The ancient Greeks and Romans viewed natural law as a function of the orderly operation of the universe. This belief was premised on the fact that "chaos and unreason cannot explain the order of nature"; therefore, "rules of conduct must rest on certain universal norms that are fixed and permanent in nature" (Rosenblatt, 2003, p. 2130). As Christianity spread through Europe during the Middle Ages, a theological conceptualization of natural law took hold. Largely due to the works of St. Augustine (354–430) and St. Thomas Aquinas (1225–1274), natural law became viewed as the "will of God" (Rosenblatt, 2003, p. 2135). As the power of the Roman Catholic Church grew, God's law as expressed in Catholic ecclesiastical (i.e., religious) law, blended with secular (i.e., nonreligious) law such that the distinction between the two became almost impossible to discern. Criminal law trials became searches for the "truth" of God's will in a particular case. Perhaps the best example of this belief was the notion of **trial by ordeal**.

In trial-by-ordeal, the accused was made to hold a scalding or burning object and the verdict would depend on the degree of injury—which reflected God's intervention. The judge [often a religious official] would wait for three days to see if the hand had healed, and, if it did, the accused was cleared. In cases where this seventy-two-hour delay seemed too long for the crowd to wait, the trier-of-fact would employ trial by water. This carried immediate results. The accused who floated was guilty. If the accused sank, it was a sign of innocence, even though it might have had other consequences. (Rosenblatt, 2003, pp. 2135–2136)

CRIMINAL LAW IN EARLY ENGLAND

Trial by ordeal was the norm in England at the turn of the second century. But the Norman invasion of England in 1066 marked a major change in the philosophy and administration of law (see Pennington, 1993). William the Conqueror blended Germanic tribal justice with English traditions, much of which had been influenced by Catholic theology and earlier conceptualizations of crime and punishment. By the time Henry II ruled England in the mid- to late-twelfth century, English common law began to develop. Under this approach, crimes were no longer private matters but instead were viewed as offenses against the Crown (Rosenblatt, 2003). Because of this shift, the law of the land began to become harmonized into a "common law"—one law that applied consistently throughout the king's lands.

In 1215, King John agreed to the **Magna Carta**, Latin for "great charter." Article 39 of that document provided: "No free man shall be taken, imprisoned, disseised, outlawed, banished, or in any way destroyed . . . except by the lawful judgment of his peers and by the law of the land." The next clause went on to state: "To no one will We sell . . . deny or delay right of justice." Originally, these protections were meant for noblemen, but they quickly grew to apply to all citizens. Once so interpreted, it should be clear that these statements formed the basis of the due process guarantees in the U.S. Constitution (see Chapter 8).

FROM ENGLISH COMMON LAW TO MODERN PENAL LAWS

Tracing the evolution of English common law (see Hale, 1971/1713) to its maturation in the United States is beyond the scope of this book (see Holmes, [1881] 1991; Langbein, 2003). We note, though, that modern criminal law largely depended on how crimes were defined, and defenses were fashioned in England from the period of Henry II to the time of the American Revolution. Those legal concepts have continued to mature, with modern criminal law being a mixture of the common-law tradition and a series of statutory changes that have been made over the years. The most significant changes to American criminal law occurred from the mid-1960s through the mid-1980s as a result of the American Law Institute (ALI) publishing the **Model Penal Code (MPC)** in 1962 and updating it in 1981.

The ALI is a think tank devoted to simplifying and harmonizing the common law across the 50 states to lead to more consistency among states. Comprised of judges, lawyers, and scholars from a variety of disciplines, the ALI researches and writes "model" sets of laws governing penal codes, probate codes (the law of wills, trusts, and estates), foreign relations, unfair competition, property, torts, contracts, employment law, and criminal law. Although none of these model sets of laws is the actual law of any particular state, they are highly influential. For example, the ALI's *MPC* has served as the basis for replacing or updating the criminal laws of more than two-thirds of all U.S. states (Robinson, 2008).

> What do you think of the concept of retributive punishment? Does it achieve justice through revenge, or do you think it is cruel and vengeful? Defend your position.
>
> In reviewing the brief history presented in this section, what common themes can you find that are illustrated across the historical legal systems described? Have they influenced the American justice system?
>
> Given the significant influence that the *MPC* has had on statutory criminal law across the United States, why do you think we do not have a single criminal code based on it that applies in all states throughout the country? Should we?

Common Elements of Modern Criminal Law

FOCUSING QUESTION 9.2

Explain the four primary components of modern criminal law.

Under both the common law and the *MPC*, crimes generally consist of a combination of two or more of four components: *actus reus*, *mens rea*, attendant circumstances, and a result.

ACTUS REUS

Every crime establishes some act or conduct that is prohibited—the "thing" you are not allowed to do under the criminal law. Such proscribed conduct is called the ***actus reus*** (Latin for the "evil act"). For example, taking the personal property of another (if coupled with the mental state of intent to steal) is the crime of theft. The *actus reus* is the actual taking of the property.

An *actus reus* must be the result of either a voluntary act or a qualifying omission. A "voluntary act" is a bodily movement performed consciously as a result of effort. For example, punching someone is a voluntary act that would qualify as the *actus reus* for the crime of battery. Similarly, shooting someone is a voluntary act that would qualify as the *actus reus* for a homicide if the victim died. Even speaking certain words may be a voluntary act upon which a criminal prosecution may be based if the words spoken are prohibited. Criminal solicitation and using fighting words to incite a riot are examples. In contrast, an involuntary act does not qualify as an *actus reus*. Involuntary acts are bodily movements that are not produced by conscious effort, such as reflexes, spasms, or spontaneous convulsions.

An omission—a failure to perform an act of which a person is physically capable—may also qualify as an *actus reus* if the law places an affirmative duty on (i.e., requires) someone to act. Assume that the law tells you that you must do something, but then you fail to do it. Your failure to have done what the law indicated you were supposed to do is an omission that can qualify as an *actus reus*. Examples include failure to yield the right of way and failure to file and pay income taxes. A legal duty to act may also be imposed by relationship. For example, a parent has a legal duty to care for his or her child. A failure to provide for the reasonable health, safety, and welfare of a child is an omission that qualifies as the *actus reus* for the crime of child neglect. A legal duty to act can also be created by contract. Babysitters, lifeguards, and bodyguards agree to act to protect those under their care. If they fail to do so, then such a failure to act could qualify as an *actus reus*.

MENS REA

Most crimes do not impose a criminal sanction for doing an *actus reus* unless it is done with a culpable state of mind referred to as the **mens rea** (Latin for "evil mind"). *Mens rea* is concerned with the level of intent to commit an *actus reus*. In most cases, if there is no intent to commit the *actus reus*, then there is no crime. Compare two situations. If you were to accidentally and unknowingly pick up a classmate's copy of a textbook while gathering your materials at the end of class and then leave the classroom, you would most likely not have committed a crime. You would have completed the *actus reus* by taking someone else's property, but you would have had no *mens rea*, or intent to do so. If, on the other hand, you saw your classmate's book and purposefully decided to take it because it was in better condition than yours, you would have completed the *actus reus* of taking someone else's property with the *mens rea* of having done so intentionally, therefore committing a crime.

The common-law approach to *mens rea* was quite confusing, using terms like specific intent, general intent, and acting with malice. The *MPC* identified four levels of *mens rea*: purpose, knowledge, recklessness, and negligence (see Table 9.1). The level of *mens rea* often differentiates an accident from a crime or serious crimes (with a higher level of intent) from petty ones (with a lower level of intent).

A narrow range of crimes are exceptions to the requirement of a union of *actus reus* and *mens rea*. Offenses that are punished *without regard* to the actor's state of mind are referred to as crimes of **strict liability**. A person can be convicted of a strict liability crime for having engaged in the proscribed act (the *actus reus*) even though there was no accompanying criminal intent (*mens rea*). Thus, a person acting without any *mens rea* may nonetheless be convicted

Table 9.1. Levels of *Mens Rea* Under the *Model Penal Code*

Mens Rea	Definition	Example
Purpose	A conscious objective or desire either to engage in prohibited conduct, or to cause a particular illegal result.	Defendant points and shoots a gun at a victim that the shooter intends to kill (without any legally recognized justification or excuse). Victim dies from the gunshot. Defendant acted purposefully (i.e., with specific intent to kill).
Knowledge	*Actual Knowledge:* Subjectively knowing, to a practical certainty, that one is either engaging in prohibited conduct or, alternatively, engaging in conduct that will cause an illegal result. *Constructive Knowledge:* Lacking actual knowledge but remaining willfully blind to circumstances under which a person should have known, to a practical certainty, that one is either engaging in prohibited conduct or, alternatively, engaging in conduct that will cause an illegal result.	Defendant is approached by a stranger who offers $1,000 in cash to drive a locked U-Haul from one city to another. Stranger offers $500 up front, and $500 upon successful delivery of the truck with its contents undisturbed. It turns out that the U-Haul contained marijuana. Defendant was in knowing possession of a controlled substance even though he did not have actual knowledge that the truck contained drugs. He did, however, have constructive knowledge that the U-Haul contained some contraband in light of the circumstances under which the deal was made.
Recklessness	Acting with conscious disregard of a known risk that is both substantial and unjustifiable, resulting in harm.	While drag racing at high speeds on a city street, a driver loses control of the vehicle and causes an accident that kills a bystander. The driver acted recklessly since he knew of, and consciously disregarded, the risk of a serious accident that could be caused by drag racing under such conditions.
Negligence	Unconsciously creating a risk of harm by failing to perceive a substantial and unjustifiable risk that the ordinary, reasonable, prudent person would have perceived.	While hiking, Defendant's girlfriend trips and sprains her ankle. To help her sleep that night, Defendant gives his girlfriend narcotic painkillers and sleeping pills that had been prescribed for him. She dies of an accidental overdose in light of the mixing of these drugs with other medicines she had been taking. Even though Defendant did not think about the possible consequences of giving the drugs to her, he should have been aware of the risk of giving the pills to someone for whom they were not prescribed. Accordingly, Defendant negligently killed his girlfriend.

of a strict liability crime. Strict liability most frequently attaches to offenses against the public health, safety, and welfare, such as motor vehicle laws and laws regulating the sale of drugs, food, and alcohol. Strict liability has also traditionally been applied to certain morals offenses, such as statutory rape (i.e., sexual intercourse with an underage person), adultery, fornication, and public intoxication. Assume, for example, that a 22-year-old man has consensual sexual intercourse with a female whom he reasonably believes to be 18, although she is actually 16. Further, assume that the jurisdiction sets the age of consent at 18 years of age. Although she was a willing participant, the man would be guilty of the crime of statutory rape in that jurisdiction because he committed the *actus reus,* and statutory rape has traditionally been punished as a strict liability offense that does not require *mens rea.* Finally, strict liability also may be applied to elements not central to the criminality of an act, such as to attendant circumstances, discussed in the following section.

ATTENDANT CIRCUMSTANCES

The third major component of crime is **attendant circumstances**. These are circumstances which must surround the occurrence of an *actus reus* for a crime to have occurred (or for it to be punished in a particular manner). For example, the crime of speeding does not take place unless one is traveling on a public roadway. Hence, it is not a crime to race in the Indianapolis 500 because the attendant circumstance of being on a public roadway is not present. Theft is another example. Taking the personal property of another, if coupled with the *mens rea* of specific intent or purpose to steal, constitutes the crime of theft. The *actus reus* is taking property. That taking of property must occur under two attendant circumstances. First, the property must be personal property as opposed to real property like real estate. Second, it must be the property of another person. Thus, if you took property that was actually yours, but you mistakenly believed it to be someone else's, you have not committed the crime of theft because the attendant circumstance of the property belonging to someone else was not met. You may, however, be guilty of attempted theft (more on attempt later).

As has been stated, strict liability often attaches to attendant circumstances. Assume, for example, that a jurisdiction makes it a felony to "purposefully or knowingly distribute, sell, or dispense narcotics." Assume that a defendant was arrested and charged with violating this statute when an undercover police officer witnessed the defendant selling cocaine. The *actus reus* of the crime would be the sale or distribution of the cocaine—a controlled and dangerous substance. Such a drug transaction was purposeful, so the *mens rea* of the statute would be satisfied and the defendant could be properly convicted. But assume that the punishment for the offense is higher (e.g., a longer prison term) if the drugs are sold within 1,000 feet of a school. This would make being within 1,000 feet of a school an attendant circumstance for the higher punishment.

Even if the defendant did not know there was a school nearby, he or she would nonetheless be properly convicted of distributing drugs within a school zone and could be sentenced to the longer prison term. The fact that the defendant did not know she was selling drugs within a school zone would be irrelevant because the location of the sale is not central to the criminality of the act itself. The intentional sale of cocaine is what is central to the criminality of the act (i.e., the union of *actus reus* and *mens rea*).

CAUSATION OF RESULT

The final major component of crime is the **result**—that which actually occurred because of the commission of the *actus reus*. Certain crimes require that a particular result occur. All forms of homicide are an example. One cannot be convicted of any type of homicide unless one's act caused a particular result—namely, the death of another human being.

When a crime requires a particular result, the prosecution must prove that the defendant's *actus reus*, performed with the requisite *mens rea*, actually *caused* the required result. This process involves the technicalities of the doctrine of causation. Causation in the law requires proof of two distinct types of causation: cause in fact and proximate cause. **Cause in fact** is what we normally think of as "causing": if a person does some act that directly brings about a particular result, then the person is said to have caused the result. To determine cause in fact, ask yourself, "Would the result have occurred *without* the defendant's conduct?" If so, the conduct is not cause in fact because the result would have occurred anyway, other than through the defendant's actions. In contrast, if the answer to the question is "no," then conduct is the cause in fact of the result because the result would not have occurred had it not been for the defendant's act.

Consider the drag racing case in Table 9.1. Assume that, after recklessly disregarding a known risk, the driver of a car in a drag race strikes and injures a pedestrian. Recklessness is the *mens rea*, and striking the pedestrian is the *actus reus*. To determine cause in fact, we would ask: Without the defendant's conduct, would the pedestrian have sustained his or her injuries? The answer is most likely "no." The injuries were sustained as a direct result of the collision with the vehicle and otherwise would not have occurred had the race not taken place. Therefore, the defendant's conduct was the cause in fact of the victim's injuries.

The law requires more than the direct causation embodied in cause in fact to impose criminal liability. The law also requires what is known as proximate cause. **Proximate cause** is concerned with whether there were any other causes (*besides* the defendant's conduct) that *contributed* to the result. If there were no other causes contributing to the result besides the defendant's actions, then proximate cause is established and criminal liability can be imposed. But if there were factors other than the defendant's acts that contributed to the result, a careful proximate cause analysis must be undertaken. When factors other than the defendant's *actus reus* contribute to the result, criminal liability may only be imposed if the result of the *actus reus* was "foreseeable."

Let's consider an example, again returning to a racing car that strikes a pedestrian. Assume that the pedestrian is seriously injured and taken to the emergency department of a hospital. If, due to a mistake by the treating physician, the pedestrian dies, can homicide charges be filed against the driver of the vehicle? The answer is most likely "yes." At least two factors contributed to the pedestrian's death: first, the individual was struck by a vehicle driven by a person in a reckless manner, and second, the physician erred. Had either of these factors not occurred, the pedestrian would probably still be alive. However, errors in emergency treatment of a crime victim are foreseeable, and it was the initial collision that led to the need for emergency treatment. Accordingly, in this example, there is proximate causation, and the driver could be charged with some form of homicide.

On the other hand, assume a different scenario in which the victim sustained only a minor injury. At the hospital, for whatever reason, the physician deliberately mistreated the victim, causing the death. Here, there would not be proximate causation because it would not be reasonable to foresee deliberate malpractice that causes death in the course of treatment for a minor injury. Thus, the perpetrator would likely still face battery charges for causing (even minor) injury but not homicide charges.

> Presume a statute reads: "A person commits a misdemeanor in the first degree if the person operates or controls a vehicle while under the influence of intoxicating liquor, drugs, or toxic substances if the person is impaired to the slightest degree." Break this crime into its component elements by specifying the *actus reus*, *mens rea*, result (if any), and attendant circumstances (if any).
>
> Recall the FBI warning regarding criminal copyright infringement that we discussed at the start of this chapter. Break this crime into its component elements by specifying the *actus reus*, *mens rea*, result (if any), and attendant circumstances (if any).
>
> What do you think of strict liability? Does imposing criminal liability without any *mens rea* seem fair to you? Why or why not?

Types of Crimes

FOCUSING QUESTION 9.3

What are the major classifications of criminal offenses?

The criminal law divides criminal offenses into four major categories: crimes against the person, crimes against property and habitation, inchoate offenses, and other offenses. We shall explore each of these classifications. Keep in mind that the crimes are presented using very general descriptions; the particulars vary by jurisdiction.

Crimes in which people are physically victimized are considered the most serious of criminal offenses. Such crimes include homicide, forcible rape, assault, battery, and robbery. These are **crimes against the person**, and their basic elements are summarized in Table 9.2.

Crimes against property account for the most common types of criminal offenses. Rather than harming people physically, these crimes harm individuals' property, including real estate, goods, and financial resources. This category of crime includes burglary, criminal trespass, arson, fraud, forgery, uttering, receiving stolen property, and a wide variety of theft offenses. These are **crimes against property**, and their basic elements are summarized in Table 9.3.

Crimes that occur as part of the preparation for committing another crime, or in an attempt to commit another crime, are referred to as **inchoate crimes**. This category of crime includes attempt, solicitation, facilitation, aiding and abetting, and conspiracy. These inchoate crimes and their basic elements are summarized in Table 9.4.

There are many other criminal offenses that do not fit neatly into one of the three categories of crime just described. Table 9.5 provides some examples of the ways in which these other offenses are often classified.

> Critique the classification of crimes in Tables 9.2 to 9.4. Does it make sense for crimes to be organized in this manner? What other ways might crimes be categorized?
>
> Why do you think we criminalize attempted or preparatory crimes as inchoate offenses?
>
> As stated earlier, crimes against the person are considered the most serious of crimes and are therefore punished the most severely. But there is a good argument to be made that certain crimes against property, especially major "white-collar offenses" (e.g., corporate negligence, large-scale fraud, etc.) have a much more dramatic effect on society than a single assault or homicide. Where do you stand on this debate? How should white-collar crimes be classified?

Defenses to Crimes

FOCUSING QUESTION 9.4

What are the major types of criminal defenses?

Sometimes, the commission of a crime may be excusable and not require punishment. For example, the intentional killing of a person normally constitutes criminal homicide, but it may be justifiable in war or in self-defense. Similarly, *mens rea* might be formed defectively due to mental illness or mistaken circumstances. The various reasons people should *not* be held criminally responsible

Table 9.2. Summary of the Elements of the Major Crimes Against the Person

Crime	Actus Reus	Mens Rea	Result	Attendant Circumstances
Murder	Any act or omission that kills	Purpose or Knowledge (i.e., intent to kill or intent to cause serious bodily harm)	Death of a human being	None
Depraved Heart Murder	Any act or omission that kills	Gross recklessness (i.e., conscious disregard of a known risk of death or serious bodily harm)	Death of a human being	Conduct must manifest an extreme indifference to the value of human life
Voluntary Manslaughter	Any act or omission that kills	Purpose or Knowledge (i.e., intent to kill)	Death of a human being	Killing must have taken place in the heat of passion prompted by legally adequate provocation
Involuntary Manslaughter	Any act or omission that kills	Recklessness or gross negligence (i.e., negligence with a deadly weapon)	Death of a human being	None
Felony Murder	Commission of a qualifying felony that unintentionally kills	Whatever the mens rea is for the underlying felony	Death of a human being	(1) Underlying felony must be inherently dangerous; (2) Death must occur during the commission or attempted commission of the felony, or during immediate flight therefrom

Rape	Forcible sexual intercourse	At least recklessness (with regard to whether consent existed)	The penetration, however slight, of a sexual orifice (vagina, anus, mouth)	Without the consent of the victim
Assault and Aggravated Assault	The creation of the immediate apprehension of bodily harm (simple assault) or severe bodily injury (aggravated assault)	Purpose	Victim must have been in apprehension of immediate bodily harm (simple assault) or severe bodily injury (aggravated assault)	Actions must have included more than mere words
Battery and Aggravated Battery	The application of force to the person of another	At least recklessness	Victim must have been touched in an unwanted manner (simply battery), or have been minorly injured (simply battery), or significantly injured (aggravated battery)	None
Robbery	The forcible taking of personal property from a person (or in a person's physical presence)	Purpose (i.e., specific intent to steal)	Property must be taken	(1) Must be personal property; and (2) theft must have been accomplished by force or the threatened use of force

Table 9.3. Summary of the Elements of the Major Crimes Against Property

Crime	Actus Reus	Mens Rea	Result	Attendant Circumstances
Burglary	The unlawful breaking and entering	Purpose (to commit a felony or theft once inside)	Unlawful entry must be into the "structure of another"	"Of another" means the unlawful entry cannot be into one's own premises
Criminal Trespass	Unlawfully entering into or remaining on another's property without the owner's consent	Knowledge (i.e., knowing you have no privilege to enter or remain)	Either the initial entry had to be illegal, or the person must fail to leave when lawfully asked to do so	The entering or remaining on property had to be nonconsensual (i.e., without any legal entitlement to enter or remain on the premises)
Arson	The unlawful burning of a structure	At least recklessness	Structure must be burned, even if just minimally, by fire or explosion damage	The thing burned must be a "structure"
Fraud	Committing any dishonest act (deceit, falsehood, or other fraudulent means) to deprive a victim of his/her property or a lawful right	Purpose (i.e., intentional deception)	The fraud must cause a "deprivation"—some loss, detriment, prejudice, or risk of prejudice to the economic or legal interests of the victim	None

Forgery	Making or altering (by drafting, adding, or deleting) a document	Purpose (i.e., intent to defraud)	None	The document must be a writing with some apparent legal significance (e.g., a check or a contract, not a painting)
Uttering	Offering as genuine any forged document	Purpose (i.e., intent to defraud)	None	The document must be false
Receiving Stolen Property	Receiving possession and control of the stolen personal property of another	Knowledge (i.e., knowing that the property is stolen)	None	The personal property (i.e., not real or intangible property) must have been stolen from a victim by someone other than person receiving the stolen property
Criminal Damage	Damaging or destroying the property of another	At least recklessness	The property must have been damaged by the act of the defendant	The property must have belonged to someone other than the defendant
Theft	The unlawful taking the personal property of another without consent of the rightful owner	Purpose (i.e., intent to steal)	The rightful owner must be deprived of the property	The personal property (i.e., not real or intangible property) must have belonged to someone other than the defendant

Table 9.4. Summary of the Elements of the Major Inchoate Crimes

Crime	Actus Reus	Mens Rea	Result	Attendant Circumstances
Attempt	Attempted to commit a substantive crime	Purpose (i.e., specific intent to commit a substantive criminal offense)	The defendant must have tried but failed to have actually committed the target offense	The attempt must involve the defendant having taken "substantial steps" toward the commission of the crime; mere preparation is insufficient
Solicitation	Inducing or inviting another person to commit a crime	Purpose (i.e., specifically intended that the other person commit the specified crime)	None	None
Facilitation	Proving the means or opportunity for someone else to commit a crime	Knowledge (i.e., knowing that someone intends to commit a crime)	None	None
Aiding and Abetting (Complicity)	Providing aid or encouragement to another person to commit a crime	Purpose (i.e., with the specific intent that the aid or encouragement help or cause the other person to commit a crime)	None	None
Conspiracy	Agreeing to commit a crime or set of crimes with one or more other people	Purpose (i.e., specifically intended that the group commit the specified crime or crimes)	An agreement must be formed	None

Table 9.5. A Sample Classification of Other Types of Crimes

Types of Crimes	Examples
Crimes Against Public Administration	Contempt. Perjury. False swearing. Tampering with witnesses or evidence. Obstruction of justice. Bribery. Failure to appear. Tax evasion. Voting fraud.
Crimes Against Public Order	Unlawful assembly. Disturbing the peace. Public drunkenness. Disorderly conduct. Vagrancy. Drug-related offenses. Criminal traffic offenses.
Crimes Against Morality	Adultery. Bigamy. Prostitution. Illegal forms of gambling (i.e., excluding casinos, lotteries, etc.). Obscenity. Statutory rape. Indecent exposure. Public sexual indecency.

for the commission of acts that usually would otherwise constitute crimes are called criminal **defenses**. Defenses to crimes are generally classified in three categories: defenses of excuse, defenses of justification, and procedural defenses.

The **defenses of excuse** are those in which a defendant admits to having committed a criminally proscribed *actus reus* but asserts that he or she did so under special circumstances that mitigate or even excuse criminal liability. Thus, excuse defenses are arguments about why an individual person should not be responsible for what might otherwise constitute criminal behavior because of unique *personal* circumstances that diminish *mens rea*. The major defenses of excuse are infancy of age, insanity, mistake, intoxication (both involuntary and voluntary), and duress. A summary of these defenses appears in Table 9.6.

The **defenses of justification** are those in which a defendant admits to having committed a criminally proscribed *actus reus*, and did so with *mens rea*, but asserts that circumstances surrounding the *act* render it justifiable under the law. The major defenses of justification are self-defense, defense of others, defense of property, consent, and execution of public duties. A summary of defenses of justification appears in Table 9.7.

It is important to note the difference between defenses of excuse and defenses of justification. Defenses of excuse suggest that the *person* should be excused for an inability to have a fully formed *mens rea*. Defenses of justification assume that the act was deliberate but argue that it was committed for a reason deemed justifiable under the law.

Procedural defenses are technical defenses created under the law for public policy reasons. Factual guilt, criminal culpability, or situational circumstances are irrelevant to these defenses. Rather, procedural defenses are rooted in concern for due process and other forms of procedural justice. In Chapter 8, you learned about a number of such defenses, such as the right to a speedy trial (and the related defense of the passage of time specified in statutes of

Table 9.6. Defenses of Excuse

Defense	Brief Explanation of the Defense
Infancy of Age	Children under the age of 7 are conclusively presumed to be incapable of forming *mens rea*. Accordingly, they are excused from criminal liability for committing acts that would result in prosecution if they were older.
	Children between 7 and 14 are similarly presumed to be incapable of forming *mens rea*, but that presumption may be rebutted by relevant evidence to the contrary. If rebutted (i.e., if children between 7 and 14 are shown to be able to form *mens rea*), they usually face delinquency proceedings under the civil jurisdiction of a juvenile court.
	Children over the age of 14 are rebuttable, presumed to be able to form *mens rea*. Assuming that the capacity to form *mens rea* is not rebutted, children over 14 may be handled in juvenile court or, under certain circumstances, may be transferred to adult court for formal criminal prosecution. Each state has its own provisions for determining when a juvenile may be tried as an adult.
Insanity	In most U.S. jurisdictions, the insanity defense excuses criminal liability if, as a result of a qualifying mental disease or defect, a person lacks the substantial capacity to appreciate the wrongfulness/criminality of his or her actions.
	In a small number of jurisdictions, conduct may also be excused if the person was unable to control his conduct due to a qualifying mental illness, even though the person understood the conduct was wrong.
	Four states have abolished the insanity defense and, as a result, limit the admissibility of evidence regarding mental illnesses to the question of whether the defendant was mentally capable of forming *mens rea*.
Mistake	Factual mistakes that negate *mens rea* may excuse criminal liability if the defendant was actually (subjectively) mistaken and if that mistake was objectively reasonable. Mistakes concerning the meaning or applicability of the law, however, generally do not constitute a criminal defense absent some very rare and highly limited circumstances.
Involuntary Intoxication	Excuses criminal liability if a person lacks the substantial capacity to appreciate the wrongfulness/criminality of his or her actions because the person ingested an intoxicant neither knowing nor having reason to know that he or she was consuming something intoxicating. Alternatively, this defense may also be invoked if someone was forced to take an intoxicating substance under duress.
Voluntary Intoxication	Excuses criminal liability if a person is incapable of forming the requisite *mens rea* of a crime as a result of being significantly intoxicated. Nearly all U.S. jurisdictions limit this defense to mitigate crimes of specific intent (i.e., those requiring purpose or knowledge as the requisite *mens rea*) down to lower levels of criminal liability, to crimes which carry recklessness or negligence as their *mens rea*. Some states, however, do not recognize this defense at all.
Duress	Excuses or mitigates criminal conduct committed out of necessity arising from an emergency situation to avoid serious, imminent bodily harm. The defendant must not have been responsible for having created the emergency giving rise to the necessity to act. The crime committed, however, must have been the lesser of two evils. That is, the harm avoided by committing the crime must be more substantial or more serious than that harm caused by committing the crime. Accordingly, this defense is not available for homicides.

Table 9.7. Defenses of Justification

Defense	Brief Explanation of the Defense
Self-Defense	Allows a person who reasonably believes it necessary to use force to defend against an unlawful, imminent attack. The amount of force used must be reasonable. Thus, physical attacks may be repelled by the use of physical force without criminal liability for assault and battery. Similarly, when faced with imminent attack involving deadly force, someone may use deadly force in self-defense without criminal liability for homicide. The use of deadly force, however, is limited in many states by requirements to retreat if the person may do so in safety and/or by requirements to give notice that deadly force will be used in self-defense unless such a warning would be futile.
Defense of Others	People are generally permitted to use force to defend someone else against unlawful, imminent attack to the same extent that the person under attack would have been permitted to use force in self-defense.
Defense of Property	A reasonable amount of nondeadly force may be used to protect one's property. As a general rule (unless a jurisdiction specifically has a law to the contrary), deadly force may not be used to defend property because life is valued more than material possessions.
Consent	A small number of crimes require a lack of consent from the victim as a core element of the offense. Rape, for example, punishes only sexual penetrations that were accomplished without the consent of the victim. Similarly, a theft occurs only if the person whose property was taken did not consent. For such crimes, consent is a defense. Consent may also be a defense to the crime of simple battery. The "victim" of a battery can consent to minor bodily injury as long as that consent was given knowingly, intelligently, and voluntarily. For example, when two boxers enter the ring, they consent to be battered.
Execution of Public Duties	Governmental actors are often permitted to do things that private persons are prohibited from doing under the criminal law. Fire and emergency medical personnel are permitted to violate a number of motor vehicle laws to carry out their official duties. Police officers may use a reasonable amount of force to make a lawful arrest without that force constituting an assault or battery. Police and correctional officers are even permitted to use deadly force under limited circumstances, such as to prevent a dangerous felon from fleeing. And military personnel are permitted to kill in defense of national security.

limitations), the bar against double jeopardy, and the use of the exclusionary rule to prevent illegally obtained evidence from being used to convict someone. Selective prosecution based on race, sex, or a similar characteristic that violates the Equal Protection Clause of the Fourteenth Amendment also constitutes a procedural defense.

Immunity is another procedural defense that gives a defendant freedom from criminal prosecution due to his or her status as a foreign diplomat or as a cooperating witness for the government in a larger prosecution (e.g., low-level criminals in drug deals or organized crime rings).

Finally, procedural defenses also include outrageous governmental conduct, such as entrapment. Entrapment occurs when law enforcement agents induce someone to commit a crime that he or she was not predisposed to commit. For example, assume that an undercover officer solicited a man who has never used a drug before to buy and use drugs. Assume that he initially refused multiple times, but after weeks of applying pressure, he finally was convinced, so he bought and tried the drug. If the undercover officer then arrested him, he would likely assert entrapment as his defense, arguing that the only reason he tried the drug was because of the officer's repeated actions. Outrageous governmental conduct, however, is not limited to entrapment. It can constitute a defense whenever the conduct of law enforcement agents is so outrageous that due process principles would absolutely bar the government from invoking judicial processes to obtain a conviction. For example, the defense was successful in *Metcalf v. Florida* (1994), a case in which police manufactured crack cocaine and then arrested the people who bought the crack from them.

> Why do you think we have criminal defenses? What would be the consequence of convicting every person who engages in prohibited conduct with the required mental state and then imposing less severe sentences on those who have some justification or excuse for their actions?
>
> Do you think it is appropriate to excuse criminal conduct because of youth, mental illness, duress, and the like? Why or why not?
>
> Do you think there are any circumstances, other than those listed here, that should serve as a defense to criminal activity?

Constitutional Limitations on Criminalization

FOCUSING QUESTION 9.5

What limits does the U.S. Constitution place on the ability to criminalize conduct?

The U.S. Constitution places certain limits on what behaviors may or may not be criminalized. These limits will be discussed in the following sections.

THE FIRST AMENDMENT

The First Amendment to the U.S. Constitution states: "Congress shall make no law respecting an establishment of religion, or prohibiting the free exercise thereof; or abridging the freedom of speech, or of the press; or the right of the people peaceably to assemble, and to petition the Government for a redress of grievances." This Amendment provides several protections that place limits on the power of government to criminalize speech, religious practices, and the ability to assemble and demonstrate peacefully.

Free Speech and Peaceable Assembly. The free speech protections of the First Amendment generally allow people to speak or write about any topic. People may exercise these liberties alone. Alternatively, people may exercise these rights in small or large groups to share their ideas with others as long as they do so peacefully. For example, a law banning speech critical of governmental policies would be unconstitutional. That would even hold true if people expressed their dissatisfaction with the government by using offensive or profane language (e.g., *Cohen v. California*, 1971). The First Amendment even protects **symbolic speech**—conduct that expresses an idea or opinion, like wearing certain clothes or styling one's hair in a particular unconventional way, accessorizing using buttons or armbands, or picketing or marching in a parade. Even symbolic hate speech, like burning a cross, may receive some First Amendment protection as symbolic speech depending on the circumstances under which such an act occurs (see *Virginia v. Black*, 2003).

In light of the First Amendment, it is quite rare for a law to ban any type of protected speech or expression. However, criminal statutes may run afoul of the First Amendment by being overbroad. **Overbreadth** occurs when a law "sweep[s] unnecessarily broadly and thereby invade[s] the area of protected freedoms" (*Zwicker v. Koota*, 1972, p. 250). This typically occurs in cases involving symbolic speech. For example, a law criminalizing flag burning was determined to be unconstitutionally overbroad in *Texas v. Johnson* (1989). The Court held that the law infringed upon people's right to express their dissatisfaction with the government through the symbolic speech embodied in the action of burning the flag.

As with all constitutional rights, there are limits to free speech. Certain categories of speech receive no First Amendment protection. These include defamatory writing and speech (i.e., libel and slander—falsehoods that damage another person's reputation), obscenity, and the use of words "directed to inciting or producing imminent lawless action" (*Brandenburg v. Ohio*, 1969, p. 447). Moreover, the government may limit the time, place, and manner in which the rights to free speech and peaceable assembly are exercised in order to prevent fires, health hazards, obstructions and/or occupations of public buildings, or traffic problems. For example, no one has the right to "insist upon a street meeting in the middle of Times Square at the rush hour as a form of freedom of speech" (*Cox v. Louisiana*, 1965, p. 554).

Freedom of the Press. The First Amendment generally forbids censorship or other restraints on speech or expression by the media whether in print or in broadcasting (e.g., radio, television, and movies). However, like with free speech, there are limits to this protection. As mentioned earlier, neither defamation nor obscenity receives First Amendment protection. Similarly, limits on the media's dissemination of information may be permitted if it concerns a matter of national security, such as the location of troops and their combat plans (see, e.g., *New York Times Co. v. United States*, 1971). And as with free speech, the time, place, and manner in which broadcasts are made can be limited. For example, the FCC can bar the broadcast of profane language and sexually explicit material on public airways that may be accessed by children (see *FCC v. Pacifica Foundation*, 1978).

Freedom of Religion. The First Amendment contains two clauses relevant to the freedom of religion. The first is known as the **Establishment Clause**, which the Supreme Court has interpreted as providing a "wall of separation between church and state" (*Everson v. Board of Education*, 1947, p. 16). It prevents local, state, and the federal governments from enacting any law that establishes an official church or from favoring one religion over another (or over none at all). For example, laws that criminalized failure to go to weekly religious services or failure to tithe (donate money to a religious organization) would be unconstitutional exercises of the state's police power in light of the protections of the Establishment Clause.

The First Amendment also protects people's rights to act on their beliefs (or to believe nothing at all) in the **Free Exercise Clause**. For instance, the Supreme Court struck down a local ordinance that prohibited the ritual killing of animals because it infringed upon the religious beliefs of a group that practices animal sacrifice (see *Church of Lukumi Babalu Aye v. City of Hialeah*, 1993). However, as with other constitutional rights, the freedom to act on religious beliefs is not absolute. With few exceptions, no one may violate otherwise valid laws in the name of freely practicing religion. For instance, laws criminalizing polygamy are valid even if one's religion condones having multiple spouses (see *Reynolds v. United States*, 1878). Some governmental restraint on the free exercise of religious beliefs is also permissible in settings where people's rights are already curtailed to some extent, such as in the military or in correctional settings.

DUE PROCESS CONCERNS

Limiting the Reach of Strict Liability.
Mala in se crimes (Latin for evil "unto itself") are common-law crimes against the person (e.g., murder, rape, aggravated assault) and crimes against property (e.g., theft and arson)

that are clearly morally wrong in and of themselves. In contrast, *mala prohibita* offenses are not necessarily inherently bad or evil acts. Rather, *mala prohibita* crimes are those created by statutes or regulations that exist to address public health, safety, and welfare.

As discussed earlier, strict liability imposes criminal penalties for doing a proscribed act without regard to whether there was any corresponding *mens rea*. The Supreme Court has limited strict liability to crimes that are *mala prohibita;* strict liability may not attach to crimes that are *mala in se* (*Morissette v. United States*, 1952). Accordingly, a state could not criminalize a truly accidental killing. However, the criminal law can punish a bartender who serves alcohol to an underage person whom the bartender reasonably believes is over the legal drinking age because the person produced a fake (but realistic) driver's license. Criminalizing such an act without even any negligence may seem harsh, but it is lawful because serving alcohol to a minor is a *malum prohibitum* crime.

Substantive Due Process. Substantive due process is the notion that certain rights and liberties are so fundamental to the American notion of justice that any governmental infringement upon those rights and liberties should not be tolerated, absent the most serious and compelling reasons. In *Washington v. Glucksberg* (1997), the Supreme Court explained its approach in identifying fundamental rights.

> First, we have regularly observed that the Due Process Clause specially protects those fundamental rights and liberties which are, objectively, "deeply rooted in this Nation's history and tradition," and "implicit in the concept of ordered liberty," such that "neither liberty nor justice would exist if they were sacrificed." Second, we have required in substantive due process cases a "careful description" of the asserted fundamental liberty interest. (pp. 720–721)

The substantive rights contained in the First Amendment discussed earlier, such as the freedoms of speech, peaceable assembly, and freedom of religion, are all fundamental rights. Other fundamental rights and liberties are not listed in the Constitution but are based on rulings in Supreme Court decisions. The right to privacy is the best example of this. The Supreme Court has interpreted substantive due process to protect a number of privacy rights, ranging from access to contraceptives (e.g., *Griswold v. Connecticut*, 1965) and abortion services (*Roe v. Wade*, 1973) to the right to marry (*Loving v. Virginia*, 1967) and the liberty for adults to engage in certain types of private, consensual sexual conduct (*Lawrence v. Texas*, 2003). The right to privacy is explored in more detail in Box 9.1.

> Given the First Amendment right to free speech, do you think the government should be able to criminalize the use of foul language in public? Why?

BOX 9.1

WHAT IS THE SCOPE OF THE RIGHT TO PRIVACY?

For most of U.S. history, sodomy was illegal. Sodomy laws criminalized oral and anal sex. These laws were incorporated into U.S. criminal law from English common law. They banned these sex acts between consenting adults even in private. As such, they applied to those who were married or single, whether heterosexual or homosexual, and to both the active performers and the passive recipients of the acts. The penalties could be quite severe; Georgia classified sodomy as felony punishable by up to 20 years in prison. That law was unsuccessfully challenged in 1986 in *Bowers v. Hardwick*. Over a substantive due process challenge, the Supreme Court rejected the argument that the right to privacy should protect such private, consensual sexual acts. The Court distinguished prior privacy cases like *Griswold* and *Roe* by reasoning those cases did not create rights to sexual privacy but rather recognized that the decision to procreate was a private one that ought to lie beyond the reach of the government. In contrast, the Court said, acts of sodomy did not involve procreation. Oral and anal sex, therefore, could be criminalized without violating substantive due process to enforce what the Court believed was the widely shared belief in the immorality of these acts.

Seventeen years later, the Supreme Court overruled *Bowers* when it decided *Lawrence v. Texas* (2003). Reversing its earlier premise that criminal law could be used to enforce the moral will of the majority without regard to harm (the classic Hart-Devlin debate as you should recall from Chapter 3), the Court stated that its decision in *Bowers* had failed "to appreciate the extent of the liberty [interest] at stake" (p. 567). The Court reasoned that sodomy laws "have more far reaching consequences, touching upon the most private human conduct, sexual behavior, and in the most private of places, the home," and in doing so, "seek to control a personal relationship that . . . is within the liberty of persons to choose without being punished as criminals" (p. 567). Reasoning that "liberty presumes an autonomy of self that includes freedom of thought, belief, expression, and certain intimate conduct" (p. 562), the Court declared all of the remaining sodomy laws in the United States unconstitutional, finding that they violated the substantive due process right to liberty.

With which approach to sexual privacy do you agree—the one taken in *Bowers* or the one taken in *Lawrence*? Why?

In light of the holding in *Lawrence*, do you think that substantive due process should extend to and invalidate any of the following criminal laws? Explain your reasoning for each.

- laws criminalizing fornication (i.e., premarital sex) and/or the cohabitation of unmarried persons
- laws criminalizing adultery
- laws criminalizing bestiality (sexual contact with an animal)
- laws criminalizing incest
- laws criminalizing indecent exposure, such as public nudity or public urination
- laws criminalizing public sexual acts

Given that the right to privacy is a fundamental right that encompasses "autonomy of self," do you think euthanasia (i.e., assisted suicide) should be legalized on substantive due process grounds? Explain your answer.

One of the great debates in contemporary society is the degree to which church and state should be separated. In light of the religion clauses in the First Amendment, do you think "faith-based" rehabilitation programs in prisons should be funded by public tax dollars?

Are crimes like adultery, insider trading, drug possession and use, gambling, and prostitution *mala in se* or *mala prohibita*? Why?

Conclusion

This chapter has traced the evolution of criminal law across several millennia to its current form. It also summarized the major elements common to all types of crime, the classifications of leading crimes and defenses, and the major limitations on criminalization. But the appropriate limits of the criminal law are often subject to deep philosophical differences of opinion. Debates centered on the harm principle, Hart's legal positivism, and Devlin's legal moralism (as described in Chapter 3) continue to this day, as experts and laypersons consider what should (or should not) be criminalized. For example, Luna (2005) compiled a list of dozens of examples of overcriminalization which included arrest and detention for failing to wear a seat belt, jail time for failing to return a library book, and criminal sanctions for frightening pigeons from their nests. Although some of these laws may appear trivial, people punished under them surely do not find them so. It is to the topic of punishment that the next chapter will turn.

Criminal Justice Problem Solving: THIRD-PARTY POLICING

Third-party policing is a strategy "to persuade or coerce organizations or non-offending persons, such as public housing agencies, property owners, parents, health and building inspectors, and business owners to take some responsibility for preventing crime or reducing crime problems" (Mazerolle & Ransley, 2006, p. 191). This strategy recognizes that there are limits to what police can do to control or prevent crime and calls upon others in the community to become involved in crime prevention and reduction activities—that is, for third parties (i.e., persons other than the police) to help police the community. Note that the definition states "to persuade *or* coerce." In some cases, civic-mindedness may be sufficient motivation, such as when residents agree to join a neighborhood watch program. Programs that use the law to require third-party crime prevention have been controversial, such as holding parents legally accountable for the actions of their children. Often formulated in response to concerns about juvenile crime (Davidson, 1996), these efforts fall under the umbrella of third-party policing because they require parents (the third parties) to account for their children's behavior, which in theory would strengthen social control. Consider the Trenton, New Jersey, "parent responsibility ordinance" as an example.

Trenton's ordinance was fairly straightforward. If twice within one year a juvenile was found guilty of an offense, the *parents* could be convicted of violating the ordinance and fined up to $500. Offenses that could trigger the ordinance included delinquent (i.e., criminal) acts as well as status offenses, meaning acts that are prohibited only for minors (e.g., truancy, curfew violations, running away, underage drinking). The law required parents to be given notice of their child's first offense. Then, "if at any time within one year of the giving of such notice, such minor shall be charged with a violation of the public peace, and shall again be adjudicated delinquent, it shall be presumed, subject to rebuttal by competent evidence that the parents of said minor during said period of time, allowed, permitted, or suffered said minor to commit a violation of the public peace" (*Doe v. City of Trenton*, 1976, p. 131).

Explain how *actus reus, mens rea*, attendant circumstances, and causation would apply to this ordinance.

Do you think the ordinance, as written, is a good idea? Why or why not? Laws of this sort were not found to actually reduce delinquency. Does that make a difference in your analysis?

Do you think the presumption stated in the law has a legitimate basis? Why or why not? What kind of evidence do you think parents could assemble to show that they did *not* "allow, permit, or suffer" their child to commit a violation?

This ordinance was challenged in New Jersey's appellate courts on the grounds that it violated parents' due process rights. How would you rule on this issue?

Criminal Punishment

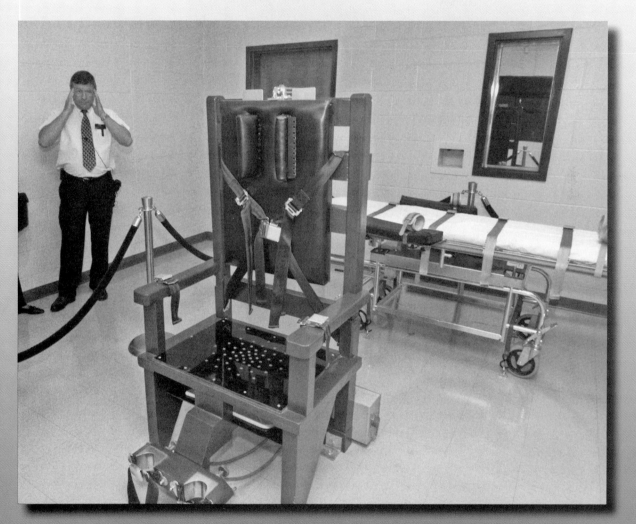

The electric chair and lethal injection gurney, used to carry out the death penalty. What do you think are the purposes of punishment?

Key Terms

punishment

retribution

just deserts

expiation

general deterrence

specific deterrence

hedonism

rehabilitation

incapacitation

reintegrative shaming

disintegrative shaming

dangerous classes

perceptual shorthand

culpability

legality

void for vagueness

bail

fines

cruel and unusual punishment

proportionality

day fines

Key People

Gresham Sykes

John Locke

Graeme Newman

Jeremy Bentham

Cesare Beccaria

Sigmund Freud

B. F. Skinner

John B. Watson

Robert Martinson

John Braithwaite

Jerome Skolnick

CASE STUDY

Three-Strikes Laws

Leandro Andrade was detained by security personnel at a Kmart store in California for stealing five videotapes valued at $84.70. Two weeks later, Andrade was detained at a different Kmart store after security personnel discovered four videotapes valued at $68.84 in the waistband of his pants. Andrade was arrested and charges were filed against him for petty theft.

Andrade did have a criminal past. In fact, he had been in and out of state and federal prisons for a number of offenses, including misdemeanor theft, residential burglary, transportation of marijuana, and a state parole violation. A heroin addict, Andrade confessed to stealing the videotapes and admitted that he had done so to obtain money to buy the drug.

In cases of petty theft in which the offender has prior convictions, California law allows the offense to count either as a misdemeanor or as a felony (in California, these are known as "wobbler" offenses). It is up to the prosecutor to make that decision. In this case, because Andrade had prior convictions, the prosecutor decided to charge him with a felony. Although the trial judge has the authority to reduce the charge to a misdemeanor, the judge in this case did not do so.

The choice between misdemeanor and felony is important because California has a strict three-strikes law. If an offender has two prior convictions for violent or serious felony offenses, then any third felony conviction carries a mandatory prison sentence of 25 years to life. At trial, a jury found Andrade guilty of two counts of petty theft, resulting in a felony conviction. Consistent with the three-strikes law, the judge sentenced Andrade to two consecutive prison terms of 25 years to life.

> If you were the prosecutor, would you have charged Andrade's thefts as a felony or misdemeanor? Why? Do you think prosecutors should be able to decide whether an act should count as a felony or misdemeanor? Why or why not? _____
>
> Do you believe that Andrade's punishment was appropriate? Why or why not? _____
>
> What do you think are the advantages and disadvantages of three-strikes laws? _____

Conceptualizing Punishment

FOCUSING QUESTION 10.1

What is punishment?

As described in Chapter 4, social control is a tool used to regulate behavior and, in particular, to ensure that individual behaviors conform to laws and social norms. This chapter explores penal social control, in which the force of law and government-imposed punishments are used to regulate behavior. This chapter's opening case study illustrates the complexities that come with the study of criminal punishment.

Punishment is most simply defined as a form of deprivation imposed on a person. That is, punishments deprive or take away something that a person desires or values. There are many possible deprivations, including freedom, which is deprived by sending a person to prison; family and friends, contact with whom may be deprived through banishment or social isolation; bodily integrity, which may be deprived through corporal or physical punishments; money, which may be deprived through fines; and life, which may be deprived through the use of the death penalty. In each of these cases, something that a person values is removed as a punishment for wrongdoing.

The concept of deprivations has been important in the study of punishment. In 1958, Gresham Sykes wrote what is considered one of the most important studies of prison life. From his observations of a New Jersey state prison, Sykes reported that prison inmates suffer five deprivations by virtue of being behind bars. These are the deprivation of their liberty, deprivation of goods and services that would be available in the outside world, deprivation of heterosexual relationships, deprivation of individual autonomy, and deprivation of personal security. More than 50 years later, Sykes's observations still hold true as accurate descriptors of prison life.

In addition to imposing a deprivation, penal social control must come as a consequence to criminal behavior. That is, criminal punishment may only occur in response to a violation of the criminal law. You may recall legal philosopher H. L. A. Hart from the discussion of law and morality in Chapter 3. Hart (1968, pp. 4–5) noted that punishment must meet the following five criteria:

1. must involve pain or other consequences normally considered to be unpleasant;
2. must be for an offense against legal rules;
3. must be of an actual or supposed offender for his offence;
4. must be intentionally administered by human beings other than the offender; and
5. must be imposed and administered by an authority constituted by a legal system against which the offense is committed.

Hart's second and fifth criteria differentiate criminal punishment from other sanctions involving similar deprivations. For instance, deprivation of liberty would occur in both of the following situations: a judge imposing a prison term for an offender who committed an armed robbery and a parent grounding a child for not cleaning his room. However, only the former would be considered penal social control, because it is a deprivation in response to a violation of law imposed by a judge within the legal system.

Although this discussion provides a basic definition of punishment, there is wide variation in terms of what specific *types* of punishments are viewed as acceptable. The concept of punishment is socially constructed with variations across time and place. This means that people within a particular society determine which actual punishments will be used and for which criminal offenses. These determinations may be based on factors including political ideology, finances, societal characteristics (i.e., the "mood" of society during that particular point in time), religious beliefs and values, and advances in science (e.g., the latest behavioral modification techniques), to name a few.

For instance, in some countries, legal codes based on religious principles specify that certain offenses should be punished through death by stoning. In other countries, the death penalty has been completely abolished and is viewed as an abuse of a government's power. As another example, consider how a society deals with drug offenders. Perhaps the political ideology favors rehabilitating drug offenders, and scientific advances provide the technology to do so. Judges could then send drug offenders to treatment centers. However, if citizens were reluctant to pay higher taxes to finance those treatment centers, other alternatives would need to be developed. Therefore, many factors enter into a society's decisions about how to structure criminal punishment, and this results in differences among cities, states, and nations.

Punishments also vary based on factors related to the actual offense, such as its seriousness, the number of victims involved, whether weapons were used, and so on. For instance, consider two hypothetical armed robbers, both of whom entered a bank during business hours, demanded money, and escaped with $12,000. The first armed robber fired a handgun into the ceiling, causing a customer to faint, and took a teller hostage. The second armed robber walked up to the counter, handed the teller a note reading, "I have a gun, give me all the money or I'll use it," and left without further incident. Would the two offenders receive the same punishment? Probably not—the first would likely receive the harsher sentence based on the circumstances of the offense. Therefore, punishment can be individualized to account for the specific actions of an offender.

> How did Andrade's punishment under California's three-strikes law meet the characteristics described in this section?

> If you were the judge, would you request additional information before announcing a punishment for the hypothetical armed robbers just described? If so, what factors would influence your decision and ultimate punishment?

Justifications for Criminal Punishment

FOCUSING QUESTION 10.2

What are the five justifications for criminal punishment?

When people break the law, it is the government that has the right—some would even say the obligation—to punish them. This gives the government the power to fine, imprison, and in some cases, even kill offenders. Think back to the Hart-Devlin debate in Chapter 3. Even though the two sides disagreed about what constituted a crime, they both agreed that the government should punish crimes, however defined.

Consider the irony of this power. Depriving a person of money, liberty, or life would be viewed as something criminal and immoral if done by an ordinary person. In fact, when done by an ordinary person, deprivation of money is robbery, deprivation of liberty is kidnapping, and deprivation of life is murder. Yet, when done by the government, it would be a fine, imprisonment, and execution, respectively—all within the bounds of the law. So, what gives the government the right to take these actions as a form of criminal punishment when ordinary citizens cannot?

A government "is the only group of people entitled to make decisions that everyone in the state has a duty to accept and obey" (Shively, 1999, p. 134). That is, by its very definition, the government has the unique authority to punish those who do not accept and obey its laws. According to political theorist John Locke, in the absence of government, individuals within the society would have to decide who would be punished and how they would be punished. However, drawing upon the social contract metaphor from Chapter 2, people form an agreement to be governed by a set of rules under the authority of a government. When people make such an agreement, they also delegate the power to punish rule violators to the government (Locke, [1690] 1963). Therefore, the institution of government holds unique powers.

Historically, governments embraced these powers. In fact, many early punishments were deliberately harsh and were carried out in public view. Offenders were beaten, tortured, and gruesomely executed in deliberate shows of force intended to demonstrate and establish the government's strength and power. As governments mature and stabilize, they tend not to make such public displays of force, as citizens become willing to accept the government's authority. At that point, and as the public perceives the government as legitimate, punishments often become more humane (Spierenburg, 1984).

In exercising the power to punish, the American criminal justice system relies on five common justifications or goals of punishment. They are retribution, deterrence, incapacitation, rehabilitation, and restitution. The popularity of each justification, like the definition of punishment itself, has varied over time.

RETRIBUTION

Retribution is grounded in the notion that offenders deserve to be punished. There are three competing views of retribution. The first is revenge, which may be conceptualized as "the impulse to get even in the face of injustice" (Barton, 1999, p. xiv). As you learned in Chapter 9, this view of retribution has its roots in ancient legal codes. According to biblical principles articulated in Exodus 21:24, if there is a serious injury, you are to take "life for life, eye for eye, tooth for tooth, hand for hand, foot for foot, burn for burn, wound for wound, bruise for bruise." This is similar to the Code of Hammurabi (c. 1800 B.C.E.) which stated, among other things, "If a man has destroyed the eye of a free man, his own eye shall be destroyed," and "if he has broken the bone of a free man, his bone shall be broken" (Edwards, 1906, p. 26). Thus, if a victim is wronged, punishment should be designed to get even by imposing the same hardship onto the offender.

The second view of retribution is **just deserts**. This, too, is a payback but with less emphasis on individual revenge and one-for-one correspondence between crime and punishment. A person advocating for just deserts would believe that the offender should be punished not only because he or she committed a bad act against an *individual* but also because all criminal acts are viewed as offenses against *society as a whole*. The resulting punishment should be proportional to the crime; that is, the punishment should be equally severe to the offender as the offender's criminal act was to the victim. Therefore, just deserts focuses on the idea *that the punishment should fit the crime* but without resorting to one-on-one revenge (i.e., doing *exactly* the same thing to the offender as the offender did to the victim) or group-based vengeance like blood feuds.

The third view of retribution is **expiation**, which refers to atonement through suffering. St. Thomas Aquinas, a medieval theologian, was an advocate of this form of punishment. Expiation is based on the idea that crime causes pain to the victim, so the only way for the criminal to repent and learn his or her lesson is through experiencing his or her own pain. Note that expiation introduces an element not found in revenge or just deserts. The pain experienced by the offender should not be imposed solely to get even (be it with an individual or with losses to society) but also to cause the offender to repent and be forgiven. Although expiation is often associated with religious punishment, criminologist Graeme Newman (1983) proposed the use of painful electric shocks as a form of criminal punishment.

Retribution has long been a part of justice systems. However, in the United States today, just deserts is the only form of retribution practiced.

DETERRENCE

To *deter* means to discourage someone from doing something. For a punishment to deter, it should have the effect of convincing people not to commit crime. This is usually accomplished through fear of punishment. If a person understands what punishment would likely occur if he or she were caught committing a crime, then that person might choose not to commit the crime. We would then say that person was deterred from committing the crime.

There are two types of deterrence: general and specific. **General deterrence** is intended to deter all people from committing crime by making an example out of others who have. The idea is that as members of the public see punishments meted out, they will decide not to commit crime out of a fear of being punished themselves. For instance, general deterrence theory would suggest that California's three-strikes law may serve as a deterrent to repeat offenders. Every repeat offender who is sentenced to a 25-year to life prison term becomes an example of what might happen to others. Would-be repeat offenders might then decide that a 25-year to life prison sentence is too much to risk and would thus avoid crime and turn to a law-abiding lifestyle.

Specific deterrence, sometimes referred to as individual or special deterrence, is not targeted at the general public. Rather, it is designed to discourage or prevent an individual offender from committing any *additional* crimes beyond those for which he or she has already been punished. Specific deterrence would occur if the offender decided that the punishment he or she already experienced was unpleasant and something to avoid in the future. To avoid future punishment, the offender would decide to live a law-abiding lifestyle. This specific offender would then have been deterred from future criminal activity.

The two people who most influenced deterrence theory were Jeremy Bentham ([1789] 1988) and Cesare Beccaria ([1764] 1995). Recall from Chapter 6 that Bentham's theory of justice was based on an analysis of pleasure and pain. This extends to deterrence theory because Bentham believed that offenders, or potential offenders, are rational. This means that people, when deciding on a course of action, consider the potential for both the pleasure and the pain it would produce. If the pleasure outweighs the potential pain, Bentham argued that the person will likely engage in the act. This is known as **hedonism**. If the pain outweighs the pleasure, he or she will be deterred from the action. For example, if you had to choose between attending a study session for an upcoming criminal justice exam or skipping the study session to go to a movie, which would you choose? A rational choice would require you to weigh the pleasure of going to the movie against the pain of doing poorly on the upcoming exam. The fear of doing poorly on the exam might then deter you from going to the movie.

Beccaria believed that three things are necessary for deterrence to be effective. First, the punishment should *swiftly* follow the crime. This is important because the more distance there is between the criminal act and the punishment, the less likely the offender is to associate the punishment with the crime. Second, the punishment should be *certain*. This means the offender must know that he or she will be punished instead of believing that he or she can get away with the crime. After all, if an offender truly believes that he or she will get away without being caught, then concerns about potential punishments become moot. Third, much like just deserts, the punishment must be *proportional* to the harm caused by the crime. Although Beccaria was an advocate for deterrence, he strongly believed that there are limits to the severity of punishment. Punishments that are too severe can actually be counterproductive to deterrence. For instance, Beccaria opposed the death penalty as well as the torture of prisoners.

There is great debate over the effectiveness of deterrence (see Nagin, 1998). To illustrate, assume you are driving your vehicle over the posted speed limit. You glance in your rear-view mirror and notice a police cruiser rapidly approaching your car. Your heart starts to beat rapidly, and you appear to be paying more attention to what is behind you than what is ahead. The police officer activates the vehicle's emergency equipment (lights and siren), and you begin to pull your vehicle over, when the officer passes you and stops the vehicle in front of you. You are relieved. You now make a promise: "I will never speed again." Does the fear of being caught deter you from ever speeding again?

Based on this example, do you believe that deterrence is effective? If not, you are not alone. There are a number of reasons deterrence is often ineffective. First, as suggested earlier, deterrence assumes that people think rationally, but this is not always the case. Mental illness sometimes clouds rational thinking. For instance, a person with schizophrenia suffering from (false) delusions that he is under personal attack may not be deterred from committing harm against another person because he strongly believes that his actions are in self-defense.

It is also important to realize not all decisions are made on a rational basis; in fact, much of human behavior may be motivated by irrational factors. Some psychologists believe this to be the case. For instance, Sigmund Freud believed that human behavior, including criminal behavior, is the product of forces in the unconscious mind. Behaviorists, such as B. F. Skinner and John B. Watson, believed that behavior is produced through a combination of both punishments for negative behavior *and* rewards for good behavior, suggesting that punishment, or the threat of punishment, *by itself* is insufficient to produce change; a system of rewards is also necessary. Neuropsychology is exploring new frontiers in terms of how the biology of the brain may influence behavior. Therefore, it becomes clear that deterrence theory's reliance on rationality as the primary basis for human behavior is likely misplaced.

Second, punishment is usually not swift; it may take years before a criminal case comes to trial, particularly for complicated legal cases, such as those involving murder or other serious crimes. Third, punishment is not certain. There is just no way to predict *if* an offender will be caught and punishment enforced, let alone *how* punishment will be administered. Recall from Chapter 1 that many crimes are not reported to the police, and of those that are reported, most are never cleared or solved. Fourth, punishment is not always proportional. As illustrated earlier, judicial discretion plays a major role in how offenders are sentenced. For similar offenses, one judge may offer probation to the offender, whereas another judge may impose the maximum penalty allowed by law. Fifth, offenders are not always aware of the punishments. You may be thinking that ignorance of the law is no excuse; true enough, but under Bentham's argument, a person must know the potential punishment to enter into the calculus of pleasure versus pain that can lead to deterrence.

INCAPACITATION

Incapacitation is a form of punishment that removes or reduces the offender's ability to commit criminal activities. The most common form of incapacitation is imprisonment. Under this justification of punishment, a person who is confined in prison will be unable to commit crimes against *society*. Notice that the key word here is "society." Crimes can and do occur in a prison setting; for the most part, those crimes are committed by inmates against other inmates, such as physical assaults, thefts, robberies, and so forth. Even in prison, inmates can be placed into solitary confinement (now known as "administrative segregation"), which is like a jail within the prison. In such a setting, an inmate would be physically separated from other inmates, which would, in turn, render it more difficult for him or her to commit criminal activities in the prison setting. Accordingly, the idea of incapacitation is that removing an offender to prison, or to administrative segregation units within a prison, eliminates or reduces the opportunity for that offender to commit crimes in society—at least for the time that he or she is in prison.

Incapacitation is currently a principal goal of the American criminal justice system. Faith in rehabilitation (discussed below) declined in the 1970s, which provided political momentum for a move toward incapacitation. President

Ronald Reagan, elected in 1980, believed that society needed to "get tough" on crime. As a result, the use of prisons as a form of punishment expanded dramatically. This has resulted in what some criminologists have called "the new penology" (Feeley & Simon, 1992, p. 449), in which prisons are viewed merely as warehouses to hold and incapacitate offenders until they have to be released back into the community.

Incapacitation is not limited to confinement in a prison. It can be argued that the death penalty is a form of incapacitation. Execution certainly removes the opportunity for the individual offender to commit another crime. In earlier times, banishment and transportation were popular methods of incapacitation. Banished offenders were expelled from their towns and counties and told never to return. Offenders who were "transported" were sent by ship (the means of transportation at the time) to a penal colony. A penal colony is a colonial location or settlement where prisoners were sent to live. Most, if not all, of the penal colonies relied on the prisoners to perform free labor that would benefit the nation's economy. For instance, Great Britain sent offenders to the American colonies and later to Australia to produce goods that were shipped back to Great Britain for sale. Both banishment and transportation assumed that as long as offenders were not in the immediate area, they could do no harm to society.

Incapacitation can also include removing the instrumentalities of the crime—that is, tools or capabilities that made the crime possible in the first place. For instance, some DUI offenders must forfeit their driver's licenses (and in some cases, their cars), which could render them unable to commit another DUI offense. Likewise, some sex offenders undergo chemical castration, which is meant to reduce or remove their physical ability to commit a sexual offense. While not relying on prison, these examples also have the effect of incapacitation.

REHABILITATION

Rehabilitation is an attempt to *correct* an offender's behavior to make it conform to the norms of society. To be effective, rehabilitation must be offender specific. Unlike the philosophy of *just deserts*—letting the punishment fit the crime—the viewpoint here is *let the punishment fit the offender*. The focus is on "treating" the offender through therapy, vocational or work-release programs, or educational training, to mention just a few. In theory, if rehabilitation is successful, the violator will return to society "cured" of his or her criminal ways and thereby become a productive member of the community.

It is interesting to note that the very first prison in the United States, Eastern State Penitentiary, opened in Philadelphia in 1829, was designed to promote the rehabilitation of offenders. In that prison, offenders were locked in a cell and permitted no human contact for the duration of their sentence. They were provided with a Bible to read, and the idea was that isolated reading and reflection would lead inmates to repent and change their ways.

However, it was not until the mid-twentieth century that rehabilitation gained widespread popularity in the United States. Advocates of rehabilitation strongly believed that treatment of the offender was more humane than other forms of punishment. Furthermore, criminology had advanced to a point where treatment of the offender was possible based on theories of what caused, and could prevent, crime. Rehabilitation was also viewed as useful to society by preparing reformed offenders to rejoin society as fully productive members.

In the 1970s, rehabilitation began to lose its popularity. This was in part due to a landmark study by Robert Martinson (1974), which stated, "with few and isolated exceptions, the rehabilitative efforts that have been reported so far have had no appreciable effect on recidivism" (p. 25). That is, the study suggested that rehabilitation programs were not effective. This result was quickly accepted by the public and politicians, and it coincided with the beginning of the get-tough era (discussed above), as states moved away from rehabilitation. This was based in part on political trends, in part on a suspicion of the discretion applied in correctional decisions about the provision and evaluation of inmate rehabilitation, and in part on the interpretation of Martinson's results as suggesting that nothing could ever work (Cullen, 2005).

At the same time, correctional experts began a research program focused on rehabilitation. A follow-up study by Martinson, himself, found that rehabilitation still held promise. Additional evidence mounted to show that rehabilitation could be effective if rehabilitative efforts were properly designed. For instance, keys to success included identifying the behaviors or factors that were most amenable to treatment, designing programs that specifically target those behaviors and patterns, and then determining which programs were most appropriate for which offenders. As a result, experts now know that rehabilitation can be effective (Cullen, 2005).

The new penology continues, but rehabilitation has made a resurgence as well. Interestingly, the public seems to simultaneously support punitive policies and rehabilitation (Cullen, Fisher, & Applegate, 2000). In addition, rehabilitative efforts have been justified as cost-saving correctional alternatives (e.g., Pallone & Hennessy, 2003), as offenders who can be rehabilitated are offenders for whom the state does not have to pay for long-term incarceration. As states experience budget cuts, this may become more important.

RESTITUTION AND RESTORATION

Restitution is a justification for punishment that requires the offender to pay back the victim—whether an individual, family, or society—for the harm caused by the offender's criminal behavior. More often than not, restitution involves some type of financial payback. It can also come through community service. Rather than paying the victim back directly with money, community service can symbolically provide restitution by requiring the offender to do something that betters the community harmed by the offense.

Restitution has evolved into a popular strategy called restorative justice. Recall from Chapter 6 that restorative justice goes beyond a mere personal financial settlement; it is a process to restore the health of the community while focusing on the needs of both the victim and the offender. For restorative justice to be effective, the offender must play an active role in the healing process by taking responsibility for his or her actions. By accepting and repaying the harm caused by his or her actions, the offender may be "restored" to society.

Restorative justice includes a variety of strategies, including the use of mediation or even apologies between victim and offender. For instance, a community dispute resolution center in Durham, North Carolina, provides mediation for low-level criminal complaints, such as "harassment, assault, and related problems among relatives, neighbors, and acquaintances" (McGillis, 1998, p. 3). In cases when both parties agree to participate, the process can provide several advantages over a traditional criminal proceeding. "Mediation provides disputants with the opportunity to communicate face to face, enables disputants to see each other as human beings rather than abstract opponents, and provides opportunities to identify common ground that can lead to the resolution of conflict" (McGillis, 1998, p. 13). This is at the center of what restorative justice encourages—collaborations to address the needs of, and thus heal, both parties and the community as a whole. The role that apologies may play in healing has led to increased discussion of their use (see Lazare, 2004), and in fact, apology has played an important form of dispute resolution in some societies, including Japan (Wagatsuma & Rosett, 1986).

One controversial form of restorative justice is shaming. John Braithwaite (1989) argues that there are two forms of shaming. The first and perhaps most effective is **reintegrative shaming**. This is a strategy whereby the offender is publicly shamed or scolded for his or her actions. The community will then, theoretically, forgive the offender and accept him or her back.

Realistically, reintegrative shaming is difficult to implement because members of society rarely forgive and reaccept the offender back into the community. As a result, most modern shaming punishments take the form of **disintegrative shaming**. Disintegrative shaming labels offenders as deviant, thereby separating them from the community rather than integrating them back into it. For instance, some states use disintegrative shaming as part of their sentences for driving under the influence. Under such a sentence, the offender found guilty of driving under the influence would display a specialized license plate (usually donning a special color). This labels the driver as a violator of the drunken driving statute, shaming that offender. As another example, some judges have required offenders to stand in public places wearing placards that announce their crimes—such as "I am a thief" or "I commit mail fraud." However, in either of these instances, there is no effort to reintegrate the offender through forgiveness and acceptance. Rather, the shaming simply labels the offender and stigmatizes him or her further.

What do you think are the advantages and disadvantages of each justification for punishment? Which philosophy of punishment do you think is most promising? Least promising? Explain your answer.

Describe how the Andrade case could have been handled under each of the five justifications for punishment. Which do you think is preferable? Why?

Do you believe offenders/criminals can be rehabilitated? Explain your reasoning. If you believe that some criminals cannot be rehabilitated, which ones fall into that category? Explain.

The Politics of Whom We Punish

FOCUSING QUESTION 10.3

Who is selected for punishment?

Now that you understand what punishment is and the justifications for it, the question remains, whom do we punish? You could answer this question by saying that we punish lawbreakers. However, this may be too simplistic a response. There are certain groups of people who are targeted for punishment far more often than the general population. These groups of people are labeled as the **dangerous classes** (see Shelden, 2001).

As with the definition of punishment, determining who is included among the dangerous classes changes with time, location, circumstances, and so on. Persons placed into the category of "dangerous classes" may be labeled as unworthy of equal treatment, as posing a threat to society, or as otherwise undesirable. However, it is important to note that these individuals are *not necessarily* criminal or inherently bad. They are only *perceived* as dangerous, generally by persons with social or political power, and then labeled accordingly. This is another example of social construction and labeling within the criminal justice system.

Although the dangerous classes may include persons from selected races, ethnic backgrounds, religious affiliations, sexual orientations, and/or regions, they certainly are not limited to those groups. For instance, police officers often attempt to identify those among the population who fall within the dangerous classes. For example, some, though not all, police officers are quick to attach a label to law violators. These officers may include among the dangerous classes persons who they believe may cause harm to society or to them personally, such as social deviants, illegal drug users, mentally ill subjects, and juvenile status offenders (i.e., truants, runaways, curfew violators, or others whose offenses are based on their status as juveniles).

According to Jerome Skolnick (1966), police officers develop a **perceptual shorthand** to assist in the immediate identification of persons believed to pose a personal danger or harm to society. These *symbolic assailants*, when observed, are routinely subjected to higher levels of social control than other persons. For example, assume you are a police officer on patrol and you observe two groups loitering on the sidewalk at night. One is a group of religious clergy conversing on a street corner, and the other is a group of teenagers leaning against a building. To which group would you pay more attention? Would you ask either group what their business is or even to move along? Juveniles have traditionally posed problems for the police, and the police have labeled them as members of the dangerous classes.

The point is that some groups are deemed dangerous by those with political, legal, or social power and have accordingly been subject to higher levels of law enforcement. Again, this is based on perceptions, biases, and sometimes discrimination, rather than actual levels of danger.

The importance of understanding the concept of the dangerous classes cannot be overstated. Being labeled as a member of the dangerous class is a means by which society and government can identify, control, and punish those targeted individuals and groups. Once tagged as members of a dangerous class, laws can then be established to constrain them. This can result in policies that foster inequality. For instance, when some drug laws were created, certain groups were labeled as dangerous classes and targeted for greater enforcement based on their race. According to Shelden (2001), Hispanics and African Americans were the focus of marijuana drug enforcement during the 1930s; during the 1950s, African Americans were the target of heroin enforcement; and from the 1980s (and up to the time of this writing), African Americans were the center of attention for the enforcement of crack cocaine. Other racial groups were not so vigorously targeted for drug enforcement, although other racial groups were involved in drug use and drug law violations. Therefore, labeling a group as a member of a dangerous class is not a drug law issue; it is a human rights issue that results from prejudice and group stereotyping.

> Can you think of other groups that have been identified as a member of the dangerous classes? If so, which groups? How have those groups experienced higher levels of law enforcement and punishment than others? Explain your reasoning.

Limitations on Criminal Punishment

FOCUSING QUESTION 10.4

Under what circumstances can punishment not be given?

Punishment does not occur without some limits. In fact, there are three philosophical principles that limit punishment under the criminal law: culpability, legality, and proportionality. Punishments may not be given if an individual is not culpable, if criminal laws are not properly constructed, or if the punishment itself violates the Eighth Amendment.

CULPABILITY: A FAIRNESS PRINCIPLE REQUIRING BLAMEWORTHINESS

The criminal law usually requires some level of **culpability**, or blameworthiness, as a prerequisite to criminal punishment. That is, only when individuals are actually guilty of a crime as defined under the law are they subjected to punishment. Recall the discussion of substantive criminal law in Chapter 9. Culpability generally requires both *actus reus*, or a criminal act, and *mens rea*, or criminal intent. The criminal law generally does *not* seek to punish persons who commit acts when they lack free will, such as people who commit acts involuntarily or under duress. The criminal law also generally does not seek to punish persons who lack rationality, such as very young or severely mentally ill offenders. In either case, imposing a punishment would be unjust because the offender would not have had the intent to commit a crime. Recall, however, that there is a class of crimes called strict liability offenses, which punish certain acts even if *mens rea* is lacking. Might these crimes be exceptions to the principle of culpability? Should they be?

NOTICE AND THE PRINCIPLE OF LEGALITY

People must be given fair notice of what is expected of them before they can be punished for not having lived up to those expectations. This is the principle of **legality**, which is based on a Latin phrase introduced in Chapter 1: *nullum crimen sine lege, nulla poena sine lege*, meaning there can be no crime without a law that defines it, and there can be no punishment without a law that allows it. This principle is central to notions of fairness and due process, and three implications flow from it.

First, under the principle of legality, no one can be punished for an act that is not expressly labeled as a criminal act by a penal code. Generally speaking, no act can be defined or punished as a crime until a legislature (or the public) vote to include it in their jurisdiction's criminal code. This is important because it ensures advance notice of what is and is not a crime. A police officer cannot make up a law on the spot and arrest a person for it, nor may a court make up a law and then punish a person for it. Laws must be specified before they can be enforced and their violators punished.

Second, criminal laws must be interpreted according to their plain meaning. If the meaning of a criminal law is unclear, most states will interpret it by using common sense and by considering what the lawmakers wanted to accomplish (see *United States v. Brown*, 1948). Some states go a step farther and require their courts to apply only what is precisely stated within a law, bypassing interpretation altogether. This is important because for fair notice to be given, the laws must clearly specify what conduct is being prohibited.

Third, the principle of legality prohibits governments from punishing someone if a criminal law is written too vaguely. A law is deemed **void for vagueness**, and therefore unenforceable, when it is written in such a way that "men of common intelligence must necessarily guess at its meaning and differ as to its application" (Robinson, 2005, p. 356). This is important because it prevents police officers, judges, and citizens from having to guess at the meaning of the law. It also prevents police officers and judges from making up the meaning of law—and from applying made-up meanings unfairly and unequally to groups labeled as the dangerous classes.

PROPORTIONALITY AND THE EIGHTH AMENDMENT

The Eighth Amendment of the U.S. Constitution reads: "Excessive bail shall not be required, nor excessive fines imposed, nor cruel and unusual punishment inflicted." This single sentence raises many important issues and debates, some of which are described next.

Bail. Bail is not a form of punishment. However, to someone who must post bail, it may feel as though it is a punishment. **Bail** is a financial or property-based pledge to ensure that the accused will appear in court. An accused person provides a sum of money or a property title to the court in exchange for being released into the community prior to trial. If the accused person appears in court at the required date and time, the money or property is returned. If the accused fails to appear (FTA) in court, he or she will forfeit the money or property, which will then belong to the court. In addition, an FTA remains on a person's record, and if caught, that person will be compelled to return to court—and almost certainly will not be granted bail again.

Persons who are unable to post their full bail amount may seek the services of bail bond agents. For a fee, usually in the amount of 10% of the bail, the bail bond agent will post the full amount to the court on behalf of the accused. The 10% fee is a cost that is not returned to accused persons, whether or not they appear in court or are found guilty or not guilty, but it does allow them to remain in the community prior to trial. The Supreme Court suggested in 1872 that bail bond agents have wide latitude to pursue those persons who fail to appear in court after securing their services (*Taylor v. Taintor*, 1872), which has given rise to controversies about the authority of bail bounty hunters and has led to laws in some jurisdictions that place limits on their activities.

Note that the Eighth Amendment does *not* require bail to be granted; it simply states that bail shall not be *excessive*. In some cases, dangerous persons or those whom the judge believes are likely to flee will not be granted bail at all (see *U.S. v. Salerno*, 1987). The prohibition against excessive bail is designed to protect accused persons from being unnecessarily incarcerated prior to trial when there is not a public safety reason for doing so. When considering the amount of bail and whether or not it is excessive, there are a number of factors that judges may consider.

- *The type of offense committed*. A person who has been arrested for murder may have substantially higher bail, or even be denied bail, than someone arrested for theft. The more serious the crime, the greater potential the accused person will attempt to flee. Therefore, bail is higher for serious offenses.

- *The circumstances surrounding the offense.* Because they are more blameworthy and thus more likely to FTA, higher bail might be set for the "instigators" or initiators of a criminal act.
- *Behavior of the accused.* If the accused resisted arrest or was belligerent to the arresting officer, that can signal a judge that the person might be risky to release, in which case bail may be set at a higher level or denied.
- *The ability of the accused to pay the bail.* Does the accused possess the financial and/or property means to post bail? If so, bail may be set at a level that is affordable to the individual, yet high enough to compel attendance at trial. Some low-risk persons may also be released before trial without having to offer money or property in exchange. This is called release on recognizance (ROR).
- *The accused's chances of not returning for trial.* Bail might be set higher or denied altogether if the accused does not live or work in the area or if the accused does not have immediate family or close friends in the jurisdiction. Individuals without community ties may be more likely to flee.

Excessive Fines. The Eighth Amendment also provides that excessive fines not be imposed. Unlike bail, **fines** are financial penalties that are imposed after the accused has been found guilty of a crime. As such, fines are a form of punishment. The law often provides an upper limit that a fine may not exceed. For instance, a state criminal code might specify that the maximum fine for a Class D (low-level) misdemeanor is $250. Otherwise, imposing fines generally depends on judicial discretion, with judges imposing whatever fines—within the legal limit—they believe are appropriate. Fines are usually applied for minor offenses, such as traffic offenses and some misdemeanors.

The Eighth Amendment prohibition against excessive fines is difficult to define. This is because it remains unclear as to what "excessive" really means. For an interesting example, consider the use of day fines as described in Box 10.1.

Cruel and Unusual Punishments. The Eighth Amendment to the U.S. Constitution prohibits the imposition of **cruel and unusual punishments**. The Eighth Amendment was written to ban inhumane punishment and to ensure fair and equal treatment of offenders. But what is "cruel"? What is "unusual"? As an example, you will probably agree that capital punishment (i.e., the death penalty) for motor vehicle theft is too extreme, but what is it that makes this punishment unusual or even cruel?

One answer is the principle of **proportionality**, which is the idea that the punishment should "fit the crime." Recall that proportionality is important to both just deserts and deterrence as justifications for punishment. It is also important from a legal perspective, as punishments may be unconstitutional

BOX 10.1

DAY FINES

Should the American criminal justice system make a greater use of fines? Consider this. In the United States, fines are primarily assigned for traffic offenses and for low-level criminal violations (i.e., misdemeanors). However, in many European countries, fines are utilized much more frequently, even for serious criminal offenses and crimes of violence (i.e., felonies).

One problem with fines is determining the proper amount. Fines that are too high may go unpaid by offenders, and fines that are too low may diminish the seriousness of an offense. One solution, again common in European countries but not in the United States, is the use of the day fine. **Day fines** allow judges to assign a fine that is proportional to an offender's "daily" income. Here's how they work. First, the government assigns a number of fine units based on the severity of each offense. Let's use motor vehicle theft as an example and assume that it is worth 30 fine units. Second, the government determines the value of each fine unit. Let's assume that each fine unit is valued as half of an offender's daily income. Finally, judges do the math. If an offender who makes $80 per day commits motor vehicle theft, that offender's fine would be $1,200 (each fine unit = $40; $40 × 30 fine units = $1,200). If an offender makes $1,000 per day, that offender's fine would be $15,000 (each fine unit = $500; $500 × 30 fine units = $15,000).

Therefore, day fines vary based on an offender's income. In one case, a wealthy driver in Finland who was going 25 miles per hour over the posted speed limit received a $204,000 penalty in a day fine system (Moore, 2007).

Why do you think the United States relies on punishments other than fines for serious criminal offenses?

Is a $204,000 traffic ticket unreasonable in this case? Why or why not?

What arguments can you make for and against day fines? What philosophies of punishment do they illustrate?

If day fines were utilized in the United States, do you think they would violate the Eighth Amendment?

Is it possible to develop a "fair" system of fines?

when they are grossly excessive in relation to the crime committed. In *Weems v. United States* (1910), the U.S. Supreme Court first signaled that the principle of proportionality was a part of Eighth Amendment jurisprudence.

Of course, this begs the question of how proportionality is determined. Unfortunately, there is no easy answer. Think back to the case study at the beginning of this chapter. Andrade appealed his two 25-years to life sentences, and the Supreme Court ultimately ruled that they were not so disproportionate to the crime as to be unconstitutional (*Lockyer v. Andrade*, 2003). Consider the implications of this. For theft of approximately $150 worth of videotapes, Andrade will likely spend the remainder of his life in prison. Of course, Andrade's sentence was based in part on his prior criminal history. However, compare this to a case heard by the Supreme Court 20 years before Andrade's. In *Solem v.*

Helm (1983), the defendant had six prior felony convictions, all for nonviolent offenses (burglary, grand larceny, driving while intoxicated, and obtaining money under false pretenses). Upon his seventh felony conviction, which was for check fraud, the defendant was sentenced to life in prison without parole. In that case, however, the Supreme Court ruled that the punishment was cruel and unusual, stating that the defendant "has received the penultimate sentence for relatively minor criminal conduct . . . [and] his sentence is significantly disproportionate to his crime." As you can see, there is an apparent inconsistency between these two cases. Unfortunately, this has left lawyers, scholars, and justice professionals wondering what disproportionate punishment actually means.

In addition to ensuring that punishments are proportional, the Eighth Amendment was also intended to ban inhumane punishment. This, too, raises a question: what kinds of punishments are inhumane and unacceptable? The first Supreme Court case to explore this issue was *Wilkerson v. Utah* (1878). Here, the Supreme Court upheld executions by firing squad but prohibited burning, disemboweling, and drawing and quartering. In reaching its decision, the Supreme Court wrote, "Difficulty would attend the efforts to define with exactness . . . cruel and unusual punishments; but it is safe to affirm that punishments of torture . . . and all others in the same line of unnecessary cruelty, are forbidden." Thus, even the Supreme Court acknowledged that it is difficult to define cruel and unusual or inhumane punishments beyond banning those of "unnecessary" cruelty.

Box 10.2 provides further background about the Eighth Amendment and cruel and unusual punishment. Try your hand at deciding what is and is not cruel and unusual punishment based on actual court decisions. Some will require you to consider proportionality, and others will require you to consider the humanity or cruelty of the punishment itself.

WHAT CONSTITUTES CRUEL AND UNUSUAL PUNISHMENT?

BOX 10.2

In 1789, one reader of the Eighth Amendment observed that "the clause appears to express much humanity, as such, he liked it; but as it appeared to have no meaning, he did not like it" (Veit, Rowling, & Bickford, 1991, p. 180).

Has the Supreme Court been able to find the meaning of cruel and unusual punishment? You be the judge. In *Ingraham v. Wright*, the Court noted that it "limits the kinds of punishment that can be imposed of those convicted of crimes"; in *Solem v. Helm*, the Court indicated that "a criminal sentence must be proportionate to the [offender's] crime"; in *Gregg v. Georgia*, the Court specified that "the punishment must not involve the unnecessary and wanton infliction of pain"; in *Rhodes v. Chapman*, the Court applied it to "conditions [that] . . . deprive inmates of the minimal civilized measure of life's necessities"; and in *Trop v. Dulles*, the Court prohibited punishments that violate "evolving standards of decency that mark the progress of a maturing society."

(continued)

BOX 10.2 (continued)

How would you define what constitutes cruel and unusual punishment? Can you develop a test or set of criteria that would help you identify instances of cruel and unusual punishment? How would you apply your definition to the following issues?

Is it cruel and unusual . . .

- to execute offenders who are mentally retarded? The Supreme Court ruled "yes," cruel and unusual, in *Atkins v. Virginia*, 536 U.S. 304 (2002).
- to execute offenders who were under 18 when their crime was committed? The Supreme Court ruled "yes," cruel and unusual, in *Roper v. Simmons*, 543 U.S. 551 (2005).
- to execute offenders who rape but do not kill an adult? The Supreme Court ruled "yes," cruel and unusual, in *Coker v. Georgia*, 433 U.S. 584 (1977).
- to execute offenders who rape but do not kill children under 12 years of age? The Supreme Court ruled "yes," cruel and unusual, in *Kennedy v. Louisiana*, 128 S. Ct. 2641 (2008).
- to give a sentence of life without parole for possession of 672 grams of cocaine? The Supreme Court ruled "no," not cruel and unusual, in *Harmelin v. Michigan*, 501 U.S. 957 (1991).
- to give a sentence of life without parole to a juvenile being tried as an adult, when the crime is something other than murder? The Supreme Court ruled "yes," cruel and unusual, in *Graham v. Florida*, 130 S. Ct. 2011 (2010).
- to punish a person who falsified a document to defraud the government with 15 years of hard labor in chains? The Supreme Court ruled "yes," cruel and unusual, in *Weems v. U.S.*, 217 U.S. 349 (1910).
- to sentence a 17-year-old male who had consensual oral sex with a 15-year-old female to ten years in prison including registry as a sex offender, for life? The Georgia Supreme Court ruled "yes," cruel and unusual, in *Humphrey v. Wilson*, 282 Ga. 520 (2007).
- to punish a natural-born U.S. citizen by revoking his or her citizenship rights? The Supreme Court ruled "yes," cruel and unusual, in *Trop v. Dulles*, 356 U.S. 86 (1958).
- to use corporal punishment (i.e., whipping) on prison inmates? The 8th Circuit Court of Appeals ruled "yes," cruel and unusual, in *Jackson v. Bishop*, 404 F.2d 571 (1968).
- to use corporal punishment (i.e., spanking) on students in public schools? The Supreme Court ruled "no," not cruel and unusual, in *Ingraham v. Wright*, 430 U.S. 651 (1977).
- to punish an individual for a medical condition (i.e., addiction to narcotics)? The Supreme Court ruled "yes," cruel and unusual, in *Robinson v. California*, 370 U.S. 660 (1962).

After considering your own opinion on each case, review the list above.

How closely did your judgments match those of the courts? Do you see any patterns in what is or is not ruled as "cruel and unusual"?

A bartender who serves alcohol to an underage person can be criminally punished for doing so even if the person produced a fake ID. Is that fair? Would the bartender's punishment violate the principle of culpability? Why or why not?

The City of Chicago passed an ordinance "which prohibits 'criminal street gang members' from 'loitering' with one another or with other persons in any public place" (*Chicago v. Morales*, 1999). Do you think this law gives adequate notice of what conduct is prohibited? How would you interpret what this law means? Alternatively, would you rule it void for vagueness? Explain.

Do you agree with the decision in *Lockyer v. Andrade?* In *Solem v. Helm?* Explain your answers.

The Future of Punishment

FOCUSING QUESTION 10.5

How might punishment change in the future?

Although punishment may initially seem to be a simple concept, it can be quite complex. Consider these questions:

- What is punishment? How do we define it?
- What do we hope to accomplish through punishment? That is, what is the purpose of punishment?
- Should there be any limits on what kinds of punishments a society can impose? If so, what should those limits be?

After reading this chapter and considering the various issues that have been raised about the philosophy of punishment, how would you answer these questions? Bear in mind that philosophers, legal scholars, and social scientists have struggled with these very questions for centuries and have not been able to distill any absolute answers on which all can agree.

Punishment represents one of the ultimate powers held by the government in any society. Only government has the power to impose criminal punishments, and those punishments can take away rights commonly held by citizens, including the various deprivations noted at the beginning of the chapter. Criminal punishment can go further as well. Even after an offender is released from prison or probation, he or she may be denied the right to vote, to own firearms, to be licensed in certain professions, and even to live in certain areas. In short, the power to punish is precisely that—a far-reaching power of the state that merits close scrutiny.

Punishment is also ever changing. Philosophies about punishment change over time; the United States moved from rehabilitation as a guiding philosophy in the 1960s to incapacitation as a guiding philosophy in the 1980s. Notions of the dangerous classes change over time, given each era's biases and discriminations, but the idea that some groups are under closer surveillance than others has been constant across history. Ideas of the acceptability of certain punishments also change; the death penalty is much less acceptable now than it has been previously in American history, but there may be an increased tolerance for lengthy prison sentences even for nonviolent offenders.

Finally, technological advances may change the landscape of punishment in the future. Fabelo (2000) writes of "technocorrections," in which new technologies may enable more sophisticated control of offenders. For instance, global positioning systems (GPS) allow probation officers to track the real-time movement of persons on probation. As tracking systems and computer technologies advance, could the future be a scenario where all known offenders may be tracked in real time on a publicly accessible Internet site? What would be the implications of this in terms of the justifications of punishment, the dangerous classes, and the Eighth Amendment? Ponder this question. Let it serve as an illustration of the importance of reflecting carefully on ideas about punishment.

How would you answer the questions posed in this section?

One concern about the future of corrections is that the reliance on incapacitation (and the new penology) costs too much money. What alternative punishment strategies could be used to maintain public safety while reducing costs?

If you were to design a system of punishment, what would it look like? Which ideas from this chapter would you incorporate? Which would you avoid? Why?

Conclusion

The power to impose punishment is arguably one of the most significant powers held by the state and federal governments. Following conviction for a crime, the government, through the criminal justice system, may compel individuals to surrender their money (through fines), their freedom (through jail and prison), or their lives (through the death penalty). Although punishments may be structured to accomplish a variety of objectives—retribution, deterrence, rehabilitation, incapacitation, or restoration—they must also comply with constitutional provisions primarily grounded in the Eighth Amendment. Like many elements within criminal justice, this illustrates the need for a balance between the achievement of punishment objectives, the protection of society, and the protection of rights. As we move to Unit V, we will turn to an exploration of the agencies within the criminal justice system—the police, courts, and corrections—who must work not only to enforce the law but also to strike the balances required by the Constitution, by notions of justice, and by concepts of law and morality. Their work is indeed challenging but necessary for an orderly society.

Criminal Justice Problem Solving:
THE DEATH PENALTY

The most controversial current issue pertinent to criminal punishment deals with the death penalty. The very existence of the death penalty raises philosophical questions about the right of the government to take a human life. Concerns about the death penalty are varied, including:

1. The disproportionate use of the death penalty against members of minority groups;
2. Debates about the death penalty's effectiveness as a deterrent;
3. Concerns about whether or not defendants receive adequate legal representation;
4. Strong international pressure to abolish capital punishment; and
5. Fear of executing innocent persons.

Drawing on the ideas raised throughout this chapter, structure an argument both for *and* against the death penalty. What are the key issues of disagreement and debate? Go to the library and do some research about these issues.

How would you answer what is quickly becoming the most pressing issue facing the criminal justice system: what should we do about the death penalty?

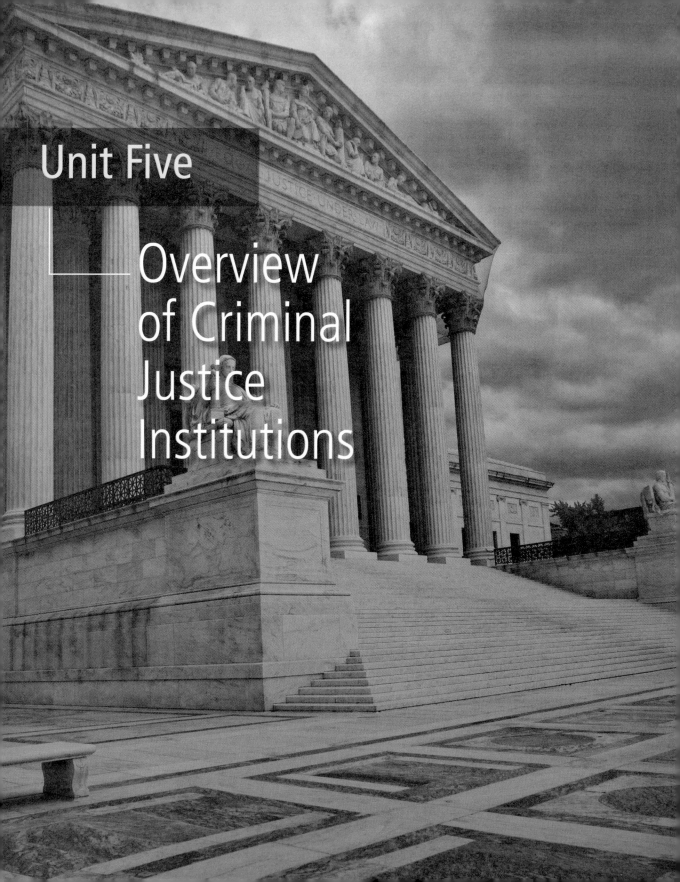

Unit Five

Overview
of Criminal
Justice
Institutions

Photo Essay: Toward the Future of Criminal Justice

Unit IV addressed the complexities of criminal law and punishment. This unit turns to an examination of the three primary components of the criminal justice system: the police, courts, and corrections. These are the agencies charged with enforcing the criminal law and determining and applying punishments. The work of the actors in the criminal justice process is profoundly shaped by the concepts in each of the previous units. As you read on, consider how issues of morality, deviance, justice, law, and punishment help to shape the role of the police, courts, and corrections.

Each of the chapters that follows provides some historical context for the development of the criminal justice system. Certainly, the criminal justice system is a dynamic entity, adapting to reflect new laws, new technologies, and new social challenges. The following examples are only a few of the innovative programs that are shaping criminal justice toward the future.

A simple truism of law enforcement is that it is not possible to place a police officer on every corner. However, technology can be used to supplement police coverage. London has a very well-developed closed circuit television (CCTV) system with CCTV cameras covering many city streets. The cameras have assisted police in lowering crime rates and reducing fear of crime (Gill & Spriggs, 2005). Some of the cameras are even equipped with speakers so that camera operators may caution potential offenders not to commit deviant acts. There has been debate about whether CCTV systems should be implemented on the streets of American cities. What do you think? Does CCTV raise privacy concerns, or is it an effective use of police technology?

Hot spots policing provides a new way of thinking about how to allocate police resources. Crime is not evenly distributed across space; rather, there are some (often relatively small) areas that experience crime at a higher rate than other parts of a community. Sophisticated computer

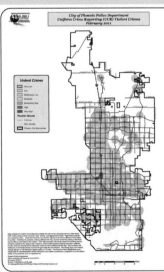

crime mapping techniques can identify concentrated areas of high crime called hot spots. Then, policing resources, often coupled with aggressive enforcement efforts, can be assigned to those areas. This has been found to reduce crime in hot spot areas (Weisburd & Braga, 2006). What potential benefits do you see from this strategy? What potential challenges do you see?

Mental health courts are designed to provide services to mentally ill offenders. The mentally ill are overrepresented in the criminal justice system and often do not have access to the services they need, which can exacerbate offending. In one form of probation, offenders referred to mental health courts are supervised by a probation officer while also receiving mental health services in the community. Progress is monitored through regular appearances before a judge, when each offender's status is reviewed. The courts have been found to dramatically reduce reoffending (Schwartz, 2008). Do you think the criminal justice system has an ethical or legal obligation to provide mental health services to offenders? Why do you think the mental health courts have been successful?

Most inmates who are sent to prison or jail will be released. This raises the question, what can the criminal justice system do to prepare inmates for their

reentry into society? This becomes a question of interest to public safety, as offenders who are well prepared for reintegration into society are less likely to recidivate. Reentry efforts received enhanced attention following President George W. Bush's 2004 State of the Union Address, in which he stressed their importance (U.S. Department of Justice, n.d.). What challenges do you think offenders face upon release from prison? What do you think could be done to help inmates successfully reenter society?

Operation Night Light is a program that was developed in Boston. Police officers and probation officers work together in teams to make unannounced

visits during the nighttime hours to the homes of persons on probation, to ensure that curfew requirements are being followed. In addition to verifying that offenders are where they are supposed to be, the program allows the police and probation officers to more easily share information about persons on probation. The program also allows probation officers and police to communicate with offenders and their families and to identify any areas of concern or any services that might be needed. The program has been credited with reducing crime rates, homicide in particular (Reichert, 2002). What elements of the program do you think help to make it successful? How does this illustrate formal and informal social control?

At first blush, prisons would seem an unlikely place for pets. However, a number of facilities have recognized that Prison Pup Programs can benefit inmates and the community alike (Harkrader, Burke, & Owen, 2004). In the programs, inmates are taught to train service dogs. During training, the dogs spend some time in the prison receiving training and some time with caregivers in the community. After being trained, the dogs enter the community and are paired with persons who benefit from the services they can provide. As a correctional administrator, how would you assess this program?

The work completed by police, court, and correctional personnel forms the backbone of the criminal justice system in the United States. As the examples presented illustrate, the criminal justice system constantly strives to develop new programming alternatives that can help to achieve goals including the maintenance of public safety, the enforcement of the law, and the rehabilitation of offenders. The chapters in Unit V will further explore the origins, development, and current practices of the agencies within the criminal justice system.

Core Concepts of U.S. Policing

Officers on bicycle patrol in a community. What role do you think the police should play in society?

Key Terms

police
Bobbies
political era
decentralization
professional era
thin blue line
community era
disorder theory
crime control theory
class control theory
urban dispersion theory
watchman style
legalistic style
service style
working personality
ethics
corruption

rotten apples
rotten pocket
grasseater
meateater
pervasive unorganized corruption
pervasive organized corruption
gratuity
professional courtesy
misuse of authority
Dirty Harry problem
team policing
community-oriented policing (COP)
problem-oriented policing (POP)
scanning, analysis, response, and
    assessment (SARA)
Compstat

Key People

William Muir
Sir Robert Peel
George Kelling
Mark Moore
James Q. Wilson
William Westley

Arthur Niederhoffer
Lawrence Sherman
Carl Klockars
Samuel Walker
Herman Goldstein

CASE STUDY

Policing a Housing Development

The New Briarfield Apartments are located in an East Coast city with 155,000 residents. The city police department has 234 officers and 46 civilian employees. The apartment complex consists of 400 one-story wooden units, each containing 4 to 16 apartments arranged in linear groups. Built in the 1940s, the apartments were originally designed and built as temporary housing facilities for workers at a World War II era shipyard. The apartments later served as public housing for low-income families. By the 1980s, the apartments were regarded as one of the worst housing developments in the city.

The residents are primarily low-income African Americans living in female-headed households. Residents live in fear of crime, sometimes afraid to leave their individual apartments. The apartments have a high crime rate, particularly burglary; for instance, 23% of the occupied units are broken into each year. Twenty percent of the units are vacant, some of which provided hiding places for drug users or dealers. With such a high vacancy rate, it is nearly impossible for the owners of the complex to make a profit; in fact, the owners were facing foreclosure of the property. Over time, the property has physically deteriorated as the temporary structures became run down, making it appear as though the facility was operated with a "who cares" approach to housing management. Litter, abandoned vehicles, and potholes mark the landscape.

The police have tried to respond with traditional strategies—such as patrol, response to calls for service, and occasional efforts by special task forces—but they have proven ineffective (Eck & Spelman, 1987; Wilson & Kelling, 1989). You are now the commander of the police district in which the apartments are located, and your chief, the fire chief, and other city agencies are demanding that you "do something" to improve the area and make it safer.

> What additional information would you want about the New Briarfield Apartment Complex before taking action? Why would this information be useful?
>
> _____
>
> What are some potential strategies you could use to improve the apartment complex? Why do you think these strategies would have the potential to be successful?
>
> _____
>
> What other agencies or groups (public or private) could you collaborate with to improve the New Briarfield Apartment Complex? How would working together help improve the situation?

Philosophies of Policing

FOCUSING QUESTION 11.1

How has the police role in society changed over time?

The very mention of the word *police* evokes a response, sometimes positive, sometimes negative. These responses are often shaped by personal contacts with the police, whether as a victim seeking assistance or as an offender arrested under a police officer's authority; by stories from friends and relatives, relating their accounts with police officers; by media portrayals of police activities, whether through the news or through entertainment programming; and by philosophies of moral and ethical behavior and how they might apply to the law enforcement function.

This chapter explores the institution of policing in American society by examining how conceptions of police duties have changed over time, the philosophies of policing that officers bring to the job, the organization of the law enforcement function in the United States, ethical issues faced by police officers, and strategies used by law enforcement agencies to respond to crime and disorder. As you read this chapter, consider how the concepts of law, morality, and justice discussed earlier in the book might apply to the policing function.

The police role in society is shaped by two key concepts: order maintenance and the legitimate use of force. Policing scholar Jerome Skolnick (1966) observed that "the **police** in a democratic society are required to maintain order and to do so under the rule of law" (p. 6). To return to the concept of social control described in Chapter 4, the police are agents of formal social control, ensuring that society's laws are enforced. Functioning under the rule of law also means that the police must follow legally prescribed procedures in enforcing law and order, such as those established in the Bill of Rights, as described in the coverage of procedural justice in Chapter 8.

When enforcing law and maintaining order, the "police are . . . given the right to use coercive force by the state within the state's domestic territory" (Klockars, 1985b, p. 12). This means that a police officer acting within his or her official capacity to maintain order can use whatever force is reasonable and necessary, up to and including deadly force, to protect a citizen or officer from imminent harm.

As noted in Chapter 1, the presence of discretion is a fundamental attribute of the criminal justice system. In their daily work, police officers must make many discretionary decisions, and these often relate to distributive justice (as defined in Chapter 6). Discretion is common in policing for a variety of reasons, including the following: limited resources and agency priorities make it impossible to enforce all laws equally all of the time; citizen demands may lead police agencies to focus more extensively on some laws at the expense of others; and there is sometimes a need for professional judgment made by police officers on a case-by-case basis (consider whether there is ever an "excusable" reason for speeding, for instance). Quite simply, discretion is not unusual; in fact, it is an everyday occurrence in police work (Klockars, 1985b). At the same time, making discretionary decisions is a substantial power held by the police officer on the street which, in part, led William Muir (1977) to describe the police as "streetcorner politicians" (p. 271).

For centuries, the police function has been defined by the duty to enforce law and maintain order with the ability to use force in doing so, all while exercising discretion. However, the application of these principles has changed over time. To better understand the philosophy of policing, we need to explore its history.

POLICING IN ENGLAND

We begin our journey in London, England, during the early nineteenth century. London is significant because much of the American criminal justice system was heavily influenced by the English model and because it was the location of the first, modern, organized police department.

In 1829, the first metropolitan police department was formed in England by Sir Robert Peel. Robert Peel was the Home Secretary, responsible for internal security in England, not unlike the U.S. Departments of Justice and of Homeland Security. London was having its share of public disorders, including riots. Peel's goal was to develop a police force that would effectively and efficiently curtail riots, public disorder, and crime. Furthermore, Peel's officers, named **Bobbies** after his first name, were to accomplish these goals without the use of firearms. For personal protection, Bobbies only carried a small truncheon (club) under their coat. To this day, with a few exceptions, English Bobbies do not carry firearms.

Peel strongly advocated for proactive policing, believing that Bobbies should work to "prevent" crime before it occurs rather than "react" to crime after it is committed. A positive police–community relationship was also central to Peel's vision, as he argued that the police patrol should provide opportunities for police–public interactions and that the police should act respectfully toward citizens. Finally, Peel believed that officers should be carefully selected and well trained to fulfill their duties (Roberg, Crank, & Kuykendall, 2000).

Peel's law enforcement philosophy proved quite successful in England. Although policing developed around the same time in the United States, it took a very different form. In fact, early policing in the United States was nothing short of chaos, and it took more than 100 years for American policing to aspire to Peel's principles. According to police scholars Kelling and Moore (1988; see also Fogelson, 1977), three historical eras helped shape the role of the police in the United States: the *political era* (1830s to early 1900s), the *professional era* (1930s to 1970s), and the *community era* (1970s to present). It was only in the community era that American policing began to meet all of Peel's principles.

THE POLITICAL ERA (1830s–EARLY 1900s)

The **political era** was America's introduction to policing (for a comparison of English and American policing in this time period, see Miller, 1975). As its name implies, early policing in the United States was characterized by political undertones bordering on all-out corruption. The police and local politicians frequently had an intimate relationship encouraged by decentralization.

Decentralization means that there is not one central law enforcement agency but rather that each geographic area, whether city, town, or county, has its own police force. This also means that there is not a central philosophy accepted by all law enforcement agencies. Fearful of a strong central government, Americans found local policing more acceptable than having a single national agency.

Having individual agencies with little centralized control allowed for early police forces to be controlled by local politicians, often town council members or the mayor. Rather than serving the public good, the police often engaged in favoritism, sustaining those who supported them. In some departments, officers obtained their jobs by bribing political leaders. For instance, in New York City, promotions once went to the highest bidder: "The going rate in New York was $1,600 for sergeants and $12,000–$15,000 for captains . . . More often the party leaders gave promotions to political favorites" (Fogelson, 1977, p. 29).

Early police officers often lacked professionalism. Reports range from regular evasion of duty and drunkenness on the job to "mutual disrespect and brutality . . . between the police and the public" and overlooking criminal activity in exchange for bribes (Walker, 1980, p. 63).

The police were sometimes used as pawns in larger political disputes as well. In 1853, the New York State legislature became concerned about the amount of power that New York City had accumulated under its mayor at the time, Fernando Wood. In response, the state government established a new New York City police force, under state control (the "Metropolitans"), but did not disband the old police force, which was under city control (the "Municipals"). A riot occurred between the two police forces on the steps of City Hall and "whenever a cop of one force made an arrest, a cop of the other would set the culprit free, and the competing forces routinely raided each other's station houses and freed en masse the prisoners in each other's jails" (Sante, 1991, p. 239).

Some have suggested that the police were able to build community relations during the political era. Police were often selected and assigned to their patrol detail based on their political affiliation, personal contacts, and ethnicity (e.g., Italian officers patrolled the Italian district, Irish officers patrolled the Irish district, etc.). As a result, the police were familiar with their communities and their respective power structures. The police sometimes provided social assistance, such as providing housing and food for the homeless and needy (see Wagner, 2008). However, this was often done for political benefit. If the police helped citizens in the neighborhood, citizens would feel appreciative toward the police, who could then encourage them to support their local politicians at election time. As was typical of the political era, benefits for local politicians were a primary interest (Fogelson, 1977; Kelling & Moore, 1988).

A significant problem that arose during the political era was police discrimination against strangers to the community and members of different ethnic and racial groups. Officers treated these individuals as members of the "dangerous classes," often using brutal force against them. Simply stated, in the political era, it was nearly impossible to maintain a sense of organizational control, leading to police agencies that were ineffective, inefficient, disorganized, and corrupt (Fogelson, 1977; Kelling & Moore, 1988).

Walker (1984) unflatteringly summarized the priorities of police officers in the political era as follows:

> The first was to get and hold the job. The second was to exploit the possibilities for graft [bribery and payoffs] that the job offered. A third was to do as little actual patrol work as possible. A fourth involved surviving on the street, which meant establishing and maintaining authority in the face of hostility and overt challenges to that authority. Finally, officers apparently felt obliged to go through the motions of 'real' police work by arresting occasional miscreants (p. 87).

Clearly, it was time for policing to change.

THE PROFESSIONAL ERA (1930s–1970s)

Political era police agencies were in need of reform, and several factors led to their reform. First, muckraking journalists published articles about the corruption of local governments and advocated reform (e.g., Steffens, [1904] 1992). Second, there was an emerging public philosophy promoting good government, which came to be known as the Progressive Movement. Supporters of the movement promoted civil service (i.e., selection of government employees based on qualifications rather than favoritism), dismantling local political corruption and encouraging government professionalism. Third, technology led to tactical change. Patrol in automobiles became the central new strategy used by police agencies, made possible in part by radio communication and dispatch. The justification was simple: criminals increasingly had cars, so police should have them as well. The move to motorized patrol replaced the neighborhood-centered policing networks that had been a defining feature of the political era.

The professional era was led by noted reformers such as former Berkeley, California, police chief August Vollmer, his protégé O. W. Wilson, and Federal Bureau of Investigation Director J. Edgar Hoover. The primary goal of the **professional era** was to remove the political element from policing. This was accomplished in part by organizational changes, such as adopting a military model for police agencies, creating hierarchies that allowed more effective supervision of officers, and developing specialized units (e.g., detective bureaus) to focus on key tasks.

During the professional era, police agencies also strived to become more professional. Policing was to be viewed as a profession with training programs, a public service motivation, and an ethical code (similar to doctors, lawyers, teachers, and engineers). Police officers were expected to meet high admission standards, to undergo extensive training, and to be free from corruption.

The professional era's focus was on crime control, crime prevention, and offender apprehension characterized by rapid responses to calls for police service and the use of preventive patrols. It was assumed that the faster the officer responded to a call for service, the greater the chance of apprehending the violator. In addition, police presence was believed to serve as a visual deterrent to potential law violators.

Officers were encouraged to distance themselves from the community to minimize the potential for favoritism. This style of policing was often characterized by television's *Dragnet* character Sergeant Friday, who coined the phrase "just the facts, ma'am; just the facts." The role of the police was to respond to a call, learn the facts, respond to them, and leave, without an emphasis on community interaction.

During this time and even to the modern day, policing in the United States has remained decentralized. In the professional era, the Federal Bureau of Investigation and other national law enforcement agencies developed, but the majority of police work was and continues to be accomplished at the local level. Yet, even with decentralization, there was a greater emphasis on consistency of professional practice through the efforts of organizations such as the International Association of Chiefs of Police and through the Supreme Court's role in resolving cases about what are and are not proper police practices from a constitutional perspective (many of which focus on the procedural justice concerns described in Chapter 8).

The professional era certainly was an improvement upon the corrupt political era, but it was not without its limitations. By creating an impersonal, detached police officer and an officer who worked primarily from the confines of a police vehicle, the police and the public were isolated from one another. This created an "us" versus "them" mentality, sometimes known as a **thin blue line** between the police and public. Furthermore, by reducing foot patrol, personal contact between the police and the community was effectively limited to police responses to calls for service. This meant that police–citizen contacts were limited to negative situations in which citizens only saw the police when they were victimized by or accused of committing a crime.

According to Kelling and Moore (1988), the professional era was successful during the 1940s and 1950s because social stability prevailed in those decades. However, the 1960s and 1970s were a time of social change, including "the civil rights movement; migration of minorities into cities; the changing age of the population (more youths and teenagers); increases in crime and fear; increased oversight of police actions by courts and the decriminalization and deinstitutionalization movements" (p. 85). As a result of these changes, police administrators and scholars began to consider the value of promoting better police–community relations.

THE COMMUNITY ERA (1970s–PRESENT)

The goals of **community era** policing are broader than those of the professional era, consisting of crime control, crime prevention, and police–community problem solving, including the use of community-oriented policing (COP) and problem-oriented policing (POP) (discussed later in this chapter). Two government reports in the 1960s emphasized the importance of police–community relations: the *Report by the President's Commission on Law Enforcement and Administration of Justice* (1967) and the *Report of the National Advisory Commission on Civil Disorders* (1968).

It is also worth noting that the values of the community era are politically popular. For instance, in 1994, President Bill Clinton promised in his State of the Union Address to provide funding to communities to put 100,000 new police officers on the street to be deployed in community policing roles.

The success of the community era of policing is predicated on cooperation and communication between the police and the community. Under this strategy, effective policing cannot be accomplished with detached, impersonal officers; thus, police agencies must adapt their operating philosophies and training programs for community era strategies to be successful.

A community era strategy includes revisiting the days of foot patrol. When foot patrol was the primary means of police patrol, the officer was able to form social bonds within the community. This provided an opportunity for information sharing between the officer and community members. Kelling and Moore (1988) note that in addition to foot patrol, the community era is characterized by

> problem solving, information gathering, victim counseling and services, community organizing and consultation, education, walk-and-ride and knock-on-door programs, as well as regular patrol, specialized patrol, and rapid response to emergency calls for service. Emphasis is placed on information sharing . . . to increase the possibility of crime solution and clearance. (p. 91)

Although the community era is a work in progress, it is designed to aid law enforcement, improve the quality of life of its citizenry, and promote citizen satisfaction.

DEVELOPMENTAL THEORIES OF POLICING

As you can see, policing has changed substantially over the past 200 years. Thus far, the discussion has explored *how* policing has changed. A related question is, *why* did we need police in the first place? There is not agreement on the answer to this question. Roberg et al. (2000) provide four theories to explain the development of the police as an institution; scholars disagree about which most accurately explains the emergence of policing. The four theories are disorder theory, crime control theory, class control theory, and urban dispersion theory.

Similar to London, many cities in the United States were plagued by riots in the early 1800s. The **disorder theory** focuses on large-scale disruptive events, suggesting that police agencies were developed to suppress this sort of mob violence. Simply stated, police were needed to curtail large-scale public disorder.

Crime control theory focuses on more "routine," though widespread, forms of disorder. Advocates of the **crime control theory** believe that as crime increased, social order and systems of informal social control were threatened. This created a public fear of crime, and the police were needed to curb both crime and the fear of crime. This theory supports the notion that as informal social control becomes less effective, formal social control takes over. In this case, as informal social control was perceived to diminish, law enforcement filled the void to provide social order.

The **class control theory** suggests that as urban and industrial growth increased, people from various social and ethnic backgrounds competed for jobs to improve their social status. Similar to conflict theory presented in Chapter 5, class control theory suggested that the modern police were created by the rich and powerful to control the "dangerous classes" and to prevent their upward mobility in society. Policing efforts sometimes targeted the working class. In some cities, the police disrupted strikes, in which workers were advocating for improved working conditions, and aggressively enforced laws regarding issues such as alcohol and gambling in working-class establishments (see Harring, 1983).

Finally, the philosophy behind the **urban dispersion theory** asserted that as cities grew, both predators and potential victims moved to the city, increasing vulnerability to urban crime. Therefore, crime became identified as an urban problem. To combat it, the police were necessary as integral components of urban society to ensure stability (Monkkonen, 1988).

Do you believe that politics still plays a role in policing? If so, how?

A key assumption of the professional era is that education benefits police officers. What are the advantages and disadvantages of requiring a college education for police officers?

How would you implement community era strategies to address the New Briarfield Apartment situation described at the beginning of the chapter?

How would police strategies differ based on each developmental theory noted in this section?

The Culture of Policing

FOCUSING QUESTION 11.2

How does occupational culture influence the police role?

To better appreciate the philosophy of policing, it is important to return to the concept of organizational culture, as described in Chapter 1. As Wilson (1989) observed, "Every organization has a culture, that is, a persistent, patterned way of thinking about the central tasks of and human relationships within an organization. Culture is to an organization what personality is to an individual" (p. 91). Aspects of organizational culture include an agency's norms, values, language, mission, and more. Scholars have studied police organizations to better understand not only their organizational cultures but, more important, how their organizational cultures influence police practice and behavior.

WILSON'S STYLES OF POLICE BEHAVIOR

In his classic book, *Varieties of Police Behavior*, James Q. Wilson (1974) describes three styles of policing. They are the watchman style, the legalistic style, and the service style. In some cases, an entire department may orient itself toward one of these styles; in other cases, individual officers within a department may approach their work drawing upon one of these styles.

The central theme of the **watchman style** of policing is keeping the peace and not making waves. Watchman officers are passive and reactive. They will likely ignore many infractions, especially minor ones, and are not concerned about community relations or service calls. The watchman police use whatever discretionary powers are deemed appropriate to maintain order, including the use of informal intervention rather than exercising formal legal authority (e.g., confiscating alcohol from a juvenile rather than charging the juvenile with underage possession). "A watchman-like department is as interested in avoiding trouble as in minding its own business" (Wilson, 1974, pp. 147–148); officers functioning under such a model do not want to draw attention to themselves. Although they certainly will respond to major incidents with their full authority, their overarching goal is to maintain a low profile as long as things in their jurisdiction are doing reasonably well.

The other extreme of policing is the **legalistic style**. Whether a minor infraction or a major crime, officers strive to enforce the law with the full force of their authority in every case. Success is measured by productivity; productivity is measured by statistics. Therefore, the greater the number of arrests and traffic tickets, the more productive the officer and the more successful the agency. Under the legalistic style philosophy, officers enforce the law because they believe it is the right thing to do—morally, ethically, and legally. Legalistic officers might be heard to say, "We don't make the laws; we simply enforce them." And enforce them they do, with vigor and enthusiasm and with little interest in exercising discretion. Here, "the law is the law," and it must be enforced without consideration of individual circumstances. In this system, the police are detached from the public; they treat everyone similarly.

The **service style** falls somewhere between the watchman and legalistic styles. Consistent with the values of the community era, service style policing is based on the use of discretion to determine the most appropriate response to a situation. Officers are willing to enforce the law aggressively and make arrests when necessary. However, they are also likely to view arrests as a last resort and to prefer seeking alternative solutions to problems. Like the watchman style, officers utilize informal social control to solve problems. Unlike the watchman style, officers are actively engaged with the community, performing routine police work, crime prevention activities, and community service activities, all the while striving to use all of the resources at their disposal to make a community a safe and pleasant place to live.

Box 11.1 discusses broken windows policing. Consider how the three styles just described would apply to the strategy.

POLICE OFFICER PERSONALITIES

Wilson's styles of policing explain three different approaches to police work. Other research has explored attributes of officers themselves, which can influence how they approach the job. Several studies are described in this section.

BOX 11.1

BROKEN WINDOWS

Is there a relationship between crime and the physical environment? Numerous theories suggest that there is. One of the best known is "broken windows" theory, which was advanced by policing scholars James Q. Wilson and George L. Kelling (1982). The theory suggests that visible signs of disorder can lead to more serious crime. Signs of disorder include physical characteristics of an area, such as broken windows, or actions that occur there, such as loitering. When a neighborhood has signs of disorder, it reflects a lack of caring. This can signal to potential offenders that the neighborhood is ripe for victimization. In addition, if residents perceive their neighborhood as disorderly, they may become fearful and avoid interacting with others outside their homes, resulting in weakened informal social controls. The culmination of these effects is that crime in the area will increase, and the cycle will repeat itself, with the disorder and resulting crime increasing in severity with each repetition.

Broken windows theory does suggest a solution to the foregoing cycle—namely, that if the signs of disorder can be addressed early, then more serious criminal activity can be prevented. Broken windows policing is a strategy to reduce disorder in neighborhoods. One form of broken windows policing involves officers *"paying attention to minor offenses that were essentially ignored in the past"* (Sousa & Kelling, 2006, p. 89). This can be done by making arrests, but as described in New York City, "officers . . . were much more likely to informally warn, educate, scold, or verbally reprimand citizens who violated minor offenses . . . officers were mindful of the moral complexities behind their activities" (Sousa & Kelling, 2006, p. 89).

Another form of broken windows policing, much more controversial, is a zero-tolerance approach (see Taylor, 2006) in which *all* perceived disorders are addressed through *formal* police action (arrests or citations). For example, residents may be told to keep their lawns cut or face mandatory fines. Or the police might aggressively enforce laws against all instances of loitering or vandalism.

What are signs of disorder that you think could be targeted by this form of policing? Do you think the types of disorder you have identified lead to more serious crime?

What are the advantages and disadvantages of each form of broken windows policing described in this box? Would you utilize this strategy if you were a police chief?

How could this theory be applied to the New Briarfield case? Should it be?

Certainly, not all officers demonstrate all attributes described, but taken together, the attributes create what has come to be known as the police officer personality.

Jerome Skolnick (1966) noted several qualities of police work that, taken together, make up an officer's "**working personality**" (p. 42). These qualities include:

- Danger, referring to the risks inherent in police work;
- Authority, reflecting an officer's legal right to make arrests and to use force in appropriate circumstances;

- Social isolation, indicating that police officers often find themselves isolated or removed from other members of the public; and
- Solidarity, in which officers associate primarily with other officers, viewing their colleagues as members of a family bound together by their work.

These values often overlap in police work. For instance, due to the dangerous nature of policing (e.g., confronting armed subjects), police will seek to control situations by creating social distance or separation from the public to more dispassionately exert an atmosphere of authority. This can lead officers to become isolated or detached from the public. The resulting social isolation generates police solidarity whereby officers frequently associate with other officers because only fellow officers can truly understand the job and its challenges, fostering an "us" (police) versus "them" (everyone else) mentality.

Skolnick adds that police officers, as a function of their authority, are sometimes responsible for enforcing unpopular laws (laws against drunkenness, drugs, gambling, prostitution, etc.). This can lead to perceptions of hypocrisy by the public. "The policeman is apt to cause resentment because of the suspicion that policemen do not themselves strictly conform to the moral norms they are enforcing" (Skolnick, 1966, p. 56). When members of the public hold this belief, it can serve to further isolate the police from the community.

William Westley (1970) concurs with Skolnick, adding that a *code of secrecy* promotes solidarity. "Secrecy among the police stands as a shield against the attacks of the outside world . . . Secrecy is loyalty . . . Secrecy is solidarity" (p. 111). That is, there is often an informal code among police officers that "what happens on the streets, remains on the street." This philosophy is reinforced throughout an officer's career: "Never rat against a fellow cop." Westley further states that the code of secrecy becomes a part of an officer's morality and therefore a part of the police personality.

The police officer's personality is also shaped by anomie and cynicism (Niederhoffer, 1967). Anomie includes frustration, alienation, despair, and a sense of powerlessness (see Durkheim, 1965). Cynicism is a distrust and pessimistic attitude toward life and career. According to Niederhoffer, officers begin their career with a sense of commitment and idealism, looking forward to their work as an opportunity to fight crime, vanquish evil, and protect American society. Over time, however, the initial enthusiasm may be followed by failure (recognizing that not all crime can be prevented or solved), disenchantment (recognizing that policing is sometimes less about crime fighting than about public relations), cynicism (coming to dislike the work), alienation (social isolation), and finally anomie ("I just don't care anymore").

Finally, Lefkowitz (1975, 1977) identified a cluster of personality traits centered on authoritarianism. This is the notion that the police may come to see themselves as the societal embodiment of the authority of the state (thinking "I am the law"). This can lead to both a rejection of anything different as "abnormal" and a corresponding belief in the need for punishment and discipline for norm breakers. This also involves a near-blind acceptance of authority figures, high pressure for conformity (to "fit in"), and a tendency to think rigidly and in oversimplified ways (seeing things as black or white, right or wrong, with no middle ground). Some scholars argue that individuals with an authoritarian personality are attracted to police work; others argue that police work causes persons to become more authoritarian (for a comprehensive review, see Owen & Wagner, 2008). Regardless of its origins, authoritarianism is a concern because it has been associated with prejudice, a reduced interest in constitutional rights, and a willingness to "accept unfair and illegal abuses of power by government authorities" (Altemeyer, 1996, p. 300).

Many of these values may strike you as negative. However, in a study of the Los Angeles Police Department, Herbert (1997) found that officers' work was guided by a set of six principles, as described here:

> Law, which by legislative fiat defines the permissible parameters of police action; bureaucratic regulations, which seek to determine police procedures more finely through a set of rules that establish a chain of command; adventure / machismo, which constitutes the police as courageous individuals who embrace danger as a test of individual ability; safety, which establishes a set of practices to protect the police from undue harm; competence, which suggests that police should be able to control the public areas for which they are responsible; and morality, which infuses police practice with a sense of right and goodness, in essence because it helps protect society from the "bad guys." (p. 3)

Herbert suggests that an examination of these values can be used as a way to analyze police activities. When all goes well, the six values may act in concert to lead to the appropriate resolution of a situation. When problems arise, it is perhaps because one value becomes too strong and eclipses or dominates the others.

Again, not all of the characteristics apply to all police officers. Over the course of a career, different elements may come and go depending on an officer's assignment, individual attributes, supervisory expectations, and life experiences. As the personality of the officer changes, so may his or her style of patrol. For instance, a police officer with a legalistic approach to policing may soon become disenchanted with the job when suspects are released back into society without serving punishment, thereby growing very cynical. The officer may decide it's just better to do the bare minimum, maintain order (watchman style), and wait it out until retirement. Conversely, an officer initially operating under the watchman style may later find meaning through interactions with neighborhood residents in community policing activities and become very involved with service style crime prevention. The police personality is dynamic and varies by officer.

Describe how each style of policing could be used in the situation at the New Briarfield Apartments. After reviewing your response, which style would you prefer? Why?

If you were a police chief, what steps could you take within your agency to promote the positive attributes of the police personality and to help remedy the negative attributes?

What similarities and differences do you see among the police personality traits described in this section?

The Structure of American Law Enforcement

FOCUSING QUESTION 11.3

How is law enforcement in the United States organized?

Policing in the United States is fragmented. That is, there are many different police agencies, and historically, there has been little coordination among them, although interagency communications and collaborations have improved over time. For this reason, it is difficult to identify a single police subculture, a single set of policing strategies, or a single definition of police role; all of these features may vary between agencies. In this section, we examine three levels of law enforcement: local, state, and federal.

In many countries, there is one national police force. This is not the case in the United States (the FBI is one of many federal law enforcement agencies; it is not our national police force). If you recall our discussion of federalism from Chapter 7, we have multiple levels of government—federal, state and local. Likewise, police agencies are also separated into multiple levels. Like snowflakes, each level of policing and each agency within those levels differs. For example, two local police departments just miles apart may have separate hiring standards, promotional opportunities, starting salaries, mission statements (the philosophy of law enforcement used to represent community interest), and practices.

According to the 2004 Census of State and Local Enforcement Agencies (Reaves, 2007), the United States has approximately 780,000 sworn officers (those with the authority to make arrests and use force) in roughly 18,000 public law enforcement agencies. Of those 18,000 agencies, about 13,000 (72%) are local police agencies.

LOCAL POLICE AGENCIES

As just indicated, the vast majority of policing in America is performed by local police. Surprisingly, most police agencies are not the large city police agencies (e.g., New York City with approximately 36,000 sworn officers) such as those featured on television dramas. In fact, they are more akin to the fictional North Carolina town of Mayberry, as most police agencies employ fewer than 10 officers (Reaves, 2007).

Depending on the mission of the local agency, law enforcement goals may differ. However, most local police agencies perform similar duties found in the acronym PEPPAS including: *P*rotecting life and property; *E*nforcing the criminal law; *P*reventing crime; *P*reserving the peace; *A*rresting violators; and *S*erving the community. Most local (city, town, county, etc.) police agencies rely on the military rank structure. For instance, most agencies' hierarchy, from lowest to highest, might look something like this: police officer, sergeant, lieutenant, captain, assistant chief, chief, and perhaps, police commissioner.

Often included within local law enforcement are sheriffs' departments. Not included in the local law enforcement statistics listed previously, there are 3,067 sheriffs' offices in the United States (Reaves, 2007). Unlike local police chiefs, sheriffs are often elected to their position, and they may or may not have actual law enforcement experience. Sheriffs and their deputies (law enforcement officers hired by the sheriff) are often responsible for court duties, such as running the local jail, transporting prisoners, serving warrants (and other court documents), and security within the courtroom (serving as a bailiff), and traditional law enforcement duties, including responding to calls for service and conducting investigations.

STATE POLICE AGENCIES

There are 49 state police agencies, also known as the highway patrol in some jurisdictions. Only Hawaii does not have a state police agency (Reaves, 2007). The hierarchical structure in most state police organizations is similar to the military model noted earlier. In fact, state agencies operate more militaristically than local agencies, and many state police academies have been compared to military style training.

While their legal mandate focuses on violations of state law, including state highway traffic enforcement and accident investigation, the duties of the state police are similar to local law enforcement, but state police officers have greater jurisdictional freedom; they can investigate criminal activity anywhere within the state.

Sometimes, the lack of jurisdictional boundary setting generates conflict between local and state police officers. For example, who has jurisdiction when state police and local police bust a drug ring in the local town? Who receives the recognition for the arrests (which may influence promotion decisions and measures of agency effectiveness)? Other than these occasional jurisdictional issues, state police agencies typically are not concerned about local political influence in their day-to-day operations.

FEDERAL AGENCIES

Of the approximately 105,000 sworn federal agents in the United States, most are employed either within the U.S. Department of Homeland Security (just over 40%) or the U.S. Department of Justice (nearly 35%) (Reaves, 2006).

Within each of these federal departments, there are multiple law enforcement agencies. For a listing of the top federal law enforcement employers, see Table 11.1. Although federal agencies have a hierarchy of command, it differs significantly from local and state police. For instance, the first-level supervisor in a local or state police agency may be a "sergeant," whereas in a federal agency, a similar ranking supervisor's title may be "agent-in-charge."

The legal mandate of federal officers is the enforcement of federal law, including interstate crimes. Federal agents can investigate federal crimes anywhere across the nation, and sometimes abroad, if they affect national security.

Table 11.1. Federal Agencies Employing 500 or More Full-Time Officers with Authority to Carry Firearms and Make Arrests, September 2004

Agency	Full-Time Officers
U.S. Customs and Border Protection	27,705
Federal Bureau of Prisons	15,214
Federal Bureau of Investigation	12, 242
U.S. Immigration and Customs Enforcement	10,399
U.S. Secret Service	4,769
Drug Enforcement Administration	4,400
Administrative Office of the Courts	4,126
U.S. Marshals Service	3,233
U.S. Postal Inspection Service	2,976
Internal Revenue Service, Criminal Investigation	2,777
Veterans Health Administration	2,423
Bureau of Alcohol, Tobacco, Firearms & Explosives	2,373
National Park Service	2,148
U.S. Capitol Police	1,535
Bureau of Diplomatic Security	825
U.S. Fish & Wildlife Service, Div. of Law Enforcement	708
USDA Forest Service, Law Enforcement & Investigations	600

Source: Reaves, B. (July, 2006). *Federal Law Enforcement Officers, 2004*, Table 1, p. 2. (Washington, D.C.: Bureau of Justice Statistics Bulletin).

Unlike state and local police officers, federal agents rarely concern themselves with order maintenance. Their duties are much more specific, based on agency, and are usually based on investigation rather than patrol. For instance, the Drug Enforcement Administration (DEA) focuses primarily on drug crimes, the Bureau of Alcohol, Tobacco, and Firearms (BATF) focuses primarily on violations of alcohol, tobacco, and firearm laws, and so on.

The vast majority of collaborative law enforcement efforts prove quite successful, but tensions may still arise. In the drug bust example provided earlier, what if the DEA participated in the drug bust in addition to state and local police? Determining which agencies have authority, and what the roles of those agencies are in a particular operation, can become complicated.

> What do you think are the advantages and disadvantages of having multiple local law enforcement agencies rather than a single national agency?
>
> Assume that, for a single incident (e.g., the drug bust described), multiple local, state, and federal agencies respond. How should it be determined who is in charge of the response and who will receive credit for the case (for the arrests, for clearing the crime, etc.)?
>
> Of the three levels of policing (local, state, and federal), if provided the opportunity, which agency would you prefer to work for? Why?

Ethical Issues in Policing

FOCUSING QUESTION 11.4

What ethical dilemmas may arise in police agencies?

As you recall from Chapter 2, a consideration of morality is essential to the study of criminal justice. Determining what is (or is not) moral is a foundation for professional ethics. In this section, we explore ethical considerations in policing.

Ethics may be viewed as the application of a set of moral thoughts and ideas to determine the right thing to do, often in a professional setting. Questions of ethics are separate from questions of legality. For instance, an action may be legal but unethical (e.g., failing to attend a roll-call briefing prior to a police shift). Although the vast majority of police work is conducted ethically, we will focus on a few police behaviors that violate the ethical standards of law enforcement, many of which fall into the category of police corruption.

Police **corruption** may be defined as an act involving the misuse of authority, often for some personal gain (personal gain may also include a gain for others, such as friends, colleagues or family members). Keep in mind that personal gain does not necessarily mean *financial* rewards, as you will see in a moment.

LEVELS OF CORRUPTION

Police corruption is not isolated to the street officer. In fact, there have been plenty of media accounts of police supervisors, including police chiefs, who have committed unethical and illegal behavior (e.g., a police chief stealing drugs from the property room to support his addiction).

Although all are unethical, not all corrupt events are equally severe in terms of how deeply they pervade a police organization. Lawrence Sherman (1974) identified four levels of police corruption: (1) rotten apples, (2) rotten pockets, (3) pervasive unorganized corruption, and (4) pervasive organized corruption.

Rotten apples occur when one or more officers independently participate in some form of corrupt activity. For instance, assume a motorist bribes a police officer $20 to avoid a traffic summons. Meanwhile, a fellow officer receives $100 from a local business owner to allow customers to double-park their vehicles, without the fear of a parking citation, in front of her store to improve her business sales. Neither officer knows of the other's illegal activity. On the other hand, if the officers worked as a team and split the total money they received during their patrol shift, they would be known as a **rotten pocket**, which is a small group of officers working together for unethical purposes.

Often associated with rotten apples and rotten pockets are grasseaters and meateaters (see Knapp Commission, 1972). **Grasseaters** are officers who accept illegal benefits as a result of some corrupt activity but do so passively. That is, they do not seek out corruption, but may take advantage of it if the opportunity presents itself. Also included in this category are officers who know that corruption is taking place but refuse to report it as part of the *code of secrecy* described earlier. **Meateaters** are officers who aggressively solicit illegal favors. For instance, if a motorist offered a police officer a $20 bribe to avoid a traffic summons and the officer accepted it, that officer would be considered a grasseater. On the other hand, if upon making the stop the officer told the motorist that he would be willing to accept a bribe or actively demanded a bribe payment, that officer would be considered a meateater.

Sherman (1974) identified two additional levels of police corruption. **Pervasive unorganized corruption** goes beyond basic grasseaters and a few rotten apples. This occurs when a large number of rotten apples participate in illegal activity. For example, in an agency of 100 officers, there may be 10–15 officers accepting illegal favors independently of one another. **Pervasive organized corruption** occurs when meateaters and rotten pockets join forces. Corruption and unethical behavior are not only well organized but may involve greater numbers of officers, potentially including supervisors and executives.

TYPES OF CORRUPTION

Unfortunately, the types of unethical behavior and corrupt activities in policing are almost endless. We will discuss several in this section. For each, consider what you would do in the situation—you make the call.

A **gratuity** is a benefit that a police officer receives simply because he or she is a police officer. This generally takes the form of a police officer being given something, often a financial discount or something tangible, which would not be given to the general public. For instance, a police officer buys a cup of coffee at a convenience store and starts to pay the clerk. The clerk waves the money away and says, "You guys protect the rest of us from crime; your coffee is free." The officer accepts the coffee and leaves.

Professional courtesy occurs when a police officer provides a courtesy or special treatment to another law enforcement officer; this sometimes extends to officers' families or other emergency service personnel. For example, Officer Speedy Sam, while off duty in his personal vehicle, is stopped for speeding by Sergeant Lock M. Up. When the Sergeant approaches the vehicle, Speedy flashes his off-duty badge. The sergeant does not cite Speedy, only because he is a police officer in a neighboring jurisdiction. Had he not been a fellow police officer, the sergeant would have issued a citation.

Misuse of authority occurs when a police officer uses his or her position for some sort of personal gain. This is distinguished from passively accepting a gratuity or bribe. For instance, while working a traffic detail, an officer observes a vehicle driven lawfully by a person he or she finds attractive. The officer stops the vehicle simply to meet the driver and obtain contact information by running the license through Central Records.

There are numerous other acts that may also represent unethical and corrupt behavior. These include officer theft, breaking and entering, unnecessary use of force, planting evidence, sexual favors (e.g., a citizen offers to perform sexual activity with an officer in exchange for not receiving a citation), kickbacks (e.g., referring an arrestee to a bail bondsman who provides the officer payment for each referral), shakedowns (e.g., meateater demanding money for a monthly payoff from a bar owner to ignore potential violations, such as overcrowding), and racial profiling (enforcing the law against a person or group of people based solely on their race or ethnicity), to name just a few.

THE DIRTY HARRY PROBLEM

As discussed in Chapter 2, moral judgments influence police discretion. Ethics also help to guide officer discretion. But when does a police officer cross the line between good police work and unethical behavior?

In discussing the **Dirty Harry problem**, Carl Klockars ([1980] 1985a) asks, "when and to what extent does the morally good end warrant or justify an ethically, politically, or legally dangerous means for its achievement?" (p. 50). The Dirty Harry problem takes its name from the 1971 movie starring Clint Eastwood as "Dirty Harry" Callahan, a fictional San Francisco police inspector who will do whatever it takes to apprehend a psychopathic killer, who calls himself "Scorpio."

In one scene, Harry tracks Scorpio to an abandoned football stadium. Scorpio is already suffering from a deep knife wound delivered by Harry in an earlier scene. Harry shoots the unarmed Scorpio in the leg with his .44 Magnum. With his gun still drawn, Harry approaches Scorpio, who is alive but disabled from the shooting. Harry demands to know the location of a kidnapped girl who Scorpio bragged was buried alive. Without regard to constitutional rights, Harry tortures Scorpio by stomping on Scorpio's open leg wound until he obtains the information necessary to locate the girl, who was dead when found. This is an example of illegal means (i.e., unconstitutional interrogation and inappropriate use of force) used for a morally good end (i.e., locating and attempting to rescue a victim).

Situations such as this pose a conundrum, as Klockars ([1980] 1985a) notes: "a police officer, at least in this specific case, cannot be both just and innocent" (p. 58). Obtaining the information could lead to justice, but the officer's actions were clearly illegal; conversely, a police officer acting within the bounds of the law might not be able to extract the confession from Scorpio that would allow the victim to be found, potentially contravening justice. Ultimately, however, police officers are expected to err on the side of the law, consistent with the requirements of constitutional criminal procedure as described in Chapter 8.

CONTROLLING UNETHICAL BEHAVIOR

The vast majority of police officers perform their duties ethically and legally. However, even a few unethical officers or a single high-profile case of police corruption can tarnish the reputation of policing as a whole and lead to a loss of legitimacy for the criminal justice system.

Regardless of the level of policing (local, state, or federal), controlling ethical behavior, misconduct, and corruption is critical for maintaining effective police service. "Exacting ethical standards and a high degree of honesty are perhaps more essential for the police than for any other group in society . . . Nothing undermines public confidence in the police and the process of criminal justice more than the illegal acts of officers" (Task Force Report [1967] 1990, p. 208). So, what can be done to minimize unethical behavior in policing?

First and foremost, police administrators must be willing to recognize and address unethical behavior and corruption. A strategy to address these issues is completing thorough background checks and hiring the proper police candidates, providing effective ethics education and training in the police academy, and continuing to monitor officer behavior throughout their careers. Departments should maintain an effective Internal Affairs Department, or Citizen Review Board, whose responsibility includes investigating police misconduct. Additionally, written policy can specify departmental ethical expectations, and police colleagues can be encouraged to report unethical and illegal police behavior, as it reflects negatively on the entire agency and all its members.

Earlier, you were asked to consider what you think would be the most appropriate response to the New Briarfield Apartment situation. What ethical problems could potentially emerge during the implementation of your strategy? What could be done to prevent them?

Can you think of other strategies to control or monitor unethical and/or illegal police behavior? Explain.

Is it ever appropriate to use unethical (or illegal) police tactics to achieve a desirable outcome? Explain.

Policing Strategies

FOCUSING QUESTION 11.5

How have policing strategies developed over time?

In addition to being ethical, policing strategies should also be effective. For the past half century, scholars have devoted substantial attention to the effectiveness of police operations. Some police strategies appear to be common sense, yet upon closer examination, they have proven to be ineffective. We will address four of the most classic studies that identified myths of policing. These studies motivated agencies to find creative and more effective methods of policing and helped lead the transition to the community era.

MYTHS ABOUT POLICING

Myth 1: The Number of Police Officers Affects Crime. Loftin and McDowall (1982) examined the relationship between reported crime and the number of officers in Detroit during the years 1926 to 1977. Their general conclusion was that the number of officers does not affect crime. That is, increases and decreases in the number of sworn personnel do not, by themselves, lead to an increase or decrease in crime. This suggests that police strategy and tactics are more important than the sheer numbers of officers.

Myth 2: Routine Patrol Deters Crime. For many years, routine preventive patrol was assumed to deter crime. Routine preventive patrol refers to police officers patrolling their assigned beat and watching for signs of trouble or disorder when not responding to calls for service. Kelling, Pate, Dieckman, and Brown (1974) examined variations in the level of patrol in 15 Kansas City, Missouri, patrol beats. They randomly assigned the beats to one of three groups: In the group 1 (reactive) beats, officers did not patrol their beats and only entered their assigned areas when dispatched to calls for service; in group 2 (control) beats, officers patrolled their areas normally; and in group 3 (proactive) beats, the level of patrol was doubled or tripled. Results indicated that variations in the level of preventive patrol did not have an effect on crime or the fear of crime. The results of this study required police administrators to rethink the notion that routine preventive patrol can deter crime.

Myth 3: Rapid Response Time Is Essential. Is quicker better? A study of response time in Kansas City, Missouri (Bieck & Kessler, 1977), examined three time intervals. The first was the time between the crime itself and a citizen's call to the police to report it. The second was the time it took for the police to process the call and dispatch a unit to the scene. The third was the time it took for a unit to arrive on the scene after being dispatched. The results found that the latter two time intervals had little impact on solving a crime. The more critical time period was the time between the commission of the crime and reporting it to the police. The average time was 41 minutes—far too long for a rapid response to make much of a difference. Accordingly, unless there is an emergency in progress that is reported immediately, response time is not as significant as it may seem.

Myth 4: The Resourceful Investigator Solves Crimes. Greenwood and Petersilia (1975) examined police investigations of reported serious crimes, including homicide, rape, robbery, aggravated assault, and grand theft (larceny). They discovered that the vast majority of crimes that police investigate were brought to their attention by the public, who also provided officers with suspect identification. That is, the majority of cases were solved with information supplied by the victim to the responding patrol officer rather than requiring in-depth investigations, such as those portrayed on television.

As you can see, commonly held beliefs about policing may be false. It is important to note, however, that these studies were subject to much scrutiny, review, and challenge; future studies may paint a very different picture. These studies did, however, lead the police administrators to consider new strategies, including team policing, community-oriented policing (COP), and problem-oriented policing (POP).

TEAM POLICING

Team policing served as the front-runner to today's community-oriented policing philosophy. **Team policing** was developed in Scotland in 1946 but did not become popular in the United States until the early 1970s. The basic concept of team policing is best summarized by Smith and Taylor (1985): "Team members are assigned to a specific neighborhood with total responsibility to perform full duties and develop a better relationship with the public. Police–citizen interaction is encouraged. The teams provide 24-hour coverage for that area and officers are assigned on a semi-permanent basis" (p. 40). Thus, each area of the city had its own team to provide all policing services, and the officers on each team worked to build strong relationships with the members of the community. This strategy essentially decentralized policing even further by creating "minidepartments" that served each area of the city.

This sounded great; what could go wrong? According to Samuel Walker (1993), there were a number of problems. First, there was opposition from middle management; with greater responsibility placed on local sergeants and patrol officers, lieutenants and captains resented their loss of authority. Second, some street officers were never informed about the new police strategy and resented those who were selected to participate in it. Third, team policing was designed for decentralization, whereas dispatch technology remained centralized, leading to implementation difficulties. Fourth, the goals of team policing were never made clear: initial planning and implementation were poor. As quickly as team policing arrived, it departed.

COMMUNITY-ORIENTED POLICING

Lessons learned from team policing were later incorporated into **community-oriented policing** (COP), whose basic philosophy is to foster a positive working relationship between the police and the community. While COP strategies may vary depending on agency and community needs, some common themes include: (1) using foot patrol when practical to encourage citizens and police to positively interact and communicate; (2) establishing community action groups (e.g., Neighborhood Watch) to allow officers and community members to listen, reflect, and respond to neighborhood issues and concerns; and (3) decentralizing police agencies to allow for easier community accessibility (e.g., by creating police substations). Largely, though, community policing is a *philosophy* that shapes how the police approach their tasks, recognizing members of the community as participants in the law enforcement function.

PROBLEM-ORIENTED POLICING

Developed by Herman Goldstein (1990), **problem-oriented policing** (POP) is a problem-solving strategy designed to involve the police and the community. According to Goldstein, the police need to: (1) become more flexible in problem solving; (2) become more proactive in addressing community problems; (3) maximize the contributions from citizens; (4) empower the patrol officer in the decision-making process; and (5) rethink the organizational structure to become less resistant to change.

A commonly used problem-solving method is **scanning, analysis, response, and assessment (SARA)**. When used properly, it is a very flexible strategy. It can be used by the patrol officer on the street to address minor problems, and it can be used by police administrators to address citywide problems.

Scanning is examining the environment to identify, confirm, and prioritize problems. Community groups, patrol officers, the news media, or others may bring problems to the attention of the police. Then, police administrators examine the list of problems and determine which need to be addressed first.

Analysis refers to understanding the problem and, in particular, the conditions that led to the problem. This makes POP proactive. The police strive

BOX 11.2

COMPSTAT

Compstat (short for "compare statistics") was developed as part of a problem-oriented policing strategy integrating computerized crime data and advanced crime mapping to analyze crime patterns. It provides police supervisors and police executives with the means to share critical information regarding criminal activity in their jurisdiction through regular meetings at which the data are presented and discussed. Supervisors are expected to develop goals and programs for crime reduction in their areas based on the crime data. As such, they are empowered to engage in problem solving in their jurisdictions and are given the autonomy to do so. They are also regularly evaluated on and held accountable for their progress.

Compstat originated in New York City after Police Commissioner William Bratton took office in 1994. Bratton found it disturbing that top police administrators were not fully aware of current crime patterns and statistics. As a result, he held mandatory meetings with jurisdictional police supervisors twice a week requesting (actually, demanding) to know what actions were being taken to reduce crime in their area (see Bratton, 1998).

What are the advantages and limitations of holding police supervisors accountable to Compstat?

Do you think Compstat would be effective in smaller police agencies?

Would Compstat have proved useful in the New Briarfield Apartment example?

to understand why a problem happened, so its underlying causes can be addressed. If the underlying causes are not addressed, the problem will continue. The analysis stage generally requires careful research and analysis of data. See Box 11.2 for discussion of Compstat, a program aimed at the analysis of crime trends.

Response is the development and implementation of solutions to the problem based on attacking its causes. In the response, the police often seek the assistance of other private or public agencies who can contribute to a solution. This is important because it acknowledges that crime prevention involves many facets of society beyond law enforcement.

Assessment refers to the evaluation of the strategy. Was the problem solved? If so, there was success. If not, the police may go back to the analysis stage once again and work on a new response to the problem.

With a focus on community policing and problem solving, today's police leaders better understand the importance of police–community cooperation. Creative police strategies have been developed, incorporated, and debated to meet community needs and demands. Increased attention has been devoted to the examination of the police subculture and its effect on police and community values. This allows police agencies to best serve citizens in their communities.

Do you think there is a way to address the four myths identified to enhance the effectiveness of police practice?

How could the various strategies described in this section be applied in the New Briarfield Apartments?

Conclusion

An exploration of police history reveals that the police role in society has changed over time. Policing strategies have also changed over time, particularly in light of research about what does (or does not) work in police practice. As the front-line enforcers of the law, the police are often a person's first point of contact with the criminal justice system, whether that person is a victim or an offender. No doubt policing will continue to change in the future as new priorities and technologies emerge. Indeed, Oliver (2006) suggested that American policing has entered a new post-September 11 era focused around "Homeland Security" and marked by a greater focus on crime control because "it is through crime control, enforcement of the criminal law, traffic law, etc., that many potential threats can be exposed and intelligence gathered" (p. 54). Regardless of the focus or the technologies, police agencies and police professionals must maintain their commitment to providing ethical and effective public service. The next chapter turns to the courts, which are responsible for hearing criminal cases, many of which are referred to them through the work of the police.

Criminal Justice Problem Solving: **FAMILIAL DNA**

A current debate in law enforcement focuses on the use of familial DNA. Familial DNA analysis is based on the similar genetic makeup shared by relatives and has become a technique whereby police officers could use the DNA from a family member of a suspect to link a suspect to a crime.

For instance, what if a police officer suspects that a suspect has committed a rape but lacks probable cause to arrest the suspect? Further suppose that the officer observes the suspect's brother, Brian, at the mall drinking a soft drink with a straw. After Brian discards the straw in the trash, the officer retrieves it and sends the straw to the crime lab for DNA analysis. Results indicate that, while not an identical match, there is a partial match of the DNA from the straw to the DNA collected from the crime scene. This would strongly indicate that a close relative of Brian's committed the rape. This could give the officer reason to believe that Brian's brother may have been involved in the crime.

> Do you believe the collection of familial DNA, if done as described here, is ethical?

> Should the partial DNA match be sufficient to secure a search warrant or an arrest warrant against the suspect in this case?

Core Concepts of U.S. Court Systems

A trial in progress. How do you think courtroom decisions should be made?

Key Terms

adjudication
jurisdiction
hierarchical jurisdiction
subject matter jurisdiction
geographic jurisdiction
courtroom workgroup
judges
prosecutors
defense attorneys
felony
misdemeanor
initial appearance
complaint
indictment
information
grand jury
preliminary hearing
arraignment

discovery
exculpatory evidence
plea bargaining
motion
bench trial
summons
venire
voir dire
peremptory challenges
petit jury
presumption of sanity
presumption of innocence
evidence
beyond a reasonable doubt
indeterminate sentencing
determinate sentencing
presentence investigation report
 (PSI)

appeal
harmless error
prejudicial or reversible error
certiorari
habeas corpus
Supremacy Clause
judicial review
legal reasoning
legal formalism
legal realism
legal process theories
law and economics
jurisprudence of rights
critical legal studies (CLS)
critical race theory
feminist jurisprudence
postmodern jurisprudence
voting disenfranchisement laws

CASE STUDY

Shipwreck

In 1884, a small yacht set sail from England to Australia carrying four crew-men—three grown men and a boy. A storm capsized the yacht, causing it to sink. The crew escaped on a small lifeboat. At first, they survived on rainwater, some turnips they had brought with them, and a turtle they captured at sea. But by the 18th day, they had gone without food for a full week and were hundreds of miles from land. The captain suggested to one of his crewmen that they draw lots so that one of them could be killed and the others could survive by eating the sacrificed member of the crew. Although the idea was initially rejected, two men eventually agreed to kill the boy in the hopes of fostering their own survival. They selected the boy because he was, in their opinion, the closest to death from starvation. They also took into account that the grown men had families, whereas the boy had not yet married or fathered children. The captain stabbed the boy in the neck, and for the next four days, the three men survived by eating the boy's body and drinking his blood. The three men were then rescued by a passing ship.

The three men were charged with and convicted of murder because they premeditatedly killed the boy when he was not threatening any danger to them. The court rejected the notion that people should be able to kill others out of necessity, outside of self-defense. Not only did the judges find no precedent to support a necessity defense for murder, but they also refused to create such a defense. While the judges were sympathetic to the men's plight, they were concerned with recognizing a defense in which individuals could choose who lived and who died because someone perceived it necessary to kill. The judges also pointed out that the defendants "might possibly have been picked up the next day by a passing ship, or they might possibly not have been picked up at all; in either case it is obvious that the killing of the boy would have been an unnecessary and profitless act" (*Regina v. Dudley & Stephens*, 1884, Opinion of Coleridge, C. J., para. 2).

> If you had been the prosecutor in the case, would you have charged the defendants with murder or some less serious crime? Explain your reasoning.
>
> Do you agree with the decision of the appeals court to convict the defendants of murder? Do you find the reasons offered by the judges in support of their decision to convict the defendants (and reject the defense of necessity) persuasive? Why or why not?
>
> The defendants were originally sentenced to death on the murder charge. The queen later commuted their sentences to six-months' imprisonment. Which sentence do you prefer? Why? How is "justice" achieved under either sentence?

The Structure of the U.S. Court System

FOCUSING QUESTION 12.1

How are U.S. courts organized?

Adjudication is the formal process for resolving legal disputes in courts of law. The court system in the United States is fragmented. The federal government has its own court system, and each of the 50 states also has its own court system. **Jurisdiction** refers to the authority given to a court to hear and adjudicate a particular dispute. There are multiple forms of jurisdiction, including hierarchical, subject matter, and geographic. It is important to understand the different types of jurisdiction because they determine which court (among the many that exist) will ultimately be responsible for issuing a verdict or making a ruling in a particular case.

HIERARCHICAL JURISDICTION

State and federal courts are organized in a hierarchy, as illustrated by Figure 12.1. Assume that a defendant is arrested for assault. We will follow his case through the hierarchy.

A court with *original jurisdiction* is where a case begins. Courts with original jurisdiction consider evidence and make both factual and legal determinations in a case. That is, these courts decide what happened and how the law should apply to the situation. These are also known as trial courts, in which a single judge presides over the proceedings. The primary function of trial courts

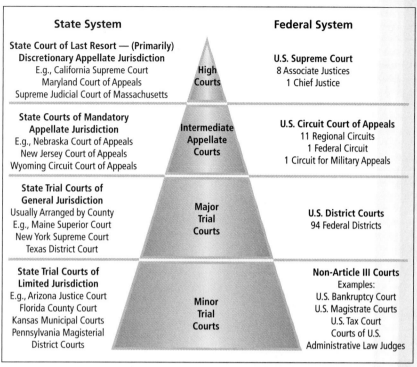

State System		Federal System
State Court of Last Resort — (Primarily) Discretionary Appellate Jurisdiction E.g., California Supreme Court Maryland Court of Appeals Supreme Judicial Court of Massachusetts	**High Courts**	**U.S. Supreme Court** 8 Associate Justices 1 Chief Justice
State Courts of Mandatory Appellate Jurisdiction E.g., Nebraska Court of Appeals New Jersey Court of Appeals Wyoming Circuit Court of Appeals	**Intermediate Appellate Courts**	**U.S. Circuit Court of Appeals** 11 Regional Circuits 1 Federal Circuit 1 Circuit for Military Appeals
State Trial Courts of General Jurisdiction Usually Arranged by County E.g., Maine Superior Court New York Supreme Court Texas District Court	**Major Trial Courts**	**U.S. District Courts** 94 Federal Districts
State Trial Courts of Limited Jurisdiction E.g., Arizona Justice Court Florida County Court Kansas Municipal Courts Pennsylvania Magisterial District Courts	**Minor Trial Courts**	**Non-Article III Courts** Examples: U.S. Bankruptcy Court U.S. Magistrate Courts U.S. Tax Court Courts of U.S. Administrative Law Judges

Figure 12.1. Overview of the Structure of the Dual Court System in the United States

is to resolve factual disputes. Thus, at hearings and trials, trial courts usually hear testimony from witnesses, examine physical and scientific evidence, make judgment about the credibility of the witnesses and other evidence, and then reach a decision that resolves the facts that are in dispute. In the case of the assault, the prosecutor would present evidence arguing that the defendant committed the assault, such as testimony from witnesses at the scene, images recorded by video cameras at the scene, testimony from medical professionals about the nature of the victim's injuries, and more. The defense attorney would challenge the evidence introduced by the prosecutor and perhaps call other witnesses testifying that the defendant was not even in town on the night of the incident. The judge would ensure that the trial proceeded fairly and according to legal rules, and a jury would determine whether or not the evidence was sufficient to convict the defendant. If the defendant were found guilty, the judge would issue a sentence (e.g., for jail, prison, probation, or fines).

The trial courts of original jurisdiction in the federal system are called Federal District Courts. As of the writing of this book, there are 94 federal districts—one or more per state and in various territories such as the District of Columbia, Puerto Rico, Guam, and the Virgin Islands (see Figure 12.2). The

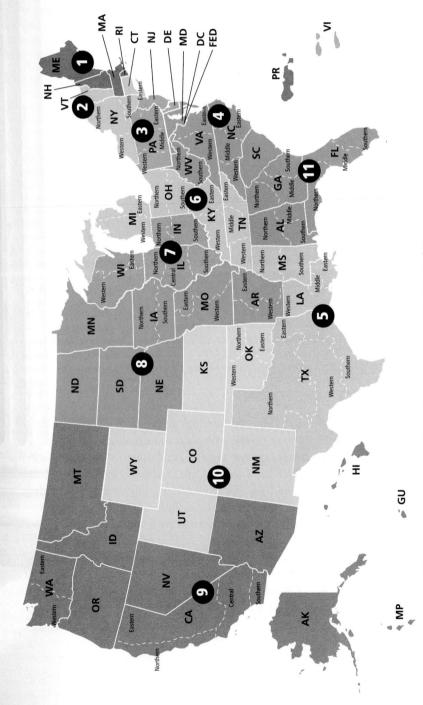

Figure 12.2. Geographic Boundaries of the Federal Court System of the United States

trial courts of original jurisdiction in the various state court systems go by many different names, as illustrated by Figure 12.1.

In contrast, courts with *appellate jurisdiction* review the proceedings of a lower court of original jurisdiction. Unlike trial courts, appellate courts do not conduct trials and rarely make factual determinations about the events surrounding an alleged criminal offense. Rather, a panel of judges reviews the transcripts from a trial court and the legal arguments offered by each party (the prosecution and the defense) to rule on whether the decision is in accordance with applicable law. That is, the work of appellate courts concerns questions about the interpretation or application of laws, not questions of fact. If the defendant charged with assault was found guilty, he might choose to appeal, and the appellate court would review issues such as whether he had a fair trial, whether the evidence was obtained legally, and whether the law had been applied correctly—all matters of interpretation and application of the law. The appellate court would not attempt to determine whether the defendant had actually been in the fight.

In the federal system and in approximately 40 U.S. states, there are enough appeals that the appellate courts are divided into two layers. The losing party in a court of original jurisdiction has the right to appeal the case to the intermediate court of appeals. In the federal system, this court is called the U.S. Circuit Court of Appeals. There are 14 federal judicial circuits: eleven are based on geographic divisions across the United States (see Figure 12.2), one is in the District of Columbia to hear appeals related to the many federal agencies located there, one handles patent and customs claims (the U.S. Circuit Court of Appeals for the Federal Circuit), and one hears appeals from military courts (the U.S. Court of Appeals for the Armed Forces). Most states also call their intermediate appellate court some variation on the term *court of appeals*.

All states have a court of last resort—the highest court in the state which serves as the final decision maker on all appeals concerning matters of state law. The federal system also has a high court of last resort, the U.S. Supreme Court, which is the final arbitrator of all cases concerning questions of federal law and constitutional interpretation.

There are some rare exceptions to the hierarchies just described. For example, U.S. district courts (ordinarily courts of original jurisdiction) have appellate jurisdiction over federal courts that were not established under Article III of the U.S. Constitution, such as bankruptcy courts, magistrate courts, and the courts of various administrative federal agencies. Similarly, the U.S. Supreme Court (ordinarily an appellate court of last resort) serves as a court of original jurisdiction in a small number of cases, such as those involving foreign ambassadors and cases in which one U.S. state sues another. In these cases, the Supreme Court does make factual determinations in the case rather than function strictly as an appellate court.

OTHER FORMS OF JURISDICTION

The type of case that may be adjudicated by a court of original jurisdiction is called **subject matter jurisdiction**. Courts of *limited subject matter jurisdiction* are specialized, hearing cases only on certain topics. Courts of *general subject matter jurisdiction* hear all other types of cases.

All federal courts are courts of limited subject matter jurisdiction, meaning that they can adjudicate only certain types of disputes. Federal courts have the subject matter jurisdiction to hear cases presenting *federal questions*. These include violations or interpretations of federal laws or regulations, such as federal crimes, social security, taxes, broadcasting, international trade, and bankruptcy. Federal courts may also adjudicate certain state law claims when *diversity of citizenship* exists (i.e., the parties to a lawsuit are all from different states and the dispute involves at least a certain amount of money). Federal appellate courts may also hear cases requesting the appellate review of state court decisions, policies, or laws (often to determine whether or not they are constitutional).

Cases that do not fall within the subject matter jurisdiction of the federal courts are adjudicated in state courts. But even within a state court system, the trial courts of original jurisdiction are usually split between two layers: minor trial courts and major trial courts. Minor trial courts typically have limited subject matter jurisdiction over traffic cases, civil cases involving "small claims" (relatively small amounts of money), municipal ordinance violations, juvenile offenses, probate matters (the administration of the estates of people who have died), and family law (e.g., divorce, adoption, child custody). In contrast, major trial courts have general subject matter jurisdiction over all cases that are not specifically assigned to a court of limited subject matter jurisdiction. This includes major criminal offenses, personal injury or contract lawsuits for larger sums of money than the small claims limit, real estate disputes, workers' compensation claims, and most issues involving the internal governance of business entities such as trusts, partnerships, and corporations.

Geographic jurisdiction refers to the geographic area where a court is located and over which it is empowered to adjudicate cases. In most state systems, those geographic areas tend to run along the county line boundaries. In the federal system, the geographic jurisdiction of federal courts is set by district (see Figure 12.2).

Do you think the U.S. court systems are well organized? Explain.

If the shipwreck case had occurred in the United States, what courts do you think might have been involved? Why?

Research the court structure in your state. What are the courts of original jurisdiction? What are the appellate courts? What courts have special subject matter jurisdiction? How is geographic jurisdiction assigned?

The Courtroom Workgroup

FOCUSING QUESTION 12.2

Who are the members of the courtroom workgroup and what do they do?

The **courtroom workgroup** refers to the working relationship among court employees (Eisenstein & Jacob, 1977). Rather than having an adversarial relationship, as often portrayed in novels and television, attorneys and judges in criminal courts frequently know one another from repeat encounters in professional and social circles. Through their interactions, attorneys and judges develop informal norms that help guide the processing of cases. Although each person is dedicated to his or her role—the prosecutor representing the state, the defense representing the accused, and the judge serving as legal referee of the proceedings—over time, each comes to know the style of the other to the point where all can anticipate how a case will be processed. This helps the courtroom function smoothly and leads to an efficient system of handling cases. Police officers also may become part of the courtroom workgroup because they regularly testify in court, often in similar cases before the same judges and attorneys.

The judge, prosecutor, and defense attorney are the three primary actors in criminal cases, but courthouses employ a wide range of professionals who keep the courthouse running. Court security staff help ensure that the courthouse and the people in it are kept safe. Court clerks file cases, manage case dockets, and attend to financial and human resource administration. Law clerks help judges conduct research and write opinions. Court reporters transcribe court proceedings so that a written record is maintained in the event of an appeal. Translators make sure that language barriers do not prevent people from understanding the courtroom proceedings. Bailiffs help maintain order in courtrooms. Secretaries schedule hearings, trials, and coordinate the calendars of judges and attorneys. It takes the coordinated efforts of all of these members of the courtroom workgroup to make the justice system function properly.

JUDGES

Judges preside over state and federal courts. Their primary role is to serve as a referee, enforcing the rules of procedure and evidence. Sometimes, however, judges are faced with tough decisions about what the law means. This is especially true for appellate judges whose decisions often set public policy. Although judges are supposed to be completely impartial, there is no doubt that their particular judicial philosophies affect their decision making (see Carter & Burke, 2006).

Methods of selecting judges vary dramatically. In the federal system, all judges (including those who serve on the U.S. Supreme Court) are nominated by the president and must be confirmed by a majority vote of the U.S. Senate. If confirmed, the judges enjoy life tenure, meaning that they remain federal judges until they die or retire (unless they do something so unethical that they are impeached from office by the Senate, which is very rare). As you might imagine, given the process of becoming a federal judge, nominees tend to have highly accomplished legal careers even before they are nominated (Goldman, 1999).

Five states grant the power to appoint judges to the governor or the legislature. Sixteen states use a merit selection process for selecting judges. That means a nonpartisan nominating committee screens applicants for judgeships and then makes recommendations (depending on the state) to the state bar association, the justices of the state high court, the members of the state legislature, or the governor, who then fills judicial vacancies based on the recommendations of the committee. In the remaining states, judges are elected either in partisan (affiliated with a political party) or nonpartisan elections. Once on the bench, rather than enjoying life tenure as their federal counterparts do, most state judges are subject to formal reelection or voter recall through retention elections (in which voters indicate whether a judge should or should not remain in office rather than voting in an open contest with multiple candidates). The method of selection does not seem to affect the quality of judges (Choi, Gulati, & Posner, 2010).

PROSECUTORS

Crimes are considered offenses against the state. Governmental officials called **prosecutors** are responsible for prosecuting violations of criminal law. Prosecutors go by many names in different states, including district attorneys, commonwealth's attorneys, state's attorneys, and county attorneys. In the overwhelming majority of states, prosecutors' offices are arranged by county, with each county having a lead prosecutor who is elected to local office. The lead prosecutor employs a staff of lawyers who litigate cases in court.

In the federal system, each federal district has a chief prosecutor called the *U.S. Attorney*. These positions are political appointments made by the President of the United States and confirmed by the Senate. Each U.S. Attorney's office employs a cadre of lawyers called *Assistant U.S. Attorneys*, who hold their positions regardless of the political party in power at the time; they assist the U.S. Attorney in preparing cases and presenting them in court.

Although prosecutors report to the attorney general of their state (and U.S. Attorneys report to the U.S. Attorney General), most prosecutors' offices enjoy a great deal of autonomy. Prosecutors may exercise a great deal of discretion when making decisions like whom to charge with which crimes and whether to agree to a plea bargain or take a case to trial. Prosecutors are sometimes called the "gatekeepers" of the criminal justice system because of their power to determine who will appear in court and on what charges. Because of this discretionary ability, prosecutors are the most powerful of the primary court actors.

DEFENSE ATTORNEYS

The Sixth Amendment to the U.S. Constitution provides that "[i]n all criminal prosecutions, the accused shall enjoy the right . . . to have the Assistance of Counsel for his defence." The interpretation of that language, however, has changed over time. The right to have a **defense attorney** (also known as defense counsel) was not recognized under English common law or in colonial America (Finnegan, 2009). The Sixth Amendment was originally intended to protect wealthy people from being told that they could not hire lawyers to represent them. It was not until well into the twentieth century that the U.S. Supreme Court began to interpret the Sixth Amendment in the way that we understand it today. In fact, it was not until *Gideon v. Wainwright* (1963) that the Court declared that criminal defendants facing felony charges in state courts had the right to the assistance of an attorney even if they could not afford to hire one for themselves. In *Argersinger v. Hamlin* (1972), the Court extended the right to counsel to defendants in misdemeanor cases who were facing a potential sentence of incarceration (jail).

A defendant who can afford to do so may hire his or her own private attorney. This occurs in roughly 20% of all criminal cases (Neubauer & Fradella, 2011). In the remaining criminal cases, defendants cannot afford to hire defense counsel; accordingly, the government provides a lawyer at no expense to the defendant. Unlike people who hire their own lawyers, indigent defendants (i.e., those who cannot afford their own representation) typically have little or no say in who represents them. Rather, a lawyer is appointed by the state in one of three ways in order to represent an indigent defendant. In jurisdictions that have busy enough criminal court systems to make it economically feasible to run a public defender's office, the state employs a group of criminal defense attorneys whose full-time job is to represent indigent defendants. In other jurisdictions, the state hires private attorneys on a case-by-case basis to represent criminal defendants. And in sparsely populated areas, the state may even take bids from attorneys in private practice who are willing to represent criminal defendants.

Whether defense counsel is privately retained or appointed, Walsh and Hemmens (2008) explain that defense attorneys have five primary roles.

> (1) to ensure that the defendants' rights are not violated (intentionally or in error); (2) to make sure the defendants know all of their options before they make a decision; (3) to provide the defendants with the best possible defense, without violating ethical and legal obligations; (4) to investigate and prepare the defense; and (5) to argue for lowest possible sentence or best possible plea bargain. (p. 103)

The Sixth Amendment right to counsel only applies when triggered by the occurrence of a critical stage of a criminal prosecution, such as postindictment lineups, arraignments, preliminary hearings, trials, and sentencing hearings (Marcus, 2009). The right does *not* apply in civil cases, including *habeas corpus* or immigration proceedings; individuals who can afford to do so may hire an attorney in civil cases, but indigent persons are not provided with an attorney by the state.

> What do you think are the advantages and disadvantages of each method of selecting judges? Which does your state use? Which do you most prefer? Why?
>
> What do you think are the advantages and disadvantages of selecting local prosecuting attorneys through elections? Do you think prosecutors should be selected through election or by other means? Why?
>
> What do you think are the advantages and disadvantages of having a state-funded public defender's office? Of contracting with private attorneys? Which method do you think is preferable for appointing an attorney for an indigent defendant? Why?

Criminal Pretrial Processes

FOCUSING QUESTION 12.3

What judicial processes occur before a criminal trial?

Criminal offenses are broadly classified into two categories: felonies and misdemeanors. The distinction between the categories is based on the seriousness of the crime and the maximum possible punishment that can be given for it (see Table 12.1 for an example from one state). **Felonies** are the most serious crimes, and they can be punished by a sentence of a year or more in prison and/or a substantial fine. **Misdemeanors** are less serious offenses, and they are punished by a sentence of less than a year in jail and/or a small to moderate fine. For instance, robbery is generally a felony, whereas disorderly conduct is generally a misdemeanor. Lawmakers, when writing legal codes, specify whether acts are classified as felonies or misdemeanors.

The following discussion outlines steps in processing a *felony* case. Misdemeanor cases are often handled less formally through assembly-line justice as described in Chapter 8. However, trials can—and do—occur in misdemeanor cases. When a misdemeanor is processed, though, grand juries are not used, and there is not always a right to a trial by jury, as you will learn later (you may also wish to refer to Figure 1.5, in Chapter 1).

INITIAL APPEARANCE

When someone is arrested, the law requires that the person be taken before a neutral judicial officer for an **initial appearance**. The initial appearance is also known as a *Gerstein* hearing after the U.S. Supreme Court case that mandated it, *Gerstein v. Pugh* (1975). The initial appearance protects the rights of an arrested person by reviewing the law enforcement officer's decision that there was probable cause for an arrest, which is required by the Fourth Amendment.

Table 12.1. Punishments for Felonies and Misdemeanors in Virginia (from Most Serious Offenses to Least Serious Offenses)

Offense Category	Authorized Punishments
Class 1 Felony	Death or life in prison and a fine up to $100,000
Class 2 Felony	20 years to life in prison and a fine up to $100,000
Class 3 Felony	5 to 20 years in prison and a fine up to $100,000
Class 4 Felony	2 to 10 years in prison and a fine up to $100,000
Class 5 Felony	1 to 10 years in prison *or* up to 12 months in jail and a fine up to $2,500
Class 6 Felony	1 to 5 years in prison *or* up to 12 months in jail and a fine up to $2,500
Class 1 Misdemeanor	Up to 12 months in jail and a fine up to $2,500
Class 2 Misdemeanor	Up to 6 months in jail and a fine up to $1,000
Class 3 Misdemeanor	A fine up to $500
Class 4 Misdemeanor	A fine up to $250

See Punishment for Conviction of a Felony (2008) and Punishment for Conviction of a Misdemeanor (2000).

The initial appearance is supposed to occur within 48 hours of a person's arrest. Delays beyond 48 hours require the government to prove "extraordinary circumstances" for the longer delay (*County of Riverside v. McLaughlin*, 1991).

Several other things typically occur at an initial appearance, although technicalities differ by jurisdiction. The defendant is always informed of charges and possible penalties. The defendant is usually provided with a copy of any charging documents and informed of the right to retain counsel or, if indigent, to have an attorney appointed. In addition, bail may be preliminarily granted or denied; a full bail hearing usually occurs later as a separate proceeding. And in more than 75% of all *misdemeanor* cases, a defendant pleads guilty to the offense charged at the initial appearance (Neubauer & Fradella, 2011).

CHARGING

Criminal defendants may be formally charged with committing a crime in three primary ways: by a **complaint** filled out by a police officer or private citizen accusing a person of committing a crime; by an **indictment** returned by a grand jury; or by an **information**, which is a document presented by a prosecutor to a judge at a preliminary hearing. Regardless of which method is used, a charging document must include the crime being charged; the person being charged; when and where the alleged acts occurred; the possible penalties; and most important, a written statement of the facts of the offense. A complaint is commonly used for *misdemeanor* charges. Indictments and informations are used primarily for *felony* charges.

Before standing trial on felony charges, an accused has the right to have the evidence against him or her reviewed to make sure there is sufficient evidence to warrant moving forward with a trial. There are two distinct judicial processes used to achieve this goal: grand jury proceedings and preliminary hearings. Defendants are entitled to have one or the other but not both.

Recall from Chapter 8 that the Fifth Amendment to the U.S. Constitution guarantees the right to a grand jury indictment in all federal felony prosecutions. About half of the states also provide this right. A **grand jury** is a group of citizens that typically ranges in size from 16 to 23 people (although a handful of states use grand juries as small as 3 to 5 people). Its purpose is to serve as a check on prosecutorial power by listening to evidence of criminal wrongdoing presented by a prosecutor and to determine whether that evidence is sufficient to make someone stand trial. If the grand jury finds, by a simple majority vote, that there is probable cause to believe a person has committed the offense, it issues an indictment (also known as a *true bill*), and the case moves forward. If, on the other hand, the grand jury finds insufficient evidence to issue an indictment, it issues a *no bill*, the case does not move forward, and the accused person does not have to stand trial for the alleged offense.

Grand juries usually sit for a fixed period ranging from 1 to 18 months. In spite of their purpose of restraining unbridled prosecutorial authority, grand juries rarely return a no bill. Instead, they tend to rubber-stamp the requests of prosecutors (see Washburn, 2008), meaning that virtually all cases brought to a grand jury result in an indictment that sends the case forward. This is largely because grand jury proceedings are held in secret (not in open court) and only the prosecutor presents evidence; neither the defendant nor his or her counsel is usually present. In fact, a defendant may not even know that a grand jury is investigating his or her alleged involvement in a crime.

A **preliminary hearing** is another proceeding designed to determine if a defendant must stand trial on felony charges. Preliminary hearings are used as checks on prosecutorial authority in jurisdictions that do not use grand juries. They are also used in grand jury jurisdictions when a defendant waives the right to a grand jury indictment. Unlike grand jury proceedings, preliminary hearings are held in open court before a judge. Both the prosecution and the defense may present evidence and arguments. A judge then determines if there is probable cause. If the judge finds there is probable cause to believe the defendant committed the felony or felonies charged, then the judge *binds over* the defendant for trial. If, however, the judge determines that probable cause is lacking, the judge may reduce felony charges to misdemeanor charges or may dismiss the charges completely, depending on what the evidence warrants.

ARRAIGNMENT

After a defendant is indicted by a grand jury or bound over for trial by a judge at a preliminary hearing, the next step is to hold an arraignment. An **arraignment** is a formal proceeding in which the charging document is read to the defendant in open court, and the defendant is asked to enter a formal plea on each charge. Defendants generally have two options: guilty or not guilty. If the defendant pleads not guilty, the case is scheduled for trial. If the defendant pleads guilty—something that usually only occurs if the prosecution and defense have agreed to a plea bargain (discussed later)—then the case is scheduled for sentencing. In some jurisdictions, a defendant may be permitted to plead *nolo contendere* (no contest), which allows a defendant to admit that there is sufficient evidence such that a conviction at trial is highly likely. However, unlike with a guilty plea, with a *nolo contendere* plea the defendant is not required to actually admit guilt. In some jurisdictions, this means that a *nolo contendere* plea cannot be used against a person in a civil (noncriminal) court trial pertaining to the same set of facts (recall from Chapter 7 that a single incident may result in both criminal and civil actions). Finally, in most U.S. jurisdictions, a mentally ill defendant may enter a plea of not guilty by reason of insanity. Contrary to popular belief, such pleas occur in less than 1% of all felony cases. Moreover, when insanity pleas are entered, they are unsuccessful approximately 75% of the time (Perlin, 1997).

DISCOVERY

Discovery is the process by which the parties exchange relevant information about a case. Although there is no constitutional right to discovery in criminal cases, a series of statutes, judicial decisions, and court rules have established obligations to disclose certain information as part of a defendant's due process rights to a fair trial. For example, both sides must disclose a list of witnesses who may be called at trial. Similarly, the parties must disclose relevant evidence, including results or reports of physical examinations, scientific tests, or experiments on evidence. Additionally, the prosecution must disclose all **exculpatory evidence** to the defense (*Brady v. Maryland*, 1963). Exculpatory evidence is any evidence that may be favorable to the defendant at trial either by tending to cast doubt on the defendant's guilt or by tending to mitigate the defendant's culpability. The prosecution must also disclose any prior inconsistent statements of prosecutorial witnesses so that the defense may conduct meaningful cross-examinations of the prosecution's witnesses (see Demands for Production of Statements and Reports of Witnesses, 1970, also known as the Jencks Act). Collectively, all of the information disclosed is supposed to prevent unfair surprises at trial.

PLEA BARGAINING

Contrary to the jury trials favored in television and film portrayals, the vast majority of criminal cases never go to trial. Rather, they are resolved by a plea bargain.

Plea bargaining is the process by which a defendant agrees to plead guilty in exchange for some consideration from the government. "Plea bargaining dominates the modern American criminal process. Upwards of 95% of all state and federal felony convictions are obtained by guilty plea" (Covey, 2008, p. 1238).

Plea bargaining usually takes one of three forms. In *charge bargaining*, the defendant pleas guilty to a less serious charge than the one in the charging document. For example, someone charged with the felony of aggravated assault may plead guilty to a misdemeanor assault charge to avoid not only the felony conviction but also the increased prison time that would come with the more serious charge. In *count bargaining*, someone charged with multiple offenses pleads guilty to only some of the charges in exchange for the others being dropped. This, in turn, reduces the overall sentence the defendant will receive. For example, someone charged with eight counts of bank robbery may plead to one or two counts and face punishment just for those counts rather than for all of the robberies. Finally, *sentence bargaining* occurs when a defendant pleads guilty to the crime originally charged but does so in exchange for a lesser sentence than would likely have been imposed if the defendant had been convicted at trial. For example, someone facing the death penalty for a homicide might plead guilty to murder if a sentence of life is recommended as part of a plea bargain.

Whatever form of plea bargaining is used, the plea agreement in any case must be agreed upon by the prosecutor, defense counsel, and the defendant. Once a plea agreement is negotiated, it is ultimately up to a judge to accept the plea and enter judgment in accordance with the agreement. If the judge refuses to accept the terms of a plea bargain, the defendant may withdraw from the plea agreement and seek a trial.

PRETRIAL MOTIONS

A **motion** is a formal request asking a court to make a specific ruling. Motions may be made orally or in writing and may concern any number of substantive or procedural issues. In criminal justice, however, the most important motion that can be made before a trial is the *motion to suppress*. In such a motion, a criminal defendant asks a judge to suppress (or prohibit) certain evidence from being considered at trial because it was gathered in violation of the defendant's constitutional rights. Recall from Chapter 8, for example, that searches for and seizures of evidence must comply with the requirements of the Fourth Amendment. Similarly, custodial interrogations that lead a suspect to make incriminating statements (sometimes even full confessions) must have been obtained in accordance with the rights in the Fifth and Sixth Amendments to the U.S. Constitution. If evidence was obtained in violation of any of these constitutional rights, then a defendant may file a motion to suppress the evidence. If granted by a judge, the suppressed evidence is excluded and may not be used to establish the defendant's guilt at trial. Thus, granting a motion to suppress may

seriously affect the outcome of a criminal case. However, such motions are relatively rare. They are filed in less than 8% of all criminal cases (Nardulli, 1983).
Moreover, such motions are granted in less than 2% of the cases in which they
are filed (Uchida & Bynum 1991).

> Why do you think initial appearances must be held within 48 hours,
> barring exceptional circumstances?
>
> If you were a criminal defendant facing felony charges, which process
> would you prefer to protect your rights—the grand jury process or a
> preliminary hearing? Why?
>
> Do you think "surprises" should be allowed at criminal trials? Explain.
>
> What are the advantages and disadvantages of plea bargaining?

Criminal Trial Processes

FOCUSING QUESTION 12.4

What happens during and after a criminal trial?

The Sixth Amendment to the U.S. Constitution guarantees the right to a speedy,
public, and impartial trial by jury for defendants who stand accused of crimes.
The Supreme Court, however, has carved out two significant exceptions to this
rule. First, because juvenile cases are civil actions as opposed to being truly
criminal in nature, juveniles in most states do not have a right to a trial by jury
(see *McKeiver v. Pennsylvania*, 1971). Second, the right to a jury trial does not
apply to petty charges, defined by the Supreme Court as any case in which the
punishment is a fine, community service, the loss of a privilege such as one's
driver's license, or incarceration for fewer than six months (*Baldwin v. New York*,
1970; *Blanton v. City of North Las Vegas*, 1989).

When the right to trial by jury does not exist or when a defendant elects
to waive his or her right to a trial by jury (as they often do in cases when they
believe a jury would be biased against them for some reason), a judge assumes
the role of the jury as the trier of fact. Such proceedings are called **bench trials**
because the case is tried by the judge, who sits on "the bench."

JURY SELECTION

In jury trials, the jury must be selected before a trial can begin. Jury selection is
a complicated process that varies significantly not only from state to state, but
even from courtroom to courtroom within the same courthouse. However,
there are several steps that commonly occur almost everywhere. First, court
personnel need to assemble a group of potential jurors. This task is usually executed by a jury administrator or clerk of the court who issues summonses to
potential jurors. A **summons** is a court order that directs a recipient to appear
in court at a specific time on a specific date. The group of people who respond

to the summons by coming to court to participate in the jury selection process are called the **venire**.

Next, the venire is questioned in court in a process known as *voir dire*, a Latin term meaning "to speak the truth." During *voir dire*, the venire is sworn to tell the truth and is then asked a variety of questions designed to screen out people who cannot make a fair and impartial decision in the case. Some judges allow the lawyers in the case to ask the questions; other judges prefer to ask the questions themselves. Either way, the questions are supposed to help the court determine who should be excused from serving on the jury because they are partial to one side of the case or because they are biased about the nature of the case. These parties are excused from jury service for cause (also known as being stricken for cause). For example, people who were the victims of significant thefts may not be able to be fair and impartial jurors in a burglary case. In some jurisdictions, each side may also be permitted to excuse a few potential jurors without cause. These are called **peremptory challenges**. Peremptory challenges may be used for nearly any reason, ranging from the prosecution or defense not liking the way someone looked at them to thinking that the potential juror may not believe the arguments they plan to make during trial. Peremptory challenges may not, however, be used in a discriminatory manner. It violates the constitutional guarantee of equal protection of the law for lawyers to use their peremptory strikes to exclude potential jurors on the basis of race or gender (*Batson v. Kentucky*, 1986; *J. E. B. v. Alabama ex rel. T. B.*, 1994).

Once the *voir dire* process is completed, the judge will impanel and swear the **petit jury**—the people who will listen to the evidence over the course of the trial and then render a verdict. In most states, criminal juries are comprised of 12 petit jurors. However, some states use juries composed of fewer than 12 jurors. The U.S. Supreme Court approved of juries as small as 6 persons in *Williams v. Florida* (1970). As indicated in Table 12.2, the size of a jury affects whether or not verdicts that are not unanimous may be permitted under the law.

PRESUMPTIONS AND EVIDENCE

At the start of a criminal trial, the jury is guided by two presumptions, which are conclusions that the jury is *required* to make in the absence of sufficient evidence being introduced at trial to overcome or *rebut* the presumption. The **presumption of sanity** applies in all criminal trials. All defendants are presumed to be sane—legally responsible for their actions—unless they are proven insane at trial. Because sanity is an issue in only a miniscule number of criminal cases, the presumption of sanity is rarely even mentioned. The second is the **presumption of innocence**. All criminal defendants are presumed innocent until proven guilty beyond a reasonable doubt. This means the defendant does not have to prove his or her innocence. Rather, the prosecutor bears the burden of proof to overcome or rebut the presumption of innocence by introducing sufficient evidence to prove the defendant guilty beyond a reasonable doubt.

If the prosecutor does not or cannot introduce such evidence or if the defense attorney is able to introduce reasonable doubt, then the defendant is acquitted (found "not guilty").

Evidence is anything that helps to prove or disprove a fact. Most people tend to think of evidence as *real* or *physical evidence*—tangible objects like clothes, weapons, drugs, documents, and so forth, but there are three other types of evidence that are commonly used in criminal trials. Evidence also includes *testimony*, or the responses of sworn witnesses to the questions posed to them by attorneys or the judge, and *scientific evidence*, or the results of scientific or forensic testing on real or physical evidence. *Demonstrative evidence* includes maps, photos, diagrams, computer simulations, and other aids designed for use at trial to help demonstrate some fact to the judge or jury.

Prosecutors try to build a case by using all of the types of evidence they have to rebut the presumption of innocence. Their goal is to prove all elements of a crime **beyond a reasonable doubt**. This term is difficult to define. It cannot be quantified; rather, it is an inherently qualitative concept. The Federal Judicial Center offered the following definition of reasonable doubt—one that U.S. Supreme Court Justice Ruth Bader Ginsburg thought was clear enough to understand that she cited it favorably in *Victor v. Nebraska* (1994, p. 27):

> Proof beyond a reasonable doubt is proof that leaves you firmly convinced of the defendant's guilt. There are very few things in this world that we know with absolute certainty, and in criminal cases the law does not require proof that overcomes every possible doubt. If, based on your consideration of the evidence, you are firmly convinced that the defendant is guilty of the crime charged, you must find him guilty. If on the other hand, you think there is a real possibility that he is not guilty, you must give him the benefit of the doubt and find him not guilty.

TRIAL

Although the order in which a criminal trial unfolds varies somewhat from state to state, most trials proceed in the order presented in Table 12.2. The ultimate goal of a criminal trial is to reach a verdict. In criminal cases, the two possible outcomes are either "guilty" or "not guilty." In insanity defense cases (which, recall, are very rare), there is also the possibility of a verdict such as "not guilty by reason of insanity" or "guilty except insane" (see Fradella, 2007).

SENTENCING

If a defendant is convicted, the trial court judge must sentence the defendant to some sort of criminal punishment (see Chapters 10 and 13). Although sentencing is technically a part of the judicial process, it is important to note that all three branches of government play a role in the process. In the penal code of a given jurisdiction, the legislature sets the permissible range of punishments

Table 12.2. **Order of Presentation at Trial**

Procedure	What Happens
Opening Statements	The parties present an overview of their case. This normally includes their "theory" of the case and an outline or road map of the evidence they plan to present over the course of trial. The prosecution usually goes first because it bears the burden of persuasion.
Prosecution's Case-in-Chief	The prosecution calls witnesses and presents other evidence in an attempt to prove the defendant's guilt. When a prosecutor calls a witness, a *direct examination* is conducted. Direct examinations are comprised of a series of open-ended questions (e.g., who, what, when, where, how, why). When the prosecutor finishes the direct examination of any witness, the defendant is guaranteed the right to conduct a *cross-examination*. Questions on cross-examination tend to be closed ended in that they typically ask for a "yes" or "no" answer. Cross-examination questions usually focus on undermining the credibility of the witness by exploring inconsistencies, inaccuracies, biases, or inadequacies of observation.
Motion for Judgment of Acquittal	While not required, the defense may move for a *judgment of acquittal* at the end of the prosecution's case-in-chief. This motion asks the judge to dismiss the case because no reasonable jury could find the defendant guilty in light of the evidence presented by the prosecution. These motions are rarely granted.
Defense's Case-in-Chief	The defense conducts direct examination of its witnesses and presents other evidence in an attempt to create reasonable doubt about the defendant's guilt. The prosecution can then cross-examine witnesses called by the defense.
Renewed Motion for Judgment of Acquittal	The defense may (but is not required to) renew its motion for acquittal after presenting its case-in-chief. Again, these motions are rarely granted.
Rebuttal Case by Prosecution	While not routine, the prosecution may be permitted to introduce additional evidence after the defense has closed its case-in-chief. Such evidence is usually limited to rebutting evidence presented by the defense.
Closing Arguments	Both the prosecution and the defense are permitted to summarize their respective cases to the jury and present arguments why the verdict should be in their favor. Usually, the prosecution makes its closing argument first, then the defense makes it closing argument, and finally, the prosecution gets the "last word" during rebuttal.
Jury Instructions	The judge instructs the jury as to the applicable law that is relevant in the case. The timing of jury instructions varies and may be at the start of the trial, before closing arguments, or after the closing arguments have been made.
Jury Deliberations	The jury leaves the courtroom to conduct their deliberations in private.
Verdict	In most criminal trials, the jury deliberates until all members of the jury vote to either convict or acquit the defendant. A handful of states allow 12-person verdicts that are not unanimous. If a 6-person jury is used, the verdict must be

Verdict (continued)	unanimous. If the jury cannot reach consensus to agree on a verdict, a judge may declare a *hung jury*, which results in the jury being discharged and the case being retried or dismissed.
Postverdict Motions	The parties may (but are not required to) introduce various motions. For example, if the defendant is convicted, defense counsel might move to allow the defendant to remain free on bail pending sentencing. Alternatively, the defense may move for a new trial or for a judgment of acquittal.
Sentencing	The imposition of sentence upon a convicted defendant normally takes place at a sentencing hearing a number of weeks after the verdict. The court must impose a sentence that is authorized under the governing criminal statutes.
Judgment	The case formally ends when the clerk of the court enters a final judgment in the case. In a criminal case, the judgment reveals whether the defendant was acquitted or convicted on each count charged and, if convicted, what sentence was imposed.

that a judge may impose (as illustrated in Table 12.1). When a jurisdiction uses an **indeterminate sentencing** scheme, the statute sets a range of permissible sentences for a given offense (usually a minimum and a maximum) and leaves it to the sentencing judge to impose whatever sentence he or she feels is fair under the particular facts of a case. Because this can lead to great disparities in sentences, some jurisdictions have adopted **determinate sentencing** schemes. In their strictest form, determinate sentencing schemes may require a judge to impose a particular sentence for a given crime; such sentences are called *mandatory sentences*. In their more common form, however, determinate sentencing schemes use *sentencing guidelines* that specify a minimum, maximum, and presumptive term for each crime. The sentencing judge is supposed to impose the presumptive sentence in the case, adding to it only if there are aggravating circumstances and subtracting from it only if there are mitigating circumstances.

The executive branch exercises a significant role in the sentencing process through the recommendations of the prosecutor. The executive branch can also control sentences by pardoning offenders or commuting their sentences through the actions of a governor, the president, or through agencies like a clemency board or a parole board. The executive branch's primary influence over criminal sentencing, though, is through the recommendations of probation officers. In the federal courts and in most states, after a defendant is convicted, a sentencing hearing is scheduled, perhaps four to six weeks after the trial. In the meantime, probation officers prepare a **presentence investigation report (PSI)**. This report summarizes the circumstances leading up to the commission of the offense; the defendant's social, educational, family, and financial background; the existence of any mitigating factors, such as drug or alcohol dependence; and the defendant's criminal history. The report may also contain the probation officer's perceptions of the defendant's level of remorse, the officer's professional judgment about the defendant's risk of reoffending (Spohn, 2008), and the officer's recommendation for sentencing the offender. This report gives the sentencing judge a great deal of information that the judge can then use when deciding how to impose a just sentence within the applicable type of sentencing scheme. These reports are very influential, as judges often agree to impose sentences in accordance with the sentencing recommendations made by probation officers in the PSI (Spohn, 2008).

POSTCONVICTION REVIEW

After a sentence has been imposed and a final judgment has been entered in a case, a convicted defendant has the right to file an **appeal**. Recall that appellate courts rarely focus on issues of guilt or innocence but most often consider whether the law was properly applied, whether the pretrial and trial processes were fair, and so on. Unlike at trial, no evidence is presented at an appeal. Rather, appeals are decided by panels of judges who review the case record (i.e., the transcripts of trial testimony, the documents received into evidence at trial, and the rulings of the trial court judge) as well as the arguments that lawyers make on appeal. These legal arguments are usually made in written form in a document called a *brief*. Sometimes, appeals courts will also hear *oral arguments* from the lawyers in the case. The judges on an appellate court review all of these materials to make sure that the criminally accused received a fair trial and a legal sentence. If minor legal errors were made that were unlikely to have affected the overall outcome of the case, appeals courts call such mistakes **harmless error**. Such errors do not result in the reversal of a conviction on appeal. If, however, significant mistakes were made at trial that likely contributed to an unfair verdict, then the court will rule these mistakes to constitute **prejudicial or reversible error** and overturn the conviction on that basis. Such an outcome is rare. In fact, criminal convictions are reversed on appeal in less than 8% of cases (Neubauer & Fradella, 2011). The overwhelming majority of cases end after the first appeal is resolved because every defendant is entitled to one appeal as a matter of right. After an initial appeal is decided, subsequent appeals to even higher levels of appellate courts are not guaranteed as a matter of right.

The high courts of most states are able to pick and choose which cases they want to hear; the same is true in the federal system with the U.S. Supreme Court. People seeking appellate review of their case *after* their initial appeal may ask a higher court to hear their case by filing a petition for a writ of **certiorari**. Such a writ is an order from a higher appellate court to a lower appellate court to send the record of the case to the higher court for review. *Certiorari* is rarely granted. Unlike intermediate appellate courts whose primary function is error correction, discretionary appeals at high courts are usually selected for public policy reasons or to resolve disagreements in how lower courts have ruled on constitutional questions. In fact, the U.S. Supreme Court typically hears only 80 to 90 cases each year, rejecting between 7,000 and 15,000 other petitions for *certiorari* that the Court receives each year.

When all appeals are exhausted, a criminal defendant might still be able to turn to the civil justice system to seek relief through applications for a writ of ***habeas corpus*** (see Chapter 8). A person in custody may seek a writ arguing that one or more errors of constitutional dimension (i.e., not merely procedural mistakes) occurred at trial that subsequent appeals failed to correct. As you might imagine, courts grant such postconviction relief rather infrequently.

> If you had been one of the defendants in the shipwreck case, would you have preferred a jury trial or a bench trial? Why?
>
> What type of person would you have wanted on the jury if you had been the prosecutor in the shipwreck case? What if you were the defense attorney? Explain your reasoning.
>
> If you were a judge, which type of sentencing scheme would you prefer? Why?
>
> If you were imposing sentence on the defendants in the shipwreck case, which facts of the case, if any, would you consider to be aggravating factors that would cause you to impose a harsher sentence? What mitigating factors would cause you to impose a more lenient sentence?

Judicial Review

FOCUSING QUESTION 12.5

How can judicial review impact public policy?

High courts often hear cases that involve the use of judicial review, which can profoundly affect justice policy. Recall from Chapter 7 that Article VI of the U.S. Constitution contains the **Supremacy Clause**, which declares that the Constitution is the "Supreme Law of the Land." What happens if Congress or a state legislature were to enact a law that conflicts with a provision of the Constitution? In the 1803 landmark case of *Marbury v. Madison*, the U.S. Supreme Court declared that it is the role of the courts to resolve such conflicts. When courts invalidate laws enacted by a legislature or rules made by an executive agency, they exercise the power of **judicial review**.

Advocates of judicial review argue that the Constitution's protections "of particular rights or privileges would amount to nothing" without judicial review because there would be no means for enforcing them (Hamilton, Madison, & Jay, [1788] 2003, p. 379). Moreover, they assert "[t]he United States is a more just society" because it has a judicial review than it would have been if constitutional rights had been left to more political government institutions (Dworkin, 1986, p. 356). Critics counter that judicial review amounts to judges substituting their own judgments for those of elected officials and for the will of the public. Disagreements about which "rights" ought to exist in a just society, as illustrated by ongoing debates regarding abortion, same-sex marriage, and euthanasia, have led some modern commentators to reject judicial review on the grounds that such disputes should be resolved through the legislative process and based on the public's preferences.

But what happens when the will of the majority is wrong? For example, when the United States was founded, slavery was legally acceptable. Even when slavery was abolished after the Civil War, the law still allowed discrimination against African Americans. Had the U.S. Supreme Court not invalidated the concept of "separate, but equal" in *Brown v. Board of Education* (1954), segregation would have remained legal until legislators corrected this injustice. Because courts are in a unique position to address inequality in society, defenders of judicial review argue that it is fundamental to the functioning of a just democracy. In fact, the courts have frequently been the branch of government to which minority groups have turned, often successfully, in their struggles for equality (Frymer, 2003).

Clearly, the power of judicial review affects public policy. When the Supreme Court ruled that the death penalty may not be given to persons who were under 18 at the time of their offense (*Roper v. Simmons*, 2005), it was a policy decision that impacted state sentencing laws. When the Supreme Court ruled that the Second Amendment right to "keep and bear arms" applied to the states (*McDonald v. City of Chicago*, 2010), state and local governments had to revisit their laws about firearms to determine if they were in accordance with the Supreme Court's ruling; the full implications of the case remain to be seen.

In short, the Supreme Court does make policy through the power of judicial review. Whether addressing injustices or inequalities or issuing constitutional rulings, the decisions of the Supreme Court have the potential to shape federal, state, and local laws, criminal justice agency practices, justice system policies, and more.

> Should courts have the ability to invalidate a law enacted by a legislative body because the judges believe that the law violates someone's rights? Explain your answer.
>
> Do you think judicial review is fundamental to democracy or inconsistent with it? Explain your position.

Legal Reasoning

FOCUSING QUESTION 12.6

How do judges decide cases?

Judges interpret and apply the law, whether a trial court judge ruling on the admissibility of a piece of evidence or a Supreme Court justice ruling on the constitutionality of a police practice. However, it is misleading to speak of "the law" as a simple set of rules whose meaning is clearly understood; "law is a language, not simply a collection of rules" (Carter & Burke, 2006, p. 5). When grappling with the language of the law, judges must engage in careful decision making to ensure that the law is properly understood and applied. Doing so is central to the legitimacy of the courts in a democracy. At its most basic level, **legal reasoning** concerns the processes by which judges "justify how and why they use their power" when interpreting and applying the law (Carter & Burke, 2006, p. 8). We expect such decisions to be coherent, logical, and well reasoned. But judicial philosophies clearly play a role in the adjudication process.

PHILOSOPHIES OF LEGAL REASONING

The traditional view of legal reasoning is called **legal formalism**. It states that "judges apply the relevant law to the relevant facts and arrive at a decision" (Friedrichs, 2006, p. 53), such that: law + facts = decision. Logic lies at the heart of this theory of legal reasoning. In fact, legal formalism rejects the notion that ethical, political, philosophical, or policy considerations should play any role in judicial decision making, even if applying the law precisely as it is written may result in an outcome judges think undesirable. This assumes that there is little role for discretion in the law; whatever the law says is what should happen. Legal formalism was criticized as too mechanical, especially because the facts of a case are often in dispute and the law is sometimes unclear or imprecise. Moreover, legal formalism assumes that there is a single "correct" answer when, in fact, there may be no such thing.

Legal realism suggests that legal reasoning is an act of interpretation involving the evaluation of arguments made by opposing parties. This analysis may require judges to consider factors *beyond* the law to resolve uncertainties in cases. This does not mean that judges simply guess or that they select an answer that suits their personal values. Instead, legal realism suggests that judges should be guided by certain basic principles, such as fairness, when deciding how the law should be applied in a case. Some legal realists go further. Those who advocate *legal instrumentalism* think that judges should make decisions that promote "good" or "desirable" outcomes. With this approach, judges craft decisions to achieve justice, serve broad social interests, and foster good public policy.

Legal realism remained the dominant school of legal reasoning from the turn of the twentieth century to the late 1940s. By the 1950s, other schools of thought began to emerge. **Legal process theories** tried to harmonize legal formalism and legal realism by offering "neutral principles" that judges could use to resolve unclear cases. Some legal process theorists believe that judges should try to understand the *original intent* of a constitution or statute (Fallon, 1994; Young, 2005). Others argue that judges should consider "general ethical principles and widely shared social goals" (Hart & Sacks, 1958, pp. 158–159). Still others maintain that judges should consider government structure, such as the separation of powers and federalism, and how that would affect decisions (Wechsler, 1954). Many of the legal process approaches still have influence today, although they have been critiqued for allowing judges to draw upon their own ideologies (Wells, 1991). Determining which neutral principles to use, and then how to use them, is in part a value decision leading to inconsistencies between judges.

The **law and economics** movement emerged in the 1970s, primarily from classic utilitarian assumptions that people are rational decision makers who will maximize their own best interest. This approach advocates that the law should be interpreted (and cases should be decided) in a way that distributes economic costs and benefits to promote economic efficiency and maximize wealth (Friedman, 2000; Polinsky, 2003; Posner, 1990). Although this approach was popular through the 1980s, it has been criticized for its focus on economic interests over noneconomic interests, most notably social justice (Edelman, 2004; Friedrichs, 2006). It still remains, however, a leading conservative theory of legal reasoning.

The leading liberal theory is called the **jurisprudence of rights**, a modern extension of legal realism. Those who subscribe to the jurisprudence of rights, most notably Ronald Dworkin (1977, 1986), argue the primary extralegal consideration that should guide judges is an ethics of "rights." This school of thought advocates going beyond the text of constitutions or statutes to examine the moral implications of the adjudication *process*. Moreover, the moral questions are examined from a perspective that promotes equality—both of opportunity and of outcome. That is, fairness for all, especially for those least able to protect their own rights and interests, is the guiding principle judges use when deciding cases under this approach.

Based on neo-Marxist notions of power, **critical legal studies (CLS)** began in the late 1970s and has gained influence since then. It argues that law *is* politics. As such, law is "hegemonic"—designed to maintain the status quo in society, meaning that it perpetuates the privileges and disadvantages that come with people's standing in the social hierarchy. Critical legal studies critiques legal reasoning that serves the interests of the wealthy and powerful at the expense of the poor and less powerful (see Kelman, 1987; Kennedy, 1997). The CLS movement produced several offshoots that focus on ways the legal system has systematically oppressed particular groups in society. **Critical race theory** focuses on the experiences of racial and ethnic minorities with the legal system (see Crenshaw, Gotanda, Peller, & Thomas, 1995; Delgado & Stefancic, 2001; Lawrence & Matsuda, 1997). The school of **feminist jurisprudence** focuses on gender inequality in society as a function of law (see Baer, 1999; MacKinnon, 2007; West, 1988). And **postmodern jurisprudence** borrows from all of these critical schools to focus on the intersection of race, gender, gender identity, religion, social class, sexual orientation, and the like to study structural inequalities in law and society, often by using literary theory to deconstruct the meaning of words in legislation and judicial decisions (Douzinas, Warrington, & McVeigh, 1993; Minda, 1996).

Critical and postmodern theories remain controversial and out of the mainstream for two reasons. First, they reject the notion of any objective truth or reality and the empirical methods of science and social science. Rather, they use the methods of literature, such as discourse analysis, narrative, storytelling, and rhetoric. Second, they focus on criticism without corresponding ideas for workable reform (Farber & Sherry, 1997). Yet critical and postmodern legal theories have undoubtedly exposed some of the shortcomings of more traditional approaches to legal decision making. This, in turn, has helped to sensitize legal actors (especially through changes in legal education) to social justice concerns about racism, sexism, homophobia, and other issues.

THE PROCESS OF LEGAL REASONING

Regardless of their philosophy of adjudication, philosophy of law, or philosophy of justice, we expect that all judges will explain *how* they arrived at their ultimate decision in a case. Carter and Burke (2006) constructed a model that explains the four primary criteria that judges may consider. Their model is presented in Figure 12.3. As you see, the facts of a case and the applicable law are only two of the factors; social background facts and value judgments also play a role.

Figure 12.3. The Four Primary Components of Legal Reasoning

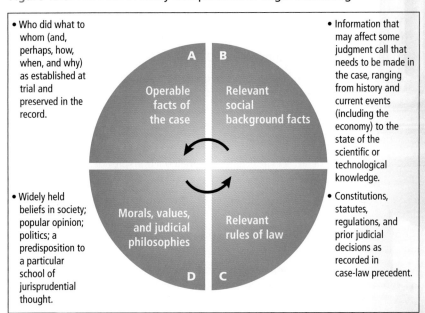

Adapted from: Carter, L. H., & Burke, T. F. (2007). *Reason in Law* (7th ed.). New York: Pearson/Longman.

The degree to which any of these factors might influence a judge's decision varies from case to case and also varies based on the judge's legal philosophy. For an example of legal reasoning, see Box 12.1.

> How would each legal philosophy described address the shipwreck case study? Be sure to include analyses of the charge, the conviction, the original sentence, and the actual punishment.

BOX 12.1

AN EXERCISE IN LEGAL REASONING

Consider the following hypothetical scenario, variations of which have been debated by legal scholars and students for years (see Hart, 1958; Schlag, 1999):

> Assume that a law prohibits bringing a vehicle into a city's park. Individuals who break the law must pay a fine not to exceed $1,000. The law was passed out of concern for the well-being of the park. You are a judge, and you are well aware of this law. You now have to rule on the following incidents:

1. A townsperson driving through town decides to take a shortcut through the park.
2. An ambulance driver takes his ambulance in the park to rescue a sick park visitor.
3. A local veterans' group donates a jeep as part of a war memorial in the park.
4. A child brings a motorized remote-control car into the park.

How should "vehicle" be defined?

What does it mean to "bring a vehicle" into the park?

Compare and contrast how each of these cases would be resolved by a legal formalist, a legal realist, and a legal process theorist who subscribes to the notion of original intent.

How would you resolve each of these cases? In each, which elements from Figure 12.1 would be most important in your decision? Why?

Legal reasoning is related to perceptions of law and justice. Review material from previous chapters, as necessary, to answer these questions:

What was your preferred theory of law from Chapter 3? How would it apply to the four incidents listed above?

What was your preferred theory of justice from Chapter 7? How would it apply to the four incidents listed above?

Consider the consistencies between your preferred resolution to the preceding cases, your preferred philosophy of law, and your preferred philosophy of justice. Compare your results to those of your classmates. Your conversations should help illustrate how and why different jurists may approach the same case in different ways.

Conclusion

The courts are often one of the first institutions that individuals think of when they hear "criminal justice" because of the role the courts play in adjudicating criminal cases. Although trials are rare, with plea bargains far more common, the courtroom workgroup plays an essential role in the resolution of criminal cases. Prosecuting attorneys, defense attorneys, and judges work to see cases through the pretrial and, if necessary, trial processes described in this chapter, all the while maintaining an emphasis on justice. Appellate courts also have a significant impact on criminal justice, particularly through the power of judicial review and constitutional interpretation, which results in decisions that can shape criminal justice policies and practices nationwide. The topic of the next chapter is the correctional system in the United States, which is (not surprisingly) directly affected by the courts. Judges determine how offenders are sentenced to the various correctional alternatives, and the power of judicial review establishes the limits of punishments that correctional agencies may impose.

Criminal Justice Problem Solving: VOTING RIGHTS

According to The Sentencing Project (2011), roughly 5.3 million U.S. citizens—about 60% of whom are black or Hispanic—are unable to vote in elections due to **voting disenfranchisement laws**. Consider the following:

- 48 states and the District of Columbia prohibit inmates from voting while incarcerated for a felony offense.
- Only two states—Maine and Vermont—permit inmates to vote.
- 35 states prohibit persons on parole from voting and 30 of these states exclude persons on probation as well.
- Four states deny the right to vote to all persons with felony convictions, even after they have completed their sentences. Eight others disenfranchise certain categories of ex-offenders and/or permit application for restoration of rights for specified offenses after a waiting period. . .
- Each state has developed its own process of restoring voting rights to ex-offenders but most of these restoration processes are so cumbersome that few ex-offenders are able to take advantage of them. (p. 1)

Disenfranchisement laws have ancient Greco-Roman roots; they were used throughout Europe and incorporated in the laws of U.S. colonies (Varnum, 2008). But "over time, these laws became both more common and more severe" (p. 116). Indeed, when African American men were granted the right to vote after the Civil War, "many Southern states tailored their criminal disenfranchisement laws, along with other voting qualifications, to increase the effect of these laws on black citizens" (Shapiro, 1993, p. 540). Today, nearly 13% of African American men in the United States are barred from voting due to criminal convictions (that is as high as one-third of all black men in some states, like Florida and Alabama)—"a rate seven times the national average" (Sentencing Project, 2008, p. 1). The United States is the only democracy in the world where some states disenfranchise convicted felons for the rest of their lives, even after they have fully served their sentences.

In *Richardson v. Ramirez* (1974), the U.S. Supreme Court upheld California's felony disenfranchisement law, rejecting the argument that the laws violated the Equal Protection Clause of the Fourteenth Amendment to the U.S. Constitution. Eleven years later, though, the Court revisited the matter in *Hunter v. Underwood* (1985). In that case, two men had been convicted of passing bad checks—a misdemeanor under state law. Yet, they were denied the right to vote under a provision of the Alabama State Constitution that disenfranchised those convicted of any "crime involving moral turpitude." In that case, the Court found that the law had been intentionally designed to disenfranchise African Americans. Accordingly, the Court declared the law unconstitutional as a violation of the Equal Protection Clause of the Fourteenth Amendment.

> Many scholars and commentators have called for either the repeal of voting disenfranchisement laws or their invalidation by the courts. Do you think the federal constitutional guarantee of the "equal protection of the laws" serves as a legitimate basis for invalidating the nation's felony disenfranchisement laws? Why or why not?

Core Concepts of U.S. Correctional Theory and Practice

The "Roundhouse" at Stateville Correctional Center in Illinois. What purposes do you think prisons serve in American society?

Key Terms

corrections	classification
incarceration	total institution
recidivism	mortification
mission statement	pains of imprisonment
culture of control	contraband
governing through crime	prisonization
essential tension	importation hypothesis
conflict theory	deprivation hypothesis
prison-industrial complex	panacea phenomenon
correctional boot camps	transportation
quantitative scales	mark system
revocation	parole
correctional institution	probation
jail	suspended sentence
prison	Great Society
debtor's prison	truth in sentencing
banishment	intermediate sanctions
stocks	halfway house
solitary system	day reporting center
congregate system	electronic monitoring
farm system	house arrest
reformatory system	drug court
pod-style design	intensive supervision probation (ISP)
unit management	split sentence
security level	justice reinvestment

Key People

Jonas Hanway	Erving Goffman
John Howard	Gresham Sykes
Hans Toch	Donald Clemmer
David Garland	Alexander Maconochie
Michel Foucault	Walter Crofton
Jonathan Simon	John Augustus
Thomas Kuhn	

CASE STUDY

Weightlifting in Prison

Should inmates in correctional institutions be permitted to participate in weightlifting as a form of recreation? Consider the following information.

Research suggests that the public does not strongly support weightlifting in prison (see Applegate, 2001). Reasons for objecting vary. Some believe it makes prisons too pleasant and less of a deterrent to crime; others believe "weight lifting simply permits inmates to become more physically dangerous"

(Lenz, 2002, p. 517). Still others are concerned about the cost of weightlifting equipment, although Lenz (2002) found that the public is more likely to support weightlifting when it is paid for by the inmates instead of by tax dollars.

Partly in response to these concerns, Congress passed a bill including the Zimmer Amendment (named for its sponsor, Republican Congressman Dick Zimmer from New Jersey) in 1996. "Provisions of this 'no-frills' bill directly affect prison recreation activities by prohibiting the purchase and replacement of weightlifting equipment and musical instruments and the showing of R-rated movies" (Kahler, 2008, p. 92). As a federal law, the Zimmer Amendment only applies to federal prisons and not those operated by state or local governments. However, other states have pursued similar legislation (Lenz, 2002).

The views of correctional administrators, however, differ from those of the public and of politicians. In fact, two-thirds (66.7%) of correctional administrators in one study supported maintaining prison weightlifting activities (Tewksbury & Mustaine, 2005). The American Correctional Association also supports prison weightlifting (Kahler, 2008). Like other recreational activities, weightlifting keeps inmates busy, which is important for the orderly operation of a prison. In addition, weightlifting can be used as a reward or incentive for good inmate behavior (Lenz, 2002).

Furthermore, weightlifting "reduces tension, builds self-esteem, and teaches the necessity of cooperation [e.g., through inmates 'spotting' for each other]" (Kahler, 2008, p. 92). Research has found that weightlifting in prison can reduce inmates' levels of aggression and anger (Wagner, McBride, & Crouse, 1999) and is also associated with lower levels of depression and stress among inmates (Bukaloo, Krug, & Nelson, 2009). As a result, it is possible that weightlifting could be beneficial not only for institutional management but also for rehabilitating offenders.

> Should prison inmates be permitted to lift weights? How is your answer shaped by your opinions of what correctional institutions ought to accomplish? How would you respond to the arguments raised by the opposing side?
>
> Recall from Chapter 2 the discussion of idealism and pragmatism. Compare and contrast how an idealist and a pragmatist would address the issue of prison weightlifting.

The Scope and Purpose of American Corrections

FOCUSING QUESTION 13.1

How large is the American correctional system, and what goals should it accomplish?

In the American criminal justice system, correctional agencies are responsible for carrying out sentences imposed by the criminal courts. Sentences may range from probation to prison to execution, depending on the crime and jurisdiction. The federal government maintains its own correctional agencies (e.g., the Federal Bureau of Prisons and U.S. Probation and Pretrial Services) as do each of the 50 states (generally through a state Department of Corrections). Individuals sentenced in federal court are under the jurisdiction of federal agencies, and those sentenced in a state court are under the jurisdiction of that state's correctional agency or agencies. Local jurisdictions (cities and counties) may also operate correctional systems, primarily for misdemeanor offenders from their local areas.

Corrections is a huge industry in the United States. In 2008 alone, total spending on corrections in the United States totaled $75 billion (Schmitt, Warner, & Gupta, 2010). This annual expenditure funded the supervision of more than 5 million probationers and parolees (Glaze & Bonczar, 2009), approximately 1.6 million inmates in state and federal prisons (West & Sabol, 2009), and more than 785,000 inmates in local jails (Minton & Sabol, 2009). The distinctions between probation, parole, jails, and prisons will be clarified later in the chapter. For now, one key point is that the correctional component of the criminal justice system entails significant expenditures and directly affects many people.

There is another key point to draw from this discussion. The United States makes extensive use of **incarceration** (prison and jail sentences) as a form of punishment. In fact, the United States has the world's highest incarceration rate, with 753 residents per 100,000 confined in prison or jail. Even the next highest, Russia, is substantially lower, at 629 per 100,000. For a point of comparison, the incarceration rate in England and Wales is 153 per 100,000 (Schmitt, Warner, & Gupta, 2010). If incarceration rates remain constant, it is estimated that one person out of fifteen (or 6.6% of the population) will spend some time in a state or federal prison, and that does not even include those who will spend time in local jails (Bonczar, 2003).

It is important to dispel the popular notion that the United States is the world's leader in incarceration because crime is so prevalent. Gottschalk (2006) observed, "the fact is that mass imprisonment [in the United States] is only weakly related to the underlying crime rates" (p. 26). As described in Chapter 1, overall crime rates in the United States are not dramatically higher than those in other industrial democracies. Although lethal violence is more common in the United States, this by itself does not account for the degree to which U.S. incarceration rates eclipse those of other nations. The incarceration rate was 138 persons per 100,000 in 1980, after which it increased dramatically to 753, as noted above. Some factors contributing to the increase included fear of crime, political campaigns and legislation focused on "getting tough" on crime, and the use of imprisonment as a strategy in the War on Drugs (Austin & Irwin, 2001; Pratt, 2009).

With corrections accounting for such a large share of the government's budget and affecting so many people, what should it seek to accomplish? The very name—corrections—suggests a degree of optimism, with a hope that offenders could be rehabilitated or corrected so that they would no longer engage in illegal activity. Indeed, in the eighteenth century, correctional reformers such as Jonas Hanway and John Howard advocated for the development and use of prisons instead of the death penalty and other physical punishments common at the time. Their rationale was that the prison was an instrument of rehabilitation and a place where inmates would reflect on their deeds and "discover the right principles to guide [their] life" (McGowen, 1995, p. 86), based in part on religious introspection.

Two millennia earlier, Plato made a similar argument. While imprisonment was not a common punishment at all in ancient society, in Book 10 of the *Laws*, Plato recommended that certain offenders should be imprisoned for a sentence of five years or more but with a goal of rehabilitation. During their time in prison, inmates would "have no intercourse with the other citizens, except with members of the nocturnal council [a moral authority], and with them let them converse with a view to the improvement of their soul's health" ([360 B.C.E.] 1892, p. 286). Ideally, reform would occur as a result.

Unfortunately, the contemporary correctional system does not fully meet the goal of offender reformation. The **recidivism** rate is a measure of how often former offenders commit new crimes. A study of inmates released from prison found that recidivism rates were fairly high. Within three years of release, almost half (46.9%) were convicted of a new crime, and one-quarter (25.4%) were sent back to prison (Langan & Levin, 2002). Persons on probation fared better, as only 17% of them in 2008 were returned to prison or jail either for committing a new crime or for violating the rules of probation supervision (Glaze & Bonczar, 2009). Still, these data suggest that the correctional ideal is not easily achieved.

There are five frequently acknowledged philosophies of punishment. One is rehabilitation, which is the most closely linked to the concept of correction. As described in Chapter 10, support for rehabilitation has declined over time. The other philosophies are retribution, or the idea that offenders deserve unpleasant punishment; deterrence, or the idea that the threat of punishment should discourage the public from committing crimes and that punishment should discourage offenders from repeating criminal acts; incapacitation, or removing an offender's ability to commit crimes against society, generally by confining the offender in prison; and restitution, or compensating a victim or society for losses caused by crime. The challenge for correctional agencies is to determine which of these philosophies (or other ideas) should underlie correctional practice and how much to emphasize each.

A **mission statement** is one way correctional agencies articulate the philosophies and goals to which they subscribe. This can help us make sense out of competing philosophical perspectives. Consider the following mission statements:

Nevada Department of Corrections (2010): "Protect the public by confining convicted felons according to the law, while keeping staff and inmates safe" (para. 1).

Illinois Department of Corrections (2002): "Protect the public from criminal offenders through a system of incarceration and supervision which securely segregates offenders from society, assures offenders of constitutional rights and maintains programs to enhance the success of offenders' reentry into society" (para. 1).

Arkansas Department of Correction (n.d.): "Provide public safety by carrying out the mandates of the courts; provide a safe, humane environment for staff and inmates; provide programs to strengthen the work ethic; provide opportunities for spiritual, mental, and physical growth" (para. 2).

Note that there are similarities and differences among the mission statements. This is precisely the point of the discussion. It is difficult to identify a single or uniform philosophy that expresses the precise nature or purpose of corrections across agencies and jurisdictions.

This leaves the dilemma as expressed by correctional luminary Hans Toch (1997): "Those who look for philosophical consistency in prison policies are apt not to find it" (p. 4). Likewise, David Garland (2001) sees little philosophical consistency in contemporary corrections, arguing that "we lack any . . . agreement, any settled culture, or any clear sense of the big picture" (p. 4). Garland also argues that a new vision is emerging based on the "culture of control."

The **culture of control** is marked by a "desire for security, orderliness, and control, for the management of risk and the taming of chance" (Garland, 2001, p. 194). Garland argues that this idea currently dominates the thinking of the public, politicians, and some correctional personnel. As a result, the agents of formal social control (i.e., the criminal justice system) take on more and more authority to use rules, technology, and surveillance to control deviant behaviors of any sort—and the severity of punishments for deviant behavior escalates during the process.

This is similar to an argument advanced by French philosopher Michel Foucault (1977). Foucault viewed the development of the prison as motivated by a desire to limit government power by limiting its ability to issue arbitrary and excessive punishments. As prisons became popular (in place of other, more brutal, punishments), they came to be used as tools of discipline, creating "docile bodies" (p. 135) through a system of surveillance and control. For instance, constant surveillance ultimately led to total control over persons. As Foucault noted (drawing upon an idea posed earlier by Jeremy Bentham), if individuals knew that at any moment they could (unknowingly) be under the observation of an authority figure with the power to punish them for wrongdoing, then they would always act as though they were under observation—and this would mean acting in a positive or law-abiding manner to avoid being detected or punished for violating a rule. Foucault observed that similar techniques of control came to be used in other areas of society, an argument echoed by Jonathan Simon's (2007) description of "**governing through crime**" (p. 5). Simon argues that efforts for control and surveillance have extended beyond the criminal justice system to also impact families, schools, and workplaces, where individuals are subject to an increased amount of monitoring, regulation, and zero-tolerance policies. As such, the notion of a culture of control may be felt in other areas of society besides corrections.

However, as control and surveillance increase, so does the potential for conflict with constitutional rights. The Constitution is a benchmark for what is or is not legally permissible within corrections, as policies are judged against its provisions about rights and liberties. Lawsuits alleging constitutional violations have historically been a significant force for reform in the correctional system and have helped to define acceptable correctional philosophies and to discard unacceptable practices (see Feeley & Rubin, 1998).

> If you were the leader of a correctional agency, what philosophy or mission of corrections would you emphasize? Why? How would your answer influence weightlifting in prisons?
>
> Do you think the lack of consistency in current correctional practice is a problem? Why or why not?
>
> Can you identify any examples of a culture of control or of governing through crime? What are the pros and cons of the culture of control as a purpose of corrections?

Four Essential Tensions Underlying Correctional Philosophy and Policy

FOCUSING QUESTION 13.2

How do essential tensions explain conflicts about correctional policy?

If correctional policy is not based on one single philosophy, how does it develop? The concept of an **essential tension**, or a conflict between ideals of *what should be* and the observable world *as it actually is*, can help us here. This is a concept developed by philosopher of science Thomas Kuhn (1977), and it is very useful as a framework to understand the way corrections policy develops in actual practice.

THE ESSENTIAL TENSION OF FINANCE

Money and budgets are the most profound of the essential tensions. Correctional agencies are funded by tax dollars allocated by legislatures. A correctional agency may have impressive goals or ideas for innovative programs, but without money to fund them, those goals or programs will go unrealized. For instance, changing economic conditions have had a dramatic effect on correctional policy:

> financial crisis, complicated by the rise in correctional expenses and in their relative share of the budget, has yielded a new set of correctional

discourses and practices, fueled by a language of scarcity. Under this framework, perceptions are changed, and policies are created, with short-term savings in mind . . . correctional techniques are chosen and discussed mainly through their impact on taxpayers' wallets. (Aviram, 2010, pp. 2–3)

Budgetary concerns can become a de facto guiding philosophy by allowing the budget to be the primary driver of correctional policy. In response to budget reductions, states have closed prisons, shifted priorities (e.g., reducing treatment programs, even those required by law), and changed laws so that fewer persons are sentenced to prison (Gramlich, 2010). In fact, for the first time since 1972, state prison populations decreased slightly (by 0.3%) in 2009. Budgetary concerns were one contributor to the decrease, as "states began to realize they could effectively reduce their prison populations, and save public funds, without sacrificing public safety" (*Prison Count 2010*, 2010, p. 3). Of course, it is logical that finances are important. But viewed as an essential tension, it is the reality of finance—rather than idealistic goals or values—that can sometimes drive correctional practice.

There is also a **conflict theory** perspective of finance as a driver of correctional policy. Conflict theorists argue that decisions are made to benefit (financially or otherwise) those who hold power in society (see generally Siegel, 2001). The conflict perspective is perhaps best exemplified by the notion of a **prison-industrial complex**, meaning "a set of bureaucratic, political, and economic interests that encourage increased spending on imprisonment, regardless of the actual need" (Schlosser, 1998, p. 54).

From 1960 to 1995, the American prison population increased dramatically, and 829 new prisons were constructed. Supporters of new prison construction argue that it brings economic benefits, jobs, and growth to the communities where the prisons are built (Hooks, Mosher, Rotolo, & Lobao, 2004). Critics of new prison growth argue that "the use of prisons as money-makers for struggling rural communities has become a major force driving criminal justice policy . . . regardless of [other] policy rationales" (Huling, 2002, p. 213). However, research has found that new prisons do not tend to produce economic benefits for the communities in which they are built (Hooks, Mosher, Genter, Rotolo, & Lobao, 2010; Hooks et al., 2004).

In short, financial concerns can and do drive correctional policy decision making. This creates the essential tension between what corrections ought to do (based on goals and philosophies) and what corrections actually does (driven by finances).

THE ESSENTIAL TENSION OF RESEARCH

Regardless of the funding available, pragmatic thinkers would hope that correctional policy is justified based on solid research about strategies and tactics that work versus those that do not. Even in times of fiscal stress, agencies can maximize effectiveness by conducting research to inform their decisions.

Sadly, this is not always the case. Steven Lab (2004), former president of the Academy of Criminal Justice Sciences, argues that criminal justice research is, at best, not actively sought and, at worst, totally ignored when criminal justice policy is made. Lab places part of the blame on scholars themselves for not disseminating research results more broadly and more clearly and for not making the effort "to step forward when bad decisions are being made [to] discourage the adoption of ill-conceived policies" (p. 692).

Indeed, correctional policy is sometimes based on inaccurate perceptions grounded in "common sense" rather than on empirical evidence (Cullen, Blevins, Trager, & Gendreau, 2005, p. 53). However, common sense is not always correct. **Correctional boot camps** provide an example. The idea of a boot camp is that offenders who are at moderate risk for committing additional crimes should be placed into a program lasting several months. In the program, offenders live in a military-style environment, subject to drills with confrontational strategies and physical labor designed to build discipline (e.g., a "drill sergeant" correctional officer yelling at an inmate and then requiring him to do 50 pushups). Justifications for boot camps were largely grounded on the common-sense belief that such a program *ought* to work.

The problem was that the program did *not* often work. In fact, prior research (largely ignored in the development of correctional boot camps) had found that military service, in general, was not an effective tool for rehabilitating offenders. Research on the correctional boot camps themselves similarly found that they were not effective in reducing recidivism (MacKenzie, 2006). When research on the ineffectiveness of boot camps in Georgia was released, a spokesperson for the governor stated, "we don't care what the study thinks," and a correctional administrator stated "that academics were too quick to ignore the experiential knowledge of people 'working in the system' and rely on research findings" (Vaughn, 1994, in Cullen et al., 2005, p. 60). Yet, it is the systematic collection and analysis of empirical data—that is, research—which leads to conclusions about what is or is not effective. Such evidence was lacking for boot camps, as one report stated: "research on adult boot camps in Georgia and Illinois found no difference in recidivism [between boot camp participants and a comparison group]. An evaluation of Washington's Work Ethic Camp (WEC) actually found higher rates of recidivism, from high rates of revoked parole" (Parent, 2003, p. 7). It is also interesting to note, however, that the same report found that boot camps may be more effective *if* they "offered more intensive treatment and postrelease supervision" (p. 9). But the treatment and supervision were key, rather than the military model of the camps, which was *not* shown to be effective.

Could a process that more deliberately included the input of researchers have resulted in a better correctional alternative than boot camps? This question illustrates the essential tension that emerges when there is research pertaining to a policy decision, but that research is disregarded in the policy-making process. In such cases, idealistic notions or popular ideas may instead justify correctional policy, leading to policies that may not maximize effectiveness.

THE ESSENTIAL TENSION OF DISCRETION

Recall from Chapter 1 the discussion of criminal justice both as bureaucracy and profession. These concepts form the basis for the third essential tension: discretion. Bureaucracies are driven by rules and procedures that all personnel are expected to follow carefully and deliberately. On the other hand, a profession is comprised of individuals who are expected to exercise their own judgment when determining how to resolve a situation.

There are pros and cons to either approach. A reliance on *rules and procedures* helps to ensure fairness and consistency while grounding decisions in agreed-upon principles that may not be overruled by an individual employee. A reliance on *professional judgment* allows for the unique circumstances of each individual case to be considered while allowing the professional to draw upon past experience and expertise in solving a problem (Schneider, Ervin, & Snyder-Joy, 1996). Many agencies have developed **quantitative** (numbers-based) **scales** to limit discretion. Deviations from the recommended outcomes must usually be justified in writing. Examples pertinent to corrections include:

- *Probation Supervision.* Some offenders, rather than being sent to prison, serve their time on probation. While on probation, they may live and work in the community, but they also must follow some special rules and report regularly to a probation officer. When determining how much supervision a person on probation needs from a probation officer, many agencies use a numerical scale (e.g., see Domurad, 1999).
- *Classification.* When an offender is sentenced to prison, the Department of Corrections must decide which prison is most appropriate for him or her (e.g., minimum, medium, or maximum security). Numerical scales are often used to guide this decision (e.g., see Federal Bureau of Prisons, 2006).
- *Parole Release.* In some states, prison inmates may be released on parole before the end of their sentence. To receive parole, inmates must be approved by a parole board, which determines if the inmate has been rehabilitated. Some parole boards use numerical scales to help them make parole release decisions (e.g., see Keilin, 2001).
- *Revocation.* If a person on probation violates a law or a rule of probation (e.g., leaving the state without permission of the probation officer), then the probation may be revoked and the person sent back to prison. Some states use numerical scales to determine whether or not a violation is serious enough to send the person to prison (e.g., see Virginia Criminal Sentencing Commission, n.d.).

Research has found that officers do not perceive numerical scales to be particularly effective, and that they would prefer more discretion rather than being constrained by the results of a scale (Schneider et al., 1996). Herein lies the essential tension. Some may feel that the most appropriate decision making occurs when well-trained professionals are able to provide individualized attention to the specifics of each case. On the other hand, correctional case processing often relies on a bureaucratic approach that minimizes discretion. This may lead to philosophical differences and disagreements about policy between those who approach corrections work from a bureaucratic model and those who view it as a profession.

THE ESSENTIAL TENSION OF INVISIBILITY

Right now, how much specific information do you know about the workings of prison and probation? For most people, the answer is "not much." Of the three primary criminal justice agencies—the police, courts, and corrections—correctional agencies are most hidden from public view. Through the study of civics and American government in high school, people generally have an idea about what the courts do. People generally have an idea about the nature and purpose of police work through officers' work in the community. Of course, the ideas about the courts and policing may not be fully developed or entirely accurate, but they are often better than the public understanding of corrections. As Farrington (1992) observed, "We 'put our criminals behind bars.' We 'send them down the river.' . . . All of these phrases are suggestive of a general out-of-sight, out-of-mind mentality regarding our nation's penal institutions and those who inhabit them" (p. 18).

The information the public holds about corrections usually comes from the media. Although some excellent documentaries exist about correctional institutions (prisons and jails), the news media rarely explore the range of issues facing correctional agencies (see Welch, Weber, & Edwards, 2000). Correctional alternatives besides prison are infrequently covered in the news, public affairs documentaries, or popular entertainment.

With the billions of dollars spent annually on corrections, it is ironic that correctional agencies are so far removed from public awareness. This leads to the essential tension at stake here. With corrections being an invisible and unknown entity to most persons, meaningful conversations about correctional policy become both challenging and uncommon. This compounds the difficulty of attempting to seek policies that articulate a guiding philosophy for correctional practice.

SUMMARY OF THE CONCEPT OF ESSENTIAL TENSIONS

Much correctional policy is shaped by the four essential tensions that have been discussed. Each involves a give and take, as people with differing opinions advocate to have their preferred policies adopted. These essential tensions also shape other areas of criminal justice, such as policing and the courts. However, they are particularly important for corrections because of the lack of correctional theory. Were there a sound, constitutionally valid, well-established, and empirically verified uniform philosophy guiding contemporary correctional practice, the four essential tensions would be less important because that philosophy could then guide key correctional decisions.

> How would each essential tension influence policy about weightlifting in prison?
>
> _____
>
> Are there remedies to the conflicts posed by the essential tensions? Why or why not?
>
> _____

History and Practice of Institutional Corrections

FOCUSING QUESTION 13.3

How have correctional institutions changed over time?

Correctional institutions are secure facilities designed to house persons accused or convicted of a crime. There are two types of correctional institutions. A **jail** is a short-term facility usually operated by a county sheriff. Jails hold persons accused (but not convicted) of crimes who are awaiting trial as well as convicted offenders who have short sentences, usually less than one year. A **prison** is a long-term facility operated by the state or federal government. Prisons hold convicted offenders who have been sentenced to longer terms, usually a year or more.

A HISTORICAL SURVEY OF CORRECTIONAL INSTITUTIONS

In the colonial era and the early years of the American republic, correctional institutions were not widely used for punishment. In fact, there were no prisons to speak of, and jails were used for one of two purposes: to hold persons awaiting trial or punishment (but not as punishment itself) or to hold persons who could not pay their debts (a **debtor's prison**). Typical punishments included the death penalty, physical beatings, banning offenders from an area (**banishment**), fines, or public shaming (discussed in Chapter 10). In shaming, offenders were placed in the town square and restrained by an apparatus known as the **stocks**, which secured the person's hands or feet so he or she could not move or leave (Rothman, 1995).

It was against this backdrop that correctional institutions developed. In 1776, the Walnut Street Jail opened in Philadelphia. The jail was influenced by reforms introduced in England and also by Quaker philosophies (popular in Pennsylvania at the time) that decried the death penalty and instead sought rehabilitation of inmates. The jail was no longer viewed as a place to wait for punishment; it became a place to send offenders for the specific purposes of punishment and reform. Correctional institutions also helped to increase the power of the state government. Walnut Street Jail was ultimately transformed into a Pennsylvania state prison in 1794, clearly establishing the state as having primary responsibility for offenders who committed serious crimes (i.e., felonies). This demonstrated that state authority for social control exceeded that of local governments (Takagi, 1975).

Three models of correctional institutions developed in nineteenth-century America: the solitary system, based on Eastern State Penitentiary in Pennsylvania; the congregate system, based on Auburn State Prison in New York; and prison farms, common in the southern United States. Each is described in the following paragraphs (see Box 13.1 for a discussion of a fourth system that enjoyed limited popularity).

The **solitary system** was modeled on practices at the Walnut Street Jail. The goal of the solitary system was to promote offender rehabilitation through self-introspection. Eastern State Penitentiary opened in Philadelphia, Pennsylvania, in 1829 and was focused on completely isolating the offender. The utter silence of the institution was remarkable (Friedman, 1993). Inmates had no human contact. They even wore hoods when taken to their cells, so they could not interact with staff or with any inmates who happened to be out of their cells. Inmates stayed in their cells for the duration of their sentences (each cell did have a small private exercise yard attached to it, so inmates could see the outdoors periodically; Friedman, 1993). Inmates could read the Bible and reflect on their past deeds, working toward rehabilitation. They also could engage in some work projects that could be completed without leaving the cell (Rothman, 1995).

The **congregate system** was based on Auburn State Prison, opened in 1816 in Auburn, New York. Auburn was promoted as a less expensive alternative to the solitary system and one that could generate revenue for the state through inmates' work in prison factories (Rothman, 1995). Like the solitary system, absolute silence was expected in congregate prisons. However, the inmates were not completely isolated from one another. At night, inmates lived in solitary cells. During the day, they moved from their cells to a dining hall for meals and then to work in factories (Friedman, 1993). Inmates who broke the rule of silence received harsh physical punishments (Rothman, 1995).

A very different system emerged in some southern states, which developed **farm systems**. It is important to note that some prisons today have farms that are operated by inmates, but the concept of a farm system is very different from any current practice. In a farm system, inmates lived together in large bunkhouses similar to barracks. Farms were largely operated by the inmates themselves. With few civilian employees, certain inmates were selected to guard others and were even armed to do so. Very little money was invested in the prison farms, but they were expected to generate revenue for the state by selling produce. Very few services were provided for inmates, and some had to

BOX 13.1

THE REFORMATORY SYSTEM

The **reformatory system** provided an alternative to the harsh environments of many nineteenth century prisons. Elmira Reformatory, one of the most recognized, opened in New York in 1876. Its founder, Zebulon Brockway, envisioned it as a more effective alternative to other prisons, particularly for young adult offenders. Inmates who were successful in the institution's programs could earn early release, and inmates progressed through grades toward this goal. Designed as a rehabilitative institution (Rotman, 1995), the elements of Elmira Reformatory included the following (excerpts quoted from Brockway, 1910, pp. 99–101):

1. "[The structure] should be salubriously situated and, preferably, in a suburban locality . . . The whole should be supplied with suitable modern sanitary appliances and with an abundance of natural and artificial light."
2. "Clothing for the prisoners, not degradingly distinctive but uniform, yet fitly representing the respective grades or standing of the prisoners . . . For the sake of health, self-respect, and the cultural influence of the general appearance, scrupulous cleanliness should be maintained and the prisoners kept appropriately groomed."
3. "A liberal prison dietary designed to promote vigor . . . Deprivation of food, by a general regulation, for a penal purpose, is deprecated . . . More variety, better quality and service of foods for the higher grades of prisoners is serviceably allowed . . ."
4. "A gymnasium completely equipped with baths and apparatus; and facilities for field athletics."
5. "Facilities for special manual training sufficient for about one-third of the resident population . . . [including] mechanical and freehand drawing; sloyd in wood and metals; cardboard constructive form work; clay modeling; cabinet making; chipping and filing; and iron molding."
6. "Trades instruction . . . conducted to a standard of perfect work and speed performance that insures the usual wage value to their services."
7. "A regimental military organization of the prisoners with a band of music, swords for officers, and dummy guns for the rank and file of prisoners . . . The regular army tactics, drill, and daily dress parade should be observed."
8. "School of letters with a curriculum that reaches from an adaptation of the kindergarten . . . through various school grades up to the usual high-school course."
9. "A well-selected library for circulation, consultation, and under proper supervision, for occasional semi-social use."
10. "The weekly institutional newspaper, in lieu of all outside newspapers, edited and printed by the prisoners under due censorship."
11. "Recreating and diverting entertainments . . . provided in the great auditorium; not any vaudeville nor minstrel shows, but entertainments of such a class as the middle cultured people of a community would enjoy."
12. "Religious opportunities, optional."
13. "Definitely planned, carefully directed, emotional occasions . . . for a kind of irrigation [utilizing] music, pictures, and the drama."

What elements of the reformatory system do you think are useful? What elements do you dislike? Explain your answer in the context of what you believe are the goals of corrections.

sell their blood to earn money for items such as clothing, health care, and other essentials. Inmates who violated the few rules that existed were punished (often by other inmates) by whippings, electric shock, or by other physical means. The farm system was marked by high levels of violence and questionable security (see Feeley & Rubin, 1998; *Holt v. Sarver*, 1970).

Over time, each of these three systems was abandoned. The prison farm system was ruled unconstitutional and replaced with more traditional correctional institutions (e.g., *Holt v. Sarver*, 1970). The solitary system was criticized because complete isolation could cause mental distress and because separate cells and yards for each individual inmate were expensive. The congregate system was the one most adopted by other states, but the system of strict silence and the practice of housing only one inmate per cell were abandoned due to overcrowding (Rothman, 1995).

CURRENT PRACTICE IN CORRECTIONAL INSTITUTIONS

In a contemporary prison, inmates typically live with a cellmate, have opportunities for work or programming (including recreation, religious services, counseling, education or vocational training, and more) during the day, and interact regularly with other inmates and correctional staff. There is, however, substantial variation in prisons in terms of their design, programs offered, and security level.

You may visualize a prison as containing cell blocks arranged in long rows with cells on one or both sides of a long corridor. Some prisons are designed this way. However, many newer prisons utilize a **pod-style design** in which cells surround a central day room, as illustrated in Figure 13.1 (each grouping

Figure 13.1. Pod-Style Design

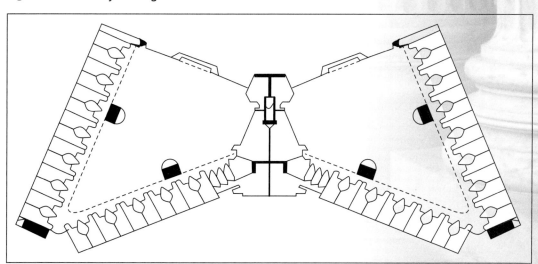

Source: Goldman, 2003

of cells and day room is known as a "pod"). Inmates may gather for recreation, programming, or other prosocial activities in the large open day room. In addition, inmates and correctional staff may interact there. These characteristics facilitate a strategy known as **unit management**, in which multiple activities are contained within the pod and staff can work more closely with inmates to promote meaningful counseling. The unit management philosophy is associated with reductions in inmate violence and other rule violations (Bayens, Williams, & Smykla, 1997).

It is also important to note that there are different types of prison facilities. Perhaps the most familiar distinction is that based on **security level**. Within each state and the federal government, there are low (minimum), medium, and high (maximum) security prisons. Differences between security levels center on issues such as how much freedom inmates have within the institution, what types of programming opportunities are available to inmates, and how much security is incorporated into the facility (fences, towers, number of correctional officers, etc.). Offenders who are sentenced to prison go through an initial **classification** process in which the Department of Corrections determines their security level and assigns them to a prison. It is common for offenders to be reclassified multiple times during their sentences based on their adjustment and their behavioral record. For instance, inmates who began in maximum security can be moved to medium security if their record has been positive.

THEORETICAL PERSPECTIVES ON PRISON LIFE

Regardless of the type of institution, there are two theoretical perspectives that provide a context for understanding correctional institutions and life within them. They are the work of Erving Goffman (1961) on "total institutions" (p. 4) and the work of Gresham Sykes (1958) on the "pains of imprisonment" (p. 63).

The concept of a **total institution** is a powerful descriptor of the prison. Consider life outside an institution as Goffman (1961) describes: "A basic social arrangement in modern society is that the individual tends to sleep, play [i.e., recreation], and work in different places, with different co-participants, under different authorities, and without an over-all rational plan" (pp. 5–6). For instance, an individual might sleep at home and work in an office. While at home, he might interact with family members and while at work he might interact with office colleagues. At home, the family unit develops a system for making decisions and resolving conflicts, while at work a boss takes on these tasks.

A total institution is the exact inverse. The inmate in a prison sleeps, engages in recreation, and works in the same place—the prison. The inmate does these activities with the same coparticipants (all other inmates) while under the supervision and direction of the same authorities (correctional officers supervise the inmate's cell, the recreational areas, and the work areas). The institutional experience as a whole is designed to accomplish some goals (although as noted earlier, there is not easy agreement in American corrections as to what those goals are).

The scope of control includes aspects of life that would not be regulated on the outside, such as acceptable hair styles, what food can be consumed, and what materials may be read. Inmate misconduct in one area of life—for instance, work in a prison factory—can result in negative consequences in another area of life—such as revoked recreational privileges or even moving the inmate to a higher security prison. Thus, the control over the inmate is total in a total institution.

Inmates entering the total institution undergo what Goffman (1961) refers to as **mortification**, which essentially means a loss of personal identity. The name is replaced with an inmate number, institutional clothing replaces individual attire, personal property that reflects one's interests is limited, institutional rules diminish individualism and unique identity, and others at the institution—staff and inmate alike—quickly become aware of the inmate's most personal information, as documented in official records (the contents of which quickly spread through the institutional grapevine).

It is within this setting that inmates experience the **pains of imprisonment** as described by Sykes (1958), which take the form of five things (tangible and intangible) that are withheld from inmates. These include:

- *Deprivation of Liberty.* Most obviously, the inmate is not at liberty in society due to incarceration in a prison. Contacts with the outside world are also limited, as mail is inspected, telephone calls are monitored, visits are subject to numerous regulations, and the Internet is not available.
- *Deprivation of Goods and Services.* Sykes suggests that, in a culture that values possessions as signs of affluence and status, "material possessions are so large a part of the individual's conception of himself that to be stripped of them is to be attacked at the deepest layers of personality" (p. 69). Prison rules specify items that inmates may not possess. Any item that inmates are not permitted to possess is called **contraband**, which includes items that are illegal for anyone (e.g., illegal drugs), items that are prohibited only to inmates (e.g., R-rated movies are prohibited under the Zimmer Amendment), and items that inmates may have only in limited quantities (e.g., if an inmate has 11 books but the rules only allow him to have 10, then the 11th book is contraband).
- *Deprivation of Heterosexual Relationships.* Prisons are usually segregated by gender. Sykes suggests that this results in the inmate being "figuratively castrated by his involuntary celibacy" (p. 70). However, sexual activity does occur in prison—sometimes consensually and sometimes by force, sometimes between inmates and sometimes between inmates and staff (see Beck, Harrison, Berzofsky, Caspar, & Krebs, 2010).
- *Deprivation of Autonomy.* This deprivation is closely related to the concept of a total institution, as it refers to the many rules and regulations governing virtually all aspects of the inmate's life. The rules make decisions for inmates, meaning that inmates lose the autonomy to decide such things

as when and where to eat, what to read, what to wear, when to exercise, and so on.

- *Deprivation of Security.* One irony of the prison was expressed by Sykes: "However strange it may appear . . . society has chosen to reduce the criminality of the offender by forcing him to associate with more than a thousand other criminals for years on end" (pp. 76–77). Although correctional staff do their best to ensure the safety of the prison, the fact remains that violence and acts of aggression can and do occur against both inmates and staff.

The nature of the total institution and its associated deprivations combine to result in **prisonization**, a term used by Donald Clemmer (1940) to describe an inmate's acceptance of the unique culture of the prison environment, including (but not limited to) its norms, jargon, lifestyle, conditions, and so on. Although some degree of prisonization may be unavoidable with time spent in a prison environment, a concern is that prisonization may lead inmates to reject positive social norms and be at greater risk for reoffending. Two competing hypotheses have been used to explain prisonization. The **importation hypothesis** holds that inmates bring their attitudes and life experiences from the outside into prison, which shape their behavior in the prison environment. The **deprivation hypothesis** holds that the nature of the prison environment and its deprivations shape inmate behavior. In actuality, both contribute to inmates' behaviors in prison (e.g., Jiang & Fisher-Giorlando, 2002), but the deprivation model has been found to be the stronger influence (e.g., Paterline & Petersen, 1999).

What do you think are the greatest challenges facing modern correctional institutions? Why?

What factors do you think should be considered in the classification process? Explain.

What lessons can modern corrections learn from studying the history of correctional institutions?

History and Practice of Community Corrections

FOCUSING QUESTION 13.4

How have community corrections changed over time?

Finckenauer and Gavin (1999) describe a cycle they call the "**panacea phenomenon**" (p. 13):

1. An intervention is proposed as the latest and greatest plan but with deeply unrealistic expectations (e.g., working for *all* offenders, preventing *all* crime);
2. The intervention is implemented but does not meet the unrealistic goals;

3. Frustration builds, and the program is labeled a failure; and
4. Finally, policy makers return to the proverbial drawing board to develop a new intervention that will be labeled the next great thing, and the cycle will repeat itself.

You may be asking, how is this related to community corrections? From its inception, the use of imprisonment as a correctional alternative has fallen into the panacea phenomenon cycle. Early prison systems were developed as an alternative to other punishments with great hopes for success. The solitary and congregate systems proved unworkable and generally ineffective, leading to a quest for the next great correctional alternative. As experts and practitioners have become dissatisfied with prisons—partly because of finances but also in the hope of finding more effective alternatives—community-based correctional programs have been proposed and implemented.

A HISTORY OF COMMUNITY CORRECTIONS

Historically, little attention was devoted to preparing for an offender's release from prison. In the 1840s, Alexander Maconochie was superintendent of the Norfolk Island prison colony in Australia. The island's residents were offenders who had been sent from their homes in England to live at the colony as a punishment for their crimes (a practice known as **transportation**). Maconochie created the **mark system**, in which inmates accumulated marks or points for positive behaviors and, upon collecting a sufficient number of marks, could receive special privileges and eventual release. The system's goal was to make inmates accountable for their own reformation. The program was successful in reducing recidivism, although it was later dismantled because it was perceived as being too soft on crime (Cullen & Gilbert, 1982).

Walter Crofton directed the Irish prison system in the 1850s. Inmates in Crofton's institutions also earned marks for good behavior. "Once a sufficient number of marks had been accumulated, offenders would progress to an open-prison in which guards were unarmed and few restrictions were imposed on the inmates' lives" (Cullen & Gilbert, 1982, p. 69). This institution was designed to enable a transition from prison to the community. After satisfactory performance in the open prison, inmates were released. However, if they subsequently violated the law, they could be returned to prison.

Maconochie and Crofton created systems that were the forerunners of modern **parole**. In the United States, parole has been used to encourage inmate rehabilitation and to provide early release for inmates who have demonstrated that they are in fact rehabilitated. Inmates generally must make application to and be interviewed by a parole board. The parole board releases inmates that they believe have reformed and pose a low risk to society. Upon release, parolees must abide by the law and by special rules of parole (reporting to a parole officer, maintaining employment, not crossing state lines without permission, etc.). If they do not, the parole board may revoke the parole and return the offender to prison. In the late 1800s and early 1900s, many states adopted parole systems.

Parole was intended as another humanizing reform in corrections consistent with the goal of using the prison to rehabilitate offenders. However, some—including John Augustus, a Boston shoemaker—wondered if prisons were really necessary for all offenders. In the mid-1800s, Augustus regularly attended criminal court proceedings and sometimes volunteered to supervise offenders who otherwise would be sent to prison. Soon, other citizens volunteered their services as well, monitoring offenders who remained in the community under their supervision instead of going to prison (Friedman, 1993). John Augustus is recognized as the nation's first probation officer. In the late 1800s and early 1900s, many states adopted probation systems.

Probation is a punishment given by a judge that allows the offender to remain in the community instead of being sent to jail or prison. Probation is often issued as a **suspended sentence**, in which a judge gives an offender a prison sentence but sets the prison sentence aside to allow the offender to serve his or her time on probation instead. While on probation, offenders must abide by the law and obey the special rules of probation (essentially, the same rules that parolees follow). If they violate the law or fail to abide by the rules, a judge may revoke the probation and require the offender to serve the original prison sentence. For instance, a judge might sentence an offender to five years in prison but then suspend the prison sentence and allow the offender to serve her time on probation. If the offender successfully completes her period of probation, then she has avoided prison. However, if the offender violates the rules of probation or commits a new offense, then she could have her probation revoked and be required to serve the original five-year prison term.

In 1967, President Johnson's Commission on Law Enforcement and Administration of Justice offered recommendations for improving criminal justice practice. Community corrections was one area of emphasis, as the report noted: "for the large bulk of offenders, particularly the youthful, the first or the minor offender, institutional commitments can cause more problems than they solve" (p. 165). Instead of relying on prisons, the report recommended increased support for probation and other correctional programs that would be based in the community. It is important to place the report in its context, coming on the heels of the **Great Society** programs promoted by President Johnson that were aimed at eradicating a variety of social problems, including poverty, inadequate health care, racial injustice, pollution, and more (Boyer, Clark, Kett, Salisbury, Sitkoff, & Woloch, 1993).

CURRENT PRACTICE IN COMMUNITY CORRECTIONS

All states currently utilize probation, and it is in fact the most common criminal sentence (see Glaze & Bonczar, 2009). However, parole is less common than it once was. In the 1990s, many states adopted **truth in sentencing**, which stipulates that offenders sentenced to prison must serve a certain portion of their time—usually 85% (see Rosich & Kane, 2005)—with no release (on parole or otherwise) prior to that time. This conflicts with parole's presumption that offenders may be sufficiently rehabilitated to earn release much earlier in their sentences. As a result, some states have abolished parole, and many inmates now serve close to their full sentence regardless of participation in programs or rehabilitative efforts. This represents the panacea phenomenon, as parole and early release were viewed as problematic and mandatory sentences were imposed as a new solution (although mandatory sentences have now come to be viewed as problematic due to the essential tension of finance).

In addition to probation and parole, many other correctional alternatives have been developed since the 1960s. Because these alternatives fall on a continuum between probation at one end and prison at the other, they are known as **intermediate sanctions**. Boot camp, discussed earlier in this chapter, is an intermediate sanction. Various community-based facilities, similar in premise to Crofton's open prison, also exist. For instance, offenders may live at a **halfway house**, a facility that provides various educational and counseling programs in a setting that is more homelike and has greater freedoms than a prison or jail. Offenders may be required to attend a **day reporting center**, which is similar to a halfway house in the programs that are offered, but inmates are only required to check in daily rather than live there.

An intermediate sanction that has increased in popularity is **electronic monitoring**. Offenders sentenced to this program must wear a device, usually in an ankle bracelet, which monitors their location. This may be used for offenders who are given curfews, for offenders who are prohibited from being in certain locations (e.g., sex offenders may not be allowed on school grounds), or for offenders who are under **house arrest** (meaning they may not leave their homes). Some additional intermediate sanctions are described in Box 13.2.

American corrections has come a long way from the time of confining offenders in stocks in the public square. Shaped by competing philosophies and the essential tensions described earlier, correctional policy continually strives to discover the next panacea for responding to crime. However, as Dean-Myrda and Cullen (1998) noted, a rational, thoughtful, and informed approach to correctional policy is necessary. Such an approach would seek to retain and improve upon the positive aspect of programs, even those that are not perfect: "In the end, we should contemplate the wisdom of entering a post-panacea period in which simple solutions are forfeited in the pursuit of meaningful, if incremental, progress in an arena—crime control—that has been stubbornly resistant to the quick fix" (p. 15).

In what cases do you think probation, parole, and intermediate sanctions are appropriate? Why?

BOX 13.2

ADDITIONAL COMMUNITY-BASED CORRECTIONAL PROGRAMS

The full variety of intermediate sanctions is too lengthy to list, but consider three programs involving variations on traditional probation.

Drug Court

A **drug court** program is a collaborative, team-based effort that includes a drug offender and the prosecuting attorney, defense attorney, probation officer, substance abuse treatment counselor, and judge. Rather than simply sentencing an offender and moving on, the court meets regularly and offenders report often on their progress. At each progress report, the judge may offer rewards to offenders who have shown progress and sanctions to offenders who have not. The concept is unique in that it creates a courtroom partnership centered on providing rehabilitation that is individualized to meet each offender's needs. Offenders who successfully complete the program may have their charges dropped or may receive lesser charges or penalties than offenders who do not go through the program. Evidence suggests that drug courts effectively reduce recidivism (MacKenzie, 2006).

Intensive Supervision Probation

Designed for offenders who are high risk or who have not been successful on regular probation, **intensive supervision probation (ISP)** is a much more structured form of probation. Traditional probation requires only weekly or monthly meetings between the offender and probation officer, but ISP requires more regular meetings several times per week with much closer monitoring of the offender's activities. Although regular probation officers may supervise up to 100 (or more) offenders at one time, ISP officers are responsible for much fewer—around 25 or 30—again enhancing surveillance. Unfortunately, ISP has not been found to reduce recidivism; in fact, offenders on ISP are found to violate probation rules more often, possibly because the increased surveillance increases the likelihood of being caught (MacKenzie, 2006).

Split Sentence

In a **split sentence**, offenders first spend some time in prison or jail and are then released to serve a probation sentence in the community. One rationale is that the experience of serving time in prison or jail will deter the offender and impress upon him or her the importance of successfully completing the probation sentence. Split sentencing is not associated with reductions in recidivism (Sherman, Gottfredson, MacKenzie, Eck, Reuter, & Bushway, 1998).

Why do you think drug courts are successful at reducing recidivism? Why do you think ISP and split sentences are not? Can they be improved? Explain your answers.

What do you think are the advantages and disadvantages of community corrections?

Can you identify examples of the panacea phenomenon? Is Dean-Myrda and Cullen's recommendation possible? What would be necessary to make it so?

Conclusion

As we close this text, we hope that you have found the study of criminal justice to be a dynamic and interesting pursuit. In Chapter 1, we defined criminal justice as society's response to crime. A simple and broad definition, it perhaps obscured the true complexity of a field to which you have now given considerable thought. As you move forward, we hope you are a more sophisticated observer of criminal justice than before you began reading this text. We leave you with a challenge—one that all students, scholars, and practitioners of criminal justice should consider: what will be your contribution to the field of criminal justice? Striving for justice is an ancient pursuit and one in which the criminal justice system is but a single component, but it is through careful thought and reflection that the system ultimately advances. The future is yours.

Criminal Justice Problem Solving: **JUSTICE REINVESTMENT**

In the opening scenario of Chapter 1, you were asked to consider how you would spend $10 million on criminal justice initiatives. We now return to the theme of justice expenditures by exploring the concept of **justice reinvestment**.

The premise of justice reinvestment is that the money spent on incarceration (sending offenders to prison or jail) could be better spent on other initiatives. Justice reinvestment advocates suggest that "there is no logic to spending a million dollars a year to incarcerate people from one block in Brooklyn—over half for non-violent drug offenses—and return them, on average, in less than three years stigmatized, unskilled, and untrained to the same unchanged block" (Tucker & Cadora, 2003, p. 2). Instead, justice reinvestment suggests the following place-based approach:

1. Think of public safety as entailing more than incarceration. Although prisons may be one component of a public safety model, it is also necessary to reinvest in neighborhoods and redevelop communities that lack fundamental services and crime prevention programs.
2. Make the provision of justice and public safety a local function. Empower local areas to make their own decisions about how offenders should be handled and how to meet the needs of the community—whether for public safety, crime prevention, social services, or other needs.
3. Allocate a sum of money to communities based on the projected cost (based on data from prior years) of incarcerating offenders from that community.
4. Allow the local jurisdiction to spend the money in any way they see fit as long as the end result is a safer community. If some high-risk offenders need to be incarcerated, the community pays the state back for the cost of doing so. The dollars that remain can be allocated to items such as "job training, drug treatment programs, preschool programs . . . a locally run community loan pool to make micro-loans to create jobs or family development loans for education, debt consolidation, or home ownership and rehabilitation, transportation micro-enterprises for residents commuting outside the neighborhood, a one-stop shop for job counseling and placement services" (Tucker & Cadora, 2003, p. 5), or other suitable initiatives.
5. Make the offenders partners in community redevelopment. Community service sentences, or conditions of parole or other postrelease supervision, could require offenders to spend time implementing programs and redeveloping the neighborhood while working alongside other community residents. This is consistent with principles of restorative justice.

The justice reinvestment model has been implemented in several jurisdictions, including Deschutes County, Oregon. There, the model was applied to juvenile offenders. For each juvenile offender who would otherwise be incarcerated, the state allocated $50,000 (the annual cost of confinement for juveniles) to the county. The county decided some of the offenders should be incarcerated, and they returned the appropriate amount of money to the state to do so. For other offenders, the county created an intensive public service program in which juveniles "serve[d] their sentences by landscaping local parks, constructing bunk beds for families in need, or partnering with Habitat for Humanity to build homes" (Tucker & Caldora, 2003, p. 6). Surplus funds were spent on "schools, libraries, healthcare, and parks" (Tucker & Caldora, 2003, p. 7). Results were mixed. The juveniles made restitution to the community at a higher rate than other offenders and completed much community service (211 hours per juvenile compared to 4 hours per juvenile for those not in the program). This produced tangible results while building skills, creating a positive relationship with the community, and fostering a sense of public service. Victims also reported greater satisfaction with the program than with the typical approach to juvenile crime. However, the program did not result in a reduction in recidivism (see Bradbury, 2002).

> Assess the advantages and disadvantages of justice reinvestment programs.
>
> Do you think anything could be done to improve the results regarding recidivism?
>
> Would you recommend this type of program? If not, why? If so, under what circumstances?

References

Introduction Photo Essay

Arrest for Violation of Order–Penalties–Good Faith Immunity for Law Enforcement Officials, Missouri Revised Statutes, § 455.085 (2010).

Bureau of Justice Statistics. (2011). *Intimate partner violence in the U.S.: Victim characteristics*. Available: http://bjs.ojp.usdoj.gov/content/intimate/victims.cfm

Dixon, J. (2008). Mandatory domestic violence arrest and prosecution policies: Recidivism and social governance. *Criminology and Public Policy, 7*, 663–670.

Hess, K. M., & Wrobleski, H. M. (2003). *Police operations: Theory and practice* (3rd ed.). Belmont, Cal.: Wadsworth.

Sherman, L. W., & Berk, R. A. (1984). The specific deterrent effects of arrest for domestic assault. *American Sociological Review, 49*, 261–272.

Thurman v. City of Torrington, 595 F.Supp. 1521 (U.S. District Court for the District of Connecticut, 1984).

Chapter 1

Blumstein, A., & Wallman, J. (Eds.). (2000). *The crime drop in America*. New York: Cambridge University Press.

Brown, J. S. (1952). A comparative study of deviations from sexual mores. *American Sociological Review, 17*, 135–146.

Bureau of Justice Statistics. (2008). *Justice expenditure and employee extracts, 2006*. Available: http://bjs.ojp.usdoj.gov/index.cfm?ty=pbdetail&iid=1022

Bureau of Justice Statistics. (2010). *The justice system*. Available: http://bjs.ojp.usdoj.gov/content/justsys.cfm

Cantor, D., & Lynch, J. P. (2000). Self-report surveys as measures of crime and criminal victimization. In D. Duffee (Ed.), *Criminal justice 2000: Vol. 4. Measurement and analysis of crime and justice* (pp. 85–138). Washington, D.C.: U.S. Department of Justice. Available: http://www.ncjrs.gov/criminal_justice2000/vol4_2000.html

Christie, N. (2004). *A suitable amount of crime*. New York: Routledge.

Clear, T. R., Cole, G. F., & Reisig, M. D. (2009). *American corrections* (8th ed.). Belmont, Cal.: Thomson Higher Education.

Cohen, D. (1996). Law, social policy, and violence: The impact of regional cultures. *Journal of Personality and Social Psychology, 70*, 961–978.

Cohn, A. W. (1974, June). Training in the criminal justice nonsystem. *Federal Probation*, pp. 32–37.

Cohn, E. G., Rotton, J., Peterson, A. G., & Tarr, D. B. (2004). Temperature, city size, and the southern subculture of violence: Support for social escape/avoidance (SEA) theory. *Journal of Applied Social Psychology, 34*, 1652–1674.

Conklin, J. E. (2003). *Why crime rates fell*. Boston: Allyn & Bacon.

Criminal Victimization in the United States, 2007 Statistical Tables. (2010). Washington, D.C.: U.S. Department of Justice. Available: http://bjs.ojp.usdoj.gov/content/pub/pdf/cvus07.pdf

Cunningham, W. C., Strauchs, J. J., & Van Meter, C. W. (1990). *The Hallcrest Report II: Private security trends 1970–2000*. Stoneham, Mass.: Butterworth-Heinemann.

Dworkin, R. (2000). *Must our judges be philosophers? Can they be philosophers?* Presentation for the New York Council for the Humanities Scholar of the Year Lecture.

Eaton, D. K., Kann, L., Kinchen, S., Shanklin, S., Ross, J., Hawkins, J., Harris, W. A., Lowry, R., McManus, T., Chyen, D., Lim, C., Whittle, L., Brener, N. D., & Wechsler, H. (2010, June 4). Youth risk behavior surveillance—United States, 2009. *Morbidity and Mortality Weekly Report, 59*(SS-5), 1–142. Available: http://www.cdc.gov/mmwr/pdf/ss/ss5905.pdf

Federal Bureau of Investigation. (2009a). *Crime in the United States by volume and rate per 100,000 inhabitants, 1989–2008.* Available: http://www.fbi .gov/ucr/cius2008/data/table_01.html

Federal Bureau of Investigation. (2009b). *Offenses cleared.* Available: http://www2.fbi.gov/ucr/ cius2008/offenses/clearances/index.html

Federal Bureau of Investigation. (2009c). *Region.* Available: http://www.fbi.gov/ucr/cius2008/ offenses/standard_links/regional_estimates.html

Felson, M. (2002). *Crime and everyday life* (3rd ed.). Thousand Oaks, Cal.: Sage Publications.

Friedman, L. M. (1993). *Crime and punishment in American history.* New York: Basic Books.

Gabor, T. (1994). *Everybody does it! Crime by the public.* Toronto: University of Toronto Press.

Geller, W. A., & Morris, N. (1992). Relations between federal and local police. *Crime and Justice, 15,* 231–348.

Gest, T. (2001). *Crime and politics: Big government's erratic campaign for law and order.* New York: Oxford University Press.

Goldstein, H. (1990). *Problem-oriented policing.* New York: McGraw-Hill.

Goodnow, F. J. (1997). Politics and administration. In J. M. Shafritz & A. C. Hyde (Eds.), *Classics of public administration* (4th ed., pp. 27–29). Fort Worth, Tex.: Harcourt Brace College Publishers. (Original work published 1900)

Gostin, L. O. (2006, April 26). Physician-assisted suicide: A legitimate medical practice? *Journal of the American Medical Association, 295*(16), 1–3.

Governors Highway Safety Association. (2010, June). *Cell phone and texting laws.* Available: http:// www.ghsa.org/html/stateinfo/laws/cellphone _laws.html

Grinnell, M. S., & Burke, T. W. (2005, December). An examination of national and international DNA databases (Part 1). *Campbell Law Observer, 26*(10), 3–4.

Hahn, P. H. (1998). *Emerging criminal justice: Three pillars for a proactive justice system.* Thousand Oaks, Cal.: Sage Publications.

Henry, N. (1995). *Public administration and public affairs* (6th ed.). Englewood Cliffs, N.J.: Prentice Hall.

Hoffmann, D. E., & Weber, E. (2010, April 22). Medical marijuana and the law. *New England Journal of Medicine, 362,* 1453–1457.

Huff-Corzine, L., Corzine, J., & Moore, D. C. (1986). Southern exposure: Deciphering the South's influence on homicide rates. *Social Forces, 65,* 904–924.

Kade, W. J. (2000). Death with dignity: A case study. *Annals of Internal Medicine, 132,* 504–506.

Kirp, D. L., & Bayer, R. (1999). The politics of needle exchange. In E. B. Sharp (Ed.), *Culture wars and local politics* (pp. 178–192). Lawrence: University Press of Kansas.

Laband, D. N., & Heinbuch, D. H. (1987). *Blue laws: The history, economics, and politics of Sunday-closing laws.* Lexington, Mass.: D. C. Heath.

Lipsky, M. (1980). *Street-level bureaucracy: Dilemmas of the individual in public services.* New York: Russell Sage Foundation.

Lynch, J. P., & Addington, L. A. (2007). *Understanding crime statistics: Revisiting the divergence of the NCVS and the UCR.* New York: Cambridge University Press.

MacCoun, R. J., & Reuter, P. (2001). *Drug war heresies: Learning from other vices, times, and places.* New York: Cambridge University Press.

Morn, F. (1995). *Academic politics and the history of criminal justice education.* Westport, Conn.: Greenwood Press.

Muir, W. K. (1977). *Police: Streetcorner politicians.* Chicago: University of Chicago Press.

Murray, J. (2005). Policing terrorism: A threat to community policing or just a shift in priorities? *Police Practice and Research, 6,* 347–361.

Owen, S. S., Fradella, H. F., Burke, T. W., & Joplin, J. (2006). Conceptualizing justice: Revising the introductory criminal justice course. *Journal of Criminal Justice Education, 17,* 3–22.

Pratt, T. C., Gaffney, M. J., Lovrich, N. P., & Johnson, C. L. (2006). This isn't CSI: Estimating the national backlog of forensic DNA cases and the barriers associated with case processing. *Criminal Justice Policy Review, 17,* 32–47.

Rafter, N. (2010). Silence and memory in criminology—the American Society of Criminology 2009 Sutherland address. *Criminology, 48,* 339–355.

Reiman, J. (2001). *The rich get richer and the poor get prison: Ideology, class, and criminal justice* (6th ed.). Boston: Allyn & Bacon.

Rosenfeld, R., Messner, S. F., & Baumer, E. P. (2001). Social capital and homicide. *Social Forces, 80,* 283–309.

Sharp, E. B. (2005). *Morality politics in American cities*. Lawrence: University Press of Kansas.

Skogan, W. G., & Hartnett, S. M. (1997). *Community policing, Chicago style*. New York: Oxford University Press.

Sport England. (2002). *Positive futures: A review of impact and good practice, summary report*. London: Sport England. Available: www.sportengland.org

Steinbrook, R. (2008). Physician-assisted death—from Oregon to Washington State. *New England Journal of Medicine, 359*, 2513–2515.

Sykes, G. M., & Matza, D. (1957). Techniques of neutralization: A theory of delinquency. *American Sociological Review, 22*, 664–670.

Thornberry, T. P., & Krohn, M. D. (2000). The self-report method for measuring delinquency and crime. In D. Duffee (Ed.), *Criminal justice 2000: Vol. 4. Measurement and analysis of crime and justice* (pp. 33–83). Washington, D.C.: U.S. Department of Justice. Available: http://www.ncjrs.gov/criminal_justice2000/vol_4/04b.pdf

Tucker, S. B., & Cadora, E. (2003, November). Justice reinvestment. *Ideas for an Open Society, 3*(3), 1–8. Available: http://www.soros.org/resources/articles_publications/publications/ideas_20040106/ideas_reinvestment.pdf

van der Does, L., Newman, S., & Dawson, A. (2004). *High-quality pre-kindergarten: The key to crime prevention and school success in Tennessee*. Washington, D.C.: Fight Crime: Invest in Kids. Available: http://www.fightcrime.org/sites/default/files/reports/TNprek.pdf

Weber, M. (1997). Bureaucracy. In J. M. Shafritz & A. C. Hyde (Eds.), *Classics of public administration* (4th ed., pp. 37–43). Fort Worth, Tex.: Harcourt Brace College Publishers. (Original work published 1946)

Welsh, B. C., & Farrington, D. P. (2009). Public area CCTV and crime prevention: An updated systematic review and meta-analysis. *Justice Quarterly, 26*, 716–745.

Wilson, J. Q. (1989). *Bureaucracy: What government agencies do and why they do it*. New York: Basic Books.

Wilson, W. (1997). The study of administration. In J. M. Shafritz & A. C. Hyde (Eds.), *Classics of public administration* (4th ed., pp. 14–26). Fort Worth, Tex.: Harcourt Brace College Publishers. (Original work published 1887)

Wolfe, N. T. (1981). Mala in se: A disappearing doctrine? *Criminology, 19*, 131–143.

Wright, K. N. (1981). The desirability of goal conflict within the criminal justice system. *Journal of Criminal Justice, 9*, 209–218.

Zimring, F. E., & Hawkins, G. (1997). *Crime is not the problem: Lethal violence in America*. New York: Oxford University Press.

Unit I Photo Essay

Carlson, P. M., & Garrett, J. S. (2008). *Prison and jail administration: Practice and theory* (2nd ed.). Boston: Jones and Bartlett.

de Beaumont, G., & de Tocqueville, A. (1964). *On the penitentiary system in the United States and its application in France* (F. Lieber, Trans.). Carbondale: Southern Illinois University Press. (Original work published 1833)

Friedman, L. M. (1993). *Crime and punishment in American history*. New York: Basic Books.

Morone, J. A. (2003). *Hellfire nation: The politics of sin in American history*. New Haven, Conn.: Yale University Press.

Rothman, D. J. (1995). Perfecting the prison: United States, 1789–1865. In N. Morris & D. J. Rothman (Eds.), *The Oxford history of the prison: The practice of punishment in Western society* (pp. 110–129). New York: Oxford University Press.

Chapter 2

American Civil Liberties Union. (2003). Surveillance under the USA PATRIOT Act. Available: http://www.aclu.org/safefree/general/17326res20030403.html

Atwater v. City of Lago Vista, 532 U.S. 318 (2001).

Bailey, W. C. (1998). Deterrence, brutalization, and the death penalty: Another examination of Oklahoma's return to capital punishment. *Criminology, 36*, 711–733.

Bales, W. D., & Mears, D. P. (2008). Inmate social ties and the transition to society. *Journal of Research in Crime and Delinquency, 45*, 287–321.

Boyer, P. S., Clark, C. E., Kent, J. F., Salisbury, N., Sitkoff, H., & Woloch, N. (1993). *The enduring vision: A history of the American people* (2nd ed.). Lexington, Mass.: D. C. Heath.

Death Penalty Information Center. (2011). *Facts about the death penalty.* Available: http://www.deathpenaltyinfo.org/documents/FactSheet.pdf

Durkheim, É. (1938). Rules for distinguishing between the normal and the pathological. In É. Durkheim, *Rules of the sociological method* (pp. 64–75). New York: Free Press.

Fain, P. (2008, August 22). News analysis: Will drinking-age fight elevate role of university leaders? *Chronicle of Higher Education.* Available: http://www.chronicle.com

Gelman, A., Liebman, J. S., West, V., & Kiss, A. (2004). A broken system: The persistent patterns of reversals of death sentences in the United States. *Journal of Empirical Legal Studies, 1,* 209–261.

Goldstein, H. (1990). *Problem-oriented policing.* New York: McGraw-Hill.

Grube, G. M. A. (Trans.). (1992). *Plato's Republic.* Indianapolis, Ind.: Hackett.

Hobbes, T. (1963). Leviathan or the matter, form, and power of a commonwealth ecclesiastical and civil. In J. Somerville & R. E. Santoni (Eds.), *Social and political philosophy* (pp. 139–168). New York: Anchor Books. (Original work published 1651)

Isaacson, W. (2003). *Benjamin Franklin: An American life.* New York: Simon & Schuster.

Johnson, L. M. (2008). A place for art in prison: Art as a tool for rehabilitation and management. *Southwest Journal of Criminal Justice, 5,* 100–120.

Jolley, J. (2008, April 3). 21's a bust? Seven states debate lowering drinking age. *ABC News.* Available: http://abcnews.go.com

Kant, I. (2002). *Groundwork for the metaphysics of morals* (A. W. Wood, Trans.). New York: Vail-Ballou Press. (Original work published 1785)

Langan, P. A., & Levin, D. J. (2002). *Recidivism of prisoners released in 1994.* Washington, D.C.: U.S. Department of Justice. Available: http://www.ojp.usdoj.gov/bjs/pub/pdf/rpr94.pdf

Locke, J. (1963). An essay concerning the true original extent and end of civil government. In J. Somerville & R. E. Santoni (Eds.), *Social and political philosophy* (pp. 169–204). New York: Anchor Books. (Original work published 1689)

Lucas, P. (2009, July 27). Businesses using music to deter crime and loitering. *Seattle Times.* Available: http://seattletimes.nwsource.com/html/entertainment/2009543344_music27m.html

MacCoun, R. J., & Reuter, P. (2001). *Drug war heresies: Learning from other vices, times, and places.* New York: Cambridge University Press.

MacKenzie, D. L. (2006). *What works in corrections: Reducing the criminal activities of offenders and delinquents.* New York: Cambridge University Press.

Maryland Commission on Capital Punishment. (2008). *Final report to the General Assembly.* Available: http://www.goccp.maryland.gov/capital-punishment/documents/death-penalty-commission-final-report.pdf

McCollough, T. E. (1991). *The moral imagination and public life: Raising the ethical question.* Chatham, N.J.: Chatham House Publishers.

Mooney, C. Z., & Lee, M. (2001). The temporal diffusion of morality policy: The case of death penalty legislation in the American states. In C. Z. Mooney (Ed.), *The public clash of private values: The politics of morality policy* (pp. 170–183). New York: Chatham House Publishers.

Morone, J. A. (2003). *Hellfire nation: The politics of sin in American history.* New Haven, Conn.: Yale University Press.

Newman, D. W. (2003). September 11: A societal reaction perspective. *Crime, Law and Social Change, 39,* 219–231.

Owen, S., & Burke, T. (2003, February). The Court of Appeals made the correct decision. *Campbell Law Observer,* pp. 3, 16.

Peirce, C. S. (1877, November). The fixation of belief. *Popular Science Monthly, 12,* 1–15. Available: http://www.peirce.org/writings/p107.html

Richardson, L. E., & Houston, D. J. (2009). Federalism and safety on America's highways. *Publius: The Journal of Federalism, 39,* 117–137.

Rousseau, J. J. (1963). The social contract. In J. Somerville & R. E. Santoni (Eds.), *Social and political philosophy* (pp. 205–238). New York: Anchor Books. (Original work published 1762)

Stimson, G., Grant, M., Choquet, M., & Garrison, P. (2007). *Drinking in context: Patterns, interventions, and partnerships.* New York: Routledge.

Turow, S. (2003). *Ultimate punishment: A lawyer's reflections on dealing with the death penalty*. New York: Picador.

Virkkunen, M. (1987). Metabolic dysfunctions among habitually violent offenders: Reactive hypoglycemia and cholesterol levels. In S. A. Mednick, T. E. Moffitt, & S. A. Stack (Eds.), *The causes of crime: New biological approaches* (pp. 292–311). New York: Cambridge University Press.

Widom, C. S., & Maxfield, M. G. (2001, February). An update on the "cycle of violence" [National Institute of Justice Research in Brief]. Available: http://www.ncjrs.gov/pdffiles1/nij/184894.pdf

Williams, M. R., & Holcomb, J. E. (2001). Racial disparity and death sentences in Ohio. *Journal of Criminal Justice, 29*, 207–218.

Zimring, F. E. (2003). *The contradictions of American capital punishment*. New York: Oxford University Press.

Chapter 3

Adler, M. (1947). The doctrine of natural law in philosophy. *University of Notre Dame Natural Law Institute Proceedings, 1*, 65–84.

Associated Press. (2002, July 10). *ACLU fights Pennsylvania police on profanity arrests*. Available: http://www.firstamendmentcenter.com/news.aspx?id=3680

Brents, B. G., & Hausbeck, K. (2001). State-sanctioned sex: Negotiating formal and informal regulatory practices in Nevada brothels. *Sociological Perspectives, 44*, 307–332.

Deitrick, S., Beauregard, R. A., & Kerchis, C. Z. (1999). Riverboat gambling, tourism, and economic development. In D. R. Judd & S. S. Fainstein (Eds.), *The tourist city* (pp. 233–244). New Haven, Conn.: Yale University Press.

Devlin, P. (1977). Morals and the criminal law. In K. Kipnis (Ed.), *Philosophical issues in law* (pp. 54–65). Englewood Cliffs, N.J.: Prentice Hall. (Original work published 1965)

Dworkin, R. (1966). Lord Devlin and the enforcement of morals. *Yale Law Journal, 75*, 986–1005.

Dworkin, R. (1978). *Taking rights seriously*. Cambridge, Mass.: Harvard University Press.

Feinberg, J. (1971). Legal paternalism. *Canadian Journal of Philosophy, 1*, 105–124.

Friedman, L. M. (1993). *Crime and punishment in American history*. New York: Basic Books.

Hart, H. L. A. (1958). Positivism and the separation of law and morals. *Harvard Law Review, 71*, 593–629.

Hart, H. L. A. (1971). Immorality and treason. In R. A. Wasserstrom (Ed.), *Morality and the law* (pp. 49–54). Belmont, Cal.: Wadsworth. (Original work published 1959)

Hart, H. L. A. (1994). *The concept of law*. New York: Oxford University Press. (Original work published 1961)

Jay, T. (1992). *Cursing in America: A psycholinguistic study of dirty language in the courts, in the movies, in the schoolyards and on the streets*. Philadelphia: John Benjamins.

Kappeler, V. E., & Potter, G. W. (2005). *The mythology of crime and criminal justice* (4th ed.). Long Grove, Ill.: Waveland Press.

Koo, J., Rosentraub, M. S., & Horn, A. (2007). Rolling the dice? Casinos, tax revenues, and the social costs of gaming. *Journal of Urban Affairs, 29*, 367–381.

Kyllo v. United States, 533 U.S. 27 (2001).

Lipsky, M. (1980). *Street-level bureaucracy: Dilemmas of the individual in public services*. New York: Russell Sage Foundation.

Michigan v. Boomer, 250 Mich. App. 534 (2002).

Mill, J. S. (1981). On liberty. In M. Curtis (Ed.), *The great political theories* (Vol. 2, pp. 190–204). New York: Avon Books. (Original work published 1859)

Parkes, H. B. (1932). Morals and law enforcement in colonial New England. *New England Quarterly, 5*, 431–452.

Paterson, T. G., Clifford, J. G., & Hagan, K. J. (1991). *American foreign policy: A history since 1990* (3rd ed., Rev.). Lexington, Mass.: D. C. Heath.

Pierce, P. A., & Miller, D. E. (2004). *Gambling politics: State government and the business of betting*. Boulder, Col.: Lynne Rienner Publishers.

Posner, R. A. (1993). *The problems of jurisprudence*. Cambridge, Mass.: Harvard University Press.

Posner, R. A. (2003). *Law, pragmatism, and democracy*. Cambridge, Mass.: Harvard University Press.

Raes, K. (2001). Legal moralism or paternalism? Tolerance or indifference? Egalitarian justice and the ethics of equal concern. In P. Alldridge & C. H. Brants (Eds.), *Personal autonomy, the private sphere and the criminal law: A comparative study* (pp. 25–47). Portland, Or.: Hart.

Reiman, J. (2001). *The rich get richer and the poor get prison: Ideology, class, and criminal justice*. Boston: Allyn & Bacon.

Room, R., Turner, N. E., & Ialomiteanu, A. (1999). Community effects of the opening of the Niagara casino. *Addiction, 94*, 1449–1466.

Sabatier, P. A., & Jenkins-Smith, H. C. (1993). *Policy change and learning: An advocacy coalition approach.* Boulder, Col.: Westview Press.

Segal, J. A., & Spaeth, H. J. (1993). *The Supreme Court and the attitudinal model.* New York: Cambridge University Press.

Tamanaha, B. (2004) *On the rule of law.* New York: Cambridge University Press.

White Tail Park v. Stroube, 413 F.3d 451 (2005).

Wolfenden Report: Report of the Committee of Homosexual Offenses and Prostitution. (1963). New York: Stein and Day.

Unit II Photo Essay

Associated Press. (2006, March 25). Bear wrestler insists critics are off-base. *USA Today.* Available: http://www.usatoday.com/news/nation/2006–03–25-bearwrestling_x.htm

Bear Wrestling, Revised Missouri Statutes, § 578.176 (2010).

Egan, K. (2007). Morality-based legislation is alive and well: Why the law permits consent to body modification but not sadomasochistic sex. *Albany Law Review, 70*, 1615–1642.

Koppel, N. (2007, August 30). Are your jeans sagging? Go directly to jail. *New York Times.* Available: http://www.nytimes.com/2007/08/30/fashion/30baggy.html

Peltz, J. (2010, April 1). "Stop the Sag" billboards battle low-slung pants. Available: http://www.msnbc.msn.com/id/36132246/ns/us_news-life/

Straus, M. A. (2001). *Beating the devil out of them: Corporal punishment in American families and its effects on children.* New Brunswick, N.J.: Transaction Publishers.

Vogel, N. (2007, February 23). Spanking ban plan revisited. *Los Angeles Times.* Available: http://articles.latimes.com/2007/feb/23/local/me-spank23

Willis v. State, 888 N.E.2d 177 (Supreme Court of Indiana, 2008).

Yates, J., & Gillespie, W. (2002). The problem of sports violence and the criminal prosecution solution. *Cornell Journal of Law and Public Policy, 12*, 145–168.

Chapter 4

Abercrombie, N., Hill, S., & Turner, B. S. (2006). *Dictionary of sociology* (5th ed.). New York: Penguin Books.

AFL-CIO. (2008). *Discrimination: Sexual orientation and gender identity.* Available: http://www.aflcio.org/issues/jobseconomy/workersrights/rightsatwork_e/disc_sexorient.cfm

Akers, R. L. & Jensen, G. F. (2007). *Social learning theory and the explanation of crime: Advances in criminological theory series* (new ed.). Edison, N.J.: Transaction Publishers.

Anderson, E. A. (2005). *Out of the closet and into the courts: Legal opportunity, structure, and gay rights litigation.* Ann Arbor: University of Michigan Press.

Applegate, B. K., Cullen, F. T., Link, B. G., Richards, P. J., & Lanza-Kadue, L. (1996). Determinates of public punitiveness toward drunk driving: A factorial survey approach. *Justice Quarterly, 13*(1), 57–79.

Baker-Brown, I. (1866). On the curability of certain forms of insanity, epilepsy, catalepsy, and hysteria in females. London: Robert Hardwicke.

Black, D. (1976). *The behavior of law.* New York: Academic Press.

Black, D. (1984). *Toward a general theory of social control* (Vol. 1). Orlando, Fla.: Academic Press.

Black, D. (1989). *Sociological justice.* New York: Oxford University Press.

Black, D. (1998). *The social structure of right and wrong* (Rev. ed.). New York: Academic Press.

Bureau of Justice Statistics. (1992). *Survey of inmates of local jails. Special report: Drunk driving.* Washington, D.C.: U.S. Government Printing Office.

Butterfield, F. (1998, March 5). Asylums behind bars: A special report: Prisons replace hospitals for the nation's mentally ill. *New York Times*, p. A1.

Clark v. Arizona, 548 U.S. 735 (2006).

Cochran, J. K., & Bromley, M. L. (2003) The myth (?) of the police sub-culture. *Policing: An International Journal of Police Strategies and Management, 26*(1), 88–117.

Conrad, P., & Schneider, J. W. (1980). *Deviance and medicalization: From badness to sickness.* St. Louis: C. V. Mosby.

Conrad, P., & Schneider, J. W. (1992). *Deviance and medicalization: From badness to sickness* (2nd ed.). Philadelphia: Temple University Press.

Curra, J. O. (1999). *The relativity of deviance.* Thousand Oaks, Cal.: Sage Publications.

Dawson, M. (2006). Intimacy and violence: Exploring the role of victim–defendant relationship in criminal law. *Journal of Criminal Law and Criminology, 96,* 1417–1449.

Deflem, M. (2006). *Sociological theory and criminological research: Sociology of crime, law, and deviance* (Vol. 7). San Diego, Cal.: Elsevier/JAI Press.

Dershowitz, A. M. (1994). *The abuse excuse and other cop-outs, sob stories, and evasions of responsibility.* Boston: Little, Brown.

Eitzen, D. S., & Baca-Zinn, M. (Eds.). (1998). *In conflict & order: Understanding society* (8th ed.). Upper Saddle River, N.J.: Pearson/Allyn & Bacon.

Falk, P. J. (1996). Novel theories of criminal defense based upon the toxicity of the social environment: Urban psychosis, television intoxication, and black rage. *North Carolina Law Review, 74,* 731–811.

Florida v. Zamora (Dade County Circuit Court 1977), aff'd, 361 So.2d 776 (Florida District Court of Appeals 1978), cert. denied, 372 So.2d 472 (Florida 1979).

Fradella, H. F. (2000). Minimum mandatory sentences: Arizona's ineffective tool for the social control of DUI. *Criminal Justice Policy Review, 11,* 113–135.

Fradella, H. F. (2007). From insanity to beyond diminished capacity: Mental illness and criminal excuse in the post-*Clark* era. *University of Florida Journal of Law and Public Policy, 18,* 7–92.

Heitzeg, N. A. (1996). *Deviance: Rulemakers and rulebreakers.* Belmont, Cal.: Wadsworth.

Human Rights Campaign. (2011). *LGBT equality at the Fortune 500.* Available: http://www.hrc.org/ issues/workplace/fortune500.htm

Lamb, H. R., & Bachrach, L. L. (2001). Some perspectives on deinstitutionalization. *Psychiatric Services, 52,* 1039–1045.

Lawrence v. Texas, 539 U.S. 558 (2003).

Luther, S., & Herrschaft, D. *The state of the workplace for gay, lesbian, bisexual, and transgender Americans 2006–2007.* Washington, D.C.: Human Rights Campaign. Available: http://www.hrc.org/ documents/State_of_the_Workplace.pdf

McCaghy, C. H., Capron, T. A., Jamieson, J. D., & Harley Carey, S. H. (2007). *Deviant behavior: Crime, conflict, and interest groups* (8th ed.). Upper Saddle River, N.J.: Pearson/Allyn & Bacon.

Miller, R. D. (1997). The continuum of coercion: Constitutional and clinical considerations in the treatment of mentally disordered persons. *Denver University Law Review, 74,* 1169–1214.

Mohr, L. B. (1996). *The causes of human behavior: Implications for theory and method in the social sciences.* Ann Arbor: University of Michigan Press.

National Coalition of Anti-Violence Programs. (2005). *Anti-lesbian, gay, bisexual and transgender violence in 2004.* New York: National Coalition of Anti-Violence Programs. Available: http:// www.ncavp.org/common/document_files/ Reports/2004NationalHV%20Report.pdf

National Conference of State Legislatures. (2011, February). *Same-sex marriage, civil unions and domestic partnerships.* Available: http://www.ncsl .org/default.aspx?tabid=16430

Parsons, T. (1951). *The social system* (new ed.). New York: Free Press.

Reinarman, C. (1988). The social construction of an alcohol problem: The case of Mothers Against Drunk Drivers and social control in the 1980s. *Theory and Society, 17,* 91–120.

Ross, E. A. (1901). *Social control: A survey of the foundations of order.* New York: Macmillan.

Ross, H. L., McCleary R., LaFree, G. (1990). Can the threat of jail deter drunk drivers? The Arizona case. *Journal of Criminal Law and Criminology, 81,* 156–170.

Saracho, O. N., & Spodek, B. (2007). *Contemporary perspectives on socialization and social development in early childhood education.* Charlotte, N.C.: Information Age.

Schiro v. Clark, 963 F.2d 962 (7th Circuit 1992), aff'd, 510 U.S. 222 (1994).

Sharkey, J. (1999, December 19). Mental illness: Defining the line between behavior that's vexing and certifiable. *New York Times*. Available: http://query.nytimes.com/gst/fullpage.html?res=9400E1D81330F93AA25751C1A96F958260

Sinha, D. (1996). Culture as the target and culture as the source: A review of cross-cultural psychology in Asia. *Psychology and Developing Societies, 8*(1), 83–105.

Slate, R. N. & Johnson, W. W. (2008). *The criminalization of mental illness: Crisis and opportunity for the justice system*. Durham, N.C.: Carolina Academic Press.

Stone, T. H. (1997). Therapeutic implications of incarceration for persons with severe mental disorders: Searching for rational health policy. *American Journal of Criminal Law, 24*, 283–358.

Talbott, J. A. (2004). Deinstitutionalization: Avoiding the disasters of the past. *Psychiatric Services, 55*, 1112–1115. (Original work published 1979)

Van Maanen, J. (1974). Working the street: A developmental view of police behavior. In H. Jacob (Ed.), *The potential for reform of criminal justice* (pp. 83–129). Beverly Hills, Cal.: Sage Publications.

Walshok, M.L. (1971). The emergence of middle-class deviant subcultures: The case of swingers. *Social Problems, 18*(4), 488–495.

Chapter 5

Agnew, R. (1992). Foundations for a general strain theory of crime and delinquency. *Criminology, 30*, 47–87.

Akers, R. L. (2000). *Criminological theories: Introduction, evaluation, and application* (3rd ed.). Los Angeles: Roxbury.

Akers, R. L., & Sellers, C. S. (2008). *Criminological theories: Introduction, evaluation, and application* (5th ed.). New York: Oxford University Press.

American Psychiatric Association. (2000). *Diagnostic and statistical manual of mental disorders* (4th ed., text revision). Washington, D.C.: American Psychiatric Association.

Arrigo, B. A. (1999). *Social justice/criminal justice: The maturation of critical theory in law, crime, and deviance*. Belmont, Cal.: Wadsworth.

Austin, J. (2003). Why criminology is irrelevant. *Criminology and Public Policy, 2*, 557–564.

Bandura, A., Ross, D., & Ross, S. A. (1961). Transmission of aggression through imitation of aggressive models. *Journal of Abnormal and Social Psychology, 63*, 575–582.

Ben-Yehuda, N. (1985). *Deviance and moral boundaries*. Chicago: University of Chicago Press.

Bentham, J. (1970). *An introduction to the principles of morals and legislation* (J. H. Burns & H. L. A. Hart, Eds.). London: Athlone Press. (Original work published 1789)

Best, J., & Luckenbill, D. F. (1994). *Organizing deviance* (2nd ed.). Upper Saddle River, N.J.: Prentice Hall.

Bracey, D. H. (2006). *Exploring law and culture*. Long Grove, Ill.: Waveland Press.

Buck v. Bell, 274 U.S. 200 (1927).

Caporael, L. R. (1976). Ergotism: The Satan loosed in Salem? *Science, 192*(4234), 21–26.

Christiansen, K. (1977). A preliminary study of criminality among twins. In S. Mednick & K. Christiansen (Eds.), *Biosocial bases of criminal behavior* (pp. 89–108). New York: Gardner.

Cloward, R. A., & Ohlin, L. E. (1960). *Delinquency and opportunity: A theory of delinquent gangs*. New York: Free Press.

Cohen, A. (1955). *Delinquent boys: The culture of the gang*. New York: Free Press.

Cohen, L., & Felson, M. (1979). Social change and crime rate trends: A routine activities approach. *American Sociological Review, 44*, 588–608.

Conklin, J. E. (1998). *Criminology* (6th ed.). Boston: Allyn & Bacon.

Dugdale, R. (1877). *The Jukes: A study in crime, pauperism, and heredity*. New York: Putnam.

Durkheim, É. (1980). The rules of sociological method. In S. H. Traub & C. B. Little (Eds.), *Theories of deviance* (pp. 3–21). Itasca, Ill.: F. E. Peacock Publishers. (Original work published 1938)

Elev, T. C., Lichtenstein, P., & Moffitt, T. E. (2003). A longitudinal behavioral genetic analysis of the etiology of aggressive and nonaggressive antisocial behavior. *Development and Psychopathology, 15*, 383–402.

Erikson, K. T. (2005). *Wayward Puritans: A study in the sociology of deviance*. Boston: Allyn & Bacon. (Original work published 1966)

Eysenck, H. J. (1964). *Crime and personality*. Boston: Houghton Mifflin.

Feinberg, J. (1965). The expressive function of punishment. *Monist, 49*(3), 397–423.

Friedman, L. M. (1993). *Crime and punishment in American history.* New York: Basic Books.

Forsyth, C. J. (1992, October–December). Parade strippers: A note on being naked in public. *Deviant Behavior, 13,* 391–403.

Glantz, S. A., & Balbach, E. D. (2000). *Tobacco war: Inside the California battles.* Berkeley: University of California Press.

Gottfredson, M. R., & Hirschi, T. (1990). *A general theory of crime.* Stanford, Cal.: Stanford University Press.

Guo, G., Roettger, M. E., & Cai, T. (2008). The integration of genetic propensities into social-control models of delinquency and violence among male youths. *American Sociological Review, 73,* 543–568.

Hickey, E. W. (2010). *Serial murderers and their victims* (5th ed.). Belmont, Cal.: Wadsworth / Cengage Learning.

Hines, D. A., & Saudino, K. J. (2004). Genetic and environmental influences on intimate partner aggression: A preliminary study. *Violence and Victims, 19,* 701–718.

Hirschi, T. (1969). *Causes of delinquency.* Berkeley: University of California Press.

Ishikawa, S. S., & Raine, A. (2002). Behavioral genetics in crime. In J. Glicksohn (Ed.), *The neurobiology of criminal behavior* (pp. 81–110). Norwell, Mass.: Kluwer Academic Publishers.

Katz, J. (1988). *Seductions of crime.* New York: Basic Books.

Kelling, G. L., & Coles, C. M. (1996). *Fixing broken windows: Restoring order and reducing crime in our communities.* New York: Free Press.

Lab, S. P. (2004). Crime prevention, politics, and the art of going nowhere fast. *Justice Quarterly, 21,* 682–692.

Lanier, M. M., & Henry, S. (1998). *Essential criminology.* Boulder, Col.: Westview Press.

Lemert, E. (1951). *Social pathology: A systematic approach to the theory of sociopathic behavior.* New York: McGraw-Hill.

Levack, B. P. (Ed.). (2001). *Gender and witchcraft.* New York: Routledge.

Mendelsohn, B. (1963) The origin of victimology. *Excerpta Criminologica, 3,* 239–256.

Merton, R. K. (1968). *Social theory and social structure.* New York: Free Press.

Miller, W. B. (1958). Lower class culture as a generating milieu of gang delinquency. *Journal of Social Issues, 14,* 5–19.

Pepinsky, H. (1999). Peacemaking primer. In B. A. Arrigo (Ed.), *Social justice, criminal justice: The maturation of critical theory in law, crime, and deviance* (pp. 51–70). Belmont, Cal.: Wadsworth.

Quinney, R. (1970). *The social reality of crime.* Boston: Little, Brown.

Riemer, J. W. (1981). Deviance as fun. *Adolescence, 16,* 39–43.

Rowe, D. C. (2002). *Biology and crime.* Los Angeles: Roxbury.

Rowe, D., & Osgood, D. W. (1984). Heredity and sociological theories of delinquency: Reconsideration. *American Sociological Review, 49,* 526–540.

Seigel, L. (2002). *Criminology: The core.* Belmont, Cal.: Wadsworth.

Serial killers and murderers. (1991). Lincolnwood, Ill.: Publications International.

Shaw, C. R., & McKay, H. D. (1942). *Juvenile delinquency in urban areas.* Chicago: University of Chicago Press.

Shoemaker, D. J. (2004). *Theories of delinquency: An examination of explanations of delinquent behavior* (5th ed.). New York: Oxford University Press.

Smith, A. B., & Pollack, H. (1994). Deviance as crime, sin, and poor taste. In P. A. Adler & P. Adler (Eds.), *Constructions of deviance: Social power, context, & interaction* (pp. 11–25). Belmont, Cal.: Wadsworth. (Original work published 1976)

Sutherland, E. H. (1947). *Principles of criminology.* New York: Harper & Row.

Sykes, G. M., & Matza, D. (1957, December). Techniques of neutralization: A theory of delinquency. *American Sociological Review, 22,* 664–670.

Tannenbaum, F. (1938). *Crime and the community.* New York: Ginn.

Vold, G. B., Bernard, T. J., & Snipes, J. B. (1998). *Theoretical criminology* (4th ed.). New York: Oxford University Press.

Walker, S. (2006). *Sense and non-sense about crime and drugs: A policy guide* (6th ed.). Belmont, Cal.: Wadsworth.

Unit III Photo Essay

Ferguson v. City of Charleston, 532 U.S. 67 (U.S. Supreme Court, 2001).

Katz v. United States, 389 U.S. 347 (U.S. Supreme Court, 1967).

People v. Diaz, 51 Cal. 4th 84 (Supreme Court of California, 2011).

State v. Smith, 124 Ohio St.3d (Supreme Court of Ohio, 2009).

United States v. Garcia, 474 F.3d 994 (U.S. Court of Appeals for the 7th Circuit, 2007).

United States v. Maynard, 615 F.3d 544 (U.S. Court of Appeals for the D.C. Circuit, 2010).

United States v. Warshak, 10a0377p.06 (U.S. Court of Appeals for the 6th Circuit, 2010).

Wald, M. L. (2010, January 12). Mixed signals on airport scanners. *New York Times*. Available: http://www.nytimes.com/2010/01/13/us/13scanners.html

Chapter 6

Altemeyer, B. (1996). *The authoritarian specter*. Cambridge, Mass.: Harvard University Press.

Argersinger v. Hamlin, 407 U.S. 25 (1972).

Aristotle. (2000). *Nicomachean ethics* (R. Crisp, Trans.). New York: Cambridge University Press.

Arrigo, B. (1995). The peripheral core of law and criminology: On postmodern social theory and conceptual integration. *Justice Quarterly, 12*, 447–472.

Arrigo, B. A. (Ed.). (1999). *Social justice, criminal justice: The maturation of critical theory in law, crime, and deviance*. Belmont, Cal.: West/Wadsworth.

Bentham, J. (1776). *A fragment on government*. Available: http://www.efm.bris.ac.uk/het/bentham/government.htm

Blake, R., & Mouton, J. (1964). *The managerial grid: The key to leadership excellence*. Houston, Tex.: Gulf.

Bohm, R. M. (2000, November–December). The future of capital punishment in the United States. *ACJS Today*, pp. 1, 4–6.

Brown, R. M. (1969). The American vigilante tradition. In H. D. Graham & T. R. Gurr (Eds.), *Violence in America: Historical and comparative perspectives* (pp. 144–218). New York: Signet Books.

Castellano, T. C., & Gould, J. B. (2007). Neglect of justice in criminal justice theory: Causes, consequences, and alternatives. In D. E. Duffee & E. R. Maguire (Eds.), *Criminal justice theory: Explaining the nature and behavior of criminal justice* (pp. 71–92). New York: Routledge.

Cohen, M. A. (1988). Pain, suffering, and jury awards: A study of the cost of crime to victims. *Law and Society Review, 22*, 537–555.

Fealy, J. (2006). *Eliminating overt drug markets in High Point, North Carolina (application for the 2006 Herman Goldstein Award)*. Available: http://www.popcenter.org/library/awards/goldstein/2006/06-20(F).pdf

Feeley, M. M. (1992). *The process is the punishment: Handling cases in a lower criminal court*. New York: Russell Sage Foundation.

Gideon v. Wainwright, 372 U.S. 335 (1963).

Hafer, C. L., & Bègue, L. (2005). Research on just-world theory: Problems, developments, and future challenges. *Psychological Bulletin, 131*, 128–167.

Hahn, P. H. (1998). *Emerging criminal justice: Three pillars for a proactive justice system*. Thousand Oaks, Cal.: Sage Publications.

Haley, J. O. (1986). Comment: The implications of apology. *Law and Society Review, 20*, 499–507.

Jordan v. City of New London, 1999 U.S. Dist. LEXIS 14289 (1999).

Judge lets victim take from thief. (1992, April 10). *Wilmington Morning Star*, p. 3B.

Karp, L. N. (2009). *Truth, justice, and the American way: What Superman teaches us about the American dream and changing values within the United States*. (Thesis submitted to Oregon State University). Available: http://ir.library.oregonstate.edu/jspui/bitstream/1957/11926/1/Thesis_LKarp.pdf

Kaufman, B. (1991). *Up the down staircase*. New York: HarperPerennial.

Kennedy, D. M. (2006). Old wine in new bottles: Policing and the lessons of pulling levers. In D. Weisburd & A. A. Braga (Eds.), *Police innovation: Contrasting perspectives* (pp. 155–170). New York: Cambridge University Press.

Kohlberg, L. (1984). *Essays on moral development: Vol. 2. The psychology of moral development*. San Francisco: Harper & Row.

Lazare, A. (2004). *On apology*. New York: Oxford University Press.

Lewis, A. (1964). *Gideon's trumpet*. New York: Vintage Books.

Marrus, M. R. (1997). *The Nuremberg War Crimes Trial, 1945–1946: A documentary history*. New York: Bedford/St. Martin's.

McGillis, D. (1998). *Resolving community conflict: The Dispute Settlement Center of Durham, North Carolina (National Institute of Justice Program Focus)*. Available: http://www.ncjrs.org/pdffiles/172203.pdf

Mill, J. S. (1981). On liberty. In M. Curtis (Ed.), *The great political theories* (Vol. 2, pp. 190–204). New York: Avon Books. (Original work published 1859)

Muir, W. K. (1977). *Police: Streetcorner politicians*. Chicago: University of Chicago Press.

Nozick, R. (1974). *Anarchy, state, and utopia*. Malden, Mass.: Blackwell.

Owen, S., & Wagner, K. (2008). The specter of authoritarianism among criminal justice majors. *Journal of Criminal Justice Education, 19*, 30–53.

Paterson, T. G., Clifford, J. G., & Hagan, K. J. (1991). *American foreign policy: A history since 1990* (3rd ed., Rev.). Lexington, Mass.: D. C. Heath.

Peirce, C. S. (1877, November). The fixation of belief. *Popular Science Monthly, 12*, 1–15. Available: http://www.peirce.org/writings/p107.html

Pennell, S., Curtis, C., Henderson, J., & Tayman, J. (1989). Guardian Angels: A unique approach to crime prevention. *Crime and Delinquency, 35*, 378–400.

Range, F., Horn, L., Viranyi, Z., & Huber, L. (2009). The absence of reward induces inequity aversion in dogs. *Proceedings of the National Academy of Sciences, 106*, 340–345.

Rawls, J. (1999). *A theory of justice* (Rev. ed.). Cambridge, Mass.: Harvard University Press.

Rawls, J. (2001). *Justice as fairness: A restatement*. Cambridge, Mass.: Harvard University Press.

Roskin, M. G. (2004). *Countries and concepts: Politics, geography, culture* (8th ed.). Upper Saddle River, N.J.: Pearson/Prentice Hall.

Sargent, L. T. (1996). *Contemporary political ideologies: A comparative analysis* (10th ed.). New York: Harcourt Brace College Publishers.

Schmidtz, D. (2006). *Elements of justice*. New York: Cambridge University Press.

Seiter, R. P., & West, A. D. (2003). Supervision styles in probation and parole: An analysis of activities. *Journal of Offender Rehabilitation, 38*, 57–75.

Sentencing circles. (n.d.). Available: http://www.nij.gov/topics/courts/restorative-justice/promising-practices/sentencing-circles.htm

Stampp, K. M. (1991). *The causes of the Civil War* (Rev. ed.). New York: Simon & Schuster.

Stone, D. (2002). *Policy paradox: The art of political decision making* (Rev. ed.). New York: W. W. Norton.

Teitel, R. G. (2002). *Transitional justice*. New York: Oxford University Press.

Truth and Reconciliation Commission of South Africa. (1998). *TRC final report* (Vol. 5). Available: http://www.justice.gov.za/trc/report/finalreport/Volume%205.pdf

Velasquez, M. (2002). *Philosophy: A text with readings* (8th ed.). Stamford, Conn.: Wadsworth.

Walzer, M. (1984). *Spheres of justice: A defense of pluralism and equality*. New York: Basic Books.

Wasserman, G. A., Keenan, K., Tremblay, R. E., Coie, J. D., Herrenkohl, T. I., Loeber, R., & Petechuk, D. (2003). *Risk and protective factors of child delinquency* (Child Delinquency Bulletin Series). Available: http://www.ncjrs.gov/pdffiles1/ojjdp/193409.pdf

Webster, D. (1914). *The great speeches and orations of Daniel Webster*. Boston: Little, Brown.

Zimring, F. E. (2003). *The contradictions of American capital punishment*. New York: Oxford University Press.

Chapter 7

Almond, G. A., & Verba, S. (1989). *The civic culture: Political attitudes and democracy in five nations*. Newbury Park, Cal.: Sage Publications.

Aos, S., Miller, M., & Drake, E. (2006). *Evidence-based public policy options to reduce future prison construction, criminal justice costs, and crime rates*. Olympia: Washington State Institute for Public Policy. Available: http://www.wsipp.wa.gov/rptfiles/06-10-1201.pdf

Archibold, R. C. (2010, April 23). Arizona enacts stringent law on immigration. *New York Times*. Available: http://www.nytimes.com/2010/04/24/us/politics/24immig.html?scp=1&sq=arizona%20enacts%20stringent%201aw%200n%20immigration&st=cse

Arrigo, B. A. (1999). In search of social justice: Toward an integrative and critical (criminological) theory. In B. A. Arrigo (Ed.),

Social justice, criminal justice: The maturation of critical theory in law, crime, and deviance (pp. 253–272). Belmont, Cal.: West/Wadsworth.

Assault in the First Degree, Maryland Criminal Law Code, § 3-202 (2011).

Baumgartner, F. R., & Jones, B. D. (1993). *Agendas and instability in American politics.* Chicago: University of Chicago Press.

Beckett, K., & Sasson, T. (2004). *The politics of injustice: Crime and punishment in America* (2nd ed.). Thousand Oaks, Cal.: Sage Publications.

Beckwith v. State of Mississippi, 707 So.2d 547 (Supreme Court of Mississippi, 1997).

Bess, M. (2008, October). Assessing the impact of home foreclosures in Charlotte neighborhoods. *Geography and Public Safety, 1*(3), 2–5. Available: http://www.cops.usdoj.gov/files/RIC/Publications/GPS-V011_iss3.pdf

Brents, B. G., & Hausbeck, K. (2001). State-sanctioned sex: Negotiating formal and informal regulatory practices in Nevada brothels. *Sociological Perspectives, 44,* 307–332.

Brickey, K. F. (1996). The Commerce Clause and federalized crime: A tale of two thieves. *Annals of the American Academy of Political and Social Science, 543,* 27–38.

Brown, E. G. (2008, August). *Guidelines for the security and non-diversion of marijuana grown for medical use.* Sacramento: California Department of Justice. Available: http://www.ag.ca.gov/cms_attachments/press/pdfs/n1601_medicalmarijuanaguidelines.pdf

California Department of Public Health. (2010, March 29). *Medical Marijuana Program (MMP) facts and figures.* Sacramento: California Department of Public Health. Available: http://www.cdph.ca.gov/programs/MMP/Documents/Web%20Fact%20Sheet%203-29-10.pdf

Callaghan, K., & Schnell, F. (2001). Assessing the democratic debate: How the news media frame elite policy discourse. *Political Communication, 18,* 183–212.

Custer, L. B. (1978). The origins of the doctrine of *parens patriae. Emory Law Journal, 27,* 195–208.

Dye, T. (1984). *Understanding public policy.* Englewood Cliffs, N.J.: Prentice Hall.

Edelman, M. (1988). *Constructing the political spectacle.* Chicago: University of Chicago Press.

Estelle v. Gamble, 429 U.S. 97 (U.S. Supreme Court, 1976).

Ferraiolo, K. (2007). From killer weed to popular medicine: The evolution of American drug control policy, 1937–2000. *Journal of Policy History, 19,* 147–179.

Friedman, L. M. (2002). *American law in the twentieth century.* New Haven, Conn.: Yale University Press.

Harmelin v. Michigan, 501 U.S. 957 (U.S. Supreme Court, 1991).

Inciardi, J. A. (1992). *The war on drugs II: The continuing epic of heroin, cocaine, crack, crime, AIDS, and public policy.* Mountain View, Cal.: Mayfield.

Information for Voters: The 2008 ballot questions. (2008). Boston: Mass. Secretary of the Commonwealth. Available: http://www.sec.state.ma.us/ele/elepdf/IFV_2008.pdf

Johnson, B. D., Ream, G. L., Dunlap, E., & Sifaneck, S. J. (2008). Civic norms and etiquettes regarding marijuana use in public settings in New York City. *Substance Use and Misuse, 43,* 895–918.

Kingdon, J. W. (1995). *Agendas, alternatives, and public policies* (2nd ed.). New York: HarperCollins.

Kyllo v. United States, 533 U.S. 27 (U.S. Supreme Court, 2001).

Lab, S. P. (2004). Crime prevention, politics, and the art of going nowhere fast. *Justice Quarterly, 21,* 681–692.

Lawrence, R. G., & Birkland, T. A. (2004). Guns, Hollywood, and school safety: Defining the school-shooting problem across public arenas. *Social Science Quarterly, 85,* 1193–1207.

Lipsky, M. (1980). *Street-level bureaucracy: Dilemmas of the individual in public services.* New York: Russell Sage Foundation.

Lowi, T. (1967). The public philosophy: Interest-group liberalism. *American Political Science Review, 61,* 5–24.

Madison, J. (1982). The Federalist No. 51. In G. Wills (Ed.), *The Federalist Papers by Alexander Hamilton, James Madison, and John Jay* (pp. 261–265). New York: Bantam Books. (Original work published 1788)

Miller, D. (1999). *Principles of social justice.* Cambridge, Mass.: Harvard University Press.

Miller, L. L. (2008). *The perils of federalism: Race, poverty, and the politics of crime control.* New York: Oxford University Press.

Mooney, C. Z., & Lee, M. (1999). The temporal diffusion of morality policy: The case of death penalty legislation in the American states. *Policy Studies Journal, 27*, 766–780.

National Coalition for the Homeless. (2009a). *Domestic violence and homelessness.* Available: http://www.nationalhomeless.org/factsheets/domestic.pdf

National Coalition for the Homeless. (2009b). *Foreclosure to homelessness: The forgotten victims of the subprime crisis.* Available: http://www.nationalhomeless.org/factsheets/foreclosure.pdf

National Coalition for the Homeless. (2009c). *Hate crimes and violence against people experiencing homelessness.* Available: http://www.nationalhomeless.org/factsheets/Hatecrimes.pdf

National Coalition for the Homeless. (2009d). *How many people experience homelessness?* Available: http://www.nationalhomeless.org/factsheets/How_Many.pdf

National Organization for the Reform of Marijuana Laws. (2006). *State by state laws.* Available: http://norml.org/index.cfm?Group_ID=4516

New State Ice Co. v. Liebmann [Brandeis dissent], 285 U.S. 262 (U.S. Supreme Court, 1932).

Otterbein, K. F., & Otterbein, C. S. (1965). An eye for an eye, a tooth for a tooth: A cross-cultural study of feuding. *American Anthropologist, 67*, 1470–1482.

Ravin v. State, 537 P.2d 494 (Supreme Court of Alaska, 1975).

Reinarman, C. (1988). The social construction of an alcohol problem: The case of Mothers Against Drunk Drivers and social control in the 1980s. *Theory and Society, 17*, 91–120.

Richardson, L. E., & Houston, D. J. (2008). Federalism and safety on America's highways. *Publius: The Journal of Federalism, 39*, 117–137.

Robertson, D. B., & Judd, D. R. (1989). *The development of American public policy: The structure of policy restraint.* Glenview, Ill.: Scott, Foresman.

Rochefort, D. A., & Cobb, R. W. (1994). Problem definition: An emerging perspective. In D. A. Rochefort & R. W. Cobb, *The politics of problem definition: Shaping the policy agenda* (pp. 1–31). Lawrence: University Press of Kansas.

Ruiz v. Estelle, 503 F.Supp. 1265 (U.S. District Court for the Southern District of Texas, 1980).

Ryan, P. S. (2003). Revisiting the United States application of punitive damages: Separating myth from reality. *ILSA Journal of International and Comparative Law, 10*, 69–93.

Sabatier, P. A., & Jenkins-Smith, H. C. (1993). *Policy change and learning: An advocacy coalition approach.* Boulder, Col.: Westview Press.

Schuetz, J., & Lilley, L. S. (1999). *The O. J. Simpson trials: Rhetoric, media, and the law.* Carbondale: Southern Illinois University Press.

Senate Bill 1070 [Senate Engrossed], Arizona State Senate (2010). Available: http://www.azleg.gov/legtext/491eg/2r/bills/sb1070s.pdf

Shively, W. P. (1999). *Power and choice: An introduction to political science* (6th ed.). Boston: McGraw-Hill.

Sotirovic, M. (2001). Affective and cognitive processes as mediators of media influences on crime policy preferences. *Mass Communication and Society, 4*, 311–329.

Tyler, T. R. (2006). *Why people obey the law.* Princeton, N.J.: Princeton University Press.

U.S. v. State of Arizona, No. 10-16645 (U.S. Circuit Court of Appeals for the Ninth Circuit, 2011).

Walker, S. (2006). *Sense and nonsense about crime and drugs: A policy guide* (6th ed.). Belmont, Cal.: Thomson Higher Education.

Welsh, B. C. (2006). Evidence-based policing for crime prevention. In D. Weisburd & A. A. Braga (Eds.), *Police innovation: Contrasting perspectives* (pp. 305–321). New York: Cambridge University Press.

Chapter 8

Argersinger v. Hamlin, 407 U.S. 25 (1972).

Baldwin v. New York, 399 U.S. 66 (1970).

Barker v. Wingo, 407 U.S. 514 (1972).

Boumediene v. Bush, Nos. 06–1195 & 06–1196 (June 12, 2008).

Brinegar v. United States, 338 U.S. 106 (1949).

Brown v. Board of Education, 347 U.S. 483 (1954).

Burdeau v. McDowell, 256 U.S. 465 (1921).

California v. Greenwood, 486 U.S. 35 (1988).

Carroll v. United States, 267 U.S. 132 (1925).

Coolidge v. New Hampshire, 403 U.S. 443 (1985).

Crawford v. Washington, 541 U.S. 36 (2004).

Cruzan v. Director, Missouri Department of Health, 497 U.S. 261 (1990).

Davies, T. Y. (1999). Recovering the original Fourth Amendment. *Michigan Law Review, 98*, 547–750.

Deutsch, M. (2000). Justice and conflict. In M. Deutsch & P. T. Coleman (Eds.), *The handbook of conflict resolution: Theory and practice* (pp. 41–64). San Francisco: Jossey-Bass.

Estelle v. Williams, 425 U.S. 401 (1976).

Gideon v. Wainwright, 372 U.S. 335 (1963).

Gitlow v. New York, 268 U.S. 652 (1925).

Hamdan v. Rumsfeld, 548 U.S. 507 (2006).

Hamdi v. Rumsfeld, 542 U.S. 507 (2004).

Harris v. Nelson, 394 U.S. 286 (1969).

Holmes v. Poskanzer, 2007 U.S. Dist. LEXIS 3216 (N.D.N.Y, 2007)

Holmes v. Poskanzer, 2008 U.S. Dist. LEXIS 13545 (N.D.N.Y., February 21, 2008).

Hurtado v. California, 110 U.S. 516 (1884).

In re Winship, 397 U.S. 358 (1970).

Justices of Boston Municipal Court v. Lydon, 466 U.S. 294 (1984).

Katz v. United States, 389 U.S. 347 (1967).

Kentucky v. Stincer, 482 U.S. 730 (1987).

Lasson, N. B. (1937). *The history and development of the Fourth Amendment to the United States Constitution.* Baltimore: Johns Hopkins University Press.

Lawrence v. Texas, 539 U.S. 558 (2003).

Lockhart v. Fretwell, 506 U.S. 364 (1993).

Maclin, T. (1997). The complexity of the Fourth Amendment: A historical review. *Boston University Law Review, 77*, 925–974.

Maiese, M. (2004). Procedural justice. In G. Burgess & H. Burgess (Eds.), *Beyond intractability.* Boulder: Conflict Research Consortium, University of Colorado. Available: http://www.beyondintractability.org/essay/procedural_justice/

Mapp v. Ohio, 367 U.S. 643 (1961).

Maryland v. Buie, 494 U.S. 325 (1990).

Maryland v. Craig, 497 U.S. 836 (1990).

McKeiver v. Pennsylvania, 403 U.S. 528 (1971).

Michigan v. Long, 463 U.S. 1032 (1983).

Miranda v. Arizona, 384 U.S. 436 (1966).

Moran v. Burbine, 475 U.S. 412 (1986).

Neubauer, D. W., & Fradella, H. F. (2011). *America's courts and the criminal justice system* (10th ed.). Belmont, Cal.: Wadsworth/Cengage.

New Jersey v. T. L. O., 469 U.S. 325 (1985).

O'Hear, M. M. (2007). Plea bargaining and procedural justice. Available: http://ssrn.com/abstract=982220

Packer, H. L. (1968). *The limits of the criminal sanction.* Palo Alto, Cal.: Stanford University Press.

Payton v. New York, 445 U.S. 573 (1980).

Peterson, R., Krivo, L., & Hagan, J. (2006). *The many colors of crime: Inequalities of race, ethnicity, and crime in America.* New York: New York University Press.

Pound, R. (1998). *Criminal justice in America.* New Brunswick, N.J.: Transaction Publishers.(Original work published 1930)

Rasul v. Bush, 542 U.S. 466 (2004).

Rawls, J. (1971). *A theory of justice.* Cambridge, Mass.: Belknap/Harvard University Press.

Raz, J. (1972). Legal principles and the limits of law. *Yale Law Journal, 81*(5), 823–854.

Reynolds, J. (2005). The rule of law and the origins of the bill of attainder clause. *St. Thomas Law Review, 18*, 177–205.

Rhode Island v. Innis, 446 U.S. 291 (1980).

Sadurski, W. (2005). *Law's legitimacy and "democracy-plus"* (EUI Working Papers in Law No. 2005/18). San Domenico di Fiesole, Italy: European University Institute Department of Law. Available: http://www.iue.it/PUB/LawWPs/law2005–18.pdf

Sholar, J. A. (2007). *Habeas corpus* and the war on terror. *Duquesne Law Review, 45*, 661–700.

Silverthorne Lumber Co. v. United States, 251 U.S. 385 (1920).

Smith v. Maryland, 442 U.S. 735 (1979).

Solum, L. B. (2004). Procedural justice. *Southern California Law Review, 78*, 181–321.

Strickland v. Washington, 466 U.S. 668 (1984).

Terry v. Ohio, 392 U.S. 1 (1968).

Thibaut, J., & Walker, L. (1975). *Procedural justice: A psychological analysis.* Hillsdale, N.J.: Erlbaum.

Thompson v. Keohane, 516 U.S. 99 (1995).

Tyler, T. R., & Huo, Y. J. (2002). *Trust in the law: Encouraging public cooperation with the police and courts.* New York: Russell Sage Foundation.

Tyler, T. R., & Huo, Y. J. (2003). Procedural justice, legitimacy, and the effective rule of law, *Crime and Justice, 30*, 283–357.

United States v. Jacobsen, 466 U.S. 109 (1984).

United States v. Kyllo, 533 U.S. 27 (2001).

United States v. McConney, 728 F.2d 1195, 1199 (9th Circuit), *cert. denied*, 469 U.S. 824 (1984).

United States v. Miller, 425 U.S. 435 (1976).

United States v. White, 401 U.S. 745 (1971).

Weeks v. United States, 232 U.S. 383 (1914).

West, A. (2007). The Georgia legislature strikes with a vengeance! Sex offender residency restrictions and the deterioration of the *ex post facto* clause. *Catholic University Law Review, 57,* 239–268.

Wolf v. Colorado, 338 U.S. 25 (1949).

Youngberg v. Romeo, 457 U.S. 307 (1982).

Unit IV Photo Essay

Assault in the Third Degree, Missouri Revised Statutes, § 565.070 (2010).

Board of Education—Specific Powers and Duties—Safe Schools, Colorado Revised Statutes, § 22–32–109.1 (2010).

Harassing Communications, Kentucky Revised Statutes, § 525.080 (2008).

Lyons, W., & Drew, J. (2006). *Punishing schools: Fear and citizenship in American public education.* Ann Arbor: University of Michigan Press.

Stanley, P., Small, R., Owen, S., & Burke, T. (in press). Humanistic perspectives on addressing school violence. In M. B. Scholl, A. S. McGowan, & J. T. Hansen (Eds.), *Humanistic perspectives on contemporary counseling issues.* New York: Routledge.

Chapter 9

American Law Institute. (1981). *Model penal code.* Washington, D.C.: American Law Institute. (Original work published 1962)

Bowers v. Hardwick, 478 U.S. 186 (1986).

Brandenburg v. Ohio, 395 U.S. 444 (1969).

Calhoun, G. M. (1927). *The growth of criminal law in ancient Greece.* Berkeley: University of California Press.

Church of Lukumi Babalu Aye v. City of Hialeah, 508 U.S. 520 (1993).

Cohen, D. (2005). Crime, punishment, and the rule of law in classical Athens. In M. Gagarin & D. Cohen (Eds.), *The Cambridge companion to ancient Greek law.* Cambridge, UK: Cambridge University Press.

Cohen v. California, 403 U.S. 15 (1971).

Cox v. Louisiana, 379 U.S. 536 (1965).

Davidson, H. (1996). No consequences—re-examining parental responsibility laws. *Stanford Law and Policy Review, 7,* 23–30.

Doe v. City of Trenton, 143 N.J. Super. 128 (Superior Court of New Jersey, Appellate Division, 1976).

Everson v. Board of Education, 330 U.S. 1 (1947).

FCC v. Pacifica Foundation, 438 U.S. 726 (1978).

Fish, M. J. (2008). An eye for an eye: Proportionality as a moral principle of punishment. *Oxford Journal of Legal Studies, 28,* 57–71.

Griswold v. Connecticut, 381 U.S. 153 (1965).

Hale, M. (1971). *The history of the common law of England*, C. M. Gray (Ed.). Chicago: University of Chicago Press. (Original work published 1713)

Holmes, O. W. (1991). *The common law.* Mineola, N.Y.: Dover. (Original work published 1881)

Langbein, J. H. (2003). *The origins of adversary criminal trial.* New York: Oxford University Press.

Lawrence v. Texas, 539 U.S. 558 (2003).

Leeds, J. (2007, October 7). Labels win suit against song sharer. *New York Times*, p. C1.

Lindgren, J. (1996). Why the ancients may not have needed a system of criminal law. *Boston University Law Review, 76,* 29–57.

Loving v. Virginia, 388 U.S. 1 (1967).

Luna, E. (2005). The overcriminalization phenomenon. *American University Law Review, 54,* 703–743.

MacDowell, D.M. (1978). *The law in classical Athens.* Ithaca, N.Y.: Cornell University Press.

Mazerolle, L., & Ransley, J. (2006). The case for third-party policing. In D. Weisburd & A. A. Braga (Eds.), *Police innovation: Contrasting perspectives* (pp. 191–206). New York: Cambridge University Press.

Metcalf v. Florida, 635 So. 2d 11 (Fla. 1994).

Milsom, S. F. C. (1976). *The legal framework of English feudalism.* Cambridge, UK: Cambridge University Press.

Morissette v. United States, 342 U.S. 246 (1952).

New York Times Co. v. United States, 403 U.S. 713 (1971).

Pennington, K. (1993). The prince and the law, 1200–1600: Sovereignty and rights in the Western legal tradition. Berkeley: University of California Press.

Reynolds v. United States, 98 U.S. 145 (1878).

Robinson, O. F. (1990). *Criminal law of ancient Rome.* Baltimore: Johns Hopkins University Press.

Robinson, P. H. (2008). *Criminal law: Cases and controversies* (2nd ed.). New York: Aspen.

Roe v. Wade, 410 U.S. 113 (1973).

Rosenblatt, A. M. (2003). The law's evolution: Long night's journey into day. *Cardozo Law Review, 24,* 2119–2147.

Roth, M. T., Hoffner, H. A., & Michalowski, P. (1997). *Law collections from Mesopotamia and Asia Minor* (2nd ed.). Atlanta: Scholars Press.

Tappan, P. W. (1947) Who is the criminal? *American Sociological Review, 12*(1), 96–102.

Texas v. Johnson, 491 U.S. 397 (1989).

U.S. Department of Justice. (2008, September 19). *Member of music piracy group sentenced to 18 months in prison* (U.S. Department of Justice press release). Available: http://washingtondc.fbi.gov/dojpressrel/pressre108/wf091908b.htm

Virginia v. Black, 538 U.S. 343 (2003).

Washington v. Glucksberg, 521 U.S. 702 (1997).

Zwicker v. Koota, 389 U.S. 241 (1972).

Chapter 10

Barton, C. K. B. (1999). *Getting even: Revenge as a form of justice.* Chicago: Open Court.

Beccaria, C. (1995). On crimes and punishments. In R. Bellamy (Ed.), R. Davies & V. Cox (Trans.), *On crimes and punishments, and other writings* (pp. 1–114). New York: Cambridge University Press. (Original work published 1764)

Bentham, J. (1988). *The principles of morals and legislation.* Amherst, N.Y.: Prometheus Books. (Original work published 1789)

Braithwaite, J. (1989). *Crime, shame and reintegration.* New York: Cambridge University Press.

Chicago v. Morales, 527 U.S. 41 (1999).

Cullen, F. T. (2005). The twelve people who saved rehabilitation: How the science of criminology made a difference. *Criminology, 43,* 1–42.

Cullen, F. T., Fisher, B. S., & Applegate, B. K. (2000). Public opinion about punishment and corrections. *Crime and Justice, 27,* 1–79.

Edwards, C. (1906). *The oldest laws in the world.* London: Watts.

Fabelo, T. (2000, May). "Technocorrections": The promises, the uncertain threats. *Sentencing and Corrections: Issues for the 21st Century* (No. 5). Washington, D.C.: National Institute of Justice.

Feeley, M. M., & Simon, J. (1992). The new penology: Notes on the emerging strategy of corrections and its implications. *Criminology, 30,* 449–474.

Gregg v. Georgia, 428 U.S. 153 (1976).

Hart, H. L. A. (1968). *Punishment and responsibility: Essays in the philosophy of law.* New York: Oxford University Press.

Helland, E., & Tabarrok, A. (2007). Do three strikes deter? A nonparametric estimation. *Journal of Human Resources, 42,* 309–330.

Ingraham v. Wright, 430 U.S. 651 (1977).

Lazare, A. (2004). *On apology.* New York: Oxford University Press.

Locke, J. (1963). An essay concerning the true original extent and end of civil government. In J. Somerville & R. E. Santoni (Eds.), *Social and political philosophy* (pp. 169–204). New York: Anchor Books. (Original work published 1690)

Lockyer v. Andrade, 538 U.S. 63 (2003).

Martinson, R. (1974, Spring). What works?—Questions and answers about prison reform. *Public Interest, 35,* 22–54.

McGillis, D. (1998, September). *National Institute of Justice Program Focus: Resolving community conflict: The dispute settlement center of Durham, North Carolina.* Washington, D.C.: U.S. Department of Justice.

Moore, L. (2007, March 18). Sticking it to the scofflaw. *U.S. News & World Report, 142,* 47.

Nagin, D. S. (1998). Criminal deterrence research at the outset of the twenty-first century. In M. Tonry (Ed.), *Crime and justice: A review of research* (Vol. 23, pp. 1–42). Chicago: University of Chicago Press.

Newman, G. (1983). *Just and painful: A case for the corporal punishment of criminals.* New York: Macmillan.

Pallone, N. J., & Hennessy, J. J. (2003). To punish or to treat: Substance abuse within the context of oscillating attitudes toward correctional rehabilitation. *Journal of Offender Rehabilitation, 37,* 1–25.

Rhodes v. Chapman, 452 U.S. 337 (1981).

Robinson, P. H. (2005). Fair notice and fair adjudication: Two kinds of legality. *University of Pennsylvania Law Review, 154,* 335–398.

Shelden, R. G. (2001). *Controlling the dangerous classes: A critical introduction to the history of criminal justice.* Boston: Allyn & Bacon.

Shively, W. P. (1999). *Power and choice: An introduction to political science* (6th ed.). New York: McGraw-Hill.

Skolnick, J. (1966). *Justice without trial.* New York: John Wiley.

Solem v. Helm, 463 U.S. 277 (1983).

Spierenburg, P. C. (1984). *The spectacle of suffering.* New York: Cambridge University Press.

Sykes, G. (1958). *The society of captives: A study of a maximum security prison.* Princeton, N.J.: Princeton University Press.

Taylor v. Taintor, 83 U.S. 366 (1872).

Trop v. Dulles, 356 U.S. 86 (1958).

United States v. Brown, 333 U.S. 18 (1948).

United States v. Salerno, 481 U.S. 739 (1987).

Veit, H. E., Rowling, K. R., & Bickford, C. B. (Eds.). (1991). *Creating the Bill of Rights: The documentary record from the First Federal Congress.* Baltimore: Johns Hopkins University Press.

Wagatsuma, H., & Rosett, A. (1986). The implications of apology: Law and culture in Japan and the United States. *Law and Society Review, 20,* 461–498.

Weems v. United States, 217 U.S. 349 (1910).

Wilkerson v. Utah, 99 U.S. 130 (1878).

Unit V Photo Essay

Gill, M., & Spriggs, A. (2005, February). *Assessing the impact of CCTV.* Home Office Research Study 292. Available: http://rds.homeoffice.gov.uk/rds/pdfs05/hors292.pdf

Harkrader, T., Burke, T. W., & Owen, S. S. (2004, April). Pound puppies: The rehabilitative uses of dogs in correctional facilities. *Corrections Today,* pp. 74–79.

Reichert, K. (2002, March). *Police-probation partnerships: Boston's Operation Night Light.* Washington, D.C.: University of Pennsylvania Jerry Lee Center on Criminology Forum on Crime and Justice. Available: http://www.sas.upenn.edu/jerrylee/programs/fjc/paper_mar02.pdf

Schwartz, E. (2008, February 7). Mental health courts: How special courts can serve justice and help mentally ill offenders. *U.S. News & World Report.* Available: http://www.usnews.com/news/national/articles/2008/02/07/mental-health-courts

U.S. Department of Justice. (n.d.). *Reentry.* Available: http://www.ojp.usdoj.gov/reentry/

Weisburd, D., & Braga, A. A. (2006). Hot spots policing as a model for police innovation. In D. Weisburd & A. A. Braga (Eds.), *Police innovation: Contrasting perspectives* (pp. 225–244). New York: Cambridge University Press.

Chapter 11

Altemeyer, B. (1996). *The authoritarian specter.* Cambridge, Mass.: Harvard University Press.

Bieck, W., & Kessler, D. A. (1977). *Response time analysis.* Kansas City, Mo.: Kansas City Board of Police Commissioners.

Bratton, W. (1998). *Turnaround: How America's top cop reversed the crime epidemic.* New York: Random House.

Durkheim, É. (1965). *The division of labor in society.* Glencoe, Ill.: Free Press.

Eck, J. E., & Spelman, W. (1987). *Problem-solving: Problem-oriented policing in Newport News.* Washington, D.C.: U.S. Department of Justice.

Fogelson, R. M. (1977). *Big-city police.* Cambridge, Mass.: Harvard University Press.

Goldstein, H. (1990). *Problem-oriented policing.* New York: McGraw-Hill.

Greenwood, P. W., & Petersilia, J. (1975). The criminal investigation process: Vol. 1. Summary and policy recommendations. *RAND.* Santa Monica, Cal.: Department of Justice (R-1776).

Harring, S. L. (1983). *Policing a class society: The experience of American cities, 1865–1915.* New Brunswick, N.J.: Rutgers University Press.

Herbert, S. (1997). *Policing space: Territoriality and the Los Angeles Police Department.* Minneapolis: University of Minnesota Press.

Kelling, G. L., & Moore, M. H. (1988). The evolving strategy of policing. In S. G. Brandl & D. E. Barlow (Eds.), *Classics in policing* (pp. 71–95). Cincinnati, Oh.: Anderson.

Kelling, G. L., Pate, T., Dieckman, D., & Brown, C. E. (1974). *The Kansas City preventive patrol experiment: A summary report.* Washington, D.C.: Police Foundation.

Klockars, C. B. (1985a). The Dirty Harry problem. In F. A. Elliston & M. Feldberg (Eds.), *Moral issues in police work* (pp. 55–71). Lanham, Md.: Rowman & Littlefield. (Original work published 1980)

Klockars, C. B. (1985b). *The idea of police.* Beverly Hills, Cal.: Sage Publications.

Knapp Commission report on police corruption. (1972). New York, NY: Braziller.

Lefkowitz, J. (1975). Psychological attributes of policemen: A review of research and opinion. *Journal of Social Issues, 31,* 3–26.

Lefkowitz, J. (1977). Industrial-organizational psychology and the police. *American Psychologist, 5,* 346–364.

Loftin, C., & McDowall, D. (1982, June). The police, crime & economic theory: An assessment. *American Sociological Review, 47,* 393–401.

Miller, W. R. (1975, Winter). Police authority in London and New York (1830–1870). *Journal of Social History,* pp. 81–101.

Monkkonen, E. H. (1988). *America becomes urban: The development of U.S. cities and towns 1790–1980.* Berkeley: University of California Press.

Muir, W. K. (1977). *Police: Streetcorner politicians.* Chicago: University of Chicago Press.

Niederhoffer, A. (1967). *Behind the shield: The police in urban society.* New York: Anchor Books.

Oliver, W. M. (2006). The fourth era of policing: Homeland security. *International Review of Law, Computers and Technology, 20,* 49–62.

Owen, S. S., & Wagner, K. (2008). The specter of authoritarianism among criminal justice majors. *Journal of Criminal Justice Education, 19,* 30–53.

Reaves, B. A. (2006, July). *Federal law enforcement officers, 2004.* Washington, D.C.: Bureau of Justice Statistics.

Reaves, B. A. (2007, June). *Census of state and local law enforcement agencies, 2004.* Washington, D.C.: Bureau of Justice Statistics.

Report by the President's Commission on Law Enforcement and Administration of Justice. (1967). Washington, D.C.: U.S. Government Printing Office.

Report of the National Advisory Commission on Civil Disorders. (1968). New York: Bantam Books.

Roberg, R., Crank, J., & Kuykendall, J. (2000). *Police and society* (2nd ed.). Los Angeles, Cal.: Roxbury.

Sante, L. (1991). *Low life: Lures and snares of old New York.* New York: Vintage Books.

Sherman, L. W. (1974). Toward a sociological theory of police corruption. In L. Sherman (Ed.), *Police corruption: A sociological perspective* (pp. 1-39). New York: Anchor Books.

Skolnick, J. (1966). *Justice without trial: Law enforcement in democratic society.* New York: John Wiley.

Smith, R., & Taylor, R. (1985, December). A return to neighborhood policing: The Tampa, Florida experience. *Police Chief,* pp. 39–44.

Sousa, W. H., & Kelling, G. L. (2006). Of "broken windows," criminology, and criminal justice. In D. Weisburd & A. A. Braga (Eds.), *Police innovation: Contrasting perspectives* (pp. 77–97). New York: Cambridge University Press.

Steffens, L. (1992). *The shame of cities.* New York: Hill and Wang. (Original work published 1904)

Task Force Report. (1990). Salem, N.H.: Ayer. (Original work published 1967)

Taylor, R. B. (2006). Incivilities reduction policing, zero tolerance, and the retreat from coproduction: Weak foundations and strong pressures. In D. Weisburd & A. A. Braga (Eds.), *Police innovation: Contrasting perspectives* (pp. 98–114). New York: Cambridge University Press.

Wagner, A. (2008). *Good order and safety: A history of the St. Louis Metropolitan Police Department, 1861–1906.* St. Louis: Missouri History Museum.

Walker, S. (1980). *Popular justice: A history of American criminal justice.* New York: Oxford University Press.

Walker, S. (1984). "Broken windows" and fractured history: The use and misuse of history in recent police patrol analysis. *Justice Quarterly, 1,* 75–90.

Walker, S. (1993). Does anyone remember team policing? Lessons of the team policing experience for community policing. *American Journal of Police, 12*(1), 33–56.

Westley, W. A. (1970). *Violence & the police: A sociological study of law, custom, and morality.* Cambridge, Mass.: MIT Press.

Wilson, J.Q. (1974). *Varieties of police behavior.* New York: Athenaeum Press.

Wilson, J. Q. (1989). *Bureaucracy: What government agencies do and why they do it.* New York: Basic Books.

Wilson, J. Q., & Kelling, G. L. (1982, March). Broken windows: The police and neighborhood safety. *Atlantic Monthly, 211,* 29–38.

Wilson, J. Q., & Kelling, G. L. (1989, February). Making neighborhoods safe. *Atlantic Monthly,* pp. 46–52.

Chapter 12

Argersinger v. Hamlin, 407 U.S. 25 (1972).

Baer, J. A. (1999). *Our lives before the law: Constructing a feminist jurisprudence.* Princeton, N.J.: Princeton University Press.

Baldwin v. New York, 399 U.S. 66 (1970).

Batson v. Kentucky, 476 U.S. 79 (1986).

Blanton v. City of North Las Vegas, 489 U.S. 538 (1989).

Brady v. Maryland, 373 U.S. 83 (1963).

Brown v. Board of Education, 347 U.S. 483 (1954).

Carter, L. H., & Burke, T. F. (2006). *Reason in law* (7th ed.). Upper Saddle River, N.J.: Pearson/Longman.

Choi, S. J., Gulati, G. M., & Posner, E. A. (2010). Professionals or politicians: The uncertain empirical case for an elected rather than appointed judiciary. *Journal of Law, Economics, and Organization, 26,* 290–336.

County of Riverside v. McLaughlin, 500 U.S. 44 (1991).

Covey, R. D. (2008). Fixed justice: Reforming plea bargaining with plea-based ceilings. *Tulane Law Review, 82,* 1237–1290.

Crenshaw, K., Gotanda, N., Peller, G., & Thomas, K. (Eds.). (1995). *Critical race theory: The key writings that formed the movement.* New York: New Press.

Delgado, R., & Stefancic, J. (2001). *Critical race theory: An introduction.* New York: New York University Press.

Demands for Production of Statements and Reports of Witnesses, 18 U.S.C. § 3500 (1970).

Douzinas, C., Warrington, R., & McVeigh, S. (1993). *Postmodern jurisprudence: The law of text in the texts of law.* New York: Routledge.

Dworkin, R. (1977). *Taking rights seriously.* Cambridge, Mass.: Harvard University Press.

Dworkin, R. (1986). *Law's empire.* Cambridge, Mass.: Harvard University Press.

Edelman, L. B. (2004). Rivers of law and contested terrain: A law and society approach to economic rationality. *Law and Society Review, 38,* 181–97.

Eisenstein, J., & Jacob, H. (1977). *Felony justice: An organizational analysis of criminal courts.* Boston: Little, Brown.

Fallon, R. H., Jr. (1994). Reflections on the Hard and Wechsler paradigm. *Vanderbilt Law Review, 47,* 943–987.

Farber, D. A., & Sherry, S. (1997). *Beyond all reason: The radical assault on truth in American law.* New York: Oxford University Press.

Finnegan, S. (2009). Pro se criminal trials and the merging of inquisitorial and adversarial systems of justice. *Catholic University Law Review, 58,* 445–499.

Fradella, H. F. (2007). *Mental illness and criminal defenses of excuse in contemporary American law.* Bethesda, Md.: Academica Press.

Friedman, D. D. (2000). *Law's order: What economics has to do with law and why it matters.* Princeton, N.J.: Princeton University Press.

Friedrichs, D. O. (2006). *Law in our lives: An introduction* (2nd ed.). Los Angeles: Roxbury.

Frymer, P. (2003). Acting when elected officials won't: Federal courts and civil rights enforcement in U.S. labor unions, 1935–1985. *American Political Science Review, 97,* 483–499.

Gerstein v. Pugh, 420 U.S. 103 (1975).

Gideon v. Wainwright, 372 U.S. 335 (1963).

Goldman, S. (1999). *Picking federal judges: Lower court selection from Roosevelt through Reagan.* New Haven, Conn.: Yale University Press.

Hamilton, A., Madison, J., & Jay, J. (2003). *The federalist (with letters of Brutus),* (T. Ball, Ed.). Cambridge, UK: Cambridge University Press. (Original work published 1788)

Hart, H. L. A. (1958). Positivism and the separation of law and morals. *Harvard Law Review, 71,* 593–629.

Hart, H. M., & Sacks, A.M. (1958). *The legal process: Basic problems in the making and application of law.* Cambridge, Mass.: Tentative edition, mimeographed copy.

Hunter v. Underwood, 471 U.S. 222 (1985).

J. E. B. v. Alabama ex rel. T. B., 511 U.S. 127 (1994).

Kelman, M. (1987). *A guide to critical legal studies.* Cambridge, Mass.: Harvard University Press.

Kennedy, D. (1997). *A critique of adjudication [fin de siècle].* Cambridge, Mass.: Harvard University Press.

Lawrence, C. R., III, & Matsuda, M. J. (1997). *We won't go back: Making the case for affirmative action.* Wilmington, Mass.: Houghton Mifflin.

MacKinnon, C. A. (2007). *Women's lives, men's laws.* Cambridge, Mass.: Belknap/Harvard University Press.

Marbury v. Madison, U.S. (1 Cranch) 137 (1803).

Marcus, P. (2009). Why the United States Supreme Court got some (but not a lot) of the Sixth Amendment right to counsel analysis right. *St. Thomas Law Review, 21,* 142–189.

McDonald v. City of Chicago, 561 U.S. ___ (2010).

McKeiver v. Pennsylvania, 403 U.S. 528 (1971).

Minda, G. (1996). *Postmodern legal movements: Law and jurisprudence at century's end.* New York: New York University Press.

Nardulli, P. F. (1983). The societal cost of the exclusionary rule: An empirical assessment. *American Bar Foundation Research Journal, 8*(3), 585–609.

Neubauer, D. W., & Fradella, H. F. (2011). *America's courts and the criminal justice system* (10th ed.). Belmont, Cal.: Wadsworth/Cengage.

Perlin, M. L. (1997). The borderline which separated you from me: The insanity defense, the authoritarian spirit, the fear of faking, and the culture of punishment. *Iowa Law Review, 82,* 1375–1426.

Polinsky, A.M. (2003). *An introduction to law and economics.* Chicago: Aspen Publishers.

Posner, R. A. (1990). *The problems of jurisprudence.* Cambridge, Mass.: Harvard University Press.

Punishment for Conviction of a Felony, Code of Virginia § 18.2–10 (2008).

Punishment for Conviction of a Misdemeanor, Code of Virginia § 18.2–11 (2000).

Regina v. Dudley & Stephens, 4 QB D 273 (1884).

Richardson v. Ramirez, 418 U.S. 24 (1974).

Roper v. Simmons, 543 U.S. 551 (2005).

Schlag, P. (1999). No vehicles in the park. *Seattle University Law Review, 23,* 381–389.

Sentencing Project. (2011, March 11). *Felony disenfranchisement laws in the United States.* Washington, D.C.: Sentencing Project.

Shapiro, A. L. (1993). Challenging criminal disenfranchisement under the Voting Rights Act: A new strategy. *Yale Law Journal, 103,* 537–566.

Spohn, C. C. (2008). *How do judges decide? The search for fairness and justice in punishment* (2nd ed.). Thousand Oaks, Cal.: Sage Publications.

Uchida, C. D., & Bynum, T. S. (1991). Search warrants, motions to suppress and lost cases: The effects of the exclusionary rule in seven jurisdictions. *Journal of Criminal Law and Criminology, 84*(4), 1034–1066.

Varnum, T. G. (2008). Let's not jump to conclusions: Approaching felon disenfranchisement challenges under the Voting Rights Act. *Michigan Journal of Race and Law, 14,* 109–142.

Victor v. Nebraska, 511 U.S. 1 (1994).

Walsh, A., & Hemmens, C. (2008). *Law, justice, and society: A sociolegal introduction.* New York: Oxford University Press.

Washburn, K. K. (2008). Restoring the grand jury. *Fordham Law Review, 76,* 2333–2388.

Wechsler, H. (1954). The political safeguards of federalism: The role of the states in the composition and selection of the national government. *Columbia Law Review, 54,* 543–560.

Wells, M. (1991). Behind the parity debate: The decline of the legal process tradition in the law of federal courts. *Boston University Law Review, 71,* 609–644.

West, R. (1988). Jurisprudence and gender. *University of Chicago Law Review, 55,* 1–72.

Williams v. Florida, 399 U.S. 78 (1970).

Young, E. A. (2005). Institutional settlement in a globalizing judicial system. *Duke Law Journal, 54,* 1143–1261.

Chapter 13

Applegate, B. K. (2001). Penal austerity: Perceived utility, desert, and public attitudes toward prison amenities. *American Journal of Criminal Justice, 25,* 253–268.

Arkansas Department of Correction. (n.d.). *Goals.* Available: http://www.adc.arkansas.gov/goals_objectives.html

Austin, J., & Irwin, J. (2001). *It's about time: America's imprisonment binge* (3rd ed.). Belmont, Cal: Wadsworth.

Aviram, H. (2010). Humonetarianism: The new correctional discourse of scarcity. *Hastings Race and Poverty Law Journal, 7,* 1–52.

Bayens, G. J., Williams, J. J., & Smykla, J. O. (1997, September). Jail type and inmate behavior: A longitudinal analysis. *Federal Probation, 61*(3), 54–62.

Beck, A. J., Harrison, P. M., Berzofsky, M., Caspar, R., & Krebs, C. (2010). Sexual victimization in prisons and jails reported by inmates, 2008–2009. Washington, D.C.: U.S. Department of Justice. Available: http://bjs.ojp.usdoj.gov/content/pub/pdf/svpjri0809.pdf

Bonczar, T. P. (2003, August). Prevalence of imprisonment in the U.S. population, 1974–2001. *Bureau of Justice Statistics Special Report.* Available: http://bjs.ojp.usdoj.gov/content/pub/pdf/piusp01.pdf

Boyer, P. S., Clark, C. E., Kett, J. F., Salisbury, N., Sitkoff, H., & Woloch, N. (1993). *The enduring vision: A history of the American people* (2nd ed.). Lexington, Mass.: D. C. Heath.

Bradbury, B. (2002, June 28). Deschutes County delinquent youth demonstration project (Report No. 2002–29). Salem: Oregon Secretary of State. Available: www.sos.state.or.us/audits/pages/state_audits/full/2002/2002–29.pdf

Brockway, Z. R. (1910). The American reformatory prison system. In C. R. Henderson (Ed.), *Correction and prevention: Vol. I. Prison reform* (pp. 88–107). New York: Russell Sage Foundation.

Buckaloo, B. J., Krug, K. S., & Nelson, K. B. (2009). Exercise and the low-security inmate: Changes in depression, stress, and anxiety. *Prison Journal, 89,* 328–343.

Clemmer, D. (1940). *The prison community.* New York: Holt, Rinehart and Winston.

Cullen, F. T., Blevins, K. R., Trager, J. S., & Gendreau, P. (2005). The rise and fall of boot camps: A case study in common-sense corrections. *Journal of Offender Rehabilitation, 40,* 53–70.

Cullen, F. T., & Gilbert, K. E. (1982). *Reaffirming rehabilitation.* Cincinnati, Oh.: Anderson.

Dean-Myrda, M. C., & Cullen, F. T. (1998). The panacea pendulum: An account of community as a response to crime. In J. Petersilia (Ed.), *Community corrections: Probation, parole, and intermediate sanctions* (pp. 3–18). New York: Oxford University Press.

Domurad, F. (1999). So you want to develop your own risk assessment instrument. *Topics in Community Corrections,* pp. 11–16. Available: http://nicic.gov/pubs/1999/period160.pdf

Farrington, K. (1992). The modern prison as total institution? Public perception versus objective reality. *Crime and Delinquency, 38,* 6–26.

Federal Bureau of Prisons. (2006, September 12). *Inmate security designation and custody classification* (Policy P5100.08). Washington, D.C.: Federal Bureau of Prisons. Available: http://www.bop.gov/policy/progstat/5100_008.pdf

Feeley, M. M., & Rubin, E. L. (1998). *Judicial policy making and the modern state: How the courts reformed America's prisons.* New York: Cambridge University Press.

Feeley, M. M., & Simon, J. (1992). The new penology: Notes on the emerging strategy of corrections and its implications. *Criminology, 30,* 449–474.

Finckenauer, J. O., & Gavin, P. W. (1999). *Scared straight: The panacea phenomenon revisited.* Prospect Heights, Ill.: Waveland Press.

Foucault, M. (1977). *Discipline and punish: The birth of the prison.* New York: Pantheon Books.

Friedman, L. M. (1993). *Crime and punishment in American history.* New York: Basic Books.

Garland, D. (2001). *The culture of control: Crime and social order in contemporary society.* Chicago: University of Chicago Press.

Glaze, L. E., & Bonczar, T. P. (2009, December). Probation and parole in the United States, 2008. *Bureau of Justice Statistics Bulletin.* Available: http://bjs.ojp.usdoj.gov/content/pub/pdf/ppus08.pdf

Goffman, E. (1961). *Asylums: Essays on the social situation of mental patients and other inmates.* New York: Anchor Books.

Goldman, M. (2003, July). *Jail design review handbook.* Washington, D.C.: U.S. Department of Justice. Available: http://nicic.gov/pubs/2003/018443.pdf

Gottschalk, M. (2006). *The prison and the gallows: The politics of mass incarceration in America.* New York: Cambridge University Press.

Gramlich, J. (2010, May 19). For state prisons, cuts present new problems. *Stateline.* Available: http://www.stateline.org/live/printable/story?contentID=485663

Holt v. Sarver, 309 F.Supp. 362 (U.S. District Court for the Eastern District of Arkansas, 1970).

Hooks, G., Mosher, C., Genter, S., Rotolo, T., & Lobao, L. (2010). Revisiting the impact of prison building on job growth: Education, incarceration, and county-level employment, 1976–2004. *Social Science Quarterly, 91,* 228–244.

Hooks, G., Mosher, C., Rotolo, T., & Lobao, L. (2004). The prison industry: Carceral expansion and employment in U.S. counties, 1969–1994. *Social Science Quarterly, 85,* 37–57.

Huling, T. (2002). Building a prison economy in rural America. In M. Mauer & M. Chesney-Lind (Eds.), *Invisible punishment: The collateral consequences of mass imprisonment* (pp. 197–213). New York: New Press.

Illinois Department of Corrections. (2002). *Illinois Department of Corrections—Mission Statement.* Available: http://www.idoc.state.il.us/mission_statement.shtml

Jiang, S., & Fisher-Giorlando, M. (2002). Inmate misconduct: A test of the deprivation, importation, and situational models. *Prison Journal, 82,* 335–358.

Kahler, H. L. (2008). Recreation. In P. M. Carlson & J. S. Garrett (Eds.), *Prison and jail administration: Practice and theory* (2nd ed., pp. 91–98). Sudbury, Mass.: Jones and Bartlett Publishers.

Keilin, S. (2001, December). *An overview of Texas parole guidelines.* Austin, Tex.: Criminal Justice Policy Council. Available: http://www.bop.gov/policy/progstat/5100_008.pdf

Kuhn, T. (1977). *The essential tension: Selected studies in scientific tradition and change.* Chicago: University of Chicago Press.

Lab, S. P. (2004). Crime prevention, politics, and the art of going nowhere fast. *Justice Quarterly, 21,* 681–692.

Langan, P. A., & Levin, D. J. (2002, June). Recidivism of prisoners released in 1994. *Bureau of Justice Statistics Special Report.* Available: http://bjs.ojp.usdoj.gov/content/pub/pdf/rpr94.pdf

Lenz, N. (2002). "Luxuries" in prison: The relationship between amenity funding and public support. *Crime and Delinquency, 48,* 499–525.

MacKenzie, D. L. (2006). *What works in corrections: Reducing the criminal activities of offenders and delinquents.* New York: Cambridge University Press.

McGowen, R. (1995). The well-ordered prison: England, 1780–1865. In N. Morris & D. J.

Rothman (Eds.), *The Oxford history of the prison: The practice of punishment in Western society* (pp. 78–109). New York: Oxford University Press.

Minton, T. D., & Sabol, W. J. (2009, March). *Jail inmates at midyear 2008—statistical tables.* Washington, D.C.: Bureau of Justice Statistics. Available: http://bjs.ojp.usdoj.gov/content/pub/pdf/jim08st.pdf

Nevada Department of Corrections. (2010). *State of Nevada Department of Corrections.* Available: http://www.doc.nv.gov

Parent, D. G. (2003). *Correctional boot camps: Lessons from a decade of research.* Washington, D.C.: U.S. Department of Justice. Available: http://www.ncjrs.gov/pdffiles1/nij/197018.pdf

Paterline, B. A., & Petersen, D. M. (1999). Structural and social psychological determinants of prisonization. *Journal of Criminal Justice, 27,* 427–441.

Plato. (1892). *Laws.* In B. Jowett (Trans.), *The Dialogues of Plato* (Vol. 5, pp. 1–361). London: Oxford University Press. (Original work published 360 B.C.E.)

Pratt, T. C. (2009). *Addicted to incarceration: Corrections policy and the politics of misinformation in the United States.* Los Angeles: Sage.

President's Commission on Law Enforcement and the Administration of Justice. (1967). *The challenge of crime in a free society.* Washington, D.C.: U.S. Government Printing Office.

Prison count 2010: State population declines for the first time in 38 years. (2010, April). Pew Center on the States. Available: http://www.pewcenteronthestates.org/uploadedFiles/Prison_Count_2010.pdf?n=880

Rosich, K. J., & Kane, K. M. (2005, July). Truth in sentencing and state sentencing practices. *NIJ Journal, 252,* 18–21.

Rothman, D. J. (1995). Perfecting the prison: United States, 1789–1865. In N. Morris & D. J. Rothman (Eds.), *The Oxford history of the prison: The practice of punishment in Western society* (pp. 110–129). New York: Oxford University Press.

Rotman, E. (1995). The failure of reform: United States, 1865–1965. In N. Morris & D. J. Rothman (Eds.), *The Oxford history of the prison: The practice of punishment in Western society* (pp. 168–197). New York: Oxford University Press.

Schlosser, E. (1998, December). The prison-industrial complex. *Atlantic Monthly*, pp. 51–77.

Schmitt, J., Warner, K., & Gupta, S. (2010, June). *The high budgetary cost of incarceration*. Washington, D.C.: Center for Economic and Policy Research.

Schneider, A. L., Ervin, L., & Snyder-Joy, Z. (1996). Further exploration of the flight from discretion: The role of risk/need instruments in probation supervision decisions. *Journal of Criminal Justice, 24*, 109–121.

Sherman, L. W., Gottfredson, D. C., MacKenzie, D. L., Eck, J., Reuter, P., & Bushway, S. D. (1998, July). Preventing crime: What works, what doesn't, what's promising. *National Institute of Justice Research in Focus*. Available: http://www.ncjrs.gov/pdffiles/171676.pdf

Siegel, L. J. (2001). *Criminology: Theories, patterns, and typologies* (7th ed.). Belmont, Cal.: Wadsworth.

Simon, J. (2007). *Governing through crime: How the war on crime transformed American democracy and created a culture of fear*. New York: Oxford University Press.

Sykes, G. M. (1958). *The society of captives: A study of a maximum security prison*. Princeton, N.J.: Princeton University Press.

Takagi, P. (1975, December). The Walnut Street Jail: A penal reform to centralize the powers of the state. *Federal Probation, 39*, 18–26.

Tewksbury, R., & Mustaine, E. E. (2005). Insiders' views of prison amenities: Beliefs and perceptions of correctional staff members. *Criminal Justice Review, 30*, 174–188.

Toch, H. (1997). *Corrections: A humanistic approach*. Monsey, N.Y.: Criminal Justice Press.

Tucker, S. B., & Cadora, E. (2003, November). Justice reinvestment. *Ideas for an Open Society, 3*(3), 1–8. Available: http://www.soros.org/resources/articles_publications/publications/ideas_20040106/ideas_reinvestment.pdf

Vaughn, M. (1994, Fall). Boot camps. *The Grapevine, 2*, 2.

Virginia Criminal Sentencing Commission. (n.d.). *Sentence revocation report*. Richmond: Virginia Criminal Sentencing Commission. Available: http://www.vcsc.state.va.us/worksheets_2007/SSR_booklet2007.pdf

Wagner, M., McBride, R. E., & Crouse, S. F. (1999). The effects of weight-training exercise on aggression variables in adult male inmates. *Prison Journal, 79*, 72–89.

Welch, M., Weber, L., & Edwards, W. (2000). "All the news that's fit to print": A content analysis of the correctional debate in the *New York Times*. *Prison Journal, 80*, 245–264.

West, H. C., & Sabol, W. J. (2009, March). *Prison inmates at midyear 2008—statistical tables*. Washington, D.C.: Bureau of Justice Statistics. Available: http://bjs.ojp.usdoj.gov/content/pub/pdf/pim08st.pdf

Glossary

adjudication. The formal process for resolving legal disputes in courts of law. (Chapter 12)

a posteriori. Reasoning that is based on empiricism, grounded in observations, data, and experiences. Most associated with pragmatism. (Chapter 2)

a priori. Reasoning that occurs without empiricism and which may stem from sources including tenacity, authority, or common-sense arguments offered without evidence. Most associated with idealism. (Chapter 2)

actus reus. One component of the legal definition of crime, expressed in a Latin phrase meaning "evil act." The *actus reus* of a crime is the actual act, conduct, or behavior that is prohibited under law. (Chapter 9)

agenda setting. The process by which an issue is identified as one that needs to be addressed through policy or law. This is often a political process. (Chapter 7)

agents of direct social control. Those who attempt to punish or neutralize organizations and individuals who deviate from society's norms. Such agents include social welfare agencies, science and medicine, and government. Compare to **agents of ideological social control**. (Chapter 4)

agents of ideological social control. Those who attempt to shape the consciousness of people in society by influencing ideas, attitudes, morals, and values. Such agents include the family, educational institutions, religion, organized sports, the media, and the government and help to maintain the status quo by persuading citizens to willingly comply with laws. Compare to **agents of direct social control**. (Chapter 4)

antisocial personality. A personality type associated with criminal activity and marked by failure to conform to norms, deceitfulness, impulsivity, aggressiveness, disregard for safety, irresponsibility, and lack of remorse. Also known as *psychopath* or *sociopath*. (Chapter 5)

apartheid. A former policy in South Africa, abolished in the 1990s, of state-sanctioned racial segregation in which the all-white government repressed the rights, freedoms, and political participation of the majority of the population, who were black. (Chapter 6)

appeal. In criminal cases, the defendant has the right to file an appeal requesting that an appellate court review the decision made by a lower court. Appeals may be filed after a sentence has been imposed and final judgment entered in a case and primarily focus on substantive due process and procedural justice rather than on factual issues of guilt or innocence. (Chapter 12)

arraignment. A judicial proceeding at which a person accused of a crime is formally advised of the charges by the reading of the charging document in open court, advised of his or her rights, and asked to enter a plea (e.g., guilty, not guilty, *nolo contendere*) to the charges. (Chapters 1, 12)

atavism. A historical theory of criminology holding that persons were born criminals as the result of inherited traits. This theory has been discredited by modern criminologists. (Chapter 5)

atavistic. Under the theory of atavism, the term referred to persons who were born criminals. (Chapter 5)

attendant circumstances. One component of the legal definition of crime, related to specific circumstances which must surround the *actus reus* (criminal act) for a crime to occur or for it to be punished in a particular manner. (Chapter 9)

attitudinal model. A model of judicial decision making which suggests that courts decide cases based on the judges' attitudes and values. (Chapter 3)

authoritarian model. A model of justice that focuses on the needs of society but not on the needs of the offender. Under the model, outcomes are highly important but process is not important. (Chapter 6)

bail. A financial pledge to ensure that a person accused of a crime will appear in court for trial. The accused person posts a sum of money (or a property title) to the court in exchange for being released prior to trial; if the accused appears for trial, the money or property title is returned. Bail bond agents may post the bail for an accused person in exchange for a fee that is not returned. (Chapter 10)

banishment. A type of punishment in which offenders were banned, and prohibited from returning to, an area. (Chapter 13)

bench trial. A trial in which the judge, rather than the jury, acts as finder of fact (e.g., determining guilt or innocence). Bench trials may occur for some misdemeanors for which trials by jury are not available or when a defendant waives his or her right to a trial by jury. Compare to **trial by jury**. (Chapters 1, 8, 12)

beyond a reasonable doubt. The burden of proof necessary to find a defendant guilty of a crime, whether in a trial by jury or a bench trial. Although a higher standard than probable cause but a lower standard than absolute certainty, there is no precise way to quantify how much proof it takes to reach the standard of beyond a reasonable doubt. (Chapter 12)

bill of attainder. A legislative act that declares someone guilty of a crime and imposes punishment for it in the absence of a trial. The U.S. Constitution prohibits bills of attainder. (Chapter 8)

Bill of Rights. The first 10 amendments to the U.S. Constitution, which identify rights and liberties and restrain the powers of the government through both substantive and procedural due process. (Chapter 8)

blue laws. Laws that required businesses to be closed, and prohibited other activities, on Sundays. Over time, most of these laws have been repealed. (Chapter 1)

Bobbies. The name given to police officers in England in the 1800s; named for Sir Robert Peel, who created the first metropolitan police department in 1829. (Chapter 11)

bureaucratic agency. An organization that is governed by rules and procedures, is organized in a hierarchy with clear lines of supervision, requires substantial amounts of paperwork, and requires training of employees. Criminal justice agencies are bureaucratic agencies. (Chapter 1)

bureaucrats. Persons who work within the executive branch of government and agencies that comprise it. They are responsible for implementing policies. (Chapter 7)

cause in fact. One type of causation recognized by the law when linking an *actus reus* with a result. Cause in fact has occurred if a person commits an act that directly brings about a particular result and may be determined by asking the question, would the result have occurred without the defendant's conduct? If the answer is "no," cause in fact exists. Compare to **proximate cause**. (Chapter 9)

certiorari. Persons seeking appellate review of their case after their initial appeal may ask a higher court to hear their case by filing a petition for a writ of *certiorari*. *Certiorari* is rarely granted. (Chapter 12)

civil justice. A process, separate from criminal justice, in which private wrongs are addressed through legal action. This generally occurs through the filing of lawsuits by one person, organization, group, etc. against another. A tort is one common type of civil justice action. (Chapter 7)

class control theory. A developmental theory of American policing suggesting that the police were created by the rich and powerful to control and prevent the upward mobility of those (often members of the working class) perceived as dangerous classes. (Chapter 11)

classical criminology. A set of explanations for crime based on the concept of free will, or the idea that individuals simply choose whether or not to commit a criminal act. (Chapter 5)

classification. The process by which the Department of Corrections determines the prison and security level to which an inmate should be assigned. (Chapter 13)

clearance rate. A statistic indicating the percentage of cases that are solved, or cleared, usually through the arrest of a suspect. (Chapter 1)

code of ethics. A statement that guides employees about moral questions and ethical expectations specific to a particular workplace or working environment. Professions have codes of ethics that can guide professionals in discretionary decision making. (Chapter 1)

Code of Hammurabi. A well-known codification of ancient Babylonian laws from around 1800 B.C.E. The code focused heavily on retribution and the principle of *lex talionis*. (Chapter 9)

Code of Ur-Namma. The earliest known set of written laws from Sumer around 2100 B.C.E. The code used monetary fines as the predominant form of punishment. (Chapter 9)

collective judgment. The consensus that members of a society would reach about which behaviors are morally acceptable and which behaviors are morally unacceptable. This was instrumental to Patrick Devlin's theory of legal moralism. (Chapter 3)

Commerce Clause. A clause in the U.S. Constitution that gives the federal government the power to regulate commerce with other nations and among the states. This clause has allowed the federal government to make and enforce a variety of criminal laws surrounding issues that involve interstate commerce, which may be very broadly defined. (Chapter 7)

community era. The era of policing from the 1970s to the present when the goals of the professional era were broadened to include not only crime control but also crime prevention and strengthened police–community relations and collaborations. (Chapter 11)

community-oriented policing. A policing strategy with the basic philosophy of fostering a positive working relationship between the police and the community. Also known as COP, there are many approaches to community-oriented policing, and it is currently popular in the United States. (Chapter 11)

commutative justice. Defines justice as proportionality. Suggests that justice has been met when outcomes are allocated proportionally. (Chapter 6)

compassionate model. A model of justice that places a higher emphasis on the offender's needs than on society's needs. The model suggests that justice is best achieved by identifying and correcting the needs of the offender that led him or her to commit crime. (Chapter 6)

compensatory social control. Focuses on providing restitution to the victim of a harmful act. This is typically accomplished through the civil justice system. (Chapter 4)

complaint. A document completed by a police officer or private citizen accusing a person of committing a crime. (Chapter 12)

concentric zone theory. Explains criminality in cities by suggesting that multiple zones, diagramed as concentric circles, emerge from the city's center. The theory holds that crime is most likely to occur in the transitional zone, which is described as a residential community undergoing transition to commercial or industrial uses and marked by social disorganization. (Chapter 5)

conciliatory social control. Attempts to create and preserve social harmony via dispute resolution. This is accomplished through practices such as mediation. (Chapter 4)

conflict criminology. Suggests that crime is a consequence of the oppression of the lower classes by rich and powerful elites. (Chapter 5)

conflict theory. Argues that decisions are made to benefit (financially or otherwise) those who hold power in society. (Chapter 13)

Confrontation Clause. The portion of the Sixth Amendment to the U.S. Constitution which guarantees that, in a trial, witnesses must provide their testimony in open court and be subject to cross-examination. (Chapter 8)

congregate system. An early method of incarceration in which inmates lived in individual cells during the night but worked in factories and had meals in dining halls during the day. Absolute silence was required of inmates, even when outside their cells. (Chapter 13)

contraband. Any item that prison or jail inmates are not permitted to possess. (Chapter 13)

correctional boot camps. A punishment alternative in which offenders live in a military-style environment, subject to drills with confrontational strategies and physical labor designed to build discipline. (Chapter 13)

correctional institution. A secure facility designed to house persons accused or convicted of a crime. Jails and prisons are the two primary types of correctional institutions. (Chapter 13)

corrections. The component of the criminal justice system responsible for carrying out sentences imposed by the criminal courts. May include prisons, jails, probation, parole, and other alternatives. (Chapter 13)

corruption. Occurs when professional ethics are disregarded or when professionals engage in illegal activities. (Chapter 11)

courtroom workgroup. The working relationship that develops among court employees, including judges, prosecutors, defense attorneys, and others. (Chapter 12)

craft. A career field in which entry into and training for the occupation are accomplished through an apprenticeship model, with current practitioners mentoring others into the field. Some have debated whether criminal justice is a profession or a craft. (Chapter 1)

crime. Any behavior that the government chooses to regulate by passing a law prohibiting it (punishing those who engage in the behavior, called a *crime of commission*) or by passing a law requiring it (punishing those who do not do so, called a *crime of omission*). A more formal definition of crime is an intentional act or omission in violation of the criminal law, committed without defense or justification, and penalized by the government as a felony or misdemeanor. (Chapters 1, 9)

crime control model. Assembly-line justice with a focus on getting an offender through the criminal justice process as quickly and efficiently as possible. This is one of Herbert Packer's two models of the criminal justice process. Compare to **due process model**. (Chapter 8)

crime control theory. A developmental theory of American policing suggesting that police agencies were created to address an increase in crime and disorder as informal systems of social control were perceived to become less effective. (Chapter 11)

crimes against property. Offenses that cause harm to an individual's property but do not physically harm the individual. (Chapter 9)

crimes against the person. Offenses in which individuals are physically victimized or harmed. These are viewed as the most serious of criminal offenses. (Chapter 9)

criminal justice. The study of society's response to crime, including crime prevention and the work of the criminal justice system. (Chapter 1)

criminal justice system. The collection of criminal justice agencies (e.g., police, courts, corrections) and how they are structured to work together in processing criminal cases. (Chapter 1)

criminologist. A scholar of criminology, studying crime trends and why persons commit criminal acts. (Chapter 5)

criminology. The scientific study of crime trends, the nature of crime, and explanations for why persons commit crimes. (Chapters 1, 5)

critical legal studies. A theory of legal reasoning which emerged in the 1970s and argues that law is politics and designed to maintain the status quo in society. Critical race theory, feminist jurisprudence, and postmodern jurisprudence are variations of critical legal studies. (Chapter 12)

critical race theory. A perspective of legal reasoning drawing upon critical legal studies and focusing on the experience of racial and ethnic minorities with the legal system. (Chapter 12)

critical theories of law. A legal philosophy holding that the law was created and is used by powerful individuals to help them remain in power. (Chapter 3)

cruel and unusual punishment. Prohibited under the Eighth Amendment of the U.S. Constitution. However, there are differing legal interpretations as to what constitutes cruel and unusual punishment. (Chapter 10)

culpability. Guilt or responsibility for a criminal offense. Only individuals with culpability may be punished. (Chapter 10)

culture of control. The idea described by David Garland suggesting that American correctional systems, and the criminal justice system in general, are marked by a desire for security, order, control, and risk management, with an increased use of rules, technology, and surveillance to control deviant behaviors. (Chapter 13)

custody. Includes situations when someone is under formal arrest and also situations in which a reasonable person would not feel free to end questioning and leave. Miranda warnings must be given prior to custodial interrogation. *See also* **interrogation**. (Chapter 8)

dangerous classes. Groups of persons who are targeted for punishment more often than the general population because they are labeled as deviant or dangerous by society. The label may be based on untrue perceptions or discrimination rather than on actual threats. (Chapter 10)

dark figure of crime. Refers to the amount of crime that is not reported to the police or other authorities. An example is the gap between the official Uniform Crime Report crime rates and those suggested by the National Crime Victimization Survey. (Chapter 1)

data. Careful and systematic observations that are analyzed to draw a conclusion about a research question. Examples of data include statistics, interviews, survey responses, and more. (Chapter 2)

day fines. A type of fine that is scaled according to an offender's income rather than being the same for all persons who commit an offense. (Chapter 10)

day reporting center. A facility offering programs for offenders, but rather than living at the facility, offenders are only required to check in daily. Day reporting centers are an intermediate sanction. (Chapter 13)

debtor's prison. A type of facility (no longer in current use) used in the colonial era to hold persons who could not pay their debts. (Chapter 13)

decarceration. A movement in the 1960s and 1970s emphasizing a reduced use of jails and prisons, instead focusing on community-based, sometimes therapeutic, forms of social control. (Chapter 4)

decentralization. The lack of a single centralized national police force; instead, each geographic area, such as a state, city, town, or county, has its own police force. Related to federalism, this reflects the structure of American policing. (Chapter 11)

defense. Various reasons, recognized under the law, individuals should not be held criminally responsible for the commission of acts that are defined as crimes. If a defendant charged with a crime successfully argues that his or her conduct falls under a recognized defense, then he or she may be found not guilty. (Chapter 9)

defense attorneys. Lawyers who represent persons accused of a crime. Defense attorneys may be private attorneys hired by accused persons who can afford to do so, private attorneys appointed by the court to represent indigent persons, or state employees whose full-time job is to represent indigent persons. (Chapter 12)

defense of excuse. Defenses in which a defendant admits to having committed an *actus reus* prohibited under the law but asserts that he or she did so under special circumstances that mitigate or excuse criminal liability. These defenses center on suggesting that the defendant was unable to have a fully formed *mens rea*. Defenses of excuse include infancy of age, insanity, mistake, intoxication, and duress. (Chapter 9)

defense of justification. Defenses in which a defendant admits to having committed an *actus reus* prohibited under the law but asserts that circumstances surrounding the act itself render it justifiable. These defenses assume that an act

was deliberate, with *mens rea,* but argue that the reasons for the act were justifiable under the law. Defenses of justification include self-defense, defense of others, defense of property, consent, and execution of public duties. (Chapter 9)

deinstitutionalization. A movement in the 1960s and 1970s in which persons were released from mental hospitals in favor of community-based, often therapeutic, social control. (Chapter 4)

delinquent subcultures. A criminological theory suggesting that some youth create their own system of values and norms, or their own subculture, to acquire the status they seek. In doing so, members of the subculture may turn to crime. (Chapter 5)

democratic socialism. A model of government in which a democracy seeks to use taxes and regulation to achieve goals of a socialist ideology. (Chapter 6)

demonology. A historical perspective on criminology that attributes criminal behavior to the influence of evil spirits of demons. This theory has been rejected by modern criminologists. (Chapter 5)

deprivation hypothesis. An explanation for prisonization suggesting that the nature of the prison environment and its deprivations shape inmate behavior. Compare to **importation hypothesis**. (Chapter 13)

determinate sentencing. A method of sentencing that limits judges' discretion by requiring specific sentences for a particular crime (as in a mandatory sentence) or by providing sentencing guidelines that use numerical scales and tables to arrive at the recommended sentence for a particular case. Compare to **indeterminate sentencing**. (Chapter 12)

deviance. Behaviors that violate society's expectations, beliefs, standards, or values. As such, deviance refers to any departure from behaviors that are typical, acceptable, or accepted. Therefore, deviant behaviors violate social norms and generate negative reactions from the agents of social control. Crime is one form of deviance. (Chapters 1, 4, 5)

differential association theory. Suggests that criminal behavior occurs because offenders learn it from others. (Chapter 5)

Dillon's Rule. The principle that local governments are creations of the legislature, meaning that local governments only have as much power as state governments decide they should have. This means that local governments are not as important as the state and federal governments under American federalism. (Chapter 7)

Dirty Harry problem. A dilemma faced by law enforcement officers when considering whether it is ever acceptable to use an ethically inappropriate method to achieve a morally good result. The Dirty Harry problem is the subject of many discussions about police ethics and procedural justice. (Chapter 11)

discovery. The process by which the parties (defense and prosecution) to a criminal case exchange relevant information about that case. The purpose of discovery is to prevent unfair surprises at trial. (Chapter 12)

discretion. A criminal justice professional's ability to use professional judgment rather than being constrained by rigid rules when making decisions about how to handle a case. Discretion is common throughout the criminal justice system. (Chapter 1)

disintegrative shaming. A form of shaming that, as a result of public shaming or scolding, labels offenders as deviant, thereby separating them from the community rather than reintegrating them into it. Compare to **reintegrative shaming**. (Chapter 10)

disorder theory. A developmental theory of American policing that suggested large-scale disruptive events and the need to suppress mob violence led to the development of police agencies. (Chapter 11)

dissenting opinion. An opinion in a Supreme Court (or other appellate court) case written by justices who disagree with the majority opinion. Although a dissenting opinion does not become law, it does serve as a statement of a justice's beliefs. (Chapter 3)

distributive justice. A perspective on justice that focuses on what individuals are due. As such, distributive justice focuses on the end results of how outcomes are distributed. (Chapter 6)

DNA database. Files maintained by state and federal governments that archive DNA (deoxyribonucleic acid) samples from known offenders. When DNA is retrieved in an unsolved case, it can be compared to the samples in the database to see if there is a match. (Chapter 1)

double jeopardy. Bars the same governmental entity from criminally prosecuting someone twice for the same offense or from giving multiple punishments for the same offense. However, there are some exceptions to the general principles of double jeopardy. (Chapter 8)

drug court. A collaborative, team-based program designed to help drug offenders in which the prosecuting attorney, defense attorney, probation officer, substance abuse treatment counselor, and judge meet regularly to review and reward (or punish) each offender's progress (or lack thereof). (Chapter 13)

Due Process Clause. The provision in the Fourteenth Amendment to the U.S. Constitution that makes nearly all of the criminal procedural rights contained in the Bill of Rights applicable to the states. Also serves as an independent source for other procedural justice rights or substantive due process rights not otherwise listed in the Constitution or Bill of Rights. (Chapter 8)

due process model. Focuses on the rights of the accused and advocates formal decision-making procedures, drawing upon the assumption that the accused is innocent until proven guilty. This is one of Herbert Packer's two models of the criminal justice process. Compare to **crime control model**. (Chapter 8)

effective assistance of council. Guaranteed by the Sixth Amendment to the U.S. Constitution. If a lawyer's performance falls so far below the standard of reasonable competence that the outcome of the case is likely to be unfair or unreliable, then a defendant has been denied effective assistance of council and a new trial may occur. (Chapter 8)

electronic monitoring. A program in which offenders must wear a device, usually in an ankle bracelet, that monitors their location. Often used in combination with house arrest. Electronic monitoring is an intermediate sanction. (Chapter 13)

emergency management. The study of preparation for, response to, and recovery from disaster or crisis situations. (Chapter 1)

empiricism. The notion that the answers to questions should be grounded in the collection and analysis of data. This approach guides criminal justice and other scholars. (Chapter 2)

equal protection. In legal terms, treating persons consistent with the concept of equality. (Chapter 8)

Equal Protection Clause. The provision in the Fourteenth Amendment to the U.S. Constitution that serves to guarantee equality, requiring that the law treat similarly situated people in a similar manner without discrimination. (Chapter 8)

Equality. Refers to protections that promote equal rights for all persons without discrimination regardless of characteristics such as race, gender, religion, disability status, veteran status, sexual orientation, income, and more. Equality

is a fundamental component of American political culture. (Chapter 7)

essential tension. A concept described by Thomas Kuhn that reflects a conflict between ideals of what should be and the observable world as it actually is. (Chapter 13)

Establishment Clause. One of two clauses in the First Amendment to the U.S. Constitution relevant to religious freedom. The Establishment Clause prohibits laws that establish an official state religion or that favor one religion over another. Compare to **Free Exercise Clause**. (Chapter 9)

ethics. The application of morality in a professional setting. Often codified in professional codes of ethics. (Chapter 11)

eugenics. The study of genetic factors that may influence future generations. Was also a term used to refer to programs, since discredited, that used medical interventions to sterilize persons who were labeled as having bad genes. (Chapter 5)

evidence. Anything that helps prove or disprove a fact. May include physical evidence, sworn testimony, scientific evidence, or demonstrative evidence. (Chapter 12)

ex parte. A proceeding that takes place without all parties to the case, such as without a defendant or detainee and his or her counsel. (Chapter 8)

ex post facto. A law punishing an act or behavior that was not criminal when it was committed. *Ex post facto* laws are prohibited under the U.S. Constitution because fairness requires that punishments can only be given when offenders have the opportunity to know that their behavior was criminalized. (Chapter 8)

exclusionary rule. Stipulates that illegally seized evidence may not be admissible at trial. Established by Supreme Court interpretations of the

Fourth Amendment. There are, however, many exceptions to the exclusionary rule. (Chapter 8)

exculpatory evidence. Any evidence that may be favorable to the defendant in a criminal trial, either by casting doubt on the defendant's guilt or mitigating the defendant's culpability. The prosecution must disclose all exculpatory evidence to the defense as part of the discovery process. (Chapter 12)

exigent circumstances. Emergency circumstances when a reasonable person would believe prompt action was necessary to prevent harm, the destruction of evidence, escape, or other such consequences. Exigent circumstances may permit exceptions to Fourth Amendment requirements. (Chapter 8)

expiation. A view of retribution based on the idea of atonement through suffering. Expiation is based on the idea that crime causes pain to the victim, so the only way for the offender to repent or learn a lesson is through experiencing pain. (Chapter 10)

external/relational social control. A type of informal social control that depends on a person's interactions with others, in which positive or negative reactions from others lead individuals to conform to social norms. Compare to internal or self-control. (Chapter 4)

farm system. A historical method of incarceration used primarily in the American South in which inmates lived and worked on large prison farms. The prison farms were operated primarily by the inmates themselves, some of whom served as guards over the other inmates. Severe physical punishment was common at the prison farms. (Chapter 13)

federalism. Having more than one level of government, as in the United States, which has a national government as well as 50 state governments in addition to counties and cities. (Chapter 7)

felony. The most serious crimes, which may be punished by a sentence to a year or more in prison and/or a substantial fine. Compare to misdemeanors and infractions. (Chapter 12)

feminist criminology. A criminological perspective that examines the relationship between gender inequality, male dominance, and the exploitation of women under capitalism. Feminist criminologists focus on gender differences in crime, female offenders and victims, and gender inequities in the division of labor. (Chapter 5)

feminist jurisprudence. A perspective of legal reasoning drawing upon critical legal studies and focusing on gender inequality in society as a function of law. (Chapter 12)

fines. Financial penalties imposed when an offender has been found guilty of a crime. (Chapter 10)

folkways. Norms that are less formal and that tend not to be based on moral foundations. Compare to mores. (Chapter 4)

forensic science. The application of scientific principles to cases progressing through the legal system, generally to aid in investigations and to prepare evidence for trials. (Chapter 1)

formal social control. Mechanisms exercised by the government to control human behavior and to cause persons to conform to norms and obey laws. Criminal justice and criminal law are the most important tools of formal social control. Compare to informal social control. (Chapter 4)

Free Exercise Clause. One of two clauses in the First Amendment to the U.S. Constitution relevant to religious freedom. The Free Exercise Clause protects individuals' rights to act upon or practice their religious beliefs. Compare to Establishment Clause. (Chapter 9)

fruit of the poisonous tree. A doctrine stipulating that further evidence acquired as a result of previously illegally obtained evidence may not be admissible in court. (Chapter 8)

general deterrence. A justification for punishment holding that the imposition of punishment, in general, will prevent (or deter) all persons in the public from committing criminal acts because they will fear being punished if they do so. (Chapter 10)

geographic jurisdiction. A type of jurisdiction based on location, in which a court is empowered to hear cases that originated within the geographic area (whether county, district, or other geographic unit) over which that court has authority. (Chapter 12)

governing through crime. An idea described by Jonathan Simon suggesting that efforts for control and surveillance once reserved to the criminal justice system have extended to families, schools, and workplaces, where individuals are subject to an increased amount of monitoring, regulation, and zero-tolerance policies. (Chapter 13)

grand jury. A group of citizens impaneled to hear evidence presented by a prosecuting attorney with the purpose of determining whether sufficient evidence (probable cause) exists to bring to trial a person accused of committing a crime. If such evidence is found, the grand jury issues an indictment. Failure to find such evidence results in dismissal of a case. (Chapters 1, 8, 12)

grasseaters. Police officers who accept illegal benefits as a result of corrupt activity but who do so passively rather than actively seeking opportunities for unethical conduct. Compare to **meateaters**. (Chapter 11)

gratuity. A situation in which a police officer is given a benefit (e.g., a discount or something for free) that is not available to other members of the general public. Gratuities are a subject of debate in discussions of police ethics. (Chapter 11)

Great Society. A collection of social programs promoted by President Johnson aimed at eradicating a variety of social problems, including poverty, inadequate health care, racial injustice, pollution, and more. (Chapter 13)

Guardian Angels. A citizen group created in 1979 to combat crime in the New York City subway system. Since that time, the group has expanded to other cities and other venues. (Chapter 6)

habeas corpus. In a legal context, a writ of *habeas corpus* is a court order directed at someone who has custody of a person ordering the release of that person because his or her incarceration was achieved through unlawful processes. This provides the mechanism by which unlawful incarcerations may be challenged. (Chapters 8, 12)

halfway house. A type of correctional facility that provides educational and counseling programs in a homelike setting and offers offenders greater freedoms than a prison or jail. Halfway houses are an intermediate sanction. (Chapter 13)

harm principle. The idea advanced by John Stuart Mill that a society (through the law) should only concern itself with actions that pose a direct harm to others. (Chapter 3)

harmless error. Minor legal errors that were unlikely to have affected the overall outcome of a case. If appealed, harmless errors do not result in the reversal of a conviction. (Chapter 12)

harmony. The idea that when things are in their proper order, it represents beauty. (Chapter 2)

Hart-Devlin debate. An intellectual exchange between British legal philosophers H. L. A. Hart and Patrick Devlin focused on the role of morality in the law. (Chapter 3)

hedonism. The idea that individuals will commit an act if the potential pleasure outweighs the potential pain but will not commit an act if the potential pain outweighs the potential pleasure to be gained. This was instrumental to Jeremy Bentham's theories and to the ideas of general and specific deterrence. (Chapter 10)

hegemony. The influence that is exercised by powerful groups in society. (Chapter 7)

hierarchical jurisdiction. The organization of state and federal court systems in which a case begins in a court of original jurisdiction where factual determinations are made. These decisions may be appealed to a court of appellate jurisdiction, which reviews the proceedings of the court of original jurisdiction to ensure that laws and procedures were properly applied. (Chapter 12)

homeland security. The identification of and response to threats to national security, with a particular emphasis on terrorism. (Chapter 1)

house arrest. An intermediate sanction in which offenders may live at home but are not permitted to leave their home. Electronic monitoring is generally used to enforce house arrest. (Chapter 13)

idealist. A philosophical perspective that evaluates actions and decisions based on how well they meet broad goals or theoretical ideas. Compare to **pragmatist**. (Chapter 2)

idealistic theories of law. Theories of law grounded in the idealistic perspective. The theories include legal naturalism, rights and interpretive jurisprudence, critical theories of law, and legal paternalism. Common ideas underlying idealistic theories include a strong connection between law and morality and the use of law to draw upon history and tradition in pursuit of ultimate truths. (Chapter 3)

ideology. A worldview to which a person subscribes. Under ideological justice, supporters of an ideology argue that society will not be able to achieve justice until policies are enacted that support their desired ideology. (Chapter 6)

imperfect procedural justice. A model of procedural justice described by John Rawls in which a criterion is identified for determining what a fair outcome is, but procedures do not guarantee that the fair outcome will be accomplished. Imperfect procedural justice balances sometimes competing interests, such as due process and crime control. (Chapter 8)

importation hypothesis. An explanation for prisonization suggesting that inmates bring their attitudes and life experiences from the outside into prison, and these shape their behavior in the prison environment. Compare to **deprivation hypothesis**. (Chapter 13)

incapacitation. A justification for punishment in which punishment is used to remove or reduce the offender's ability to commit criminal activities. The most common form of incapacitation is the use of prison or jail, with the idea that removing the offender from society will reduce the offender's ability to commit crime. (Chapter 10)

incarceration. The use of sentences to correctional institutions (prisons and jails) as a form of punishment. (Chapter 13)

inchoate crimes. Crimes that occur as part of the preparation for committing another crime or in an attempt to commit another crime, including such acts as attempt, solicitation, facilitation, aiding and abetting, and conspiracy. (Chapter 9)

indeterminate sentencing. A method of sentencing in which a statute sets a broad range of permissible sentences for an offense (usually a minimum and a maximum) and leaves it to the sentencing judge to impose whatever sentence he or she feels is fair, given the particular facts of a case. Compare to **determinate sentencing**. (Chapter 12)

indictment. A written statement issued by a grand jury to indicate that sufficient evidence (probable cause) exists to bring to trial a person accused of a crime. Also known as a true bill, the indictment indicates the specific offense with which the accused is charged, including a description of the facts and circumstances surrounding the crime that led the grand jury to find probable cause. (Chapters 1, 8, 12)

indigent. In criminal justice, refers to defendants who are unable to afford legal representation. (Chapter 6)

individual justice. Focuses on whether outcomes that apply to individual persons are just. (Chapter 6)

informal social control. Tools used to control behavior in everyday social life, including social control exercised by peers, communities, families, and groups. This forms the basis of the socialization process. Compare to **formal social control**. (Chapter 4)

information. A formal, written document accusing a person of a crime. The document is prepared by the prosecuting attorney and submitted to a judge for his or her consideration at a preliminary hearing. (Chapters 1, 12)

infraction. Low-level offenses that are violations of laws or ordinances but are not classified as either felonies or misdemeanors. Many traffic violations are infractions. Compare to **felony** and **misdemeanor**. (Chapter 1)

initial appearance. When a judge or magistrate informs an accused person of the charges against him or her, the possible penalties, and the right to retain counsel or have an attorney appointed if indigent. A decision may also be made about whether to grant bail. The initial appearance is to occur within 48 hours of a person's arrest. (Chapters 1, 12)

initiative/referendum elections. Elections in which the public, as a whole, votes directly on whether or not certain laws should be passed. (Chapter 3)

intensive supervision probation. A highly structured form of probation designed for high-risk offenders or offenders who have not been successful on regular probation. Also known as ISP, it requires more frequent meetings and closer supervision than traditional probation. (Chapter 13)

interest groups. Organized groups of individuals who advocate for a particular policy outcome. (Chapter 7)

intermediate sanctions. A range of correctional alternatives that lie on a continuum between probation and prison. (Chapter 13)

internal or self-control. A type of informal social control related to conscience in which an individual internalizes norms and acts according to them. Compare to **external or relational social control**. (Chapter 4)

interrogation. Questions, statements, or actions that are designed to elicit an incriminating response from a suspect. Miranda warnings must be given prior to custodial interrogation. *See also* **custody**. (Chapter 8)

jail. A correctional institution holding persons accused of a crime who are awaiting trial and offenders who are sentenced to less than one year. Jails are short-term facilities usually operated by a county sheriff. (Chapters 1, 13)

judges. Those who preside over state and federal courts. The primary role of the judge is to enforce the rules of criminal procedure and criminal evidence. (Chapter 12)

judicial review. The power of the courts to invalidate laws enacted by a legislature or rules made by an executive agency if they violate or conflict with the U.S. Constitution. In criminal justice, judicial review is often focused on issues of substantive due process or procedural justice. (Chapter 12)

jurisdiction. The authority given to a court to hear and adjudicate a particular dispute. There are multiple forms of jurisdiction, including hierarchical, subject matter, and geographic. (Chapter 12)

jurisprudence. The academic and philosophical study of law. (Chapter 3)

jurisprudence of rights. A modern extension of legal realism which argues that the primary consideration, other than the law, that should guide judges is an ethics of rights, in which fairness is the guiding principle to be used when deciding cases. (Chapter 12)

just deserts. A view of retribution focusing on the idea that punishment should be proportional to the crime; that is, punishment should be equally severe to the offender as the offender's criminal act was to the victim. (Chapter 10)

just world. A world where individuals receive what they deserve. The concept of and belief in a just world has been important in the psychological study of justice. (Chapter 6)

Justice. That which is just. There is no single agreed-upon definition of justice. Rather, conceptions of what does or does not constitute justice have been influenced by culture, history, philosophical perspectives, and more. (Chapter 6)

justice reinvestment. Programs based on the idea that money spent on incarceration could be better spent on other initiatives to prevent crime. (Chapter 13)

labeling theory. Assumes that once society places a label on a person, that individual will self-identify with the label and behave accordingly. If a person is labeled as a delinquent, deviant, or criminal, the theory suggests that the person will accept that label and therefore engage in delinquent, deviant, or criminal activity. (Chapter 5)

law and economics. A movement emerging in the 1970s advocating that the law should be interpreted (and cases decided) in a way that distributes economic costs and benefits in a manner that promotes economic efficiency and maximizes wealth. (Chapter 12)

law and legal studies. The study of legal issues in law school or prelaw programs of which criminal law is one component. Also included are civil law, constitutional law, jurisprudence, legal research, philosophy of law, and more. (Chapter 1)

Law Enforcement Assistance Administration. An agency created by Congress to distribute funds to improve criminal justice administration and practice. Known as LEAA, the agency was created in 1968 and abolished in 1982; the Office of Justice Programs has continued some of LEAA's functions. (Chapter 1)

Law Enforcement Education Program. A program created by the Law Enforcement Assistance Administration to fund college-level criminal justice education. Known as LEEP, the program was restructured in 1979 and discontinued soon thereafter. (Chapter 1)

legal formalism. The traditional view of legal reasoning holding that judges apply law to the facts of the case to arrive at logical decisions separate from any ethical, political, philosophical, or policy considerations. (Chapter 12)

legal moralism. The idea that popular notions of morality should influence decisions about what behaviors the law ought to regulate. This was the perspective held by Patrick Devlin in the Hart-Devlin debate. (Chapter 3)

legal naturalism. A legal theory espousing a belief in the concept of natural law. (Chapter 3)

legal paternalism. A legal theory holding that the government creates and enforces law to protect individuals from engaging in risky behaviors or making decisions that might harm them. (Chapter 3)

legal positivism. A philosophy that views the law solely as a human creation rather than as an attempt to discover, confirm, or enforce higher moral standards. This was the perspective held by H. L. A. Hart in the Hart-Devlin debate. (Chapter 3)

legal pragmatism. A legal theory arguing that the law should be based on empirical evidence rather than on grand concepts such as morality. (Chapter 3)

legal process theories. An approach to legal reasoning that attempts to harmonize legal formalism and legal realism by offering neutral principles that judges could use to resolve unclear cases. However, determining which neutral principles to use and how to use them is a value decision which can lead to inconsistencies between judges. (Chapter 12)

legal realism. A legal theory with a primary focus on the decision-making processes of the courts. The theory holds that the courts create law through their accumulated decisions, meaning that the law becomes whatever the courts say it is. Legal realism suggests that legal reasoning is an act of interpretation, requiring judges to consider factors beyond the law to resolve uncertainties in cases. In this approach, judges craft decisions to achieve justice, serve broad social interests, and foster good public policy. (Chapters 3, 12)

legal reasoning. The processes by which judges make decisions about how to interpret and apply the law. (Chapter 12)

legalistic style. A style of police behavior described by James Q. Wilson in which the purpose of policing is to enforce all laws with the full force of police authority in all cases. Officers operating under the legalistic style enforce all laws strictly with little exercise of discretion and measure productivity by statistics, such as number of arrests or tickets. (Chapter 11)

legality. In punishment theory, legality means that punishment can only be given for crimes as defined by the law and that the punishments given must be within the bounds of the law. (Chapter 10)

legitimacy. Exists when citizens accept that their government has the right to govern them. Governments without legitimacy may face protest, disobedience, or revolution. (Chapter 2)

lever pulling. A policing strategy with a three-step process. First, groups of offenders are told by family and community leaders how their actions have caused harms to the community. Second, offenders are offered resources to help them stop offending. Third, offenders are told that if they do not stop offending, an aggressive enforcement campaign will be launched against them by the police. (Chapter 6)

lex talionis. The retributive principle of punishment illustrated by the phrase "an eye for an eye, a tooth for a tooth . . ." This was the idea that offenders should have the same harm applied to them as they applied to their victims. (Chapter 9)

libertarian. An ideological perspective holding that society should respect individual rights with only minimal government influence, particularly the right to own and do as one wishes with property. (Chapter 6)

liberty. The freedom and the protection of rights as enumerated in the Constitution and Bill of Rights. Liberty is a fundamental component of American political culture. (Chapter 7)

life course theory. Explores how involvement in criminal activity changes as offenders grow older and encounter new life circumstances. (Chapter 5)

Magna Carta. A document signed by King John in England in 1215. The document established basic rights of procedural justice for citizens accused of a crime and was one source for the types of due process protections granted under the U.S. Constitution and Bill of Rights. *Magna Carta* is Latin for "great charter." (Chapter 9)

majority opinion. The opinion in a Supreme Court (or other appellate court) case providing the Court's ruling, which becomes the law of the land. (Chapter 3)

mala in se. A Latin phrase for crimes prohibiting acts that are universally (or nearly universally) viewed as being inherently evil or bad, such as murder or rape. Compare to *mala prohibita*. (Chapter 1)

mala prohibita. A Latin phrase for crimes prohibiting acts that have been made illegal not because they are viewed as being inherently wrong but because a legislature or government has chosen to criminalize them nonetheless. Compare to *mala in se*. (Chapter 1)

Marijuana Tax Act. A federal law passed in 1937 that had the effect of outlawing marijuana nationwide by imposing a series of strict restrictions and taxes on its distribution. (Chapter 7)

mark system. Used by Alexander Maconochie at the Norfolk Island prison colony; inmates accumulated marks or points for positive behaviors and, upon collecting a sufficient number of marks, could receive special privileges and eventual release. (Chapter 13)

Marxist criminology. A form of conflict criminology which argues that there is a strong relationship between capitalism, class conflict, and crime. The theory suggests that persons with political power and wealth create laws to suppress the lower class. (Chapter 5)

meateaters. Police officers who actively solicit corrupt or unethical activities. Compare to **grasseaters**. (Chapter 11)

mechanical model. A model of justice focusing neither on the needs of society nor on the needs of the offender. The intent of the model is to rigidly and rapidly follow laws and processes without discretion and without consideration of the outcomes they produce. (Chapter 6)

medical collaboration. A form of medical social control that occurs when the medical profession works with other institutions of social control. (Chapter 4)

medical ideology. A form of medical social control referring to the implications that result from defining a behavior in medical terms. This can include the ideological consequences of labeling a behavior as a disease and how doing so reflects dominant social values. (Chapter 4)

medical model of deviance. A way of explaining deviance that underlies therapeutic social control. Under the model, deviance is defined objectively as a disease, and treatment of the disease is sought in accordance with the therapeutic style of social control. (Chapter 4)

medical technologies. A form of medical social control referring to the actual techniques available to treat forms of illness and/or deviance. Examples include the administration of medication or the use of medical procedures, such as surgery. (Chapter 4)

medicalization of deviance. Defining a deviant behavior as an illness or a symptom of an illness and then providing medical intervention to treat the illness. Incorporates elements of the medical model of deviance and therapeutic formal social control. (Chapter 4)

mens rea. One component of the legal definition of crime expressed in the Latin phrase meaning "evil mind." The *mens rea* of a crime is the level of intent the offender had to commit the criminal *actus reus*. Levels of intent include committing a crime with purpose, knowledge, recklessness, or negligence. (Chapter 9)

mesomorphs. Under the criminological theory of somatotypes, persons who are muscular, active, and aggressive and therefore viewed as more likely to engage in delinquent behavior. (Chapter 5)

Miranda rights. In 1966, the Supreme Court ruled in the case *Miranda v. Arizona* that suspects must be advised of the following rights prior to custodial interrogation: You have the right to remain silent. Anything you say can and will be used against you in a court of law. You have the right to have an attorney present during questioning. If you cannot afford an attorney, one will be appointed for you. (Chapter 8)

misdemeanor. Less serious offenses that may be punished by a sentence of less than a year in jail and/or a small to moderate fine. Compare to **felony** and **infraction**. (Chapter 12)

mission statement. A written statement of the philosophies that guide an agency or organization. (Chapter 13)

misuse of authority. Occurs when a police officer uses his or her position for some sort of personal gain. Generally viewed as a violation of police ethics. (Chapter 11)

Model Penal Code (MPC). A set of model criminal laws developed by the American Law Institute in 1962 and updated in 1981, which has formed the basis for revisions to the criminal laws in two-thirds of the American states. By being a model, the code stands as the American Law Institute's conception of what criminal laws ought to look like. (Chapter 9)

morality. Judgments about what behaviors or actions societies or individuals view as right or wrong, good or bad. Morality may also be viewed as an ongoing process in which society or individuals continually reflect on norms, values, and standards when determining the best solution to a dilemma. (Chapters 1, 2)

mores. Norms that are formally expressed and that tend to have moral underpinnings. Compare to **folkways**. (Chapter 4)

mortification. The loss of personal identity that comes with admission to a total institution, such as a prison or jail. (Chapter 13)

motion. A formal request asking the court to make a specific ruling on an issue or question. Motions may address any number of substantive or procedural issues, but the most significant is a motion to suppress evidence that was gathered in violation of a defendant's constitutional rights. (Chapter 12)

National Crime Victimization Survey. A survey conducted by the Bureau of Justice Statistics to determine how many persons have been the victims of criminal acts. Also known as the NCVS, this is an example of a victimization survey. (Chapter 1)

National Incident-Based Reporting System. Crime data collected by the Federal Bureau of Investigation with more detailed information than available in the Uniform Crime Reports. Also known as NIBRS, the data are often used by researchers to analyze crime patterns. (Chapter 1)

National Supremacy Clause. A clause in the U.S. Constitution that identifies the federal government as the supreme law of the land. This means if there is a conflict between a federal law and a state law, the federal law will take priority. (Chapters 7, 12)

natural law. A belief that there are universally accepted principles of human behavior meant to apply to all persons in all places and that law should discover, reflect, and enforce these principles. (Chapter 3)

neutralization theory. Suggests that crime occurs because offenders justify their criminal behavior through a series of neutralizations or excuses, including denial of responsibility, denial of injury, denial of the victim, condemnation of the condemners, and appeal to higher loyalties. (Chapter 5)

nolle prosequi. A Latin term referring to a prosecutor's decision to drop criminal charges after initially attempting to prosecute a case. (Chapter 1) *nolo contendere*. A Latin term for a plea in which a person accused of a crime does not challenge the charges and accepts a penalty but without admitting guilt for the offense. (Chapter 1)

nonsystem. An idea expressing lack of coordination between criminal justice system agencies. This may be due to fragmentation between agencies, the prevalence of discretion, and lack of agreement on criminal justice goals and philosophies. (Chapter 1)

nulla poena sine lege. A Latin phrase meaning that no punishment can be given by a court unless there is a law that authorizes it. (Chapter 1)

nullum crimen sine lege. A Latin phrase meaning that no behavior can be considered a crime unless there is a law enacted that prohibits it. (Chapter 1)

original position. A state achieved under the veil of ignorance in which one has a lack of knowledge about his or her personal background. John Rawls argues that this is the starting point from which government and policy should be developed, as it minimizes a focus on self-interest. (Chapter 6)

overbreadth. Occurs when a law intrudes upon constitutionally protected freedoms, in which case the law may be ruled invalid, unconstitutional, and unenforceable. (Chapter 9)

pains of imprisonment. As described by Gresham Sykes, five deprivations, or things that are withheld from inmates: liberty, goods and services, heterosexual relationships, autonomy, and security. Taken together, these deprivations partially define the prison experience. (Chapter 13)

panacea phenomenon. The cycle in which a new criminal justice intervention is proposed but with unrealistic expectations; the intervention is implemented but does not meet the unrealistic goals set for it; frustration builds and the program is labeled a failure; and policy makers

develop a new intervention, at which point the cycle repeats itself. (Chapter 13)

paradigm. Philosophical tendencies or worldviews held by individuals that they use to help them make decisions. (Chapter 2)

parens patriae. A metaphor suggesting that the law (or the government through law) acts as a parent and protector to its subjects. This notion, grounded in the belief that society has a moral obligation to protect its citizens, underlies the theory of legal paternalism. (Chapters 3, 7)

parole. A process allowing the early release of an offender after serving part of his or her sentence. Release may be granted by a parole board if the inmate has demonstrated that he or she is rehabilitated and poses a low risk to society. (Chapter 1)

participatory model. A model of justice that places a high value on both the needs of society and the needs of the offender. In this model, a variety of participants must work together to create, understand, and apply the law. (Chapter 6)

peacemaking criminology. A perspective arguing that the encouragement of communication and relationships can promote justice and heal social wrongs. Views traditional forms of punishment, such as incarceration, as counterproductive because they reflect an imbalance of power. (Chapter 5)

penal social control. Views the violator of a social norm that has been codified into criminal law as an offender who is deserving of official condemnation and punishment. This is accomplished through the criminal justice system. (Chapter 4)

perceptual shorthand. A concept described by Jerome Skolnick, in which police officers use labels and perceptions to make rapid judgments about which persons are believed to pose a personal danger or harm to society. Persons so identified are known as symbolic assailants and may routinely be subjected to higher levels of social control than other persons, whether or not an actual threat exists. (Chapter 10)

peremptory challenge. Allows the prosecution or defense to excuse a potential juror during the *voir dire* process without specifying a cause. Each side is typically permitted only a limited number of peremptory challenges, and they may not be used to exclude jurors on the basis of race or gender. (Chapter 12)

perfect procedural justice. A model of procedural justice described by John Rawls in which a criterion is identified for determining what a fair outcome is, and then procedures are put into place to achieve that fair outcome. Perfect procedural justice strives for accuracy when searching for the truth. (Chapter 8)

pervasive organized corruption. A level of police corruption identified by Lawrence Sherman describing agencies where corruption and unethical behavior are well organized and involve many officers, potentially including supervisors. (Chapter 11)

pervasive unorganized corruption. A level of police corruption identified by Lawrence Sherman where a large number of rotten apples in an agency participate in illegal activity. (Chapter 11)

petit jury. The group of jurors impaneled to hear a particular criminal case, at the conclusion of which they render a verdict. In most states, petit juries in criminal trials are composed of 12 jurors. (Chapter 12)

phrenology. A historical theory in criminology that was the study of personality traits as revealed by an examination of the bumps and grooves in the skull. This theory has been discredited by modern criminologists. (Chapter 5)

plea bargaining. The process by which a defendant agrees to plead guilty in exchange for some consideration from the government, such as a lower charge, fewer counts, or a reduced

sentence. Approximately 95% of felony cases are resolved by plea bargaining. (Chapter 12)

pod-style design. A modern style of prison design in which cells surround a central day room where inmates may gather for recreation, programming, or other prosocial activities. Each grouping of cells and day room is known as a *pod*. (Chapter 13)

police. A formal agent of social control and component of the criminal justice system responsible for law enforcement and the maintenance of order. (Chapter 11)

policy window. Based on John Kingdon's theory of public policy, it refers to a time when policy change is most likely to occur for an issue. For a policy window to open for any particular issue, that issue must have been identified as a problem, a solution must be available, and the political climate must support making a change. (Chapter 7)

political culture. The broad set of values that underlie a particular political system. As such, political culture shapes the development of law and policy. (Chapter 7)

political era. The era of American policing from the 1830s to the early 1900s, in which policing was characterized by political undertones and police officers and agencies often fell under the control and influence of local politicians. The era was marked by high levels of corruption. (Chapter 11)

postmodern jurisprudence. A perspective of legal reasoning drawing upon critical legal studies and focusing on the intersection of race, gender, gender identity, religion, social class, sexual orientation, and other perspectives to study inequalities in law and society, often using literary theory to interpret legislation and judicial decisions. (Chapter 12)

postmodernism. A philosophical perspective holding that there are multiple equally valid realities, as individuals create their own narratives and understandings of what is real. Postmodern perspectives on justice recognize these differences and have as a goal helping to understand why different persons and groups have differing conceptions of what is just. (Chapter 6)

pragmatist. A philosophical perspective in which actions and decisions are evaluated based on empiricism and the analysis of data. Compare to **idealist**. (Chapter 2)

prejudicial/reversible error. Significant mistakes made in a criminal trial that are likely to contribute to an unfair verdict. These errors may result in overturning a conviction. (Chapter 12)

preliminary hearing. A hearing held in front of a judge to determine whether or not there is probable cause to believe that a person committed the crime of which he or she stands accused. If probable cause is found, the judge binds over the defendant for trial. If probable cause is not found, the case may be dismissed. (Chapters 1, 8, 12)

preponderance of evidence. The burden of proof used in deciding cases heard through civil justice processes (it is also used in some criminal justice hearings and in some administrative hearings). It means that the judge or jury believes it is more likely than not that an incident occurred or that one party caused harm to another. (Chapter 7)

prescriptive norms. Norms that specify what individuals should or are encouraged to do. Compare to **proscriptive norms**. (Chapter 4)

presentence investigation report. A report prepared by probation officers containing information about the offender and the nature of the offense. Commonly known as PSI, its purpose is to aid a judge in determining the sentence for a case. (Chapter 12)

presumption of innocence. Presumes that all criminal defendants are innocent until their guilt has been proven beyond a reasonable doubt. This is a presumption that the jury (or

judge in a bench trial) is required to make at a criminal trial. (Chapter 12)

presumption of sanity. Presumes that defendants are sane (i.e., legally responsible for their actions), unless they are proven insane at trial (through successful use of the insanity defense). This is a presumption the jury (or judge in a bench trial) is required to make at a criminal trial. (Chapter 12)

pretrial release. A decision to allow a person to remain free rather than held in jail prior to a trial in criminal court. (Chapter 1)

prison. A correctional institution holding persons who are sentenced to more than a year. Prisons are long-term facilities operated by the state or federal government. (Chapters 1, 13)

prison-industrial complex. A conflict theory perspective of corrections, suggesting that increased spending on incarceration is not driven by need but rather by political and economic interests. (Chapter 13)

prisonization. An inmate's acceptance of the unique culture of the prison environment, including (but not limited to) its norms, jargon, lifestyle, and conditions. Prisonization has been explained by the importation hypothesis and the deprivation hypothesis. (Chapter 13)

privilege against self-incrimination. Specifies that a person may not be compelled to provide testimony against himself or herself. The Miranda warnings are given prior to custodial interrogation to ensure that suspects are aware of the privilege against self-incrimination. (Chapter 8)

probable cause. A fair probability based on facts and known circumstances. Probable cause is required for an arrest, for the issuance of search and arrest warrants, and for a case to proceed beyond the grand jury and preliminary hearing stages, among other decisions. (Chapter 8)

probation. A punishment given by a judge that allows the offender to remain in the community instead of being sent to jail or prison. Often part of a suspended sentence. (Chapter 13)

problem definition. Refers to attempts by interested individuals and groups to advocate how a problem ought to be understood. This often occurs after an issue has been placed on the public agenda (through agenda setting), as individuals and groups debate the causes of and solutions to the problem in question. (Chapter 7)

problem-oriented policing. A policing strategy designed to help the police identify and respond to the root causes of problems that lead to crime. The emphasis is on making police proactive rather than reactive through use of the SARA model. Also known as POP, it is currently a popular strategy in the United States. See also **scanning**, **analysis**, **response**, and **assessment**. (Chapter 11)

procedural defense. Technical defenses in which guilt, level of intent, or characteristics of the offense are irrelevant. Procedural defenses include those related to violations of procedural justice rights, immunity, and entrapment. (Chapter 9)

procedural justice. Holds that justice is achieved when the proper procedures are followed and addresses the fairness of the procedures used when applying the law. Procedural justice is grounded in the idea that fair procedures are the best guarantees for fair outcomes. (Chapters 6, 8)

profession. A career field that meets criteria including a common educational background, adoption of an ethical code, performing specialized tasks, having mechanisms for quality control, prestige as a member of the profession, and lifetime membership in the profession. Some have debated whether criminal justice is a profession or a craft. (Chapter 1)

professional courtesy. Occurs when a police officer provides a courtesy or special treatment to another law enforcement officer (e.g., not giving an officer a ticket if he is stopped for speeding). Professional courtesy is a subject of debate in discussions of police ethics. (Chapter 11)

professional era. The era of policing from the 1930s to the 1970s focused on reform, professionalism, and removing political influence from policing. (Chapter 11)

Prohibition. The time in American history from 1920–1933 when alcohol use was banned by the 18th Amendment to the U.S. Constitution. Prohibition was repealed by the 21st Amendment to the U.S. Constitution. (Chapter 1)

proportionality. The idea that the punishment should fit the crime. Punishments may be ruled unconstitutional if they are grossly excessive in relation to the crime committed. (Chapter 10)

proscriptive norms. Norms that specify what individuals should not or are encouraged not to do. Compare to **prescriptive norms**. (Chapter 4)

prosecutors. Government officials who are responsible for prosecuting (charging and bringing to trial) violations of criminal law. Prosecutors are sometimes called the "gatekeepers" of the criminal justice system because of their power to determine who will appear in court and on what charges. (Chapter 12)

protective sweep. An examination of the premises after making an arrest, including areas outside the arrestee's immediate control or reach. Reasonable suspicion must exist to conduct a protective sweep. (Chapter 8)

proximate cause. One type of causation recognized by the law when linking an *actus reus* with a result. Proximate cause asks whether there were any other causes that could lead to the result. If not, the defendant may be criminally liable for the result; if so, the defendant may be liable only if a reasonable person would have foreseen that the defendant's specific *actus reus* would lead to the result. Compare to **cause in fact**. (Chapter 9)

psychodynamic theory. A theory of crime suggesting that human behavior, including crime, is controlled by a variety of mental processes. The theory was developed by Sigmund Freud based on the dynamics of the id, ego, and superego. (Chapter 5)

public policy. The individual and accumulated decisions made by governments (local, state, or federal) about what should be done to address any issue, including crime. (Chapter 7)

punishment. A form of deprivation imposed upon a person as a result of committing a criminal act. Punishments may include, but are not limited to, incarceration (deprivation of freedom), fines (deprivation of money), or physical punishments (deprivation of bodily integrity). (Chapter 10)

pure procedural justice. A model of procedural justice described by John Rawls that focuses on creating a system with fair procedures that, if followed, are likely but not guaranteed to produce fair outcomes. Pure procedural justice is based on a participation model in which persons affected by a decision have the opportunity to participate in the process (e.g., a trial) by which that decision is made. (Chapter 8)

putative backlash. May occur after a formerly deviant behavior has been vindicated. Occurs when the behavior is either recriminalized or redefined as deviant. (Chapter 4)

quantitative scales. Numerical scales. In criminal justice settings, the results of quantitative scales are used to guide decisions and thereby limit discretion. (Chapter 13)

rate. A standardized measure that allows comparison of data between areas with different populations. Often used when reporting crime data, crime rates are calculated by dividing the number of offenses by the population of an area and then multiplying by 100,000. The resulting number indicates how many offenses occur per 100,000 persons in a particular location. (Chapter 1)

rational choice theory. An explanation for crime suggesting that offenders use a strategic thinking process to evaluate the potential rewards and risks from committing a crime and make their decision accordingly about whether or not to commit the crime. (Chapter 5)

reasonable expectation of privacy. Refers to an expectation of privacy that society views as a reasonable one. Significant because, for the protections of the Fourth Amendment to apply, there must be a governmental intrusion upon a reasonable expectation of privacy. (Chapter 8)

reasonable suspicion. A lower burden of proof than probable cause in which officers can articulate facts and make inferences from them that criminal activity may be afoot. Required for stop and frisks and protective sweeps. (Chapter 8)

recidivism. A measure of how often former offenders commit new crimes. (Chapter 13)

reformatory system. An early method of incarceration designed for young offenders, with an emphasis on education, vocational instruction, and rehabilitation. (Chapter 13)

rehabilitation. A justification for punishment that views the purpose of punishment as attempting to correct an offender's behavior so it will conform to the law and to social norms. Rehabilitation involves the use of programming (counseling, treatment, education, etc.), rather than fear or pain to correct behavior. (Chapter 10)

reintegrative shaming. A form of shaming in which the offender, after being publicly shamed or scolded, is forgiven and accepted back into the community. Compare to **disintegrative shaming**. (Chapter 10)

restitution. The payment of money to a victim by an offender to compensate the victim for the losses caused by the offender. This concept was present in some ancient Greek legal codes and also is utilized as part of restorative justice models today. (Chapter 9)

restorative justice. Focuses on restoring the victim, offender, and society to the desirable conditions that existed before a criminal offense occurred. (Chapter 6)

result. One component of the legal definition of crime related to the requirement that the prosecution must prove that the defendant's behavior (*actus reus*) caused the prohibited result. **Cause in fact** and **proximate cause** are two types of causation that can be used to link an *actus reus* with a result. (Chapter 9)

retribution. A justification for punishment grounded in the notion that offenders should be punished because they deserve it. Forms of retribution include revenge, just deserts, and expiation. (Chapter 10)

revocation. Occurs when a person on probation or parole commits a new crime or violates the rules of probation or parole and is removed from probation or parole and sent to prison as a result. (Chapter 13)

rotten apples. A level of police corruption identified by Lawrence Sherman in which one or more officers independently participate in some form of corrupt activity. (Chapter 11)

rotten pocket. A level of police corruption identified by Lawrence Sherman in which a group of officers work together for corrupt or unethical purposes. (Chapter 11)

routine activities theory. Views crime and victimization as a function of people's everyday behavior, habits, lifestyle, living conditions, and social interactions. Suggests that crime occurs when three elements converge: a motivated offender, suitable target, and lack of capable guardians. (Chapter 5)

scanning, analysis, response, and assessment. The four steps used in problem-oriented policing. Commonly referred to as SARA. (Chapter 11)

security administration. The identification and management of risk in public, commercial, or residential settings. This provides the basis for the private security industry. (Chapter 1)

security level. In corrections, the differences between prisons centering on issues such as how much freedom inmates have within the institution, what types of programming are available, and how many security features are incorporated into the facility. Typical security levels include minimum, medium, and maximum. (Chapter 13)

self. A philosophical concept that represents how one views humanity. (Chapter 2)

self-report study. One way of measuring the amount of crime in society by administering surveys that ask persons to report whether or not they have committed certain criminal acts. (Chapter 1)

serial murderer. Offenders who have killed two or more victims over time. (Chapter 5)

service style. A style of police behavior described by James Q. Wilson in which policing is understood to draw upon the use of discretion to determine the most appropriate response to any given situation. Officers operating under the service style view each situation in its own context and prefer to resolve problems with arrest as a last resort. (Chapter 11)

six concepts of law. A framework for understanding the role of law in society by considering the foundation, rationale, formation, application, focal point, and use of discretion in law. (Chapter 3)

sneak and peek warrants. Warrants authorized under the USA PATRIOT Act which, in some circumstances, allow law enforcement officers to search a person's property without notifying the person whose property is being searched. (Chapter 2)

social bond theory. Suggests that crime occurs when an individual's bonds to society are weak or broken. Bonds include attachment to prosocial persons and organizations, commitment to prosocial goals, involvement in prosocial activities, and belief in a common set of prosocial values and morals. (Chapter 5)

social capital. Patterns of social relationships among people. Areas with high social capital have strong social relationships among community members. (Chapter 1)

social contract theory. A philosophical explanation for the origins of government, in which individuals willingly give up complete freedom to do as they please in exchange for a more secure society governed by laws enforced by a government. (Chapter 2)

social control. The processes by which society controls individual and group behaviors. The term is now often used to refer to the ways deviant behaviors are controlled, both informally and formally. (Chapter 4)

social disorganization theory. Focuses on the community environmental factors that may lead to crime, including poverty, breakdown of family and social institutions, high turnover of residents, and lack of attachment to the community. (Chapter 5)

social justice. Considers issues of equality and inequality in society and whether benefits and risks are distributed in a manner that is fair and without discrimination. Argues that the pursuit of justice is the pursuit of equality. (Chapter 6, 7)

social norms. Societal judgments about what individuals should or should not do. Norms are based on widely shared values about what are good or bad, correct or incorrect, behaviors. (Chapter 4)

socialist. An ideological perspective favoring a society with a large government structure that manages public ownership of industries viewed as most necessary for a productive society and that provides many public services to all members of society. (Chapter 6)

socialization. The process by which individuals learn a society's or culture's norms and also learn to conform to them. (Chapter 4)

socially constructed. The idea that societies and individuals construct their own understandings about what certain ideas mean. This helps to explain why different societies or different localities define crimes in different ways, as each may have its own understanding of what crime means. (Chapter 1)

solitary system. An early method of incarceration in which inmates remained in individual cells with little to no human contact for the duration of their sentence. The goal was to promote offender rehabilitation through self-introspection. (Chapter 13)

somatotypes. A historical theory of criminology suggesting that a person's height and weight were associated with criminal behavior and that individuals with different physical builds, or somatotypes, possess different temperaments. This theory has been discredited by modern criminologists. (Chapter 5)

specific deterrence. A justification for punishment that is designed to discourage or prevent individual offenders from committing additional crimes out of fear for being punished again if they do so. (Chapter 10)

spirituality. Refers to belief in organized religion or to a personal spirituality separate from a specific religious tradition. Notions of spirituality may affect how people make moral decisions. (Chapter 2)

split sentence. A sentence in which offenders first spend some time in jail (or prison) after which they are released to serve a probation sentence in the community. (Chapter 13)

standing. A requirement in law that only persons whose direct interests have been involved, or whose rights have been violated, may bring a case or a challenge to evidence in a case. That is, individuals cannot bring a lawsuit or challenge evidence on behalf of someone else. (Chapter 8)

state of nature. A philosophical idea describing an environment in which there is little order because there is no justice system or government. (Chapter 2)

statute of limitations. A legal provision that sets time limits on how long after an incident court processes can be initiated. (Chapter 7)

stocks. An apparatus located in a public area for the purpose of shaming offenders. The device restrained offenders by securing their hands or feet so they could not move or leave, thereby placing the offender on public display. (Chapter 13)

stop and frisk. Briefly detaining a person and performing a limited pat-down of the outer clothing when there is reasonable suspicion of criminal activity. (Chapter 8)

strain theory. Suggests that crime occurs when members of society, predominantly the lower socioeconomic class, are unable to achieve goals valued by society (principally, the accumulation of wealth). Failure to achieve goals results in frustration, leading some to turn to criminal activity to achieve goals. (Chapter 5)

strategy. The overall approach that an agency or organization uses to address a problem or issue. A strategy is a broad plan that is put into effect through the use of various specific tactics. (Chapter 2)

stratification. Differences between members of a society that occur when persons and groups are divided in a hierarchical manner. This results in levels of inequality from which persons at the top of the hierarchy benefit, whereas those at the bottom suffer. (Chapter 4)

strict liability. Crimes that do not require criminal intent, or *mens rea,* on the part of the offender. These offenses can therefore be punished without regard to the offender's level of intention (or lack thereof) at the time of the crime. (Chapter 9)

subculture. A group that shares a set of norms that are different from those of the larger society. (Chapter 4)

subject matter jurisdiction. A form of jurisdiction based on the subject matter of a case. Courts of limited subject matter jurisdiction hear cases only on certain topics; courts of general subject matter jurisdiction hear all other types of cases. (Chapter 12)

subpoena. A court order commanding a witness to appear in court at a specific date to provide sworn testimony in a case. (Chapter 8)

substantive criminal law. The area of criminal law that lists and defines specific criminal offenses and the punishments that may be administered to those who violate them. (Chapter 9)

substantive due process. Protects against governmental infringement of fundamental rights, such as freedom of speech, freedom of religion, and the right to privacy. The rights protected under substantive due process include those specified in the Constitution and Bill of Rights as well as those held through the Due Process Clause. (Chapters 8, 9)

summons. A court order that directs a recipient to appear in court at a specific time on a specific date. Among other uses, the summons is the mechanism by which potential jurors are compelled to appear in court to participate in the jury selection process. (Chapter 12)

suspended sentence. A type of sentence in which a judge gives an offender a prison sentence but sets the prison sentence aside to allow the offender to serve his or her time on probation instead. If the offender violates the terms of probation or commits a new crime, the judge may revoke the probation and require the offender to serve the original prison sentence. (Chapter 13)

symbolic speech. Conduct that expresses an idea or opinion. Although not verbal or written speech, symbolic speech receives First Amendment protection. (Chapter 9)

tactics. Specific actions that are taken to implement the broad idea outlined in a strategy. (Chapter 2)

team policing. A policing strategy developed in Scotland in 1946 in which a team of police officers was assigned to a specific neighborhood with the responsibility for performing all police services for that neighborhood. The strategy proposed decentralizing policing by creating numerous mini-departments within a city. The strategy was attempted but never became popular in the United States. (Chapter 11)

teleology. A philosophical concept suggesting that a vast and purposeful universe with an underlying order creates meaning. (Chapter 2)

therapeutic social control. Views the deviant person as someone who needs help to become nondeviant or "normal." This is often accomplished through science and medicine. (Chapter 4)

thin blue line. In policing, a division between the police and the public stemming from limited contact between police and public and from an "us" versus "them" mentality sometimes held by police officers. Also associated with the solidarity that emerges among police officers. (Chapter 11)

third-party policing. A strategy in which persons other than the police are held accountable under the law for maintaining order and preventing crime. (Chapter 9)

tort. A harm that is classified as a civil wrong and that forms the basis for action under civil justice processes. (Chapter 7)

total institution. A concept described by Erving Goffman in which an institution controls all aspects of a person's life. Correctional institutions are one example of a total institution, as the institution controls all aspects of an inmate's life. (Chapter 13)

transitional justice. Applies in the unique set of circumstances when a country's government changes and the new government seeks to move away from human rights abuses that occurred under the old government. The transition between governments is marked by a focus on human rights and just outcomes. (Chapter 6)

transportation. A practice used through the 1800s in England in which offenders were sent to live in overseas colonies and prohibited from returning to England. (Chapter 13)

treason. The only crime defined in the U.S. Constitution, which defines treason as making war against the United States or providing aid and comfort to enemies. (Chapter 8)

trial by jury. A trial in which guilt or innocence is determined by a jury of one's peers. The right to a trial by jury exists for felonies and some misdemeanors. Compare to **bench trial**. (Chapter 8)

trial by ordeal. A type of criminal trial once used in which offenders had to perform physical feats or tests, the results of which were used to determine guilt or innocence. (Chapter 9)

truth in sentencing. Stipulates that offenders sentenced to prison must serve a certain portion of their time, usually 85%, and no early release (on parole or otherwise) may occur prior to that time. The federal government and many states have adopted truth in sentencing. (Chapter 13)

typical crime. A crime in which one individual or group victimizes another individual or group, usually through direct physical harm or property loss. Also known as *street crime*, this stands in contrast to white-collar crimes committed in the arena of finance or by corporations. (Chapter 1)

ultimate truth. A belief held by idealists that there are certain absolute notions or ideas (i.e., truths) that guide or should guide human action. (Chapter 2)

Uniform Crime Report. An annual report of the number of crimes reported to the police, prepared by the Federal Bureau of Investigation. Also known as the UCR, this stands as the official source of crime data in the United States. (Chapter 1)

unit management. A modern strategy of correctional management implemented in prisons with pod-style design. Under unit management, multiple activities are conducted within the pod, and staff can work more closely with inmates, promoting meaningful counseling and reducing inmate violence and rule violations. (Chapter 13)

urban dispersion theory. A developmental theory of American policing suggesting that the growth of cities led crime to be identified as an urban problem and that the police were necessary to ensure the stability of urban society. (Chapter 11)

utilitarian justice. Defines justice as that which provides the greatest good for the greatest number. Also draws upon cost–benefit analysis, comparing the costs and benefits of an action. (Chapter 6)

veil of ignorance. A thought experiment used by John Rawls, in which a person is to assume that he or she knows nothing about his or her background. When under the metaphorical veil, individuals are in an original position. *See also* **original position**. (Chapter 6)

venire. The group of persons who are summoned to court as potential jurors and who then participate in the *voir dire* process for jury selection. (Chapter 12)

victimless crime. A category of crime in which no direct victim is readily identifiable. This includes crimes such as drug possession, prostitution, illegal gambling, and others. (Chapter 7)

victimology. The study of why persons or entities (e.g., businesses, organizations) become victims of crime. (Chapter 1)

vigilante justice. Occurs when individuals bypass the criminal justice system in resolving a conflict by taking the law into their own hands. (Chapter 6)

vindication. Occurs when a behavior once viewed as deviant is no longer viewed as deviant. (Chapter 4)

void for vagueness. Laws so vague that persons must guess at their meaning, and as a result, such laws are unenforceable. Laws may be struck down under judicial review if they are void for vagueness. Based on the principle that laws must provide clear descriptions of the conduct that is prohibited. (Chapter 10)

voir dire. A Latin term for the process in which the venire of potential jurors is sworn to tell the truth and then questioned to screen out persons who may not be able to make a fair and impartial decision in the case (this is known as being stricken for cause). Potential jurors can also be excused with peremptory challenges. (Chapter 12)

voting disenfranchisement laws. Laws that prohibit persons convicted of a felony from voting. States differ in the type and extent of disenfranchisement laws they have, if any. (Chapter 12)

waiver. An instance in which a person knowingly, intelligently, and voluntarily gives up his or her constitutional rights, such as when allowing law enforcement officers to conduct a search or when choosing to answer questions after being advised of Miranda warnings. (Chapter 8)

watchman style. A style of police behavior described by James Q. Wilson in which the purpose of policing is viewed as keeping the peace and not making waves. Officers operating under the watchman style are passive and reactive. (Chapter 11)

Wolfenden Report. A report issued by a British government commission in 1963 regarding the legal status of homosexuality and prostitution. The report formed the basis for the Hart-Devlin debate. (Chapter 3)

working personality. Refers to the occupational culture of policing, reflecting elements of police work including danger, authority, social isolation, and solidarity. (Chapter 11)

Youth Risk Behavior Study. A survey of high school students administered regularly by the Centers for Disease Control to measure the frequency of high-risk behaviors. (Chapter 1)

Index

Photo Credits